A PHILOSOPHY OF FREEDOM

OTHER BOOKS BY LOUIS AARON REITMEISTER

PARADISE FOUND
IF TOMORROW COMES
GIST OF PHILOSOPHY
A PHILOSOPHY OF LOVE
MUSIC AND PHILOSOPHY
WHEN TOMORROW COMES
WHAT LIFE MEANS TO GREAT PHILOSOPHERS
THE CRISIS OF 1940: BEING AN APPEAL
   TO COMMON SENSE
THE NATURE OF POWER
THE GODS AND MY FRIENDS
BY THE WAY
A PHILOSOPHY OF TIME

In preparation

THE NATURE AND PHILOSOPHY OF FRIENDSHIP
MY MOTHER—A BIOGRAPHY

Louis Aaron Reitmeister

FELLOW
INTERNATIONAL INSTITUTE
OF ARTS AND LETTERS

A PHILOSOPHY

OF *FREEDOM*

an attempt to explain
the natural basis
of freedom

1970
New York
Poseidon Books, Inc.

To

My Friends

DAVID B. KRISER
and
MAXWELL LEHMAN

ACKNOWLEDGMENT

The author is grateful to the publishers of the following works and for the granting of permissions to quote from them: *In the Beginnings,* H. R. Hays (Putnam, 1963); *The Dangerous Sex,* H. R. Hays (Putnam, 1964); *Prehistory and the Beginnings of Civilization,* Hawkes and Woolley (Harper & Row, 1963); *Freedom in the Ancient World,* Herbert J. Muller (Harper & Row, 1961); *Reflections on Religion,* Mark Twain (Hudson Review, 1963); *Book of Indians,* William Brandon (American Heritage, 1961); *Hebrew Myths,* Robert Graves and Raphael Patai (Collins-Knowlton-Wing, 1964); *Book of Bird Life,* A. A. Allen (Van Nostrand Reinhold, 1961); *People's Padre,* Emmett McLoughlin (Beacon, 1954); *Paths of Culture,* Kaj Birket-Smith (University of Wisconsin, 1965); *Mankind Evolving,* Theodosius Dobzhansky (Yale University, 1962); *The Hummingbird and the Hawk,* R. C. Padden (Ohio State University, 1967); *This Fascinating Animal World,* Allan Devoe (McGraw-Hill, 1951); *My Wilderness: East to Katahdin,* William O. Douglas (Doubleday, 1961); *Why I Am Not a Christian,* Bertrand Russell (Simon & Schuster, 1957); *The Future of Unbelief,* Gerhard Szczesny (Braziller, 1961); *Power,* Bertrand Russell (Allen & Unwin, 1962); *Sex, Culture and Myth,* Bronislaw Malinowski (Harcourt, Brace & World, 1962); *This View of Life,* George Gaylord Simpson (Harcourt, Brace & World, 1964); *Book of the Hopi,* Frank Waters (Viking, 1963); *Masks of God: Oriental Mythology,* Joseph Campbell (Viking, 1962); *The Golden Bough,* 1 vol. ed., James G. Frazer (Macmillan, 1922); *Authority and the Individual,* Bertrand Russell (Simon & Schuster, 1960); *African Genesis,* Robert Ardrey (Atheneum, 1961).

PREFATORY NOTE

SNOOKY

Snooky, my German Shepherd, died on April 25, 1969. He had lived for thirteen years, a good full life for his kind. Snooky was my buddy for all these years, a constant companion during the time this book was written. He was never too far from my typewriter and in many ways I can say that *we* wrote this book. For his life was a symbol of innocent freedom dedicated to love, devotion and, in many ways, a very real and genuine commitment of responsibility for and toward each other. It is very befitting that this page be set to consecrate our partnership in this undertaking, that I am not alone here. My co-author, Snooky, is here with me. The memories of his love, his gentleness and his closeness, will always be a mark of my gratitude as long as I am able to remember, and as long as people may remember me, they will also remember Snooky.

L.A.R.

CONTENTS

BOOK ONE

BOOK TWO

BOOK THREE

BOOK FOUR

BOOK FIVE

PART I

PART II

Out of the earth to rest or range
Perpetual in perpetual change,
The unknown passing through the strange.

—John Masefield

". . . an enchanted loom where millions of flashing shuttles weave a dissolving pattern, always a meaningful pattern though never an abiding one. . . ."

—Sir Charles Sherrington

BOOK ONE

THE NATURE OF FREEDOM

THE NATURE OF FREEDOM

FREEDOM IS PROBABLY the sweetest word in any language. It is also the most affirmative. It is cherished by all, more or less, or should be; fought for by all, more or less; abused at times by the few, at other times by the many; used by the few to help or deceive the many and used by the many to get rid of the few. At times it has been used as a torch to lead the many to more or less satisfying ways of life, to change places with former tyrants or bring salvation to people out of desperation. Very often its banner has been used as a Judas goat to lure the many or the few to misery, slavery, and even death.

Like the word GOD, it means varied values and sentiments according to each individual, but unlike God it is purely limited to the world we live in and try to know and understand. It is purely constricted to *this* world, as neither in heaven nor in hell could people be free; in each place one's soul is "forever" tied to bliss or fire without reprieve or change. Besides, freedom, being more or less a voluntary thing, fallible and limited, cannot be handled or understood in terms of "eternity." Whenever it is expressed, it is in the *now,* not later. If people believe in immortality, it seems very obvious that it really is not that people realize or know anything about what such a "forever" could mean; they want to believe in immortality becausce they continually do not want to die today or tomorrow.

Man teaches but what he teaches is what he knows or thinks he knows, and teaching is the division of experience and things in categories, classes, particulars, and our judgments thereof according to our desires and goals. Some of the greatest errors in history, some of the greatest deceptions and misconceptions, with their trailing traffic in miseries, have often been hailed as "objectives" and considered in the realm of "objectivity." All these goals, all these destinies and destinations which people seek, do not appear to exist save in the processing of the present, and it is in the pres-

3

ent only that reality exists, regardless of what it may consist of.
Therefore, time is not an existent factor within itself alone; nor
does it partake of the past or the future. It comes when we are
conscious of it, aware of it; it leaves us when we cannot be conscious of it. Its values and its realness depend upon *our* values and
the realness *we* place upon the present in which we live. It is in
the *process,* the continual present, that time could possibly take
place, and in the present only can we express our philosophy and
it is the only time we really have to *live* it.

Like the word LOVE, we need it to live and yet so often deny it
to ourselves needlessly and unwisely. There was love in the world
long before man came, long before man made rules—and there
will be love when man has gone. Without love, as without freedom, all the rules seem empty things in an empty world. "There
are few ways in which man can be more innocently employed than
in making love."[1]

Like the word HAPPINESS, we want it and we seek it, or we
should, and when we are fortunate to have it in our hands, we
all too often crush it by our selfishness, by our gullibilities, by our
dominance, by our being seduced and blinded by false and super-
fiicial concepts, by our neurotic frustrations and ignorance of our
own being and experiences. "One cannot have pleasure without
giving it, and that every gesture, every caress, every touch, every
glance, every single part of the body has its secrets which can
give pleasure to one who can understand."[2]

In everyone's life there fall some beautiful things, happy things,
and also sad and unpleasant things. It all depends where one
stands when they fall. "Every day of the Egyptian year was divided
into three parts, each of which was lucky or unlucky."[3] When we
understand how these things occur, never fully understanding
why, we cannot hate life or hate the lives of others for then we
would be hating the reflection of ourselves. Rather, we should
build courage to receive eventualities, whenever they do come;
fortitude and some wisdom to avoid, if we can, the sad; and
persuade, if we can, the happy things to greet us. We cannot all
be lucky. No matter how wise we think we are or how cautiously
we tread, we cannot all be lucky, no matter how strong we are,
for we all stand under the same sky. As Manuel says (in *The*

Children of Sanchez): "To those of us who are born to be *tamale eaters,* heaven sends only *tamales*."[4]

Like the word SECURITY, we are in need of it constantly, and yet, like the dog dropping the bone into the pond to snatch at an inflated image of the real, we sell it short and count our profits in our own self-made prisons.

Like the word FRIENDSHIP, it gives good meaning and joyful purpose in our lives and relationships, and yet so often we betray it for a mirage we can never reach. And, of course, it often happens that a person's friendship can mean that his freedom indicates that the extent of his friendship is as far as his hand can reach into your pockets.

CONCEPTS OF TRUTH

LIKE TRUTH, WE revere it but all too often forget to practice it. While freedom appears to be *a* truth, truth as we see it is what we think a thing "actually" is, and whether we are right or wrong indicates an attitude, not a certainty. Truth, which is *Mantra* in India, *Chen Yen* in China, and *Shingon* in Japan. Whether a thing is true or not may be opinionated correctly, but the identity of it as truth is subject to processes of verification. *Real* is what a thing *actually* and *verifiably* is. To be rational is a way of thinking out a perspective or an opinion of what we think it is, which may be real or not real. Man will always continue to build newer knowledge or "truths" upon the cumulative pile of experience. There can be no regress or remission to before-the-present. This can no more be undone than the past can be relived in time. Pure knowledge, which attempts to establish or identify what is presumed to be an already existent reality, is of itself meaningless, unless it is, or can be, applied to the betterment and satisfaction of living more reasonably secure and free. The reason why the ancient Greeks argued the notion of proof in establishing the truth is that very few of them trusted one another. The mountains separated their loyalties, not their suspicions.

KNOWLEDGE, being a manifestation of human judgment, follows

its own line of imperfection toward an ever perfecting end, which, as long as humans exist, is endless. Thus, knowledge reveals *knowledge-in-process*. It is the understanding and identity of this process which identifies, in turn, the continuing search.

All knowledge is on a *finite* basis. Perfections and universals are merely human values and judgments in stretching the imagination, nurtured by hope and dream, beyond the possibility of perception. The attempt by the Patristic theologians to mold the Aristotelian potentiality and actuality into universals of eternal perfections was the attempt to state that two plus two adds up to *ad infinitum*.

Knowledge is perception-in-process. Error is the same perception-process. Both are changeable, correctifiable, reversible, and never irrevocable. Arguments and dissent identify this process. So long as process exists there can be no idea or concept of perfection or perfectionism. What could possibly remain is the *idea* of the idea of perfection.

The consequences of hypothesis as well as the appearances of opinion and judgment identify the fluxions and continuums of process, which is, in the nature of itself, never stable. While it may be argued that the "stability" of process, as an "all," may be considered as stable, this argument falls to the ground because we cannot know its measurement, limitation, and verifiability, and, therefore, it becomes mystical and meaningless. Stability is merely the illusion of appearance that process is at "rest," but there is no rest, eternally and forever, so long as existence exists in any form whatsoever.

Form, like quality and potentiality, identifies matter, like quantity and actuality, in process. Form and matter, individually abstractions, become jointly as process, for there is no form without matter and no matter without form. To accept the idea that a thing remains static forever without change, even men's concepts of God, is the attempt of vanity to soothe purpose, not the search for reality.

Knowledge does not imply that it is necessarily true, because knowledge, although it may contain the possibility of truth, is also a *means* of reflection, a process of identity, and a symbol to act by or upon. Both *pragmatism* and *utilitarianism* consider or hold the view that truth or righteousness determine themselves by the consequences of any act or principle. Both these viewpoints seem to be highly volatile when rationalized to justify acts or ends which can be arbitrary, unilateral, good for one and bad for another. Bertrand Russell sums it up nicely: "Pragmatist theory that a belief is true if the consequences are pleasant. Pleasant for whom? Belief in Stalin is pleasant for him but unpleasant for Trotsky. Belief in Hitler is pleasant for the Nazis, but unpleasant for those whom they put in concentration camps. Nothing but naked force can decide the question: Who is to enjoy the pleasant consequences which prove that a belief is true? . . . Belief in pragmatism, if wide-spread, leads to the rule of naked force, which is unpleasant; therefore, by its own criterion, belief in pragmatism is false."[5] To establish truth or an ethic on such a flimsy, pragmatic basis is to provide the fuel to establish the reverse.

Very often in literature we read the orations of great scholars and public men in which *truth* is raised high as a *virtue,* as something of a *divinity,* which we should worship as some sort of pinnacle-goddess. The actual truth is that it is very obvious from experience that *absolute* truth is most often unreachable for the reason that whatever we accept as truth is *human* concepts of truth, and whether a human truth is applicable to some basis of absoluteness or a certainty of knowledge is again subject to verifying processes of objective and scientific method and procedure. Edmund W. Sinnott: "Truth, about which we once could feel so sure, today is often very hard to find. Axioms have lost their old authority. Natural law is based on probability. Truth, like so many other things, may turn out to be a relative, not an absolute thing."[6]

The pursuit of truth for its own sake is meaningless, but the pursuit of truth as a basis for value to benefit us and the world has meaning. While it is important for the sake of *knowledge* that we seek the truth, it is more important that we systematize or construct this knowledge into a method of values based on such knowledge and experience as to make it possible to secure, extend, or improve our level of security, peace of mind, happiness, and general life satisfaction. The rational pursuit of truth is not for truth's sake, but for *our* sakes, and it is rational for one to consider his own sake in terms of happiness, security and satisfaction. Archibald MacLeish: "After Hiroshima it was obvious that the loyalty of science was not to humanity but to truth—its own truth—and that the law of science was not the law of the good— what humanity thinks of as good, meaning moral, decent, humane —but the law of the possible."[7] Truth need not lead to despair, as we note in the philosophers of existentialism; here the *fear* of the truth preceded the invitation to despair, as the *fear of the truth* has preceded so many illusions in the psychological history of humanity.

Karl Jaspers states that "To be genuinely true, truth must be communicable. . . . Truth therefore cannot be separated from communicability. . . . The movement of communication is at one and the same time the preservation of, and the search for, the truth. . . . That which is not communicable is as though it were not at all."[8] Jaspers obviously attempts to establish truth as the exclusive asset of the human mind; that man alone, being the agent to communicate and receive communication, is the only vehicle for the revelation of truth. Such an egocentric attempt makes even God unnecessary, as heretofore it has been assumed by the theologians that God alone has and reveals the truth to mankind through His revelations. Undoubtedly man has found out much by the means of communication. Man's world today is the result of it. All his histories, his sciences, even all his religions and beliefs, are the result of his ability to communicate and understand communication, but this does not mean that communication has always enabled him to discover the truth. A liar also communicates, so does the con man, the deceptor, even the preacher, who preaches much he does not understand himself or is sure of. Who among us have been so lucky that we have not been, at some time or other, taken in by the means of communication? Communication is a means by which we can convey our thoughts to others and they to us; it does not necessarily, by the expression of this means, set up, *ipso facto,* any such communication as truth. Whether a certain communication is a truth or not depends upon sequences of experience and verification to confirm its particular status as truth or untruth. Unfortunately for man, language has been more often used to beguile and deceive than to reveal truths, and the nature of our courts' procedures and practices confirms that our jurisprudence, in order to try to render justice, cannot accept communication as the *sole* judge of truth and fact.

Truth existed long before man grew a brain, a thought, and a tongue to speak with. It existed without communication throughout the world, and still does. Man would learn more truths if he had the courage to shed his self-made bloated god-shell, extricate himself from the wordy maze of his metaphysics, and look about this world more silently. Perhaps then he might find some truth outside his own ephemeral and fragile phrases. Too many of us have become proficient in emitting nebulous sentences without *real* meaning. Regardless of how we try, we will not make Nature become like us. If mankind ceases to exist, Nature will continue to exist, in one fashion or another, with or without communication, with or without language, without culture, even without the sciences and all their intricate formulae of communication and knowledge, and what will remain will also be a truth—if perhaps without a witness. Man, for all his communication, does not always tell the truth, nor does he always find out what the truth actually is. Man's concept of truth is man's *idea* of a truth. Man's mind represents the man, not the world. And with this we are stuck. Man cannot be *all*, regardless how he may try. David Reisman makes the point in another way: "I believe that the processes of communication are inherently ambiguous, since we understand other people's symbols in terms of our own character and the experience it has let us have. Therefore even those people who are sure they know what the truth is may not succeed in communicating it, but something quite the opposite, as the history of every reform movement testifies."[9] The syllogism of Jaspers, that truth can be identified or established by communication—therefore all communication is truth—is a false a priori deduction from the original correct premise that truth may possibly emanate from communication.

History reveals that whenever and wherever societal organization, military power, or religious dogma held down the individual and his right to dissent in his own pursuit of the truth, genuine advance stopped and there was stagnation in the social order.

Hudson Hoagland states the case from the view of the scientist:
"The individual who seeks the truth must be independent and
free from coercion, and the society that values the truth must
safeguard his independence. In a scientifically oriented society,
excellence, independence, and originality are esteemed assets and
must be protected by respect for the right of dissent. . . . The high
spots in our Western civilization have been great moments of
dissent—the Declaration of Independence, the writings of Milton,
the sermons of John Wesley. In science the open challenges of
men like Copernicus, Galileo, Newton, Darwin, and Einstein
have brought fresh insights and surges of social progress in their
wakes. Dissent is thus an instrument of social evolution. All
scientists must be heretics and dissenters against accepted views
in science if science itself is to advance. Freedom is thus essential
to a scientific society, one in evolution. It is merely a nuisance
to be discouraged in a static, authoritarian society."[10]

Many scholars, like Bergson, have attempted to establish the
idea that intuition is the ultimate key to truth, since reason is not
capable, in an inward as well as in the cosmological sense, to establish the certainty of truth. However, Bergson overlooked the particularized nature of intuition, that it is the effect of a cause that
is individualistic. There seems to be no such thing as collective
or group intuition. An intuition of an individual may contain
knowledge that is true, but of itself it has no such proof.

Intuition, of any nature, is based upon the cumulative effect
of previous experiences, of oneself and/or others, and therefore
is not exactly intuition in the full sense of the word. Intuition is
a "hunch" made possible by a momentarily mentally activated
decision to act of a sort. Pure intuition, completely unattached
and inconcordant with some operable consciousness of reason, is
a myth. "Bergson holds that the intellect is to be condemned as
unduly passive and merely contemplative, and that we only see
truly during vigorous action such as a cavalry charge. He believes
that animals acquired eyes because they felt that it would be
pleasant to see; their intellects would not have been able to
think about seeing, since they were blind, but intuition was able
to perform this miracle. All evolution, according to him, is due
to desire, and there is no limit to what can be achieved if desire

is sufficiently passionate. The groping attempts of biochemists to understand the mechanism of life are futile, since life is not mechanical, and its development is always such as the intellect is inherently incapable of imagining in advance; it is only in action that life can be understood. It follows that men should be passionate and irrational; fortunately for Bergson's happiness, they usually are."[11]

If only philosophers and scientists would make some effort to minimize the use of language to incite the enjoyment of linguistics and instead use language to admit, in the rational and scientific sense, a certain and inevitable quantum of ignorance and with it the possibility of "newer" truths, they would start moving onward into the light, not necessarily to agree or to submit to agreement, but with more firmness and more honesty. Bertrand Russell: "The more serious of my objections is that the new philosophy seems to me to have abandoned, without necessity, that grave and important task which philosophy throughout the ages has hitherto pursued. Philosophers from Thales onward have tried to understand the world. Most of them have been unduly optimistic as regards their own successes. But even when they have failed, they have supplied material to their successors and an incentive to new effort. I cannot feel that the new philosophy is carrying on this new tradition. It seems to concern itself, not with the world and our relations to it, but only with the different ways in which silly people can say silly things. If this is all that philosophy has to offer, I cannot think that it is a worthy subject of study."[12] This is Russell's reaction to modern linguistics, polemics, semantics, and pedantics. It is time to get back to the body and the world it lives in—for a little while, at least—and to get back to the body while it still lives. Epitaphic philosophy, even in the most beautiful prose, is both too late and meaningless.

H. T. Costello states that "truth is a property of judgment."[13] This, no doubt, is a pragmatic view. However, regardless of our wishes, truth remains the verified reality of an object, state, or condition, or combinations of them; judgment is purely *our* view of such things, and varies according to our likes and dislikes, our cultures, our characters and objectives, our habits and hopes, and the nature and substance of our knowledge. So long as we consider truth as that which a thing *actually* is, we cannot presume that such truth is the property of *human* judgment, as this would imply and necessitate the acquisition of omniscience into the already cosmocentric mind of man. Loren Eiseley: "There is one dubious answer to this buoyant optimism: science is human, it is of human devising and manufacture. It has not prevented war, it has perfected it. It has not abolished cruelty or corruption. It has enabled these abominations to be practiced on a scale unknown before in human history."[14]

Mr. Costello goes on to say: "The greatest privilege of the human mind, and peculiarly of the philosophic and artistic mind, is to be able to rise above the world as it is, and compare what is with might be and might have been."[15] Regardless of our logical and emotional hopes, our beautiful imaginations and our ideas of universals, we *do not* really rise above the world, and all our thoughts, as philosophers and artists, are still pretty much wholly and completely of the world as it is. We may dream and hope and visualize, but we do all this in a natural way, in a worldly way from which we cannot escape, nor should we, even in a poem or with a prayer. Whatever we know or imagine about heaven and hell comes from no other place than the world we live in.

There has been too much stress on the nature of knowledge, as a particular and as a universal, whether *neo* or *critical* realism, and not enough stress placed upon the uses of knowledge for the happiness of man and the peace of the world. The academic field has been, and is presently, unduly loaded with polemics using too much of their precious time and lives in polemics. The idea is not to eliminate or discourage the need for free and full opinion and disputation; I cannot deny something which I am privileged to use for myself, but there must be some reasonable sense in acknowledging that life is much more than an argument over the facets of a word. Language came about as a means of communication in order to feel and live better; perhaps now that this is not so essential, it has become more essential to use up life as a means of communication. Academics might finally evolve into a vast cluster of bobbing heads without bodies, each head jabbering away with every word weapon to prove its point, and all heads acknowledging that each one is logical but untenable, true but not real, possible but not probable, rationally feasible but vulnerable, and all of it not moral! Process is experience, experience is process, and knowledge, a judgment and a subject-status, is always in process. Horace M. Kallen: "The 'body of knowledge' I saw was an ever changing body in which truths of the past become errors of the present, and truths of the present are struggling not to be reduced to errors of the future."[16]

EQUITY AND POWER

LIKE EQUITY, WE demand freedom for ourselves and all too often deny it to others. Most often equity is something we extend because at the moment it is something we can *afford* to part with. In the broader and public sense, it is a word used to beguile ourselves, coming out of the "moral" fabric or soul of man that sets him apart from all the other creatures he has to live with. Not only has he eaten almost all of them in order to survive; he has exterminated many of them needlessly and cruelly, and continues to do so, even if it threatens his own survival. The drive to kill seems to be greater than the drive to live.

Like POWER, freedom has been used to bring wealth, achievement and prestige; also tyranny, slavery, poverty, and war. When the first human despot-to-be managed to hold arbitrary power over the life and death of the first slave-to-be, *power politics* departed from the natural expression of power in "territorial" dominance among animals and rose in the new technique of forcing people to become submissive and to resign themselves as slaves. When this occurred, freedom bowed its head between its knees and took its first defeat with both resignation and hope of deliverance. This resignation is the story of human slavery in its many forms, and this hope of deliverance is the story of rebellion in its many forms. Perhaps one can say that both resignation and hope of deliverance is culture itself. The ancient Greeks believed in freedom, but purely for themselves and not for those they conquered. The Romans believed in freedom, but also for themselves and not for those they conquered. They ended up as the Greeks did. Aristotle felt that the Greeks were by nature free people and the "barbarians" by nature slaves. What happened in a Greek's mind when a barbarian enslaved him is not in the record, but the Greek must surely have been amazed by this error in the cosmic scheme. It seems that people's sense of equity is first approved by what is good *for them;* when it also happens to be good for others, then one can become a philosopher and set principles. The Catholic Church, while laying down its scholastic catechisms of "goodwill to all men," made sure that every heretic was promptly done away with in order to maintain its "goodwill." Every country in history that felt the same way—freedom for it and not for its neighbors—always ended up enslaved by others or by themselves. Freedom is a reciprocal program that necessitates a naturally unconscious or rationally justifiable impartiality in its distribution. Like light, once lit, it radiates impartially in all directions.

It is essential as well as natural for every human being, and even for every other creature, to look out for itself, to possess a sufficient essence of physical and psychological power in order to preserve itself and carry on its functions and to satisfy its normal wants and desires. It is also very natural for anyone, including most other animals, to gain or enjoy a certain satisfaction in being admired by others. As the more or less helpless child feels or senses a feeling of security in being loved, in having the affection and safeguard of its parents or elders, so does the grown-up feel a satisfying pleasantness in being admired by others, in being "cradled" by group or community participation and acceptance. This is understandable, and in many ways a favorable and good factor. It appears, when we apply our focusing sense of analysis a bit closer, that power and admiration are not so strange to each other, and that there is an affinity of causation and of consequences which makes them very close relatives if not altogether offshoots of the same stem.

The possession or accretion of power most often results in some self-satisfaction to the possessor of the power, which it is reasonable to understand: this is another way of describing self-admiration. When a person seeks group-admiration of himself he usually falls more or less into the category of egotism. When a person seeks and is oversensitive, oversusceptive to the admiration of himself by others, we might state that he is receptive to flattery, to an exaggerated sense of himself he accepts as true because it suits him to accept it as such. When, as a result of a rationalistic introspection of the nature of certain events and actions, a person feels a sense of satisfaction or pleasantness about himself, we can reasonably identify this consequence as probably real and possibly good, because the consequence, in itself, qualifies him accordingly and does not reasonably include the probability of regret or disillusion. When, as a result of an intuitive or emotional thought or action, a person concludes that he is greater, more powerful, more handsome, or more wise than others, and accepts this picture of himself as a truth, we may reasonably deem this "truth" to be probably unreal and possibly compounded of regret and disillusion, depending upon the nature and intelligence of the person and the substance of his judgment.

Inasmuch as power and admiration are both complementary manifestations of the human character and experience, it does not necessarily follow that they should be subordinated to, or alienated from, each other. When a person *attempts* to rationalize an objective analysis of his own character—which requires, if it is at all possible, a great deal of courage as well as intelligence—he may realize that, in order to have any sense of power or any pleasantness owing to admiration on a real basis, he cannot subordinate his character to go counter to its own judgment, cannot truly know the satisfaction of admiration so long as there is any feeling that it is founded on superficial grounds and not *actually* acknowledged by him, rightly or wrongly, to be merited. It all depends on whether a person wants to remain an individual or get lost in the coagulated mass of groupism wherein intellectual integrity and self-identity are practically lost. Unqualified subordination surrenders the individuality of a person. Rather, it is more reasonable, considering the innate and inner nature of the individual to remain one, to seek a process of coalescence with society in which coordination takes place for mutual ends. These ends should have value and meaning to the individual and a preserving, stabilizing, yet progressive process for the society or state. Such a process does not imply either a dogmatic person or a dogmatic society; this all depends upon the character and intelligence of the individuals and the extent of the flexible and inflexible traditionalism of the society. To achieve these necessary flexible, coalescent ends for both individual and society is to provide the proper education for the individual and an empirical process for the society, so that the individuals may be able to find fruition of their knowledge, intentions, and wants in a grounded order open and flexible to judge and receive them, holding in mind as a constant factor that any order of society is only a medium or process, not an end, a process by which any number of individuals may provide for themselves a workable and an orderly way of life without diminishing the satisfactions they might possibly be able to realize within such an orderly society. Thus, freedom implies a quantum of power, true; but not all expressions of power are expressions of freedom. John Dewey wrote: "A philosophy which accepts the denotative or empirical method accepts at full value the fact that reflective thinking transforms confusion, ambiguity and discrepancy into illumination, definiteness and consistency."[17]

A completely isolated person, if we can find one, has no need of power and surely no opportunity of being admired. One who has more or less completely subordinated himself to the "will" of the community has also lost the need, to this degree, for individual power and has resigned himself to think of admiration only in terms of his society. Thus, the individual, to this extent, wastes his life away by subordination and submergence, and society becomes for him an impersonal structure for awe and reverence. "For although few man can be happy in solitude, still fewer can be happy in a community which allows no freedom of individual action."[18]

There is another facet to the nature of power. In stating that "the function of reason is to dominate experience,"[19] Santayana adds that reason should always be open to the new impressions and reinterpretations by which the principles of such reason do its reasoning. Even *reason,* though it has made us what we are today, and though it has and will always have a constant influence upon our groping nature, our decisions, and our events, should rather enlighten our way according to our natures than act as some enthroned authority to dominate the course of our events and experiences. Someone said that the heart has its reasons which reason knows not. Life is more than mere mental calculations. I feel that the function of reason cannot possibly dominate any experience, as experience seems to be dominated, so to speak, by the *idea* of domination by which the reason is being processed in any such mind. Reason itself is the result of continuums of experience, which cumulatively and concomitantly result from each other, and the "moral," or human, prerogative of dominance seems to be absent in the actual dimensional factors of the experience itself. It is the human *mind* that creates for itself this dimensional factor of dominance in the interpretation of experience and thus finds itself as the barometer of truth, while, in actuality, what is meant here is *human truth* or conceptual truth, and the observable truth according to what *we* see, feel, hear, smell, or touch. A thing which is transient like reason cannot be understood as dominating experience which has been creating the power of reason to judge it. The function of reason is not to dominate, but rather to make a thing explainable, understood, describable, evaluable. By so doing a possible reasoning may ensue that can possibly give it some identity, meaning, and value in human values, but human values that concern human beings, that can be transcended and applied to other values if a truly existentially-moral base is to be created.

Domination of any kind is averse to freedom of any kind. In the life of freedom no form of domination can be accepted or made acceptable, except to the weak, the exploited, or the sick who feed on it. The brain of man evolved to benefit the body and life of man; that it further evolved to become an instrument of domination, using reason to dominate experience or the course of events, we can easily see from how it has operated these last few thousands of years and the results of it in the world today.

Like TOLERANCE, freedom implies the spirit of good will, understanding, neighborliness, kindness, and sympathy, and yet all too often it has been used to create hate, further persecution, murder, and invent the rack, the thumbscrew, the stake, the guillotine, and the concentration camp. Paul Blanshard gives us a clear picture of tolerance in Spain today: "I was able to see for myself the

physical proof of the constant discrimination practiced against
Protestants by the Franco regime with the systematic and open
collaboration of the Catholic hierarchy."[20] Those who publicly
preach charity, goodwill and peacefulness towards others are not
always the true carriers of good intent. "The Church, as late as
the 1890s, excommunicated Catholics who ate a meal with Protestants."[21] "The textbooks in the national schools still carry openly
anti-Semitic diatribes."[22] Arthur Whitaker tells us that "there is
less religious freedom in Spain today for non-Catholics than in
any European country."[23] Faith and the Sword, the historical
twin-partners of power, have always extended the cherub trumpets
of heaven in one hand and robbed, misled, enslaved, and murdered with the other. It is written that Jesus said unto his brethren
and disciples: "Think not that I am come to send peace on the
earth: I came not to send peace, but a sword."[24] I am inclined to
feel that the one who wrote these words carried a sword, but he
was not Jesus.

Like the word PEACE, we always cherish it and all too often
overcome it because we seem not to want it, to be peaceful, and
bring conflict to our restless traits. This may be the result not of
the dominance by reason but of dominated reason.

CONCEPTS OF FREEDOM

LIKE ALL THESE words and more, freedom is a conglomerate,
affording a generous supply of particular viewpoints, purposes,
uses, explanations, excuses, and philosophies. It is hardly simple
to define, and yet it begs definition by the pointing of a finger
and saying—*This is it!*

There seems to be no life wherein the natural expression of
freedom does not exist, no matter how limited or related. Life—
"that infinitesimal ripple on the ocean of eternity"[25]—is the
Siamese twin of freedom. Michel de l'Hôpital so aptly said: "Liberty and life walk hand in hand." But while freedom identifies
the movement of life and its drive for preservation, this life also
overlays deeper-rooted multicellular drives for propagation, fu-
sion, and eventual disintegration of the individual, the continual

sacrifice for the continual overall chain of life. Thus, life becomes a continuum detonator of death, and death, or partial death, that is, the forced acceptance of undesirable conditions and situations, is what freedom, speaking for the *Ego,* does not want. As Brigid Brophy muses about life: "For the remarkable thing about life is that it not only lives but dies: and not only dies but, during life, is limited to a Self."[26]

One may say that freedom denotes the absolute, unconditional, and natural expression of pure volitionism, which is instinctive and innate in both the physical and mental manifestations of life. Another may state that freedom indicates the "divine" right of humans to move about "freely," that is, without any, or the least, external resistances or controls; his neighbor might add that this is all right provided the other does not get any bright ideas of invading his home or wanting to rob or kill him. Still another might add that he has come to the conclusion that freedom belongs only to the intelligent, the learned, the aristocratic, the crafty, or the elite, who can best use it for the "general" good; and yet the more common poor, who are supposed to be below the elite, might cry out that freedom does not imply this right to rule and exploit the many for the benefit of the few, and that it includes the right to resist, to rebel, to make the underdog an aristocrat. To try to apply the essence of freedom itself to any definition should include, as a prerequisite of its own nature at least, in terms of civilization, the merited right of freedom for all kinds of minds and all kinds of people to define, describe, or denote its nature and meaning according to their particular viewpoints and desires; and, equally, for others to accept, modify, change, reject, oppose, deny, or destroy any of these concepts. James G. Frazer, searching for some common indicator of the human psyche, wrote: "Man is a very curious animal, and the more we know of his habits the more curious does he appear. He may be the most rational of the beasts, but certainly he is the most absurd."[27]

To the primitive shaman freedom meant the opportunity to be independent by the dependence of others upon his magical charms and powers, whether sincere or deceptive, while the ordinary tribal members felt their freedom unconsciously by their more or less uncontrolled movement and deeds, so long as these were in order with tribal custom and law and were for the common good.

To the ancient despot, tyrant, or ruler who possessed naked power to do with his subjects as he pleased, freedom meant exactly this *for him,* while for his subjects it meant his death, assassination, or overthrow by another.

To the theologian freedom might mean that it really belongs to a god or gods, and the only freedom that men have is the freedom to be on trial for some mystical purpose or other, as a result of being born, or to fulfill the god's aims or rules, or to oppose the god through "sin," nonconformance, or nonacceptance, in which case the god has the freedom to reward or punish. Gerhard Szezesny writes on this subject: "A theologian is a man who never questions God, but talks about him as though divinity were an irreversible truth. He is a person who takes his stand on a certain answer before his searching, and the answers to them, have actually reached the limit of his power to question and find answers. This leaves him with a residue of unused intellectual energy, which he is free to expend on the artistic elaboration of his theses, developing ideas to ripeness as he sees fit and discarding those he thinks false."[28]

Man should cease worshipping the gods, though he is naturally free to worship them if he pleases to do so. Man should cease worshipping man, yet he can if he wants to. Man should cease worshipping, though he should have the freedom to do so, even though "a persuasive explanation for God as an autonomous personality has yet to be invented."[29] Bertrand Russell: "Every man would like to be God, if it were possible; some few find it difficult to admit the impossibility."[30] "I do not pretend to be able to prove that there is no God. I equally cannot prove that Satan is a fiction. The Christian God may exist; so may the Gods of Olympus, or of ancient Egypt, or of Babylon. But no one of these hypotheses is more probable than any other: they lie outside the region of even probable knowledge, and therefore there is no room to consider any of them."[31] Joseph Campbell: "No one of adult mind today would turn to the Book of Genesis to learn of the origins of the earth, the plants, the beasts, and man. There was no flood, no tower of Babel, no first couple in paradise, and between the first known appearance of men on earth and the first building of cities, not one generation (Adam to Cain) but a good two million must have come into this world and passed along."[32] Wallace I. Matson: "There cannot exist, compatibly with this world, a Being who is at once omnipotent, omniscient, and benevolent, where benevolence is taken in a sense intelligible to men."[33] Michael Scriven: "The most exhaustive study of all the proofs, indeed, of all the evidence for the existence of God, has thus far failed to reveal any grounds for rational belief in theism."[34] F. H. Heinemann: "The mediaeval problem whether angels are male or female no longer moves us in any way because we no longer believe in angels."[35] Edmund R. Leach: "Everyone now knows that the cosmology that is presupposed by the language of Christian utterance is quite unrelated to any empirical reality. . . . Today when the molecular biologists are rapidly unraveling the genetic chemistry of all living things—while the radio astronomers are deciphering the program of an evolving cosmos—all the marvels of creation are seen to be mechanisms rather than mysteries. Since even the human brain is nothing more than an immensely complicated computer, it is no longer necessary to invoke metaphysics to explain how it works. In the resulting mechanistic universe all that remains of the divine will is the moral consciousness of man himself."[36] George Gaylord Simpson: "We no longer live in a capricious world. We may expect the universe to deal consistently, even if not fairly, with us. . . . That is, perhaps an act of faith, but it is not superstition. Unlike recourse to the supernatural, it is validated by thousands of successful searches for verifiable causes. This view depersonalizes the universe and makes it more austere, but it also makes it dependable."[37] Goethe succinctly poeticized it:

> As anyone is,
> So is his God:
> And thus in God
> Oft strangely odd.

All this worship is not sacred, nor is the act of worshipping necessary to a respectful and well-principled life, nor to a happy and coordinative society or community. Santayana puts it clearly: "The gods are demonstrable only as hypotheses, but as hypotheses they are not gods. . . . They are symbols, not extensions, for the experience we know."[38] Gods are the good or evil of people who have lived before them. They are the mirrors wherein people can see their own reflections, not as they really are, but as they imagine themselves to be or would like to be. The mirrors of promises and hopes are the images of the gods. The real reason that the ancient Greek gods settled in Greece is because the Greeks were there before them, and the gods decided to stay because the people were so kind to them, understanding, hospitable, gay, and affectionate.

In the long historical trek of human thought and action, there appears clear that man, in his earnest plea and dream to achieve life satisfaction in *thought,* has very often denied himself, in *action,* the very satisfaction he desires. His religions, emerging from the magical ooze of protoprimitive psychic search of elemental need and desire, being in content no different from their parent and source, have misled him into nefarious philosophies that lifted his feet off the gravitated hold of earthly rationalism, elemental common sense, and simple observation onto a self-cherubed height, from which he lost sight, as he continues to do, of the life he is supposed to live, not *de*-live.

Born to eat, grow, mate, search, and laugh, he cultivated self-imposed dogmas to fast, abstain, escape, isolate, resign, and weep himself away from the natural, normal, wholesome needs that living a life demands. Instead of allowing himself to receive the openness and endlessness of the skies as his temple, he has built himself holy mausoleums to sepulcher his being and mumble words without reality or meaning to metamorphose his deluded ego into a something that can only maintain itself as a delusion at the expense of living.

"It is not the gods who have created man," wrote August Bebel, "but man who has created the gods."[39] "As far as science is concerned," wrote Richard A. Proctor, "the idea of a personal God is inconceivable."[40] Walter Russell: "There is no created universe."[41] Andrew D. White: "Just as the line of astronomical thinkers from Copernicus to Newton had destroyed the old astronomy, in which the earth was the centre, and the Almighty sitting above the firmament the agent in moving the heavenly bodies about it with his own hands, so now a race of biological thinkers had destroyed the old idea of a Creator minutely contriving and fashioning all animals to suit the needs and purposes of man."[42] Joseph K. Hart: "It was long assumed—by certain religious traditions, at any rate—that man was external to Nature: that he had been created and put *into* the world, set over against Nature, with the command to make war on Nature, to subdue and reduce to control the resources which alien Nature offered him. But . . . history and philosophy attest that man has had a natural history: he bears in his body the marks of the cosmic processes out of which have come the world, and all that is in or of the world, including himself."[43] Philip Wylie: "Only a brave man will dare to think with solemnity that he is an animal and there is in consequence no human God."[44] Ralph Waldo Emerson: "As men's prayers are a disease of the will, so are their creeds a disease of the intellect."

Whether it is pleasantly acceptable or not, we have to face up to the reality that organized and formal religion, that is, the priesthoods and their complements, in their basic frame and function, is a method of *selling*, by the priest who is the god's intercessor or *salesman*, of the favors of rewards and the fears of punishment by the god, for which man has to pay, preferably with money, but acceptable in the form of services or gifts, in addition to the usual coincidental requirements of conformance. For the wealth and existence of any priesthood cannot grow and survive on conformance or good intentions alone, but depends for its material sustenance on its followers. The many kinds of worship, as well as the god or gods worshipped, are idealistic forms of no intrinsic value to the individual or to the community, nor have these forms any necessary relationship to the esthetic and psychological enjoyments derived from the arts, nor in the forms of appreciation of beauty, symmetry, and harmony, which are derived from *natural* situations and influences. As Goethe wisely wrote: "Man is born not to solve the problem of the universe, but to find out where the problem begins and then to restrain himself within the limits of the comprehensible." Or, as the philosophical Dr. Peck wrote in his salubrious little book, *Life With Women and How to Survive It:* "People were not put on earth to achieve the ideal—only to pursue it."[45]

So great has been the impact of the sciences, especially in the Western world, moving forward together with the liberal arts and general education at an ever accelerating velocity of progression on a miraculous scale, that the neo-theologians of our present time see the writing on the wall for theology itself. Even though man may always need some tranquilizer to overcome the anticipation of death and the fear of eventual non-selfness, the confrontation with reality will necessitate an enlightenment and a scale of values that traditional theology simply can no longer provide. Religion itself is beginning to realize its own futility. Thomas J. J. Altizer writes in his essay on *America and the Future Theology:* "A theology that chooses to meet our time, a theology that accepts the destiny of history, must first assess the theological significance of the death of God. We must realize that the death of God is an historical event, that God has died in our cosmos, in our history, in our Existenz. . . . Never before has faith been called upon to negate all *religious* meaning, but it is the very radical nature of this negative movement which can prepare the way for the deepest epiphany of faith. . . . In the presence of a vocation of silence, theology must cultivate the silence of death. To be sure, the death to which theology is called is the death of God. Nor will it suffice for theology to merely accept the death of God. If theology is truly to die, it must *will* the death of God, must *will* the death of Christendom, must freely choose the destiny before it, and therefore must cease to be itself. Everything that theology has thus far become must now be negated; and negated not simply because it is dead, but rather because theology cannot be reborn unless it passes through, and freely wills, its own death and dissolution."[46]

Of course, this is obviously a negative attitude on the part of some theologians who have applied the stethoscope and declared God dead. To begin with, this is a postmortem on a prior fantasy. It is rationally absurd to declare one dead whom it has not been possible to establish as having lived. It seems to appear that the "God is dead" movement is the wailing lament of theologians

who, realizing that God is no longer here to safeguard their
securities and dignities as theologians, it is now wise and practical
to dump him in favor of something else more social, political, or
economic to sustain them. It is the death pang not of God but
of theology itself.

If man must worship anything, he should worship *life*. This
can be called sacred. Albert Schweitzer calls this the "reverence
for life." The breath we breathed a moment ago will never return. Gods, religions, theologies, are ideas in the mind of man
and exist only as long as the ideas persist in maintaining them.
Relating to the history of the gods, Homer W. Smith states: "Historians may debate the relative importance of ideas as against
other factors in the shaping of this history; but any application
of the principle of determinism implies that history would have
been different had the determinants been different—among other
things had man's ideas been different."[47]

CONCEPTS ON LIVING

LIFE, IN ITS naked objectivity, is the reality we cannot
afford to gamble with, to sacrifice in order to sustain ideality.
The ultimate ideal, if we have to have one, is the sacredness and
regard we attach to life, in which our body, being a transient,
happens to participate. This participation demands our reverence
for it in order to allow it to permeate its flow within and about
us. Science may lead us into the house where life lives and where
we may come to see its face more closely, its nakedness, its parts,
but the intellectual enjoyments and all their attributes in trying
to encompass a wise fullness of living are things which we cannot
depend upon science to hand us. Science can lead us, show us,
make it known to us, but we, gaining this knowledge and intelligence through science and its reflections, must find its meaning
and value, if there is any. In its meaning we may find its value,
with sufficient fortitude to try to understand its vicissitudes and
eventualities, and enjoy whatever good it offers as much as we
can—while we can. We cannot be permanent residents in this
house of life, regardless of our ideals and imagery. At least let us

live as good and wise tenants. There seems to be no rent to pay when we leave nor any rent to collect in departing.

Michael Scriven: "A more interesting way of supporting the idea that death is an illusion is the usual religious claim that we achieve personal immortality through the survival of a spirit or soul conceived as the essence of personality. . . . There is not only no shred of evidence to support such a claim, but it is clearly contrary to the evidence that greets our eyes and instruments if we care to watch the entity we have known dissolve in its component parts in the process of decay. . . . A person is one particular combination of his components, with a certain gradually varying character, memories, skills, form, and actual history. When that combination no longer exists, the person does not exist either. . . Memories are memories of a man who is dead, and the existence of those memories is not his existence. . . . Fascinating though the literature of survival research is, then, it does not provide us with anything more than a thorough education about the experimental investigation of allegedly supernatural phenomena. And there is no other source of evidence to support belief in our survival of bodily death. We die, and then we rot; and that is the only reward or retribution for our life as a whole that we shall ever receive. The meaning of man's existence lies within his life and not beyond the grave."[48]

I think Loren Eiseley expresses the point beautifully in his poem *Epitaph:*

> Stranger, be not afraid because you follow
> Fast on my heels yet know the light of day.
> The earth takes back the garment that it lent us
> To clothe the hedgehog or the bright blue jay.
>
> All this I was before the living trapped me
> And hurled me from deep night into the sun.
> I have gone home because a snowstorm called me.
> Say to my love there is no other one.[49]

To the metaphysician freedom might mean his own "moral" right, established by his own idea, to prove by logic, if he can, what the theologians believe in and what has already been exposed to be untenable and fallacious, wrong by nature and experience, and further to prove the axiom that two errors do not mean, by a combination of both, that both or either is true. A merry-go-round narration of metaphysical conjectural ideality is a linguistic vehicle on which we are taken for a ride, going nowhere. Self-awareness is the causative event of the inherent trait of a *separate* animal's biological freedom to exist as a separate unit or self, and it made possible the series of processes which eventuated in man becoming a philosopher. When he became a metaphysician, he had already and unfortunately forgotten or lost sight of his biological origin and the field in which he exists. Albert Einstein said: "The most beautiful thing we can experience is the mysterious. . . . It is the source of all art and science."[50] Einstein was not talking metaphysics; he meant by this not the mysticism of the East, of Zen, of the Essenes or the Apostles, but the humility of the human mind to realize, as its life asset, the preponderable unknowable that always lies ahead in the mists of knowledge-to-be and the provinces of man's intellect-to-be in trying to visualize its immensities, its vastnesses, and the unfolding drama of the cosmos with its seemingly never ending play. Dostoevsky wrote: "Man needs the unfathomable and the infinite just as much as he does the small planet which he inhabits." This is understandable and sustains the human drive to unlimit its efforts to extend itself, through poetry as well as his sciences, into the unknown, the mysterious, and the beckoning magnetic call of new experiences. This we have always done, whether conscious of it or not, in the course of living.

Edmund W. Sinnott, the noted botanist and biologist, writes in his *The Bridge of Life:* "In this dark mystery of death, what has the philosophy of life to offer for man's consolation?—But for a man who faces death it is small consolation to know that the reason he must go is simply to make room for someone else. . . . What makes many still believe in some sort of endless life is that mortality does not make sense to them. . . . There is something in us that rebels at such a fate."[51]

True. I also wish I could live forever. There is nothing to be gained by dying and everything to lose, the loss being so total

that one can really become fearfully stunned just thinking about
it. Here Sinnott departs from his botany and biology and turns
metaphysician and mystic. As he presents it, immortality means
that all man's thoughts, hopes, fears, aspirations, and spirituality
are based on biological explanation. He finds comfort and assurance in the belief in immortality by a pseudo-optimum that can
never escape from pretext, and in the hopeful self-solace that life
has meaning only if some immortal self-identity can be maintained to justify the psychic and intuitional aspirations of humanity.

For thousands of years the peoples of the world *have* believed
in immortality, unquestionably and fanatically. They have created multitudinous organized and formal religions for this express purpose. Yet they have not realized the brotherhood of love
Dr. Sinnott so idealistically envisions as brought about through
such belief.

Only the realization of the sacredness of the one life we can
honestly profess to know can serve as a principle of appreciation
and ethics for peaceful living, bring a surcease to mutual hostility, and lead to activated evaluation of the unrecoverable life
that is ours. Or perhaps the scientific advance of weapons of total
destruction, with their potential of total planetary disaster, may
succeed where reason and aspirations have failed in persuading
humanity, if only out of sheer hysterical fear, to police and constrain its innate desire for aggression, to channel this biological
drive into constructive and elevating values, principles, and
actions.

Sinnott proceeds further to resolve "purpose" into a creativity
of God because behind the "purpose" is the want to live forever.
In the stance of a metaphysical philosopher, he is trying, if
illogically, to find a needed key to bring humanity to its senses
and give it some wholesome and workable direction toward unity
and a universal order of peace. Unfortunately, this is purely an
a priori conclusion, stemming from desire, not knowledge. It is
the rationale that created religion and its progenitor, magic. We
see it also in the desire for, and acceptance of, mysticism and the
unknown as the optimum release to comfort man in his struggle
to refuse to lose his identity in death.

Sinnott's "purpose" is intrinsically an intent, conscious or unconscious, to use the lofty and inspired purposeness in man to signify an attempt built on rationalism and newer truths, which could, disregarding the obsolescence of traditionally religious factors, justify the belief and acceptance of some kind of god principle that has within itself an assurance of immortality for man through some mystical, if as yet unknown, psychic process. The acceptance of such an idea of immortality based on some "natural" and "scientific" probability of future "truth" still to be revealed or discovered is considered sufficient justification to warrant a philosophic outlook that offers self-comfort through faith in science both as known to us today and as to be discovered in the future.

Like Descartes, Sinnott simply cannot establish God on the principle of self-identity and idea alone. World peace and individual happiness can be founded only on present objectivity; it cannot be founded on supposition and the a priori deducing of science to sustain intuition and desire. The mind of one and the minds of many, through continued and greater education and enlightenment as to the value of *this* life, might bring about an abatement of man's fears and a relaxation of hostilities. Even this is an unpredictable factor. The sacredness of the present hour in each life can be the only objective key to any value of future indeterminabilities. Confucious advised his people not to worry about immortality or be concerned with death, since we know nothing about either, but to cultivate good living, happy days, and societal order and peace while we live. Socrates said the same. How can we fathom the mysteries of death, Confucius asks, when we have still to learn how to live better in this life? Sinnott regretfully takes the same course as Kant, from the limitations and imperfections of reason to sustain, by reason and lack of absoluteness, a visionary unknown and a probable absolute merely established on desirability. Thus, by the back way of idealistic optimism, contrary to idealistic pessimism, he becomes what he does not want to be—an existentialist *with hope* that future science may yet bear him out and prove the existentialist to be despairing needlessly and weeping in error. It brings to mind a line from a poem of Pablo Neruda: "A garden I tend whose blossoms never existed."[52]

Franklin L. Baumer gives us the apologist's and the metaphysician's view: "In consequence of the decay of religious belief in modern times there is no answer to the meaning of existence, no meaning to participate in."[53] What exactly does Professor Baumer mean by *existence?* Does he *really* know of *any* existence other than that we experience in our lives here and now, or of any other existence to which we may be related? And what exactly does he mean by *participation* in this existence? Has religion, theology, and metaphysics given him *really* and *certainly* the "answer" he is seeking? Assuredly, he *is* participating in the metaphysical solaces and hopes that religion and theology have extended to him, but any such participation is occurring right here on earth, in his very material existence in a very material earth and universe. The meaning that Professor Baumer seeks is not truth, certainty, or verifiability, but merely a *psychological assent* to his own personal desires, his own hope to extend and perpetuate, regardless of reality, his own egocentricity. His desire to make his own personality a "forever" situation seems to be the only meaning he could possibly attach to any acceptable view of existence, and he most certainly merits the freedom to feel and believe as he does, but intelligence and honesty must concede that what man thinks and believes belongs to him, and any such thought or belief does not become, *ipso facto,* a principle of certainty for the universe. Descartes identified *his* own existence by *his* own thought: by do soing, he established a *man's* thought, not God's.

Professor Baumer quotes Joad: "It is only in so far as men accept the existence of this immaterial world [i.e., a religious or metaphysical view of the universe] in their theory and seek to increase the degree of their awareness of and contact with it in practice, that the human mind advances in respect of knowledge, the human character in respect of goodness and the human spirit in respect of the perception and love of beauty."[54] I wonder if Professor Joad ever tripped over a rock and found the rock and his pain immaterial? I wonder if Professor Joad ever learned any true knowledge that was immaterial itself or came from immaterial sources? I wonder if he ever came across goodness that did not emanate from people or things, and the experiences of both, and both very material? I wonder if he ever *saw* or *imagined* anything beautiful or lovable that did not reflect some material thing or event, even his own thought of beauty from his own very material mind and body?

EXISTENTIALISM AND SOME CONCEPTS ON DEATH

To THE EXISTENTIALIST freedom is a mere word signifying nothing, since, he contends, we are all a "something about nothing." He claims we are objects without essence or sense-meaning, pointless creatures that seem to be unable to "touch" or identify a purpose or end in just "floating" about the transitional and brief period of life in a purely physical merry-go-round, which keeps going, as far as he is concerned, nowhere.

Existentialism is a psychological mechanism, modern by name but ancient in expression, which can be used as a pillow for man to cry his eyes out on. Gerhard Szczesny writes: "Existentialism is a philosophy born of Christian despair, a way of thinking that has retained Christian metapsychology while abandoning Christian metaphysics. The feeling of anxiety and lostness that is the mark of this philosophy is rooted in the fear of the secularized Christian of never being released from his subjectivity. Thus arises the alternative between an heroic nihilism, which affirms this fate, and a sentimental positivism which flees from it and which yearns to rediscover the secure refuge of the Christian notion of the world."[55]

The modern version of existentialism came about due to a European century of constant war and upheaval, despoiling people, juggling of nations and borders and populations, wastage, tragedies, during which time the constant disarrangements, dispersions, uprootings, and the knocking about of people from pillar to post, the endless problems of the squeeze between industry and human numbers, the transformation of the Continent from the individualistic laissez faire and "little village" peacefulness and cobbled roads to the complex, pressurizing, steaming, pushing, regimenting forces of modern industrialization, ultimately bringing about a more or less resigned futility and meaninglessness for people and toward things in general. Heinemann: "It [Existentialism] represents one of the essential forms of West European philosophy in the age of European collapse. German *Existenzphilosophie*, French *Existenialisme* and Italian *Esistenzialismo*, though profoundly differing in form and content, have this in common—that they arise in the wake of national catastrophes."[56] Thus Jean Wahl speaks for existentialism: "Why we are flung into the world, we do not know. . . . We are, without our finding any reason for our being; hence, we are existence without essence."[57]

Jules Henry, observing the helplessness and despair of the aged and infirm, institutionalized, losing their self-identity as persons, as people, and reflecting upon the inherent needs of people to feel secure in life and death as exemplified in primitive ancestor worship, kinships, totemistic clans, writes: "Contemporary man suffers from the certainty that when dead *he will mean nothing to everybody*, and from the anxiety that even while alive he may come to mean *nothing to anybody*."[58] This is so well stated that I sense in it a feeling of anxiety that impregnates itself within the philosophy of existentialism, a philosophy which, consciously or unconsciously, keeps brooding and finds no solution in bringing about a more stable and normal, even stoical, attitude toward life and its potential satisfactions.

Life and freedom exist in the present, in the moment, neither in the past or future. Freedom is the present field wherein the senses of man and the experiences of living things in general can carry on their normal ways of living and *continue* what Julian Huxley described as "the whole of phenomenal reality" as a single process.[59] Existentialism seems to dam up this normal flow of evolutional activity in the cultural field of man, and what interjects itself as a deterring or despairing and thus destructive force in the cultural levels affects in turn the biological field and level *within* which the cultural processes of man and of man and his ecological framework operate. The existentialist takes the past and laments upon it and thus enchains his freedom to his memories; he has become "nothing" to the present because he has submitted to the past and acknowledges his "nothingness." The monk pawns his liberty for something to receive or expect, in compensation, after he dies. He, too, enchains his freedom to a state of non-being, something supposedly nonexistent and which only exists in the resignation of his present thought to a future hope. In both such directions freedom cannot move as life normally directs it. When a person has so stifled freedom, either in memories of the past or in future expectations, as practically to void its expression for the present, we can say that the essence and power of freedom have been set in a dying condition through the principle of non-use. A continued nonuse of the power of freedom can only bring about stagnation and degeneration. The spirited sense of *wanting* to live and enjoy livingness, of *wanting* to understand and thus further the ability to accept and participate in life's various potentials and eventualities of *wantable* things and understand the necessary travail and compromises that make up the interdependencies of people and things, is stifled.

Jesuit Father Boros adds his bit to the existentialist line: "If human death has no meaning, then the whole of life is nothing but emptiness."[60] The amazing deduction from this is that life, which we know *something* about, is empty and without meaning, while death, of which we know *nothing*, has meaning. Confucius taught that it is silly to give any thought or even any meaning to death when we hardly know much about life. Father Boros continues that "to be forgetful of death is to be forgetful of life, whereas thinking of one's death is an act in which life begins once more to appear as a source of light."[61] Spinoza taught that it is stupid to waste one moment meditating about death, and Father Boros is very wasteful, especially when he knows nothing about death or about any "light" that emanates from dying. Belief and truth are hardly logical and compatible companions.

Explaining Heidegger's thought, Jean Wahl writes: "One does not need to believe oneself immortal to be afraid of death, and that finitude, the fact of disappearance and end, despite all the epicurean considerations, remains an agonizing fact. This is what Heidegger tries to unveil or make us aware of."[62] Here again we note the lament for the loss of Olympus. We *know* that death will eventually overtake us, and this awareness is certainly not pleasant; to those whose minds constantly mentate about death it becomes an agonizing experience, which often brings about, as a consequence, a neurotic and ailing psychosomatic pathology. The question arises: Why do we have to think about "death" as a constant, negative factor *while we live?* The theologian threatens us with the "judgments" that arrive with death; the existentialist wants us to weep about it while we live. Both are pessimistic and negative factors; besides, they get us nowhere. Both are anti-natural thoughts, which are not beneficial to our health and to the time we actually do manage to live. Coue, the French psychologist, advised people to say to themselves: "Every day in every way I am getting better and better!"—which is a daily reminder that there is still something wrong with them. While we live we are able to be free to express life; death cannot even be an afterthought.

Edgar Herzog, in following Jung's psychoanalytic psychology about death and dreams, writes that one matures when he becomes more conscious of the horror and fear of death; that, to the extent a person thinks of life in terms of death and death in terms of life, to this extent he becomes more human and less of a primitive. The protoprimitive and the protohominid, being indifferent and practically unconscious of the meaning and eventuality of death in the same manner as animals in general, are therefore, according to Herzog, *"pre-*human" and without the need of the emotional and mental requisitions and relaxation-comforts that came later with the advanced primitives, and still later with the evolution and establishment of the traditional and historic religions. Somewhere in the dim paleolithic stretches of time the preprimitive, by the killing of his food animals and the placating of their spirits to avoid vengeance, gradually became aware of his own death, which he considered to be an unnatural accident due to evil spirits. Professor Herzog states: "The capacity to feel horror at death is one of the most essential characteristics which distinguish man from the animals. . . . The animal does not experience death as something which confronts it like an abyss and engenders immeasurable horror because it seems beyond all comprehension . . . it is *pre-*human. It is only on the basis of horror that a man can develop an inner attitude to the fact of death, and only when he has done this can life itself emerge into consciousness."[63]

This outlook affords the Jungian school of psychology and its disciples the basis for their apologetics to justify the need of religiousness in order to "neutralize" death by its acknowledgment and acceptance "within life" or "continued life." To the Jungian, death thus becomes a possible "self-absorbing" concomitance (like the coexistence of the body and blood of Christ in the eucharistic bread); also it becomes "phasic." It may be true that man may be the only animal extant that *knows* about death, and that because of this consciousness, anticipation, and awareness of death he fears it and is horrified by it. Religion, therefore, becomes essential, the Jungians claim, because it provides peace of mind by "overcoming" the extinctional finality of death and brings it within life itself. Therefore, they feel, the contemplation of death is indicative of a rising maturity, and faith in this outlook and belief is a psychic necessity to a peaceful and requited life.

As stated above, Spinoza wrote that one should not waste life by thinking about death. Confucius, when asked about immortality, questioned the importance and need of thinking about death as something we know nothing about, while it *is* more important to learn more about life and how to live it better and more fully. Even Socrates, when asked about immortality, replied that whether there is immortality or not does not matter while we live, for we have no knowledge of it except through desired intuition, but it is essential that one live a good life. No doubt the other animals and creatures, not being aware of coming death, are better off, as whatever time they do exist is completely dedicated to living. Voltaire, comparing animals and men, wisely wrote: "Animals have these advantages over man: They never hear the clock strike. They die without any idea of death, they have no theologians to instruct them, their last moments are not disturbed by unwelcome and unpleasant ceremonies, their funerals cost them nothing, and no one starts lawsuits over their wills."

Man's brain, by becoming aware of death, has brought about more untimely death into the living time of people than any other factor. Man, as a result and to this extent, wastes away his life by the constant *pre*-dying of life by the consciousness of the

fear and horror of death and the dread of extinction of his identity as he is in life in spite of his beliefs. If the Jungians feel that
it is more "normal" to experience constantly the fear and horror
of death to reach maturity, then it would seem to be better to
try to live more fully without being so "normal" as the Jungians
would desire us to be.

The fear and horror of viewing a corpse, the desire to finalize
the physical extinction and dissolution of the dead by deep
burial, cremation, by allowing dogs and wolves (the symbols of
death-demons) to devour the dead, the murder of the aged, the
very sick and the dying, the appeasement of the animal and plant
spirits before killing and consuming them to avoid vendetta by
these spirits upon the killers and eaters, the dancing and jumping
on the fresh grave to make sure the dead stays down, the wearing
of black to imitate the darkness so that the evil spirits may not
find them, the exhumation of the dead remains to give them their
seasonal food and drink so that the dead may not complain or
reek evil upon them, and a thousand other customs and rituals—
all these signify, according to Herzog, that the primitive distrusted
the dead and so feared them that he was compelled to use magic,
utterance, and ceremony to overcome the possible evils and
demons of the underworld of the dead. This may be true, but it
is also true that this fear of the dead has not left us; the modern
as well as the primitive still fears the dead, and customs in many
parts of the world today still continue these same rituals. It would
be difficult to find anyone who would be willing to spend a night
in the middle of a cemetery, primitive or modern, parishioner or
priest, the illiterate or the intellectual, in spite of all the faith
and belief in the various religions and their assurances of phasic
elements in immortality through the consciousness of death within
living time. It is this very horror and fear of the dead that provided the physical and psychical impetus and conditions for the
origins and evolution of religion, all the way from preprimitive
times to the present day.

Man's anticipation of death, his consciousness that death will
overcome him sooner or later, the dreaded fear of losing forever
his ego-social participations and enjoyments, the very oblitera-
tion of his personality—all these fears rose out of his self-aware-

ness, when he became conscious of his own consciousness. The ensuing evolution of his intelligence gave him increasingly the ability to make reflective and conscious deductions on the basis of his experiences—the power to reason—and from this followed the extension of the mind and its adaptabilities through reason, which carried on the evolution of his mental and emotional faculties to self-awareness, the mirror of his own ego and self-identity. Bernard Campbell: ". . . it seems that human perception and human reason, acting under the competitive conditions of organic life, are the twin bases from which we may suppose the growth of human material culture to have developed. . . . Man has learned to project into a cultural form most of the activities of his own brain. Man's unique achievement was, therefore, in the first place, the extension of his motor function and, in the second place, the extension of his sensory and neural functions, all by means of a material culture."[64] One of the significant products of this process was the awareness of coming death, and because of this fear and the daily fear of survival, all his religious and theological philosophies and structures came into existence.

Alex Comfort gives his view: "When it comes to the crunch, we personally will die, and Man will eventually die out. It is to unpleasantnesses like these that religion of the factual type (by denying the facts), philosophy (by suggesting that we should not feel they matter), and intellectual demagogy of the Teilhard variety (by making an inspiring noise) have all tried to apply a salve. None have quite succeeded, partly because they fail in integrity, but also because they lack pity. It is no answer to the dislike I feel for the idea of dying that my genes will persist to produce higher achievements, or that my thoughts will join a kind of moral Van Allen belt around the human race. My dislike of the idea remains as deep-seated as that of any Australopithecine —and had an Australopithecine seen a vision of his posterity possessing the world he would still have disliked not being there to join in. Death, our own and others, means separation, and we are social animals for whom 'parting is all we know of heaven and all we need of hell.' . . . There are times when we ought to weep —and there are times when a frank admission of loneliness or fear is more 'human' than any amount of inspiring pollyanna."[65]

This awareness of death, evolved through the processes of perception, natured and nurtured out of the particular experiences of a particular animal in particular situations and environments, proceeded to use this perception and reasoning process to outwit and circumvent death. The expected separation from his social belongings and the contemplation of nonentity in death brought about an introspective and reflective sense of loneliness, caused anxieties and neuroses, in dream and in conscious life. The egg and the sperm that gave eventual birth to religion evolved out of man's mind and the fears it nurtured by the fears of uncontrollable external and internal factors interacting within and between his own organic neural system and the various environments within which and with which he was compelled to exist through necessitated compatibilities in order to survive. Loren Eiseley muses: "For the first time in four billion years a living creature has contemplated himself and heard with a sudden unaccountable loneliness, the whisper of the wind in the night reeds."[66]

One should not try to drown his sorrows in the disquieting springs of the past or etherealize his own realness into the fog of being absorbed into some blissful and fragrant veil of mysticism. One should try to live *now*, his ideas should be applicable to his present day and condition, and in this way he will express and value his freedom in terms of the present and possibly be able to gain the proper heights in freedom value. He will find that the meanings of origins and goals can be best synchronized by the *process* of the present. If we allow our stereoscopic mentality to fuse our images of the past with those of our imagination and expectancies of the future, the past giving us some deep chromes and the future the softening light pastels, perhaps our painting of the present would neither be too dark to see nor too light to see. If man has no eyes in back of his head, and if his eyes can only limit his vision of distance, perhaps it is because his natural experiences to survive forced him always to place priority upon the solution to his present needs and immediate environment.

What is death, anyway? Is it something objective, a definitive phase we meet up against, pass through or over or beyond? For thousands of years men have been told over and over again that it is something "objective," that it is a "phase" we pass through and beyond, and this "telling" came from people like ourselves, living people who knew about death as much as we do—nothing. For how can anyone know anything about anything in a state of nothingness or nonexistence? True, there are many tales, tall and short, of spirits communicating or returning from the world of the dead, but let's not kid ourselves, they remain tales for the gullible who seek to believe in them.

However, this "objectivity" of death, phasing itself into a fear of death and its possible consequences and uncertainties, gave birth to the most profitable and most cruel enterprises, which gave nothing for something, and this something was not only the material things of money and property, but this something was the very lives of people who were willing to buy a hope and a dream and waste their lives away hoping and dreaming.

What is death? It is nothing, absolutely nothing, the same nothingness we were before we were born. Why do we not ask ourselves: the world itself was born perhaps four or five billions of years ago; what were *we* doing all these billions of years before we were born? We just didn't exist, anymore than the coming newborn of next year exist today. This we can understand, observe, sense, and recapitulate. What we apply to our prebirth period we can safely apply to our afterlife period: nonexistence. Therefore, there is life and existence, and outside of existence we can only conceive nonexistence, for a thing exists or it does not. There is life or the absence of life. Dying is part of existence, but death itself indicates a state of nonexistence, or the absence of existence, and is thereby reduced to nothingness, absolutely nothing so far as *we* are concerned. Anything else will always be a mere presumption, a self-beguiling and a tendency to waste some part of our real and only existence even thinking about it. As we are transient beings, let's live while in transit, as we can do nothing else, for when we no longer exist, we cannot look back and reflect on what we should have done when we could have done it; we just will not *be*. Life is something, and all we have got. Death is nothing, and nothing to get.

This may be judged by many to be moving words about to give us, psychologically, a greater consoling or futility effect. This may or may not be so, but one thing is sure: Regardless of how we try to make concepts, believe in whatever we want to believe in, fear and submit ourselves to illusions we condition ourselves to see as if they were real and not imaginary, we are still talking about something which does not exist, and that which is not cannot be. Where before we were a whole, a throbbing, breathing, conscious, thinking, consuming, disposing whole, a thinking whole made up of unthinking parts, in dying we become the separated, unthinking, unconscious parts. This is a judgment that confines life to existence and not a predying to life. Psychologically and in reality, life is brought face to face with itself, something which exists and is real and not a dream. For life is not a dream to awaken from. Life *is* real; the self *is* real; let them always *be together,* a *living whole.* The disintegration of death is taking place, and people, especially the younger people, are beginning to realize more and more that life is the only concern for there is nothing else to be concerned about. Herein is the sprouting root of the new biophilosophy— thinking and doing about life and living—and herein is the constantly present and the constantly ultimate nexus between man, his life, and the world.

It does not seem reasonable to use philosophy as a couch to crouch on and cry, in fear of oneself, nor is it necessary. Whatever life is, it is all we have, and it is a pity to waste one moment of it exhorting lamentations and crying with words that we are not gods, that imperfect and limited living things cannot be happy, and that we should all sit under a banyan tree, like Buddhists, and beg for the void to overtake us or absorb us, Nirvana-style. Morris Raphael Cohen said wisely: "We must learn to live in an imperfect world, though we dare not relax the effort to make it better."[67] Realizing the brevity of life without immortality, Santayana wrote: "What matters then is quality. The reasonable and humane demand to make of the world is that such creatures as exist should not be unhappy and that life, whatever its quantity, should have a quality that may justify it in its own eyes."[68] Professor Cohen again tells us: "The philosopher who piously visits the cemetery of human hopes may well shake his head. And this attitude is not dismissed by calling it a counsel of despair. There is strength as well as solace in fearlessly look-

ing at things as they are. But in the end no philosophy is really
humane, or avoids needless cruelty, unless it recognizes the inevitability of human suffering, defeat, death, and destruction
and provides some anodyne through wisely cultivated resignation.
. . . So long as human beings lack omniscience they will lack
omnipotence and will therefore have to face insuperable difficulties and evils. . . . No man is as happy and energetic as the one
who is a glad slave to his beloved, whether it be a person or a
great impersonal cause. For this reason it would be hazardous
to deny that human beings have probably derived as much happiness from accepting their lot as from efforts, so often tragically
vain, to improve it. . . . Doubtless there is such a thing as unwise
submission. But who will deny that there is also an unwise ob-
stinacy in refusing to accept our limitations and thus wasting
life in efforts that are fruitless if not worse?"[69] Santayana returns
to say that "the darkest spots are in man himself, in his fitful,
irrational disposition."[70] Thus the greatest problem of man is
man himself. As Brigid Brophy notes: "What we will not do
without is *an* enemy,"[71] that man finds himself a devil or an evil
within himself. "God and Satan are projections of our contradictory emotions toward a single personage."[72]

People, especially when old, are naturally frightened when
they sense that immortality is merely a hope, a man-dreamed-up
hope. "The panic," writes Santayana, "which seems to seize some
minds at the thought of a merely natural existence is something
truly hysterical; and yet one wonders why ultimate peace should
seem so intolerable to people who not so many years ago found
a stern religious satisfaction in consigning almost the whole
human race to perpetual torture, the Creator, as Saint Augustine
tells us, having in his infinite wisdom and justice devised a special
kind of material fire that might avail to burn resurrected bodies
forever without consuming them."[73] It is not heaven that a good
Catholic is concerned about; what he fears is a miscalculation in
the masses that might deliver him to hell. As I have written in a
previous book, the God-loving people are in no hurry to meet
Him. They want to live. Pascal wrote: "When I consider the
short duration of my life, swallowed up in the eternity before
and after, the little space which I fill, and even can see, engulfed

in the infinite immensity of spaces of which I am ignorant, and which know me not, I am frightened, and am astonished at being here rather than there; for there is no reason why here rather than there, why not now rather than then. . . . The eternal silence of these infinite spaces frightens me."

This is understandable and affects us all. The brain of man has brought about many things, among them theology and the awareness and anticipation of death. We must save ourselves from being destroyed by our own brain. We must regain some balance of the biological pre-Sapian drives that may possibly collate our intelligence to bring reason within reality and return life to itself. Theodosius Dobzhansky laments: "Man no longer enjoys the certitude that he stands at the center of a universe created especially for his sake or the twin certitude that this universe is presided over by a Power which can be implored or propitiated and which cares for man, individually and collectively."[74] Kallen comments: "I do not see that, first and last, any human life requires a sanction from any other existence, human or nonhuman, natural, supernatural, or unnatural. Nor do I find this a cause for tears and not for laughter: Existentialist tearfulness seems to me as comic as perennial philosophy's cheerfulness."[75]

Jean Wahl states that "Heidegger echoes the ancient theme of wisdom: wisdom is always the acceptance of what is."[76] However, it is a matter of judgment as to what to accept, and that acceptance of the natural order does not mean that man cannot allow himself within the natural order to improve his lot and extend his freedom for his own betterment. Acceptance is merely the acceptance of something that is what we *think* it is. Our view should not be accepted as the *absolute* truth of what it may be. Acknowledging an existence is not implied approval of its content or verifying its actual reality. If men and their ideals have always accepted things as they are, we would today still be climbing the steps of ziggurats at Sumer and Babylon, burying our employees in our graves, and parading the Olympian gods on Fifth Avenue. There may be wisdom in our perspective but our perspective is peculiarly our own, conditioned by ourselves in flux with our environment and experiences; it is our own attitude towards existence; it does not necessarily identify the true aspects of *the* existence but what we are either trying to find as the "truth" or what we are trying to make it appear to be to satisfy our own wants and desires. The very existence of freedom implies a *movement* of judgments and acceptances, the potential of change and the creativity of ideality, as well as what existence may be in itself and what it means to us. We are not qualified to sit in *absolute* judgment about anything.

The existentialist is the psychological result of not being able to fill the vacant spaces made vacant with the twilight of the gods, of our inner desires not only for controlling nature but even superseding it or overcoming it with immortalities and humanly-divine images and meanings. In slowly realizing this vacuum laid bare by the flight of the angels and their heavens, and that we are just coming and going little parts of the natural realm, which is most emphatically not noble or aristocratic, and are thus forced to join the "parade" of all the parts of nature, man finds himself without an Olympian throne and demoted to the curriculum of a muskrat or a fish. Transition and change, transientness, often mean pain of parting, and this pain of parting is expressed in existentialism.

When Jean-Paul Sartre states that "a man is involved in life, leaves his impress on it, and outside of that there is nothing,"[77] we can agree or disagree with him, depending upon our religious feelings and beliefs. It would follow, to be wise, that man should make the most of his life and leave the rest to the gods. It does not matter whether we are nothing after we die; it does matter that we are something while we are alive. What constitutes making the most of life is as varied as there are individuals in the world. That people are different, even though similar, is axiomatic. Theodora Kroeber, sensing the ways of Ishi, the "wild" Indian, would have him say, "I am one; you are others. This is in the inevitable nature of things."

Sartre says: "To choose to be this or that is to affirm at the same time the value of what we choose, because we can never choose evil. We always choose the good, and nothing can be good for us without being good for all."[78] Again Ishi, the "wild" one and last remnant of his tribe, could say: "What you have chosen for yourselves in coming to California may be good for you, but your choice has exterminated my people, burned my villages, raped our daughters, driven us into the hills without food or shelter, forced our babies to wither and die and our women to kill themselves. I am the last of my kind and clan. I cannot rightly say that what you have chosen is good for anyone except for yourselves, if you consider robbery, murder, genocide and a total lack of sympathy for fellow-creatures, as being 'good'!"

Sartre continues: "If existence really does precede essence, man is responsible for what he is. Thus, existentialism's first move is to make every man aware of what he is and to make the full responsibility of his existence rest on him. And when we say that a man is responsible for himself, we do not only mean that he is responsible for his own individuality, but that he is responsible for all men."[79] Thus, Sartre exposes his own want of cosmocentricity; it is not enough that Sartre makes each person responsible as if each one of us is born with a specific G.I. package of pre-ordained responsibilities, not taking into account the infinite, fortunate and unfortunate, lucky or unlucky variations of congenital equipment and fortunate and unfortunate, favorable and unfavorable experiences of childhood, the almost infinite variety of perspectives and judgments toward any given object or event. Sartre ordains that each of us is responsible for all others—thus each one should, like Jesus dying on the Cross to save mankind, consider himself the patriarch and savior of all others. I can assure you that I would not feel good inside to be or feel responsible for what Hitler did!

Sartre states: "Man is nothing else but what he makes of himself. Such is the first principle of existentialism."[80] In a way man has really no choice but to make of himself whatever he does make of himself as each person lives his own life and nobody else can live it for him. The question arises whether man is free or unfree to do what he in his own mind and desire wants to make of himself. Man is not an isolated god looking down from the summit of the world and able to choose whatever and whichever direction he wants to, and take from the world what he wants to, and do with it what he wants to. Most people are caught in the trap of the helplessly cohesive group or pattern from which it is often most difficult to extricate oneself if one so desires. Every society, religion, culture, polity, even business, all poured into one porridge, constrain, very often emasculate, deter a person, and minimize the faculty of freedom to make the most of life. A person is not only an animal, born with natural longings and wishes; he is also a product of cultural habit, whatever it may be, for better or worse. He becomes a pattern, a helpless pattern, often neurotic and antinatural, helplessly serving a culture and not himself. To place the responsibility solely upon the individual person, notwithstanding explainable considerations, is to become blind to the potential evil that any society or culture, or for that matter, civilization itself, can make a person into. Sartre, like the Catholic God, creates man as he is, makes him responsible for his own creation, and then would condemn and hold him liable for any "evils" or "sins" inherent in the creation itself. Man can only and possibly make of himself that which he is in reality capable of being, and this is affected and determined by his heritage, his experiences and environment, even his luck (call it what you may). He has not chosen his heritage, and most often, due to economic and cultural constriction and limitation, cannot even choose his possible experiences.

It is freedom, not for freedom's sake as Sartre contends, but for our own sakes, that can make possible a greater periphery of action in which man and men can make the most of their lives and produce a field—society or culture—where freedom breathes through the consciousness of individuals to bring about more equitable levels of action and the opportunity to achieve some reasonably fulfilled want and satisfaction. A dictum of judgment could not achieve this, but education, knowledge, reason, enlightenment, political and economic liberation, and security, might. This calls not for despair and self-pity, but for constructive and objective action—if we are fortunate to know what it may be and what to do. Not even the gods know, really. But we must continue trying and this trying is human history.

Existentialism feels that Reason has robbed man of the soma that religion provided to soothe man's misfortunes, pains, and other negative factors in life; that religion has been the medium to overcome, or anesthetize him away from, the dread and tragedy of inevitable death. But now that Reason and its offspring, the

sciences, have exposed the absurdities and fallacies of superstitional belief, metaphysical, mystical, and metapsychological self-
delusions, and have blown away the ectoplasmic clouds of supernaturalism into nothingness, the Existentialist, the historical
addict to ego- and cosmocentricity, again uses the very means of
Reason, Pascal-wise, as did the primitive theologians to create
their own ancient theogonies, to subjectivize himself into a meaninglessness *during* his life because the after-death subsequences
do not *now* assure him of the continuance of the same pains,
dreads, and despairs about which he weeps as unbecoming the
grandeur of either Teilhard's Ascending Arrow or the Nietzschean
concoction of Superman and the Blond Beast.

Reason, whether activated by logical thinking, emotional needs,
or desperate urgency, has been man's tool in anything that impelled or required thought of *any* kind, subjective or objective.
Paul Roubiczek begins his book on *Existentialism* in this manner: "All experience shows that reason is part of human nature,
that it is influenced by human nature, that its powers are limited,
and that reason, therefore, cannot and must not be considered
as absolute. It is this violent, unreasonable, fundamentally irrational claim of reason which in its turn produces the violent and
now openly irrational reaction of Existentialism. . . . Existentialism is a rejection of all purely abstract thinking, of a purely logical or scientific philosophy; in short, a rejection of the absoluteness of reason."[81]

First, Roubiczek rationally admits the inconclusiveness, limitations, and the trial-and-error inevitabilities of reason, which is
both logical and historical. Then he accuses man of considering
and holding reason to be the absolute vehicle, the new god or
goddess to be worshipped, which, to begin with, is unreasonable.
The very pantheons of the *absoluteness* of the religions have
come tumbling down because of the *flexibilities* and freeing
variants of reason. Freedom itself, by its very process, is a state of
nonabsoluteness. Reason has only been *attempted* in any kind of
absolute sense by the dogmatists, the fundamentalists, the metaphysicians, theologians, and now by the Existentialists, because
all these have used reason, whether rightly or wrongly, to support,
uphold, and identify their own concepts of absolutes. Logical

thinking itself, exposing, by its very use and expression, the non-absoluteness, the innate and rooted nature to variate, differentiate, and recapitulate, is forever committed, *ipso facto,* to a state of *nonabsoluteness.* The scientific method, by the nature of its process and being *a* process, precludes at any point any state of absoluteness. Being part and parcel of man himself, the product of man's mind cannot be different from the body: a nonabsoluteness cannot give birth to an absolute, though man has beguiled himself by thinking and believing so.

Roubiczek states that "Kierkegaard insisted that philosphy should not be abstract, but based on personal experience, on the historical situation in which man finds himself, so that it could become the basis, not of speculation, but of each man's life. The only evidence to be accepted was that which both could be and had been tested by experience."[82] Here again we find the paradox of Existentialism clamoring against the sciences, and at the same time maintaining that philosophy should concern itself with experience and be tested by it. There is no such thing as personal experience being a thing in itself unrelated to the experiences of others and the enivornments in which both operate and through which they experience themselves. A man is born into a world without being asked; he is here and he grows up in a certain environment and among certain individuals and peoples, is patterned and constantly influenced by the culture and conditions that more or less govern his time. Thus, one cannot consider the individual and personal experiences of a person without concomitantly knowing something of the external factors and influences in which the person's experiences are processed. Man can think as an individual, and he does, and he can act as an individual, and he does, but he cannot escape from the world in which all this takes place, and both must be taken into account if wise and reasonable judgments are to be made.

Roubiczek states further: "For the extreme Existentialists, death supports all the negative experience upon which they concentrate; it is the final proof that life is meaningless."[83] A philosophy that tries to be consistent in its despair and badge of meaninglessness in its evaluation of the only life we know, tested by the only experiences we have experienced, is neither a sensible

nor a wholesome philosophy. Such a philosophy can only habituate the harboring of morbidity, dread, and a needless and fearfully uncourageous pessimism that withholds from itself whatever
joy, satisfaction, and even health and life, while we have it, may
possibly give us.

Existentialism reveals its own self-helplessness. Because knowledge and the sciences have taken away his theological immortality,
let down the boom forever to keep him earthly and without a
jury of saints to allow him to pass through the ordeal of death
into the continued life beyond, to him nothing matters: everything *is* nothing. Being fully conscious, he senses the "senselessness" of his own being; he is alive, yet nothing. Edward Albee
puts it thus: "Man attempts to make sense out of his senseless
position . . . in a world that makes no sense."[84]

At least Albee admits to his own Cartesian self-identity. Beyond
this everything becomes meaningless. Everything seems to become
"senseless." Whereas before theology sacrificed man's earthly
existence for the seemingly greater glory of some ethereal paradise, the existentialist is willing to sacrifice man's only life again
by "senselessness" because he is reasonably convinced there is
no future paradise awaiting him: therefore, this life is senseless.
He shudders to think about the extinction of his being, his personality, by dying. This is understandable, congruous with sympathy and forgiveness, and to this we can agree there are no
normal exceptions. Yet in actuality it becomes a process of dying
before death, dying in living experience. Thus cynicism breeds
intellectualized asceticism, which sours the spirit of freedom and
constantly spoils the uninhibited flow of possible happiness and
satisfactions that should be the content of man's time during his
life. Kallen: "I do not see that extinction by dying can in any
way render meaningless the living of life as it is lived. The living
makes its own meaning, *is* the meaning, is all the meaning there
can be. . . . To itself, no life lacks meaning, even if, like some
professors and poets, it cultivates its own meaning by charging
everybody's else's life with lacking any. For all lives, their going
on is goal enough."[85] Peter Freuchen: "Eskimos have many
strangely naïve and beautiful beliefs about death. In general,
though, they merely say that death can either be the end of it

all or a transition into something new, and that in either case there is nothing to fear. . . . It is as if they one day believe in the continuation of life after death, and the next day don't take it into consideration. Life is their essential concern. The thought of death is remote. . . . Fear of death is unknown to them, they know only love of life."[86]

When a person *can* witness the rising sun, the setting sun, the rejuvenations of spring, and the wisdoms of fall, when he *can* see and touch the oceans and its tides, the floating clouds, all that surrounds him in living things and the vistas on which all this is staged before him, and then say that *all* is meaningless and senseless, he has succumbed to his own inability to withstand the shock of theological deterioration. He has forgotten to count his blessings without necessarily being optimistic. He cannot *move* to re-evaluate life in terms of the present. He is "pining away" his present. He incarcerates his freedom in a prison-like philosophy wherein all values become nebulous, unstable, questionable, all ends vain, all efforts meaningless and all hopes illusions. His egocentricity has reached the high point of self-pity. This is the ailment that hangs like a thick fog in the interval between the dying gods and the world of today. Man cannot effect this wide jump summarily and with dispatch. It takes time and toll.

Man does not seem to be rationally conscious of his animal past and his animal present; he does not seem to be conscious of the *total symbiosis* of which he is a segment in a chain. His enlarging brain and his weakening body have lifted him for so long into the skies of dream and imagery that he seems to have lost to a great extent the sense of securely walking on the surface and enjoying it. He will have to learn all over again, like the child, to stand upright. Man is the only animal intelligent enough and free enough to degenerate and destroy his own life; all other animals, in their natural ignorance, just "know" enough to try to live *as best as possible* and *as long as possible*. Man, even with his intelligence and freedom, must learn to do this. If he is to survive, for himself, and to continue his kind, he has no other alternative. Pandora-weeping will only continue to infest the anthropomorphic and egocentric, whether with magico-religiosity or with science, or with both.

Any possible solutions are not simple as the problems are historical and deep-rooted in the very core of human evolution and
experience. The present nature of man stands in the very shadow
of the preprimitive and the preilliterate. The branches of descendancy or ascendancy of man may have extended far, but the
Igdrasil-trunk of human nature, tied to its animal and biological
roots, earthbound to its mundane nucleus, stands still. The prime
desires of animal life and the dreams of its intellectualization
remain umbilical forever. So long as humanity can revitalize its
own natural freedom through the evolved and cultured processes
of reason, so long is it possible to project hopefully some solution
that would justify the operable freedoms that are within the
human domain and within the essence of living experience. Barrows Dunham: "I do not share the existentialist pessimism which
advocates surrender before attempt. We know our future to be
uncertain, but more than this we do not know. Where nothing
is certain, nothing is doomed, and accordingly we may explore
with some confidence certain very attractive possibilities: an
abundant life, a peaceful world, all blessings shared with all
men."[87]

The psychological and neurophysiological history of man exposes and confesses a constant game played by the opposing teams
of over-internalization and over-externalization in which game
man seems to be the *ball*. In the former, people have fathomed
and succumbed themselves in innunedos, ambiguities, and word
puzzles of "spirit," "soul," "I and Thou," "Thou and I," "I-
Thou," "Ding-in-sich," "Mitsein and Dasein," "Being-in and
Being-with," "Other-as-subject," "Other-as-object," etc., etc., until
the centrifugalizing words become a dazzling whirlpool of pure
nonsense. So artful has become the application and manipulation
of words that they themselves who have done the applying and
manipulation not only become lost in their own verbose wander-
ings but consider others who get lost in trying to understand them
as people who just do not know enough, or who just cannot apply
their *cogito* sufficiently, to detect all the manifest and manifold
intersubjectivities of their premises. In the former team we find
Karl Jaspers, Martin Heidegger, Jean-Paul Sartre, Jacques Mari-

tain, Martin Buber, Soren Kierkegaard, and others. These neo-theologians of the present era confine their metaphysics to this world, true, but it is a metapsychic of despair, of Jeremian lamentation, of attempting to sedate oneself with sleep-inducing word-phrases or to drown oneself in a bottomless whirlpool of ambiguities and "intersubjectivities" until all becomes a nebulous mentated fog.[88]

In the latter, the team of overexternalization, we find that this team consists of impersonal things such as machines, methods, routines, schedules, progress reports, graphs, increased sales drives, status cultures, societal conformances, and the like. Here we find the pressures of extension and production, the lustful temptations of greater and better machines, more intricate methods and greater efficiency. These have taken away from man his heart, his closeness and affinity to nature, his personality and peace of mind, his innate desire to raise his eyes to see the waters, the forests, the sky in all its changing, moving beauties. Lewis Mumford: "It is time that our present wholesale commitment to the machine, which arises largely out of our one-sided interpretation of man's early technical development, should be replaced by a fuller picture of both human nature and the technical milieu, as both have evolved together."[89]

Man is losing the priceless pleasure and the gusto of spirit to enjoy the ecstasy of the soft flakes of snow upon his cheeks, the penetrating freshness of the wind opaqued with snowy mist, to enjoy seeing the millions of tiny green lividness breaking through the surfaces of regenerating soil in the spring and to enjoy walking upon crackling carpets of dry leaves of gold, rust and brown in the fall, to enjoy walking in the rain through forests of tall pines and smell their musk. Man is forgetting these and more and in forgetting he is losing his humanness, his arts and poetry, and becoming more like the machines he has invented. Between the former neo-theologians and the latter processes of mechanization man is becoming a psychic cripple. Man must free himself from these bondsmen of imaginations gone out of control and the drive of synthesizing the human elements into products beyond the call and need of necessity.

ZEN

THE FOLLOWER OF another philosophy, *Zen,* dreams of a freedom of mind and body so free that freedom is no longer necessary, that the mind would leave the body (if it can) while the body also "floats" in the vacuum of a totally "free" mind. Zen is a system of thought that is not supposed to think or even to be conscious of the word *Zen,* especially after one has had a good meal and can sleep it off. People who are happy do not need to *escape* into such a mysticism, and the unhappy neurotic who tries to escape into such a mixture can only meet up with frustration and a deepening of his problem.

D. T. Suzuki, the exponent of Zen, writes: "For the intellect has a peculiarly disquieting quality in it. . . . It upsets the blissful peace of ignorance."[90] He continues: "Zen has its own way of pointing to the nature of one's own being, and that when this is done one attains to Buddhahood, in which all the contradictions and disturbances caused by the intellect are entirely harmonized in a unity of higher order."[91] This is the clear legendary example of the ostrich trying to escape by burrowing its head in the sand. There is no need to outrun life; it is beautiful and wonderful, this life of ours, even with all its conflicts and eventual sad events. Besides, why try to escape from what we are and destined always to be until we die? One who cannot find some beauty and peace in the sunshine of the day will not find it by trying to conceal his identity in darkness, or by not thinking, or by concealing himself in a banyan tree. Zen is the mourning cloak of darkness one uses to deceive himself that he is being concealed from the magic of living. Suzuki continues: "A Zen master once remarked that the life of a monk can be attained only by a man of great moral strength, and that even a minister of the state cannot expect to become a successful monk."[92] But who in his right mind wants to become a monk? What is there so grandiose about being a monk, Chinese, Japanese, or otherwise? Is it not to become a parasite, begging alms from others for his next meal so as to get on with his contemplating and meditating? We have already made the gods into beggars. Should we become beggars ourselves? Truly, I would rather be a minister of the state and express an opinion that concerns the living and the daily problems of living. Zen is the attempt to reach the epitome of self-reliance through the point of nonidentity—so often a poor substitute for something unfulfilled or as an escape from something one cannot overcome or endure. Zen is a "mystical" sedation. Wallace I. Matson: "It is understandable if the nonmystic's reaction is to complain that the mystic is crazy. And evidence tending to support this conclusion is not difficult to find. The claim to possess a profound but inexpressible insight is characteristic of many psychotic states. . . . It is well known that in many cultures drug-induced hallucinations are ritually cultivated; and it is not clear how, or even whether, these states are to be distinguished from true mystic ecstasy. It is somehow unseemly that the secret of the universe should be unveiled via eating mushrooms."[93]

VARIETIES OF CONCEPTS ON FREEDOM

To the philosopher, the sense of freedom might be indicated in his own courage and intelligence to express to the world what he thinks freedom should constitute and why it could be merited and enjoyed, in his expression of pathos that history reveals constantly with its conflicts and futilities, as well as its hopes and determinations to achieve freedom. Abraham Kaplan states it this way: "Politics looks to the philosopher to define the national purpose, science expects him to serve as referee, art as interpreter, and religion as apologist."[94]

It seems that man has to attempt to simulate mentally, if possible, or to think as the most primitive primitive, in the most simple and elemental terms and phrases, and then, from this beginning, again attempt to build a rational and natural philosophy consistent and applicable to human beings and human nature and the human environment and not to angels and fantasy. We have to rationalize human action for the purposes of satisfaction, not dismal futility and ethereal reward. We have strayed too far from realities and truths, and the idealistic structures we have built with our dreams and imagery are covered and permeated with so much verbiage of little or no meaning that it seems advisable to start over again from scratch. History and experience, castings from the general overall processes of evolution in all its phases, are irreversible and irrevocable.

We have spent most of our labors in philosophy trying to fathom or prove beginnings and ends, which are obvious unknowables, while giving the least attention to the only thing we can possibly know—the processes going on between these two designations. By giving attention to these we may find not only the nature, the meaning, and the value of these processes, but the realization that beginnings and ends are only manifestations of the very processes themselves, and that the attempt to set beginnings and ends is merely to be tricked by our own rationalism and reflectively deductive curiosities into concerning ourselves with a morphology that does not exist at all within the true acquisitions of thought and its consequential products of idea and theory. It is high time that philosophy, if it desires to make of itself a practical value to the living, should relegate itself to the living. Philosophy has been a pseudo-science long enough. Let the sciences continue to search for the substance and nature of things, including beginnings and ends. Philosophy has enough on its hands merely trying to interpret them and apply any meanings and values derived to help humanity make a freedom-loving and peace-loving world—Now! Wittgenstein said that "Philosophy is not a doctrine, but an activity."[95] In a poetic vein Frazer muses: "For the thinker there is no permanent place of rest. He must move ever forward, a pilgrim of the night eternally pressing towards the faint and glimmering illumination that eternally retreats before him."[96] Freedom denotes the substance of life and exposes its restlessness; the recurring cycles of its helpless motions confess its ambivalent extension between light and darkness, between birth and death, seemingly forever moving, repeating itself according to its nature, like forever emerging, repeating sound waves circling out endlessly to the galaxies beyond.

To the Artist, freedom might mean his sense of the right to create art any way he wishes, whether we or even the artist himself likes it or not. To the viewing esthete freedom might mean his right to judge it or like it according to his own particular point of view or pleasure, regardless of whether it agrees with any or all of the experts in the world. Thus, while the effects of freedom might be relational and influential, the essence of freedom itself remains a *personal* factor, as life itself, though relational, remains a personal factor. The protoprimitive who painted and sculptured on rock and cave wall is on the same personal level as the artist throughout history and today. Jacquetta Hawkes and Leonard Woolley: "After a million years during which development, in so far as we can observe it, was so slow that hundreds of generations might live and die without making the smallest change in their culture, men began to create works of art which can rival anything that has been achieved in the last ten thousand years. This earliest painting and sculpture illuminates the truth that essentially there is no progress in art."[97] Irwin Edman: "The traditional quarrel between the artist and the puritan has been the quarrel between those who were frankly interested in the sensuous appearances and surfaces of things and those to whom any involvement or excitement of the senses was a corruption of the spirit or a deflection of some ordered harmony of reason. The history of censorship in the fine arts, if it could be told in full, would be found to revolve in no small measure around the assumed peril of the corruption of the spirit by the incitements of the flesh through beautiful things."[98]

To the Industrialist, freedom might be interpreted as the legal right to carry on a system by using labor and natural materials to increase his own personal wealth and power irrespective of its implications to the general welfare. To the Worker, with his recently collectivized power to bargain and strike, freedom means the reverse, and here, too, regardless of its implications to the general welfare.

Basically, reduced to simple elements from complex variations of degree, the economics of man and of men boil down to this classification: those who work for others, willingly or unwillingly, and those who have others work for them so that they do not have to work at all or work less because of it. In the economic history of mankind those who more or less submitted, in folly or by force, to power crafts of any kind—whether the psychological or traditional power to be worshipped, such as kings, or to lead worshippers, such as the priesthoods; military or naked power, such as tyrants, feudal lords, nobles, barons, and others; the revolutionary and emotional power of "prophets" and "deliverers" and "leaders," or the power of oligarchies and dictatorships, such as modern communism, nazism, fascism; the powers of plutocrats, such as exist in the professions, industries, military brass, or high finance; or even, more recently, the power of propaganda and fanatical excitement of intense new nationalisms, many of which are mere police states and dictatorial cliques ridden with graft, self-emulation, self-aggrandizement, opulence, waste, and arbitrary might, headed by megalomaniacs, egocentrics—were those who spent their few miserable years working for others, doing what they could to eke out some comfort, serenity, security, and satisfaction. The history of mankind is the history of slavery enslaving itself—in some form or manner—constantly. The recipients always claimed that *they* were the ones who were making the "sacrifices" and giving their lives for the common herd, while gathering the wealth in so doing. What these do with respect, dignity, authority, and legality, and even with "morality," others such as gangsters, dope-peddlers, swindlers, dishonest beggars, do without respect, against authority, and with illegality. All of these people, from the awing preacher in the pulpit to the high echelons of fancy finance and their small-print prospectuses, use the beguiling Circean verbiage of linguistic philosophy which, when boiled down to residual exposure, is plain elemental humbug. Thus the problems of freedom to security and the freedom to starve will be taken up, as the others, in later and more appropriate places.

To the Conservative, freedom might mean the freedom to restrict freedom, and to the Liberal, it might mean the freedom to restrict the conservative from accomplishing this. To the Anarchist, it might mean the freedom to get rid of both of them, so that *he,* supremely and uncontrolled, can go haywire with his ideals, at least until he gets hungry and sleepy.

To the Communist serf, freedom might mean something his leaders are trying to get him to forget, while they retain the freedom to make sure that this forgetfulness is effective in one way or another. To the Communist leader, freedom might mean his present power and to his people their present slavery to accept and serve, willingly or unwillingly, the new god of the State. To the Communist dialectician, the State is the criterion, the only repository and depository of freedom and the only "Great Mother" ovipositor of the strings of belongingness for its seedlings, the godhead and the "objective" ideal to be achieved. To the individuals of such a state, freedom could mean the indoctrinated, enculterated, caterpillared desire or resignation to attempt to uphold and continue this silly myth. To the Fascists and Nazis, freedom is a very naughty word, but a substance divinely allocated to them alone to rule over, or dispose of, other people in accordance with their own paranoias.

Freedom, in the "modern" sense, might be taken by too many individuals as the vehicle of proving their "smartness" in becoming "realists" and "practical" people, who desire to establish "ethically" the doctrine that it is "natural" and "mature" to outwit or overwhelm others for their own ends, that *the ends justify the means* regardless of the nature of the means—one of the foul eggs laid by William James in his attempt to justify the acceptance of a myth as a "practical" fact. Freedom in the modern world and modern civilization is finding it more and more difficult to be fully expressive in the reasonable sense. Modern civilization is gradually becoming a culture primarily existing under tables, as it appears that if one wants to get anywhere, he must begin to learn the art of crawling and dealing "freely" under the table.

There appears to be a rising tide of futility on the part of individuals to cope with their problems of survival and resign themselves to the impersonal power and authority of organization and the State. The individual is beginning to resign himself because of the sheer weight of numbers and the increasing obstacles of free competition, to be absorbed by organization, by the Univac, by the oligarchies and naked power of the totalitarian states. It is not a question of organizational existence: group and communal society and polity are coexistents of the human animal and of prime essentiality to his existence. It is not that the individual should desire the elimination of group or communal existence, social, economic, and political. It is simply that he feels that this communal existence has become too vast, too preponderable for him to fight back to retain some sense of self-identity as an individual. His confidence to be self-assertive, critical, to rebel, if need be, and win seems to be shattered. He has created a socialized Frankenstein out of his own despairing cries for social and economic justice. He feels futile and he seems to be relaxing from his historical struggle to be a free animal and a freedom-loving person.

To a Man, freedom might mean that woman was born into the world to make his days less laborious and his nights ecstatic; whereas, to a Woman, it might mean that man, after all, needs her for a supply of citizens and for other good immediate reasons. For thousands of years, Ottaker Nemecek tells us, "The demand for pre-nuptial chastity in the bride is closely connected with woman's position as a purchasable and purchased possession."[99] Paul Blanshard writes of Catholic equity in Spain today: "Even today a husband may desert his home from one to three years without losing his family rights, whereas a wife may lose those rights by one day's absence."[100] That man is the naturally more superior animal than his female consort is purely man's viewpoint, and if woman allows him to keep on believing it, that is probably due to her subtle wisdom. In the insect world it is surely different: "The insect world is essentially a female world in which the male plays a secondary part."[101]

To the many Children in these modern times, freedom might mean the right to anything and everything their whims and wishes desire, regardless of the consequences—and to heck with everybody else. Or to many other youngsters, in the poorer classes, freedom might be the sum of many fears, that is, the fear of freedom from security, the fear of freedom from opportunity, from having a fair chance to express and realize their hopes, talents, initiatives, creativeness, and their strivings to achieve some success and satisfactions as individuals, as persons, the fear of a freedom which grants them their minds but not a free world for their minds to think in.

In almost every community, small or large, we find the beatniks passing us by. We turn and look at them, often with amazement with their hair styles and hobo clothes. These are the modern "Lombards" (how they manage to get their pants on I will never know) who think that freedom has now been resurrected and restored to the new humanity because of their emergence. They behold themselves as the Messiahs of the New Era of uninhibited freedom and they refuse to be crucified by obsolescence and unwarranted and restraining conventions. They feel that theology reveals nothing, created by man to soothe himself with false mirrors and is now done with it; that as existentialism does reveal despair and hopelessness, therefore everything goes, regardless of where it may lead and in spite of what "ordinary" people may think.

To be modern, beatnik style, one must look filthy even if he happens to be clean; otherwise, how would one beatnik recognize and accept another one if he does not conform to the expectancies of beatnik appearance, protocol, and neglect? With all the outcries of freedom, the beatnik *is* a conformist to beatnikism in the same manner as in ancient times the saints and clerics upheld the premise that to take a bath and keep the body clean was blasphemy against God's teaching, that the body was filth, vulgar, lustful, earthy, and worthless and the only important thing is to keep the soul pure and purified by abstinence from soap, water, and girls. Today the beatnik is no longer an individualist because he has to look like a beatnik to be accepted among his kind; the appearance and costume go along with identity. This is a *style*, not an intellect. Beatnikism is the uniform of a protest against uniformity; it is a badge, not a thought; it is a rebellion against an "enemy" that makes possible any self-ordained justification to carry on as it does. The beatnik alone looks silly in his appearance and out of context but in his group he is defiant and challenging. Every beatnik is not self-sustainable; he needs psychological support. So does the klansman look silly alone in his bed-sheet mantle with peepholes, but, in a group of bed-sheeted bravados, he is again raising his voice strongly to go forward and onward in their "crusade" against the "enemy." Very often it becomes difficult to find enemies, and it becomes urgent that a few become created in a hurry as the good fortitude of defiance cannot lay dormant for too long and courage must be served. These are all beings who somehow cannot make up their minds to consider seriously the idea of growing up. If someone took away their

"toy of hostility," they would be aghast and acclaim their inse-
curities by crying and by a plea for sympathy and understanding.

Freedom, being a natural element, is used often in strange
and bizarre ways. This is the way it has always been. Like the
painted and decorated savage dancing and prancing about in all
directions to chase away the evil eye, in many ways the beatnik
today has to dress and appear likewise. What he may be chasing
and why is a multitudinous array of problems, inward and outward, but he surely attracts plenty of flies.

A beatnik is one who tries to overcome his own feelings of
inferiority and insecurity by an exhibitionism of being *different*.
What the differences consist of and whether they are salubrious
does not matter; what does matter is that they be arrogantly and
courageously different. This is the attempt to be considered apart
from the ordinary and the sedentary. He must not conform to
anything that *was* but only to that which could be, but what this
is that should be leaves him in a quandary. His freedom consists
primarily not in any logical or rational approach to what may be
intrinsically good, worthwhile or sensible, but in that which
would arouse in viewers some contempt. In his attempt to be
different the result is that he becomes indifferent. The beatnik
nourishes himself with the contempt that he expects the ordinary
to heap upon him; a sort of symbiotic relationship in which contempt is enjoyed and considered a stamp of unwilling approval.
On this point he may be easily successful, seeing that he is most
often playing solitaire with his "enemies." This makes him feel
not only brave and challenging but also as a martyr to those to
come, for he feels that he stands against the preponderance of
society itself and all that it stands for in its past ascendancy, that
he is part of the vanguard of the still unrewarded new breed of
hominids that has dedicated itself to a "full" and "raw" restoration of freedom that defies tradition and the usual acceptances of
uniformity and conformity.

He *must* be different; he must challenge; he must be looked
at; he must be admired, if not for his hairdo and dirty shoes, for
his unqualified stance of bravado. Beneath the banner of rebellious attempt to sustain individuality he, too, is a conformist to

the uniformity of beatnikism and so follows its pattern. Joining the parade of beatniks and absorbing its mass and group acceptance of what has already been established as the pattern of conforming and performing beatniks, he imagines himself alone, defiantly, like little David, challenging fearlessly and steadfastly the Goliaths of Tradition, thinking that with his little slingshot of freedom in his hand he can undo his own innate drives and change his nature from cleric to clown. He merely changes clothes. He cannot escape from the hominine compound and all its possible stupidities of self-exaggeration.

There is no escape from being human; regardless of how the beatnik boy and girl want to express their freedom of being different and opposing, they are still tied to a "tradition" much older than culture, the tradition of their own species and all its genetic and experiential endowments. Behind the long locks of hair and bushy beards is the feeble try of show and impression to gather camouflage-power to stand up to a more difficult world to grow up in and to the fears of insecurity in an increasing vortex of competitive fields for economic sustenance and personal achievement. Within this region of fears and uncertainties is born the expanding periphery of societal responsibilities. What the beatnik fails to understand is that he, too, is part of the societal structure, and, therefore, is committed, or should be, to bear his part of the whole of this responsibility, as a concomitant factor with an intelligent and rationally applied use of his freedom, even though responsibility, in actuality, is not within itself a natural accessory of the freedom-life process.

The impression of personal daring and challenge, like Cervantes' high aspirations to protect and win the lady in distress from the evil windmills, shows itself in the beatnik pattern in which the freedom, which should be used for actual and unheralded work, progress and personal satisfactions, is spent throwing pebbles at stone walls. Thus it is not unusual for the beatnik to feel that it is the world that is indebted to him and it is the society that should be made to burden the responsibilities for his securities, while he tries to scare it by making believe, beardwise, that he has, in his image, grown up.

PURPOSE, PLAN, AND DESIGN

HERBERT J. MULLER'S concept of freedom as "the condition of being able to choose and carry out purposes" is a fairly comprehensive and broad identity mark of the process of freedom, but it does not seem to fulfill more completely a plausible explanation of the natural and its offspring, the cultural freedom of man. While it seems obvious that many actions or situations are involved with or are a result of some purposive predetermination, yet in the essence or core of freedom itself there is no absolute implication that *purpose* is its prime or generic determinant or essentiality. Purpose and freedom are not always concomitant factors; they may be related factors but it seems to me that an act of freedom may not necessarily rise out of any plan, idea or wish or applied discretion in choosing, to carry out some preconscious sense of purpose. Acts or expressions of freedom are often spontaneous, erratic, spastic, even convulsive, often intensely emotional and uncontrollable. Purpose so often reveals prethought, contemplation, discretion, selectivity, and a sense of awareness of good and bad, desirable and undesirable, wrong and right, here or there, what to do and what not to do, of anticipated success or fear of failure. In deference to Mr. Muller, there seems to be a sense of direction in his definition, which may be considered as purpose or intuition, whether conscious or unconscious, but this sense of direction is but the sequence of previous determinants. Also, it would appear that any such choosing, even purposing, is qualified by its limitations of extension and fulfillment. Freedom without the possibility of some fulfillment, even though limited, becomes a pure purpose or intent, and thereby becomes limited to a freedom of purpose or intent. Purpose and choosing are natural events in the daily lives of people, and even of other animals, and yet we should realize that we must refrain from any idea or ideology which makes freedom an *ideal* or abstract situation, when it is and has always been a *natural* situation.

Free Will is not exactly free, but limited to each individual's heritage and experience to do any such willing, including the constant admixture of chance and unexpected event in the very expression and activity of freedom itself. Freedom, I think, is

much more than this. It is the innate and natural inclination of
a living thing, which, because of its very nature, desires to and
can move, express, or do things according to its very nature. It
is true that this places freedom, on a biological basis, but from
this we, as animals, with all our cultures affixed, cannot escape.
We should only try to understand it as such and build upon this
a philosophy that could possibly resolve for us a compatibility of
satisfaction and possible fulfillment. If culture cannot do this,
then we must modify or change the culture, since we cannot
change the basic nature of humans.

Now that the gods have descended past the twilight into nonentity, the restlessness of man begins to repeat the same metaphysical grind of subjectivism by attempting to replace the gods
with "patterns" and "purposes," not only to be indicated, a
priori, in the processes of "purposive directionalism" (which
Simpson rightly terms "Evolutionary Theology") in the "progressive" (from lower to higher) development by biological
forces of all micro- and macro-organisms, including man, of
course, but that the entire universe may, within its totality and as
a totality, of which man may or may not be the only conscious
part, indicate within the nature and operationalism of itself a
"purpose," a *"plan,"* a specifiable or unspecifiable direction, which
it may, like a person, "intuitively" and "objectively" (in the
classical urge of dualism) "mold" or "shape," consciously or unconsciously, in some mystical fashion into a self-directed purpose.
There are many erudite scholars who still persist in attempting
to restore the obviously still desired old theological standards in
a new pedantic though modern and rational manner.

Man knows he is intelligent to a degree—to what extent does
not really matter—and he knows he is naturally *attached* to an
objectivity that to his senses appears *real* and *materialistic*. He
also realizes that this very intelligence is a manifestation of his
personal molecular panmixis of genetic endowment operating
biologically and psychologically in ways still to be probed for
the isolated key of explanation. It is only understandable that
man, with his metaphysical-theological development of both
subjective and objective desires, as a result of his own being and
his awareness of inevitable death, now begins to shift, Buber-

fashion, where science falls short, to translate God into Purpose and immortality into cosmic Plan. Lecomte du Noüy also puts on the cloak of evolutionary theology and tries to give his fellowmen a pseudo-scientific pill he calls "telefinalism," which, according to Simpson, "is a word applied to professed ignorance."[102] Simpson explains further: "There is no fact in the history of life that requires a postulate of purpose external to the organisms themselves. It could, of course, be maintained that the whole system, purposeless itself, was created for a purpose or that purposes not required by the evidence may nevertheless exist. Such speculation is without control, incapable of validation, and therefore altogether vain. We do know, however, that purposes peculiar to and arising within organisms exist as one of the great marvels of life. We know it because we form purposes ourselves."[103]

For the pragmatic moment man does not wish to see that purpose and plan, imbedded in his cerebral capacity to express its own egocentricity, limited to himself and possibly other living things, now forms its own aurora borealis to extend itself, as it always has, onto its world and the universe beyond. The nature of this psychological inner and outer projection, as well as its limitations, can be understood, but no knowledge, intuitively honest or scientifically verifiable, can present such a premise, regardless how desirably intended, as *certain* and *real*. "A world in which man must rely on himself, in which he is not the darling of the gods but only another, albeit extraordinary, aspect of nature, is by no means congenial to the immature or the wishful thinkers. . . . Life may conceivably be happier for some people in the older worlds of superstition. It is possible that some children are made happy by a belief in Santa Claus, but adults should prefer to live in a world of reality and reason. . . . Unless *most* of us do enter it and live maturely and rationally in it, the future of mankind is dim, indeed—if there is any future."[104]

Man, for sure, exhibits and lives out, or attempts to live out, his purposes and plans, limited to himself, and the nature of these purposes and plans are not only limited by his biological development, equipment, and present endowment, conscious-wise and ego-wise, but even limited in its will to express itself on a totally free basis. Man can intuitively and subjectively take the universe on his lap, as one would take a wooden dummy, and ventriloquize purpose and plan into the dummy until it appears to him to have personality, livingness, and "human" relativeness to himself, and, to please himself, he has the freedom to do so. But he cannot admit on any intelligent or objective basis that his desire to make the dummy "talk" proves in any way its own livingness, purpose, or plan; it only proves the man's purpose and plan to make the dummy "talk" what the man wants it to "say." The limitation of this subjective potential, so far as he *knows,* is *personal* and *individual.* The nature of individuality, the individual equipage from the genetic pool, and the processing of these with the particularization of the experiences of the individual self can only make possible the issuance of a particular and individual viewpoint, similarities, coincidents and agreeableness notwithstanding.

Besides, any concept of cosmic purpose or plan, or for that matter, any purpose or plan that may be attributed to the entire species of *Homo sapiens* as an "aggregate" or "conscious sum," Durkheim- or Teilhard-wise, would imply by the nature of itself a confrontation with ethical or *sensible intent,* which would expose, as a result, its fallaciousness and untenability of "progression" in the general experience of nature, including man, its development and its inexorable and helpless ways of expression and existence. There is no question that man, regardless how objective or scientific he may desire to be, cannot wholly detach himself from the human relationship and his own psychic influence upon all his endeavors and behaviors. This does not necessarily mean that, because of his own consciousness and relatedness to all else, he can become wholly "methodolatrous" (thanks to Cooley), which is antithetic to any reasonable explanation of the causative and effectual sequences of experience, even if between a scientist and his test tube. Theology and all the mythologies and metaphorical legends it has created throughout history are the result of what Cooley calls "sympathetic introspection," and as long as man exists he has the freedom, and most probably will express it, to delight his ego, through his consciousness, in what he *wants* to see and believe to be "real," James-wise. The persistence of this subjectivity and anthropocentricity without the admission of the gods is evident in the continually despairing efforts of man to etherealize a cosmos with human psyche, purpose, and the metaphysical "progression"-goal of Teilhard's "Ascending Arrow."

Man need not be a self-beguiling optimist or take a pejorative view of despair and resignation in order to sense and express and continue his own purposes and plans. Whether it was "good" or "bad," wise or foolish, earthbound or heavenbound, he *has* always experienced and lived his purposes and plans. That he has not fully realized them or finally succeeded are indicated in the fact that the nature of man does not allow this, that he is still purposing and planning and will most probably continue to do so as long as he and his descendants hold on, or until his own purposed and planned destruction of himself and the world he exists on.

Man has, and should have, purpose and plan, and he should realize that this purpose and plan can be rationally applied to *know himself* and the world about him, and that, in doing so he can realistically and practically attempt to make it possible to better himself, solve, if possible, his problem of numbers and their biological and societal needs. Only in this way can any purpose or plan have any potential of justifying its own expression and intentions. If in doing so man restores to himself his own identity of animalness and the recognition of his biological limitations, he will also concomitantly restore the possible natural freedoms that are essential for him to fulfill some satisfaction for his existential term and his conscious sense of the element of time-specificity, which, in man's existence, is always an uncertain and uncalculable factor.

The actual translation and meaning of "sympathetic introspection" and "evolutionary theology" are the composite principle of self-love and the adoration of one's personality to such a mystical extent that everything such a person thinks or believes in becomes, to *him,* like a parade of golden angels issuing right out of God's mouth and fluttering about, too divine and too supra-worldly to be understood or valued by mere biological mechanisms. These people go about worshipping their own linguistic "sympathies" and "intuitiva," while the rest of the world keeps on cleaning up the mess they have been leaving behind for thousands of years. Their unilateral, if scholarly, condemnations of scientism as blinding to human values and leading to what they call "methodolatry" are simply a naïve and linguistic attempt to resurrect the metaphysic of unlimited self-extension, the "intuitive" desire of self-love, regardless of reality, by the neo-naïveté of the indeterministic assumption that unpredictability on the part of man's desire to innovate a super-mechanical yet purposed and planned universe to synthesize and synchronize with man's self-projection and desire. Science is simply the pursuit of truth and the open door to maintain this pursuit of truth on a free, continual and empirical basis. Science is based on the fullest possible exposure of experience, human and otherwise, and the establishment of knowledgeable materia of this experience and the environment, world, and universe about us. If not for this pursuit of truth these neo-theologians would still be living in the Dark Ages harrowing and hanging heretics and satisfying their "sympathetic introspection" by autos-da-fé. If they are not disposed to express such a power today, it is the result of their having to compromise with the ethics and responsibilities of modern and democratic localities wherein they can only use the media of debate and discourse, media which only the free processes of democratic society can make available to them. Pursuing a knowledge of ourselves and the world we live on does not preclude that the scientist has lost sense of and desire for value and meaning. And if there is to be any properly rational attempt at value and meaning, such rationalization should be based on what we *actually* know and not on what we would like to believe, regardless of knowledge and the constant exposure of experience.

Thus freedom has many connotations and these, in turn, bring as varied perspectives and concepts as there are individuals conscious enough and intelligent enough to express an opinion. Even with intelligence, it all becomes a matter of degree according to one's heritage and character and the experiences of external resistance and affluences upon them, including the nature of the intent according to the concepts to which any degree of intelligence may be applied.

CAN WE DEFINE FREEDOM?

CAN WE SUPPLY a definition of freedom that would suit or fit the phraseological regents for universal acceptance, satisfy the verbiage hunger of the linguistic philosophers, and give it ontological or teleological ideality so that it can be heralded as something of a cosmological or universal nature? I do not know. But this is not relevant or important except to the metaphysicians. What is relevant and important is what freedom means to an individual—*to you and me*. And to all the other individuals, and not as societies or mere principles rationalized as beautiful ends in themselves.

Before we can even attempt to evaluate any form of freedom— whether it is good or bad, just or unjust, wise or unwise, what we have done with it and what it might do for us—we have to know where it came from, what it is possibly made of, and how it operates in our being and other beings with whom we are related and neighbors. This is the reason we are concerned with its origins and nature.

It seems to me that only individuals—*persons*—manifest freedom, that is, considering an analysis of the human factor and its organizations. John Dewey stated that "Individuality is at first spontaneous and unshaped; it is a potentiality, a capacity for development."[105] Dobzhansky wrote: "Biology not only recognizes the absolute individuality and uniqueness of every person and every living thing but in fact supplies evidence for a rational explanation of this uniqueness."[106] He goes on to say: "Although all men now living are members of a single biological species, no two persons, except identical twins, have the same genetic endowment. Every individual is biologically unique and nonrecurrent. It would be naïve to claim that the discovery of this biological uniqueness constitutes a scientific proof of every person's existential singularity, but this view is at least consistent with the fact of biological singularity."[107] Lorus and Margery Milne put the point in another way: "No single concept of our universe can be completely convincing to all of mankind, because each of us lives in a private world. We judge every sensory impression in a peculiarly personal way, based upon our previous experiences.

No two individuals have the same experiences, even when they are brought up in one household. Nor are any two people, unless they are identical twins, exactly alike in refinements of sensory perception. Rarely are we aware how these personal differences circumscribe our views."[108] René Dubos: "All human beings have fundamentally the same anatomical structure, function through the same chemical activities, exhibit the same physiological manifestations, and even possess the same occult biological needs; yet no two human beings are alike. Clearly knowledge of the attributes that are common to mankind as a whole is not sufficient to account for the manner in which each individual person behaves as he does, develops his own peculiarities, in brief, becomes different from all other human beings. . . . Each one of us lives as it were in a private world of his own."[109]

Societies may reflect the nature and expression of freedom among its individuals, as a school of small fish reflect a moving directional shadow upon the surface of the sea; and a number of individuals in any group, community, or organization, may identify by their acts of freedom the existence or expression of certain types of freedom and the nature of the organization or group. But whether we come through the back door or the front door, we are dealing with individuals, and the principles of freedom belong to people as individuals.

Freedom covers a latitude of many intentions, needs, desires. Its *wants* vary according to each individual and his particular situations and circumstances. Many need freedom *from* something to fulfill their want or purpose; some need freedom *from* somebody to fulfill some necessity or urgency; others need freedom *for* something or somebody. Still others require freedom *to* and *toward* things or people; yet others need it *with* something else to arrange fulfillment of some kind. All people, as all animals, must have this freedom *in* themselves, as a natural and biologically voluntary process of the being, for themselves, and not necessarily for things outside of themselves. "The mark of a living organism," writes Brophy, "which distinguishes it from a dead or inanimate one, is that it *wants*. . . . Here, at the very roots of life, discernible in even the most rudimentary life-activity, is

a tremendous faculty of discrimination, whereby the self holds itself discreet from non-self."[110]

All freedoms have limitations, as nothing exists purely and
absolutely by itself alone. Life, in all its genus and nature, is
surrounded by limitations. All things are related and relatives.
As Brand Blanshard remarked, "Whatever nature's robe, it is a
seamless one."[111] Holbach held that a "man, who thinks himself
free (in the absolute sense), is a fly who imagines he has power to
move the universe, while he is himself unknowingly carried
along by it."[112] F. W. Headley wrote: "The understanding of one
makes the understanding of another possible,"[113] and Morris
Raphael Cohen follows: "In the phenomenal realm there can be
no recognition of the absolute freedom of any individual. Indeed,
it might well be asked whether any kind of plurality, or rational
society, of absolutely free individuals, is logically possible, since
the very existence of any one must in some way limit any
other."[114]

We realize, even though man or anything else is not absolutely
free, that man has no need of such absoluteness, as he would have
to be *outside* nature, as a god, to express it. Man, as every other
animal and plant, is a prisoner of the universe, confined to existing and living *within* and as *part* of nature, not outside of it.
James B. Conant writes: "The full impact of the consequences of
Man thinking about Man as a part of nature has not yet been
felt."[115] Such an earthly freedom implies, within itself, a nature
of *associated continuums:* One is free, as we have stated previously, *from* something, or *free* to join or go to something, to prevent something, or identify and acknowledge, or unknowingly
express himself as free. All these indicate relationship and some
kind of association. "Tendency toward association," writes H. R.
Hays, "is a basic force that operates at all levels of evolution and
modifies evolution."[116] The very nature of freedom within association brings about, in order to maintain itself, a certain tolerance, adaptable affinity or compromised adjustment in ratio to
pressures and resistances. This becomes an automatic and natural
limiting agent to unbridged freedom, and an unbridged freedom,
in the true sense, cannot even exist.

Freedom does not preconclude in the security and preservation of its own operating principle and nature that "all things are permissible," as stated in *The Brothers Karamazov*. In the first place, the very attempt of this premise of unlimited permissibility is the creator of conflict, opposition, and arbitrary power; secondly, if such an absurd principle could be successfully fulfilled, considering the nature of human nature, there would not be much human nature left to cope with, or to be free.

Accordingly, let us presume, as a self-searching and exploratory beginning to our analysis and philosophy of freedom, that *freedom is a natural, instinctively evolved sense of affirmative behavior that is essential for the fulfillment of the life processes and of life itself, of which freedom is a verification of its identity, variable in degree and kind, and which is favorably and necessarily required in order to process and attain a more satisfied and nonconflictive life.* We may add that this evolved behavior and sense are *determined wants compatible with the physical and psychological nature and need of the human being,* and any pressures and/or resistances opposing the fulfillment and satisfaction of this wantable behavior become deterring obstacles to the favorably desired satisfactions of living and the normal processes of animal motility, the cause of stress and strife, the chronic growth and penetration of which are some of the prime causes of individual, social and world conflict. "The mark of a living organism, which distinguishes it from a dead or inanimate one, is that it wants."[117] The experience of *want* is naturally determined by pressures and resistances, or what the physiologist may consider the processes of *conductivity* and *irritability*.[118]

AN IDENTITY OF FREEDOM: WANT

WANT IS ALWAYS attached to the *present*. It cannot belong to the past. It cannot belong to the future, because a "want" for the future is merely a wish or a hope, and such a want must be necessarily limited to the want of wishing or hoping. Want is a livable, a biological thing, whether it be nurtured from the instinctive or from the cultural. To want something means that the processes that make up and create the want, want it *now*, not before or after; even the need of wishing or hoping serves the immediate need of doing so. "Before" is forgotten (unless one wants to remember) and "later" has not arrived to gratify a want (unless one enjoys wishing, dreaming, hoping, and so derives some kind of satisfaction or relief from this way of thinking). "Life can only be understood backward," wrote Kierkegaard, "but it must be lived forward." This may sound nicely-put, even poetic, but I feel it is an error of observation, illogical, and even senseless. We *do* learn from the past, or we should, and we may hope and plan forward, but we only live *now*, not backward or forward. Whatever life offers, it is in the *now*, the present. Life is sadly and all too often wasted looking backward; planning, always planning for the future, forgetting for the *moment* the moment, that all we know of the past and all we can hope for in the future is in *process* at any point of the present. *Life is, not was or may be.*

Want indicates a desire and a consciousness of a need for gratification of something for the present, whatever it may be, even an act of remembering or wishing. A want may find present gratification in sensing or knowing that security for tomorrow, or some satisfaction or pleasantness that will be, or may be, obtained or reached tomorrow or later, permits the person to "enjoy" its future determination of expected fulfillment as some sort of anticipated experience. In such a case, the want is something rationally possible of realization, at least to the person rationalizing or sensing. Otherwise, it again turns into wishful thinking or fantasy, and while it is a form of self-beguilement, a person is in actuality still free to want it, and experience it. A free person can want, or he can wish or dream, which is really a want to wish or a want to dream, but the fact of wanting is also an action and mode of freedom.

Inasmuch as conflict is the opposite of peace, the growth or continued establishment of such conflict must lead sooner or later either to partial, often complete, submission and futility or the rise and expression of a revolutionary drive for relief and escape; to moderate, remove, or destroy this conflict that has become unbearable so that some form of *compatibility* may be restored as a natural base.

The human being, we all know, needs water, food, shelter for his necessary comfort and as security against his natural enemies. "No man can survive for three weeks if his water supply is cut off completely."[119] He also needs these fundamental things so that he can carry on his instinctive drive to mate and thus provide and propagate his kind and secure in this way some reasonable measure of success for the continuance of his species while enjoying the process of propagation. All other animals do the same. In the overall, freedom is the ability to move to accomplish or fulfill a want or desire, which includes the want of wanting something or desiring nothing. His natural wants to accomplish or fulfill these things must have concomitantly evolved certain emotional desires and mental traits which we may combine into the necessary psychological wants and needs of the human being. Anything that would enhance the enjoyment or satisfaction of these wants was instinctively sought for and accepted. This "sought for" and these acceptances may have habituated into naturally unconscious drives which evolved the integration of these wants into inherited continuums to advance growth, extension, adaptability to change, and to reduce conflict. Thus freedom evolved, no doubt, as a biological trait necessary for the human being to survive, enjoy his life, and increase in numbers. The fact that the human race has increased vastly in numbers and extended itself all over the world is reasonable verification that this natural freedom process is operating, at least in compatibility and propagation, and that the pressures against this process have always modulated, more or less, within the potential of human compatibility for compromise and endurance. Where this could not occur, extension and continuity in some way stopped, whether from within or without, and the people perished.

However, this capacity for endurance and compromise can acculturate the human animal to such an extent that it can reach a point of diminishing returns and hasten the processes of degeneration. The fact that for many thousands of years it gradually came to be justified by rational debate and the growth of man's sense of *ethos* and equity only confirms that there are certain factors in man's cultural and natural history that affirm each other favorably and as necessarily compatible principles. To realize the

significance of this viewpoint is to understand that this natural
want for freedom evolved as a biological trait and therefore later
became one of the receptive and acceptive principles of the historical progression of man. René Dubos: "While it is obvious
that man is the product of his social and cultural history, it is
equally certain, on the other hand, that everything he does is
conditioned by his biological attributes. The performance of each
human being, and of each human group, reflects biological necessities and propensities inherited from the evolutionary and experiential past. Human decisions create social and cultural history, but the raw materials of this edifice are derived from man's
biological history."[120] Fritz-Martin Engel: "Although modern
man lives in a protected environment, created by himself, which
in the course of time he has adapted more and more, he remains
nevertheless a part of nature. . . . Man's relationship to earth
and nature is equivocal. . . . Over all stands the law of nature,
governing every form of life, man not least; and man must therefore seek to play the part alloted to him in the whole complex
pattern."[121]

NATURALISM AND FREEDOM

JOHN DEWEY STATED: "Naturalism is ready at any time to
maintain the thesis that foundation within man and nature is
a much sounder basis than is or can be any foundation alleged to
exist outside the constitution of man in nature."[122] Henri Pieron
goes further: "Little by little we succeed in freeing ourselves from
the congealed concepts of traditional psychology. . . . We are
engaged in constructing a science of psychology, dynamic in spirit,
which forms an integral part of the biological sciences."[123] Professor Robert L. Sinsheimer tells us: "As we have penetrated the
processes of the living cell, as the domains of mystery have receded, it becomes ever more clear that all of the properties of
life can be understood to be simply inherent in the material
properties of the complex molecules which comprise a cell. And
thus that seemingly qualitative gap—self-evident to the most
naïve—between the living and the nonliving has in our time

been bridged. . . . I do not pretend to understand how to bridge the seeming gap between matter and conscious sensation; but I suggest that having bridged one seemingly qualitative gap will give confidence to those who will bridge the next. In time we will come to understand the molecular and organizational basis of memory and emotion and intellect, and we will comprehend the strange spectrum of sensations and the dimensions of consciousness."[124] Slowly and clearly man is investigating more and meditating less, to rediscover his own alignment with the world about him and thus recover, if possible, the freedoms by which the world moves and by which he and other creatures manage to live in it.

The difference between the primitive savage and the civilized man today is that the primitive, in ratio to the restricting limitations of his environment, was more or less free but *did not know it.* The civilized man of today, also in ratio to his limitations, cultural and otherwise, is more or less *not* free and *knows it.* Thought, in itself, is a form of objective action, even if its relative value may be very limited to the external or outside world. "Peace of mind," so to speak, is a form of evolved and more or less stabilized state of realized contentment or nonirritability of some reasonable degree which engages in a continuing condition of normal activity. Therefore, the idea that an individual's thought, which emanates from, and is part of, his body, and which is naturally a form of objectivity, cannot be fairly judged as purely subjective even where it is not identified as an act by the individual or by or induced external factors or other individuals. John Dewey: "The traditional psychology of the original separate soul, mind or consciousness is in truth a reflex of conditions which cut human nature off from its natural objective relations."[125] Bertrand Russell: "From the standpoint of philosophy, the distinction between physical and mental is superficial and unreal." Samuel F. Dunlap: "Mankind have lived for ages as forms of matter. Life and mind have only been proved to exist in animal organizations. The spirits, like the dead, manifest neither life nor mind, and, in the case of injury to the brain, if life continues, mind ceases."[126] Lester F. Ward: "There can be no mind where there is no brain or nerve ganglia, no life where there is no animal, plant, protist or protoplasm." John Herman Randall, Jr.: "Ideas, emotions, meanings are impossible without bodily functioning; no mental event has ever existed except in a body. There can be a living brain without thought, but no thought without a brain."[127] Bernard Campbell: "The potentiality for life and consciousness exists in every atom (of carbon, hydrogen, oxygen, nitrogen, etc.), and these properties are revealed to us as the atoms are combined into organic molecules of greater and greater complexity. In other words, the fundamental particles have a mental component that is only apparent when they constitute appropriate structures."[128]

The function of thought seems to have evolved from the animal neural means to protect and aid the creature in its struggle to exist, survive, and better itself. Out of thought evolved attempts to communicate—the origin of language. Thus, freedom, which thought confesses the existence of, became a concomitant tool of the animal to further its own ends naturally and affirmatively.

It may be important to observe that many great men, including brilliant and erudite philosophers, have tried to systematize the history of man's advance in certain stages, very often logically and idealistically, but history does not allow us the privilege of perfecting a methodology of humanity on a logical basis and hardly on an a priori basis. The potentials in the seed of man, evolved many millions of years ago, repeat again and again in the same manner as history so often repeats itself in similarities of pattern and event.

For this reason some thinkers feel that freedom is a thing of the mind alone, that it came with man's awareness of himself, that it was processed by man's cultures or came about with the early societal growths of primitive attempts at some embryological forms of civilization. I do not think so. I think that freedom was there to begin with, prior to the emergence of cultures, that it is in the very nature of the human animal, in the very nature of the psyche, as it is in other forms of animal life: that with awareness of self came the sense of its identity. Man discovered freedom when he discovered himself; it was there before he found out. Every discovery of science only confirms and verifies the existence of the discoverable before the discovery. With the rise of priestly and imperial power came the awareness of its values and needs, and the misery and suffering of living without these values and needs.

Santayana writes that "society has three stages—the natural, the free, and the ideal."[129] Santayana's arrangement is confusing to me. I think that the *free,* that is, freedom, already exists with the natural, not in the absolute sense but in the sense of its potential within itself and within its related continuums of limitations and extension operable, as all other things, in the natural field. I think that freedom, in its greatest extent, exists in the natural. With the rise of man's sense of self-awareness, his sense of individualism, that is, his own being as a self, the anxieties, cravings for continued life, and fear of death, the pressures of power, the awareness and anticipation of death, and, therefore, the desire to penetrate through it and reach immortality, the gradual or sudden encroachments of the necessities and exigencies of social and political order and disorder—with all of these, freedom received its first and ugly restraints and disciplines. In order to achieve the "ends" of what it now deemed paramount, even insurmountable and unrealistic, perhaps even unattainable, the ideologies of man created the great gamble of categorical imperatives, asceticisms, commands, catechismic regularities and fulfillments to reach a stage of a newly invented goal—"purity"—within either the organization or pantheon of the gods or within the social and political conglomerations of materia and idea that constantly moved, changed, or stagnated people and the things they lived with and in.

Man has had and will always have, so long as he has a mind, the desire to create ideals, for himself and others, even for the entire universe. Whether these ideals can be logically and realistically applied to the experience of men is the determination whether they properly belong in the category of poetic fantasy or as part of any constructive effort or activity in the actual and possible experiences of people. There may be ideal-ized individuals, that is, individuals with any kind or classes of ideals, but I cannot find any identity of what Santayana seeks as the ideal society. There does not seem to be any such concoction as an ideal society. There may always be the search, the desire, even the actual effort to

attempt to form or reach some kind of ideal society, but the
identity of the existence of any such attainment or the physical
forms of its outline will remain, I fear, the constant horizon of
hopeful human progression. True, Santayana does not believe
any such thing exists or might exist in the future; he recognizes
the constant search for it. "Progressive evolution in any but an
anthropocentric sense cannot be recognized."[130]

It is not in the nature of life to become perfect, or to attain a
status of perfect satisfaction for any or all the individuals who
are already, and will always be, invested with imperfect minds.
Life and the universe of which it is a part, can never be in any
ideal state. Plato played with the thoughts of ideas, ideals, and
perfections, but never touched one. So long as we can think, hope,
dream, and idealize, we will strive on to reach *that* horizon,
whatever it may be. And these strivings, these struggles to reach
beyond us, these dreams and hopes to achieve something better,
higher, finer, more beautiful, more satisfying, will continue to
portray and screen the constant parades of grandeur and intellectual pageantries of human experiences and the things these
experiences constantly create, destroy, and create again.

It is for man, rather, to realign his mind toward a re-evaluation
of the natural field and its forces, of which he is a part, to identify
its mechanisms and compositions and so to try to understand its
field and possible directions and eventualities, and upon this
knowledge realign and re-evaluate his own knowledge and experiences so that upon a more realistic synchronization can there
be rendered some coordinative and possible alignment of human
forces and aspirations within this natural field. "The first move
toward a richer and more human philosophy of life should be to
rediscover man's partnership with nature."[131]

It appears silly that man, sitting on his own idealized throne
of egocosmocentricities, still believing that the universe was especially created for *him*, hawing about his glorious ideals while he
exterminates and despoils the natural life and field, while he
continues to push his own kind around, thinking the world itself
will get bigger or smaller with his ambitions, while he identifies
himself as the cruelest animal that creeps upon the earth, even
with his great music and poetry and profound orations about the

greatness of man. There can be no laws but the laws of man and every law of man was violated and is being violated by man, and yet if not for this law man would quickly destroy himself. His societies, in actuality, are the composite resignations of people to live as best as they can, anywhere, any time, and yet if society were left to individual whim or wish, man would promptly destroy man and there would be no hole or crevice where peace could be. Society is the product of man's fears of self-destruction, of the fears of man by man, not man's fear of nature. The first walled settlement or city was not built to protect itself against the rain, the sun, or the wind, but against the invasion of men. True, the primitive people, in families, clans and tribes, formed organizations or societies as a method of mutual assistance in their use of their natural environment in order better to survive; man necessarily respects nature by his resignation to, and his use of, it. There is really nothing else he could have done, regardless of his wishes, and this relationship, the evolved symbiosis of man and nature, is the actual history of man. All his freedoms are interwoven into this fabric of experience; it is for man to weave a more durable and satisfying pattern and fabric, and this depends upon his understanding of his raw materials, his own limitations and potentials, and the natural field in which he gets born, lives a while, and then dies.

It seems logical for man to graduate various phases of man's advancement from the crude to the fine, from the naked to the clothed, from the savage to the peaceful, from the wild to the tamed, from the beastly to the orderly, from the uncontrolled to the abiding, from the ignorant to the wise, from the lean-to to the castle, from the primitive to the professor. In the same manner, many brilliant thinkers have systematized these phases in a very logical manner: Spinoza had his three stages, from emotion to understanding to the third or final stage, intellectual knowledge. Hegel had his three stages. All these stages systematized by the logical sequences of man's thinking seem to run from what has been to what is being, and the idea or ideal of what would be or ultimately will be, according to the claims or dreams of each. This may be a logical synthesis, just as Hegel thought that his idea of thesis, antithesis, and synthesis, is the key to all experience and even ultimate knowledge. For all we know, it could be the other way around. It could be that man's increasing intelligence, due to the expanding of his brain and the concomitant lessening of the use of other parts of the body, may ultimately destroy the body with its brain. For all we know, we may find out, perhaps too late, that the emotions or the instinctive processes of the living human system, evolved out of millions of years of experienced trial and error, may contain far more nonintellectualized and nonrationalized knowledge, and be far superior in some ways to the application of intelligence without such experience, and based on theoretical and logical deduction. This does not mean that man's intelligence has been a hindrance; perhaps it has been and may get worse; this is not the point in question. The problem is whether in depending more and more on logical thinking and cultivating a greater degree of intelligence man may be overlooking and gradually forgetting the main purpose as to why and how intelligence got started in the first place—to preserve and satisfy the body! Whether the process going on since then has vindicated its original purpose or not, if we could momentarily call it purpose, is open to inquiry and may be questioned. Refinement does not always mean a better quality, a better condition; often it destroys, as in the many foods of men, the rugged and undegenerated and undiluted qualities essential to the needs and life of living things.

It may be interesting to inquire into the history of man and see whether or not we have paid too high a price for being led into the more refined and fragrant ways of civilization. The Christian-Euro-American civilizations, with their ascetic-puritanical refinements and hypocrisies, on the one hand offering goodies to the "primitive" so that the primitives should suffer as they do, on the other hand extending the tools of mechanization, power aggrandizement, and economic intrigue and exploitation—these have degenerated the natural freedom of people wherever they have trod and infiltrated; they have discolored the natural green of the world with their false philosophies and are now slowly polluting it with their industrial excreta, fouling the byways of living things; these have hid the sun from our eyes and shut us away from the fresh air and the wholesomeness of natural and healthful living. These

civilizations have not brought ethics around the world; they have
brought hammers, nails, mirrors, gadgets to bribe the natives to
enslave themselves and be degenerated by the intruders. This
world of ours would be a far better place to live in if everyone
greeted each other with a Ponapean *Kasaléhlia,* and smelled the
nectar of the unadorned, the unsynthesized, and the open vistas
instead of the refuse of the complexed man and his machines.

The evolution of the principle of freedom from primitive to
modern times is the story of human conflict and the gradually
increasing portent of human tragedy to live a more or less non-
free life. Perhaps there are deep-rooted drives in the human animal that constantly deprive him of the freedom drive and set in
motion the strange dilemma of desiring negation and even self-
destruction. Buddha is an example. The ascetics are many more.

The primitive unconsciously enjoyed freedom as a natural way
of life, just as he enjoyed any of his other natural wants, just as
a child, unconscious of things and people, in the grown-up sense,
moves about as it pleases. If civilized man will use his cultivated
intelligence to re-establish this natural want of freedom on a
conscious basis as indispensable and essential to a naturally good
and happy life, then perhaps he can make something out of his
mundane existence, perhaps mankind may probably still have a
chance, slim as it may be, to move toward affirmative rationalization instead of negational despair, and take a positive attitude to
the gradual end of such conflict. The intelligent translation and
application of such biological and psychological power may enable man to naturally transform the springs of needless conflict
into streams of good and happy achievement for the individual
and his social, economic, and cultural processes and products.

The view that man's sense of freedom is a biological trait and
evolved like other things in his physical and psychological history does not imply, as Rousseau held, that man is naturally free
and good. "Man is naturally good," he wrote, "and that it is by
our institutions alone that men become wicked." This is an illusion, as man is not, in the unlimited sense, free, being attached
inexorably to all else; nor is he *per se* naturally good, this judgment being purely his own and based on bias, not observation.
Being free and being good are two different things; however, this

does not imply that freedom and goodness are naturally alienated from each other. It does mean that a free person can be bad and a good person not necessarily free, and vice versa. The natural potential of the human being contains cruelty as well as peacefulness, contains the drive for freedom and the drive to unfree the self. These counter and opposing drives make up the paradoxes of the human constitution and its involvement with the world. Alex Comfort: "Man is the only animal which is inherently able, corporately and individually, to be his own worst enemy."[132]

Hobbes held that natural man seeks only "that which pleaseth him and is delightful to himself." This is also not entirely true and not based on sufficient observation. All men are natural, true enough, to begin with, and they all end up that way. But people do not always seek the good, the delightful, or even that which pleases them. Often man seeks the opposite, even self-denial of pleasures and things his very nature craves and longs for (which he calls his religious ways of purification), even suicide which other animals do not know about or commit, and whether anything delights him is not always the object of his affections or of his search. Rationalism and the general education of the intellect may assist him to further his right to pleasure or his search for it, within a self-realizable sense of freedom that may afford him some scale of value-judgment by which he might possibly attain the good without the bad or remorseful consequences. We must remember that what is natural is not necessarily intellectual, ethical, wise, good, or good-seeking. We should also keep in mind that the evolution of the intellect and of intelligence has been a means by which man extended his physical and bodily powers beyond his personal self, the causative process involved being the drive for security, power, and greater life satisfaction.

We will have the opportunity in later pages to analyze further the various philosophic paradoxes of men and institutions regarding the many factors of human experiences for which the subject of freedom provides the "space" in which these factors exhibit and operate. In doing so we must try to be as realistic as possible so that the observable and experienced ways of man can be lucidly applied to a philosophy of freedom that might fit and apply to man's daily existence, in his surroundings, in his household, in his consciousness of his own nature to the potential of freedom. This is usually overlooked by the metaphysicians in their submergence to Osirian resurrections of absolutes and godheads. Demeter need not look for Persephone; her daughter, being the younger composite of herself, will always return in the spring. And so the metaphysicians need not grow old seeking the resurrection of that which is not possible to resurrect while they waste away their younger years by dilution into the void. Metaphysics has been theorizing so much and so long about ultimates and ultimate reality that it has forgotten all about immediate reality—*us*. It may be good to get up into the sky, and we do, but good only if we can always get back to good old solid ground—the world itself. Metaphysics has been trying to separate, as much as possible the personality and thought of man, on one side, and, on the other, his body, life, the world, man's habits, and his daily chores. It is high time they should get together for the common good. They would no doubt find out happily that they were made for each other.

A philosopher's future is always in his nostrils. There are no shortcuts or easy solutions to a panacea for humanity. The human element is a limited element with much promise, no less than much unpredictability and paradoxical surprises. It all depends on what we do, or can do, with our heritage and our search for a better life in a better world. Philosophy has cried "Eureka!" ever so often, and each "Eureka!" brought us to places unknown and new circumstances to be solved. While we can think, we also, in a way, "smell" our way to good or bad things as our minds translate odors and fragrances into principles and actions. As Bertrand Russell so soberly stated: "We must, therefore, renounce the hope that philosophy can promise satisfaction to our mundane desires. What it can do is to help us understand the general aspects of the world and the logical analysis of familiar but complex things."[133] Randall: "The philosopher who ceases to ask questions has ceased to be a philosopher."[134] The nature of inquiry proceeds endlessly so long as man remains an inquiring mind and animal. And "as long as man remains an inquiring animal, there can never be a complete unanimity in our fundamental beliefs."[135] "The human mind is uncommitted."[136]

Freedom is a quantitative and a qualitative word, both factors influencing the extent and nature of each other. In protohominid times it seems very probable that these subhuman savages were possessed of the fuller extent of freedom only limited to their own aggressiveness, wanderlust, and their environmental bounds. With the primitive, where there probably existed a wide leverage of unconscious freedom, the quantitative and qualitative factors of this freedom were more or less limited by the tribal customs, usages, and their cultural frame. No doubt, as tribes became more numerous and grew in size, and the customs of these tribes became more complex, more deep-rooted in the behavior patterns, the increasing complexities of the tribal structure and its group functions began to diminish, to some extent, the sense of freedom. This diminishment continued through human history and into modern times. Freedom, in the raw, so called, is something every wild animal possesses, and to a lesser extent many of the savage humans still prowling about in the deep recesses of the jungle; to a still lesser extent the semi-civilized man; and to the least extent, the civilized man.

MAN, THE ANIMAL

THE FACT THAT man is an animal, that he rose from savage, cruel, and merciless ancestors is, in itself, a great credit to him considering his rise from such a heritage to the great stages of his present domain, civilized cultures, his sciences, his vast structures and cities, farms and industries, his wondrous arts in all its forms of expression, his philosophies and his laws. The long historical paths he has trodden from the primitive bush of grass and branches to the magnificent edifices of today, from the stone slab, the logogramic clay tablet and stylus to the electric typewriter with interchangeable types, from the cave wall on which he cut his Aurignacian lithic pictures to the academic professor reading some encyclopedia in the college library corner: that man should and could have accomplished this must be accredited to him. This is the story of a remarkable animal with a remarkable history.

Assuredly, man might still be able, perhaps under the pressure of necessity, to go farther and higher to abide eventually in a more peaceful and more intellectual and a more equitable philosophy, which can reflect these premises, not merely in the library corner or in the teacher, but in the daily labors, leisures, and habits of the rank and file of humanity. On the basis of what has occurred in the past such an optimistic realization cannot be reasonably predicted. On the contrary, if mankind continues in the way of the past, the reverse of such an idea has more reason to be predicted. Whether man can give such meaning and value to his physical accomplishments is something that cannot be predetermined. Unless this could possibly come about—and whether it can or will is highly conjectural, even improbable—all his cultural and material accomplishments will only that much sooner degenerate his biological foundation, diminish, and eventually eliminate more of his freedom by the absence of its necessity—its *nonuse*—a cultivated, patternized, emergent inertia. Perhaps *necessity,* the parent of want and the very shadow of freedom, might still be the primer in the survival and ultimate peacefulness of the human race.

As a rule, people do not like to hear themselves called animals. But we are. Desmond Morris: "We are, despite all our great technological advances, still very much a simple biological phenomenon. Despite our grandiose ideas and our lofty self-conceits, we are still humble animals, subject to all the basic laws of animal behaviour. . . . Our climb to the top has been a get-rich-quick story, and, like all *nouveaux riches,* we are very sensitive about our background. We are also in constant danger of betraying it."[137] Douglas M. C. MacEwan: "We are accustomed to think in terms of the human environment, but in fact the environment in which we live supports not only the human race but a vast variety of other living things—both plants and animals. The human being is an animal—a remarkably successful one, though his success may possibly prove to be shortlived—and it is within the whole system of animal and plant life that human life must be considered."[138] Alex Comfort: "The shock did not lie in realizing that human beings have elements in common with the 'lower' animals—that had long been recognized. It lay in the recognition that cherished human behavior and attitudes, as well as such processes as thinking, loving, producing art and all the other activities which we traditionally accept as 'ours,' were now within the scope of the same sceptical method which could be used to elucidate the ways of animals: that Man was subject to study and experiment, not at a different rate of exchange, but at the same rate of exchange as the rest of nature."[139] Desmond Morris: "In becoming so erudite, *Homo sapiens* has remained a naked ape nevertheless; in acquiring lofty new motives, he has lost none of the earthly old ones."[140] Vernon Reynolds: "Beneath the veneer we are still animals."[141] John Steinbeck: "It is not observed that I find it valid to understand man as a animal before I am prepared to know him as a man."[142]

Civilization, in which a certain extent of ethics and decorum may express themselves, is still a thin, if opaque, veneer of pressure, insufficient by far to keep smooth even the surfaces of the seas of humanity that keep boiling, bubbling, erupting, swelling and storming, forever unstill and not silent, even though the air above be calm and the butterflies safely perched on warm, sunny leaves and the forests echo back the peaceful gibbering of the squirrels on its branches. It seems, as William Golding so brilliantly metaphrased, man must seek and be cowed by the "Lord of the Flies."[143]

The wild animal is not conscious of its freedom; it lives it. Even the primitive naked savage in the Brazilian jungle, gathering his roots, locusts, woodworms, and bitter nuts, with an occasional bird or fish to keep him alive in his constant struggle for existence from day to day, is conscious in a sense of the pressing, threatening jungle, its parasites, its venom, and its overpowering totality, against which he pits his frail naked body, his essential compromises with it in the form of resignation to magic and tribal customs, and to this extent realizes, even physically, a sense of limitation of his freedom. It is understandable that we moderns consider that we are freer than a savage in the jungle, that we can do this or that, dress, go to theaters, take a plane to faraway places and be wined and dined, travel as we feel like, think better, write and communicate freely, and in many ways may claim that we are more free than the primitive. But the modern fails

to see outside of himself, and if both the savage and the civilized
man could possibly do so, they would see that whatever they
have been acculterated and enculturated with has become part
of their natures and consequently inwardly acceptable to a certain degree sufficient to make them feel "more free." By being
brought up in their cultures and becoming part of their culture-
traits, their sense of resistance to any of these cultures becomes
minimized or eliminated, and, as a consequense, any limitation
or deprivation of freedom is not consciously felt or opposed.

The freedom of the savage, to a certain extent, has been surrendered to the jungle. The freedom of the civilized man, to a
greater extent, has been surrendered to specialization, greater
interdependency, culture and its society. The savage, in his
limited freedom, can still survive reasonably well in the jungle
so long as the civilized man does not take potshots at him. The
civilized man, now attuned and dependent upon his society to a
greater degree, cannot reasonably survive in the jungle under
the same conditions as the savage. The surrender of the biological
freedom of the civilized man has, by new adaptations and dependencies, weakened to a certain degree his natural power to survive. Mechanism has devitalized him. "The fantasy which the
religion of Science is still nightmarishly acting out is the fantasy
of the machine getting out of hand and marching on the machin-
ist."[144] As Alan Moorehead ends his book, *The Fatal Impact:*
"The noble savage, in short, is well on his way to becoming the
noble robot."[145] W. Phillip Keller, the naturalist, gives his viewpoint: "In our modern society the individual man or woman has
to wrestle with the social and scientific technology which he himself has devised to surmount his surroundings. Electricity, air
conditioning and central heating temper his climate. Mass marketing provides him with a steady food supply. Social security has
guaranteed his safety from the cradle to the coffin . . . or, at least,
so he imagines. Yet all of this comes at a price. That price is the
loss of personal freedom. For just when we would shout from our
television towers that we have mastered our world, men suddenly
discover that we have in fact become slaves to a man-made system
of gadgetry, collectivism and gross materialism. Instead of a man's
worth being measured in the integrity of his character, the

strength of his body, or the quality of his mind, it is in the pomp and prestige he can impose upon his fellows, either by possessions or position."[146]

To each human in a certain culture his particular culture seems to be the most "natural" one and other cultures somewhat strange and unacceptable to some degree or other. A man today, looking back, cannot understand how people could have possibly got along without the auto, without steam, without all the tools, gadgets, and conveniences of living we possess today. The modern housewife, in her steam-heated, air-conditioned apartment, buying her frozen meals ready to heat and eat, or just dropping in on the local restaurant of her choice, not having to fire the stove or grow or kill her own food, just could not "exist" in the conditions of a generation or two ago. How their grandmothers managed to keep house they are unable to understand or visualize. Not having lived in that period of even a short time ago, they cannot feel the contemporary pulse of that period; they are already oculated with present sights given them by their present cultures. All this has been purchased with some "money" taken from the "purse" of biological freedom. Thus, from the biological point of view, the machine is creating in man a greater fantasy of greater freedom, but what is really happening is that the machine is slowing taking away man's activity, and what man is receiving, in return for his ingenuities, is *inertia,* or what science calls *entropy.* Mechanization has enslaved him.

Whether man can mechanize the world for the good of his society, as well as for the good of his body and mind, is a problem that man's civilizations have not yet solved and that we shall try to discuss more fully later on. Whether this problem may ultimately be solved is conjectural, and if there can be some attempt at solution then man must realize and know his own nature and the nature and operableness of his freedoms and in which directions and ways these freedoms can be exhibited, motivated, and extended for his own good and that of the social and mechanical organism in which his living destiny is resigned to spend itself. Claude Lévi-Strauss stresses this point well: "From the day when he first learned how to breathe and how to keep himself alive, through the discovery of fire and right up to the invention of the atomic and thermonuclear devices of the present day, Man has never—save only when reproducing himself—done other than cheerfully dismantle million upon million of structures and reduce their elements to a state in which they can no longer be reintegrated. No doubt he has built cities and brought the soil to fruition; but if we examine these activities closely we shall find that they also are inertia-producing machines, whose scale and speed of action are infinitely greater than the amount of organization implied in them. As for the creations of the human mind, they are meaningful only in relation to that mind and will fall into nothingness as soon as it ceases to exist."[147]

There is no doubt that by the collective effort of the peoples of the world, the earthly and the only environment of mankind can be changed enormously to suit the needs of man and his expanding, exploding populations. Much can be done to "condition" the world to man's needs and ascendancy, but the cost of this project is already rearing its ugly heads: *regimentation* for the human being, and with it his loss of individualism and its natural freedoms; *destruction* of the natural balances and evolved interrelationships of man's biological nature and its symbiotic structures, which came about over hundreds of millions of years of evolved adjustments and its consequent forms. "Humanity has taken to monoculture, once and for all, and is preparing to produce civilization in bulk as if it were a sugar-beet. The same dish will be served to us every day."[148] This problem, too, we will have to consider more thoroughly later on and attempt to arrive at some constructive and realistic analysis that might engender some suggestibility for thought and action.

An analytical exposition of the nature of the historical processes of the diminishment of freedom may seem to be of introductory value and should be one of the early labors of this work. From this we might gain some beneficial critique of meanings and values, still hopeful we might be able to construct a reasonably and naturally sound philosophy of freedom which we might possibly and practically feel as part of us, as existing within our circumjacent environment and which we can consciously and actively apply with some expectation to better our lives and possibly the lives of those to come. The only opposition we can en-

counter in this effort is not nature, not the world, not the other
animals, not the skies and the stars, but man himself.

COMPATIBILITY VERSUS HARMONY

Before we enter into the misty past of our ancestors in
our efforts to reach even the outer rim and approaches of the
early arenas of life in which the natural forces helplessly polarized the pressures and resistances of living things, both plant and
animal, into the compromised chains of growth, extension, change,
specialization, and survival, we should try to discern the important differences between what is indicated as a *natural compatibility* and what is considered by some philosophers as opposing,
a purposeful, or preplanned, pattern of design, whether vitalistic
or mechanical. This might include an intelligent direction toward a perfecting process or a planned curriculum of material
and spiritual forces designed or ordered to reach ultimately a
goal of the highest good or perfection. All of these attributes indicate a "oneness," which a scientist may call Nature, a philosopher
may call the Cosmos, and the theologian may call God.

A *natural compatibility* does not necessarily imply that certain
things agree to join forces, to socialize, or to live in peace with
themselves out of some intelligent, planned, predetermined, pre-
engaged, or agreed, purposeful design of nature, by which certain things "agree" to exist or to live in a "certain" way or in a
certain compromised pattern or behavior. It does mean that in
the long trek of evolutionary time during which animal and plant
life came to be what they are, all these things existed or lived
in a certain way or pattern because of what they *were,* and all
relationships were *determined* by what they were related to. In
other words, the human animal, whether he agreed or not,
whether he liked it or not, "accepted" this natural world and
its relationships of his umbilicalized ties to it. With this as a
base, the human being proceeded to use his intelligence and intellect, evolved out of his prehensilities and the environmental
influences affecting them, to better or worsen his condition.
Which, in another way, simply means that man's thinking in

terms of what is his natural heritage and its relationships to all else about him, enabled him to make changes, when possible, to situations from a certain compatibility, whether good or bad, to another compatibility, whether better or worse. In actuality, this is the way man has *moved* through history, from the arboreal life to life on the ground and from the ground to the village, town, city and nation, and this is the only process that has advanced man materially and intellectually. Bernard Campbell: "We ourselves are primates, and the origin of our nature may be traced quite precisely to the adaptations of the primates that evolved in response to the forest environment . . . man's move from the forest to the plain made us finally into what we are and is the story of our own evolution."[149]

So great has man's image of idea become that a single individual can emotionalize millions of people to destroy others and to destroy themselves. This process of *image,* determined by previous experiences, and of *invention,* nurtured by sequences of ideas, accidental discovery, and necessity, are the two hands with which man has built his advance and sciences. Inventions are the mechanical emissarial absorbents of natural freedom. At the cost of his own reduction in biological quantum, man has made it possible for the individual to become many; he has given his body extensions and thus enabled himself to express the processes of freedom to a far greater degree, and bring about many more consequences as a result of this extended freedom. These extensions may become so vast and so distant from his physical self as eventually to make him helpless. Whether these extensions of freedom have been a real beneficence or not is a question of opinion, but they are here, and here to stay so long as man continues to stay. The chain of increasing mechanization has been set in motion and nothing will stop it except the elimination of man by man by these very extensions. Whether man can regain his biological freedom and control his newly found mechanical prehensilities is another question, the solution of which cannot be fairly predicted. Mechanization is the greatest reality of the modern age; so is neurosis, psychosomatics, stress and strain, bewildered power, and a sick humanity. So great has his inventive-

ness become that today a single person can, by choosing to press
a button, destroy the world and all that lives on it.

When man's mind in ancient times *digressed* from the process
of natural compatibility, congruity, and noncontradiction, as
occurred in the fantastic taboos and fetich-magics, shamanism,
ancient Egyptian and Sumerian life-sacrifices in "continuance"
burials, Hindu asceticisms, Buddhistic withdrawals and escapes,
Shinto absorption into the godhead, or the Christian betrayal of
life for paradise or damnation—when these things occurred, man
forced *metaphysical* compatibilities which, although part of his
natural experiences like everything else, drew him away from
life, degenerated and misguided him away from the *real* and
more rational compatibilities to *unreal,* irrational, and antinatural compatibilities. These were the psychological changes and
powers in man's history that affected the rest of the story.

When man's course of freedom was abruptly or gradually, willingly or unwillingly, changed by the force of naked, absolute or
traditional power, whether this power was psychological, rebellious, oligarchic, feudal, religious, or military, or any combination of them, the process of his natural compatibilities was
affected and thus regenerated or degenerated. New compatibilities, favorable or unfavorable, created resistances to their pressures, and then cyclic chains of conflict, until some eventually
natural or tolerable compatible level was reached. Whenever
man's mind forced or coerced his body and its experiences, willingly or unwillingly, to accept an antinatural situation, he
aborted the natural processes of compatibility and thus sowed the
seed to germinate conflict and anxiety within himself and in his
relationships with others and the world. All life is a chain of
compromises, a constant process of adjustment within the nature
of living. Whether these compromises, or any of them, are good
or bad, regenerative or degenerative, is another question of a
particular meaning and value and so determines the happiness
or misery of a person. Ruth Benedict wisely wrote: "No one has
ever developed an objective scale of values according to which all
different cultural goals may be graded as better or worse."[150] This
problem, too, will be taken up in due course.

When we give some thought to this idea of predetermined harmony or design—whether it be the Zoroastrian belief that all existence is specially and finely divided into light and darkness, good and bad, opposing each other in the constant struggle for mastery, yet predetermined that the good should win and paradise attained; or whether this harmony is a necessary coadunating pattern of nature, in which all things are fitted purposefully to carry on a particular predetermined plan or *idea* toward perfection or as a perfection in itself—we realize that if any such harmony could be true, the existence of any form of freedom would become an absurdity, as it would find no place in a scheme ideologically evolved in the mind of man but certainly not in the general experiences and ways of nature. "For all that is justified by the facts of organic history," writes Henry E. Crampton, "is the statement that the processes of nature . . . cannot be reasonably regarded as the inevitable or necessary results of a 'purposed' production."[151]

Teilhard de Chardin, a believer in more or less directed or purposeful evolution, calls the direction of evolution "the point Omega"—a "harmonized collectivity of consciousness, equivalent to a kind of superconsciousness. The earth is covering itself not merely by myriads of thinking units, but by a single continuum of thought, and finally forming a functionally single Unit of Thought of planetary dimensions. The plurality of individual thoughts combine and mutually reinforce each other in a single act of unanimous Thought . . . Man, the ascending arrow of the great biological synthesis."[152]

Teilhard de Chardin forgot to include in this "ascending arrow," which he calls man, the reinforcing thoughts, combining themselves into the great Unit of Thought, contributed by Hitler, Mussolini, by the Conquistadores of Mexico and South America, by the Inquisitors, by the Greek, Roman, Babylonian, and Chinese slaveholders, by the wholesale murder and theft by the Catholic Hierarchy in the New World as well as in the Old for many centuries, by Edwin Booth just before he shot Lincoln, by Oswald just before he shot Kennedy, and the fine thoughts uniting with the Unit of Thought of the English, Portuguese, and Spanish bishops blessing the slave ships going down to Africa to tear the natives away from their roots and sell them for animal labor in the New World. All these murderers and sadists no doubt had consciences, and most assuredly in their minds their consciences were at ease and requited for having accomplished what they thought, according to their natures, was right, just, and even for the benefit of their victims. Conscience is conditional and conditioned, and therefore depends more upon the emotions and subconscious desires and drives than on reason and rational analysis. Dr. Alex Comfort, in his book *The Nature of Human Nature,* writes: "Conscience, indeed, is always largely irrational, even when it is supporting reasonable moral judgments, and is not a very reliable guide to ethics if judgment and conscious self-mastery can be substituted—conscience, after all, made inquisitors and self-mutilating ascetics as well as saints."[153]

Teilhard de Chardin no doubt had fine thoughts, and fancied the world in keeping with his own dreams, of which his Unit of Thought is one. His error was in forcing the projection of man's thought upon the cosmos and deflecting it back in human guise and desire, then shifting the blame and praise of man's thought to the great Unit of Thought of the Universe, of which man, in his new role, is but a helplessly designed thinking part of the thinking Whole. To satisfy his idea of his own purpose in life and to fulfill, at least emotionally, his continuing dream of coalescence, in some form, rational or irrational, with the Over-Allness, of God, or the Unit of Thought, he contrived to beautify science and human evolution to lead him where theology failed, to the Holy Grail, to drink the potion which will drive away the fright of oblivion and bring eternal life. This metaphysical pseudo-sociological theory of collective superconsciousness will be taken up in later pages when we examine the work of Durkheim.

Although various degrees of intelligence appear in living parts of nature, including man, this does not imply or prove that nature as a whole is intelligent or that it contains some prearranged design or purpose or that this is contained in its processes. Can there be any intelligent purpose or design in the Mayfly that remains in a quiescent pupal stage for many years and, when mature, lives only a few hours to fulfill the need to propagate the same process again? "*Calopteryx virgo* develops in the water as a rapacious gray-brown larva for about two years, but once it has turned into a dragonfly proper (in this final stage it is called an *imago*) its span of life is rarely more than twelve days."[154] "A Mayfly may arise at noon from the water that cradled it," observes J. Arthur Thomson, "and by sundown its aerial dance of love may be over and its lifeless body be floating on the surface of the pool."[155] Commenting on the Mayfly, Benjamin Franklin mused: "Art is long and life is short." "Man must accept the fact," writes George F. Thomas, "that nature is indifferent to his ideals and values, in the sense that there is no evidence of purpose on her part to realize or support them."[156]

Freedom, like life itself, implies by the nature of itself a subjection to possible trial and error, and this exposes the absurdity and wishful thinking of natural harmony, or a completely harmonious freedom, or some form of freedom based on purposeful and/or intelligent design. "Evolution is a peculiar combination," write Carleton Ray and Elgin Ciampi in their book on *Marine Life,* "of the randomness of mutation and the orientation of natural selection. . . . Evolution has no goal, but it does have method and a reason. The necessity of life to adapt to an ever-changing and complex environment is the reason."[157]

Man, deeming himself a "moral" person, tries to conceive the nature in which he lives to be of some "moral" nature, too, or to contain some "moral" purpose. Man, being himself at times ethical, or at least attempting to be so in principle, feels that the entire order of nature was "created" or evolved out of some fine, eventually happy or good plan, that nature is basically good and will eventually lead to the good.

Horace said: *"Nihil est ab omni parte beatum"*—does good fortune exist to which no misfortune is attached?—which brings out the old moss-covered concept that with every positive there must be a negative, good and evil, heaven and hell, life and death, etc. This smacks of Zoroastrian flavor, and is firmly enculturated within the old and present formal religions. The idea is religious in character. It seems to me that a thing or act does not necessarily have to be positive or negative, good or bad, these being viewpoints and values placed upon experiences and things by different people. What is important is that an act or thing is

favorable or unfavorable to the affirmative and desirable. What
has been considered as unmoral has often been the regenerating
force of life, without which life would be empty of meaning and
beneficially natural and normal activity.

As stated above, the theologian believes that each person has
to choose between going on the road to heaven or the road to hell,
and, therefore, life and nature are processes of refinement or ultimate solution between good and bad, eventually ending up with
the enthronement of the blessedly good. Even Paul, creating a
Jesus out of Egypt's Osiris, Phrygian's Attis, and the Semitic
Adonis, had Jesus say, to explain the "free will" of the people
who crucified Him: "Father, forgive them, for they know not
what they do!" Morris Raphael Cohen gives us a clear-cut rebuttal of this Maimonidean concept: "The Kantian freedom of
the will means a form of causation, quite different from the kind
of causation in the natural world. In the natural world cause
and effect form a series in which there is no first or last term.
Cause and effect are on the same level. But in the moral determination pure reason, according to Kant, is not a temporal term
and yet it produces practical effects in time. How that is possible
or reconciliable with the universality of natural causation (on
which he always insists) we are in no way told. On the other hand,
if certain acts or social arrangements are pronounced unjust because they interfere with transcendental or noumenal freedom
are we not assuming that the phenomenal world can have causal
efficacy in the noumenal realm? And if there is this constant interaction between the noumenal and the temporal, how can we
maintain the purely rational and non-temporal character of the
former?"[158]

Of course, what is exactly good and bad as a common principle, from the viewpoint of all people and all experience, is
something the Kantians and theologians have not furnished us.
We know that there is good and bad, according to what we want
and like and what we want to avoid and do not like. But to place
this upon a universal plane, or to impose any such discretion of
desire or feeling as a cosmic standard, is something else. The
theologian feels or believes that it is good to be a theologian, and
no doubt would not discourage this attainment for all others.

If all others, that is, all the people in the world would become theologians, it would ensue that being a theologian is good so long as all the theologians agree with each other. If this should occur—and thank the gods it will not—the world would stagnate and die of boredom and agreement. When we examine the pages of religious history, especially the controversies of the early Church, it is difficult to find where *two* theologians did fully agree with each other. In those days agreement was reached by murder or banishment. Writing about the early Church, Homer W. Smith states: "The efforts of each group to exterminate dissident opinion were rendered all the more difficult by the multiplicity of theories: conflicting heresies cross-ruffed each other until the faith of Christendom was on the verge of destroying itself by its internal disagreement."[159]

When we examine nature a bit closer, we do not find these haloed high purposes in the struggle of living things. Harry A. Overstreet enlightens us: "The scientist has a gently persistent way of refusing to be awed by holies of holies. When he is told that he must not enter a particular unenterable, he quietly proceeds to make preparations to walk in and take possession. That, in brief, is the history of the development of the mechanistic theory of life in biology and later in psychology. The scientist walked into the holy of holies and *found nothing there*."[160]

If a theologian likes to eat steak—and many do, most enthusiastically, no doubt—we do not think of it as bad. But the steer must feel that this is not good, highly unethical, in fact, cruel, to say the least, and that it would be more to his liking should humans eat grass as he does and leave him alone. To order harmony or intelligent design to the totality of nature is not logical or sensible. It confesses the cosmocentricity of man. Let us take a look at a few of the "harmonies" and "purposeful" "designs" of nature:

Donald Culross Peattie writes: "Senseless might smashes in a tidal wave upon the unfeeling rocks. Forever wasting itself, the terrific energy of sea and wind is but a fraction of the power in the universe that radiates away unused, unfelt."[161] Bertrand Russell: "Instinct, like all human faculties, is liable to error."[162] Van Campen Heilner: "It appears that fish and birds continue to

follow ancestral migration routes regardless of changing conditions and in some instances to such an extent that the entire
species might be seriously depleted."[163] Elie Metchnikoff: "There
are in certain orchids organs which do not fulfill any function."[164]
"It does not follow that development always takes a progressive
march."[165] "The wide-spread results of alcoholism show plainly
the prevalent existence in man of a want of harmony between the
instinct of choosing food and the instinct of preservation."[166] The
same is true in governmental warning in the smoking of cigarettes
as the cause of lung cancer; people just go on smoking, even more
so. "Disharmony is exhibited in the human body not only by
rudimentary organs such as the wisdom teeth and the appendage,
or by degenerating organs such as the caecum. Some very large
parts of our alimentary canal must be regarded as useless inheritance, bequeathed to us by our animal ancestors."[167] "Puberty
declares itself in a woman by the beginning of menstruation at a
time when girls still possess infantile characters and when the
bones of the pelvic basis are not yet fully developed."[168] "In the
legacy acquired by man from his ancestors, there occur not only
rudimentary organs that are useless or harmful, but fully developed organs equally useless. The large intestine must be regarded
as one of the organs possessed by man and yet harmful to his
health and life."[169] "Sexual excitability appears at an age when
there is no question but that the sexual elements are unde-
veloped."[170] "Even amongst fossorial wasps, the instincts which
are so admirably developed, harmony is far from perfect."[171] The
disharmonies and waste in nature are so varied and so extensive
that it would take volumes and volumes to recite them.

NATURE AND MORALITY

Is THERE A moral purpose in nature? "Let us now examine
the motives," writes Fabre, the great French naturalist, "which
induce the philanthus to kill its bee instead of paralyzing it. The
murder once committted, it does not release its victim for a moment, but holding it tightly clasped with its six legs pressed
against its body, it commences to ravage the corpse. I see it with

the utmost brutality rooting with its mandibles in the articulation of the neck, and often also in the more ample articulation of the corselet, behind the first pair of legs; perfectly aware of the fine membrane in that part, although it does not take advantage of the fact when employing its sting, although this vulnerable point is the more accessible of the two breaches in the bee's armour. I see it squeezing the bee's stomach, compressing it with its own abdomen, crushing it as in a vise. The brutality of this manipulation is striking; it shows that there is no more need of care and skill; the bee is a corpse, and a little extra pushing and squeezing will not deteriorate its quality as food, provided there is no effusion of blood; and however rough the treatment, I have never been able to discover the slightest wound. These various manipulations, above all the compression of the throat, lead to the desired result: the honey in the stomach of the bee ascends to the mouth. I see the drops of honey welling out, lapped up by the glutton as soon as they appear. The bandit greedily takes in its mouth the extended and sugared tongue of the dead insect; then once more it presses the neck and the thorax, and once more applies the pressure of the abdomen to the honey-sac of the bee. The honey oozes forth and is instantly licked up. This odious meal at the expense of the corpse is taken in a truly sybaritic attitude: the Philanthus lies upon its side with the bee between its legs. This atrocious meal lasts often half an hour or longer. Finally, the exhausted corpse is abandoned; regretfully it seems, for from time to time I have seen the ogre return to the feast and repeat its manipulation of the body. After taking a turn around the top of the bell-glass the robber of the dead returns to the victim, squeezes it once more, and licks its mouth until the last trace of honey has disappeared."[172] Which would be the espouser of the universal moral principle or of the perfecting harmony of nature—the philanthus or the bee?

Jordan and Everman, ichthyologists, in their standard work on fishes, write about the rapaciousness of the bluefish: "It has even been maintained that such is the gluttony of this fish, that when the stomach becomes full the contents are disgorged and then again filled! It is certain that it kills more fish than it needs or can use. The amount of food they consume or destroy is incredibly great. It has been estimated at twice the weight of the fish in a day, and one observer says that a bluefish will destroy daily a thousand other fish."[173] Which would the theological advocate of the categorical imperative or of the harmonious totality of the cosmos, be—the bluefish or the herring?

"Rarely, in nature do animals die by 'natural causes.' Predators, parasites, or disease usually spell the end."[174]

Where is the harmonious factor?—in the animal or the parasite? "Sometimes, female lace-wings have been known to become hungry during the process of depositing their stalked eggs and to appease that hunger by making a meal of one of the eggs they have just laid."[175] What is part of the great harmony, the eaten egg or the voracious mother? "C. F. Hodge showed that a single pair of houseflies, which began to reproduce in April, could, if all the flies lived, be the progenitors by August of 191,010,000,-000,000,000,000 adults."[176] Does this indicate intelligent, purposeful, or divine design? Hardly, but it does mean that nature is certainly prolific, especially houseflies.

I should like to lead a tour for theologians into the hospitals, clinics, and rehabilitation centers to see for themselves the Great Harmony and the Universal Moral Law at work. Little tots in constant unbearable pain, chronic arthritics, infants with twisted and retarded minds, emotionally disturbed and shocked, frightened, frozen without the warmth of love and devotion to soothe their tiny aching bodies. This awesome review can go on endlessly. I know, as I am a director of such a clinic. We are doing all we can for them, and we are reasonably successful, but if we had to depend upon the theologians or the Universal Harmony, my heart and mind could not be so patient, nor my life so long in waiting.

Theology believes that God created man. If this is presumed, it would follow that the attributes of man, whatever they are, both good and bad, emanate, or issue from, or reflect, the attributes or nature of this God. Upon this presumption it would appear that anything that man is could come only from what God is, since God created him, and He could not possibly create him with attributes which He was incapable of creating. If God created man, then man is only that which the God made him to be, for better or worse. And if the attributes of man are classified or evaluated on a reasonable basis of what is good and bad, kind and cruel, sympathetic and merciless, unselfish and selfish, and so on, it would readily appear from the general run of human experience that God is more bad than good because, unfortunately, we find this to be so with many people. If more people are not bad, cruel, or outwardly and overtly dishonest, criminal, and vicious, it is because the *law* and its police are watching (or should be watching), and because a good number of their intended victims have the sheer luck or vigilance to get out of their way.

Coming down to earth, it would be more realistic to translate the preceding metaphor into a clearer and more verifiable observation that man and all his attributes emanate or issue from, or reflect, the nature of which he is merely a part, inexorably coalesced with what we can call the "seamless robe" of nature, or the world in which we find ourselves. By searching in almost any direction the nature of Nature, we come to learn a little more about the nature of Man. So it is in the natural origins of things, in the common experiences of the natural processes, in the rudimentary and evolutional histories of life and its environments, and the constant processes of interacting relationships, from which emerge all the physical changes, habits, patterns, and all the events of mankind's past and present. John Dewey abbreviates it this way: "Life denotes a function, a comprehensive activity, in which organism and environment are included."[177]

There never has been nor can there ever be, a true and real sense of morality in human nature such as the idealists and Kantian prophets desire, with all good intentions, to see in the human character now or in the future, or as part of some role the human being has been divinely chosen to enact. A universal, idealistic, or absolute principle of morality, like Kant's imperative, is an utter illusion in the actual and verified experiences of people. "A truly rational morality, or social regimen," says Santayana, "has never existed in the world and is hardly to be looked for. What guides men and nations in their practice is always some partial interest or some partial disillusion."[178] This is because people are always acting upon what seems or appears to be "good" and "acceptable" *to them,* according to each one's makeup, that is, his character, the product of his heritage and experience. As such it is not possible, owing to the nature of the intent, to establish a morality based either upon rational grounds or upon categorical imperatives attempting to set up universals as standard-bearers of morality and conduct. William Lillie: "In deed perhaps the most fundamental objection to Kant's theory is just that he conceived of a good will as willing in a vacuum, whereas actually the good will wills in the light of conditions and consequences."[179]

Man represents man, consciously or unconsciously, not his animal relatives, his environment, or the world. Basically and in the ultimate, depending upon the variety of circumstances, man has no choice but to look out for himself according to his instincts, his drives, and his self-preservative innateness to stay alive and satisfy himself whenever and wherever possible. And this is exactly the way he actually lives or tries to live. Man may set up beautiful exaltations, write esthetic poems about the world and the animal creatures that swim, fly, crawl, and creep in and upon it and around him, but with the first pang of hunger he will kill to get his prize, with the first gust of power he will want more and more power, and for all of these he invents a god and gods who are to carry him on a soft cushion to eternal bliss, who will preserve for him his indomitable will to keep on living and breathing and thinking and being admired for all he does. The ego of man cannot behave otherwise; it can do only what it can do; and all it wants is to keep being what it is and not to die. Whether the ego is "good" or "bad" is irrevelant, but it is certainly *right* in wanting to stay alive. Santayana elaborates this point: "Here are two flagrant instances where prerational morality defeats the ends of morality. Viewed from within, each religious or national fanaticism stands for a good; but in its outward operation it produces and becomes an evil. It is possible, no doubt, that its agents are really so far apart in nature and ideals that, like men and mosquitoes, they can stand up in physical relations only, and if they meet can only meet to poison or to crush one another."[180]

Man is a cultural and moral hypocrite. Living a natural life as he only can, he pretends to be governed by his sense of "right-eousness" while managing, nevertheless, to flex his "righteousness" to afford some compatibility to what he cannot help continuing to do. What is wrong is that he *knows* he cannot fulfill the requisites of his idealistic moralities, that it is wrong to hold them in reverence, to exalt their celestial "goodness" and eternal "blessedness." Yet he goes on doing what is natural according to his being, living as the animal he is, which is natural, and which, in the immediate or the ultimate, has little to do with what is wrong or right, but what is simply necessary in order to survive, and in surviving, to try to live well. In order to live well and extend his environment he has applied in the most *natural* way all his physical tools and his mental ingenuities to interfere with, change, improvise, and manipulate various experiences within nature, and it is this ability to manipulate and change parts of nature to suit or better himself that has gradually separated man from his other animal relatives, enabled him to build cultures and carry on as he has throughout history. Ralph de Pomerai wrote: "Ever since man first made himself a crude weapon, tattooed his body or covered it with leaves or grass or an animal skin, learned to make a fire, and artificially prepared his food, he has been consistently interfering with nature, and had he not done so he would have retained the status of his ape-like ancestors."[181]

It therefore becomes obvious that it is more rational to build any morality on a compatibility with what is natural, and to cultivate any such naturalism into some knowable goodness and social direction that can make possible a more normative satisfaction for individual and group. This approach is consistent with man's nature as he is and with his cultural and rational accumulation processed by his experience with, and as part of, the nature of his evolution and the world about him. Such a naturally compatible cohesion between order for the group and freedom for the individual might make possible the emergence and enculturation of a social growth based on realities, on our heritage, and to allow whatever culture we have to determine the relationships of people to a more healthy, clear, and a more naturally acceptable compatibility. If there are to be changes, let us not try to change the heavens or shuffle the trinities; let us change the cultures so that they can be attuned to what is best in man, what is natural in man, what is a good life for man, and upon this build our ethics on a realistic basis. Volitionism, determined by natural as well as by nature's subsistent cultural requisites, can be the instrument of the lessening of individual and group conflict, and so, also, the instrument of peaceful living and the satisfactions of living which may be nurtured and brought about. This seems to be the more practical and righteous road to take.

However, whether man is actually capable of realizing this natural compatibility without conflict, and of realizing the attainment of what can be reasonably and commonly called goodness, is merely prophetic. The unilateral drive of the ego, now thrown upon, and breast- feeding from, a cultural teat, and more or less independent of the forces of natural selection that coalesced natural social orders and compatibilities, yet, at the same time, imposed upon by the social orders and necessities of law and order, may find it difficult indeed to reach a truly natural compatibility. The brain of man may yet be the final monster that will destroy the body, and thus its own symbiotic chain of existence, including all man's fanciful ideals and imperatives.

A philosophy of morals and ethics that attempts, in any decisive sense, to sustain the principle that the human race *cannot*, because of its very nature and experience, reach a stage in which warfare and the other forms of traditional, arbitrary, and authoritarian power are reduced to a level of ethical compatibility based on the evolved conscience of man through his reason and on the instinctive fear of extinction in the absence of such a conscience, is a philosophy of defeatism and exaggerated pessimism. On the other hand, it is silly to continue an optimism based on the irrational submergence of people to dogma and power founded on the sense of an unchangeable mythic theology from which there is no escape save in conformance and self-beguiling belief, and perpetuating, as for thousands of years, the frustrations and neuroses and wasted lives of millions of people. Both give reason and conscience a sense of lowness of futility and/or fatalism. In the light of experience and history, there is little to make the heart and mind light and hopeful. In the light of the theologian, there is nothing except to throw oneself upon the mercy of an explanatory myth which is the mere man-made shadow of humanity's persistent effort to move further away from its nature and natural habitat (as if it really could), to pursue the dream of immortality through resignation to some religious order or philosophy in which the reason and conscience of man can find no justification or truth.

When things go our way, we attribute it to our intelligence, our good judgment, our foresight mixed with a little luck. When things go bad for us, we call it *fate*. Considering "fate" to be a field of possibility, we forget that it is in this field that our life exists, that we are exposed to it constantly, as other things are exposed to us. The steer may call it "fate" when we approach it with the butcher knife, and when we humans suffer or die, we may call it "fate" that we were not any luckier than the steer. But the steer has not the intelligence to give such a situation a name, whereas humans, expressing their egos through their intelligence, must necessarily allude to something called "fate" to provide resignation and explanation to the processes of life, living, and dying that are just beyond their fingers' reach, and the sudden overreaching of things unexpected, uncalculated, and unknown. Man breeds, lives, and dies in the same pond of protoplasmic experience as all else, except that man alone gives it a name, a title, a date, or a being.

THE SENSES OF FREEDOM

FREEDOM, OR THE lack of freedom to any degree, is a method of *possibility* by which man moves about within his internal and external limitations, and which, as a result, causes the constant chain of events, regardless of their intent, nature, or consequences. There seems to be no predetermined or purposeful design or plan in the nature of experience due to more or less freedom. What happns when freedom is present or absent, less or more, happens like all else. It sets up a chain of constant causation, and the conflicts, benefits, or fusions resulting therefrom are what we observe in the continual processes of evolution, where there appears to be no goal, destiny or destination, but only the constant

emerging of forms and functions resulting from and in regenerative or degenerative changes, the importance or value of which
depends upon where the opinion comes from. Therefore, whether
a certain process or event is regenerative or degenerative, or simultaneous combinations of both in process, cannot be deduced from
a universal point of view because the human being is incapable
of speaking for the universe. He can speak only for himself, and
whether he is capable of doing this is also a matter of opinion.
The essence of an experience is one thing, and its meaning and
value, another, a possible relative consequence of the experience
and not physically attached to it, although psychologically affecting the experience of both.

The illusion that free will is innate in the *whole* of a person
as a particular and unique personality, in contradistinction to the
various parts, cells, functional structure of the body in which this
personality is the expression of the whole—this illusion-attitude
seems to refuse egotistically to realize that whatever free will,
choice, and decision the *whole* or individual personality activates, or reacts to, is the result of the genetic uniqueness, experiential field, and all the interrelationships of pressures and resistances which constantly keep in flux the necessitated adaptational disciplines and rebellions of living experience and event.
The experiences of our babyhood and early childhood have a
lot to do with how we express and activate freedom for the rest
of our lives.

Freedom is thus a *process*, limited and affected by heredity,
environment, and by experience, in which chance and accident
play their roles. And this process of freedom is in the *part* as it is
in the *whole*, and the expression of freedom is exhibited in the
part as befits the part, and in the whole as it befits the whole.
But the idea that freedom appears to be a function or ability
that transcends the natural composition and experience of things,
or that it is irrelevant to molecules and atoms and the fields they
play in, is a conceptual anthropomorphism peculiar to metaphysicians, abstractionists, and theologians.

Freedom is the process that tries to compute and adjust the
wants, needs, compromises, and compatibilities that make possible the existence and survival of living things. This process is

the natural experience of life and living. If there is any such process or part of such process that appears to some to be supranatural or apart from the natural, it is yet to be proven to be part of reality. What is proven is that the idea of this concept, like all ideologies, theories, and philosophies, emanates from the *processing* of *natural* living things and their experiences. René Dubos: "There is no such thing as objective vision and representation, because each person experiences the world and responds to it in his own particular way."[182]

That freedom is not unlimited, and that it adjusts itself according to what it is and what it experiences in pressure and resistance, is nicely exemplified by a little story: It was a snowy day in the city ghetto; a policeman was leaning against the lamp post at one corner, a little boy of five was running around the block. After the boy's fifth round, the policeman stopped him and said: "What are you doing?"

The boy replied; "I'm running away from home."

"Then why are you running around the block?"

"Well, that's all I *can* do," said the little boy, catching his breath. "You see, I am not allowed to cross the street!"

We may find some justification in being critical of the anthropocentric attitudes of men. We philosophize and debate fine issues and wrangle over the meaning and use of odd words, as if man and the rest of nature were two distinct worlds of existence and experience. What man is, is natural and part of the natural realm, and to understand the potential and limitation of man and his freedom, we must take into account the nature of freedom itself *within* and as *part of* nature, of which man is a *relational, relative,* and *participating* part. In our attempt to understand the processes by which nature exhibits its experiences we may come to know the parallelisms and simultaneities of the essence and nature of freedom that are exhibited by and in man. "For natural philosophy," wrote Alfred N. Whitehead, "everything perceived is in nature. We may not pick and choose. For us the red glow of the sunset should be as much part of nature as are the molecules and electric waves by which men of science would explain the phenomenon. It is for natural philosophy to analyze how these various elements of nature are connected."[183]

It is also reasonable to feel that any part of nature, whether man, animal, or plant, if sufficiently restricted or limited in its necessary natural habit of movement or growth to survive, will wither and perish. If the restriction is partial and endurable, the forces of the survival drive may bring about adaptational changes, adjustments, or compromises to absorb these barriers and obstacles, or they may allow themselves to be absorbed in the forms that come about as a result of the interaction of the animal or plant and the restrictive pressures and resistances. When *all* freedom is eliminated, this we can call *death,* for only the dead are completely unfree in the absolute sense, and this absoluteness is limited, even in death, to the organism as a living whole. What is left of it, that is, the chemical substances minus the life it possessed, diffuses itself away into the totality of nature.

We are not concerned with the dead, and they have been relieved of being concerned with us. They no doubt deserve to be left in peace, withdrawn from the commonalty of the living, and in due time they usually are. Unfortunately the living do not always permit this. Humans keep on believing that the dead are still "alive," and are to be considered as part of the community; the custom or religion of the manes throughout history, from the crude tribal forms to the more refined and veiled catechisms of the greater religions, is only one segment of a complicated symbology of magic and superstition that concerns itself with the "living" dead and is one of the basic foundations of all modern religions. From the Freudian point of view, one might call this some sort of unconscious desire of the living to impersonate, through the dead, their own continuance by the nonacceptance of any idea that could relate to the mortality of their own egos. Narrating about the Bororo in the Mato Grosso area of Brazil, Lévi-Strauss tells us that "the imagery with which a society pictures to itself the relations between the dead and the living can always be broken down in terms of an attempt to hide, embellish or justify, on the religious level, the relations prevailing, in that society among the living."[184]

If a person feels a self-rewarding relief, fortitude, or a sense of affection in thinking about the dead, this may be good and pragmatically justifiable or needed. If people, and there are many, who, being cruel and vindictive, keep on cursing or hating the dead, or draw relief in desecrating the memory of the dead, this may be considered good *to them* also. These are the varied perspectives and sentiments of people. Freedom, as a process, is not concerned with any "moral" or "ethical" factors. And all of these perspectives and sentiments, we should realize, still belong to the living and to the living only. Only the theologians claim to "hear" the dead—via *revelation*—and this is their prerogative. If only they could manage to collect alms from the dead directly instead of from the living, the world economy would immediately take a drastic turn for the better.

It therefore becomes self-evident that, so far as we really know, freedom seems to be a concomitant factor of that which lives, grows, moves, and dies. A mountain may grow but it does not really move in the human sense, and it does not live in the same sense as an animal or plant that is born, grows, lives a while, and dies. A river moves, and it may even grow or diminish, but still we cannot consider it as a personality or as an individual like a person or some other animal. There is no consciousness or ability to think or judge in a mountain or river, as there is in ourselves and our animal relatives. The "freedom" a mountain or a river can have is purely a physical coalescence of itself and the surrounding world that comes in contact with it or affects its nature. The same equation applies to the "freedom" of the tides or, for that matter, "freedom" of the world to move and revolve around the sun. This is not the freedom we are concerned with except to the extent we realize that we are also physical things and parts of this same natural field and also limited in our movements and potentials in the circumferential arena of minimums and maximums which range within us and outside of us, and which more or less influence and affect the nature and extent of our freedom. With this exception: we are capable of *knowing* and/or *sensing* that we are free or not free, and what it means to us as to why we should or must be free, or free in some things and limited or controlled in other things, for our own good and for the good of others, or for the good of all. Of course, most of us are oblivious to these factors, and the farther we go back into the history of human beings, the more we find that they were *less and less conscious* of this freedom, and that it was as man rose in the general advance of civilization that he became *more and more conscious* of this freedom. When people felt the impact of the diminishment of freedom, they felt a sense about it, and began to think about the nature of freedom and what it meant to them. A child born into a wealthy family usually grows up never knowing what it means to be without security or money, until it finds itself on its own without any security or money.

However, it is important to understand that the sense of freedom is not a cultivated thing, or an emergence of religious, political, economic, or social life. On the other hand, these factors have constantly affected the sense of freedom; these factors have modified it, defected, affluenced, or constricted it, extended, worsened, or bettered it, even patternized it by the impress and the relationships of these factors in themselves and between themselves and their interaction with the nature and sense of freedom. Like life, freedom was there before, and it preceded all of these developments as a biological and inherent trait of animal life. If not, the freedom of man to create these factors, institutions, and cultures could never have been demonstrated; it was historically imbedded in the homogeneous and heterogeneous combinations and fusions of the animal organism; it identified the emergence of an animal as a *separate* unit and as such became an *individual* unit and motivated, within the nature of itself, the social or gregarious drive. To eat as a unit, to move as a unit, to sleep as a unit, think, laugh, cry, feel pain, fear, power, to mate as a unit—all these moved to identify the natural processes of freedom. It is thus that freedom did not emerge or evolve as a result of preceding stages of cultural evolution, but freedom evolved as a concomitant and spontaneous factor with the evolution of man, and from the beginning has never left him. He may have been unconscious of it, never thought of it—many are still not conscious of it or do not think about it—but it was there as he was there. If not we would not be here today.

Before we can properly evaluate freedom, it may be appropriate and essential to establish, if possible, the nature and essence of freedom. We have already tried to explain it as a *determined* natural want and compatibility. We should now clarify what we mean by the word *determined*.

DETERMINISM AND CHOICE

DETERMINISM MEANS SIMPLY that everything that exists or occurs is the result of previous situations and processes which are considered the causes of the thing or event. In another way we can say that whatever there is now is the result of what has been up to now. In still another way, we can say that every cause or event is an event of previous causes. The *process* experienced between causes and effects is called *determinism*. C. J. Ducasse states that "determinism, in the sense that every event has some cause and some effect, is analytically true."[185] Theodosius Dobzhansky: "The life cycle of any organism is a sequence of stages succeeding each other in a definite order. The order is there because the developmental events at a given age or stage are brought about by the preceding events. A baby learns to walk when it has achieved a certain degree of muscular control; reproduction can only occur after the hormonal system has attained some degree of maturity,"[186] which is the biologist's way of describing the process of determinism. William Lillie states: "Determinism . . . maintains that the law of causation holds in the case of human actions just as it does in the case of physical events,"[187] which is the way on ethicist would explain it.

The world of sciences, which uses the empirical method of furthering and gaining its objectives and ends, is a process of determinism. Thought, or reasoning, or reflecting, is the result of what a person inherited, acquired, the experiences of his participating and particular life and his knowledge of the experience of things and people outside himself. Thus, determinism is really a *common-sense* approach and explanation of the processes of life and its experiences. Hudson Hoagland: "I know of no scientist today who works outside of a deterministic framework."[188]

There are brilliant scholars who might consider themselves indeterminists, people who look at things, more or less, from the viewpoint of *absoluteness*, and who contend that determinism is not the final answer, that it is insufficient to answer *all* questions, and, therefore, because of it, it is lacking as a thorough and foolproof explanation of phenomena and experience. They attempt to attach to philosophy the necessity of omniscience and omnipotence, which are really metaphysical imageries and not verified in the actual nature of experience. They are more or less concerned with the solution of the problem of *ultimates* or universal ends rather than with the processes in which any such "ultimates" or "ends" might experience themselves into being. They seem to look at philosophy as an end, not as a process; as a medium of theology, not as a scientific and reasonable method of inquiry and search. Their quest is not to find out what and how, but merely to establish *what* without the *how* by insisting upon an absoluteness of *why*. Therefore, they say, unless man knows *all,* he knows nothing, as nothing can be explained without a knowledge of all.

It is true that we are all ignorant to a degree, and that total knowledge is obviously impossible to man, as man cannot contain or process all experiences within himself. This applies to the indeterminist as well as to the determinist. If the indeterminist position is considered hypothetically as logical and verifiable, there is no way, as a result, to explain the cultural, inventive and material progress of mankind. People must have learned *something* along the way of man's historical ascendancy from the cave to the city, and this cumulative process of learning is determined by its heritage and continual experiences compounding causes and events, by the succession of ideas and associations that resulted, and continues to result, in the consequences and sequences of experience. The reasonable man understands and will surely agree that the human mind has limitations and is limited in its endeavor to penetrate probabilities, expectancies, and future events. Sidney Hook states: "Unpredictability, however, does not entail indeterminism, since it is compatible with the existence of a theoretically determined system of such vast complexity that it is beyond human power to make correct predictions."[189]

The importance of the process of determinism in our philosophy of freedom is seen in the expression of freedom as a natural factor and vehicle for the processing or determining the nature and products of man, his experiences and achievements. Paul Weiss writes: "It is good common sense to say that whatever occurs is determined, and it is good common sense to say that men act freely. . . . The contention that men are determined and the contention that they are free seem opposed. They are not. Determinism applies to what has happened when all the conditions are already present and fulfilled. Freedom applies to what is happening and will happen; it concerns the creation of new conditions and thus of consequences that until then have not been necessitated."[190] Brand Blanshard: "To the objection that we always feel free, we answer that it is natural to feel so, even if we are determined, since our faces are set toward results and not toward causes, and the causes of present action always elude us. . . . To the objection that determinism would reduce us to the level of mechanical puppets, we answer that though we are puppets in part we live, as Aristotle said, on various levels. And so far as causality in reflection, art, and more choice involves control by immanent ideal, mechanism has passed into that rational determinism that is the best kind of freedom."[191]

By the application of this empirical process of induction we will be able to see how the motility and myriad expressions of freedom brought about certain sequences and further consequences. Therefore, we might be able to make some explanation of man's present situations and what he might still be able to achieve, good and bad, as a rationally and reasonably predictable series of events, by the implementation or processing of certain factors that could possibly bring about certain consequences. Hudson Hoagland: "The application of the behavioral and social sciences to testing the values men live by has, I believe, marked potentialities for the advancement of cultural evolution."[192]

Paul Weiss explains it further: "A cause must precede its effect. That is why history can cover an extensive stretch of time. This means that the cause cannot necessitate the effect. If it did, the effect would exist when the cause did. What is normally termed a cause is only an antecedent condition. The nature of the effect is defined by it, and can often be predicted in the light of what we know of it. But the cause does not produce the effect that in fact ensues. The actual effect comes about as a result of an activity that, taking its start with the cause, ends by producing an instance of the predictable effect. The causal situation, then, has not two but three components; the cause, the process of production, and the effect. Since freedom is the doing of something beyond the determination by a cause, the process of production is evidently free. An actual effort is freely produced inside a frame that necessarily binds together an antecedent cause and a predictable type of effect."[193]

In reaching a *natural* explanation of freedom, we will better understand the processes by which man "chooses" or "decides" to think, does or does not do certain things, which is the nature, substance, and process of choice, or what is more commonly thought of as "free will." Paul Edwards states: "When we call an action 'free' we never in any ordinary situation mean that it was uncaused . . . that the agent was not compelled or constrained to perform it."[194] This is in the nature of a free act. Carl G. Hempel states: "The existence of an earlier state of affairs that is a logically sufficient condition for a given act of choice surely does not mean that the act is determined in any sense that would cast doubt on the freedom of choice."[195] Arthur Pap writes: "Determinism is compatible with the occurrence of free actions, since what distinguishes free from unfree actions is the mode of causation, not the absence of freedom."[196] Brand Blanshard clarifies the nature and meaning of an act of choice: "An act of choice is an extremely complex process. It involves the idea of one or more ends, the association of that idea with more or less numerous other ideas, the presence of desires and repulsions, and the operation of habits and impulses; indeed, in those choices for which freedom is most demanded, the whole personality seems to be at work. The cortical basis for so complex a process must be extremely broad. But if it is, the great mass of cells involved must, by the physicist's admission, act with a high stability, and the correlated psychical processes must show a similar stability. But that is what we mean by action in accordance with causal law."[197]

Those people who, with all good intent, contend that determinism, whether soft, hard, medium, or medium-rare, is too nebulous a premise and that it is not really true that every event must have a cause, must fairly concede that, when they are looking at something, the actual sight they become conscious of is not the result of their eyes, optic nerve, and brain, but the result of their philosophy, which determines the indeterminism of their picture.

A person cannot separate himself from causative consequences and sequences any more than he can separate himself from life or organic totality. His character is the result of this and so contains more or less the potential of the so-called "will" to choose or make decisions. However, the extent and nature of his decisions are within this polarized area and result from his own complex structure and organism of both psychic and physical elements and combinations of both, all of which seem to be a process of determinism, although from the epistemological viewpoint it might not be as yet explained or made known. The ever recurring fact that man does not know *all* does not detract from the realization that he does know *something*. The admitted fact that it is impossible for men to *be* all, does not mean that what small part of the total he represents and its relationships to the all, cannot be reasonably verified, not only as a particular event and process, but as a process of more or less simultaneity with the entirety of nature itself.

The determinist does not assume that in order to accept the premise of determinism, one "must" know everything, macro-microphysics, all laws, etc., in order to make a "necessary" prediction, or know beforehand the sequence of events, because he sees in experience the rational as well as the scientific processes of the sequences of causality. Neither has the indeterminist the privilege of foisting upon the determinist the problem and essentiality of total knowledge and all the total combinations of possible experience that these may bring about, which is absurd, in order to preclude any meaningful basis for the determinist position. This belongs to the category of playing upon words or linguistic philosophy, and merely exposes that the indeterministic premise has been determined, by its own persistence of vaguity and contrariness, to create its own absurdity.

To verify what appears to be a process of determinism in the nature of experience and in the nature of Nature, does not imply or preconclude any appearance or affirmation of fatalism. Only the acceptance of the idea of the existence of an external-to-nature omniscience, its preknowledge and its predeterminedly controlled course of natural events, can indicate such a fantasy of unchangeability in the course of experience and event.

To deny determinism, that every event has a cause, is to claim that an experience does not contain the elements necessary for the experience to take place, to become experienced, and therefore occurs on some *ex nihilo* premise, which, of course, is also absurd.

The indeterminist, putting forth no counter explanation of phenomena, experience, and knowledge, takes a dogmatic and precocious position when he expects of the determinist a degreeless infallibility to solve all problems. Determinism is a *process* of explanation, observation, verification, not a catechism of absolutes. The doctor, in making a diagnosis, is not infallible and yet no one would preclude the doctor from the practice of making diagnoses.

The observation that causality in nature is not necessarily orderly, but often accidental and subject to experiences of chance, does not necessarily imply that these events are not causative and not subject to the orderly procedure and processes of pressures and resistances that make up the totality of nature and experience. Predictability or unpredictability is not essential to the acceptance of the premise of determinism, as both these factors lay in a "future" state not yet determined. Therefore, only the theoretical judgments or values rising out of *calculated* predictability or probability form as a result of the deterministic process. What may be considered logically predictable is merely a *judgment* of some value. Verifiability acknowledges and necessitates a knowledge of it as an experienced event.

Even imagination is a potential composed of instinctive and acquired levels of mentation as a result of previous causative associations of ideas and experiences, in a process of interacting wants within and upon each other produced in an expected, but not necessarily unpredictable, sequence. The sequence may not be necessarily rational, but it may be rationally explainable. It may even contain elements of illogical fantasy and absurdity; yet it may be logically deduced as to its origins, nature, and wantability.[198]

Indeterminism preconcludes, as a premise, that an ignorance of something, in any degree, is "proof" that intelligibility or any knowledge of this something becomes an impossibility, except, of course, the contention of the indeterminist. The indeterminist, by refusing to admit it, or in accepting any particular premise, confesses the experience of a line of causation that results in his sequence of idea. His own causative process of indeterminism, which is the sequence, is based on the process of determinism in arriving at this premise. Indeterminism *in itself* confesses to a deterministic attitude, which merely exposes that a person has *determined* by his own causative analyses that he finds himself incapable of fulfilling a certain premise because of his own inter-preted "limitations" and "improbabilities," which, even though they be empirical, theoretical, or mystical, produce a determined premise as such.

It is a simple observation that man *has* a freedom of choice, but this is a capacity not *beyond* or *outside* the natural involve-ment of his evolution. Dr. Corliss Lamont, in his *Freedom of Choice Affirmed*, errs, I believe, in attempting to make a parallel between fatalism and determinism and then attempting to recon-cile the processes of free choice with the processes of determinism. In the former he submerges natural processes into the cosmo-centric bog of man's abstract thought and theory; in the latter his attempt of reconciliation of man's capacity of free choice with determinism is to establish that this human capacity is above or apart from the deterministic base and yet naturally part of it; that, inasmuch as free choice is not determined in the same sense as other things, man has evolved in such a way that he is truly the captain of his soul and master of his destiny. With this I do not agree. Man can and should use all his abilities and capacities to change and improve his life and place on this world, and not submit himself to the metaphysical and theological egocentrici-ties of godism and fatalistic resignation in which he has so fool-ishly meandered these many thousands of years. But he must come to realize that he is a *natural* product, even in flux and constantly evolving, and all he is and all he does and all he will ever be and do is a *natural process,* whether instinctually genetic or culturally and intellectually acquired. All these emerge and evolve out of and within his natural base of origin and nature, and from this he cannot escape, nor should he. He must come to realize that his freedom of choice is part of his biological structure and not purely an accidental mutation that created itself out of extranatural factors. We cannot escape from our being as *wholly* biological. If there are many things we still do not understand about ourselves or how our nature and capacity operate in their many strange ways, how man came to think and do as he has thought and done since *Homo sapiens* emerged from the primeval mixtures and strains, it only means that we are still learning and finding, as, it is to be hoped, we always will. And whatever man may ever learn about himself, his relatives, and the universe, will show him that all that issues from what *exists,* that change comes from the pressures and resistences of *necessity,* that this necessity is the constant product of existence and experience, a continual, constant, endless *process.* All his abstract and conceptual thought, his wondrous neuronal system, evolved and structured out of billions of years of neuroplasmic processes, its origins reaching back to the earliest basophilic cytoplasm of nerve cell beginnings, must be seen as a *natural* process, within which all existence is involved, interacting, interdependent, and symbiotically tied together in all its segments.

All our theories, abstractions, and concepts are nourished from the same fluids that make possible the life and existence of our bodies as living things. A brain within a living body can make concepts, but a brain without a body cannot make concepts, nor does it continue to exist as a brain. Someday, when we may learn more about the livingness of life, we may also learn more about the processes that determine the processes of man's capacity to express his natural freedoms, including his freedom of choice.

Dr. Lamont does not deny the reality of determinism and its processes; what he attempts to do is to reconcile man's evolved differences, which include the freedom of choice factor, a factor he feels is not evolved in other animal life, with the obvious ability of man to express this freedom of choice in a way unknown in all other life on earth. In his view, this freedom of choice factor must be recognized as such, and regarded as not necessarily rising out of necessity, but out of the uniqueness of man and his capacity to be so.

Dr. Lamont thus applies the Cartesian claim that men are the only creatures with souls, and all other animals are mere machines. He seems to infer that animals have no freedom of choice, as they are "instinctually" determined. If this is so, man's "improving" upon it has certainly done in this planet of ours in many ways that may eventually not only destroy man, but also destroy the innocent animal life that has been the constant victim of his freedom of choices. He states: "The human ability to think created an altogether new level of behavior among living creatures and led to the emergence of free choice. Thinking and choosing of course have a physical base and in their causal efficacy rely continually upon a man's internal determinants. Since animals in general are not endowed with the attribute of abstract, conceptual thought, they presumably do not have freedom of choice. Their choices are *instinctually* determined."[199]

Man's freedom of choice may be far greater than that of other animals, but it is a limited choice, determined by internal and external pressures and resistances; and although these pressures and resistances are subject to chance and contingency, as well as unpredictability and uncertainty, the limitations of man and of other animals are only a matter of degree, due to processes of evolution, genetic and acquired, both constantly integrating and interacting through the continuums of experience itself. This does not crown man with any supranatural or extraterritorial powers, but it does make him the greater, and a most remarkable, animal.

Man has the freedom of choice to judge himself a god or any god's agent or as a greater or lesser god. Man, not knowing fully yet what makes him tick the way he does, what makes his marvelous brain act the way it does in freedom of choice decisions and judgments, should not take it upon himself, as a reasonable freedom of choice, to say he *fully knows* what makes the brains in other animals act as they do in expressing and actually processing, in their limited and different ways, their freedom of choice and their methods of activating and carrying out their freedom of choices and decisions. Freedom of choice is a relative factor, however limited it may be among lowly creatures or however highly advanced among these who possess the ability of abstract and conceptual thought. We find these limitations and variances among humans as well as among his animal relatives; it is not the sole domain of *Homo sapiens* alone.

Determinism does not imply by the nature of its process any fatalism or predestation; it denotes a *constant* process in experience and event from causes to effects; it tries through human eyes and minds to find out why it operates as it does, and this includes the nature of free choice wherever and whenever capable of being experienced. Fatalism and predestination preclude change and the consequences of the constant interaction, interrelativity, and processes of composition of substance and experience. Determinism merely describes the apparent process of this constant change and event. Fatalism and predestination imply external controlling or supernatural powers of design and prepatternization over natural forces; determinism merely describes the processes of these natural forces without alluding to any relationship or influence of any supposed forces beyond the natural, and from a purely objective and analytical focus.

There is no predestination in determinism; this is a mark placed by those who do not accept the principle of determinism. This is because the continual causal and consequential influences are an unknown x quantity and quality at any given point or moment, and therefore become a reasonably as well as a specifically unpredictable factor from the *absolute* view, and this is due to the experiences not processed in event.

Determinism does not preclude, because it tries to fathom the causes and consequences of people who, by their freedom of choices and decisions, do things which are obviously cruel and evil. Determinism does not imply in any way forgiving, pardoning, or accepting the inevitability of evil. Science does not undertake to replace the gods in the matter of moral and ethical judgments and punishments. Through the constant revelation and interaction of knowledge to and upon us we do or should come to understand ourselves better; even this does not mean any condonement of evil. Man may and will experience what appears to him in fact as a freedom of choice, as well as judgments of others and things, but this is as human nature allows it to process the freedom of choice as it is processed in his natural heritage and experiences.

Determinism is not a law or a cosmic absolute or a fatalistic and predestined recording tape running backard or forward to please either historian or prophet. Such an interpretation only indicates the ego- and cosmocentric, introverted, and ingenerated mirror of the human mind. Determinism denotes and describes what appears to us as a *process, a way of explaining experience.* Within *experience* we find *substance* in all its forms of existence and potentiality, that is, what a thing *is* and *could be;* the *field,* that is, the relationships that occur with and between things. This acknowledges the potential and interaction of necessitated predictables (calculated) and unpredictables (chance, contingency, and unexpectancies), and the consequences and effects *necessitated* out of such interactivity and relationships.

Change and chance are interrelated. Change lies with the constant processes of experience and this change is both predictable and unpredictable, calculated or chance, but in any event necessitated by and within experience. God's will and Man's will complement each other only through man's mind, but Nature only "knows" process being processed, determined by its own nature of experience. There can be no experience without process and no process without relationships and no relationships without existence, and there can be no existence without the potential of what is and what could be.

Causes and effects do not have to be relevant, as revelancy is a human judicator of events; in nature and the nonhuman world relevancy is unknown. It is the relating factors and the interaction of these factors that give explanation to chance, contingency, and unpredictabilities. An accident is an unexpected or unpredictable event, but because it is so does not imply or preconclude that the accident has not been an event of natural causes and effects. Unexperienced experience cannot be absolutely determined in the same manner as the future, or tomorrow remains only an expectation without certainty or the play of events to come. History is the story of causes and effects. Man's imagination and hope can envisage future events and man's awareness and reason can understand certain eventualities and inevitabilities, but the *absolute* nature of these projected events and the *if/then/ when* of these events must necessarily contain some potential of uncertainty. Man can think about the future, but he cannot live it until it becomes an experienced event in time.

I feel that we have reasonably tried to make clear what we mean when we say that a want or compatability, being natural as it is, is a *determined* want or compatability. Now we have to contend with the problem of substantiating our premise on an empirical or experienced basis, which we shall take up in our next chapter. Following this, we should see that in the study of mankind's cultures, religions, societies, its political, economic, social evolutions, institutions, and histories, wherever man roamed and made his mark, it is evident that all these affected, for better or worse, this natural inherent freedom. It is the story of these influences upon freedom with which we are concerned. This concern is essential to any reasonable analysis of its value to the individual and to the organizations he has formed.

Before concluding this first phase of our venture into the philosophy of freedom, let us realize one thing: society did not create freedom for man. Man had the freedom to create society. Nor did society, in return, give freedom to him uncompromisingly. The natural compatabilities of freedom had often to be influenced in such a way as to make itself compatibly essential to the survival of the animal unit, otherwise there could not have been any instinctive motility or primeval drive for gregariousness. The story of the gradual ascendancy of the human colony from the nomadic little families or "prides" of humanlike protohominids to the great civilizations and complex organizations of today is the story of the *conflict and compatability of freedom with environment*—and the varied intermixtures, psychical inconsistencies, divergent ideologies, and paradoxical submissions, rebellions, disharmonies for illusory harmonies.

The history of freedom is the story of the relationships between an individual animal and the world about it, and why these relationships make the animal behave the way it does. By finding, if possible, the key to this behavior, we may also find the key that could possibly open the door to meanings, values, and directions. We should bear in mind that the sense of satisfaction one may derive from a feeling of independence does not necessarily imply or require any dissatisfaction with one's environment, with other individuals, the state, or society. Nor does such independence mean that an individual, to be independent, must necessarily be at odds with external factors, relations, or situations. Neither does it imply, because one feels independent, and thus satisfied to this degree, that all or any external factors are harmonious with him or that they are conducive to his state of independence.

What the sense of independence appears to mean is that a person feels that his mind, judgments, his ethical, economic, and political principles, whatever they may be, are not subjected to a forced or coerced subordinated state or level, or in a status of submission to external situations or factors that may tend to achieve this subordination and submission by instilling various types of fear, forceful and psychological duress, emotional propaganda, and many other power vehicles or media of persuasion by which individuals are made to lose, willingly or unwillingly, rationally or unwittingly, their individuality, their sense of self-ness, their sense of being, and so their independence. The progressive evolution of the organized state is indicated where there is coordination by independent and freedom-loving individuals educated by intelligence, knowledge, and experience, and not indoctrinated by authoritarianism, to assist each other in the form of a group or organization or state that functions as a *process* for this very purpose—and not as an end in itself to become a bloated, traditional, arbitrary, or naked power growing apart from, and fattening itself upon, the collectivized regimentation of human beings as a meal for its Molochian furnace of impersonalized identity. There is a world of difference between the natural desires of a free person to express himself and the habituated movements and actions of a regimented person who has become so conscious, by fears of many kinds, of the need to cohere to the general mass of similar fear-ridden people that any surface coordinative behavior or cultural cohesion is the result of the subsurface sense of futility or gullibility, and of the resignation or relaxation of the instinctive to preserve oneself under overwhelming conditions or false concepts.

To unravel this complex story so that we may be able to accomplish as true a picture as possible of what has happened to freedom in the past, how we stand today, and the probable and possible directions in which freedom, or the lack of freedom, may take us—this is our concernment and the objective determination of our task, which we shall try to investigate, analyze, evaluate, and attempt to understand by understanding ourselves better and more clearly.

And thank the stars, we still have the freedom to do it!

REFERENCES—BOOK ONE

1. Brigid Brophy, *Black Ship to Hell*, p. 472.
2. Hermann Hesse, *Siddhartha*, p. 68.
3. Wallis Budge, *Egyptian Magic*, p. 224.
4. Oscar Lewis, *The Children of Sanchez*, p. 171.
5. Bertrand Russell, *Power*, p. 177.
6. Edmund W. Sinnott, *The Bridge of Life*, p. 35.
7. Archibald MacLeish, *The Great American Frustration*, Saturday Review, July 13, 1968, p. 14.
8. Karl Jaspers, *The Worlds of Existentialism*, ed. M. Friedman, pp. 205-7.
9. David Riesman, *Individualism Reconsidered*, p. 10.
10. Hudson Hoagland, *Science and the New Humanism*, Science Magazine, vol. 143, no. 3602, Jan. 10, 1964, pp. 112-3.
11. Bertrand Russell, *Power*, p. 175.
12. Bertrand Russell, *My Philosophical Development*, p. 230.
13. H. T. Costello, see *American Thought: A Critical Sketch*, Morris R. Cohen, p. 400.
14. Loren Eiseley, *Science and the Unexpected Universe*, American Scholar, Summer, 1966, p. 426.
15. H. T. Costello, *loc. cit.*, p. 399.
16. Horace M. Kallen, *How I Bet My Life*, Saturday Review, Oct. 1, 1966, p. 28.
17. John Dewey, *Experience and Nature*, p. 67.
18. Bertrand Russell, *Authority and the Individual*, p. 70.
19. George Santayana, *Reason in Common Sense*, vol. I, "Life of Reason," p. 54.
20. Paul Blanshard, *Freedom and Catholic Power in Spain and Portugal*, p. 54.
21. *Ibid.*, p. 61.
22. *Ibid.*, p. 86.
23. Arthur Whitaker, *Spain and the Defense of the West*.
24. see *Man and His Gods*, Homer W. Smith, p. 187.
25. Edward Westermarck, *Memories of My Life*, p. 307.
26. Brigid Brophy, *Black Ship to Hell*, p. 391.
27. James G. Frazer, *Psyche's Task*, preface, pp. vii-vii.
28. Gerhard Szczesny, *The Future of Unbelief*, p. 42.
29. *Ibid.*, p. 165.
30. Bertrand Russell, *Power*, p. 8.
31. Bertrand Russell, *Why I am not a Christian*, pp. 50-1.
32. Joseph Campbell, *Masks of God: Occidental Mythology*, p. 520.
33. Wallace T. Matson, *The Existence of God*, p. 170.
34. Michael Scriven, *Primary Philosophy*, p. 156.

35. F. H. Heinemann, *Existentialism and the Modern Predicament*, p. 4.
36. Edmund R. Leach, *We Scientists Have the Right to Play God*, Sat. Eve. Post, November, 1968. pp. 16 and 20.
37. George Gaylord Simpson, *This View of Life*, p. 5.
38. George Santayana, *Reason in Science*, vol. V, "Life of Reason," pp. 15-6.
39. August Bebel, *Woman and Socialism*, p. 438.
40. Richard A. Proctor, *Our Place Among Infinities*.
41. Walter Russell, *The Universal One*, p. 1.
42. A. D. White, *History of the Warfare of Science with Theology*, p. 49.
43. Joseph K. Hart, *Inside Experience*, p. 110.
44. Philip Wylie, *An Essay on Morals*, p. 16.
45. Joseph H. Peck, *Life with Women and How to Survive It*, p. 205.
46. Thomas J. J. Altizer, *America and the Future of Theology*, from "Radical Theology and the Death of God," pp. 11, 13, 15.
47. Homer W. Smith, *Man and His Gods*, p. 4.
48. Michael Scriven, *Primary Philosophy*, pp. 175-7.
49. Loren Eiseley, poem *Epitaph*, American Scholar, vol. 35, no. 2, Spring, 1966, p. 292.
50. Albert Einstein, quoted in *Mankind Evolving*, Dozshansky, preface xi.
51. Edmund W. Sinnott, *The Bridge of Life*, pp. 240, 243-4.
52. Pablo Neruda, poem *Truth*, Evergreen Magazine, no. 44, December, 1966, p. 20.
53. Franklin L. Baumer, *Religion and the Rise of Scepticism*, p. 14.
54. Cyril E. M. Joad, *Decadence: A Philosophical Inquiry*, pp. 248-9.
55. Gerhard Szczesny, *The Future of Unbelief*, p. 114.
56. F. H. Heinemann, *Existentialism and the Modern Predicament*, p. 3.
57. Jean Wahl, *A Short History of Existentialism*, p. 13.
58. Jules Henry, *Culture Against Man*, p. 350.
59. Julian S. Huxley, *Evolution, Cultural and Biological*, Current Anthropology, 1956, p. 3.
60. Ladislaus Boros, *The Mystery of Death*, p. vii.
61. *Ibid.*, p. viii.
62. Jean Wahl, *A Short History of Existentialism*, p. 45.
63. Edgar Herzog, *Psyche and Death*, p. 22.
64. Bernard Campbell, *Human Evolution*, pp. 357-8.
65. Alex Comfort, *The Nature of Human Nature*, p. 214.
66. Loren Eiseley, *The Immense Journey*, p. 125.
67. Morris R. Cohen, *Reason and Law*, p. 71.
68. George Santayana, *Reason in Science*, vol. V, "Life of Reason," p. 68.
69. Morris R. Cohen, *American Thought: A Critical Sketch*, pp. 377-8.
70. *Ibid.*, p. 393.
71. Brigid Brophy, *Black Ship to Hell*, p. 120.
72. *Ibid.*, p. 20.
73. George Santayana, *Reason in Science*, vol. V, "Life of Reason," p. 67.
74. Theodosius Dobzshansky, *Mankind Evolving*, p. 345.
75. Horace M. Kallen, *How I Bet My Life*, Saturday Review, Oct. 1, 1966, p. 80.
76. Jean Wahl, *A Short History of Existentialism*, p. 41.
77. Jean-Paul Sartre, *Existentialism and Human Emotions*, p. 33.
78. *Ibid.*, p. 17.
79. *Ibid.*, p. 16.
80. *Ibid.*, p. 15.
81. Paul Roubiczek, *Existentialism, For and Against*, pp. 1-10.
82. *Ibid.*, p. 53.
83. *Ibid.*, p. 114.
84. Edward Albee, Saturday Review, Dec. 16, 1963.

85. Horace M. Kallen, *How I Bet My Life*, Saturday Review, Oct. 1, 1966. p. 80.
86. Peter Freuchen, *Book of the Eskimos*, pp. 193-4.
87. Barrows Dunham, *Heroes and Heretics*, p. 469.
88. see *The Worlds of Existentialism*, ed. M. Friedman.
89. Lewis Mumford, *Technics and the Nature of Man*, from "Knowledge Among Men," p. 141.
90. D. T. Suzuki,, *Zen Buddhism*, ed. W. Barrett, p. 8.
91. *Ibid.*, p. 10.
92. *Ibid.*, p. 17.
93. Wallace I. Matson, *The Existence of God*, p. 24.
94. Abraham Kaplan, *The New World of Philosophy*, p. 199.
95. Ludwig Wittgenstein, *Tractatus Logico-Philosophicus*, Part IV, p. 112.
96. James G. Frazer, *The Worship of Nature*, vol. I, "The Golden Bough," pp. 3-5.
97. Jacquetta Hawkes and Sir Leonard Woolley. *Prehistory and the Beginnings of Civilization*, vol. I, "History of Mankind," p. 186.
98. see *The Philosophy of Humanism*, Corliss Lamont, p. 229.
99. Ottaker Nemecek, *Virginity*, p. 65.
100. Paul Blanshard, *Freedom and Catholic Power in Spain and Portugal*, p. 98.
101. Edwin Way Teale, *Strange Lives of Familiar Insects*, p. 56.
102. George Gaylord Simpson, *This View of Life*, p. 217.
103. *Ibid.*, p. 175.
104. *Ibid.*, p. 25.
105. John Dewey, *Individualism, Old and New*.
106. Theodosius Dobzhansky, *Mankind Evolving*, p. 29.
107. *Ibid.*, p. 219.
108. Lorus and Margery Milne, *The Senses of Animals and Men*, p. 272.
109. René Dubos, *Humanistic Biology*, American Scholar, vol. 34, no. 2, pp. 190-2.
110. Brigid Brophy, *Black Ship to Hell*, p. 374.
111. Brand Blanshard, *Heritage of Idealism*, from "Changing Patterns in American Civilization," p. 98.
112. Paul Edwards, *Hard and Soft Determinism*, from "Determinism and Freedom," ed. Sidney Hook, p. 121.
113. F. W. Headley. *Problems of Evolution*, p. 323.
114. Morris R. Cohen, *Reason and Law*, p. 136.
115. James B. Conant, *Man Thinking About Man*, American Scholar, vol. 33, no. 4, p. 543.
116. H. R. Hays, *From Ape to Angel*, p. 403.
117. Brigid Brophy, *Black Ship to Hell*, p. 374.
118. see *Anatomy and Physiology*, vol. I, Edwin B. Steen and Ashley Montagu, p. 8.
119. Lorus and Margery Milne, *The Senses of Animals and Men*, p. 148.
120. René Dubos, *Humanistic Biology*, American Scholar, vol. 34, no. 2, p. 179.
121. Fritz-Martin Engel, *Life Around Us*, p. 193.
122. John Dewey, *Antinaturalism in Extremis*, from "Naturalism and the Human Spirit," p. 9.
123. Henri Pieron, *Thought and the Brain*, p. 251.
124. Robert L. Sinsheimer, quoted by Joseph Wood Krutch, Saturday Review, May 4, 1968, pp. 12-3.
125. John Dewey, *Human Nature and Conduct*, p. 85.
126. Samuel P. Dunlap, *The Ghebers of Hebron*, p. 999.
127. John Herman Randall, Jr., *Introduction to Philosophy*, p. 191.
128. Bernard Campbell, *Human Evolution*, p. 365.
129. George Santayana, *Reason in Society*, vol. V, "Life of Reason," p. 158.
130. Bernard Campbell, *Human Evolution*, p. 33.

131. René Dubos, *So Human an Animal,* p. 23.
132. Alex Comfort, *The Nature of Human Nature,* p. 145.
133. Bertrand Russell, *Our Knowledge of the External World,* p. 18.
134. John Herman Randall, Jr., *Introduction to Philosophy,* p. 153.
135. Sir Arthur Keith, *Living Philosophies,* p. 141.
136. Robert Ardrey, *African Genesis,* p. 346.
137. Desmond Morris, *The Naked Ape,* pp. 240-1.
138. Douglas M. C. MacEwan, *Conservation as the Intelligent and Purposeful Control of Human Environment,* International Humanism, vol. III, no. 1, p. 1.
139. Alex Comfort, *The Nature of Human Nature,* p. 3.
140. Desmond Morris, *The Naked Ape,* p. 9.
141. Vernon Reynolds, *The Apes,* p. 20.
142. John Steinbeck, quoted in *The Radical Humanism of John Steinbeck,* Daniel Aaron, Saturday Review, Sept. 28, 1968, p. 26.
143. William Golding, *The Lord of the Flies.*
144. Brigid Brophy, *Black Ship to Hell,* p. 349.
145. Alan Moorehead, *The Fatal Impact,* p. 206.
146. W. Phillip Keller, *Under Wilderness Skies,* p. 67.
147. Claude Leví-Strauss, *A World on the Wane,* p. 397.
148. *Ibid.,* p. 39.
149. Bernard Campbell, *Human Evolution,* p. 84.
150. Ruth Benedict, *The Growth of Culture,* from "Man, Culture and Society," ed. Harry L. Shapiro, p. 188.
151. Henry E. Crampton, *The Coming and Evolution of Life,* p. 20.
152. Teilhard de Chardin, *The Phenomenon of Man.*
153. Alex Comfort, *The Nature of Human Nature,* p. 153.
154. Adolf Portmann, *Animals as Social Beings,* p. 12.
155. J. Arthur Thomson, quoted in *The Strange Lives of Famliar Insects,* p. 73.
156. George F. Thomas, *New Forms for Old Faith,* from "Changing Patterns in American Civilization," p. 138.
157. Carleton Ray and Elgin Ciampi, *Marıne Life,* pp. 72-3.
158. Morris R. Cohen, *Reason and Law,* p. 137.
159. Homer W. Smith, *Man and His Gods,* p. 221.
160. Harry A. Overstreet, *The Enduring Quest,* p. 52.
161. Donald Culross Peattie, *This is Living.*
162. Bertrand Russell, *Our Knowledge of the External World,* p. 22.
163. van Campen Heilner, *Salt Water Fishing,* p. 16.
164. Elie Metchnikoff, *The Nature of Man,* p. 30.
165. *Ibid.,* p. 18.
166. *Ibid.,* pp. 76-7.
167. *Ibid.,* p. 69.
168. *Ibid..* p. 94.
169. *Ibid.,* p. 73.
170. *Ibid.,* p. 95.
171. *Ibid.,* p. 33.
172. J. H. Fabre, *Social Life in the Insect World,* vol. I, p. 125.
173. van Campen Heilner, *Salt Water Fishing,* p. 51; also Jordan and Everman, *American Game and Food Fishes.*
174. Carleton Ray and Elgin Ciampi, *Marine Life,* p. 29.
175. Edwin Way Teale, *Strange Lives of Familiar Insects,* p. 137.
176. *Ibid.,* p. 158.
177. John Dewey, *Experience and Nature,* p. 9.
178. George Santayana, *Reason in Science,* vol. V, "Life of Reason," p. 170.
179. William Lillie, *Introduction to Ethics,* p. 158.
180. George Santayana, *Reason in Science,* vol. V, "Life of Reason," p. 158.

181. Ralph de Pomerai, *Marriage,* p. 325.
182. René Dubos, *So Human an Animal,* p. 118.
183. Alfred N. Whitehead, quoted in *American Thought: A Critical Sketch,* Morris R. Cohen, p. 410.
184. Claude Leví-Strauss, *A World on the Wane,* p. 231.
185. C. J. Ducasse, *Determinism, Freedom, and Responsibility,* from "Determinism and Freedom." ed. Sidney Hook, p. 166.
186. Theodosius Dobzhansky, *Mankind Evolving,* p. 60.
187. William Lillie, *Introduction to Ethics,* pp. 44-5.
188. Hudson Hoagland, *Science and the New Humanism,* Science Magazine, vol. 143, no. 3602, Jan. 10, 1964, p. 113.
189. Sidney Hook, *Necessity, Indeterminism, and Sentimentalism,* from "Determinism and Freedom," ed. Sidney Hook, p. 166.
190. Paul Weiss, *Common Sense and Beyond,* from "Determinism and Freedom," ed. Sidney Hook, pp. 232-3.
191. Brand Blanshard, *The Case for Determinism,* from "Determinism and Freedom," ed. Sidney Hook, p. 30.
192. Hudson Hoagland, *Science and the New Humanism,* Science Magazine, vol. 143, no. 3602, Jan. 10, 1964, p. 112.
193. Paul Weiss, *Common Sense and Beyond,* from "Determinism and Freedom," ed. Sidney Hook, p. 236.
194. Paul Edwards, *Hard and Soft Determinism,* from "Determinism and Freedom," ed. Sidney Hook, p. 118.
195. Carl G. Hempel, *Some Reflections on "The Case for Determinism,"* from "Determinism and Freedom," ed. Sidney Hook, p. 171.
196. Arthur Pap, *Determinism, Freedom, Moral Responsibility and Casual Talk,* from "Determinism and Freedom," ed. Sidney Hook, p. 212.
197. Brand Blanshard, *The Case for Determinism,* from "Determinism and Freedom," ed. Sidney Hook, p. 25.
198. see *Determinism and Freedom,* ed. Sidney Hook, p. 27.
199. Corliss Lamont, *Freedom of Choice Affirmed,* p. 45.

Go, from the creatures thy instructions take;
Learn from the birds what food the thickets yield;
Learn from the beasts the physic of the field;
Thy arts of building from the bee receive;
Learn of the mole to plough, the worm to weave;
Learn of the little nautilus to sail,
Spread the thin oar, and catch the driving gale.

—ALEXANDER POPE, *Essay on Man,* Epis. iii, 1.172

No man who has studied animal life would hold the old notion of the special creation of their species and look an animal in the face.

—David Starr Jordan

BOOK TWO

ORIGINS: THE NATURAL BASIS OF FREEDOM

ORIGINS: THE NATURAL BASIS OF FREEDOM

To PROVIDE THE necessary objective and factual material to support the premise of the natural basis of freedom as a precultural and innate process of living things, it is obviously necessary to draw upon the sciences and the scientists. In this chapter it is more important to learn, as I have, though not a scientist, what the scientists have to say that will enable us to collate their contributions to the purposes of our premise. George Gaylord Simpson: "Science itself, as a whole, is fundamentally biological. . . . It is all carried on by human beings, a species of animal. It is in fact a part of animal behavior, and an increasingly important part of the species-specific behavior of *Homo sapiens*. . . . It is now, especially through its operating arm, technology, the principal means of biological adaptation for civilized man. It is an evolutionary specialization that arose from more primitive, pre-scientific means of cultural adaptation, which in turn had arisen from the still more primitive, prehuman behavioral adaptation. . . . Biology, then, is the science that stands at the center of all science."[1] Margaret Mead puts it in another way: "At this moment in history it is useful to consider man and man's learned behavior within the entire context of the living world, without emphasizing the discontinuities between the different orders of living things, between subhuman and human, preliterate and literate, primitive and civilized man."[2] Kaj Birket-Smith: "We must see our culture not as the sole culture in existence, but as one of many, a part of the world-wide whole."[3] René Dubos: "Modern man in his sheltered environment continues to be under the influence of cosmic forces much as he was when he lived naked in direct contact with nature."[4]

Philosophy cannot ordain; it can try to interpret, explain, understand, and provide a rationalized frame of possible meaningfulness and some value to any present knowledge of things and ourselves. Philosophy cannot order or catalog truth; it can try

135

to interpret what appears to be the truth as it is given to us by those whose task it is purely to find it. Therefore, it has been essential to present some findings of people who are specialists in their various fields of investigation. Even so, I have been compelled to reduce substantially the available evidence to a much smaller extent than I might have wished, so as to avoid drifting too far afield from our prime purpose and thesis: to present the natural basis for a philosophy of freedom.

Why should we consider and accept freedom as a *natural* and *affirmative* want?

First, we should recognize the observational fact that what is naturally desirable and inherent in man, or in any part of nature, for that matter, does not imply any relevance or agreement, necessary or logical, with man's idea of goodness, badness, morals, ethics, or codes. These are individual or cultured perspectives, opinions, usages, cultivated ways and mores of a given person, group, or society, or even of the general opinion, if we can presume this, of mankind itself. Whether certain types of ethical values or standards are beneficial, desirable, or necessary, in the individual and/or general sense, applicable to a "better" or a more "beneficent" sense and practice of freedom, and bring certain meanings and values to individuals and groups, is a subject that has a more proper place in later chapters. "Biological evolution is not in itself a moral process. The word *moral* is simply irrelevant in this connection. But evolution has produced a moral and ethical animal. Man is not the 'darling of the gods,' as he thought he was before Darwin."[5]

THE ANIMAL ORIGIN OF MAN

PRESENTLY WE ARE concerned with *origins,* and in the study of origins we find that as life emerged, freedom emerged—in the separation and movement of the first amoeba, the first protozoa, the first stir of animal life. "About a billions years ago, the water in the seas had approximately reached their present level. It was in the shallow, warm waters of this sea that life arose. . . . In the sea because there is a liquid (plasma) bathing the tissues of all animals which is very much like sea water in its composition. The similarity of sea water and plasma indicates that the seas of a billion years ago, when life arose, were very similar in chemical composition to what they are today."[6] "As far as life is concerned there are no really fundamental differences between the various forms it takes. We all originated in the primeval ocean."[7] "Whoever they were, the first creatures had no choice but to live on the oceanic broth in which they arose."[8] "The sea gave birth to life and without its waters no living thing could ever survive on earth."[9] "Geologists believe that there is not a sizable area of any continent that has not at some time been beneath the sea. The sediments laid down during these floodings of large parts of the continents are the pages of the book in which paleoontologists read the history of the development of life on our planet."[10] "In the time-honored analogy of the clock, if the twenty-four hours of the day be taken as equivalent to the lapse of time since the beginning of life on earth, then man would have to be shown as appearing only within the last minutes and our own type, *Homo sapiens,* within the last few seconds of the twenty-four hours."[11] "As soon as living matter emerged, it became subject to death. . . . These two alteratnives, growth and death, set the stage for the working out of the evolutionary process."[12] C. P. Idyll, of the Institute of Marine Science, in writing about the *Birth of the Sea,* states: "In the seventeenth century an eminent Irish churchman, Archbishop James Ussher, declared with enviable assurance that the earth was created in 4004 B.C. He even named the exact day and hour: Sunday, October 23rd, at 9 A.M. . . . By analyzing rock samples to determine the proportion of uranium to the breakdown products, geologists have measured the age of the oldest rocks known. On this basis the age of the earth accepted today is approximately 4½ billion years."[13] Recently (September 5, 1967) it was reported that in South Africa Dr. J. William Schopf, a Harvard paleobotanist, discovered a chemical relic that is estimated to be about 3.1 billion years old. This relic contains evidence of twenty-two amino acids, chemical substances that act as building blocks for the protein essential to all living organisms. Dr. Kvenvolden, of the Ames Research in Biochemistry, gives his opinion about this discovery: "It tells me life processes as we know them were extant 3 billion years ago."[14]

There are certain natural ways that are specifically and generally bad for man; man considers these as such and tries, as a result, to destroy, overcome, or change them. Natural ways that are basically and potentially beneficial to man, man accepts readily (or should) and even tries to improve upon them. However, often what is natural and what is acquired and acculturated in and by man, agree or are relevant to each other, sometimes not. When it is an agreeable thing to man, he calls it good; when it is disagreeable, he calls it bad. Even here, very often what was considered bad at one time or place was considered good at another time or place, according to man's ways, needs, environments, and societies. The sun and its warmth is heaven to the Eskimos; to the Arab it is an evil; and the Moslem's heaven is in the cool shade of wafting breezes and bowing palms laden down with dates. To a bat the epitome of heaven is a cloudy swarm of delicious mosquitoes, and to some jungle Indians heaven is on the moon where there are no mosquitoes. We should note, also, the historical fact that often those in power—and this power can be military, political, economic, religious, and include the emotional and psychological, or combinations and multiples of any of them—*ordered* and *ruled* what they considered good or bad, what to do and not to do, how to serve and obey, how free or unfree people had to be, and the individuals under such subjection had to submit more or less or else endanger their security, their togetherness, their relative or limited freedom, and even their lives.

Thus, man may be, in a limited and opinionated way, the measure of man, but only from the viewpoint of man, not from any viewpoint, if there could be one, of Nature itself, of which man is merely a part. "The beauty of nature," writes Dozshansky, "refers to human feelings about certain natural objects, not to these objects themselves."[15] Joseph K. Hart: "Nature is both the *means* of life—that is, the materials for our uses—and also the *ends*—that is, the source and repository of human hopes and happiness."[16]

A surgeon, when operating upon a patient, does not take into account (or at least he should not) whether the person is a Congolese, and black, or a Scandinavian, and white; he is operating upon a *human body,* which he is supposed to understand from a natural and objective analysis and knowledge of it, not from an intellectual, racial or cultural level. "There is no evidence whatever," states Clyde Kluckhohn, "that the genes which determine skin color or hair form are correlated with genes influencing temperament or mental capacity. The idea of deducing character from color is intrinsically absurd."[17] Some people have the silly idea that colored people are inferior to whites because of the difference of pigment in their skins. These are not the medical concern of the doctor. He expects to find the stomach or the heart or the liver in its accustomed place, and generally does. The rich and the poor have the same human bodies; some may be healthier or weaker and ailing, taller or shorter, fatter or thinner, regardless of wealth, position, intellect or status. As the old proverb goes, the rain falls on good and bad alike. And death comes to all, to the cruel, the tyrant, the thief, as well as to the scholar, the genius, the "godly," the honest, and the gentle. Nature, our blind mother, has no preferences or prejudices. Only man has.

There is no rational or ethical discretion in the diffusion of nature's ways, gifts, accidents. Man's ways are obviously natural ways, in the sense that all of man is part of nature, but nature's ways may not be necessarily, or always, the ways of man. Fred Hoyle writes, "We cannot think outside the particular patterns that our brains are conditioned to. . . . It was this long evolution —not recent history, not the periods since the Romans or Greeks, for instance—that determined our basic physical and psychological characteristics."[18] Today's sons of yesterday's slaves have become great masters of music, masters in composition, painting, sculpture, poetry, great singers and dancers, inventors, doctors, judges, lawyers, ministers. Given adequate opportunity and practical freedom they can stand side by side with the white man endowed with thousands of years of Western culture. The Japanese, primitive only a few years ago, restrained, and militantly refusing to expose themselves to the outside world, have the most modern industrial expansions, scientists, and technologies, producing the finest, most delicate, and precise instruments—all this in little more than fifty years! The Eskimos, just a few years ago wandering, primitive, food-hunting, noncooking people, are today mechanics, watchmakers, and, some of them, exceptional artisans and artists. One can continue this list of peoples who have been considered savage, primitive, even dangerous only a few years ago, who, after being exposed to new things by accident, war, or penetration, have become like the white man, even addicts for profit and greed, and property-conscious. Take in savages from the Brazilian jungle, give them schooling, clothes, food, guidance, expose them to the white man's environment, customs, and usages within a periphery of confidence and security, and you will be amazed how soon they will adapt themselves and learn. Of course, like each animal in any animal group, each individual has a distinctive personality and distinctive qualities and potentials in varied degree; so it is with humans everywhere, white and all other shades, and these variations will express themselves in adaptabilities, inclinations, desires, strivings and goals. True, although we have become indoctrinated and adapted to our own cultures and times (and this has been the identifying portrait of any period), the basic nature of human nature, with all its characteristics and potentials, was determined and evolved long before the protohominid discovered a weapon in his hands and a fire with which to warm them. Desmond Morris: "Cultural developments have given us more and more impressive technological advances, but wherever these clash with our basic biological properties they meet strong resistance. The fundamental patterns of behaviour laid down in our early days as hunting apes still shine through all our affairs, no matter how lofty they may be."[19]

Freedom is the conscious or unconscious exposure of the elements in a being's makeup that tend toward any action that is impulsively or rationally considered as some sort of relieving, fulfilling, protective, or progressive *force,* which, in the ultimate, is accepted or activated as something that allows it to live according to its nature. Whether this activity is beneficial or harmful, lovable or hateful, goodness or badness, honest or dishonest, sympathetic or cruel, law-abiding or criminal, sacrificial or self-interested, ethical or unethical, is irrelevant and aside from the point, and depends upon the nature, containment, and "field" of the individual: the "outward" sequences of the process of freedom which is naturally inward in man. These sequences of freedom are not our concern at the moment. What we are concerned with in this chapter is the recognition that freedom was not handed down to man on some cultural, political or societal platter, but preceded these, and that it evolved in man as man evolved himself from the animal tree of his ancestry. Robert Ardrey states that "A bird does not fly because it has wings; it has wings because it flies."[20] Man is not free because he has a brain; he has a brain because of the natural freedom that *experienced* the brain for him.

Most assuredly, the environmental influences—the cultural, the religious, political, and socio-economic—affected, modified, advanced or retarded, and, patternized his quantitative and qualitative sense and quanta of freedom. "All species that survive, survive by adapting themselves to their environment."[21] "Each organ and system displays the same quality of adaptation in its make-up which characterizes the creature as a whole."[22] "One of the criteria of intelligence is flexibility of behavior," adds Kenneth Norris of the U.C.L.A. Zoology Department in California.[23] "Man's special capacities, his awareness, his perceptual functions, his reactability, his ability for symbolization and socialization, are all biological adaptations developed by evolution under the stress and guidance of natural selection."[24]

We should, therefore, as a prerequisite, understand that freedom appears to be a natural factor deep-rooted in the rudimentary and evolving processes of the human being, whereas his cultural and societal acquisitions and traits and patterns are acquired, as in the process of child education, parental and group guidance, indoctrination and the adapabilities of the growing young to the disciplines and customs of their particular cultures. These acquisitions, while definitely affecting the sense of freedom, are in themselves not permanent or inherited fixtures of trait or habit, but subject to greater flexibility of modification, change, fashion, philosophies, religious and societal changeabilities and innovations. A baby born of Parisian parents but brought up in India by Hindus grows up to be a Hindu; a Japanese baby brought up by white Americans in New York grows up to be a New Yorker.

Invention and modes of living affect the sense of freedom, but freedom itself was part of the human system long before the earliest tool-man chipped the first rock into an adze or an ax.

Considering the spatial field of political potential made possible by the human, and its historical elements of negotiability, communication, maneuverability, and the various intricate and complex phases of politico- logistic arrangements of people and their groups and societies, it seems to be evident that the problems of humans, nations, and ideologies are still problems not different from, on the contrary, identifiable with the elementary problems that originate, evolve, and experience themselves in the general field of living things and that, therefore, at root, they can be confronted and explained in biological terms. Kaj Birket-Smith: "Society as a whole—and, with it, culture—is based on a few qualities of so primitive a character that their roots really go down into the darkest depths of the animal kingdom."[25] René Dubos: "The urge to control property and to dominate one's peers are also ancient biological traits which can be recognized in the different forms of territoriality and dominance among most if not all animal societies. Animal behavior provides prototypes of the lust for political power, independently of any desire for financial or other material rewards, which is so common among men. Even the play instinct and certain kinds of aesthetic expression correspond to derivative but nevertheless important biological needs which exist in one form or another in animal species and which have probably always been part of man's nature."[26] Heini Hediger: "It can be assumed that the natural history of territoriality in the animal kingdom represents the first chapter of the history of property in mankind."[27] Walter Heape: "It may be held that the recognition of territorial rights, one of the most significant attributes of civilization, was not evolved by man but has ever been an inherent factor in the life history of animals."[28] And man *is* an animal.

The dress of civilization still covers the body of an animal made human through physical event; the impact of culture and science only indicates that all we are today is the result not alone of cultural and political acquisition, but that we are a product resulting from the constant interaction of an animal with its environment, both biological at base, out of which all the cultures and ideologies and political systems and sciences were slowly generated, acquired, changed, evolved, to make possible the abridgement of the caveman into the statesman of today. The potential of the present-day scientist, sociologist, philosopher, or politician was already seeded in the subhominid and in the world environment in which he lived, moved, and multiplied. The elements of human history are the elements of animal survival and power, and these elements, biological in nature, still rule in the complex changes of the human psyche and the modern world. Life identifies the nature of freedom as the nature of the animal; what is important is what we do with it, and why, and on this depends our differentiation and change from the human beasts who roamed the jungles of millions of years ago. Psychologically and consciously, at least, we have drifted far from the birds and squirrels, to have noticed that we still, with all our complex ways and things, basically continue to exist as they do. We have deified ourselves and thus estranged our minds and dreams away from the flow of the real and the good to the adverse currents of somas that so often lead to self-beguilement, power intoxication, and self-dilution. Roger A. Caras: "Man evolved into his present form concurrently with a great many other animal species. Some that preceded him have lasted miraculously into our present era. Not a few come to us from times more ancient than we can readily comprehend. Man was and is a part of this whole, vast, pulsing scene. He is legitimate heir to a natural heritage, he is an animal among animals—spirited, spiritual, inspired though he may be. His estate is the estate of rock, sea, and air, bush, fire, and earth. His stuff is the stuff of the planet, the solar system, and the universe. So it is with the worm, the fish, the eagle, and the swine. In this regard, at least, man is not unique."[29] Desmond Morris: "These five categories of interspecific relationships—prey, symbiont, competitor, parasite and predator—are the ones that can be found to exist between other pairs of species. Basically, we are not unique in these respects, but they are the same types of relationships."[30]

To distinguish between the ways of nature and the ways of man is not an easy matter seeing that our lenses of verification and our scales of meaning and value are already oculated with human vision and minds; but we can try, as the scientist does, to attempt to apply empirical tools with which to gather, as much as is humanly possible, an objective viewpoint by objective inquiry, even though this may be helplessly colored to some inevitable extent with the purposes of our search. Even the anthropocentric and egocentric tendencies of scientists expose and express themselves in the helpless *human* element of influence in research. V. G. Dethier: "Students of behavior tend to seek in other animals that which they believe exists in themselves. . . . The farther removed an animal is from ourselves, the less sympathetic we are in ascribing to it those components that we know in ourselves."[31]

Man, being a *part,* cannot possibly know or experience *all,* but we can try to encompass as great a knowledge as we can and so be enabled to evaluate as much experience as is possible for us. The way to do this seems to be by the empirical or scientific method of inquiry, investigation, analysis, and projection. Here the essence of freedom itself is to keep the door of inquiry open and the freedom to change one's convictions as plausible and as desirable. Only freedom can wind the clock of education. Only freedom can allow our eyes to see without blinds, our minds to think without subjection, regimentation, or indoctrination, our feet to walk firmly in the light and safely in the darkness and firmly on the ground. History, *the freedom to look back,* is essential to verifiable diagnosis; a rational and scientific approach, and *the freedom to look around and ahead,* is essential to any realistic and meaningful prognosis.

IDENTITIES OF FREEDOM: GENETIC

THE IDENTITIES AND verifications of freedom as a *natural* and *affirmative want* may be classified into several categories: *Genetic, Evolutional, Analogical,* and *Relational.* These we will briefly explore here in more or less random fashion. The identities and verifications of freedom as a natural compatibility, its role and history of confliction and adaptational latitudes and range of applicable judgments, will be classified and discussed later in their appropriate places. In the meantime, it is important to know something about the nature of man himself, whose freedom is the pursuit of our present task. "To understand human nature it is necessary first to give an account of the origin of man."[32] "From seashore and jungle, from ant-heap and travertine cave have been collected the inflammable materials that must some day explode our most precious myths."[33] George Gaylord Simpson: "Man was certainly not the goal of evolution, which evidently had no goal. He was not planned, in an operation wholly planless. He is not the ultimate in a single constant trend toward higher things, in a history of life with innumerable trends, none of them constant, and some toward the lower rather than the higher."[34] "It is obvious that the great majority of humans through history have had grossly, even ridiculously, unrealistic concepts of the world. Man is, among other things, the mistaken animal, the foolish animal. Other species doubtless have much more limited ideas about the world, but what ideas they do have are much less likely to be wrong and are never foolish. White cats do not denigrate black, and dogs do not ask Baal, Jehovah, or other Semitic gods to perform miracles for them."[35] "Perception of the truth of evolution was an enormous stride from superstition to a rational universe."[36]

William Blake clamored that "Nature is the work of the devil. The devil is in us as far as we are nature." Blake forgot to mention that he, too, was part of nature, including his utterance, and what he stated was the result of his own natural thinking. On the other hand, Schopenhauer countered by saying, "There is only one untruthful creature on earth, and that is man. All the others are honest and upright in that they openly declare their nature and do not simulate emotions they do not feel." William Saroyan came closer when he wrote: "Man is an actor. He acts all manner of men, and each one is a lie. Only the animal in him is real." Brand Blanshard, explaining the naturalistic philosophy of Santayana, writes: "The roots that man has in nature are very long roots that run down through the animal mind; indeed we are all animals whose science and poetry, religion and art, disguise it as we may, are the flowering of animal impulse."[37]

Santayana himself reiterated, in a letter to Warren Allen Smith, in 1951, his basic principle of naturalism: "My naturalism is fundamental and includes man, his mind, and all his works, products of the generative order of Nature."[38] Harry Overstreet, appreciating the historic fact that man is the product of comparatively recent evolution, said: "Man is far more a child of nature than any of the animals or plants around him."[39] Baron d'Holbach wisely stated: "The unhappiness of man is due to his ignorance of nature."

Democritus, considering that he lived around 400 B.C., made a sharp deduction about the world when he said, "In reality there is nothing but atoms and space." "So small are nature's building blocks," writes Allan C. Fisher, Jr., "that you could put 36 billion billion atoms on the head of a pin."[40] Organic life is an observable part of existence in general, though in pure science it would be difficult to mark the line where organics end and inorganics begin. Science sees the organic and inorganic as the descriptions of certain elements in certain states, the elements being the composition of matter or forms of matter, which can lead, in certain chemical processes and evolutions, to organic and inorganic identities or appearances. "Virtually all biochemists agree that life on earth arose spontaneously from non-living matter."[41] "Organic life is a form of energy, and is subject to the same laws that determine the motions of electrons and of heavenly bodies."[42] So far as man is concerned, "there can be little doubt now that man has been in existence upon the earth much longer than the million years assigned to the Pleistocene Period."[43] So far as the diversification of the evolution of animal life is concerned, "at the lowest estimate, the number of different species of animals now living all around us is at least three million."[44] Man is but *one* of them.

Regarding genetic origins, it is needless to establish what the sciences have already established very well and conclusively: that man is an animal, and a destructive and self-destructive animal at that, yet capable of goodness and some order; that he evolved, like all other animals, from a common origin; that his anatomical structure and functions are factually similar and related to other animals and organic life in general; that he is part of the food chains common to all organics, outside of which he cannot exist; that there is a symbiotic relationship and union between animal and plant life; that plant life preceded and made animal life possible; that there exist today many organisms and species which are both animal and plant in structure and function; that the body and mind of man evolved over a period of many millions of years; that during this long trek of time man's brain grew from a small diencephalon controlling the instinctive and protective self-preserving drives of the animal, later evolving the expanding brain box of the cortical system. Sinnott: "The unity of life must impress itself on every thoughtful biologist. Protoplasm is very constant in character wherever we find it, and genes are chemically much the same in the simplest plants as they are in man. . . . From the simplest creatures up to man the web of life has been continuous and unbroken, and though lowly ones lack many qualities that we possess, there is in them the germ from which all these things have come."[45] Peter Zollinger: "Life is synonymous with organisms, from whose singular nature is derived the concept of organization."[46] A. Ingelman-Sundberg, the noted obstetrician, writes: "We all start as one-celled beings. The sperm and ova of sea urchins and man are, at a hasty glance, strikingly alike. A fish embryo swims around with a yolk sac hanging down from its belly and also has six arches—gill arches—between the mouth and the heart. There is not even very much difference between the chick embryo in the egg and the human embryo in the chorionic cavity on the day when their hearts start beating, though it takes the chicken only two days to get to that point. Could it be that at an early stage the child is a fish or a frog or a young bird? . . . Of course it has several features in common with most living organisms, for all creatures have the same origin."[47] "Darwin's ideas are now on so solid a basis as to be regarded as part of our scientific knowledge."[48] René Dubos: "The paradox is that while man unquestionably occupies a unique place in creation, his responses to environmental stimuli have their counterparts in the life of one or another animal species. Man's physiological urges, including the need to play, are common aspects of animal life in nature; most of his social activities and organizations are also represented in the different types of animal communities; even the ability to express attitudes and desires through symbolic sounds, postures, objects and other representations is widespread among animals."[49] Fred S. Hulse: "The fact that man is a social animal is inseparable from the fact that he is a biological organism. Culture has added a new dimension to human life, but it has not abolished the dimensions which already existed."[50] Robert Evans Snodgrass: "Insects, for example, are not curiosities; they are creatures in common with ourselves bound by the laws of the physical universe, which laws decree that everything alive must live by observing the same elemental principles that make life possible. . . . Many sincere people find it difficult to believe in evolution. Their difficulty arises largely from the fact that they look to the differences in structure between the diverse types of living things and do not see the unity in function that underlies all physical forms of life."[51]

The progress in the genetic sciences, and especially in the new experimental extensions in the study of DNA and its field and play upon heredity, and the probable ensuing possibilities of the still-to-be-born technology of controlled and selective heredity, is so revolutionary and volatile in the future social sciences and all its applications, that man has taken upon himself, because of this knowledge, greater freedom of choice and, therefore, greater responsibility in its eventual potential regarding himself and the world that is his home. Whether such advance of man to improve his own nature is dangerous or will tend to create unforeseeable and unpredictable problems is something that only experienced event and its sequences can reveal. Whether such control, selection, and hybridization will be able to preserve the individualization and individuality of a person, or whether it will tend to "mechanize" him to suit the socio-politico-cultural structure cannot be reasonably and clearly predicted. Richard A. Yarnell: "It is possible that we are entering an era in which we will acquire knowledge requisite to influencing many of the cause-and-effect relationships of our own cultural evolution in significant respects, but the vision of man in *control* of his own destiny is a dim one and one which has the effect of obscuring, rather than enlightening, our view of ourselves."[52]

So far as we are here concerned, we should note that when man was not yet human but a wild animal half erect and not completely free from the treetops, he already was as free as any wild animal could be, limited, of course, to his animal nature and his movement within the sphere and potential of his environment. Outside of his immediate desires and his instinct to mate, guard over his consort and probably his offspring, there was no society, rules, taboos, totems, religions, cultures. The only culture he could have possessed was his thirst, appetite for food, drive for sex satisfaction, and a place to sleep, no different from any wild animal today. "Eating, drinking, sleeping, and breeding will ever remain the most important functions of human life. The rest is nearly all mere extrinsic, superficial ornamentation."[53] Albert Einstein: "Feeling and desire are the motive forces behind all human endeavor and human creation, in however exalted a guise the latter may present itself to us."[54] "Hunger is the first and most universal experience. Its cry is not to be denied. When the parent bluejays decide that their chicks must fly, they will starve them off the bough. After the first terrified flutter, the youngsters will be rewarded with a morsel."[55] "All organic beings have two essential needs: that of nutrition and that of propagating the species. The former brings them to a struggle and to mutual extermination, while the needs of maintaining the species bring them to approach one another and to support one another."[56]

At this stage of wildness man was as independent and as free as any creature could be. As the species grew in numbers, the filial habit evolved the gregarious instinct, and herds, prides, and colonies of these preprotohominids evolved or cultured gregarious instincts out of the automatic processes of self-preservation against common natural enemies. In the evolution of the group or colony the subhuman animal had to abide with the evolved necessities that became essential to the preservation of the *individual* through the colony or group *mass:* here he had to lose, unconsciously and instinctively, some individual freedom. It is possible, the subhuman not being a nocturnal feeder and prowler, that simple fear of the darkness and of isolated attack could have at least partly motivated the gregarious instinct to group for common protection and psychological shelter. The fear of darkness, through which the eyes of man cannot ordinarily penetrate, persisted in the ancient foundations of religion, to become the abode of evil spirits, the environmental stage for hells, devils, witch parties. Regarding the attitude of birds to darkness, W. C. Allee writes: "The crowded roosts to which certain birds return not only for one season but sometimes for years are widely known. Here we are concerned with a positive social appetite which grows stronger with the approach of darkness; the details as to why and how it operates are not known."[57] It is also possible that these sparsely-haired humans closeted together for body warmth during periods of coldness, or were induced to group because of limited shelter within a specific area, or because of natural accidents and catastrophes. Gronefeld gives us another view: "When an ape goes to sleep, it does not usually just sit on a branch or use a tree-trunk as a back-rest and squat down. Perhaps it needs a sense of security which only comes from having some kind of shelter around it. Do we humans also not feel something similar? Is it not true that we only feel really safe when we are unseen, safe within the four walls of our home? Is it not such a big step from the nest of the apes to the human bedroom?"[58]

Still, at this stage our ancestors existed in pure animalism, not much different than the troops of baboons, monkeys and chimpanzees today. The distance from animalism to animism is a trek of many hundreds of thousands of years. The genetic origin of freedom became operable in the purely free movement of an individual unit as a self-sustaining and self-preserving "colony" of specialized cells united and functioning as a body, in contradistinction to the ant formicary or beehive wherein the ants and bees could only exist as unconscious, physically detached but psychically united parts of a colony without which the insect would immediately degenerate and perish. The insect had existed and evolved for many scores of millions of years before man's origin; the insect had already lost his individuality, if it ever had any, eons of time prior to the emergence of the humanlike animal. The insect's society had already been established and more or less stabilized, and the insect had become forever "lost" into the social mechanism of its society, never again to regain any possibility of individualization. Only the formicary or hive, or cycle, was "free" within its own limitations and existence. Professor Snodgrass: "We can not help but remark how often parallelisms are to be discovered between things in the insect world and affairs in the human world."[59]

The genetic freedom of a single cell is "free" in the sense that it possesses *anima,* the living urge and ability to move itself; it is free to exert any movement or drive for food and reproduction limited to its own natural containment within its nature and field. This continued with the multicellular unit. Environmental constancy may variate in time a genotypic inherited factor or trait, wherever compatibly possible, as part of the general genetic adaptational force to adjust itself in its automatic processes of maintaining its self-preservative and self-reproducing compulsions of survival. This is the operableness of evolution and a basic impetus for change, mutation, and extension—*natural selection.* Therefore, we see that, in the strict sense, freedom has never been an unlimited or absolute prerogative of life, as the theologian would have us believe, but limited within the nature of itself. This genesis of the individual unit, of the natural freedom of the cell, the nucleus of *anima,* Morgan *called* "the particulate composition of the germplasm and of particulate inheritance." No divinity operates in the evolutionary process, nor do we see the affirmation of purpose or supernatural control in the process. Dobzhansky, in his *Mankind Evolving,* states that "Natural selection is, however, a blind, mechanical, automatic, impersonal process."[60] Looking at it from the ethical point of view, Santayana wrote: "Only in its relative capacity can the universe find things good, and only in its relative capacity can it be good for anything."[61]

The biological genesis of freedom emanates from "the primal stir in the single cell in the morning of the world,"[62] and identifies the origin of a *self,* in its simplest form, to the complex *individual* of today. Freedom is rooted genetically and evolutionally in the self, the self-moving unit, the individual. The genus of the very nucleus of freedom necessitates the existence of a unit capable of being coalescently drawn to, or of withdrawing, out of its own spontaneous action, from, something else. Whether this freedom is mindless, that is, incapable of acknowledging, *sensing,* or *knowing* its own process, is irrelevant in the same sense as an infant instinctively moves its arms and legs and begins to crawl and grasp things in its reach, and instinctively activates its curiosity about or toward things, or spontaneously and compulsively withdraws its finger when it accidentally touches something very hot; yet we cannot deny that the infant is free, limited to itself and its environment, and automatically responds to, and operates, the process of freedom in so doing. This is what we mean by the genetic origin of freedom. Freedom, being a natural and biological trait, is a genetic constant predetermined in the evolution of man and his animal ancestry. It preceded the emergence of cultural and social patterns. While this freedom varies in different individuals and peoples, it is still of genetic origin, and "genetically determined differences have little, if anything, to do with culture."[63]

IDENTITIES OF FREEDOM: EVOLUTIONAL

THE *evolutional* NATURE of freedom, prior to man's appearance on the historical stage, was a concomitant and congruous factor more or less attached to man's preprimitive tribal habitat. With an expanding cortical brain, man became "courageous," left the tree and the hole in the hillside, and "challenged" the open plain. To do this he left behind some part of his instinctive process of the isolated unit of family group and "massed" his courage with that of his fellow creatures; otherwise he could not have ventured forth in confidence and achieve the results which only collective mutual-assistance could have brought about. "The observed variation in intelligence has both genetic and environmental components."[64] One of the conclusions that Ardrey draws in his *Territorial Imperative* is: "We must know that while the human brain exceeds by far the potentialities of that possessed by any other animal species, its psychological processes probably differ not at all from those of other higher animals, and from those of lower animals perhaps as well."[65]

In many parts of the world today this primitive mutual-assistance pact is at work, although the individual members may not be conscious of it. In doing this he exchanged or "sold" a certain quantum of freedom for a certain quantum and type of new power, which is also a freedom potential. This power was very realistic because it actually realized what he could not realize alone: expansion, extension, greater security, better protection against attack, newfound pleasure in communication and expression, competitive spiritedness, wider range of mating selectivity, better homes by cooperative "kibbutz" effort, innovations of play, etc. He was no longer "on his own." He now "belonged" to something bigger. Thus, besides the actual accretion of physical and economic power, he found a new oasis of psychological power, which soothed and pleased his cortical system, that part of his brain which favored somehow a relaxation more or less of the primeval "look out for yourself" instincts of his diencephalon. His unconscious instinctual drive of living to preserve himself as best he could, and yet satisfy the natural cravings of his physical and emotional makeup, in which his greatest extent of natural freedom unconsciously expressed and manifested itself, now joined with others to create a collectiveness out of the sheer necessities of numbers and conditions. "The will to live," wrote Metchnikoff, "to preserve health, to satisfy the instincts and to make them act in unison, have driven mankind, in the very earliest days of reflection, to invent remedies for the imperfection of the human constitution."[66]

Freedomwise, man became "greater," "bigger," "stronger," and *less fearful*. By becoming less fearful, he became *less careful*. Civilization processed the reduction of fears at the expense of caution, only to revert to fear when the traditional power of the shaman and king established their dominion of the few over the many. Yet, previously, his natural fears, as a more or less isolated entity on its own, became dissolved in the aggregate new powers of the kinship or tribal family group. With less fears and more security, the human brain relaxed a little from its ways of purely instinctive action based on appetite, alertness, alarm, and flight, a unit compelled to save itself constantly or perish, to adopt the newly discovered benefits of group coordination and cohesion. What he did not anticipate was that his individual fears as an animal were being exchanged for the acceptance of a *mass* fear in the group, which turned away from his more natural ways of individual animal life and evolved the earliest forms of shamanism, the great-grandfather and lineal ancestor of monarchial, theocratic, and political domination.

From that point on the physical evolution of man, to strengthen and automatically and gradually modify his body to meet individual drives, began a slow relaxation, while, on the other hand, his brain evolved the necessary emotional and "reasoning" impulses and thinking habits emerging out of his efforts to communicate, to specialize, to meet the demands and needs of his social and group drive. Thus, in the union of the group, the unconsciously freer individual let down his physical and instinctive guard to become eventually a being conscious of its own enslavement. That he needed the group to survive seems to be a biological admission of fact; otherwise the human species would probably have diminished in numbers and possibly become extinct in time. The gradual enslavement of man to the group or the favored few, and its historical events, are also admissions in the story of man and have to be reckoned with.

Before attempting to analyze the prehistoric and primitive tribal periods of man, another factor should be stressed in this transition from a one-ban business to the misty, dawnlike beginnings of the corporate structure of primitive society. In the earlier and freer fields of animal nature and behavior, there existed, and still exists, the biological (from which stemmed the psychological and the cultural) struggle for survival, and its constant arterial flow generated the natural processes of selection. This biological "eliminating" and competitive process brought a *parallelism* of psychological power as a necessary appendage in the "higher" animals, in whom a growing cerebral capacity can combine the needs of the instinctive processes with the compromising needs of the species to exist within a limited area and its unconscious struggle to carry on its kind. We find this *power* factor of *territory* or *territorial* power still intensely expressive not only in man but in almost all kinds of animals and plant life, even today. "The tumult of bird song in early spring is in the nature of a territory-proclamation."[67] "Dominance—beyond any comprehension—is related to the mystery of the fundamental life force."[68] "The spot from which the male bird sings becomes the center of his territory, which he guards against all other male buntings. There can be no doubt that the song itself serves mostly as a notice that this particular bit of territory is already occupied and that any bird which disregards it is in for a fight."[69] "Self-regard is the primary quality of living matter."[70] Describing the reef fish in the Maldives Atolls, Irenäus Eibl-Eibesfeldt relates: "In general, however, the free-living fish is by no means as free as one often thinks. It cannot usually move at will into any territory but is tied to a definite living area, in which it lives according to a closely outlined daily plan. The area in which the fish lives is the animals' field of activity *(Aktionsraum)* and any part of it that it can defend against other members of the same species is its territory. . . . *Aktionsraum* and territory are often further subdivided. . . . Thus there are pastures, hunting grounds and cleansing stations, where others are tolerated, and there are residential holes which are strenuously defended against members of the same species but which are also sometimes shared with members of its own family. . . . Many fish are however very intolerant. They take up residence in a certain area of reef, either singly or in pairs and defend it against every strange member of their own species."[71]

Without this instinctive drive it is doubtful whether any creature could have continued to exist. Where this process was halted or degenerated, either by natural accidents, "drifts," whether climatic, geological, cataclysmic, or from other causes, the species vanished. Without this drive, which essentially identifies and attaches man to his animal ancestry and his interdependence with the rest of nature, it would not have been possible for all parts of nature to have evolved as they have, as the result of pressures and resistances in the general causative process of determinism, and to form the particularized dependent and interdependent symbioses and relationships which make up the totality of nature and experience.

This is a basal trait in the relationships of individual animals to survive in their environments, and it exposes the natural freedom which is a biological function of the animal to move or extend itself, within its nature and limitations, but affording to itself, because of its nature, an adaptive surge to benefit itself, and thus to lessen limitation and increase potential and a wider field of movement and habitat. Therefore, the *relational* identity of one animal to another, of one living thing to another, whether it be macrocosmic or microcosmic, is in the nature of some degree of *force* which exhibits itself in *freedom,* and the relative processes of pressures and resistances of this force have evolved the processes and products, that is, the constant, sudden, or gradual, substance of myriad animal and plant life in the general arena of nature's experience and existence. "Storm and stress are the mothers of evolution."[72]

It is obvious, therefore, that evolution is not a thing of the past, some stay-put accomplishment. The nature of evolution, in itself, denotes a process and a constant processing. Evolution has been, is now, and will be, the concomitant expression of nature itself. Like *being,* it is forever a state of *becoming.* "Man has not only evolved; for better or for worse, he *is* evolving. Our not very remote ancestors were animals, not men; the transition from animal to man is, on the evolutionary time scale, rather recent."[73] "The evidence of biology means to most people familiar with it that the world of life, including man, is a product of an evolutionary development."[74] "The marine plants and animals of today are the successful survivors of a process of evolution that has probably lasted over a thousand million years."[75] "Out of modest, inconspicuous marine animals there had evolved the first representatives of that phylum of the animal kingdom whose ultimate representative, perhaps half a billion years later, was to be man."[76] "Those first green cells (chlorophyll) were the ancestors of all the prolific forests and grasslands that Charles Darwin marveled at on his trip around the world. Indeed, they were the ancestors of all the plant-kingdom . . . all the oxygen in the air we breathe today is completely renewed by photosynthesis every 2,000 years."[77] "The first organisms to photosynthesize became the ancestors of all the grasses, trees and sea-weeds. Green plants alone can produce the stuff of life—proteins, carbohydrates and fats— from the elements of water, soil and air. Every animal that ever lived has been dependent on them, directly or indirectly, for its existence."[78] The principle of evolution, from the simple to the complex, is the same principle of the biology of freedom, from the simple to the complex.

We have noted that the evolution of forces and functions became processed, and is still being processed and processing, not because of any rigidity or changelessness in the character of things, but because of the helpless *motivism* to grow or shrink, to move about, toward or away from something, to separate from or to join something, to take from or give to, and that this motivism in nature is in the relativity of its parts and the coalesced separatedness of things, individualized but inexorably attached to, and with, the processes of nature and its experiences, its constant innovations, "imperfections," or "errors" causing permutations and mutations and all their sequences. Life is fluid, unstable, in constant sensitivity within itself and from the relentless reception of impressions from the outside world. The fact that life is changeable, flexible, plastic, modifiable, and contains within its nucleus the gene of voluntary movement and choice, even though these forces are predetermined by heredity and experience, implies the rooted biology of freedom in the very nature of all animal life, regardless of the measure of limitation and potential. "The discovery of radio-activity . . . has shown us that the atom is not completely indivisible and changeless, but can break up and modify its elemental structure."[79]

We will try to determine later if man's political, social, religious, economic, or even cultural philosophies and traditions, which have more or less caused "rigidities" of dogmatisms and ingrained usages and customs, have eventually accelerated this force and brought about some movement and change. Whether these have been "good" or "bad" for man is another problem, and whether freedom in itself is "good" or "bad" is another problem again; both are irrelevant to the play of natural forces. Here we are primarily concerned with the origins and nature of freedom itself, and we cannot logically and reasonably realize these origins unless we also begin to understand the origin of man. William C. Boyd, the geneticist, states the case in his preface to his *Genetics and the Races of Man:* "The present world crisis has made it very clear that unless mankind acquires deeper and more intimate information about the nature of man and the human societies he forms and their mechanisms of action, civilization as we know it may come to an end in the only too foreseeable future."[80] Roy Pinney gives a warning: "We attack the world around us. We obliterate one species after another. We turn forests into dusty plains and fertile lands into barren deserts. We turn rivers into sludge heaps. We pollute the very air we breathe. If we continue, the earth will not be fit for any living creature—even man."[81] "In re-arranging the world to suit himself, man has initiated a complex series of chain reactions which may one day make the earth uninhabitable."[82] Rachel L. Carson: "The first recognition of malignancies traceable to the age of industry came during the last quarter of the 19th century. . . . By the end of the 19th century a half-dozen sources of industrial carcinogens were known; the 20th century was to create countless new cancer-causing chemicals and to bring the general population into intimate contact with them. . . . Judging by the present incidence of the disease, the American Cancer Society estimates that 45,000,000 Americans now living will eventually develop cancer. This means that malignant disease will strike two out of three families. . . . Today, *more American school children die of cancer than from any other disease.* . . . Twelve per cent of all deaths in children between the ages of one and fourteen are caused by cancer."[83] "Today we find our world filled with cancer-producing agents."[84] Pat McGrady: "For some time cancer has been epidemic, and the epidemic is growing. It seems hardly reasonable to ask the public and Congress to let industry and business have their way, unmolested by the press or governmental inquiry, for an entire human generation. The fact is that the average person is exposed constantly not so much to a single carcinogen but to multiples of them."[85] "The atmosphere is being polluted by countless new compounds, many of them foreign to the chemical requirements of life and toxic to the systems they touch. . . . More and more, it is becoming difficult to hide from, or survive, the trend of the times as directed by the inventiveness of the human mind. Sadder still, the trend has only begun. . . . The air gets dirtier all the time. Its annual pollutants would bury the cities under 21 feet of dangerous debris. Among the pollutants are numerous carcinogens."[86] W. Phillip Keller describes what happens to the environment after an atomic testing blast: "In the Pacific, where atomic tests have produced unusual levels of 'fall-out' in a short space of time, nature has been maimed beyond measure. Birds nest and lay eggs—but the eggs are sterile and the nests stand empty of fledglings for a future race. Sea turtles exposed to heavy 'fall-out' forget to return to the sea whence they came and perish in the sand of their waterless atolls."[87] René Dubos: "We do not hesitate to spoil our surroundings and human associations for the sake of efficiency in acquiring power and wealth. Our collective sense of guilt comes from a general awareness that our praise of human and natural values is hypocrisy as long as we practice social indifference and convert our land into a gigantic dump. . . . Aggressive behavior for money or for prestige, the destruction to scenic beauty and historic landmarks, the waste of natural resources, the threats to health created by thoughtless technology—all these characteristics of our society contribute to the dehumanization of life."[88] Andreas Feininger: "No thoughtful person can fail to speculate about the causes of Western man's selfishness, shortsightedness, and destructiveness. And it seems to me that the underlying motivation—and justification—has its roots in his religious beliefs. Flattering himself that he is created with godlike powers, gifted with godlike wisdom, the master of his environment, of everything that is and lives—his to use, his to exploit, and his, if he wishes, to destroy. And so he goes on raping the land, killing its animals, cutting down its trees, dumping his waste into the rivers, and polluting the air until he destroys his life-giving environment and in his abysmal ignorance, vanity, and greed endangers his very existence."[89] Ricketts and Calvin: "If the naturalist has anything to contribute to human culture and well-being beyond the aesthetic and emotional delight that comes from pretty books and bird-watching, it is the knowledge that nature is an interrelated system that should not be lightly tampered with. This ought to mean more to man's survival on this planet than towering pyramids of technology and a knowledge of what moon dust is made of. To discard lightly the admonition of the naturalist to admit that we are not very far from the caves, and perhaps to hasten the day when we will join the dinosaurs in their fossil beds. . . . As a species, we must not forget that our continued well-being is in turn dependent on the well-being of our ecosystem."[90] Caras: "We are about to commit ourselves once and for all time either to a planet rich in wonderment and beauty or to a planet that is a mockery of itself, drenched in poisons, littered with metal junk heaps, and stripped of lumber, an ugly planet that will soon enough strangle itself on its own reeking gases and gag itself on its self-spawned contaminated juices. This is *mankind's* last chance on earth. From here on, the world will be a heaven or hell of our own choosing."[91]

The nature of change indicates the *necessity* and *essentiality* of freedom, though of relational limitation and conditioned by the relativity of things to each other. The natural selectivity and the unconscious struggle to survive, the innate drive to adapt to a possibly widening periphery of existence or to a defensive constraining perimeter of self-preservation: these processes and products could not have been possible without the simultaneous and concomitant biological or natural freedom underlying the nature of living things. Kaj Birket-Smith: "It is therefore a difference of degree, and not one of essence, that separates us from primitive man. Every cultural element denotes a certain growth and thus represents a progressive step, even though it may sometimes have paradoxical results."[92]

As we shall see later, the rise of human society and civilization, in its various phases, intermixed and interdependent, brought about, by the nature of these processes, a diminishment or series of evolutive changes of this natural freedom in order to "self-create" or determine methods and orders of kinds and degrees that made possible the adaptational grouping or "living together" of masses of humanity. The nature of these changes and the trends effected by these mobilities we shall endeavor to trace and analyze. We shall also make an effort to confront the problem of evaluation and meaningfulness of it all: whether there is any rationality in it, whether our directional trend not only is rational, but whether it is *good,* and whether its goodness, lack of goodness, or evil ways are compromisable with some degree of natural freedom; whether man "can," "should," or "must" eventuate some orderly methodology by which the needs of this *living together* and the natural and unconscious drives of individual freedom might be coalesced in such a way that society, *impersonal,* as a whole, can be operable for the good and welfare of the individuals comprising it, who are the *personal* units and the basic criteria of any social structure. We should gradually attempt to understand how society emerged. For only then will we understand that all the images and imaginations of men and their societies are parts of the only realm we know, the *natural* realm, in which we are born, live, and die. Should we find that praise or blame, freedom or slavery, peace or violence, are separate drives or simultaneities, we will realize that these, like all else, are with *us* and with the gods whom we have created to burden with our problems of love and hate, of feeling and power; of building and destroying, of relieving and frustrating. And should we be so fortunate as to find some beneficent and encouraging key to the solution of these problems, we will find it *within* and *about* us, not in the image-scapegoats we have so holistically manufactured to soothe our egos or give fuel to the seething restlessness of our natures and all the adversity and tragedy they have wrought.

The evolutional process of freedom rests, therefore, not solely upon the particular or individual thing, but upon three concomitant and simultaneous factors, which in their constant relational associations with each other carry on the process of evolution affecting all three, and which cause continuums of what seem to be stability and continuums of change depending upon the nature of the pressures and resistances by and between the three factors. These factors are: the individual being; the area, or spatial potential or field; and other beings that have existed and exist now. What we call *experience* is the *interplay,* the interacting flow, and the consequences of this process. The interaction and interdependence between and within these factors are the result of, the causes of, and the continual "stage and cast" of, the processes of what we generalize by the name of *Nature.*

IDENTITIES OF FREEDOM: ANALOGICAL AND RELATIONAL

REGARDING THE *analogical* and *relational*, there is, in fact, a great commonality and communality of and between all living things, of which man is just one segment. Albert Schweitzer: "We must explain to ourselves and understand that everything that lives is related to us."[93] Royston Clowes: "Gradually over the past few decades, it has been realized that beneath this bewildering diversity of life that surrounds us is concealed an underlying unity. It is a unity which exists at the microscopic and biochemical level. The first step in the recognition of this essential interrelationship was the realization that the smallest living part of all things—the cell—has an inherent similarity in all plants and animals. This was followed almost a century later by the discovery that the basic living processes in all cells depends upon intrinsically similar chemical units that are assembled and function to the same basic pattern. . . . In this way it becomes apparent that the outward complexity of the living world, which we see as made up of a widely divergent variety of plants, animals and micro-organisms, conceals a fundamental similarity at the microscopic level."[94] Regarding this interdependence and interrelationship of living things, Leslie Reid writes: "So it goes on, this dynamism of give and take, this omnipresent nexus of mutual dependence. It goes on not merely between crust, air, water and life, not merely between plants and animals, but also between one plant and other plants, between one animal and other animals, until the strands of the web cross, bifurcate and return upon themselves with a complexity to excite wonder and baffle analysis. This mutualism is the very stuff of ecology, a principle; one of two principles, of which the other is change. The web of things and the flow of things."[95] René Dubos: "To be fully relevant to life, science must deal with the responses of the total organism to the total environment. . . . Heraclitus, who taught that everything is flux, may well replace Democritus as the precursor of the new scientific humanism."[96]

The communality is evident throughout the world in the nature-worship, totemism, and animal-worship-ancestor interchangeabilities. The deer dance of the Yaqui Indians, the fish dances of the Michoacans, the Crows' bear, bird, and snake dances, the bear dances of the Ainu, the African animal dances, the crow dances of many Indian tribes, are just a few instances; the list is long and almost endless. Frank Waters, in his book about the Hopi, describes how these Indians were bound to animal and plant, the eagle and its feathers, the spruce tree and its needles.[97] H. R. Hays: "In North America there is in particular the idea of an ancient time in which there was no distinction between men and animals."[98] Richard A. Martin: "The Egyptians believed that a god incarnate assumed the form of an animal. Nearly every deity was associated in their minds with a certain bird or beast. . . . The animals were mummified. . . . There are mummies of jackals, cats, ibises, snakes, lizards, gazelles, hawks, bulls, sheep, baboons, crocodiles—in fact, almost every conceivable kind of animal known to Egypt."[99] George Gaylord Simpson: "The Kamarakoto Indians quite believe that animals become men and men become stones; for them there is neither limitation nor reason in the flux of nature. . . . It is nevertheless superior in some respects to the higher superstitions celebrated weekly in every hamlet of the United States. The legendary metamorphoses of my Indian friends are grossly naïve, but they do postulate a kinship through all of nature. Above all, they are not guilty of teleology. It would never occur to the Indians that the universe, so largely hostile, might have been created for their benefit."[100]

The commonality is the constant array of similarities of degrees, if not in kind; it brings to light the *necessary* and *determined* interdependence of all the parts and kinds, as a result of the interrelated and constant processes of evolution. There is hardly a type of human emotion, impulse, compulsion, instinctive or what is often called "insighted" intelligence, that is not found in other creatures. In getting about this world of ours and observing people of various kinds in various places, I have come to the conclusion that many people, in spite of being human, do not seem to have or express the intelligence that many other animals possess. Both human and other animals are born limited in instinct but equipped with sufficient neural-brain apparatus to acquire, in ratio to such equipment, a certain degree of intelligence, whether conscious or unconscious, as they experience these

possibilities in their living time. It is high time that man should
cease anthropomorphizing all creation and begin *animalizing*
himself for self-identify, analysis, and self-protection. Man,
through his gods, did not create the world, but the world created
him and all his other animal relations. "The relationships between mankind and animals are of endless diversity, for the road
along which they have traveled together leads back into the gray
mists of pre-history."[101] "All animaldom is related."[102] "A robin,
a coyote, or even the cricket on the hearth, is at least in some
degree, after its fashion, akin to us."[103] "Jellyfish and sea anemones may not appear at first sight to resemble us more closely,
but they do."[104] "Any human embryo demonstrates this. The
wormlike shape, the gill slits, the tail, all to be seen at various
stages of embryonic development, clearly reveals the animal ancestors of the lord of the earth."[105] "Indeed one might say that
it is a hangover from our fishy ancestry that we have ears, eyes
and noses in our heads and not in some other part of our body. . . .
Our teeth and our Eustachian tubes are the oldest relics in our
bodies, reminders of our shark-like ancestors."[106]

Evolution and relationship are both verifications of the individuality of things, and the processes by which these are carried
on are expressed in the primordial and biological principle of
freedom. Man differs from his animal relatives in that he can
reflect, introspect, count, make judgments, philosophize (although
whether other animals and creatures possess to any exent any of
these capabilities cannot be dogmatically excluded or ruled out).
In so doing, man and the sequences of his mind may have wan-
dered off too far from the prime and generic events which originally motivated and activated his intellect as such. It is high
time he should try to reconstrue and reconstruct the meaning,
purposes and values of the intellect. Perhaps then he may yet
become sufficiently free intellectually to recover other freedoms
that are necessary and essential to a normally and even orderly
happy life. Robert Briffault so wisely stated: "Intellectual honesty
is of the essence of the biological mechanism."[107]

By the *analogical* viewpoint we mean the common, obvious,
observational, anatomical, psychological, and other verifiable
similarities between man and the other animals, and the curious

commonalities, the genetic, embryological, and maturing phases, the instincts and traits of these creatures. By the analogical we mean the similarities and interdependent interactivities of man and the world about him, the processes and consequences of which are both overt and covert. If man is to rediscover the nature of freedom he must seek its roots, not in his rational and intellectual processes, which are the results of this freedom and the methodological and fruitional growths above his physiological surfaces, but below in the roots and soil of his beginnings and in the common beginnings of things and beings. The common origin of plants and animals are so tied together in the genesis of organic life that "down in the very lowest life levels, in the elementary ooze . . . animals and plants are so almost indistinguishably alike that it seems hardly possible that the one life line leads to oaks and redwoods and the other one to rabbits and foxes."[108] Sir D'Arcy Thompson in his book *On Growth and Form,* states: "So the living and the dead, things animate and inanimate, we dwellers in the world and this world wherein we dwell—are bound alike by physical and mathematical law."[109] Gerhard Szczesny: "Western man's emancipation from the spiritualistic and dualistic Christian metaphysic is basically characterized by a discovery of the unity of all being, which revelation has spilled over into the general awareness."[110] Donald Culross Peattie laid his hand on a beech tree and said, "We be of one blood, brother, thou and I!"[111] Albert Schweitzer: "Formerly, people said: Who is your neighbor? Man. Today we must no longer say this. We have gone further and we know that all living things on earth who strive to maintain life and who long to be spared pain—all living things on earth are our neighbors."[112]

Jules H. Masserman tells us about the common biodynamic roots of man and his animal relatives: "The contention has been advanced that animals differ from man in two major respects: (1) they do not project, modify, or enhance their power through cherished tools, and (2) they lack, or are not interested in, 'artistic creativity.' But ethologists can reply that the first of these shibboleths simply distinguishes those who refuse to believe that sand spiders use pebbles to tamp their tunnels, that Geospizas pick cactus spines with which to dig out their insect prey from the bark of trees, that chimpanzees in the wild use specially fashioned twigs for probes and shovels, leaves for dishes and napkins (Goodall, 1963, 1964), and sticks and stones for defense against leopards (Kortland, 1962). In organisms with more highly potentiated nervous systems, exploration of the physical universe, presumably with view to its control and manipulation—i.e., a technology—may take precedence over all other motivations. Thus, Butler (1954), Yerkes (1943), and others to the effect that monkeys and apes—particularly young ones—would leave food and other rewards to indulge in individual and conjoint exploration and 'play activities' that consisted essentially in the development of increasing knowledge about, and control of, the physical milieu. When required to do so, monkeys thus learn to open cage locks with keys and work for differently colored 'coins' with which to secure grapes from vending machines (the 'value' of the token, in terms of the number of grapes it can secure, determining the effort and ingenuity the monkey will put forth to earn it), and apes can be taught to assemble complex tools and drive motorcycles. Ferster (1964) taught chimpanzees to recognize numerals, write in ordinal numbers, and otherwise demonstrate high intellectual capacities, including 'abstract thought.' . . . No human engineer confined to the raw materials available to a spider, bee, or beaver, can improve the plan or construction of a spiderweb, a beehive, or a beaver dam. In the field of architecture combined with domestic decoration only one of numerous examples need be cited. The bower birds of Australia and New Guinea, as reported by A. J. Marshall (1956), build elaborate landscapes, tunnels, and may poles out of sticks, pebbles, seashells, or other materials, paint them with berry juice or charcoal mixed with saliva, and decorate them with flowers. Others construct towers up to nine feet high with tepee-like roofs and internal chambers, and improve their environs with circular lawns that they tend carefully and embellish with golden resins, garishly colored berries, iridescent insect skeletons, and fresh flowers that are replaced as they wither."[113]

Wherever we turn, in the study of animal life, we find a homologous pattern of similarities, in the mammals, the insecta, the arachnids, in birdlife, the reptilians, etc. Also we find a same structural and functioning homology in plant life, from the tall trees to the tiniest mosses. Their analogical resemblances and similarities in the processes of generic, growing, reproducing, and living cycles, may vary in some degree, but not in principle or kind, within their particular phylum and class. All this could not be mere coincidence and dressed-up uniformity of creation *ex nihilo* as poet or theologian may depict. A. I. Oparin, in his *Origin of Life,* wrote: "One must first of all categorically reject every attempt to renew the old arguments in favor of a sudden and spontaneous generation of life."[114] Allan Devoe: "The animals didn't just abruptly *be,* in a dramatic instant of completed creation. They have *become.* What we see now, when we look at the animals, is final animals shaped by almost immeasurably long, slow workings of the process of evolution."[115]

INSTINCT AND INTELLIGENCE

WHILE INSTINCT IS an established and transmissible pattern in animals, in all *anima,* there is no sacred border where instincts end and where consciousness and sensory or self-conscious awareness begins, where some degree of intelligence of the kind that humans possess is being born, activated, and carried on as modes and habits of living adaptation and experience. All animals, including humans, of course, have the relative ability to *learn* by experience, by trial and error, by accident, by urgency, by continual repetition of certain ways of necessitated behavior. Innovation, invention, and ingenuity belong relatively to all living things and not to humans alone. Many animals not only innovate and invent to meet certain conditions and circumstances; they even seem to be aware of what they are doing, to understand why, which would indicate a certain practical intelligence and a basic ability to modify and adapt to meet some situations. Lewis Mumford: "In any comprehensive definition of technics, it should be plain that many insects, birds, and mammals had made far more radical innovations in the fabrication of containers than man's ancestors had achieved in the making of tools until the emergence of *Homo sapiens:* consider their intricate nests and bowers, their beaver dams, their geometric beehives, their urbanoid anthills and termitaries. In short, if technical proficiency were alone sufficient to identify man's active intelligence, he would for long have rated as a hopeless duffer alongside many other species."[116] Andreas Feininger: "Man is not the only architect and engineer on earth. A large number of animals, from mammals and birds down to insects, spiders, and others still lower on the evolutionary ladder, build structures which, considering the size and equipment of their builders, are as interesting, beautiful, and worthy of admiration as New York's Verrazano Bridge or the Taj Mahal."[117]

All creatures are more or less educable by new types of experience and apply themselves accordingly, some more, some less, to modify, or momentarily adapt themselves to, new conditions. Many experiments have shown that animals can even "reverse" their instinctive drive in order to accomplish or overcome something. J. S. Szymanski proved this point with a cockroach. "Bees can be trained to recognize time, place and scent: that is, they learn."[118] The human being is not alone in making new decisions. If anyone steadfastly believes that only humans have intelligence, have minds to think with, and that man's world is a completely different world from that of the other animals, he should read two books, *Born Free* and *Living Free* by Joy Adamson.[119] Fredric C. Appel, in his *The Intellectual Mammal*, writes: "The porpoise brain appears to be as large and complex as the human brain, and many aspects of porpoise behavior—in freedom and in captivity—suggest an extremely high order of intelligence."[120] Porpoises, in freedom as well as in captivity, play games, play jokes on one another, and even spit water or small stones at people they do not like. In captivity they have been taught to play baseball, run bases, play basketball, do acrobatics, jump through flaming hoops. In Honolulu, a young porpoise called Keiki has been trained to leave his friend-teachers and go out alone into the open ocean completely free to do as he pleases. Even though he may be at a great distance away he returns promptly within seconds when the marine scientists trigger an electronic recall signal device. Research on the porpoise continues at a fast pace and an increasing knowledge of its intelligence potential is becoming an amazing and a most inspiring motive to further fathoming of the possibilities to be achieved and learned from this wonderful cousin of ours. Bubbles, the pilot whale of the Pacific Seaquarium at Palo Alto, California, will quickly captivate the onlooker with its amusing ways, indicative of a high degree of intelligence. The Hayes and Hayes experiment with Vicky, the chimpanzee, is an outstanding example of animal intelligence and adaptability. Among many words, she learned to say *mamma* and *papa!* W. Köhler's experiments proved the adaptability of animals to use their intelligence to solve new situations. Those who have animal pets know, and will often admit, that their pets understand them better than they understand their pets. This is because we make the mistake of humanizing them, whereas they cannot make this mistake, since they look upon us as animals like themselves. And they are right.

Regarding the intelligence of polar bears and their ability to improvise, devise, and habituate cooperative methods in hunting for food, Richard Perry tells us: "Polar Bears, with their relatively large brain-cases, do not lack intelligence, as we have seen again and again when studying their methods of hunting seals. . . . Haig-Thomas states that when two bears are hunting together, one will wait beisde the *aglo* (the breathing hole of the seal) while the other walks away, perhaps deceiving the seal into returning, to be caught by the waiting bear. But should the seal fail to return, then one of the bears will find and stop up all the other breathing holes in the vicinity with snow. The seal is thus compelled to return to the one open hole, beside which the other bear is waiting, or drown. Haig-Thomas and Nookapingwa watched an almost full-grown cub performing this operation while its mother sat over an *aglo* some 200 yards away. This is precisely the technique often employed by Eskimo hunters. 'If only I had the brains of a bear,' commented Nookapingwa, 'I would never go hungry for a little seal meat.' "[121] This beautiful animal, the largest carnivore in the world, may become extinct unless the airplane hunters in Alaska and the Norwegian Tourist Bureau with its Tromso ferry to Spitzbergen, among others, stop murdering them off. Unless the so-called "sportsmen" for trophies and the sadistic home decorators, who rug their floors with animal skins, become conscionable (which is unlikely), as also, zoo-keepers who do not care how they get their animals, the polar bear may become extinct within a foreseeable few years.

Man is not the only animal to make and use tools; chimpanzees do it without the aid of culture. Jane Goodall, observing the chimps for two years in the Gombe Game Preserve near Lake Tanganyika, found that they even fashion tools, modifying or changing a natural object to make it suitable for a special or specific purpose and use. She saw a chimp use a leaf for a napkin to wipe his hands and mouth; to crumple leaves and use the batch as a sponge to soak up water to drink; tear off the leaves of a small twig and then use the twig to pick out termites for food. They also have about twenty words or more, distinctive words to communicate distinctive and specific meanings. Given a few more millennia, the chimpanzee might be reading Shakespeare and orating on Hamlet![122] William A. Mason: "The task of bringing the behavior of man and the non-human primates into meaningful relationship within a comparative-evolutionary frame-work has scarcely begun. Broadly viewed, the social development of monkey, ape, and child follows the same basic pattern."[123]

Many animals use natural tools, directly and indirectly, go piggy-back on other creatures for effortless transit, carry their live lunch with them, use other creatures to bring them food or obviously to act as their defenders. "The small xanthid coral crab, *Lybia plumosa,* always carries a minute anemone in each claw. The crab eats mucus produced by the anemones' bodies and may use the anemones for defense or to catch food."[124]

Inasmuch as freedom is being here considered as a natural and affirmative want, as a natural function of an animal called *Homo sapiens,* it follows that it should be reasonable to expose not only his generic commonality with animal life but to give some thought to the communality of his usual traits, habits, and tendencies, with those of other creatures.

The all-too-common experiences of *trial* and *error* in all animal experiences, including man, expose the constant and simultaneous expression and activation of freedom. Prerational or practical intelligence, as a result, compared to rationalism in man, indicates the difficulty of drawing a fine line to mark where practical or animal intelligence ends and rational or human intelligence begins. As one zoölogist remarked, "Even protoplasm has brains." Homer W. Smith expresses it philosophically: "We must acknowledge that our kidneys constitute the major foundation of our physiological freedom. Only because they work the way they do has it become possible for us to have bones, muscles, glands, and brains. Superficially, it might be said that the function of the kidneys is to make urine; but in a more considered view one can say that the kidneys make the stuff of philosophy itself."[125]

Animals get nervous, have anxieties, feel unhappy and happy, have split personalities and frustrations. Animal babies as well as the adults cry and moan like humans do. "Crying is not only the earliest mood-signal we give, it is also the most basic. . . . Crying we share with thousands of other species. Virtually all mammals (not to mention birds) give vent to high-pitched screams, squeaks, shrieks, or squeals when they are frightened or in pain."[126] Masserman: "It is of particular significance that early familial or other stresses can produce serious and lasting deviations of conduct in animal as well as human progeny."[127] At the Walter Reed Army Institute it has been seen that monkeys take readily to alcohol when they are under stress or tension, as humans do. Animals, like humans, suffer from frustration and the subsequent acts of aggression that so often result from it. Harold E. Burtt writes: "A situation that sometimes induces aggressive behavior in people is the so-called frustration-aggression mechanism. A child wants to go outside but is not permitted to, so he smashes up some toys or furniture, taking out his frustration by aggressive behavior. There are a few cases resembling this mechanism in birds. A bluebird, for example, frustrated by a recording of a bluebird song and unable to find the rival, simply tore up its own nest as an outlet for the frustration. Similarly, a shrike punctured its own eggs. A cowbird may solicit preening by some other bird, but if its friend does not cooperate, then it turns around and attacks."[128]

SYMBIOSIS, CONTROL, AND CONSERVATION

ALL NATURE SEEMS to be an evolved coalition of symbiosis, and obviously without any moral basis. Man's place and attachment to the relationships and relativeness of other animals and plant life are indispensable and a necessary frame to secure his survival and the preservation of his kind. More and more modern man tends to become oblivious of this need and the truth of his place in nature. S. H. Skaife reveals to us the symbiotic chain existing between the parasitic flagellate protozoa and the termite.[129] Franz A. Roedelberger and Vera Groschoff, in their *The Wonders of Wildlife*, relate the process of symbiosis between the Mediterranean Sombrero Jellyfish and its usual accompaniment of a swarm of horse mackerel. The mackerel attract larger predator fish who seek it for food, and when the attacker nears the horse mackerel close to the jellyfish, the jellyfish grasps the attacker only to ingest it. The mackerel get the protection of the jellyfish, which uses the mackerel to attract its own food.[130] The hippopotami allow birds to enter their cavernous mouths to pick their teeth; the moray eel allows the banded shrimp to do the same; and brain coral allow the tiny neons to harbor themselves in its crevices in a symbiotic exchange of amenities.

As man attempts more and more to create a mechanical world, or as Arthur Koestler so aptly calls it, the "coca-colonization," he seems more and more to lost sight of the living natural realm, and attempts more and more to create a mechanical man. Allan Devoe: "We forget to be feeling the sunlight on us. We don't hear any more all the astonishing little earth-musics, such as, say, crickets. We tend to lose what in a beautifully exact phrase we call our animal spirits."[131] This does not mean, like Rousseau, that it is best for man to take off his clothes, grow more hair, and run back to a cave. It does mean that man should be conscious that he is a natural product as well as an intellectual product, and not merely a metaphysical brain with a halo of mystic ectoplasm or a Pythagorean puzzling number scaling a theoretical ladder of universals. By combining both the natural and intellectual products he can still synthesize a way of thinking and acting that can keep him intellectually natural and naturally intellectual. "The intellectual life is *natural*. It is an organic development of the life of man."[132] "Human thought is founded in our animal endowment."[133]

If freedom is to come of age, then the biological need of freedom can be rationally understood and intelligently processed in human experience for the prime benefit of the human being as an individual living thing, and of humanity as a social order for the prime purpose of making the former realizable. To accomplish this man must not destroy this natural balance, this unconscious mutual-assistance pact, this almost-osmotic symbiosis which makes of nature her "seamless robe." Rachel L. Carson's *Silent Spring,* is a beaming light of warning to man that nature should be understood, not destroyed; controlled where necessary, but not contaminated; assisted for the benefit of all, not contaminated to poison all. "As man proceeds toward his announced goal of the conquest of nature," she writes, "he has written a depressing record of destruction, directed not only against the earth he inhabits but against the life that shares it with him. The history of the recent centuries has its black passages—the slaughter of the buffalo on the western plains, the massacre of the shorebirds by the market gunners, the near-extermination of the egrets for their plumage. Now, to these and others like them, we are adding a new chapter and a new kind of havoc—the direct killing of birds, mammals, fishes, and indeed practically every form of wildlife by chemical insecticides indiscriminately sprayed on the land."[134] The biologist and the philosopher view the potentials of the sciences with some dread unless these potentials are reasonably controlled for peaceful and beneficial means. Sir MacFarlane Burnet: "Science having freed a large portion of the human race from every type of pestilence, and being potentially capable of doing it equally effectively for the rest, now stands poised to create a new more lethal and more uncontrollable plagues than ever sprang from nature."[135]

Bernhard Grzimek, whose son Michael gave his life to salvage and protect the animal life in the Serengati, reports from Africa: "When Tanganyika came under British control after the First World War, hunters from the older British colony of Kenya soon came into the Banagai region because Serengati was so conveniently close. Nobody felt scruples about massacring the lions since they were simply regarded as dangerous pests. Some hunters returned from such safaris having killed one hundred lions on a single trip. Since they could not carry so many skins they merely hacked off the tails as trophies."[136] Mervyn Cowie defends the lion: "Why should the lion be labelled as a brute, why should he have to be killed on sight merely to add to the list of trophies of this intrepid [sic] hunter who, with the advantage of a precision weapon, merely had to ensure that the sights of his rifle and the lion on the rock were in a straight line at the moment he pulled the trigger? Why, in any event, should the lion be scorned because he had got away, and got away perhaps with a broken leg, to die of starvation or be killed by hyenas." The only brute in this picture is *man,* and natural history attests to the fact that he has been and still is the cruelest brute of all the animals in the world. "The early pioneers and farmers, as a poor adaptation of the Masai custom, encouraged every young man to bag his lion to prove his manhood."[137]

David Kenyon Webster, in his story about sharks, states: "What other creature kills his own kind in such vast quantities as man, in a thing as vile as war, and for so little reason? The shark at least kills only in self-defence, to eat, and perhaps in battling for a mate. Man, on the other hand, kills for pleasure and for the shabbiest reasons propounded by his priests and politicians. Nevertheless, with the arrogance that characterizes his judgments on other animals, he designates his vilest spawn as sharks."[138] Hartmut Bastian adds his bit in appealing to some sense of discretion in the wasteful and heartless killing-off of some of our oldest relatives: "The sight of the floating factories of the present-day whaling fleets, with their super-efficient modern weapons, will make it plain to anyone that *Homo sapiens* is well on his implacable way to the eventual extermination of these ocean mammals. It will not take much longer."[139] George Bernard Shaw so wisely remarked: "When a man wants to murder a tiger he calls it sport; when the tiger wants to murder him he calls it ferocity."

Justice Douglas appeals for the salvation of both man and his animal relatives: "One of our deepest conflicts is between the preservation of wild life and the profits of a few men. The coyote, with his wise, doglike face and his haunting call, is gone. Fox, marten, and bear have been sacrificed. Mountain sheep are doomed. Is there no place left for any life except man and his greed? Must we see our wild animals only in zoos? Is there no place left for mountain sheep and coyotes? The thought of their eradication was as dismal as the prospect that all trails would be paved, that man will go only when a machine will take him."[140] Mr. Douglas continues: "Man is crowding everything but himself out of the universe. . . . Why must we be so destructive? What of people who want to hear the whir of sage grouse, who thrill at the white, saucy rump of the antelope as it makes its getaway? How about those who, wanting to fish, find a beaver a stout ally? What is to be said for people who love the sight of moose in willow? Must we sacrifice all of these for the Almighty Dollar that goes into the pockets of the privileged few?"[141] And thus he concludes: "Man is the worst predator of all!"[142]

Roy Pinney presses his warning in *Vanishing Wildlife*: "Even if we choose to suppress our physical and psychological yearnings for the peace and beauty in nature, even if we ignore the fading cries of her wild creatures, we can never escape the fact that we, like every other animal on earth, are dependent upon the life-giving properties of the world around us."[143] "We do not own the world; our place in it is merely leased to us by nature. If we persist in waging war against our natural landlord—if we continue in our efforts to reduce the world to a sterile desert—our leave will soon expire."[144] Where man settles, he exterminates indiscriminately. On Kodiak Island, Alaska, they have been shooting down the dwindling numbers of Kodiak bears by gunfire from airplanes, even with the discreet consent of the authorities. The persuasion of the dollar is more effective than human kindness and wise judgment.[145] Schaller reports: "One reliable authority told me that in about 1948 officials organized the killing of some sixty mountain gorillas near Angumu to obtain eleven infants for zoos. One mining official near Utu bragged to me of having shot nine of the strictly protected animals for sport."[146]

Surely man can improve nature, and he very often does beautify it, modify it, even change it for his own good, so long as he does not try to abduct his body and mind to some asphalt jungle in which he incarcerates himself as a mechanical, anthropocentric doll in a prison so removed from his natural habitat that it could stifle him, dehydrate him away from his free-flowing protoplasmic pond, and bury him in his own self-made maze of Pythagorean etherized *etherea*. Archibald MacLeish: "Wildness and silence disappeared from the countryside, sweetness fell from the air, not because anyone wished them to vanish or fall but because through-ways had to floor the meadows with cement to carry the automobiles which advancing technology produced first by the thousands and then by the thousand thousands. Tropical beaches turned into high-priced slums where thousand-room hotels elbowed each other for glimpses of once-famous surf not because those who loved the beaches wanted them there but because enormous jets could bring a million tourists every year—and therefore did."[147]

In our own country the wolf has been almost exterminated. In Canada it still manages to hold onto life and continue its own kind. Man kills for fun, but a wolf kills only for food. Farley Mowat relates from his personal observation of the wolf: "The wolf never kills for fun, which is probably one of the main differences distinguishing him from man. I know of no valid evidence that wolves kill more than they can use, even when the rare opportunity to do so arises." He goes on to tell us that they mate for life, that they do not quarrel, have a well-developed code of ethics, are patient and affectionate in their habits, that they find delight in each other and have a sense of responsibility for other wolves outside their own den. Dr. Benson Ginsburg, at a meeting of the American Institute of Biological Sciences in Corvallis, Oregon, reported that "he considers them highly social and intelligent. . . . Some of his wolves are uncannily bright. They have learned to work switches and faucets; their cages must be fitted with locks operated from outside lest they unfasten the inside latches and roam the lab building."[148] Dave Mech: "The claim that wolves are dangerous to man has never been authenticated anywhere in North America."[149] Sterling North: "For many years there was a sizable reward offered in Canada for convincing proof that any wolf in the wilderness had ever bitten a human being. There was never a taker. . . . Little Red Ridinghood and her grandmother had little reason to fear any wolf. But every wolf has reason to fear mankind. Bounties on their scalps still disgrace the legal codes of states where wolves have been hunted to the point of extinction. . . . Archeologists, studying the drawings, artifacts, and bones found in ancient caves, believe that wolf puppies, brought home to cave children after the mother wolf had been slain, became the first domesticated pets of the human race. . . . Reared with kindness and enough food, the wolf can be trained to be as gentle as any domestic dog."[150]

But man continues relentlessly and cruelly to exterminate the wildlife of the world. "On 'Draga Lund' in the Faeroes tens of thousands of brooding birds are pulled out of their nesting holes every year by sticks with hooks on the end."[151] "From 1851 to 1900 thirty-one kinds of mammals and some of the world's most beautiful birds were exterminated. Most of these losses occurred in North America and the West Indies."[152] "From 1901 to 1944, forty forms of mammals were wiped out." "In succeeding decades, the situation grew still more alarming."[153] "Since the time of Christ about 100 kinds of mammals and about the same number of birds have become extinct—wild creatures, evolved over millions of years, which suddenly disappeared off the face of the earth because of the stupidity and selfishness of man."[154] Ian McTaggart Cowan: "In nineteen hundred years the world has lost 107 kinds of mammals and close to 100 kinds of birds. The extent of extinction of plants and the lesser animals is not known but probably vastly exceeds that of birds and mammals. Nearly 70 percent of these losses have occurred in the past century and mostly through the activity of man. Here and there throughout the world, on every continent and on many of the remotest islands, a host of other species, more than 1000 strong, face the imminence of complete and final passage from the world's fauna." . . . "The worst example of the failure of conservation, not for want of biological information but from bad faith, commercial avarice, and political iniquity, is to be seen in our treatment of the marine mammals of the world. Completely adequate demonstration has been available for at least a decade that species after species among the larger whales is being reduced to the point of extinction. . . . Despite this, the responsible international organization of whaling nations has been repeatedly prevented from establishing the essential conservation measures through the political interests bent only on retiring an investment as quickly as possible."[155]

Caras, in his sad and appealing book, *Last Chance on Earth,* tells us: "In American history, and perhaps in all the heartless story of man against nature, the bloody history of the Eskimo curlew is second only to the story of the passenger pigeon. Masses of gunners would assemble along the flyway and blast upward into the flocks for hours. A dozen or more birds could be had for a single shot shell if the gunner waited until the birds were in the right position overhead. They were carried off to market by the wagon load to be sold for a few pennies apiece. Thousands were left to rot where they fell."[156] It is doubtful if any of them exist today; the greater probability is that the curlew is now extinct. "The killing of birds for their feathers is not in any way parallel with the killing of livestock for food. There is not a shred of necessity in the feather business; it is one of the greatest evils man has perpetrated against our natural world."[157] This evil almost resulted in the extinction of the egret and heron in Florida.

Pinney describes the extermination of the Great Auk: "Several crews stayed on Funk Island off the coast of Newfoundland where the birds were particularly abundant, and devoted all their time and energy to the profitable slaughter. It was easy work, for there was no need to fire a shot. The birds were simply clubbed to death, a task made easy by the fact that they made no attempt to escape, refusing to leave their eggs or young. Unfortunately, the Great Auks laid only one egg each year, making it impossible for them to counteract their tremendous losses. Also, as even the egg was edible, the auks' extinction was inevitable. In Europe, the slaughter ended in 1834, when the last European auk was killed on the Waterford coast, off Ireland. The last living specimen was taken off Edley Rock, off the coast of Ireland, in 1844. Nine years later, a dead auk was found at Trinity Bay, Newfoundland. That was the last ever seen of the birds."[158] "It was the bad luck of the great auk to taste good and to live within the reach of man."[159]

One would think that after all the wanton killing of animals in the nineteenth century and in our own twentieth century, after extinguishing the passenger pigeon among many others and still killing off many animals presently on the verge of extinction, people would be so aroused as to demand some abatement of the constant slaughter. But man keeps on sadistically shooting, murdering, maiming, and torturing any animal he can put his sights to. Today Canada is guilty of one of the worst crimes against one of the most beautiful and intelligent of animals—the Harp Seal. Each March the slaughter begins, especially the murder of the baby seal. In 1966, within a week or so, 81,000 whitecoat pups were murdered, in addition 41,000 young and not fully grown seals! At this rate within a few years the Harp Seal will be extinct, because of the petty greed of heartless and cruel people without compassion and foresight. Prime Minister Pearson was indifferent to the aroused public sentiment against the colossal killing, but Hédard Robichaud is guiltiest of all. As High Commissioner in charge of the Fisheries Department, he thwarted every attempt to prevent any change in the rules that would ban the killing. The documentary film *Artek*, depicting this slaughter, which can be seen only by those of stout hearts and strong stomachs, should be distributed and shown in every city and village of the world.

Peter Lust, a courageous Montreal writer, describes the fight to save the Harp Seal from extinction, witnessing, at the risk of his life, the murder of the baby pups in the Magdalen Islands of Canada. In his book, *The Last Seal Pup,* he writes pleadingly: "The problem of cruelty in sealing becomes a question of ethics. Canada is a highly civilized country which has, during the past decade, passed a Bill of Rights for its citizens. Her standards of justice to humans are based on the principles of Magna Carta. Does our government have the right to tolerate cruelties which the most primitive society would not practice? Has a Canadian Minister the right to stand idly by and permit small, charming animals of comparatively high intelligence to be brutally beaten, skinned alive, wounded, tortured and treated in a manner forbidden by the criminal code of the land? Canadian law maintains that it is an offense to cause needless suffering to animals. May a member of the Canadian government fail to act, if completely helpless newborn animals are skinned alive in front of their

mothers' eyes? Can income or money ever excuse brutalities
common to the annual seal hunt? Most citizens whom I have told
about my observations of the 1966 seal hunt were outraged. I have
yet to meet a disinterested witness of these appalling cruelties
who endorsed the continuation of the seal hunt. But sealing
goes on. No ban has been issued against it, and none is presaged
for the 1967 season. One month before millions will visit Montreal's World's Fair, the blood of hundreds of thousands of seal
pups will flow in the very province playing host to the rest of the
world. . . . Germany actually made the mass-killing of seal pups
possible. German furriers bought the largest number of white-
coats—78 percent of the entire crop. Yet almost all Germans were
deeply shocked by the discovery of the Magdalen crimes and
would outlaw sealing. Why this strange paradox?"[160] Gavin Maxwell, in his *Seals of the World*, states: "Perhaps no other group
of animals has suffered as much as the seals, their mass destruction involving a degree of horror and brutality that is without
parallel. . . . The Eskimo killing of seals, though it involved the
very high degree of cruelty entailed in harpooning a warm-
blooded living creature and playing it as a man may play a fish,
was a question of survival only; there was no question of mass
financial exploitation. . . . Few people who are aware of the facts
even in broadest principle can view the sealing industry as anything but a degradation to human nature."[161]

Man's cruelty to animals is not merely the province of the
"sportsmen" for trophies or the market gunner for a buck; it
shows up in the high echelons of the most civilized people, among
the scientists in their temples of science. According to a bulletin of
the Virginia Federation of Humane Societies, issued in May, 1963,
we note the following: "Within the past decade medical research
has mushroomed into a giant industry which demands the sacrifice of several hundred million animals a year. . . . In the national
capital area alone, comprising Washington, Northern Virginia
and nearby Maryland, eight million animals give their lives annually in research. . . . Dogs and cats are confined year in and
year out in cages so small that the larger dogs are unable to either
stretch out or to stand up. Monkeys have been photographed
chained by an eighteen-inch chain to a wall. Resting boards are

rarely provided; the animal has to sleep on the wire mesh flooring of its cage. Sometimes its feet are cut and bleeding from walking on the wire; sometimes the wiremesh is so coarse that the animal cannot stand at all, but spends its entire life lying down."[162] Claire Booth Luce has called the laboratories "the Buchenwalds, the Auschwitzes and Dachaus of the animal world." Dr. Robert Gesell, Professor of Physiology at the University of Michigan, states: "We are drowning and suffocating unanesthetized animals—in the name of science. We are determining the amount of abuse that life will endure in unanesthetized animals—in the name of science. We are observing animals for weeks, months or even years under infamous conditions—in the name of science. This may well prove to be the blackest spot in the history of medical science."[163] Albert Schweitzer: "Those who test medicines or operating techniques on animals or who inoculate them with illnesses in order to help mankind through the results they hope to obtain in this way must never quiet their conscience with the general excuse that in practicing these cruel methods they are pursuing a lofty purpose. . . . How many crimes are committed in laboratories where anesthesia is often omitted to save time or trouble!"[164] Man's inhumanity to man is only one phase of his cruelty; it extends into every part of the natural world; unless this cruelty is controlled and channeled into intelligent, peaceful, and restorative processes and thus the force of cruelty changed to a force of benevolence, man may yet succeed, by destroying his surroundings, in destroying himself.

Why, in a philosophy of freedom, the stress on conservation and guardianship over the world ecology that is so clearly an imperative to man's survival? Of what good is freedom if man himself is no longer here to express it, to live it; or if, having succeeded in adapting himself to a malignant environment, he lives only to endure, starve, suffer, and commit worldwide disasters? Robert Silverberg: "Now the world is in our hands. We could choose to cut down the last redwood tree for its timber, harpoon every whale for its oil, and turn every open tract of land into a row of houses. We could hand on to our successors a world in which all wildlife was gone, every stream fouled with wastes, and natural beauty was only a memory."[165] "The only way wildlife can survive on this planet is through the conscious effort of mankind.

We who are crowding all other forms of life into extinction must take steps to save the creatures that remain, lest we find ourselves inhabiting a world in which we are alone."[166] Anthony Storr: "Whilst it is of course true that animals destroy each other, killing is only habitual when the relationship between the animals is that of predator to prey. In other words, although animals may kill each other for food, they seldom do so for any other reason. Even the relation between predator and prey is less 'aggressive' than is commonly supposed. At the collective level, predators never exterminate the animals on whom they prey, for to do so would of course endanger their own survival."[167]

If man, by his intelligence and power, and the freedom to use both, in his blinded and blinding race of overwhelming things, tearing up the natural balances made possible by many thousands of millions of years of man-undisturbed evolution, wasting away the timberlands and causing floods to erode the plains, spreading concrete and asphalt jungles, despoiling natural resources wantonly, burying the green grass with gray cement and the round purplish hills with blocks of squared steeled stone, polluting the brooks, streams, rivers and bays with filth and chemical debris, poisoning the fish and fowl that inhabit them, destroying the feeding and nesting grounds of the diminishing and dying migratory birdlife, greedily netting up vast schools of fish before they have a chance to lay their spawn and provide more fish, pushing back what is natural and all the life it contains and replacing it with the mechanical, the artificial, the lifeless, substituting the natural chain of dependence and even affection with a fabricated chain of greed, indifference, spoilage, and self-interest: If man, in his reckless advance, finally kills off every creature[168] and puts to the saw every living tree—from that moment on the human race will have sealed its own tomb and fulfilled its own certainty of extinction. Beauty, living color and its freshness will be gone. Man and his freedom would become nothing without their natural relatives and the relational sequences of his habit.

Man is losing sight and sound of the freer and more natural experiences of open nature, and he is being slowly ground up and indoctrinated into the unwarm processes of civilization. Heinz Heck, of the Hellabrunn Zoological Gardens in Munich, ponders over the future of animals: "Mass destruction of animal life commenced with the age of discovery. Many lovely species of birds, including several varieties of the bird of paradise, have vanished for ever. . . . Already we can see far fewer of the works of nature than our fathers saw, and despite all the efforts now being made our grandchildren will only be able to enjoy pitifully small remnants of the free life of the world as we know it."[169] Thus, civilization is slowly aborting its original premise of bettering man and, instead, it is turning man into a Univac, segmentalized as a termite nest yet functioning as a nest, just as the termites do. Perhaps that might have been the way the termites evolved.

All life is tied together in an almost endless chain of symbiosis in so many complex and myriad ways as to defy ordinal and categorical procedures. The accumulation of objective material that identifies this process in living existence, both plant and animal, is tremendous and unceasing. From every department of the biological and, in particular, from the physiological and zoological sciences come the verified realization that man cannot exist alone, even if he would, without the around-the-world umbilical cord that resolutely and inexorably makes possible the life and containment of all that lives on this planet. Aldo Leopold, a defender of wildlife, makes his plea: "We now know what was unknown to all the previous generations: that men are only fellow-voyagers with other creatures in the odyssey of evolution. This new knowledge should have given us, by this time, a sense of kinship with fellow-creatures; a wish to live and let live; a sense of wonder over the magnitude and duration of the biotic enterprise."[170]

Jack McCormack, in *The Living Forest,* writes: "The members of the forest community, from microscopic bacteria whose life may span but a few minutes to gigantic trees which may live for several centuries, are bound together by their feeding habits."[171] Douglas tells about the *gambusia,* a tiny inch-long tropical fish that thrives principally on mosquito larvae: "The gambusia starts the chain of life that maintains the Everglades. The gambusia is food for larger fish. They are in turn food for garfish, bowfin, and bass. They are in turn food for the wading birds. They are the mainstay of the alligator. Yet the alligator, whose only enemy in its adult stage is man, is more than the end product of this food chain. He makes a distinct and vital contribution. When the waters recede, he wallows in the mud; and this wallowing creates a hole. It is enlarged by the wallowing of other alligators, until a slough is formed. The slough is the salvation of all life during the dry season and the droughts. So it is that, while the alligator is dependent on others for his existence, all the others are in turn dependent on him. There is as much interdependence among the creatures of the Everglades as there is among men in our industrial age."[172] "Practically without exception, all animals live at the expense of some other organism."[173]

Even though it is axiomatic that larger fish eat smaller fish, especially shrimp, the fishes' gourmet delicacy, it has been observed that many kinds of fishes allow themselves to be cleaned by shrimps and smaller fishes without molesting them. "The fish to be cleaned, including such species as parrotfishes, surgeon fishes, groupers and many others, line up to await their turn at cleaning stations. Many of these are predators which commonly consume small fishes, but they usually refrain from eating the species which perform the parasite-picking service."[174] "Manta rays which are often seen in open water, visited cleaning stations on the reef with which they were evidently familiar. . . . Swarms of wrasse of the genus *Thalassoma* and also cleaner-wrasse swam up and picked around the belly and mouth flaps of the mantas."[175] "I am convinced that when Gesner described the detail of the crocodile gently moving its jaw when it wanted the cleaning process to stop, he was reporting a case of true cleaning symbiosis. The grouper warns its cleaner-fish in exactly the same way."[176]

Pictures are common of the birds scavenging about in the open mouths of hippopotami; the bird courser and the crocodile. The honey guide bird leads the badgers to the hives to collect their share of honey for the service. Pilot fish lead the large fish to their prey and collect their shares. Humans are not the only ones to have Judas goats among themselves. Acorn barnacles attach themselves to the sides of humpback whales and live out their lives taking a world oceanic tour.[177] "The flates of living things are bound together. . . . The whole long vital experiment on earth is symbiotic by chains of cause and relation past glib explaining.

. . . It is not explained why there is for us but one life, but it is plain enough that all life is one."[178]

The remora with its suction cup on its back attaches itself to the underside of large fish to join in its feast. The tiny pearl fish lives its life within the pearl oyster of the South Pacific. The deadly sting of the anemone "tentacles" do not bother the little fishes it uses as decoys to bring other fishes within its grip in exchange for morsels from the captured prey. The zebra eats the grass; the lion eats the zebra; the hyena comes in for the leavings; the carrion-birds pick the shreds and the vultures finally carry away the bare bones: nothing remains. I could go on endlessly reciting the bizarre and strange interdependencies of animals and plants, the symbiotic alliances that go on all over the world, from the high mountain peaks to the slopes and plains, in the streams and bays and in the vast oceans that cover most of the world. Man is just one species out of millions of species depending and feeding upon each other. From the "feudal" ants and their "serf" aphids to the multi-ton whales feeding upon the plankton of the sea, from all this we realize and see at work what we call the adjusted or limited natural freedom of living things.

VARIANTS, SIMILARITIES, AND PARALLELISMS

AMONG HUMANS THERE exist forms of *inquilinism,* as in their neighbor animals, where one "chisels" from another by habit and pattern, imposing and living off the fat of another's labors; we see it in many forms of exploitation and confidence games. There is also among humans as well as in plants and many animals what we can call *symbiotic parasitism.* Among humans we can recognize them as beggars, loafers, bums, tramps, hoboes, specialists in the art of getting hand-outs, relief checks, charity from every conceivable source instead of looking for a job. In the "higher" classes we note this parasitism among political ward heelers, ambulance chasers, and high finance money gougers. Animal and plant life, including our own, have these parasites in one form or another, from the unseen to the recognizable, within and without.

Assault and battery, conspiracy for theft, petty thievery—all these drives, so common among humans, are abundant among many animals. Of birds, Burtt tells us: "An eagle dives at any osprey flying with a fish in its talons, and the osprey drops the fish, which the eagle retrieves—frequently before it hits the ground or the water. . . . In another place a baldpate and a gadwall followed a coot, and when the latter surfaced with some pondweed the other two birds pounced on him. . . . Laughing gulls have been noted stealing from pelicans—sometimes taking the food directly from their pouches. Sanderlings give it a little different twist in stealing from a turnstone; when the latter turns over stones to expose food, the sanderlings rush in and seize it before the turnstone can get it himself. . . . A skua attacked a gannet, seized it by the wing until it crashed and then held it down until it disgorged some food, which the skua then ate. Robbery directed at eggs or young in the nest is practiced by wrens, grackles, crows, jays and some gulls."[179]

We may apply some kind of symbiotic explanation to the arrangements in the growing or diminishing food-chains in relation to the birthrate of predators depending upon these food-chains. Lionesses will bring more lions into the world when the herds of wild game become more abundant; bees will grow bigger hives and produce more bees if the flowering season warrants it. Yet man himself, and this includes some of the most intelligent, does not take these factors into consideration and goes on indifferently to explode his own population regardless of future limitations in the natural materials essential for life. Very often this symbiotic adjustment operates in reverse for the protection of one living thing from another. In the Galapagos, the cacti and the tortoise have kept a race going for a long time, the tortoise wanting to eat the cacti and the cacti trying to keep growing out of reach; both have been sufficiently successful to keep both alive and prospering. "The cacti and the reptiles, especially the prickly pear and the tortoise, seem to have evolved side by side within the islands, each in relation to the other."[180] While this is typical of concurrent evolution, it does portray the struggle to survive, even within the symbiotic relationships between a plant and an animal, where plants in order to survive have evolved tendencies for fast growth to avoid being exterminated by animals. While we cannot yet ascribe a form of insighted intelligence within the structure and function of a plant, it is interesting to note the expression of natural freedom even in a plant, call it plain mechanical function if you will, yet it is wonderful to see a plant able to change or "move" in order to save itself.

The struggle to survive and continue its own kind is inherent in all living things. All seem to possess the sufficient freedom to feed upon each other. There is no esthetic or moral where sufficient hunger is involved; even the theologian can recite his proclamations more fluently and reverently to the skies with his belly filled with filet mignon. Allan Devoe asks: "Is it worse that a beetle should feed on long-dead bodies than that we should feed ourselves on recently dead ones? Meat is meat, flesh is flesh, and everything in the world lives on some other things. If we don't like these terms, we are on the wrong planet."[181] The animals even have their "undertakers" who bury the dead—*Necrophorus,* the beetle.

While the fear of reprisal is very strong in nature and has its physical as well as its psychological elements in the symbiotic chain, "the idea of reciprocity was one of the most basic organizing factors in society."[182] The relationships between human individuals and between them and their societies are forms and expressions of symbiosis, and these relationships identify the natural freedoms, to this extent, of the constituents of the group, society, and in the intimate and close relationships of individuals. "Among animals, as among ourselves, devotion of the individual to other individuals goes very deep. The one subserves the many. The impulse to cooperation, to mutual help, goes down and down to the root of things, to the inmost tissue of livingness."[183] Siberian Bluejays hug together closely for warmth in very cold weather; partridges do the same, forming a covey to keep themselves from freezing. Sheep, wolves, wild horses, buffalo and many others do the same.[184]

"The conclusion seems inescapable," writes W. C. Allee, "that the more closely-knit societies arose from some sort of simple aggregation, frequently, but not necessarily, solely of the sexual-familial pattern. Such an evolution could come about most readily with the existence of an underlying pervasive element of unconscious cooperation, or automatic tendency toward mutual aid among animals."[185] The crow is an excellent example. When a porpoise is wounded, two porpoises will come to his aid, and with their flippers on each side of him, they will hold him up and carry him along to safety. We find this a usual trait among Cetacean animals in general. E. J. Slijper, the authority on whales, informs us: "The strong ties between members of a particular school often take the form of mutual aid and, particularly, of assistance to wounded animals, to an extent rarely found among terrestrial mammals, which generally leave the weak and sick to their own devices, or actually set upon them. Of terrestrial animals, only elephants have been reported to come to the aid of their wounded. When this happens, two friends hold up their comrade on either side with their bodies and tusks."[186] Roedelberger and Groschoff report: "Some sharks, the most ferocious, can communicate with each other by means of short-frequency waves, and that explains why they all come surging around when a quarry has been sighted or a whale has been wounded."[187]

Concerning the sudden unity of different species of birds ordinarily fighting between themselves, to face a common enemy, Burtt writes: "Sometimes several species combine against a comman enemy. A group of 20 birds, including towhees, two species of wren, and titmice were observed scolding collectively and moving around in the brush about four feet above the ground. It was discovered that the object of their concern was the shed skin of a large rattlesnake that they evidently did not differentiate from the real thing. At any rate, it was a common enemy. . . . This mechanism whereby individuals that are not too congenial unite against a common enemy is not confined to birds. We have it ourselves. In the old days the Scottish clans used to fight each other until the British came across the border. Thereupon they united against this common enemy and after he was taken care of, they resumed fighting each other again."[188]

It takes only ordinary common sense to see for oneself that the structural and functional forms of humans and other animals, though varied and diversified in shape, size and habitat, indicate very obviously so many basic similarities and parallelisms, in the coitus, the ova and sperm, embryo, gestation, the dependence upon oxygen, water, and other similar body requirements to live, that no longer can any premise of divine creation be entertained seriously, especially with man as the main star of the cosmic show. "The basic mechanisms of reproduction and transmission of heredity are universal. Genes and chromosomes occur in man, in all animals and plants, and in microorganisms down to bacteria and bacteriophages."[189] "Ultimately our desires and our whole character are derived from our inherited equipment and the environmental influences to which we were subjected at the beginning of our lives. It is clear that we had no hand in shaping either of these."[190] "A living being must always contain within itself the history, not merely of its own existence, but of all its ancestors."[191] "Specific heredity, which is proper to all living things, is the fundamental fact distinguishing them from all lifeless things."[192] "All proteins, whether derived from plant or animal, bacterium or virus, contain the same twenty varieties of amino-acids. The processes by which these amino-acids are synthesized seem to be common to all organisms which possess the capacity for such synthesis."[193]

That man feels he is the star of the cosmic show, in self-acknowledgment, for the time being anyway, only proves that he had specific equipment and an age-long evolved training and he had to accept, unconsciously in any event, the long patient trek that enabled him to leave the cave and build the castle.

Yet humans are not alone in perfecting specialized inherited and acquired traits, abilities, intelligence, and adaptability, and these are not the sole province of man. In many ways numerous animals are more agile, rugged, and have greater endurance than man who is by far a much weaker and fragile creature than most animals. A Graubünden steinbuck will make the world's best human mountain climbers look silly. Squirrels are more adept in wire walking the suburban cables than the most expert humans in this art. Many fowl and other birds can outdo the most clever criminals in the artistry of confusing enemies in order to escape or protect their young. The seal makes human swimmers look like strugglers in the water. Even the Eskimos cannot endure the Arctic frosts, blizzards, and storms as the polar bear, the Arctic fox, or even the little lemmings. Not too many humans have the courage of the musk-ox of the North who, forming a square with his fellow creatures, will take his turn and go forth alone to fight his enemies, and when all are killed save one little calf, this little one, alone among its dead parents and guardians, will stand up and fight. Under dire circumstances humans will do the same where there is the courage and devotion, for creatures want to live and protect their own. True, animals have their specializations in movement and habit, yet to a great extent they move and have habits and ways of living comprehensively common to humans. Any variations and differences are a matter of degree, not of kind.

It is amazing that so often we find that adopted wild animals, especially when adopted very young, adapt themselves to the ways of man, become pets, adjust themselves to living indoors, eating food their parents never ate, learning to improvise and implement their instinctive habits to modify ways and means to cultivate themselves to completely different surroundings. Even sharks and rays in aquariums have learned to depend upon their human feeders and roll up on boards out of the water and take the food out of one's hand with graciousness and with no intent to harm. Could it be that man, too, once did the same, and that all his cultures are actually and basically extensions, adaptations, and innovations of the biological frame within which his entire existence, including his cultures, is a *continuous* interaction and/or progression of the biological base, and that there is no discontinuity between biology and culture, but that culture flowed out of the biological frame and field? The Japanese anthropologist, Junichuro Itani, states that "We are now convinced that 90% of an adult monkey's behavior is acquired by learning, not instinct."[194]

One of the evident similarities, for example, in the mammalian class to which we belong is seen in the strong instinct to protect, guard, feed, and nurture the helpless infant and child in all its phases. A mother cat, nursing its kittens, mothers and feeds a baby mouse. A robin, bereft of its own, feeds worms into the gaping mouths of goldfish. The goose surrounded by baby chicks and the chicken surrounded by goslings; the human mother tenderly protects the babies of other animal mothers. A bitch will mother a squad of ducklings. Lionesses will come to the aid of a lioness in labor and in giving birth; they act as midwives for each other. Animals carry their young about, in pouches, on their backs, on their bellies, on their tails, just as people do in their own way. Richard Carrington: "Walruses are devoted parents, and if their calves are threatened will immediately do all in their power to shield them from injury, even interposing their own bodies between their young and the lances of the hunter. It is the custom of professional walrus hunters to take advantage of this trait by catching a young calf and then striking it until it begins to cry. The sounds of distress bring all the adult walruses in the vicinity to attempt a rescue, and these animals then fall an easy prey to the hunters."[195] We have already seen how the devoted auk parents were decimated by the same principle. Albert Schweitzer: "In the past we have tried to make a distinction between animals which we acknowledge have some value and others which, having none, can be liquidated when and as we wish. This standard must be abandoned. . . . Some of the more evolved animals show that they have feelings and are capable of impressive, sometimes amazing, acts of fidelity and devotion."[196]

Mother porpoises will collectively gather and surround their young to protect them from the sharks; pelicans, penguins, seals, otters do the same. C. P. Idyll informs us about the starfish; parenthood and guardianship over the fragile young is so deep-rooted that even the lowly scarlet starfish *Henricia* "is a careful parent, protecting its young during the early stages. To spawn it stands on the tips of its five arms, thereby creating a cavity under its body into which it releases its eggs. For the three weeks or so during which the eggs develop, the starfish stands guard over them. Only after they hatch and swim off as larvae does she begin to feed again."[197] We could continue to cite such examples almost endlessly.

Motherhood, the synonym of Nature herself and its composite twin—the human mother is just one among thousands of mothers of various creatures that generate the same drive and perform the same service, and commit the young to the same basic and comparable disciplines necessary for each kind to survive. Some animal mothers find it difficult to part with their dead babies, just as many humans do. "If a baby is born dead, or dies soon after birth, the (porpoise) mother may carry it around on her neck for a few weeks, or may adopt a shark or an inanimate object to carry."[198] The story of *Jambo,* the first gorilla raised by its mother in captivity,[199] describes the care and devotion of a mother for its child and the instinctive dependence of the child to his mother, Achilla, which many human mothers in modern society could do well to emulate. The "humanness" of the hugging, cuddling, kissing and exhilarating play shows plainly the natural and unsublimated happiness of the animal mother in contrast to some human civilized mothers who have been so much affected by cultural acquisition and desire as to lose to some considerable extent this close naturalness and naturally free happiness. Often the cultural impaction is so determined that either the maternal instinct is blinded and so modified and adjusted to depreciate itself for some cultural principle or societal usage. In ancient Sparta we can see this depreciating process: "The whole education of a Spartan woman was aimed to fit her for bringing forth not only a Spartan citizen but, what was in fact the same, a Spartan soldier; there was no other purpose in her life, her greatest reward was to hear of the death of her son in battle."[200] In Aztec times, "every woman who died in childbirth, giving birth to a warrior at the sacrifice of her own life, was deified and included among the divine spirits known as the Cihuateteo or woman goddesses."[201]

The difference between the human mother and other animal mothers vary in the perplexities and emotional complications due to the human enlarged cortical brain. The human mother directly or indirectly often insists on continuing to mother the adults. No longer protected by her diencephalon, and more and more exposed, through her cortical, to the emotional and sensuous illusions and intraverted imagery, the human mother has strayed somewhat from her general role, but her deep-rooted and incontrovertible maternal instinct, being tied to her life as her breath, as a flower to its seed, can never leave her.

Like humans, polygamous fathers among the other animals are not usually devoted and it is simply a matter of "seeding" and letting the females do the rest. "Natural marriage among human beings is fundamentally identical to natural marriage among the animals—especially among the anthropoids."[202] "As soon as baby animals are born, if not before, their father usually removes himself completely and reverts either temporarily or permanently, to a separate existence."[203] "A doe and her fawn are alone. A male squirrel stays with the female only long enough for mating and then is gone. Male and female bears are some-times devoted in mating time so that they have what without vul-garizing we can call a 'honeymoon,' but when that season is over they go their separate ways. There are a great many children's tales about Mama Bear and Papa Bear and the Little Bears all together, but it is hard to rid ourselves of the pictures these stories conjure up; but we have to."[204] Of course, nature is not a monotone rule; there are many exceptions and variations, but in general it can safely be said that where the male is usually polygamous he is there to propagate, and if it were left to the males to bring up the infants and rear the family to secure the species, there would be few creatures left to survive, probably some sea-horses, marmosets, Siamese fighting fish, and a few more, but *no humans.* "Of all the artificial creations of human society, the idea of the perpetually loving and responsible father of young children is probably the farthest from natural instinct."[205]

Unlike humans, with exceptions, pure monogamy for life or for the season does exist with many creatures, and where it does exist devotion and fidelity are codes never violated. Faithfulness to each other is constant, even in death. Richard Perry tells of the devotion of the polar he-bear when his mate was shot: "At such times the he-bear would put his forepaws over a she-bear that had been killed, nuzzling her gently, and allow himself to be shot rather than desert her. Pedersen confirms this behaviour, adding that a he-bear will hunger for days beside the body of his dead mate. He cites the case of one who, after remaining beside his mate's body throughout a four-day blizzard without making any attempt to leave it and hunt for food, attacked a Greenland hunter when the latter sledged out to fetch in the carcass."[206]

Monogamy in human marriage came about, most assuredly, not because of morals or social customs, but because the human female, unlike many of her mammalian relatives, is receptive to sexual union at least from the time of puberty to the time of menopause, and more or less even beyond. If the human male was only accepted for propagation twice a year as animals do in their heat, rut, or mating season, man would have no alternative but to wander about to satisfy himself; he would have had no incentive to submit to monogamy, wait patiently for the next rutting season or build a family with its establishments of relatives, kinships, and *mishpoochas*. Even with the situation as it is, most males find it affirmatively pleasant and acceptable to engage in extra-curricular performances whenever and wherever they can.

It is plain to see that different phylae of animals differ from each other in many ways. Different animals within a family or clan differ from each other, just as human individuals within a family or group, each having its own personalities, idiosyncrasies, and peculiar tendencies. Individual creatures within any particular animal type differ, just as there are no two individual humans exactly alike. The nature of the individual unit, of individuality itself, to live as a unit, of a unit to move as a unit and have its individual personality and experiences as a unit—all this implies the attachment of some freedom as a natural state, and this, in turn, indicates and brings out variances and differences of degree. "It can therefore be safely said that no two individuals in any species are ever exactly alike. This even applies to identical twins, which *may,* but do not necessarily, start out with an absolutely identical genetic pattern but are now thought to undergo some genetic differentiation during embryonic development."[207] George Gaylord Simpson: "If organisms did not vary, and had not done so for some billions of years, they would not exist at all. . . . Organisms, of course, have various characteristics in common, in degrees varying from such minimal resemblances as between, say, a man and a Sequoia to the maximal resemblances of identical twins. Nevertheless, no two organisms, not even identical twins, are exactly alike. Each is the product of a history both individual and racial, and each history is different from any other, both unique and inherently unrepeatable."[208]

Humans, however, differ from other animals in a number of peculiar ways. Humans kill each other for reasons other than sex.

Humans kill each other as strangers, on the battlefield or in crime. No animal destroys itself so needlessly as the human being. "In any event, 'murder' is a term applicable only in relation to laws of human society."[209] Humans commit suicide; other animals do not. They may sacrifice themselves for the group protection, as baboons do in safeguarding the troop, but they seem to know nothing of death by foreknowledge, reflection, intuition, or anticipation. The adult human *knows* and *anticipates* death, while the human infant or child, being not yet "human," remains its animal self, and knows neither of death nor its coming. When a human adult senses he is dying, he *knows* he is dying; the other animals, and even very young humans, do not know this and do not sense reflectively what death is or that it could happen to them. The tragedy of death is in acknowledging its eventuality, in fearing it, in *knowing* of its coming; the other animals just die, not knowing what is happening or why. "The freedom of animals' lives from the dark shadows of worry, apprehension, and fear of death—the freedom that makes animaldom such a glad kingdom, all confidence, life acceptance, and an immediacy of Now—an animal cannot know, any more than a little child, that it has a self to lose. It cannot look ahead to self-ending; it can't contemplate a coming of non-ness."[210]

Humans, in differing from other animals, are more and more dependent upon the brain, and thus forget more and more that the brain is just one part of the *body*. Humans reflect, and thus give birth to imagery besides invention. As man evolved, his expanding brain separated him increasingly from the natural interdependent symbiotic democracy of animal life, put a tiara upon his head, and seated him upon a cloud of magnifying mirrors wherein his lordship's reflections have more and more built a *new* world of illusions that had never existed in the animal fold from which he ventured. This cortical explosion and its resultant mirage became the harbingers of newborn somas, and man pawned and shelved his body to buy himself a reflecting soul in his own brainmade mirror. In so doing he also pawned and shelved his *natural* freedom.

From the genetic point of view, regarding the stream of life on our planet, there are various schools of thought on the possible origins, some claiming that plant life preceded animal life, others feeling that both plant and animal rose from some common predecessor. Many scientists think that *flagellates* are the link between plant and animal life, as they both possess the attributes of being an animal and absorb nourishment by photosynthesis, as do plants.[211] Another germ-plant, strictly neither plant nor animal, is the *Dinoflagellate*. Scientists consider the *Leptothrix* as the presently known most primitive form of life; the *Psilophton* as the earliest known plant. The *Thallus* spore plants—*Thallophyta* —are considered the *lowliest* forms of plant life.[212] "Fundamentally the hydroid structure forms the basis of the evolution of the higher phyla. In fact, all higher animals culminating in man go through what essentially may be termed a 'hydroid' stage in their development. That is, from a single-celled egg, they pass through cell-divisions which are more or less comparable with those of the hydroid."[213] "What is a plant and what is an animal? It is only in the case of the higher organisms that the distinction between the two is obvious and unquestionable. The lower in the scale of life we go, the more difficult it is to actually decide whether an organism is a plant or an animal. And there are whole groups of living things which combine enough characteristics of each so that both botanists and zoologists lay claim to the organisms in question; this is true of the flagellates, the motile green algae, the slime molds and at one time the bacteria."[214] "The appearance of the unique chlorophyll and its union with protoplasm changed the entire aspect of life, made possible food manufacture in a far more efficient manner, and resulted in many-celled organisms in the variety found in the plant world. The presence of chlorophyll was the fork in the road which has led in increasingly divergent directions along the two basic patterns of life from the ancestral bacterial and flagellate single-celled forms of life."[215]

N. J. Berrill tells us about the sea potato, an animal-vegetable creature: "When the larvae hatching from their eggs were examined, zoologists were startled to see not merely a tadpole or fish-shaped organism, but one that has the forerunner of a backbone and a nerve cord that is unmistakably the same as the spinal cord of the backboned animals. Somewhere in the inconceivably distant and murky past our own kind may have had its beginnings in such as these. Sea squirts and man are two ends of the same line."[216] The sea lily is not a plant, although it looks in every way like a plant; it is an animal, a relative of the starfish family. It has what looks like roots, a long stem and branches and leaves like a fern.[217]

There is no question, when we pursue an unbiased and scientific analysis of organics, that plants and animals are not only related in the symbiotic food chains, in the concurrent evolution of both and their survival, but also that they possess a common origin as a precursor of organic life in general. C. Stuart Gager: "Plants and animals are alike in that they are both born, feed, grow, breathe, reproduce, and move (both motion and locomotion). Contrary to a common misconception, most plants are capable of motion and some locomotion by their own efforts, while some animals (e.g., sponges and oysters) are capable of locomotion only when very young, and are as fixed as trees when mature."[218] Some "animals" continue to be plants and some "plants" continue to be animals; the *Venus Flytrap* is one among many. The *Nematode-trapping fungi* are animal-eating plants.[219] Sir Jaghadis Chunder Bose, of the Bose Institute, Calcuata, wrote: "The life of plants is a mere reflection of our own. Plants devour various insects and small mammals by dissolving them with their secretions of natural acids."[220] It seems that plants, or more probably certain plants, are affected by various types of sound. Douglas relates an interesting incident when he traveled in India: "The relation of all life in the circle of existence has been of consuming interest to philosophers as well as anthropologists. When I first visited India, I heard of Hindu epics that extol the beneficial effect of music on plant life. The ancient god Krishna was said to have made a garden blossom by playing a flute. I dismissed the idea as fanciful. But T. C. N. Singh, a botanist on the faculty of Annamalai University in Madras State, India, has shown that music does affect plant growth."[221] According to Cleve Backster and others, each living cell, whether plant or animal, regardless of its assigned biological place, identity, and function, appears to contain a *sensing* capacity, *stimulus*, and *excitation* potentials, and their effects are the carousels on which each cell rides from birth to death and is constantly influenced by inner and/or outer

pressures and resistances. This *sensing* [neuronal] flow reveals the
emission of "signals" or forms of intracellular communication.
The experimental polygraphs on philodendron plants indicate that
"staggering as it may be to contemplate, a life signal may connect
all creation."[222] More and more we are finding out that sense
organs, the *anima* of movement, growth, stimulation, excitation,
and even provocation are in the core of all living things, both
plant and animal life, and that there appears to be a common
denominator and monistic element basic to all organics. Henry
E. Crampton: "Living Nature is essentially the same throughout
its entire range in certain fundamental qualities. All organisms
agree in protoplasmic make-up, in cellular constitution, and in
physiological abilities for the purpose of individual maintenance
and for the perpetuation of their kinds."[223] C. J. Hylander: "The
plant kindom is more than a necessary background for the parade
of the animal kingdom; it is more than a colorful backdrop for
the drama of animal life. Plants are an integral part of the world
of living things whose every member is a growing, feeling, striving individual which seems very different superficially from an
animal but in reality is faced with the same vital problems of
existence."[224]

According to the biologists, life in both plant and animal rose
from the primeval sea, and not in the Garden of Eden. That the
earliest animals were fishlike creatures is proven by embryological
studies. "Comparative anatomy shows that the extremities of the
land vertebrates arose from the paired fins of their fishlike ancestors."[225] "The celebrated gill arches, which are formed in
human embryos and in those of other land-dwelling vertebrates,
are also present in embryos of fishes, but in the latter they eventually become the supports of functioning gills. Can one avoid the
inference that our ancestors had gills that were used as such?"[226]
William K. Gregory, former Curator of Fossils and Fishes of the
American Museum of Natural History and an outstanding scientist in his field, wrote: "Man's much admired face is molded upon
the fish-trap of a creature that was no higher than a shark; his
voice, which he now broadcasts over the world, issues from an apparatus originally made out of the gill-bars of a fish; his very brain,
by means of which he has discovered space-time and plumbed

the depth of the atom, began as a simple automatic mechanism for directing his motor and digestive apparatus toward his next meal."[227] Cromie: "The human embryo develops gills like a fish, a kidney like that of a shark and a stiff rod of cartilage (notochord) which is characteristic of primitive chordates."[228] Berrill says of the octopus: "I think if you asked any zoologist to select the single most startling feature in the whole animal kingdom, the chances are he would say, not the human eye, which by any account is an organ amazing beyond belief, nor the squid-octopus eye, but the fact that these two eyes, man's and squid's, are alike in almost every detail."[229] Frank W. Lane affirms: "Both have a transparent cornea, although there are differences because the squid's medium is water, and man's is air. Behind the corneas of both eyes are small chambers filled with liquid. Both have an iris diaphragm, and behind this a lens set in a ring of muscle and ligament. There are dark pigments in both eyes which act as light screens in excessive glare, and both have tough fibrous coats to keep the eyes rigidly in shape."[230] B. H. Hoyer, B. J. McCarthy, and E. T. Bolton (of the Carnegie Institute) have revealed that the DNA type in human genetic substance and that of monkeys is almost identical. Szczesny concludes: "Man would never have finally seen this planet, had he not been preceded by fish, reptile, mammal and primate."[231]

As stated previously, man is a remarkable creature with a probably still greater and remarkable future. The fact that he identifies himself with the animal world, as a product of organic evolution, does not berate him in the least. On this point he can say that he is not alone, that he is a participant, a partaker and partner in the greatest corporation of all—Nature. To realize the meaningfulness of this acceptance is the first premise of our task, the understanding that natural freedom is a congenital factor, the primeval gene of freedom that is a concomitant twin-psyche without which the animal would have no *anima* and without which a certain thing called a life could never have become a *self*. John Dewey explains the human heritage nicely: "While man is other than bird and beast, he shares basic vital functions with them and has to make the same basal adjustments if he is to continue the process of living. Having the same vital needs, man derives the means by which he breathes, moves, looks and listens, the very brain with which he coordinates his senses and his movements, from his animal forebears. The organs with which he maintains himself in being are not of himself alone, but by the grace of struggles and achievements of a long line of animal ancestry."[232]

People who believe that man and his animal neighbors are separated by divine intervention or choice are not acquainted with the subtle and esthetic ways of animals. In my home there is Snookie, the German Shepherd; three cats, Harry Weinstein, the roving tomcat, Bootsie, and his mother Mae; Joe, the dwarf parrot, and Willie, the canary. Ever since they were babies they have always heard classical music being played. Let anyone play a jazz record and Snookie and his cats will get up and leave, and Joe the parrot will cack-cack strongly until the record is taken off or finished playing. Animals, too, can cultivate a taste for a *particular* kind of sound reception. Although animals cannot in any extent improvise, by far, as readily as man and with any degree of complexity, yet many animals do often improvise and meet new situations in many ways which are outwardly recognized as intelligent. They figure out things for themselves and go into action to accomplish what they are after. It was real fun reading Gerald Durrell's account of the penguins in Patagonia, and how a neglected and very hungry baby penguin managed to fool the "next door" family mother who was tricked into feeding it before she could recognize it as a strange baby and not her own.[233] Hu Shih concludes: "Man is only one species in the animal kingdom and differs from the other species only in degree, but not in kind."[234] Robert Ardrey: "Our kingship is a limited sovereignty; we are part of all things. We stand upon creatures lost in pre-Cambrian slimes. Our genes still reflect their ambitions. We may anticipate species unborn, times beyond prediction, sovereignties beyond *Homo sapiens,* and beings that we shall never know. But we shall be part of them, influencing their destinies as others have influenced ours."[235] Hartmut Bastian: "The anatomical revolution in the development of mammals lay primarily in the increasing differentiation and final perfection of their method of bringing young into the world. This development was in three stages. The first mammals were merely animals which laid eggs like reptiles, and then unlike reptiles, suckled the young after they were hatched. . . . The next step upwards led to the marsupials . . . the third and highest step in embryonic evolution—the Placentalia, to whom Man, in this particular sense, belongs."[236]

Man is a mammal and all mammalian life on earth is less than five per cent of all animal life, as more than ninety-five per cent of all species are invertebrates.[237] Man is just one species out of some four to five thousand species of mammals: the human kinship is worldwide and quite involved with each other, appearances and appetites notwithstanding.[238] A mammal is a warm-blooded vertebrate (chordate) that grows hair, has claws, hoofs or fingernails, discernible or vertigial tails, and suckles its babies from teats or milk glands. There are many kinds of mammals: *Insectivores,* those who feed mainly on insects; *Chiropters,* the bat family, who love mosquitoes for all meals; the *Rodents;* the *Cetaceans,* such as whales, dolphins, and porpoises; the *Ungulates,* the hoofed animals, such as horses, cows, and elephants; the *Primates,* which comprise the anthropoids, lemurs, marmosets, and others; *Man,* which includes *all* human beings, of all shades and colors, wherever they may be.

Thus, the biological sciences have established beyond any doubt that man is a descendent of some subhominoid or anthropoid type of animal. Hartmut Bastian: "With the chimpanzees and their astonishing accomplishments we now come to the highest order of animals. . . . They form the evolutionary line along which Nature has developed and consummated her greatest weapon—the brain. . . . There is nothing to contradict this view, and everything is in its favour. The first pieces of fossil evidence appertaining to the advent of Man were found, quite logically, at a point in the Tertiary when the whole evolution of the mammals and particularly the apes had reached such a stage that the deviation in the direction of Man was simply inevitable."[239] "All the evidence indicates," writes A. E. Hooten, "that man was an uncompromising anthropoid ape for five million years or more, and the lowest kind of an apparently unprogressive and brutish savage at least for another million years. His acquisition of high civilization is very recent and perhaps only temporary. The period of human civilization is inconsiderable in man's cultural history as is post-glacial time in the age of the earth."[240] Forest Ray Moulton adds: "When we compare the brains of man and the apes they appear much alike except for the greater size and complexity of the human brain. No major differences are found in the nervous system or in the skeleton; even blood tests indicate the close relationship between them."[241] Cromie: "A comparison of ocean water and animal blood reveals a startling similarity. Jellyfish, lobsters, sharks, some fishes, frogs, dogs and humans all have body fluids containing the same salts in much the same proportions as sea water. . . . Our blood and the body fluids of other animals is nothing more or less than modified sea water."[242]

According to Professor Nuttall, zoologist of Cambridge University, England, biochemical reactions of the blood show definite and even more convincingly, the real relationship between man and the apes.[243] S. Zuckerman gives further confirmation: "The blood serum and red blood corpuscles of the apes, including the gibbons, respectively contain group iso-agglutinins and group iso-agglutinogens which are specifically the same as those found in human blood."[244] "In the light of the evidence of the blood groups and precipitin reactions, it would seem that, except for the presence in each of reciprocal heteroagglutinins, there is little haematological differentiation between man and the apes."[245] Grzimek: "That the great apes have the same blood groups as we do ourselves has been a source of astonishment to many, but the common nature of our heritage is even greater than this. Thanks to the Uhlenhut method . . . it is possible to tell the blood of cows from that of swine, that of a cat from that of a tiger and that of a hare from an otter and so on; but it is impossible to tell the difference between the blood of a donkey and that of a horse, between that of a dog and a wolf, because these animals are so closely akin to one another and have common ancestors. The same applies to humans and chimpanzees. It is impossible to distinguish between the blood of the two."[246] Dobzhansky affirms: "The human body is constructed on the same general plan as the bodies of other animals, in an order of increasing similarity with the vertebrates, mammals, primates, and apes. Every bone of the human skeleton is represented by a corresponding bone in the skeletons of apes and monkeys."[247] "Man shares with monkeys and apes the following specialized traits, among others: stereoscopic and color vision, loss of mobility of external ears, replacement of a muzzle by a face, reduction of the sense of smell, loss of tactile hairs, occurrence of menstrual cycle, absence of breeding season, birth usually of a single offspring, great maternal care, and dominance of adult males over females and the young."[248] "The human embryo at a certain stage has a tail formed like those of mammalian embryos that have tails as adults. Does this not suggest that our ancestors had tails?"[249] George Gaylord Simpson: "No one doubts that man is a member of the order Primates along with the lemurs, tarsiers, monkeys and apes. . . . It is pusillanimous if not dishonest for an informed investigator to say otherwise. . . . Evolution is a fully natural process, inherent in the physical properties of the universe, by which life arose in the first place and by which all living things, past or present, have since developed, divergently and progressively. . . . [Man] is in the fullest sense a part of nature and not apart from it. He is akin, not figuratively but literally, to every living thing, be it an ameba, a tapeworm, a flea, a seaweed, an oak tree, or a monkey—even though the degrees of relationship are different and we may feel less empathy for forty-second cousins like the tapeworms than for, comparatively speaking, brothers like the monkeys. This is togetherness and brotherhood with a vengeance, beyond the wildest dreams of copy writers or of theologians."[250]

Jacqueta Hawkes and Sir Leonard Woolley in their *Prehistory and the Beginnings of Civilization,* state: "The fact that the human stock grew from a creature that walked upright and was ancestral to ourselves and the great apes cannot be denied."[251] "Man belongs to the order of the Primates, which he shares with the tree shrews, lemurs, tarsiers, monkeys and apes."[252] Harry Hoijer affirms: "Apes have a bodily structure very much like our own. Like humans, they learn readily from experience and by observing and imitating the actions of others. A number of experimenters have shown that apes not only learn to use tools but also invent them."[253] Robert Ardrey: "The creator of our human

culture had not been a man but an animal . . . the link between
the world of man and the world of the animal has been definitely
established. The African highland was humanity's cradle. And
man was born of the southern ape."[254] Hawkes and Woolley: "It
is now very generally agreed that the African continent was the
birthplace of mankind."[255] H. R. Hays: "South Africa has the
distinction of having been the home of the earliest transitional
manlike life form, the man-ape or Australopithecus."[256] Bernard
Campbell: "From animals not unlike them [the shrews] of the
order of Primates is believed to have evolved, and finally man
himself."[257] "Man's body in its structure and function is very
similar to that of other mammals; his difference from them lies
in his behavior and the mechanisms determining it. Such differences are far-reaching because the environment in which man
evolved has itself changed drastically."[258] "With the early mammals we find not only the full range of sense organs that we ourselves have, which respond to changes in the external environment, but also the full range of internal homeostatic mechanisms."[259]

It is observationally true that intelligence and the ability to
learn by experience are the results of genetic and environmental
endowments and components. So it could have been that the
hands of man, and the diverse potentials of holding, grasping,
making, and using tools, were the helpful precursors of the expanding human brain, which later probably led to cultural evolution and all its sequences.[260] Jerome S. Bruner: "The evolution
of primate intelligence is only now beginning to be understood.
The evidence today is that the full evolution of human intelligence required for its movement the presence of bipedalism and
tool use in early hominids. It is subsequent to these developments
that we find a sharp increase in man's cranial capacity and in the
size of his cerebral cortex."[261]

In the general field of animal life it is amazing to what degree
of new variances and adaptational traits, even if they are temporary, that animals will acquire and adhere to under different
artificial, suggestional apparatus and simulations, as indicated in
the experiments of imprinting and conditioning. However, we
should note that, while man is an animal, not all animals are men,

and what man is today is the result of many factors that other animals do not possess, or possess so little as to become negligible and nondiffusive. Among these factors are the processes of tentation or the ability to improvise to the extent that man possesses, the diffusion of ideas from one person to another, and the ability to organize mass effort, with its resultant sharing of its benefits, to the extent that man has cultivated and cultured it.

Yet we must hold in mind that this superiority of man over his related animals is the endowment of his particular heritage and the consequential potential that it made possible. "Human behavior," writes Mark Graubard, "must not be considered as purely social behavior because it is an animal organism we are dealing with. . . . We must view human conduct as the interaction of many forces which came into being in the course of evolution and exerted a strong influence upon his behavior."[262] And this applies not only to man but to all living things in their capacities to adapt or suffer the consequences of the effects of not doing so, whatever they might be. Harry Overstreet makes the point that "human nature differs from other forms of nature simply in the greater powers through which it has released itself from too narrow areas of functioning."[263] A. J. Carlson says of the human brain: "Man has no new kinds of brain cells or kinds of brain-cell connections. On the anatomical and biochemical side, so far as present data go, the differences in brain between man and other animals is one of quantity rather than of kind."[264] It may be added that besides having a larger brain, the specific advantage in intelligence as indicated in the human brain may have been brought about by the gradual maturing or conditioning of it over long periods of utilizing the physical endowments of man's prehensile hands and feet. Whales have much larger brains than man, yet the whale could not have achieved the maturation or evolution of its brain as man has because of the lack of this prehensility; the whale could not somehow grow a thumb. Also, it is evident that many humans have about the same quantity of brain matter yet vary greatly in intelligence potential; the specific of quality seems to make its value essential in the endowment of intelligence in any one individual. Sometimes it is the overlay of genetic endowment, sometimes favorable or adverse environmental conditions and external influences, sometimes mere accidents or the events of chance; any of these or combinations of them in degree may bring about the proper conditions for increased potential in the expression of intelligence and the actions that follow. Margaret Meads adds a viewpoint: "Even in the very simplest cultures we find conditions which are favorable or unfavorable to evolution in the ways in which age, sex, and the manipulation of even very small amounts of esoteric knowledge are structured, so that the specially gifted are assured—or deprived —of a chance to exercise their gifts in any particular field."[265]

Man is not the only creature to possess a measure of common sense. George Bernard Shaw rhetorically refers to common sense as instinct, and feels that enough of it can lead to genius. Actually it is most difficult indeed to place an absolute line of division between instinct and intelligence. R. W. G. Hingston wrote that "every animal, man included, possesses two sets of mental activity: the one instinctive, automatic, innate; the other, intelligent, plastic and acquired. These two activities are always blended. They may differ immensely in degrees of development but they never completely separate from each other."[266]

If one would follow the wolves, continually wandering in their marauding packs and following their food supply—the moose, reindeer, elk, etc.—then follow the Artic Eskimos in their ways, he would find that the similarities of purpose, deed, and sequence, are startling. If anyone doubts the animalism in man he should see Robert Flaherty's documentary film, *Nanook Of The North*, filmed about forty years ago, which depicts the rugged and ceaseless struggle from day-to-day, the constant search for food, resisting the bitter unrelenting cold, and the refusal to die. The nurturing and maturation of anyone's intelligence as well as the activated force of his instinctive drive depend not only on one's inherited endowment but on pressures and resistances of environment and the interplay of both. And so it is in the Arctic. Eskimos start eating chunks of warm, bloody deer or seal meat within seconds after the animal has been caught, just as quickly as they can start cutting, and before its heart has given up its last gasping beats. Any of us would do the same if we were as hungry as Eskimos or wolves, and had to struggle as much to get something to eat. The hunt for prey is constant and repeating, and the always hazardous fight to live never ends except with death.

Every zoologist has a deep respect for the intelligence of his subjects, contrary to the general human opinion that man is in a world by himself enthroned with an intellect that indicates a divine contract between man and his gods. Animals as well as man, through their sensory and instinctive potentials, provide themselves with tools that generate decisions, changes, adaptations, and adaptabilities which can be identified as forms of intelligence. As John Burroughs once remarked, "Animals know without knowing that they know," which the zoologist can identify as a form of insighted intelligence. Referring to the Cetaceans, Professor Adam Sedgwick wrote: "Had the whale a means of recording his experience, then he would have been the master of the world. Possessing a better brain than man, bigger, more convoluted, he lacks only the reversible digit, the thumb which can grasp and hold a tool."[267] One can wonder, if the whale could have held a tool, would it have been a harpoon gun to throw into other creatures of the sea? Perhaps so, if we can assume that a whale with hands could have evolved as man has. Perhaps the whale, having thought of this possibility, preferred to roam the oceans and take its chances with its flippers. Who can tell? We can only conjecture.

However, as stated previously, it is remarkable how diverse creatures, insects among them, can *learn* from experience and apply themselves in urgencies or new situations. Edwin Way Teale relates: "That nymphs have the ability to learn from experience is illustrated by the fact that they can be trained, in an aquarium, to come for food."[268] E. P. Evans: "It has been proved conclusively that the magpie and some other birds, even in their wild state, can count to at least four, and this fact is recognized and utilized by fowlers."[269] Allan Devoe: "Mental complexity has certainly, in a rabbit or a raccoon, not attained to a degree capable of constructs of theory, intricate self-reflection, or artful juggleries of concept and idea. But it won't do to say that when a rabbit comes out from its form on a summer morning, and contemplates the universe, its experience is nothing akin to ours. It won't do to say that the nature of the midnight coon, fishing for crayfish along the sedgy brookside, is unrelated to the nature of the midnight human fisherman. We are the brother of rabbits. We are the brother of coons. All that major part of our life experience which is emotional, impulsive, sensory and, as it were, animally spontaneous, we share with the rest of nature's creaturely brotherhood. We share a kind of primal intelligence which is a sensorimotor thing. We are distinguished by an extension to intellectuality: to the abstraction of principles. That addendum does indeed transform our world of experience. It makes us, in a valid sense, a new and unique species of being under the sun. But it does not abolish the fact that an enormous, indeed major, area of the life experience, below the level of intellectuality, is common to ourselves, coons, rabbits, and all the rest of animaldom."[270]

Charles Darwin, in his celebrated *Descent of Man*, wrote: "It is certain that there may be extraordinary mental activity with an extremely small absolute mass of nervous matter: thus the wonderfully diversified instincts, mental powers, and affections of ants are notorious, yet their cerebral ganglia are not so large as the garter of a small pin's head. Under this point of view, the brain of an ant is one of the most marvelous atoms of matter in the world, perhaps more so than the brain of man."[271] Julian Huxley: "There is every reason for believing that ants have long since reached the highest level possible to them, and equally every reason for believing that man is only at the bottom of his evolutionary ladder."[27] [2]Maeterlinck tells us about the termites: "Their civilization, which is the earliest of any, is the most curious, most complex, the most intelligent and, in a sense, the most logical, and best fitted to the difficulties of existence which has ever appeared before our own on the globe. From several points of view, this civilization although fierce, sinister, and often repulsive, is superior to that of the bee, of the ant, and even of man himself."[273] S. H. Skaife: "Termites were using poison sprays long before man thought of them."[274]

Lorus and Margery Milne, in their *The Senses of Animals and Men*, have this to say about bats, butterflies and mice: "A bat which migrates year after year between Newfoundland and Georgia with no known reliance upon visual clues has a brain scarcely larger than the eraser on a lead pencil. The nervous system of a monarch butterfly could be balanced by a millet seed. The control centers of a fruit fly would scarcely cover the period at the end of this sentence. Yet these creatures are all capable of complicated actions. They have survived just as long and just as well as we. Their adaptability, moreover, seems limitless. Every time a man builds a better mousetrap, the surviving mice build better mice."[275]

Elie Metchnikoff, once director of the Pasteur Institute in Paris, tells us about the very low forms of life: "Observations on protozoa, and especially on the infusorian group of protozoa, show that these simple things, each of which is composed of no more than a single cell, possess a high degree of sensibility. They select their food, distinguish living from dead animalculae, and seek out their mates for conjugation, avoid danger, and hunt their prey."[276] *Life*, too, is a matter of degree, not of kind.

SOUND AND COMMUNICATION

Sound, the vehicle of language and communication, is composed of vibrations. These vibrations express thought and actions in utterance. Vibrations are the strings by which all animal life is tied, and not necessarily by its ears. Sound and language are not the sole properties of man; they are diffused through all living experience and creatures, from the deep sea to the highest mountain, in the rivers, bays, valleys, and in the thick jungle. Schools of shrimp and fishes, herds of whales, and families of porpoises— all keep up a constant conversation that is understandable between them. The terrestrial animals also have their peculiar sounds, some in song, some with screams and shrieks, some with sighs and hums, but whatever it is, they understand each other and the sounds of their foods, their friends, and enemies. Language is the correspondence of universal symbiosis. It reminds us constantly that in the world environment in which our lives are spent, we are not alone; it is our security from boredom and the expressed manifestation that identifies the deep-rooted genus of association and relationship which interrelates and interacts all life into one umbilicalized family. Its language in its myriad

forms and tenses is the oldest language of life, preceding by hundreds of millions of years the first shriek of man's forebears, and
it will be here when expiring man may have to give up his last
appealing cry for survival.

If not for the evolution of language, which preceded the historical period and the origins of which are lost in the labyrinth
of prehuman times, it is highly doubtful, without a system of
communication that the cultures, religions and societies, as we
know them, would ever have come into being or that man would
have theologically established any idea of a soul, spirit, or a god.
Magic could not have generated without the *Word*, and the Word
became the prayer and the prophecy. Max Müeller wisely said:
"Mythology is only a dialect, an ancient form of language."[277]
Logos, the *Word,* is also the *God.* Lewis Mumford: "The emergence of language—a laborious culmination of man's more elementary forms of expressing and transmitting meaning—was in-
comparably more important to further human development than
would have been the chipping of a mountain of hand axes. . . .
From the beginning the creation of significant modes of symbolic
expression, rather than more effective tools, was the basis of *Homo
sapiens*'s further development."[278] Mumford thus feels that *ritual*
preceded and made possible the beginnings of speech communication between humans: "For one sees primordial human ritual
against an older background of animal habits: the courting rituals
of many animals and birds, the emotional cries uttered in the
midst of sexual excitement, the howling of wolf-packs at the
moon, the singing of gibbons, which impressed Darwin, the nocturnal dances of elephants, all support the notion that ritual is
older than language in man's development and played an indispensable part."[279] He thus intimates that symbolic gestures and
protoprimitive beginnings of magic and ritual, rather than invention and tool-making reflections, gave birth to later language.
"The movements and gestures of ritual were the earliest foreshadowings of human speech."[280] Yet the question arises in one's
mind: how could ritual, being a cultural acquisition and which
was a family or group performance, have been able to be carried
out without some elemental and intelligible process of communication? No one really knows. One thing we do know: All animals

manage to communicate, some more, some less. The hominid managed, because of his enlarged brain and other factors, to communicate more so to the eventual culmination of highly integrated and complex languages and writing. This indeed marks him as a truly remarkable animal.

As it led to the earliest arts, the forerunner of writing, the language of the carved, inscribed, written or printed word became the translation of a picture into mental sound communication. Scientists have learned to listen to the "language" of the atom, to the "conversations" of the electrons and protons, and have come to know increasingly that where there is any mass of energy, there is always the possibility of sound. Language, or the ability to communicate, is the bridge that the individual crossed to reach *Homo sapiens* and the first approaches of organizational society. Language is the confession that man by nature is a social animal; assuredly, he didn't start talking all by himself, but as a means of commuication. It made it possible for freedom to express an experience of desire or fear from one individual to another or to a group experience of desire or fear; thus, *natural* freedom, supremely the *physical* tool of the individual and animal became the *social, collective,* and *cultural* tool of the group. Language implies association as freedom implies individualistic action, association being also the result of an act of being free to associate, so "it appears to be fairly certain that language arose as a result of men learning to work together toward a common end."[281] "A law of association is a causal law of mental events,"[282] without which there could be no possibility of the evolution of language in the life of man.

There are many theories regarding the origin of language. Harry Hoijer writes: "To understand how language came into being we must know how man came to establish his arbitrary and conventional habits of associating speech sounds with experience."[283] And Kroeber felt that language is something acquired, not inherited. He refers to the experiment in which children, brought up by deaf-mute nurses, spoke no language, but communicated by gestures, as deaf-mutes do. There is no question that children are taught *a* language, which they learn, as they grow up, by imitating and listening to their elders, and by associating certain familiar sounds or words with certain experiences; or that they *can* be taught other languages foreign to them by correlating foreign words to the words in their own language. Nevertheless, Kroeber seems to have overlooked the fact that such acquisition of language is not *purely* acquired, but is the effect of the natural potential inherent in the human child to give off expression by sound, just as in other animals, and that the human brain has a *relatively* greater potential than the brain of other animals for success in such acquisition.

Language is not an altogether new artificial or purely noncongenital achievement but the result of millions of years of animalistic attempt to convey thought and expression through utterance. This consistent and continuing attempt on the part of an individual human or other animal contains within itself the natural freedom to activate such a process. Language, as we know and speak it, is not present in the insect societies (except mostly in the males for mating purposes) because, in the insect world, the individual members do not contain the type of freedom in the arbitrary sense of choosing actions, but only contain a sufficient mechanical freedom to motivate and fulfill their purely instinctive processes. In like manner, when the children adapted themselves to the mute gestures of their nurses, it was not because they lacked the potential of utterance, but because they *adapted* themselves in a field given them wherein gestures were a replacement. Therefore, while language, as we know it, is an acquisition of learning by imitating or being taught, it remains only possible because the human child is *capable* of imitating sound, and because its brain has evolved enough to be able to understand it and retain a knowledge of it. With our animal neighbors, "the world in which an animal moves is a world of sensing, feeling, acting; a world less of thought than of impulse and the unrationalized wisdom of the muscles and nerves; a world of awareness and response, and not analysis. It has its own kind of language, subtle and diverse."[284]

The animals, too, "learn" the familiar sounds of their parents and the sounds of their environment and their meanings. Mice sing, rabbits scream, a cat meows, a dog barks and whimpers, the lion roars, the crow haws, the frog croaks, owls screech, the ape mutters, babbles, and ooo's, the horse whinnies, the birds perform symphonies of song, porpoises and whales talk and sing, shrimp give off noises like subtle low-rumbling distant thunder, and the list goes on in length. Every time I catch a grunt, it grunts. Besides, many animal, fish and insect sounds are not heard by man's ears, being supersonic in ratio to man's hearing ability. Bird vocabulary is extensive and birds "talk" among themselves just as we do. Crows are great conversationalists in their own society; they might even feel the same way about us. Dozshansky states that "Bird songs are in part learned. Some birds are capable of producing a great variety of vocalizations and tend to imitate the sounds that they hear other birds make, especially their parents and conspecific individuals."[285] Burtt: "If we observe closely, we may detect a considerable variety of sounds. In fact, birds are better off than many other animals in this respect. Dogs and cats have very limited vocabularies; fish grunt now and then; frogs trill; crickets chirp—but birds express alarm, distress and aggressiveness, call a group together, announce a source of food and make appropriate vocal response to a member of the opposite sex. . . . Most birds have various call notes that are simpler than a song but still transmit information to the other birds."[286]

Arthur A. Allen, in this *Book of Bird Life,* writes: "The song of a bird is primarily an announcement to the female of the presence of the male and a challenge to other males of his species to keep out of the territory which he is guarding."[287] Is there really any difference between the song of the male bird and the human lover playing his guitar beneath the window of his beloved? Allen continues: "There can be little doubt that the voice in birds has been developed, as in other animals, as a means of communication. This does not necessarily imply an elaborate thought mechanism nor even an extensive vocabulary, but merely a means of communicating their feelings. Anyone who makes an extensive study of the call-notes of one bird, however, will be impressed with the number of modulations, and these may correspond to different words. The barnyard fowl, for example, in leading her chicks about, is continually calling to them in various notes. One announces food, another announces danger, another calls them to brood, and so on. What is true of the domestic fowl is true of all birds, only most of us are not familiar enough with them to recognize the differences, and even if we do recognize differences, it is almost impossible to represent them with words."[288] Most probably the animals have the same problem with us.

Regarding the "language" of the nonhuman primates, Peter Marler tells us: "In the vocal systems of higher monkeys and apes, there is one sense in which perhaps the stage is being set for the development of the type of sound system used in human speech. Human children begin with an ability to produce a very wide range of sounds of somewhat the same type as are heard in macaques, baboons, and apes. . . . There is no evidence that any nonhuman primate has a significant ability for vocal learning. However, reflection upon the kind of sound signals from which human speech might have developed suggests that it is much more likely to have stemmed from a richly graded system such as has been found in rhesus monkeys, and perhaps in chimpanzees and gorillas."[289] Jarvis Bastian falls in line: "There are also many human auditory signaling actions that have comparable simplicity and steadiness of upper tract configuration and predominant variations in laryngeal and sublaryngeal adjustments. These are signals of the sort that may be loosely termed expletives, such as laughs, moans, shrieks, cheers, and the utterances of infants. Such signals also have properties similar to human visual signals, with which in fact they are often closely linked."[290] "Signals between members of the same species and even between creatures of different species are as common as life itself. Even the individual egg cell sends out chemical signals and attracts spermatozoa."[291]

Like humans and their consciences in human society, animals are socially conditioned, and a cry of alarm or a piercing shriek of pain or fright will shock a number of animals and put them in a state of preflight and flight, just as it will among humans. Joel Carl Welty: "Even the most casual observation shows that much bird behavior is socially conditioned; that is, one bird's behavior depends in part on how other birds behave. In colonies of gulls and terns, one alarm cry may set up a contagious panic of cries and up-flights by thousands of birds. Perhaps by the same nervous mechanism that makes yawning infectious in man, great waves of instinctive behavior may suddenly sweep a gull colony, and just as suddenly fade away."[292] Yawning, too, is infectious among many animals; I have witnessed it at home with my cats; lions do the same. Adolf Portmann: "The structure of human life in general is social, as with all higher animals. Man comes to 'sociability' not by 'arrangement,' by rational reason, but from the natural, primary disposition which he shares with all higher animals. . . .[293] That the drive to find forms of society in freedom is part of our nature, is suggested by the fact that the conditions we are born in seem directed towards this objective. . . .[294] Scent-organs, which are often 'transmitters' in the service of the sexual encounter, may with higher organisms acquire a significance leading far beyond this connection into wider social relationships. . . .[295] It is now appreciated that the life of all higher animals is basically social, that social behavior in its most different aspects is an essential feature of that life. . . . Movements, attitudes, gestures, sounds, scents, markings, ways of meeting, inconspicuous to the superficial glance and earlier unnoticed, are recognized as significant, playing their part in social life."[296]

E. J. Slijper, the authority on Cetaceans, writes about a documentary film in which whales came to the rescue of a calf that screamed for help: "In a memorable scene of this film, twenty-seven female Sperm whales came from miles away to rescue an over-inquisitive calf which had been injured by the ship's screw. In all such cases, the rescuers are unquestionably attracted by distress signals, and the crew of the *Calypso* did in fact hear the calf emitting such sounds."[297] Among porpoises, also Cetaceans, distress sounds are emitted by whistling noises and "apparently the animals used variations in this whistling sound to indicate different emotional states."[298] Eibl-Eibesfeldt: "When I swam up to an angelfish it gave a short, metallic 'tock-tock' and this warning call caused the other fish to dive down under the protective corals."[299]

Whether the art of symbology, language being one of its media, is purely a process of learning in man, that is, a learned habit, seems not to be the *whole* story and the *only* key to the origin of language. It could be that antecedent instinctive and other natural processes, including the increasingly evolved variety of sound

emissions by the stressful use of the vocal chord as a mechanism
of imitation and demonstration to relieve the emotional impulse,
and the gregarious and social drives to communicate, and to enjoy
it, might have laid down a causative line of sequences that might
have led up to the animal giving off sounds and to the talking
Homo.[300]

ANTHROPOMORPHISM AND ANIMAL WORSHIP

THE FARTHER WE go back, we find that the savages, primitives, and preprimitives felt and believed that other animals and
men were a kinship of clans, of related families, that animals have
the spirits of people, good and bad, strong and weak, and all the
other attributes and characteristics that people possess and the
attributes of animals that people would like to possess, or simulate. Every kind of animal—bug, fish, bird, reptile, insect—has
been worshipped by people all over the world; in many places
they still are. On this subject alone a large volume could easily be
written. "Natives often seem convinced that they are the sons of
crocodiles, emus, kangaroos, and even grubs."[301] This trait has
been one of the main foundations of totemism. Franz Boas
brought out brilliantly the relationships between birds, animals,
and people among the American Indians, especially in the Northwest and Canada. In India today the people still worship the cow
as sacred, and not only has every living creature a soul, but even
the plants have souls, and one must be careful not to rip the roots
of certain plants for fear of injuring their souls. When it comes to
the distribution of souls, the Hindu people at least seem to be
more equitable and magnanimous than the Christians, who re-
serve souls strictly for themselves. The Chinese and Japanese hold
the carp fish to be sacred. Animism is worldwide, and its influence
upon the cultural evolution of people and its effects upon natural
freedom will be taken up later in its proper place. But from these
few examples we can see that, as we go back into the distant past,
we find man more *consciously* attached and related to the animals
and plants, and that this phase gradually declined and degenerated and withered away with the advance of cultural institu-

tions, which brought about a greater degree of concentration of consciousness of man upon and for *man.* The gap between man and his natural environment widened with the advance of civilization.

Strangely, anthropomorphism is not the sole prerogative of man; animals have it also, which is really the process in reverse. "Have a person be the first living creature a duckling sees upon hatching, and thereafter the little bird is permanently 'imprinted' by mankind—clearly convinced that it is no duckling but another human being."[302] Welty: "Imprinting has been demonstrated in a great variety of precocial species—ducks, geese, coots, domestic chickens, turkeys, pheasants, and quail—and even in such altricial species as owls, ravens, doves, and finches. Different species of birds show varying degrees of imprintability."[303]

The intricate processes of mentation, continually mixing instinct with experience, do not belong to man alone; they are the ways and means of all life on earth. Man is really a very small stockholder in this corporation of nature, but gradually the ingenuity, power, knowledge, mechanics, and the moving powerhouse of civilization are the means with which man is succeeding in becoming the Chairman of the Board, the Board of Directors, and gathering in more and more of the shares. When Nature becomes a closed corporation held by man alone, by that time the structure will have reached the points of diminishing returns and least marginal utility, bearing no return and barring any return, for that which has been completely extinguished cannot be brought back. It reminds me of the prophetic remark of Leonardo da Vinci: "Nothing will be left. . . . All will be hunted down. . . . All exterminated."

Vernon Reynolds: "Man's attitude to the apes is still fundamentally one of exploitation. Perhaps at some time in the far distant future, man will mature sufficiently to realize how primitive this exploitative attitude is; but that day is a long way off, and the apes will probably be extinct before it arrives. . . . Anyone who doubts that urgent action is necessary to save the large apes is under a misapprehension. Anyone who doubts that it is worth the effort involved in saving them is blind to the future needs of mankind. The gorilla, the orang, the chimpanzee, and their lesser cousin the gibbon, have a right to survive. . . . Must we watch gloomily while our nearest relatives in the animal world are slowly exterminated by our more exploitative fellowmen?"[304] Rosl Kirchshofer: "One of the greatest zoological tragedies of our times is the mass slaughter of orang-utans. . . . These animals do no harm to anybody and never plunder fields or gardens. But they are persecuted by traders who capture their young for sale to zoos and private collectors. The hunter selects an adult female with a baby and shoots her down from the trees. . . . It is safe to assume that for every orang-utan baby eventually sold, four healthy adult females have been murdered and at least three young animals killed by inexpert care and exhaustion. . . . If the hunt continues at the present rate, there can be no doubt that the days of the orang-utan are numbered."[305]

COMMONALITIES OF THE SENSES, BEHAVIOR, AND SURVIVAL

A well-known zoologist once said that "even a child can see that a human and ape have many things in common. A chimpanzee spits to show his resentment; man does the same."[306] Animals, including man, can see, feel by touch, smell, taste, breathe, move about, sleep, respond to temperature changes, respond to light and darkness—in sum, animals and man are born, live, and die in a similar way and under similar circumstances.

Dancing and prancing are common in the animal world. "In many of the ape's rhythmic movements are also to be traced the crude foreshadowings of the human dance."[307] The human dance and other arts of rhythmic movements can also be traced to the primitive's imitation of similar motions of the animals in their particular environments. The American Indians have dances in which they cover themselves with bird feathers or animal skins and dance about imitating the movements of these animals. "Mimetic dancing is common throughout contemporary hunting cultures. Nearly all the North American plains Indians danced buffalo dances."[308] The ancient Ainu of Japan and Siberia had their bear dances, and these are still performed in the remote northern regions of the Japanese islands. All through the world man has imitated in his dances the movements and behavior of his animal neighbors. In Africa, a great proportion of the dances can be traced to animal simulations. The prancing, jumping, and stamping of baboons, apes, and monkeys are not distant from the same movements by the primitives in their neighborhood. The leopard dance is well known. Gerald Durrell, in his *A Zoo in My Luggage*,[309] describes the butterfly dance and the dance of the horses' tails, in which the old Fon of Bafut takes such an ex-hilarating part. All these dances are poetical, metaphorical, and artful. If not for the cultural progress of the Age of the Enlighten-ment and the advances of the nineteenth century, we would still be dancing the minuet. "There are many birds which supplement their displays with curious evolutions in the air, with what might well be called dances, and with other performances that will have to be called 'antics' for want of a better word."[310] "The rhythmic stiff-legged dance of the Sharp-tailed Grouse as they whirl about their cackling ground with erected tails and arched wings is a definite courtship performance. So are the promenades of the Cayenne Lapwing of South America. The clustering and waving of wings of the flocks of Jaçanas on the tropical marshes and the dances of the Cranes and the Albatrosses are all examples of courtship performances."[311] We see the beautiful Peacock pranc-ing about with feathers outstretched showing off his gorgeous colors in display. Is this any different from the young human lover who takes his girl to dances so he can display his own hand-someness, movement, and desire?

While man tastes with his tongue, an insect tastes with its feet. The insect lives practically on instinct while man lives by in-stinct and acquired behaviors and desires. Compared with the insect, man's legs are infantile, as "the legs of no other living creatures have as great variety in form and uses as the legs of the insects."[312] Fawns are able to stand within *ten minutes* after they are born and start nibbling vegetation on their own within a few days."[313] While the sense of smell has degenerated with man and other mammals, it is still a keen factor with most animals and in-sects. "The sense of smell is far older than the oldest hills. It preceded all other ways in which an animal can become aware of food, or a mate, or danger at a distance."[314] "The rabbit smells its way to a carrot or dandelion. The cat or dog ignores these scents, but might find interest in the rabbit's tail. The scavenging dog sniffs vigorously at manure a cat disdains, but passes by the flowers and foliage a cat often takes time to brush against and smell appreciatively."[315] Smelling and odors are lively factors with the insects, as they are with human people in manifold ways. "A home [hive] odor is very important to honeybees. Each worker leaving the hive for field duties carries a sample of this fragrance locked in a special scent sac. As she returns and alights on the sill at the hive entrance, she opens the sac as though displaying a pass badge to the guardians of the portal. Only bees with the proper hive odor are admitted."[316]

When it comes to eyesight, there are definite similarities between man and his relatives. We have seen the amazing extent of this factor in the eye of man and the eye of the octopus. It seems that almost everything that lives, both animal and plant, is *phototropic*—it has the primeval urge and surge to move toward the light. Human eyesight is subject to phototropism, as with moths; to negative phototropism, as with the queen bee; to hydrotropism, as with grubs, grand larvae, and aquatic plants; to stereotropism, as with snakes and other reptiles; and even positive thigmotaxis, as we find in the cockroach or in fish, especially the trout, moving or heading into current and tide. While birds see many colors, including the reds, yellows, and greens, even better than humans do, color blindness is general among the mammals except in man and his close cousins, the apes and monkeys. There are many justifiable and natural reasons why the sun became so often the Sun-god, the head god of many ancient pantheons of gods, and many explanatory reasons for the burning torch, later the burning tapers and candles in temples, symbolizing light in opposition to darkness, as life symbolized its own opposition to death.

Man's eyes, with all their fine and sharp uses, are still no match for the tiny eyes of insects. "An insect sees both color and movement through eyes that are far different than ours. Instead of one lens in each eye, an insect may have thousands of lenses. . . . Some dragonflies have as many as 30,000 lenses in a single eye.

Each lens is six-sided. Fitting together, they form a great compound organ of sight covering most of the insect's head. It bulges forward so the dragonfly can see ahead, behind, above and below all at the same time. . . . Some of them can see what our eyes cannot—the 'black light' of the ultraviolet."[317] "An insect breathes but it has no lungs. It hears but it has no ears on its head. It smells but it has no nose. Its heart pumps blood but it is so unlike our hearts that it often reverses itself and beats backwards."[318] "Insects, in proportion to their size, are the strongest animals on earth."[319] "For nearly 200,000,000 years before man appeared on this planet, the insects had been a feature of its fauna. . . . Of all living creatures on the face of the earth, fully nine-tenths are insects. . . . The insects are, as they have been since prehistoric times, the most widespread and successful form of animal life."[320] One historian has written that it was not man's deeds that destroyed Babylon, but mosquitoes.[321]

As for the affairs and trades of men, the insects were the precursors of most of them. They are farmers, raise "cattle," keep slaves, go to battle as warriors, hatch different classes of its people, such as laborers, nurses, soldiers, breeders, timekeepers (as the famous Clock of the Bees), arrange and maintain storage warehouses, store different kinds of food as security and capital, and even express jealousies, admiration, coquetry, and valor. Among the insects we find hunters, trappers, fishermen, scavengers, miners, funeral directors, builders, tunnel-making engineers, soldiers both loyal and mercenary. They even have hired *Samurai* fighting men, as in Japan. Are there basal relationships between the insects and man in the long generic march from periods long lost in the fogs of the story of evolution?

Animals, including man, take baths, mudbaths, wash themselves methodically, clean and sharpen their claws, lick to clean their furs, lick their wounds as human children often do. Birds, cats, dogs, and many other animals take dust baths to get rid of fleas, lice, and other vermin. In traveling about the world, when it comes to the duties of the toilet, I can safely say that most animals take to habits of cleanliness more readily than most humans. Joy Adamson tells the beautiful little story about a baby weaver bird that she rescued as it fell naked from its nest and fed it as a pet, naming it *Tam-Tam*. Weavers, unlike human babies, who are helplessly filthy unless cared for, are instinctively very clean, and even a baby weaver can take care of itself very well. She narrates a titillating story: "The little bird's instinct for cleanliness was remarkable, and every time it had to empty its intestines, it climbed to the edge of the nest, let its tail overhang the entrance, and carefully let its droppings fall to the ground below. Even when I held it in my hand, it always warned me by its restlessness that it was going to excrete until it found a finger on which to perch and from which it could relieve itself without soiling my hands. . . . George [the author's husband] noticed that every night the weavers seemed to give vent to this urge in unison. He was often waked up by their sudden sleepy twitters that were succeeded by a sound like raindrops, caused by their droppings falling on the tent canvas. This lasted for a few moments, after which all was quiet again. As this happened two or three times during the night, it seemed obvious that the weavers were gregarious even in this habit."[322] Has the human race, or any group or society of the human race, advanced to this extremely social, collective, esthetic, and therapeutic point?

Any motorist who drives through the more rural and country roads can see for himself that animals die on the highways, just as people do. Animals are subject to common diseases, inflictions, suffering, accidents, pain, and death, just as human beings are. Anyone even casually informed of the extensive and comprehensive broad plain of knowledge upon which husbandry and the practice of veterinary medicine depend knows and realizes the deep-rooted and positive commonality of animal life and its relationships and similarities to the human kind of animal. Animals, as humans, are subject to parasitism, bacterial infections, viruses, mold growths, tumors, cysts, cancers, impactions of the teeth, skin and circulatory diseases, allergies, emotional disturbances and retardations, mental imbalances and insanities. Birds get attacks of appendicitis, and sometimes hordes of migrating birds die of paratyphoid. "To go outdoors at all into animaldom is to find death happening. Death by storm, death by starvation, death by freezing, death by fire or drowning, death inflicted by an enemy. There is also death by disease."[323]

Human behavior and animal behavior have many things in common, so common and specific as to insure a definite behavioral relationship that brings to the surface many physiological and psychological similarities that cannot be written off as coincidental or imaginary. The role of dominance by the male over the female, the role of greater strength over the weaker ones, the role of power aggrandizement acted out in the territorial proclamations and struggles of animals to retain, maintain, accrete, or conquer "territory" they can feel to be their own and be master over, the resignation or the cowardice of the weaker or fearful ones, the psychological portrayal of strength of the arrogant, the tricky and chicanery of the more clever, more intelligent, the roles of masters and slaves, the shrinking away of the dubious and the aged, and the sacrifices of life by individual heroism for the group, the protection of the young and helpless, especially by the mother, even moral codes regarding fidelity and comradeship—these are merely a few of the same historical pageantries of human beings and are the common experiences and behaviors of people, the same as we find among the other animals. "The writer has observed a Redstart returning with food for its own young, to be waylaid by a young Cowbird that was being raised by a Red-eyed Vireo, and actually to give the food which it carried to the young Cowbird, so insistent were its cries."[324] Mothers and motherhood in the wild may be even more tender and expressive than in the highly civilized communities of humans.

One may recall the popular story of the chicken that gets pecked the most, and the rules of pecking accepted in the henhouse. This dominance-pecking demonstration among chickens was exposed brilliantly in the experiments of the Norwegian scientist Schjelderup-Ebbe. "The high-ranking chicken may peck left and right at the feeding pan; but there is always that lowly chicken who is pecked by all, and can peck no one in return."[325] Do we not recollect in our own experiences human counterparts of this situation?

"We may say with certainty," writes Robert Ardrey, "that the instinct for hierarchy benefits many an animal society. Wild geese are assured that on their long flight south in escape from storm and winter the strong will fly first, breaking the wind, and that the ranks of the V will remain unbroken. A herd of migrating elephants may proceed with assurance that the strong and experienced will lead the way, and the weak and unwise will follow protected. We may say with equal certainty, based on innumerable observations, that dominance brings many an unpleasantness to a society of animals. Punishment tends to be handed down the line. To be high in rank is to be privileged in all things, and to be low in rank to possess but one satisfaction, that there is probably someone worse off than yourself. Yet discontent with one's status is a scarce commodity in a state of nature. Hierarchy is a force too valuable for natural selection ever to have favored the discontented."[326] "Some birds have separate nesting and feeding territories and apparently recognize, also, certain neutral feeding areas. Thus a pair of Great Blue Herons may claim only a few feet of nesting territory in the colony while they are defending a whole lake shore as a feeding territory. A pair of Kingfishers may claim the fishing rights to half a mile of stream, their nest being in a sand bank a half mile in another direction, and they will drive away any other Kingfisher from this part of the stream. A little lower down there may be a neutral territory where several Kingfishers feed and still farther down will be the territory of another pair. Similarly with the Robins about one's garden. The whole area may be divisible into several Robin territories with a pair defending each, or there may be some neutral ground not claimed by any particular pair where all feed in peace."[327]

This *neutral* area is a form of adaptability of affirmative want wherein other forms of dominance, territory, relative fears, uncommon and regularly strange to each other, and the status levels of the strong over the weak, are sublimated to the immediate need of satisfying hunger or survival under stress or urgency. I see this at work in my own garden, where there is a large feeding station in the open. Through my study window I can see hundreds of birds representing a dozen or more varieties, all feeding together peacefully. There are sparrows, wrens, bluejays, starlings, doves, cardinals, red-winged blackbirds, an occasional crow or pheasant, and many others. Often I see a squirrel squatting down in the middle of it with the birds crowding all around him, all eating in toleration of each other, with Snookie, my German Shepherd, less than ten feet away, watching silently from inside his kennel. As in so many things, among humans and his animal relatives, *necessity* is not only the father of invention, but also the mother of reform, of compatibility, and of peacefulness. Perhaps necessity may force man, against his inner and outer drives, to eventuate such compatibility and the peace it could make possible. It succeeds nicely among wild animals. Can it succeed among civilized men and their politics? Is there not a familiar ring from all these in the actual social, religious, economic, and political life of people?

Some of the migration distances are so long that it is amazing how many birds manage to fly, some at high altitudes, and many without stopping, to destinations thousands of miles away—without a compass! "Think of the Golden Plover," writes Arthur A. Allen, "that starts on a non-stop trip from Nova Scotia to northern South Africa or from Alaska to the Hawaiian Islands, distances over 2,500 miles, with only the fat stored up on their bodies to serve as fuel."[328] Up in James Bay, Canada, I was told by the Cree Indians that the Blue Geese make a nonstop flight from that area to Louisiana, their wintering grounds, thousands of miles away.

Let us go to New Guinea and observe the same behavior and process among savages. Peter Matthiessen, in his *Under the Mountain Wall,* relates the following about the *Kurelu* people: "A man without valor is *kepu*—a worthless man, a man-who-has-not-killed. The kepu men go to the war field with the rest, but they remain well to the rear. Some howl insults and brandish weapons from afar, but most are quiet and unobstructive, content to lend the deadwood of their weapons to the ranks. The kepu men are never jeered or driven into battle—no one must fight who does not choose to—but their position in the tribe may be determined by their comportment on the field. Unless they have strong friends or family, any wives or pigs they may obtain will be taken from them by other men, in the confidence that they will not resist; few kepu men have more than a single wife, and many of them have none."[329] Is there not a familiar ring of this in the life experiences of the more civilized, in London, Paris, Rome, or New York? Do we not find this behavior and mode expressed in the relationships between nations and in the rise and fall of tidal diplomacy among smaller or weaker nations and the larger or stronger ones? The pecker-and-the-pecked trait transcends them all, and can be traced back to the primeval struggle of individual things to exist. It is rooted in the common experiences of living things and is lowly imbedded in the core of the animal ego that wants to *be* no matter what.

Is there a social drive in animals as there is in people? Is there a group behavior for the protection of all the members of the group, as among human groups? The various studies concerned with animal behavior and the nature of animal society affirm that there definitely is, and that it is very often much stronger and abiding than with humans. "When the behavior of such animals as cockroaches, fishes, birds and rats shows evidence of distinct modification as a result of more than one being present, we have another suggestion that there exists a broad substratum of partially social behavior. There are many indications that this extends through the whole animal kingdom."[330] "The densely packed communities of animals on a wharf piling can persist only if toleration for crowding is well developed."[331] Roedelberger and Groschoff write of the *Processionary* Caterpillars: "In the evenings they emerge in a long column and wind through the branches in order to feed on the succulent pine needles. During this march the leader spins an endless thread out of its body fat which is constantly being strengthened by the other caterpillars, so that later on they can find their way back to the nest by following the thread."[332]

Do animals express, make, and enjoy love as people do? The human female is not alone of her kind in using perfume or scent to lure her male; many animals and insects do the same. The deer and antelope have their *musk;* the beaver, *castoreum,* and the skunks use *sulphide* as a love lure. The elephants have theirs, the amatory potion being located in a little gland in the head. The list is too long to enumerate here. "Scents are used as aphrodisiacs by a large number of animals. Both males and females perfume themselves to attract the other sex and to increase sexual excitement. Among the favorite aphrodisias scents is musk. It is produced at mating time by alligators, musk drakes, musk rats, musk oxen, musk deer, and even by several turtles, beetles, snails, and squid."[333]

In the natural world of animals and insects, the sex drive of love, of companionship, is a clean and normal event as other animal experiences. "Except for tiny animalcules and primitive hermaphrodites, all animals engage in specifically sexual relationships. Male lies with female; amatory and reproductive impulses are aroused; sperm makes contact with ovum to fertilize it. The kingdom of animals, as we have seen, runs a great gamut. The gamut of love is nearly co-extensive."[334] Listen about the beautiful "honeymoon" of the egrets: "For days the two egrets are always together. By the hour they perch motionless, the female on a twig just below her mate's, her head pressed against his flanks. Every so often, as quiet delight surges into ecstasy, both birds raise their wings, stretch up their long necks, and then with an outburst of love-cries intertwine their necks together. The egrets' necks are so long and supple that each of them actually makes a complete turn around the other. The birds are locked together in a true lover's knot. Then each of them takes the fine plumes of the other in its beak, and nibbles them lovingly, giving each plume a long sliding 'kiss' from its base to its tip. As the egrets' love-play subsides they untwine their necks and relapse once more into their sharing of a quiet happiness; side by side, always touching one another. The honeymoon of the egrets often lasts as long as four or five days."[335] And the waxwing bird: "When waxwings are in love, the little birds caress each other tenderly, rub their beaks together after each separation of even a few minutes, and when building up to their final intimacy often spend long periods side by side on a twig, passing a ripe berry or small fruit back and forth from mouth to mouth."[336]

When it comes to hugging and kissing, there is really nothing like the *Douroucoulis,* the nocturnal monkeys of South America. Humans can take lessons from their affectionate nature; they are the gentlest of the monkeys and "they spend a lot of time clasped in each other's arms exchanging the most human kisses."[337] Describing the love life of Japanese monkeys, Denzaburo Miyadi relates: "There is also 'proposing.' A male advances toward an estrous female with a dancing gait, lips protruding and opening

and closing rhythmically. Then, together the two monkeys leave
the troop for a short time. Such rhythmic lip movement is a
sign of affection; it is also quite common among young females.
The function of behavior and gestures of this kind is one-to-one
communication, not unlike speech between individual human
beings."[338] Jean-Pierre Hallet: "Anyone who has ever seen chimpanzees hugging, patting each other tenderly on back or shoulder,
holding hands, or kissing mouth to mouth with their large sensitive lips, cannot doubt or deny that they know the spirit and the
ways of love."[339] Describing the preplay and the sex act of seals
in Patagonia, Gerald Durrell relates: "The whole act had been
beautiful to watch, and was a lesson in restrained lovemaking
which a lot of human beings would do well to emulate."[340] As
for elephants, "they caress and fondle one another with their
trunks in a most intimate way and they even put tit-bits into each
other's mouths. Devoted couples stand face to face with inter-
twining trunks occasionally bringing the tips together in a way
which is difficult not to describe as kissing. . . . And when they
walk the bull follows closely behind the cow brushing her back
gently with his trunk."[341]

Does the animal female play at romance like human females do?
"The doe uses coquetry, pretending to run away in alarm, stopping and looking back at the buck, timidly returning to just
beyond his reach."[342] "A female monkey will scramble for a bit
of fruit, seize it, then discover bearing down on her the outraged
dominant male to whom the food by all monkey law belongs. She
will promptly present her behind to him in an effort to keep him
otherwise occupied, or at least distracted, while she devours the
fruit."[343] "Highly emotional at all times, the chimpanzee habitually and spontaneously expresses affection by the very human
mediums of kissing and hugging."[344] "The fire of love burns all
through the creation, now bright in passion, now a steady flame of
quiet happiness. It is more than just sex. A pair of old apes, long
past days of passion, will sit by the hour with their arms around
each other, petting, comforting, in the quiet joy of togetherness.
A gander, while his mate broods her eggs, will lie patiently with
his long neck stretched protectively across her back. Love is a
fire of many degrees, at which all animals may warm themselves,

after their fashions. It is the central fire of life itself, and it's what makes the world go round."[345]

And yet, as in human society in many places, where legally monogamous and institutionalized marriage does not exist, we find in animals the same promiscuity and random mating as prevalent among humans. The mating habit of the *Boattail Grackle* is just one example: "At mating time the males gather on tops of shrubs around a slough and go through a fascinating display. The females come in, pick and choose, mate promiscuously, and then go off to make their nests."[346] Human primitives today behave in practically the same way.

Do animals break their own moral codes? Hardly ever. But humans do, and often. A wise man has said: "As the sense of fun is not exclusively ours, nor the gift of intelligence, neither is the moral law. What is exclusively ours is that we can elect to break it."[347] And how we do!

All the funny little episodes of human behavior, habit, and experience find their counterparts in the animal world. Animaldom has its merriment, its little good-humored trickeries, conniveries, innovations, as well as its violent, sad, and tragic events, just as in the human world. "Playing possum" is an old trick of the alert soldier when he finds himself overwhelmed by the enemy, and many a woman, as a last resort to protect herself, has fainted away in the very arms of the intruder. All these things express and exhibit forms of voluntary actions, which, in the nature of movement and decision, can be accepted as modes of freedom. Animals show glee and deep satisfaction, melancholy, loneliness, become depressed, introverted and extraverted, just as people do. Humans turn black in the tropics. Weasels, like rabbits, turn white when it gets cold and the snow falls, and turn brown when it comes springtime. Humans cannot change color as rapidly and as often as many types of animals, but if they do not change the color of their skins, they most certainly can change quickly enough to save their skins.

Animals play games and crows even play jokes on their fellow-crows. "No animal can appreciate a joke that requires understanding of principles; but crows can, in a precisely accurate phrase, *see* a joke. They can relish the upsetting of the sense-familiar

world. A Cornell ornithologist has recorded the huge and raucous
delight of his pet crow when the children's seesaw would suddenly
get out of balance, tumbling one of the teeterers to the ground."[348]
Playing and joking are not relegated solely to the land animals;
they also occur in the sea. Professor Slijper tells us again about
porpoises: "Dolphins will fetch stones and other objects for you,
and even bring up stones from the bottom of the tank to spit
them with great accuracy at bystanders. One of them is reported
to have taken an instant dislike to Roman Catholic priests, spit-
ting stones at them the moment they approached."[349]

The amazing friendships and playfulness of porpoises are almost unbelievable but they are true, considering that they have
been proven by experiment and observation. The porpoise is so
intelligent that it can be taught to *understand* language and cultivate conversation. "Dolphins in their natural state can also make
friends with man. Thus, the dolphin which died on Opononi
Beach near Auckland (New Zealand) had been the playmate of
children and adults for many years. Opo or Opononi George,
as they called him, allowed the children to ride on his back and
played ball with them. Similarly, Lamb (1954) described the
antics of an Amazonian Boutu which assisted fishermen by driving fish from deep into shallow water. It responded to the men's
whistles and would spend hours in the vicinity of the boat. A
third example of man's close contact with wild dolphins was
cited by Captain Mörzer Bruins, who reported that in the Bay
of Dakar, Bottlenose Dolphins habitually mingle with the bath-
ers, and often try to snatch fish from skin divers."[350] This should
make people proud that they *are* related to the dolphins.

SUMMATION

THUS WE HAVE surveyed, in a brief and sketchy fashion, our
animal heritage and a few similarities, variances, and relationships of creatures in living experience. We have done this to
affirm not merely our animal heritage but to make us more aware
of and to understand more deeply its *natural* freedom that is at
the foundation of the organic household, and from which *all*

forms of freedom arose and to which all things are "freely" tied. This is not a new idea, nor is it a novel discovery; but it is good, after thousands of years of culture and civilization, to remind ourselves of this heritage, and what it means, and how it is affected when intermixed and so often coagulated with the porridges and potions of modern cultural times. It is good that the true ingredients of freedom be exposed again and again to our sensitivities and to our minds. Is it because, whenever man and woman and child rebelled, it was the subconscious or unconscious drive of the human animal to regain, repossess, re-express, and relive the simple and natural elements of freedom that the nature of the animal and the human animal crave and *affirmatively want?*

Perhaps, in acquiring culture and civilization, man has become less aware of freedom and, therefore, less aware of life itself, as he has become more and more molded to the cultural patterns, indoctrinations, concepts, and regimentations of succeeding historical periods, gradually to reach the forced sedentariness of modern urban existence. Man has become, still more, a nonliving, existing *anxiety-continuum,* moving with increasing limitation within a periphery of increasing boredom. He has become a product for uses, methods, systems, ideologies—part of some total sum of some economic data in some locality. The other animals live, and with all their shortcomings, privations, constraints for extension, accidents, and constant struggles to be, they still automatically and nature-protectively *live in being.* From this natural awareness of life we have strayed too far, and we have ingeniously created for ourselves growing, complex situations, in which this sense of being is withering away, as our products, as we ourselves, are becoming larger and more dangerous. With all we have, with all our intellectuality, with all our cultures, we are the most bored animals on earth, and the most self-enslaved slaves. We have covered and surrounded ourselves with so many diverse anti-natural man-made *somas* as to result in rational pandemonium, intellectual futility, and social confusion. We are losing our sense of being, which is another way of describing our loss of natural freedom. Our biological wants have been gradually degenerated by obscurantisms, by metaphysical meanderings, and by lethargic theologies. The wants to realize a normalcy of desire and satisfaction of life have been twisted and contorted into machine-like ingenuities that are artificial. We have become entangled in the whirl of producing systems and their economically, politically disastrous directions. If man has still the chance of saving himself, he must regain his humanity. He must return to his humanness. He must become aware that he *is* human—and not a gadget or a number. To do so, he must realize, by the very power of thought and introspection, his more natural and animal bearings.

With some awareness of this natural heritage of freedom, let us now proceed into the world of man starting when man began his departure from this heritage, while the animals in the woods, in spite of the trap and hunter; the birds in the air and the fish in the waters, in spite of the poisons and pollutions that man spreads over their homes and pathways—these still persist in expressing their freedom as *living* things *living* that freedom, *nobly*.

REFERENCES—BOOK TWO

1. George Gaylord Simpson, *This View of Life*, pp. 98-9, 107.
2. Margaret Mead, *Continuities in Cultural Evolution*, p. 30.
3. Kaj Birket-Smith, *The Paths of Culture*, p. 4.
4. René Dubos, *Humanistic Biology*, American Scholar, vol. 34, no. 2, p. 187.
5. Hudson Hoagland, *Science and the New Humanism*, Science Magazine, vol. 143, no. 3602, Jan. 10, 1964, p. 114.
6. Carleton Ray and Elgin Ciampi, *Marine Life*, pp. 26-7.
7. Heinz Heck, *The Future of Animals*, from "The Survival of the Free," p. 4.
8. William J. Cromie, *The Living World of the Sea*, p. 13.
9. *Ibid.*, p. 332.
10. David B. Ericson and Goesta Wollin, *The Ever-Changing Sea*, pp. 119-120.
11. Harry L. Shapiro, *Human Beginnings*, from "Man, Culture and Society," ed. Harry L. Shapiro, p. 4.
12. Sir MacFarlane Burnet, *Natural History of Infectious Diseases*, p. 29.
13. C. P. Idyll, *Abyss, The Deep Sea and the Creatures that Live in It*, p. 3.
14. New York Times, Sept. 5, 1967.
15. Theodosius Dobzhansky, *Mankind Evolving*, pp. 214-5.
16. Joseph K. Hart, *Inside Experience*, p. 111.
17. Clyde Kluckhohn, *Mirror for Man*, p. 125.
18. Fred Hoyle, *Can We Learn from Other Planets?*, Saturday Review, Nov. 7, 1964.
19. Desmond Morris, *The Naked Ape*, p. 39.
20. Robert Ardrey, *The Territorial Imperative*, p. 7.
21. F. W. Headley, *Problems of Evolution*, p. 295.
22. Henry E. Crampton, *The Coming and Evolution of Life*, p. 6.

23. Kenneth Norris, Sat. Eve. Post, Jan. 4, 1964.
24. George Gaylord Simpson, *This View of Life*, p. 39.
25. Kaj Birket-Smith, *The Paths of Culture*, p. 24.
26. René Dubos, *Humanistic Biology*, American Scholar, vol. 34, no. 2, p. 188.
27. see *The Territorial Imperative*, Ardrey, p. 101.
28. *Ibid.*, p. 102.
29. Roger A. Caras, *Last Chance on Earth*, preface viii.
30. Desmond Morris, *The Naked Ape*, p. 224.
31. V. G. Dethier, *Microscopic Brains*, Science Magazine, vol. 143, no. 3611, Mar. 13, 1964, p. 1138.
32. Elie Metchnikoff, *The Nature of Man*, p. 40.
33. Robert Ardrey, *African Genesis*, p. 13.
34. George Gaylord Simpson, *The Meaning of Evolution*, Terry Foundation Lecture Series; see *From Fish to Philosopher*, Homer W. Smith, pp. 175-6.
35. George Gaylord Simpson, *This View of Life*, preface viii.
36. *Ibid.*, p. 4.
37. Brand Blanshard, *Heritage of Idealism*, from "Changing Patterns in American Civilization," p. 94.
38. George Santayana, *The Letters of George Santayana*, ed. Daniel Dory, p. 408.
39. Harry A. Overstreet, *The Enduring Quest*, p. 77.
40. Allan C. Fisher, Jr., National Geographic Magazine, September, 1958, p. 303.
41. George Gaylord Simpson, *The Nonprevalence of Humanoids*, Science Magazine, vol. 143, no. 3608, Feb. 21, 1964, p. 771.
42. Fridtjof Nansen, *Living Philosophies*, p. 95.
43. L. S. B. Leakey, *Adam's Ancestors*, p. 228.
44. Allan Devoe, *This Fascinating Animal World*, p. 5.
45. Edmund W. Sinnott, *The Bridge of Life*, pp. 22 and 90.
46. Peter Zollinger, *The Political Creature*, p. 29.
47. A. Ingelman-Sundberg, *A Child is Born*, p. 50.
48. James B. Conant, *Man Thinking About Man*, American Scholar, vol. 33, no. 4, Autumn, 1964, p. 541.
49. René Dubos, *Humanistic Biology*, American Scholar, vol. 33, no. 2, p. 194.
50. Fred S. Hulse, *The Human Species*, p. 11.
51. Robert Evans Snodgrass, *Insects, Their Ways and Means of Living*, preface iii.
52. Richard A. Yarnell, Science Magazine, vol. 143, no. 3611, Mar. 13, 1964, p. 1121.
53. J. H. Denison, *This Human Nature*, p. 400.
54. Albert Einstein, *The World as I see It*, p. 24.
55. Donald Culross Peattie, *This is Living*.
56. Kessler *Memoirs*, St. Petersburg Society of Naturalists, vol. XI, 1880.
57. W. C. Allee, *The Social Life of Animals*, p. 47.
58. Gerhard Gronefeld, *Understanding Animals*, p. 16.
59. Robert Evans Snodgrass, *Insects, Their Ways and Means of Living*, p. 314.
60. Theodosius Dobzhansky, *Mankind Evolving*, p. 128.
61. George Santayana, *Reason in Common Sense*, vol. I, "Life of Reason," p. 37.
62. Allan Devoe, *This Fascinating Animal World*, p. 24.
63. William C. Boyd, *Genetics and the Races of Man*, p. 4.
64. Theodosius Dobzhansky, *Mankind Evolving*, p. 21.
65. Robert Ardrey, *The Territorial Imperative*, p. 350.
66. Elie Metchnikoff, *The Nature of Man*, p. 137.
67. Allan Devoe, *This Fascinating Animal World*, p. 149.
68. Robert Ardrey, *African Genesis*, p. 112.
69. John Paul Scott, *Animal Behavior*, Am. Mus. of Natural History Series, p. 159.
70. Charles Duff, *This Human Nature*, p. 20.

71. Irenäus Eibl-Eibesfeldt, *Land of a Thousand Atolls*, pp. 69-70.
72. E. W. McBride, *Evolution*, p. 108.
73. Theodosius Dobzhansky, *Mankind Evolving*, p. 287.
74. *Ibid.*, p. 5.
75. Richard Carrington, *A Biography of the Sea*, p. 158.
76. Herbert Wendt, *The Sexual Life of the Animals*, p. 120.
77. William J. Cromie, *Exploring the Secrets of the Sea*, p. 30.
78. William J. Cromie, *The Living World of the Sea*, pp. 13-4.
79. Harry A. Overstreet, *The Enduring Quest*, p. 48.
80. William C. Boyd, *Genetics and the Races of Man*, preface xiii.
81. Roy Pinney, *Vanishing Wildlife*, p. vii.
82. *Ibid.*, p. 126.
83. Rachel L. Carson, *Silent Spring*, pp. 220-1.
84. *Ibid.*, p. 241.
85. Pat McGrady, *The Savage Cell*, pp. 31-2.
86. *Ibid.*, p. 54.
87. W. Phillip Keller, *Under Wilderness Skies*, pp. 159-160.
88. René Dubos, *So Human An Animal*, pp. 4-5.
89. Andreas Feininger, *Forms of Nature and Life*, p. 16.
90. Edward F. Ricketts and Jack Calvin, *Between Pacific Tides*, pp. 450-1.
91. Roger A. Caras, *Last Chance on Earth*, preface ix.
92. Kaj Birket-Smith, *The Paths of Culture*, p. 28.
93. Albert Schweitzer, *The Schweitzer Album*, ed. Erica Anderson, p. 161.
94. Royston Clowes, *The Structure of Life*, pp. 15-6.
95 Leslie Reid, *Earth's Company*, pp. 13-4.
96. René Dubos, *So Human an Animal*, p. 27.
97. Frank Waters, *The Book of the Hopi*, pp. 208-9.
98. H. R. Hays, *In the Beginnings*, p. 443.
99. Richard A. Martin, *Mummies*, Chicago Natural History Museum, Anthropology, no. 36, p. 17.
100. George Gaylord Simpson, *This View of Life*, p. 4.
101. Heinz Heck, *The Future of Animals*, from "Survival of the Free," p. 13.
102. Allan Devoe, *This Fascinating Animal World*, p. 14.
103. *Ibid.*, p. 3.
104. Fred S. Hulse, *The Human Species*, p. 61.
105. Herbert Wendt, *The Sexual Life of the Animals*, p. 78.
106. F. D. Ommanney, *A Draught of Fishes*, pp. 42, 71.
107. Robert Briffault, *Rational Evolution*, p. 11.
108. Allan Devoe, *This Fascinating Animal World*, pp. 1-2.
109. D'Arcy Thompson, *On Growth and Form*, ed. J. T. Bonner, p. 327.
110. Gerhard Szczesny, *The Future of Unbelief*, p. 77.
111. Donald Culross Peattie, *Flowering Earth*.
112. Albert Schweitzer, *The Schweitzer Album*, ed. Erica Anderson, p. 47.
113. Jules H. Masserman, *The Biodynamic Roots of Psychoanalysis*, from "Modern Psychoanalysis," ed. Judd Marmor, pp. 194-5.
114. A. I. Oparin, *Origin of Life*, p. 246.
115. Allan Devoe, *This Fascinating Animal World*, p. 11.
116. Lewis Mumford, *Technics and the Nature of Man*, from "Knowledge Among Men," pp. 128-9.
117. Andreas Feininger, *Forms of Nature and Life*, p. 31.
118. Burkhardt, Schleidt, and Altner, *Signals in the Animal World*, p. 12.
119. Joy Adamson, *Born Free; Living Free; Forever Free*.
120. Fredric C. Appel, *The Intellectual Animal*, Sat. Eve. Post, Jan. 4, 1964.
121. Richard Perry, *The World of the Polar Bear*, pp. 12, 147.

122. see Science Magazine, Nov. 6, 1964, pp. 801-2; also National Geographic Magazine, August, 1963.
123. William Mason, *The Social Development of Monkeys and Apes,* from "Primate Behavior," ed. Irven DeVore, p. 542.
124. Sea Frontiers, Institute of Marine Sciences, Un. of Miami, vol. 14, no. 2, March-April, 1968, inside front cover.
125. Homer W. Smith, *From Fish to Philosopher,* p. 3.
126. Desmond Morris, *The Naked Ape,* p. 115.
127. Jules H. Masserman, *The Biodynamic Roots of Psychoanalysis,* from "Modern Psychoanalysis," ed. Judd Marmor, p. 199.
128. Harold E. Burtt, *The Psychology of Birds,* p. 147.
129. S. H. Skaife, *Dwellers in Darkness,* p. 131.
130. Franz A. Roedelberger and Vera Groschoff, *The Wonders of Wildlife,* p. 97.
131. Allan Devoe, *This Fascinating Animal World,* p. 117.
132. Joseph K. Hart, *Inside Experience,* p. 225.
133. Robert Ardrey, *African Genesis,* p. 345.
134. Rachel L. Carson, *Silent Spring,* p. 85.
135. Sir MacFarlane Burnet, *Natural History of Infectious Diseases,* p. 372.
136. Bernhard and Michael Grzimek, *Serengati Shall Not Die,* p. 70.
137. Mervyn Cowie, *The African Lion,* pp. 13-4.
138. David Kenyon Webster, *Myth and Maneater, The Story of the Shark,* pp. 21-2.
139. Hartmut Bastian, *And Then Came Man,* p. 229.
140. William O. Douglas, *My Wilderness: East to Katahdin,* p. 46.
141. *Ibid.,* p. 53.
142. *Ibid.,* p. 59.
143. Roy Pinney, *Vanishing Wildlife,* pp. vii-viii.
144. *Ibid.,* p. viii.
145. see *Never Cry Wolf,* Farley Mowatt.
146. George B. Schaller, *The Year of the Gorilla,* p. 103.
147. Archibald MacLeish, *The Great American Frustration,* Saturday Review, July 13, 1968, p. 14.
148. see Science section, Time Magazine, Sept. 14, 1962.
149. Dave Mech, *The Wolf,* National Wildlife Magazine, Feb.-Mar., 1968, p. 5.
150. Sterling North, *Who is Afraid of a Little Wolf?,* Defenders of Wildlife, Aug.-Sept., 1968, pp. 289-91.
151. Franz A. Roedelberger and Vera Groschoff, *The Wonders of Wildlife,* p. 29.
152. Roy Pinney, *Vanishing Wildlife,* p. 9.
153. *Ibid.,* p. 10.
154. H. R. H. Prince Bernhard of the Netherlands, *Vanishing Wildlife,* Pinney, p. v.
155. Ian McTaggart Cowan, *Conservation and Man's Environment,* from "Knowledge Among Men," pp. 67, 71.
156. Roger A. Caras, *Last Chance on Earth,* p. 144.
157. *Ibid.,* p. 170.
158. Roy Pinney, *Vanishing Wildlife,* p. 85.
159. Robert Silverberg, *The Auk, The Dodo, and The Oryx,* p. 96.
160. Peter Lust, *The Last Seal Pup,* pp. 129-31.
161. Gavin Maxwell, *Seals of the World,* pp. 14 and 16.
162. Virginia Federation of Humane Societies, Arlington, Va., Bulletin, May, 1963.
163. Robert Gesell, *Annals of Allergy,* Mar.-Apr., 1953.
164. Albert Schweitzer, *The Schwetizer Album,* ed. Erica Anderson, p. 49.
165. Robert Silverberg, *The Auk, The Dodo, and The Oryx,* p. 21.
166. *Ibid.,* p. 227.
167. Anthony Storr, *Human Aggression,* p. 22.
168. Joy Adamson, *Living Free,* p. 136.

169. Heinz Heck, *The Future of Animals,* from "Survival of the Free," pp. **7, 11.**
170. Aldo Leopold, *Defenders of Wildlife,* vol. 40, no. 5, December, 1965.
171. Jack McCormack, *The Living Forest,* p. 14.
172. William O. Douglas, *My Wilderness: East to Katahdin,* pp. 154-5.
173. Sir MacFarlane Burnet, *Natural History of Infectious Diseases,* p. 31.
174. *Sea Secrets,* International Oceanographic Foundations, July, 1962.
175. Irenäus Eibl-Eibesfeldt, *Land of a Thousand Atolls,* pp. 64.5.
176. *Ibid.,* p. 66.
177. see *Whales,* Slijper, p. 89.
178. Donald Culross Peattie, *Flowering Earth,* p. 246.
179. Harold E. Burtt, *The Psychology of Birds,* pp. 153-4.
180. E. Yale Dawson, *The Giants of Galapagos,* Natural History Magazine, November, 1962, p. 54.
181. Allan Devoe, *This Fascinating Animal World,* p. 102.
182. H. R. Hays, *From Ape to Angel,* p. 392.
183. Allan Devoe, *This Fascinating Animal World,* p. 102.
184. see *Wonders of Wildlife,* Roedelberger and Groschoff, pp. 202-3.
185. W. C. Allee, *The Social Life of Animals,* p. 49.
186. E. J. Slijper, *Whales,* p. 193.
187. Franz A. Roedelberger and Vera Groschoff, *The Wonders of Wildlife,* p. 83.
188. Harold E. Burtt, *The Psychology of Birds,* p. 143.
189. Theodosius Dobzhansky, *Mankind Evolving,* p. 167.
190. Paul Edwards, *Hard and Soft Determinism,* from "Determinism and Freedom," ed. Sidney Hook, p. 121.
191. Clifford, *Lectures and Essays,* vol. I, p. 82.
192. Auguste Forel, *The Social World of the Ants,* vol. II, p. 317.
193. Sir MacFarlane Burnet, *Natural History of Infectious Diseases,* p. 30.
194. Junichuro Itani, quoted in *The Marvelous Monkeys of Japan,* Christopher Lucas, The Reader's Digest, November, 1968, p. 123.
195. Richard Carrington, *A Biography of the Sea,* p. 183.
196. Albert Schweitzer, *The Schweitzer Album,* ed. Erica Anderson, p. 42.
197. C. P. Idyll, *Abyss, The Deep Sea and the Creatures that Live in It,* p. 105.
198. Kenneth Norris, U.C.L.A., Zoology Dept.
199. see *The Story of Jambo,* Ernest M. Lang, National Geographic Magazine, vol. 125, no. 3, March, 1964, pp. 446-453.
200. John Langdon-Davies, *A Short History of Women,* p. 170.
201. Pedro Ramirez Vazquez, *Mexico,* pp. 108-9.
202. Ralph de Pomerai, *Marriage,* p. 6.
203. Allan Devoe, *This Fascinating Animal World,* p. 70.
204. *Ibid.,* p. 70.
205. Jacquetta Hawkes and Sir Leonard Woolley, *Prehistory and the Beginnings of Civilization,* vol. I, "The History of Mankind," p. 129.
206. Richard Perry, *The World of the Polar Bear,* p. 18.
207. Homer W. Smith, *From Fish to Philosopher,* pp. 12-3.
208. George Gaylord Simpson, *The Crisis in Biology,* American Scholar, Summer, 1967, p. 369.
209. Ronald Singer, *Emerging Man in Africa,* Natural History Magazine, November, 1962, p. 18.
210. Allan Devoe, *This Fascinating Animal World,* p. 110.
211. see *Marine Life,* Ray and Ciampi, p. 77.
212. see *The World of Plant Life,* Hylander, p. 13.
213. Roy Waldo Miner, *Fragile Creatures of the Deep, The Story of the Hydroids,* Natural History Magazine, vol. XLII, no. 4, p. 245.
214. C. J. Hylander, *The World of Plant Life,* p. 4.
215. *Ibid.,* p. 5.

216. N. J. Berrill, *The Living Tide*, p. 175.

217. see *Abyss, The Deep Sea and the Creatures that Live in It*, C. P. Idyll, p. 237.

218. C. Stuart Gager, *The Plant World*, University Series, 1st Unit, Part III, p. 3.

219. see *Nematode-Trapping Fungi*, David Pramer, Science Magazine, vol. 144, no. 3517, Apr. 24, 1964.

220. Jaghadis Chundar Bose, Bose Institute, Calcutta, India.

221. William O. Douglas, *My Wilderness: East to Katahdin*, p. 46.

222. Thorn Bacon, on *Cleve Backster*, National Wildlife Magazine, Feb.-Mar., 1969, pp. 5-8.

223. Henry E. Crampton, *The Coming and Evolution of Life*, p. 76.

224. C. J. Hylander, *The World of Plant Life*, p. 1.

225. Theodosius Dobzhansky, *Mankind Evolving*, p. 203.

226. *Ibid.*, p. 165.

227. William K. Gregory, *Introduction to Human Anatomy*, Am. Mus. of Natural History, Series 86, p. 4.

228. William J. Cromie, *The Living World of the Sea*, p. 72.

229. N. J. Berrill, quoted in *The Kingdom of the Octopus*, Lane, p. 72.

230. Frank W. Lane, *The Kingdom of the Octopus*, p. 72.

231. Gerhard Szczesny, *The Future of Unbelief*, p. 147.

232. John Dewey, *Art as Experience*.

233. see *The Whispering Land*, Durrell, pp. 56-8.

234. Hu Shih, *Living Philosophies*, p. 261.

235. Robert Ardrey, *African Genesis*, p. 32.

236. Hartmut Bastian, *And Then Came Man*, pp. 224-5.

237. see *Marine Life*, Ray and Ciampi, p. 86.

238. see *This Fascinating Animal World*, Devoe, p. 4.

239. Hartmut Bastian, *And Then Came Man*, p. 256.

240. E. A. Hooton, *Apes, Men and Morons*, p. 48.

241. Fay-Cooper Cole, *Man*, from "The World and Man as Science Sees Them," ed. F. R. Moulton, p. 487.

242. William J. Cromie, *The Living World of the Sea*, pp. 29-30.

243. G. H. F. Nuttall, Cambridge University, Eng.

244. S. Zuckerman, *Functional Affinities of Man, Monkeys and Apes*, p. 53.

245. *Ibid.*, pp. 56-7.

246. Bernard Grzimek, *Such Agreeable Friends*, pp. 29-30.

247. Theodosius Dobzhansky, *Mankind Evolving*, p. 163.

248. *Ibid.*, p. 164.

249. *Ibid.*, p. 166.

250. George Gaylord Simpson, *This View of Life*, pp. 12-3.

251. Jacquetta Hawkes and Sir Leonard Woolley, *Prehistory and the Beginnings of Civilization*, vol. I, "The History of Mankind," p. 4.

252. *Ibid.*, p. 34.

253. Harry Hoijer, *Language and Writing*, from "Man, Culture and Society," ed. Harry L. Shapiro, p. 197.

254. Robert Ardrey, *African Genesis*, p. 28.

255. Jacquetta Hawkes and Sir Leonard Woolley, *Prehistory and the Beginnings of Civilization*, vol. I, "The History of Mankind," p. 6.

256. H. R. Hays, *In the Beginnings*, p. 269.

257. Bernard Campbell, *Human Evolution*, p. 56.

258. *Ibid.*, p. 28.

259. *Ibid.*, p. 27.

260. see *Human Beginnings*, Harry L. Shapiro, from "Man, Culture and Society," pp. 6, 8.

261. Jerome S. Bruner, *The Perfectibility of Intellect*, from "Knowledge Among Men," p. 19.

262. Mark Graubard, *Man the Slave and Master*, pp. 27-8.
263. Harry A. Overstreet, *The Enduring Quest*, pp. 82-3.
264. Anton J. Carlson, *Physiological Processes*, from "The World and Man as Science Sees Them," ed. F. R. Moulton, p. 403.
265. Margaret Mead, *Continuities in Cultural Evolution*, p. 82.
266. R. W. G. Hingston, *Instinct and Intelligence*, p. 184.
267. Adam Sedgwick, *Mysteries of Natural Science*, ed. E. L. Grant Watson, p. 229.
268. Edwin Way Teale, *Strange Lives of Familiar Insects*, p. 77.
269. E. P. Evans, *Evolutional Ethics and Animal Psychology*, p. 285.
270. Allan Devoe, *This Fascinating Animal World*, p. 163.
271. Charles Darwin, *Descent of Man*, 2nd ed., p. 54.
272. Julian Huxley, *Ants*, p. 10.
273. Maeterlinck, quoted in *Dwellers in Darkness*, S. H. Skaife, p. 162.
274. S. H. Skaife, *Dwellers in Darkness*, p. 47.
275. Lorus and Margery Milne, *The Senses of Animals and Men*, pp. 273-4.
276. Elie Metchnikoff, *The Nature of Man*, p. 268.
277. Max Muller, quoted in *From Ape to Angel*, Hays, p. 76.
278. Lewis Mumford, *Technics and the Nature of Man*, from "Knowledge Among Men," pp. 131-2.
279. Lewis Mumford, *The Myth of the Machine*, p. 61.
280. *Ibid.*, p. 62.
281. Harry Hoijer, *Language and Writing*, from "Man, Culture and Society," ed. Harry L. Shapiro, p. 203.
282. Brand Blanshard, *The Case for Determinism*, from "Determinism and Freedom," ed. Sidney Hook, p. 27.
283. Harry Hoijer, *Language and Writing*, from "Man, Culture and Society," ed. Harry L. Shapiro, p. 201.
284. Allan Devoe, *This Fascinating Animal World*, p. 87.
285. Theodosius Dobzhansky, *Mankind Evolving*, p. 211.
286. Harold E. Burtt, *The Psychology of Birds*, p. 159.
287. Arthur A. Allen, *The Book of Bird Life*, 2nd ed., p. 157.
288. *Ibid.*, pp. 151-2.
289. Peter Marler, *Communication in Monkeys and Apes*, from "Primate Behavior," ed. Irven DeVore, p. 584.
290. Jarvis Bastian, *Primate Signaling Systems and Human Languages*, from "Primate Behavior," ed. Irven DeVore, p. 590.
291. Burkhardt, Schleidt, and Altner, *Signals in the Animal World*, p. 14.
292. Joel Carl Welty, *The Life of Birds*, p. 181.
293. Adolf Portmann, *Animals as Social Beings*, p. 70.
294. *Ibid.*, p. 75.
295. *Ibid.*, p. 79.
296. *Ibid.*, p. 231.
297. E. J. Slijper, *Whales*, p. 195.
298. see Natural History Magazine, January, 1940.
299. Irenäus Eibl-Eibesfeldt, *Land of a Thousand Atolls*, p. 68.
300. see *Mankind Evolving*, Dobzhansky, p. 210.
301. H. R. Hays, *From Ape to Angel*, p. 216.
302. Lorus and Margery Milne, *The Senses of Animals and Men*, p. 7.
303. Joel Carl Welty, *The Life of Birds*, p. 176.
304. Vernon Reynolds, *The Apes*, pp. 20, 267.
305. Rosl Kirchchofer, *The World of Zoos*, p. 29.
306. see *Apes and Monkeys*, E. G. Boulenger.
307. *Ibid.*, p. 54.
308. H. R. Hays, *In the Beginnings*, p. 41.
309. Gerald Durrell, *A Zoo in my Luggage*, pp. 83-88.

310. Arthur A. Allen, *The Book of Bird Life*, 2nd ed., p. 162.
311. *Ibid.*, p. 163.
312. Edwin Way Teale, *Strange Lives of Familiar Insects*, p. 40.
313. see photos by Leonard E. Rue III, Natural History Magazine, June-July, 1964.
314. Lorus and Margery Milne, *The Senses of Animals and Men*, p. 119.
315. *Ibid.*, p. 120.
316. *Ibid.*, p. 133.
317. Edwin Way Teale, *Strange Lives of Familiar Insects*, pp. 32-3.
318. *Ibid.*, p. 23.
319. *Ibid.*, p. 27.
320. *Ibid.*, pp. 18-22.
321. see *After the Seventh Day, Calder*, pp. 31-2.
322. Joy Adamson, *Living Free*, pp. 140-1.
323. Allan Devoe, *This Fascinating Animal World*, p. 37.
324. Arthur A. Allen, *The Book of Bird Life*, 2nd ed., p. 152.
325. Robert Ardrey, *African Genesis*, p. 91.
326. *Ibid.*, pp. 108-9.
327. Arthur A. Allen, *The Book of Bird Life*, 2nd ed., p. 151.
328. *Ibid.*, p. 201.
329. Peter Matthiessen, *Under the Mountain Wall*, p. 15.
330. W. C. Allee, *Social Life of Animals*, pp. 173-4.
331. *Ibid.*, p. 43.
332. Franz A. Roedelberger and Vera Groschoff, *The Wonders of Wildlife*, p. 166.
333. Herbert Wendt, *The Sexual Life of the Animals*, p. 133.
334. Allan Devoe, *This Fascinating Animal World*, p. 16.
335. *Ibid.*, pp. 20-1.
336. *Ibid.*, p. 19.
337. Gerald Durrell, *The Whispering Land*, p. 202.
338. Denzaburo Miyadi, *Social Life of Japanese Monkeys*, Science Magazine, vol. 143, no. 3608, Feb. 21, 1964, pp. 784-5.
339. Jean-Pierre Hallet, *Animal Kitabu*, p. 241.
340. Gerald Durrell, *The Whispering Land*, p. 83.
341. Rennie Bere, *The African Elephant*, p. 49.
342. Allan Devoe, *This Fascinating Animal World*, p. 21.
343. Robert Ardrey, *African Genesis*, p. 136.
344. E. G. Boulenger, *Apes and Monkeys*, p. 62.
345. Allan Devoe, *This Fascinating Animal World*, p. 23.
346. William O. Douglas, *My Wilderness: East to Katahdin*, pp. 149-150.
347. Allan Devoe, *This Fascinating Animal World*, p. 167.
348. *Ibid.*, p. 165.
349. E. J. Slijper, *Whales*, p. 185.
350. *Ibid.*, pp. 182-3.

I am as free as nature first made man,
Ere the base laws of servitude began,
When wild in woods the noble savage ran.

—DRYDEN, *Conquest of Granada,* Act I, Sc. i

Man is born free; and everywhere he is in chains.
One thinks himself the master of others, and still
remains a greater slave than they.

—JEAN JACQUES ROUSSEAU

I pronounce all this to be a fish (a meat dinner which the Cardinal wanted to eat at a friend's house on Friday).

—Cardinal Wiseman

As long as men speak of God, they will also speak of me.

—Napoleon

BOOK THREE

THE RISE OF SOCIO-RELIGIOUS FORMS

THE RISE OF SOCIO-RELIGIOUS FORMS

THE NATURE OR instinct of gregariousness in an animal indicates an inherited or innate disposition, inclination, or tendency towards expressing sympathy, to be subject to suggestibility, to imitate, to cling, to avoid isolation, and feel less free when alone and more secure and free when with others of its own kind or similar kinds.[1] In the animal world, wherever the nature is gregarious, we have seen that there is a dominance of some individuals over others, perhaps the stronger, the more aggressive, the wiser, or the less fearful, and by this dominance and the submission of others to it, a sort of *status* society of assorted levels and variances creates itself, with the stronger at the top and the weaker and more fearful ones below. This serves the individual drives of the animals at the top, the submissiveness of those below, and protects the herd, troop, or colony, in the processes of natural selection and the specific survival of the species. Thus, nature, by its own struggles and trial-by-error experiences, brings about, as a result, certain survivals where it succeeds and certain extinctions where it fails, and many compromises and adjustments between these two extremes. In animal societies, where dominance and territory proclamations play an important role, the division of spoils, that is, food, mates, and emotional requisition, becomes the beneficence and reward, and the weakest and most lowly have little or none. Nature does its own weeding and raking in the processes of struggle and elimination: this is the story of evolution. "There can, I think," writes Robert Ardrey, "be no question but that territorial rights are established rights among the majority of species of animals. . . . In fact, it may be held that the recognition of territorial rights, one of the most significant attributes of civilization, was not evolved by man but has ever been an inherent factor in the life history of all animals."[2]

Pride, a subtle expression of the ego not to give in to some dominance nor to surrender to it, becomes a psychological and

247

cultural vehicle by which an individual *strains* to keep his head high on some superficial level. It lends itself to no practical ends but to satisfy the inwardly-directed emotional and psychological tendency to sustain the ego, for the ego's sake, and to maintain this satisfaction of the ego for its own ends. This is one of the reasons that *man* came to make *God* in his own image. S. H. Skaife: "Man has been in existence as a social animal for less than one million years; ants, wasps and bees, for about seventy million years; and termites for something like two hundred million years."[3]

Human society could have started the same way, for the same principle expresses itself throughout nature and human history and into modern times. It applies to the sociological, the economic, the cultural, and religious, to the political, to the military. These are *all* forms of *biological* force, and *force,* in some form or other, expresses itself in all of them. Individuals and societies are the products of all this as *interflowing* and *interacting* forces; not as parallel or separate activities, but as arterial fretworks intermingled with, and attached to, each other, pulsating, growing or extending, shrinking or changing, forming or disappearing, outward identities of inward, unseen, bodily functions and products of the biological core, the physical, natural, and central nucleus which is both latent and expressed in the very spark of life.

Cassirer, Pavlov, and White brought out that "all human behavior originates in the use of symbols. It was the symbol which transformed our anthropoid ancestors into men and made them human."[4] *Language is symbology in sound,* as writing is graphic symbology. The first formalized art of writing a language is said to have been cultivated by the Sumerians. Music, sculpture, painting, and other forms of art are all symbolic expressions attempting to communicate, and any form of communication, at root, is basically an expression of biological force. Even mythology, when any attempt is made to analyze its origins, exposes the hard core of biological struggle of human animals to explain themselves and the world in which they struggle. Joseph Campbell: "Mythology was historically the mother of the arts. . . . Mythology is not invented rationally; mythology cannot be rationally understood. . . . A new and very promising approach is opened, however, when it is viewed in the light of biological psychology as a function of the human nervous system."[5] John Dewey: "An ideal is not an illusion because imagination is the organ through which it is apprehended. For *all* possibilities reach us through the imagination."[6] Yet we must bear in mind that the *ideal,* as well as the *imagination,* is not the only cause for continuums of thought and acting emanating therefrom, but the outgrowth of previous causes and effects rising out of the nature of a certain individual and his environment, the constant interacting play and flow of experience within it; that is, all things and all events are parts of, and operate upon and within, a natural base. H. R. Hays: "It must be remembered that individuals create mythology and these individuals may be, in the first place, merely good storytellers."[7] Gerhard Szczesny: "Imaginative thinking and inferring is characteristic of the early phase of all intellectual development."[8] Theodosius Dobzhansky: "The fact which must be stressed, because it has frequently been missed or misrepresented, is that the biological and cultural evolutions are parts of the same natural process."[9] Szczesny: "Even the 'gods,' if there were any, would be rooted, together with their divinity, in the human, the animal, the plantlife and the material. They would, in fact, be no more exclusively divine than man is exclusively human."[10] Hawkes and Woolley: "There can be no question, whatever construction we put upon them, that these mental and emotional inheritances which man received from the prehuman past were to provide a most potent force in the creation of culture."[11]

Man may call *this* sociological or *that* economic, or *that* religious or *this* political, or something else esthetic or moral or metaphysical, cultural, or what-not, but this is man's way of identifying segments or viewpoints of a process, the process of a body, a whole in which all of these are parts of its composition. Specialization of thought and effort in the various fields man has signified, in his own way, as identifiably different studies of man and the world, is a *natural* process and outcome of the growth of man and the extension of his intelligence within this growth, just as the modern sciences, in all their categories and classes, are the complexed outgrowth of the simplest tooling and grasping and think-

ing of the subhominid. James G. Frazer: "Our resemblances to
the savage are still far more numerous than our differences from
him; and what we have in common with him, and deliberately
retain as truth and useful, we owe to our savage-forefathers who
slowly acquired by experience and transmitted to us by inheritance those seemingly fundamental ideas which we are apt to
regard as original and intuitive."[12]

To engage in the attempt to understand the evolution of society, we may consider things from certain particularized or specialized viewpoints or studies, but we must *constantly* hold in
mind that all these things, social, religious, economic, political,
the arts, sciences, industries, and all their cultural products, are
in process simultaneously, interflowing and interacting as *a* process. They are the determinants of causes and effects within themselves as part of a central monistic entirety, a sort of monophony,
in which the potential and nature of sound identify themselves
in myriad vibrations of variance, tone, depth, and reception. All
these manifestations are not merely related; they are part and
parcel of each other, causing and effecting determinants and determinations that are the causes and effects of *a* process, the parts
forever tied to each other because *separately they cannot and do
not exist.* "Taking away the principle of causality from reality's
correlativeness leads only to self-contradiction. Everything that
dwells for a time in existence does so in relatedness and in a web
of necessity."[13] Only in this manner can we properly attempt to
dissect and analyze the structure and history of human society and
its meanings and values, if and when we can find any, to us as
individuals—to *you* and *me*. Read Bain: "Sociologists hold that
all social phenomena are conditioned by and organically related
to, the inorganic, organic and cultural environments. Changes in
any of these, whether produced by directed or undirected cultural
agencies or by non-human influences, will inevitably and drastically modify social phenomena."[14]

Esthetics and ethics are found only in the nature of freedom
when one is esthetic enough and ethical enough to be willing to
protect or retain it by sacrifice or rebellion, or to forego any part
of freedom to fulfill one's enjoyment or desire for compromise
or to attempt to bring about a fulfillment of what one senses or

judges to be enjoyable and just, acceptable or unacceptable, according to the viewpoint and drive of each and his kind of conscience. Edward B. Tylor: "So far as savage religion can stand as representing natural religion, the popular idea that the moral government of the universe is an essential tenet of natural religion simply falls to the ground. Savage animism is almost devoid of that ethical element which to the educated modern mind is the very mainspring of practical religion. . . . . The lower animism is not immoral, it is unmoral."[15] Arthur Koestler puts it in another way: "When reality becomes unbearable, the mind must withdraw from it and create a world of artificial perfection. Plato's world of pure Ideas and Forms, which alone is to be considered as real, whereas the world of nature which we perceive is merely its cheap Woolworth copy, is a flight into delusion."[16]

Esthetics and ethics are variables and variants, temporary or more or less permanently "imprinted," according to the nature and experiences of individuals and their desires and needs. The bare fact remains that the absolute necessity of law and its enforcement agencies indicates that if people were left to their own devices and depended solely on the ethics of human beings without law and its enforcement, the jungle of the "wild" animals would most probably be the safest place in the world. The rich can afford to allow themselves to be esthetic and ethical and yet usually are not; the poor might like to if they could, and many do in spite of poverty and pressure, but the pressing needs of daily existence, security, and the struggle to survive become overpowering and overwhelming processes that often helplessly dictate and condition the habits of the miserable. Jean Valjean felt it through the pen of Victor Hugo. In his brave little essay, "The Ground is Our Table," Steve Allen relates, in speaking of his own struggles in his youth: "I remember another time when, to speak plainly, hunger drove me to steal. I went into a grocery store in New Mexico with only enough change in my pocket to buy a loaf of bread. I paid for the bread but concealed a can of sardines in my pocket. Outside, I ducked around the corner, sat down on the sidewalk, opened the can with trembling hands, and stuffed myself with five or six sardine sandwiches. It is of enormous significance that hunger simply annihilated guilt."[17]

RECIPROCITY AND REPRISAL

THE FARTHER WE go back, the more we find, as compensatory processes in the nature of a living thing and its relationships with its environment, its food supply, its amenable neighbors and, its natural enemies, and the symbiotic chain of dependence and interdependence of its cycle, *reciprocity* and *reprisal*. The more we move to a higher state of the human animal, the more we find increased esthetic maturation in more individuals (this does not necessarily mean *civilized*) and a deeper and more unbiased sense of justice in a small but growing number of people. The great majority of humans, however, continue to live and think more or less according to the purer principles of primitivism, that is, to the basic, immediate needs of life. All individuals live out their lives today in some category between these two extremes, between more or less pure animalism and the robotismic product of civilization. Reciprocity and reprisal acted, and still act, on the principle of immediacy, depending on the nature of each animal or individual. Bernhard Grzimek: "Pastoral people, whether black or white, never consider the soil and its vegetation, they never think of the future. The barren hills of Italy, Spain and Greece, and the new deserts of India, are evidence of this."[18] Primitive people do not see the future, neither does civilized man. Erich Kahler: "The life of primitive man, like that of an animal, is a life of alertness and fear, a life that is essentially on the defensive. In his fear and defensiveness, primitive man is unable to make a distinction between the material and the immaterial, the visible and the invisible world, an animate or an inanimate object. What matters to him are only the present or potentially present sensations and effects he continually encounters."[19] George C. Valliant: "The Aztec thought of his gods as having strong material powers, but their spiritual aspect counted little with him."[20] What was important was the beneficence the gods could give him *now*, in this life, not later.

Goodwill is a word that did not exist except when it served the ends of one or both, and it is the same story today. Human nature has changed little in any basic sense. Beneath the refinements of people lay the needs of the animal to survive. So long as these needs are reasonably satisfied, the refinements continue to flourish. When this is not the case, the animal looks for relief. Thus, natural freedom asserts itself for survival and life sufficiency and satisfaction. Civilization, which generalizes the rise of increasing complexities and determinants of cultures, is the refining process of this natural freedom to adjust, adapt, limit, or extend itself within the requisites of the civilizing process and its ends. The great error, I think, of this process, in both the individual and his freedom, on the one hand, and the pressuring needs of organization and societal structure, on the other, is that it brought about, except in temporary cyclic rebellious periods of relief, a lessening or shrinking of the *personal* factor of each individual life and an increasing growth of the *impersonal* factor of organization, the forces of impelled collectivization of thought and habit, and the ensuing deterioration of the protective natural freedoms that are biologically and psychologically essential to a life normalcy of satisfaction. *Freedom is the constant process of Nature trying to remain natural.* So often freedom has become a football; where the goals are nobody seems to know, while kicking it around. Why and how these things came about is the attempt and object of this book.

SYMBOLOGY AND MAGIC IN PRIMITIVISM

James G. Frazer wrote: "The savages of today are primitive only in a relative, not in an absolute sense. They are primitive by comparison with us; but they are not primitive by comparison with truly primeval man, that is, with man as he was when he first emerged from the purely bestial stage of existence."[21] The evolution of man from animalism to animism is a long gathering mechanism of experience, a long stretch of thousands of generations of humans, during which the constant continuums of experience in the interaction and interdependence of man and his environment brought out, habituated, and functionalized new thought, new ideas, multiple and related ideas, new practical ends. This *cumulative* index prepared the savage more and more for the eventually determined road to more complex ideas, in which reason asserted itself increasingly, and which, in turn, paved the way for the primitive sciences. These primitive sciences gradually *idea-ed* through experience, upon which alone they could be based, into two principal drives in the struggle to survive and extend. First was the drive that entailed the *knowledgeable* field, and which they more or less controlled, in which improvisation, innovation, invention, and discovery through combining idea with experience or through urgency and accident, played their interrelated roles. The second drive entailed unseen powers they could not ordinarily control, command, or overcome by knowledgeable means, and which had to be approached in some other manner: in the imitation and initiation of similarities and simulations, even by the exposure of coitus to induce similar creativeness for their plantings; in the acting out in human-animal style the expression of these powers; in mimicking by dress, mask, movement, dance, cry, and song their environmental creatures and elements, whose powers were different from their own and so could be shared, added, absorbed, or solicited.

Referring to the Gravettian carvings and the animal figures painted on the walls of caves in France and Spain, Germain Bazin states in his *History of Art:* "For his [the Aurignacian primitive of the Upper Paleolithic period] the image was no mere imitation. It had the same living faculties as the being of which it was a model, a double. It was thus a work of magic by which man asserted his mastery over the world. We know that our ancestor of the Old Stone Age painted or carved natural forms with no intention of making a 'work of art': he intended, rather, to ensure the fertility of his prey, to entice it into his traps, or to acquire its strength for his own purposes. The primitive artist was a magician whose drawing had all the virtue of a magic spell, and incantation. . . . Primitive man was deeply involved in the natural world, and lost none of its inherent energy. Not a thought or deed of his failed to make contact with some power in the universe. Man's entire activity was aimed at skillfully intervening in the play of natural forces, in the hope of preserving a balance, attracting 'good' and repelling 'evil' powers. . . . The artist-magician had to enter into a ritualistic trance, during which he 'emptied' his own soul by an act of intense mental concentration: he then evoked the supernatural powers which identified him with the bison, mammoth, horse or deer, until he was possessed by the soul of the animal itself and could then portray its image on the wall of his cave."[22]

The primitive used appeasement in the same manner as a weaker animal appeals for mercy and sympathy; in offers of conciliation and mutuality, such as the animal compromises in matters of dominance and territory; compromises in feeding habits, even mating; in connivery and trickery, to gain its objectives or escape destruction; in sharing its possessions, victuals, tools, artifacts, and arts; in sharing its women as virginial offerings and its male genital prepuce; in the sacrifice, when pushed by desperation, of its own life or the lives of others as substitutes; in the use and symbology of the flame, the fire, the torch—the deepest mystery of all, later to become the central ceremonial gatherer for ritual, later to the burning urns, later the tapers in the temples, the candles of the Menorah, the fire sticks of the Chinese and the Japanese, and still later the little candles burning brightly in cathedrals to light the way for those in the darkness of purgatory and to show homage to the gods and saints. H. R. Hays: "At times we can clearly see how man's religion is shaped by his relation to the earth on which he lives, molded by the climate and the seasons. His desire and his imagination are given form and poetry by the forces of nature."[23]

John Gray, writing about the Canaanites, states: "It is probably true that in spite of other and more sober aspects of religion, what predominated in Canaan was in fact the fertility-cult relating to the recurrent seasonal crises in the agricultural year, man's efforts to enlist Providence in supplying his primary need, his daily food and the propagation of his kind."[24]

It was natural that man should try, with whatever crude and limited knowledge he had, coupled with an embryonic mind steeped in brutality, savagery and pure animism, to attempt some understanding of his life and the powers which controlled and influenced his daily precarious existence. Out of this dim and foggy age were born magic, spirits, the personification of trees, animals, stones, places, elements and what-nots as beings like himself and with whom he had to contend in order to preserve and better himself.[25, 26] Birket-Smith: "To them [the primitives] magic is just as often a necessary link in the maintenance of natural order."[27] Ruth Underhill: "A belief in spirits and a purposeful attempt to concilate them is found in every Indian tribe. . . . Other spirits were those of animals, plants, and natural phenomena. To most Indians, there was no sharp dividing line between these and human beings. . . . Every act connected with planting was a religious ceremony. Every wild thing, too, was treated with consideration. The Papago women asked permission of the plants which she plucked for basketry. The Zuñi apologized to the deer he killed. . . . Animal spirits appeared in some form in almost every [American] Indian group."[28]

The primitive lived in a world of powers he could control and of powers he could not control, or which were beyond his sphere of possible control, but he believed both to be *natural,* if we can state that the primitive believed in the confinement of both to *his* world. He did not know, nor was he conscious, intuitively or otherwise, of any other world. The idea or concept of certain powers to be *natural* and others to be *supernatural* or *supra-natural* came into the human mind only a few thousand years ago. A good portion of humanity has not yet reached this point of dualism even to the present day.

"We find magic," wrote Bronislaw Malinowski, "wherever the elements of chance and accident, and the emotional play between hope and fear have a wide and extensive range. We do not find magic wherever the pursuit is certain, reliable, and well under the control of rational methods and technological processes. Further, we find magic where the element of danger is conspicuous. We do not find it wherever absolute safety eliminates any elements of foreboding."[29] Magic and its rituals appear not to have had any deteriorating effect on the primitive's unconscious, expressive, and activated sense of natural freedom. On the other hand, in many ways it gave him an increased sense of freedom by adding confidence, greater self-containment, self-sufficiency, and psychological power which, in many ways and moods, added the unseen or spiritually beneficent powers to his own and brought his psychological inventory up to a level with which he could have openly challenged the unseen powers that were considered as evil adversaries. This sense of increased power against the otherwise uncontrollable powers of evil, and the greater security of feeling that the good spirits of nature and its concomitantly greater benefits were on his side, are both carry-overs that have been biologically evolved in the higher and more intelligent animals, especially the primates, and were at least two of the highways that could have bridged the gaps between the periods of naked animalism and the embryologically cultural approaches of the early stages of preanimism.

Magic thus served as the earliest pseudoscience, to fill in for the primitive what the sciences of today are filling in for the modern. Birket-Smith: "Thus religion and science are branches of the same ancient trunk, and on primitive levels they have not yet diverged."[30] As knowledge comes in, as it proceeds to gather greater and wider momentum in revealing realities of existence and throws its beacons of light farther and farther into the darknesses previously considered as the realms pertinent to magical power and control—as this relative quantum of knowledge proceeds to remove and dissipate the relative quantum of ignorance, with its twin sisters of fear and pragmatic gullibilities, to this extent the need for magic and its later offspring of formal theologies become less necessary. "We must try to understand that which we can no longer believe in. The freedom to develop a new scheme of existence comes only if we duly respect and understand the creedal notions handed down to us."[31]

From this it becomes clear that there is no retreat. Theology, as a dogmatic catechism upon which absolutes are instituted as unchangeable and to which man must surrender his natural freedom as the needs of surrender serve the purposes of this dogma, submit to save his soul or be doomed to eternal fire or celestial demotion, with all its mixtures and additives, is most clearly and definitely on the wane. It is all a matter of time and knowledge-integration. The new and even greater danger that faces mankind is whether knowledge and its sciences can overtake and remove the ignition caps of political and economic power, themselves a carry-over of earlier priestly and royal leaderships, which, if not removed in time, can and might become the detonators to destroy us and all else.

Both the science of knowledge and the pseudoscience of magic become interacted and interwoven to gain practical ends. Both emanated from, and pursued, a common purpose; both aimed to extend natural freedom and to gain its ends, to solve if possible their problems, to ease their daily struggles, to lessen the dangers to their physical selves, to remove illnesses and avoid accidents, to bring them offspring and good harvests, to satisfy their emotions and desires, in their tribal area, in their environment near or far, in this world and not on any other. Frazer: "Experience in general consists in the whole body of conclusions thus deduced from a comparison of all the particular sensations, emotions, and ideas which make up the conscious life of the individual."[32] John Dewey: "Experience is no infinitessimally thin layer or foreground of nature, but that it penetrates into it, reaching down into its depths, and in such a way that its grasp is capable of extension."[33] Sylvanus G. Morley: "To the ancient Maya the principal object of religion and worship was to procure for themselves life, health, and sustenance."[34] George C. Valliant: "Aztec religion was an outgrowth of the recognition and fear of natural forces and the attempt to constrain them."[35] Joseph K. Hart: "Primitive human society grew and multiplied upon the fact of the earth as part of nature, and with its habits securely riveted upon it, in the forms of customs. These customs were as old and as natural as the habits of animals. They were organized into each new individual, each new generation, by processes of 'education' established in the long experiences of group history. These customs and habits held the individual and the group to effective levels of living, to established skills, to traditional masteries of their environment, to accepted relationships with nature."[36]

The dual primitive role of science and pseudoscience gave rise gradually to *shamanism*, as the specialties and varieties of magical procedure grew, until science and pseudoscience parted company with the establishment of the shaman as the leader upon whom the group came to depend more and more. The scientists and pseudoscientists went their separate ways, and the pseudoscientists have been opposing and fighting and declaiming and frustrating the scientists ever since. The pseudoscientist became the first witch-doctor, the first priest, the first priest-king, and then the first king, a process Herbert J. Muller has described as "the blight of the sacred monarchy,"[37] the holy initiator of *eminent domain*. "All along Christianity had been taking on a cargo of prehistoric magic."[38] "Christianity is the precipitate of a conglomeration of mythic, magical and ideological notions from a variety of folk religions."[39] Even St. Augustine admitted that "the same thing which is now called Christian religion existed among the Ancients." "The *priest* is the first form of chieftain, the first form of king."[40] St. Paul was a composer and a compounder, what would be considered today an expert organizer, a compromiser in public relations, and a politician who harmonizes the dissidents and the incumbents, the poor and the rich, the free and the enslaved, the rebellious and the governments, and all of this for the good of Paul and his purposes. The priest also became the first prophet, the first pope, the guardian of the gates of heaven, and the keeper of the keys to the divine household. These keys were not sufficient to assure the permanence and wealth of these guardians: they became the god's agents in the judgments of people's lives, and thus ordained a hell and a devil to be used as a prison and warden for those *they* condemned according to *their* rules, with purgatorial periods for possible parole and good behavior, and to all this they also made keys. Between the keys to heaven and the keys to hell, they made a heaven for themselves and a hell for all others. They forbade all the freedoms that can possibly make for a normal and happy life. These postgraduated magicians have managed to keep too many people locked up in this mythical prison made "real" to their followers. Ironically, it all had to be paid for, and from those who unfortunately became their victims. "Nothing in all history," wrote Mark Twain, "remotely approaches in atrocity the invention of hell."[41] Edward B. Tylor: "The conception of hell as a fiery abyss, so familiar to the religions of the higher civilization, is all but unknown to savage thought."[42] Goethe: "I shall be well content that after the close of this life we should be blessed with another, but I would beg not to have there for companions any who have believed in it here."

Nature-worship, it seems, did not originally imply the presence of divine purpose or some personal supernatural guiding power, but simply parts of nature which, to the primitive, meant his environment, weather, food, rain and sun, the strangeness of disease by its "invisible" powers, the mystery of the non-ness of death, the lack of breath and movement, the withering away of the body, the constant subjection to chance, luck, accident, and the sudden beneficence or destruction by enemy or natural event. To the primitive all these were the things and situations that he *actually* had to cope with every day and live with. These were the things and situations that he felt were *natural* things and situations, most often beyond his capacity and knowledge to control, overpower, subdue, or enslave. He had no notion of any sphere or suprasphere outside of nature. People may die heroically, sacrificially, bravely, stoically, meekly, defiantly, cowardly, impulsively, with resignation, fortitude or shivering fear, beckoningly as surcease from pain or torture, but at all times they die unwillingly. Clyde Kluckhohn and Dorothea Leighton: "Navaho fears and avoidance reach a climax in the complex of beliefs and acts connected with death. It is believed that only witches will go near places of burial. There is some avoidance of uttering even the names of dead people."[43] Death is the prime fear of the human being. Hawkes and Woolley: "At the beginning man, like every other animal, has been forced to adapt himself to his environment; that was the condition of his survival, and such species as failed to fulfill that condition died out."[44] "Death with its emotional shock and power to stir the unconscious has always been one of the great forces behind the religious impulse and magical activities. The idea that a man's spirit should continue to live, perhaps be reborn into another body, which was to have so long and vast a history before it, appears to have been one of the first to emerge among our Palaeolithic ancestors."[45] S. G. F. Brandon: "The earliest written records that we possess afford impressive evidence that anticipation of death inspired the desire to achieve some form of security beyond the effacing flux of time. . . . This Egyptian evidence, affording our earliest documented insight into the human mind, is notable for its vivid attestation of man's aspiration, when faced with death, for some form of post-mortem survival. . . . We may reasonably assert that the various religions and philosophies of life have stemmed from the sense of insecurity that man's awareness of time has inspired."[46]

Elie Metchnikoff: "Religion is still occupied with the problem of death. The solutions which as yet it has offered cannot be regarded as satisfactory. A future life has no single argument to support it, and the non-existence of life after death is in consonance with the whole range of human knowledge."[47] Grzimek: "The missionaries have never had much success among the Masai, who believe in *Engai*, a single, benevolent deity who sends them rain. They do not believe, however, that a man's spirit lives on after his death."[48] Lewis Mumford gives his point of view: "The notion of 'eternal life,' with neither conception, growth, fruition, nor decay—an existence as fixed, as sterilized, as loveless, as purposeless, as unchanging as that of a royal mummy—is only death in another form. What is this but a return to the state of arrest and fixation exhibited by the stable chemical elements that have not yet combined in sufficiently complex molecules to promote novelty and creativity? From the standpoint of human life, indeed of all organic existence, this assertion of absolute power was a confession of psychological immaturity—a radical failure to understand the natural processes of birth and growth, of maturation and death."[49]

Today, practical and experienced missionaries know that the way to a primitive's heart is to give him the things he needs now and today, and not what he might take along after he dies. Peter Mathiessen relates of the Indians in the South American jungle: "The Indian superstitions, after all—and I hope my friends at Macauba will forgive me—are no more incredible than the miracles they are asked to accept instead, though the airplane and penicillin have made the evangelists the greatest medicine men who ever lived."[50]

The *knowable,* to the primitive as well as to the modern, represents his sciences, his capacity to identify, use, control and extend. The *unknowable,* to the primitive, as well as to the modern, was, and still is, his magic, his religion, his cult, his fortune-teller, and even, at times, his psychiatrist. As man gains more knowledge of himself and things, his new acquisitions leave the domain of the possibly religious and become part of his possible sciences. Thus, in a way religion is a sort of related limitless inventory of *belief commodities* that man creates and then believes to be true to

offset what his hopes and curiosities, through his sense of awareness and rationalism, are denied the confirmation of knowledge
and fact, and which he innately feels is essential to his own stability and peace of mind in experiencing and facing things and
situations which, in his own words, are "in the hands of God."
As man has advanced and his sciences have extended his reach
and the perimeter of knowledge, his inventory of belief commodities has declined and is still declining in most parts of the world.
"This process is occurring everywhere. The facts which make
for doubt and which force human beings to think things over
and form new ideas are reaching out into the remotest villages."[51]

Totemism is probably the oldest and earliest form of tribal
cult. It is the primitive's method of making his environment part
of the corporate and employment structure of his family, clan and
tribal entity. In totemism we see the primitive mentality at work
within nature. Seen and unseen powers and things all operate
within *one* field. All creatures, dead or alive, whether animal, fish,
bird, or bug, have the same properties of substance and spirit.
Through the mysteries of existence we are one big family of relations. Human spirits can occupy the substance of other creatures,
and these, in turn, can reside in human substance. Frazer:
"Totemism is an intimate relation which is supposed to exist
between a group of kindred people on the one side and a species
of natural or artificial objects on the other side, which objects are
called the totems of the human group. . . . Totemism is thoroughly democratic; it is simply an imaginary brotherhood established on a footing of perfect equality between a group of people
on the one side and a group of things."[52] "The savage commonly
believes that animals are endowed with feelings and intelligence
like those of men, and that, like men, they possess souls which
survive the death of their bodies either to wander about as dis-
embodied spirits or to be born again in animal form."[53] Tylor:
"The sense of an absolute psychical distinction between man and
beast, so prevalent in the civilized world, is hardly to be found
among the lower races. Men to whom the cries of beasts and birds
seem like human language, and their actions guided as it were
by human thought, logically enough to allow the existence of
souls to beasts, birds, and reptiles, as to men."[54] Sir Wallis Budge:

"The educated Egyptian never worshipped an animal as an animal, but only as an incarnation of a god, and the reverence paid to animals in Egypt was in no way different from that paid to the king who was regarded as 'divine' and as an incarnation of Ra, the Sun-god, who was the visible symbol of the Creator."[55] "The Hebrews, Greeks, and Romans never understood the logical conception which underlay the reverence with which the Egyptians regarded certain animals, and as a result they grossly misrepresented their religion."[56] The Egyptian *sistrum* and the Hopi *mongko* performed the same services.

The hunting peoples, like the Ainu and the Eskimos, desired to placate the souls or spirits of the animals they killed in order to avoid retribution and vengeance by these animal spirits. Later, as cultures and established religions emerged with the early agricultural development of primitive and ancient societies, the killing of humans as sacrifices, of kings, queens, and other royal personages, even the simulated killing of the god or gods—such killings became, in one form or another, rituals that spread all over the world. These cultured magical ceremonies were gradually absorbed into the later religions many of which still exist today. Perhaps the killing of humans as sacrifices to make the corn grow in ancient Mexico and the killing of the priest in the tiny temple of Diana at Nemi by a runaway slave originated in the basic idea of the use of the killer-death-demon as the magical means to induce fertility, good growth, and abundant harvest. Could it not be that the killing of the Christ-god, as well as the killing of Osiris, Adonis, Tammuz, and many others too numerous to mention, and their cyclic seasonal resurrections, were all mythologems metaphorically representing the need of spilling human blood, as the fluid of life force, to bring about successful plantings and harvests.

Thus, magic, the precursor of religion, dealt with the natural world, and, in all its categories of white, black, sympathetic, and so on, came to be associated with the primitive attempt to control the otherwise uncontrollable parts of the natural realm in which the primitive lived, struggled, and died. What he could not control was necessarily an *invisible* power, something he could not see, touch, smell, or hear, as the power that makes people sick,

or makes them lie still and decay, or makes the rain fall from
the sky, or the wind to blow, or the sun to shine, or that lights
the moon and the stars, makes a seed to sprout and bring fruition,
the power that makes woman produce a life, and the strange
and magnetic power of sex. These were to the primitive *part* of
his world, the *natural* world, the *only one* of which he was capable
of being aware.

RESIDENCES OF THE SPIRITS

THE INVISIBLE POWERS were, therefore, necessarily "spiritual,"
that is, nonmaterial. Inasmuch as some invisible power, a natural
occurrence or manifestation, made people die, and as living
people indicated a sense of some natural power, doing things,
expressing thought and emotion, this *"livingness"* became identified in the same sense as other invisible powers. The human
body thus contained or housed, also, an invisible power which
later became its *spirit*. Where did the spirit abide in the body
of man? The primitive imagined it to reside in the head, since
the head could talk, cry, laugh, see, smell, hear, taste, and communicate with itself and others by the awareness of thought, convey ideas and purposes, make decisions. The head saw danger
first, appreciated beauty, and aroused the body most pleasantly
and mysteriously in matters of sex and other appetites. Each head
identified a specific person, regardless of how similar, so each
head-spirit was unique, unlike every other, and only by the
spirit representing or residing in the head could the ancestor-
spirits or the gods verify and identify the spirit. "They considered
that the owner of every human head they could procure would
serve them in the next world, where, indeed, a man's rank would
be according to his number of heads in this."[57] Thus the head-
hunters believed that each head they obtained was another
"spirit," which would always be their slave in this life and in
the "continued" or "afterlife." E. O. James: "The head being
regarded as the most vital part of the body . . . its preservation
was essential for the attainment of immortality."[58] "In ancient
Egypt where the cult of the dead assumed such gigantic propor-

tions and became the characteristic feature of this remarkable civilization, the skull in prehistoric times was severed from the body and buried separately."[59] Ann C. Crawford tells us about a Vietnamese custom: "Never touch anyone on the head as this would be considered as a personal insult to the individual and perhaps even to his ancestors. Many Vietnamese believe the spirit resides there."[60] In primitive Mesopotamia it was customary in many parts to retain the head of the deceased and keep it buried beneath or within the household. However, there were periods when the heart was considered as the seat of thought and therefore the soul resided in the heart rather than in the head. In many parts of the world and in many strange cults and religions there is the belief that a person contains more than one soul. Thomas A. Dooley: "According to the Lao belief, there are thirty-two parts of the human body and each possesses a soul."[61]

When one died at the hands of some invisible power or spirit, what happened to the spirit or invisible power of the body? Where did it go? Inasmuch as the body decayed, this power must be somewhere and the only place the primitive could have imagined these spirits to be at or in would be in some part, animate or inanimate, of *his* world—his habitat, the environment, the sky, the surface, or below the surface, that is, the world they occupied and what they could see or imagine in any direction. Thus magic became to the primitive a pseudoscience, as many psychical "sciences" claim to be today, to deal with things and situations of the natural world. Magic, to the primitive, became an added vehicle of natural biological freedom, an added tool, physical in its elements and psychological in its portents, which unconsciously, at least, increased to this extent his natural and biological freedom.

AGRICULTURE AND RELIGIOUS ORIGINS

THE FIRST AGRARIANS who cultivated the fields, seeded the soil to grow crops, were the first to metamorphose the rise and fall of irrigating and inundating waters, the seasonal cycles, the sun and the rains, the drought and the harsh winds, the favorable and beneficent and the unfavorable and evil factors, into interpretations of their own physical creations and life cycles. This led to fertility rites and created imaginative cosmogonies of myth, recitation, and ritual. While the basal beginnings of society could have begun in the trees when hominoids were still aboreal and each male or troop guarded its territory and range, the earliest formations of social structure, of society as we see and try to understand it, began, it seems, when the neolithic human savages stopped roaming as hunters, scavengers, gatherers and plunderers, and settled down to become the first peasants and formed the first villages. Andreas Lommel: "The ancestors of all human beings were at one time hunters, and the hunter cultures are extremely old. From a primeval stage of simple food-gathering, man seems to have developed into a hunter, a process which we think began about 50,000 B.C., during the last Ice Age. Agriculture first appeared in the Middle East, though exactly where has not yet been determined. Excavations in Jericho and elsewhere make it likely, however, that the evolution from hunting to farming began about 8000 B.C. The agricultural communities also spread out over the whole world, slowly absorbing the hunter cultures that stood in their way. Only one continent, Australia, was untouched by the early planter cultures and remained the preserve of hunters alone. . . . It was as a hunter that man devised the earliest forms of religion, while the invention of language and the use of implements go back much earlier, to about half a million years ago when our ancestors were not even hunters but only food-fatherers."[62]

When man made his farm and began some kind of crude husbandry he made his "castle" and created his first fertility goddess. The idea of *property* evolved out of the biology of territory, and the *deed* was filed in the temple as a proclamation before the goddess. Man became his own priest, built his own family temple, and worshipped the elements to ensure his own safety and security and to bring about the procreation and sustenance that could make possible his survival and the continuance of his kind. Richard S. MacNeish: "It is generally accepted that the development of agriculture is basic to the rise of village and urban life."[63]

MAGIC, SPELLS, AND THE BIRTH OF THE GODS

WHITE AND SYMPATHETIC magics were applied to gain what the people considered good; black magic was applied to ward off what they considered evil. In many parts of the world, when a wife is about to deliver a child, the husband is subjected to various forms of sympathetic-magic exercises to induce, by participation, a quick and healthful delivery. Thomas A. Dooley: "It is said that there are some tribes over in Burma that get the husband into the act in a more meaningful way. During the wife's labor, the husband is hung by his feet, outside the house."[64] Birket-Smith: "Today it is customary only in a few parts of India for the husband to dress in female clothing as soon as labor begins, and lie down in a dark room, where he moans and groans and then stays in bed with the newborn child."[65] Douglas L. Oliver writes of the Dobu Islanders: "A person with many magical powers which result in his personal beauty, his success in love affairs and gardening and trading, is a 'good' person. Persons poor in magical powers, as manifested in personal ugliness and failure in affairs, are 'bad.' 'Good' individuals inspire consuming envy in their less fortunate fellows, who are believed to attack them with sorcery. Men who acquire knowledge of sorcery steal a thing identified with an enemy and charm it so that the enemy sickens and dies. Women practicing witchcraft can leave their sleeping bodies and strike their foes, or they can extract the spirits of enemies and leave them inanimate. Some persons, diviners, possess powers to counteract sorcery and witchcraft."[66]

These notions and practices evolved later into the good gods and the bad gods. Still later, all this evolved into the idea of one overall Universal God and his opposition of the overall Universal Satan, and the realms of heaven and hell over which each presides and predominates. Psychoanalytically, it is the reflection of these two struggling natures within the nature of man and the world about him. "The great gods of the sky played an important part in the duality of the Aztec world in which an eternal war was fought symbolically between light and darkness, heat and cold, north and south, rising and setting sun. Even the stars were grouped into armies of the east and west. Gladiatorial combats, often to the death, expressed this idea in ritual; and the great warrior orders, the Eagle Knights of Huitzilopochtli and the Ocelot Knights of Tezcatlipoca, likewise reflected the conflict between day and night. This Sacred War permeated the ritual and philosophy of Aztec religion."[67] "When the spell-weaving primitive finally became disillusioned as a result of too many failures of his spells, his attitude towards nature and the unseen powers changed to one of awe, and he commenced to worship."[68] Michael Grant tells us about the creation of the Greek gods: "It was from the poet of the *Iliad* that the gods took shape, with whatever assistance he may have received from his forerunners. This religion and this mythology are the outcome of poetic and artistic genius, conveying an euphoric vision, aesthetic not moral in its origin, of a dazzling, awe-inspiringly vital Olympian world."[69]

The life of these primitives was not exactly rosy. The prehistoric primitives, as some primitives today, were so practical in their efforts to survive and limit their numbers within a given area in ratio to the supply of needs for survival that their cruelties to resolve this problem reached abhorrent and merciless proportions, including the killing off of children and the older people in the tribe, since they were useless as contributors to the continuing material welfare. Freuchen recounts of the Eskimos: "In some tribes, an old man wants his oldest son or favorite daughter to be the one to put the string around his neck and hoist him to death."[70] In his *Book of the Eskimos,* Freuchen describes how the old, very tired, and sickly mother pleaded with her son to build her a little snow house wherein she could be sealed up to die. Mala, the son, tearfully begs his mother, Naterk, to carry on with them, and she tries, but finally orders him to prepare the snow house for her. Such stoicism may have been philosophized in the Western world, but rarely so exemplified.

Perhaps this accounts for the "culture" or traditional warfare that goes on in an internecine manner between closely related or neighboring tribes in the present-day still-neolithic savages of jungle lands, as in the vastnesses of the Amazon and in New Guinea. This may be nature's way, in a Malthusian manner, to

keep a "proper" balance between existing numbers and the potential sustenance pool available.

Theological religions, as we know them today and in their historic and ancient content and variety, gradually evolved out of
earlier magical and ritual periods of animism, totemism, ancestor-
worship, nature-worship, taboo, and the like. They also evolved
concurrently a new phase in the theocratic organization of worship, sacred tenets, and new principles by which these later religions were to influence and direct the course of human history
—the emergence of kingcrafts and priestcrafts as top echelon levels
of society—the leadership and the rule of the few over the many,
leading to the eventual establishmnt and general acceptance of
the right of *eminent domain* in its economical, political, and religious peripheries, related and intermixed, which overflowed into
the secular royalties and nobilities and into the hierarchies of the
religious. Pedro Ramirez Vazquez: "The central importance of
religion and military power are reflected in the structure of
Aztec society itself."[71] Relating about Mexico during the early
sixteenth century, R. C. Padden writes: "In both Spanish and
Indian minds sovereignty was inextricably associated with religion. And sovereignty, by virtue of its awesome power of enable-
ment, was one of the most dynamic of cultural determinants."[72]
"The Polynesia chiefs and nobles," writes Danielsson, "would
certainly never have been able to maintain their provocative
privileges in the long run if they had not had an effective support
in religion. . . . To avoid the springing up of any false doctrines
the chiefs themselves served as priests or saw that only members
of their families were appointed to priestly offices and professor-
ships of theology."[73] Lewis Mumford: "Both to establish and
maintain kingship, an infusion of divine power was essential.
But the constant intercourse with Heaven, necessary for the guidance of the king, demanded professional aid from priests, magicians, soothsayers, interpreters of dreams, and readers of cosmic
signs, who in turn were dependent upon the king's secular power
and wealth for their own status and office."[74] The history of the
papacy is the same story.

KING-PRIEST DIVINITIES

THE EARLIEST KINGS were the earliest gods, alive and dead, and being gods the welfare or destruction of the people depended upon the divinity-king. Even the king's body was holy and endowed with divine power. The sacrifices of kings, willing or unwilling, to influence the general welfare through the birth-death-resurrection ritual evolved out of the appeasement of the celestial powers that controlled the chances of harvest and the threat of starvation. "The killing of the god so that he may be reborn or so that his blood may bring benefits and fertility to the social group is, of course, a metaphysical idea which lives on in Christianity."[75] "In Egypt almost from the beginning, in Mesopotamia at intervals, the king was conceived as a god in his own right. Egyptian history, as a tale transmitted, begins at this point. By this union of cosmic and earthly powers the ruler became at once a living person and an immortal: he was born and died like other men, yet he would be reborn, like his other self."[76] "In Malabar, as late as the sixteenth century A.D., a king was observed standing on a platform slicing himself to bits and tossing the pieces about to his waiting folk, until, when about to faint, he slit his throat."[77] "One cannot overlook the fact that the chief fertility myths of later periods, like those of Osiris and Dionysus, involve the murder and the brutal dismemberment of a male deity, whose death and resurrection result in the emergence of plant life."[78] The sacrifice stories of Osiris, Adonis, Tummuz, Dionysus, Jesus, and many others, are the ancients' attempt to explain the seasons, the cycles of crops, and the birth, death, and rebirth of themselves. The idea and belief of the god dying in the winter solstice and resurrecting himself in the spring goes back thousands of years before Christ. More than two thousand years before Jesus the Egyptians had their annual Eastertime resurrection of Osiris, who is depicted as a lying mummy with stalks of wheat growing tall and upward from out of his body. The belief in a god as a son of the top echelon or father-god, symbolizing the return of fertility and fruition for food and survival, was ancient even before the beginning of Christianity. Relating to the Incas, Ubbelohde-Doering states: "Eduard Seler has already surmised that in ancient times the humming-bird was considered a sort of god of Spring or fertility god, since it disappeared in autumn to return in the spring, when rivers flowed again and the crops began to grow."[79]

Throughout human history and, in particular, in religious history, it was very common for fanatics and zealots to sacrifice their own blood by mutilation as a sort of "bartering" method to achieve some closeness to, or acceptance by, the gods, blood being the symbol and fluid of life. This ordeal of cruelty persists in many parts of the world to this very day. Today, in parts of Italy, fanatical youths mutilate their bodies with brushes of sharp needle-point nails and walk through the streets covered with their own blood; this is in celebration of some Catholic saint, in the belief that in spilling blood, their very own, they can come closer to the household of their God. Describing similar customs among some of the American Indian tribes, Peter Farb states: "Mortification of the flesh has always held a fascination for religious fanatics everywhere, for it is the most obvious way that this too, too human flesh can break its link with the world of men and approach the threshold of the gods. Among those who have groped toward deities in this way are the Jewish Essenes around the Dead Sea, the many ascetic orders of Christian monks, the whirling Dervishes of Islam, and the hermits of Buddhism."[80]

No doubt, these kings and priests were very sincere in their own theological beliefs and felt that they were living sacred lives and performing sacred acts for the general guidance and good of their peoples, and that the people must believe in and uphold the sacred "truths" as *they* saw things and believed in them themselves. But the rewards were great and increased their wealth, their social levels, their powers. They became covetous and jealous of their positions, and their gods became jealous gods, vindictive if they were not sufficiently worshipped and sacrificed for. The kings were deified, and priests became specialists as guardians of the communication and transportation systems to immortality and paradise. The Egyptian priests were monopolists in the arts of magical prayer and command directed to the gods; they became intercessors, and to this day the ministers of the various religions authoritatively and justly feel that they more or less speak, and even act, for the god or gods, as his or their appointed agents. They learned quickly that this profession not only brought them the respect and adoration of being saintly and sacred, with a badge of divine sagacity and providential judgment, but it also allowed them to lead a life of comfortable leisure and relief from the labor and hard struggling life of the masses. Any human could, and would, sooner or later, come to like this very much. Throughout history different individuals and groups, independent of the people's accepted religions, have competitively tried to share in what they felt were the "innocuous" profits of religiosity. Cultists, evangelists, healers, and all kinds of fakers go about the country like Indian-cure salesmen, offering solutions to all the ills of life, together with an extra bonus of immortality bearing a special pass to the gates of heaven, all for a fee called a "contribution to the holy work" of the specially selected. Many have become millionaires. They prefer to live on earth and enjoy beautiful estates with all the luxuries of an opulent and sensuous life. Aimee Semple McPherson in California and Father Divine in New York were two outstanding examples. Now that the public regards them with disdain and suspicion, many of their successors have become marriage-counselors, pseudopsychiatrists, or teach Zen with love lessons. The principle remains the same: taking something for nothing and with deception, whether flavored with sincerity or cupidity.

MALINOWSKI'S APOLOGETICS FOR RELIGION

YET, WITH IT all, many fine and brilliant scholars feel that the human animal, to achieve peace of mind and to face death with some sort of composure, must be fed these opiates, as they have been realistically diagnosed. Man cannot be expected to feel, they think, even with the truth, that these few years of life are all that are alloted to him, and that he is unlike other animals; that he possesses a soul given him by his deity, which animals do not possess, and, because of this soul, he can look forward to reach heaven after death. One of these fine scholars who widened the reaches of anthropological knowledge and investigation was Bronislaw Malinowski. Though he did not himself accept positive religion, he became an apologist for it, feeling that man needs religion as a pragmatic basis of life purpose and peace of mind.

Having devoted his life to the study of anthropological investigation, especially in the Far Pacific islands, having seen at first hand the intimacy and almost complete integration of the individual, the tribe, the environment, the mores and manes, that is, the living and influencing elements of interdependence of a living community, all involved in a constraining periphery of magic and religion that framed the society with purpose, meaning, hope, dreams, and psychological fortitude, it is not difficult to understand that the sympathies of Malinowski were affected and led to his feeling that magic and religion are necessary to the human being, even as blinders, and to making of his little society what otherwise it could not have been.

Malinowski described to us the primitive's viewpoint about nature and his worship of it. "Primitive man, even as civilized, feels an autonomous purpose in nature which at times rewards, at times punishes, and invariably follows its own mysterious way. Man naturally turns toward this purpose or providence; he personifies it and tries to propitiate it. This is the foundation of nature-worship, which takes various forms, of which the most primitive, perhaps, is totemism. But all nature worship implies the deification of natural forces, the admission of a purpose, a providence, a personal guidance in the universe."[81] He tells us about magic in the primitive field: "Within the context of primitive culture is also primitive magic, in which the savage tries to harness his luck and to bribe his chance, by spell, ritual, and taboo. Magic flourishes wherever man cannot control hazard by means of science. It flourishes in hunting and fishing, in times of war, and at seasons of love, in the control of wind, rain, and sun, in regulating all dangerous enterprises, above all in disease and in the shadow of death."[82]

It is not difficult to appreciate Malinowski's deep understanding of the emotional and psychical needs of the natives he wrote about; we do not have to go so far from home. I enjoy the singing of the gospel choirs of Florida, Tennessee, Kentucky, and other states. The harmonies and group singing of these jubilee presentations are really exhilarating. Again I see, feel, and respect the reverence, the slow tonal appeals of *Kol Nidre* as the temple cantor, choir, and organ lift up the worshippers to awe. Under the stars I listened to the children of Bali sing and act the Monkey Dance, and I felt good relishing the chuck-chucks of these little Balinese singing the song-story of Sita and Rama. These are all enjoyable. We can still enjoy them as poetical metaphors, beautiful dramas of primitive imagery and search to explain the wonders of life and what it is surrounded by.

Children's fairy tales are beautiful, too, and I love to read the fairy tales of the world's folk people. No one should desire to do away with these beautiful things. We can enjoy them *for what they are* as we can live the life *for what it really is.* Beauty lives in the eyes of the beholder; reality can be beautiful, too, if only we make up our minds and hearts to make it so. Man can never sustain and feel the beauty in life and in the world by cutting down his neighbors, destroying and vulgarizing the world environment while praying to the Lord; needlessly shooting down for mere trophies the beautiful and rare creatures while he sings he would like to be like Jesus, Mahomet or Shiva.

Malinowski rightly points out that out of the experiences of living, happy, tragic, struggling, the peaceful and violent primitive man slowly accumulated a knowledge of things, achieved by trial and error, by discovery, by invention, by implementation and improvisation, by innovation, by adaptation with the help of the physical tools of his own evolution; and that it was this natural cumulative property that laid the groundwork for greater organization, more complex cultures, and a wider range of habitat. Malinowski wrote: "Science, primitive as much as civilized, is the solid achievement of the human mind, embodied in the tradition of rational knowledge and put to practical purposes. As far as primitive man has really obtained the mastery of natural forces, and of the forces in his own nature, he relies on science and science alone."[83]

Yet this knowledge could not solve all the problems of the primitive. There were too many factors beyond his control, beyond his reach, beyond his comprehension and knowledge. He knew, but not enough; his sciences were young, still probing and searching elemental meanings. This gap, the gap of the natural elements, events, accidents, and uncertainties of birth, disease, and death, had to be explained and bridged, and the bridge the primitive built, in lieu of knowledge, was magic and ritual. It was this gap of the unknowable that created the beliefs and the early forms of tribal religion that persist in many of these Pacific islands, as well as elsewhere in the world, today. Jean Guiart writes of the South Pacific: "Nowhere in Oceania does the idea of death involve that of annihilation. It is rather another kind of life. The living lean upon the dead who surround them perpetually and who, in certain cases, take the visible forms of trees or animals. It is their good- or ill-will which rules the destinies of their children or grandchildren."[84]

Magic concerned itself with the natural field, not the celestial one, at least in its early causative and evolutional stages. Huxley was convinced that God and the immortality of the soul played no part in early primitive ritual; these came much later with the emergence of more or less formal religions and theological systems. Primitive man had all he could do to preserve his life every day, and his magic and worship of spiritual forces, in the forms of ancestor spirits, animal and plant spirits, the spirits of the elements and conditions, all these related to his nature and his environment.

The ways of magic were multitudinous and as varied as the imagination of the primitive could vary and extend itself. He concocted certain "sacred" words which later became the magical commands and directives of the Egyptian priests, the holy words of the Israelites and the prayers of the Jesuits. As the self-identity of the individual expressed itself more and more through a slowly growing consciousness of self during millennia of time and thousands of generations, the idea and picturization of the spirit, from the earlier general or pantheistic view of existence to the later individuated and eternal nature of the specific person or personality, are the story of the growth of religion, of the soul and the wish to fulfill the already accepted idea of personal immortality. Victor W. von Hagen writes of the Aztecs: "Poor human beings, we must needs furnish ourselves with illusions even in death. Since man, primitive or civilized, cannot endure the idea of a mechanistic interpretation of the universe, he cannot grasp the fact that when one is not, one ceases to be. Ignorance is not alone a necessary condition of happiness, it is a condition of life itself; the sentiments that make life bearable to all spring out of falsehood and are fed on illusions."[85]

The primitives and preancient peoples had gradually, over periods of thousands of years, accumulated out of their experiences a great and wide knowledge of the use of organic plant and animal parts to treat illnesses, to help the maimed and arthritic, to restore health. The word *"drug"* in ancient Greek was called *pharmakon,* which "originally designated a vegetable substance that had magic powers."[86] However, the ancient religions left the world of herbs and natural applicatives and entered more and more into the realm of "complete" dependence upon the "beneficence" of the gods and the efficacy of prayer.

Professor Henry E. Sigerist, in his *History of Medicine,* gives us an idea as to why the science of medicine lay practically retarded and hibernating until the nineteenth century, when freedom, freshened by knowledge and courage, broke the chains that had been fastened to it for thousands of years by theology and superstition. He writes: "Here is a typical example of religious medicine. A god, provoked, sends illness in his wrath. The diviners find out what caused his anger and once he is placated by religious means, by reparation for the offense committed, by prayer, sacrifice, purification rites, he arrests the disease and relieves the people."[87] The Christian Scientist, today, carries on this same denial of science and knowledge to keep himself alive; he insists, when he is sick or injured, on prayer alone—and when sick enough or injured enough, he just dies, a victim of hallucination and ignorance. Marti-Ibañez tells about the "progress" of medicine in Byzantium: "Since no one in Byzantium was able to garner the heritage of Galen and again raise the torch of experimental medicine, medicine became a matter of faith. The sick person was regarded as a potential saint; prayer was adopted as the best medicine, the priest was considered the best physician, the Church became the best hospital, and Christ was the Supreme Healer. . . . The diseased person became a privileged being, and medicine was founded on faith and miracles, the Divine Word, and prayer. Faithful Christians renounced classical hygiene. . . . The diseased body was extolled as the only possible dwelling for a healthy soul."[88]

Some investigators feel that man just did not jump from raw animalism to cultural animism without slow and gradual transitional stages bridging the two periods. The trek of evolution from animalism to animism was slow, gradual, covering a periodic range of hundreds of thousands of years. Ronald R. Marett felt that there were periods of *preanimism* that covered these situations, long periods in which the unseen and primeval lower and below-the-surface pillars of possible culture were laid and which made possible the continuing experiences of man which led him to animism and still later to the higher cultures of the prehistoric and ancient worlds of man.[89] While all this is a sort of extrapolation, as so many other theories about those times now forever beyond the reach of historical and scientific verification, still we do know that whatever culture man possessed at any time was at any period the temporary advance, as well as the debris, of the long road of natural evolution. It was not handed down to him on any celestial platter. It came about as a natural process of natural events within natural experience of natural existence.

We have noted that originally magic, which Malinowski called "religious science," was involved with mortality, not immortality. When Malinowski stated that "religion and science have existed from the very beginning,"[90] it was the beginning of some confusion, a priori theorizing, and metaphysical interpolation. While he confirms the concept that religion differed radically with magic ritual "in that it does not aim at practical ends in emergencies of ordinary life,"[91] and that "the acts of religion are not means to a practical end," he goes on to state that "although cultural determinism supplies all the final motives of behavior, culture, in turn, is determined all along the line . . . it is evident that the driving forces of all behavior are biologically conditioned."[92] He states further that "as regards the drives, man is obviously an animal; hence his organic needs will always give rise to a permanent biological determination in all behavior. . . . It is equally important to realize that human beings live not by biological drives alone, but also by physiological drives molded and modified by culture."[93] These cultural modifications too often led to the deterioration of the natural freedom of the individual and subjected his body and mind to the will and disposal of the culture-modifiers.

Herbert J. Muller tells us about the modification in the Land of the Pharaohs: "The Egyptians submitted to a distinctly harsher rule by Pharaoh, to a notoriously corrupt bureaucracy, and to a still more corrupt, immensely rich priesthood, presiding over temples that came to own one out of every five subjects of Pharaoh, and owned the souls of the rest through their possession of the ritual necessary for admission to the next world."[94] Von Hagen, regarding the Mayas: "Thus Maya religion made use of every possible device to exert control over the people, for as in all theocracies, astronomy, religion, ritual, and science were interlinked."[95] C. A. Burland, regarding the Incas: "The priests of the Sun not only arranged the calendar, but also conducted ceremonies at appropriate times to release the rains, or to dismiss the sins of individuals and communities. Their curse could kill, their blessing bring health."[96] William O. Douglas puts it well on the line, not of ancient Egypt or of the Mayas, but of the *Church* today: "In many feudal lands (today), the Church is the overlord whose voice is seldom heard on the side of justice and equality. The Christian church has in critical areas promised the villagers much in their future life, yet not helped them find a bit of heaven on earth. Churches are filled with gold; the villages, with misery."[97]

In experiencing the magical and religious ceremonies and their intense meaning in the life of the primitives, one can readily understand why Malinowski, besides putting forth whatever objective analysis he could offer, had a deep *humanist* sympathy and affinity for these primitives, and not only deeply appreciated the solemnity and rooted influences and consequences of social order at work, but even learned to cultivate an affection for these humans, who, in their wildness and wilderness, try sincerely and passionately to wrest some meaning and value out of the endless unanswerable riddles of life, living, and death. H. R. Hays: "It cannot be denied that certain determinants of man's symbolic behavior derive from his inherent biological nature. All human beings dream. Almost universally the dream plays some role in religion, ranging from the experience of the Crow warrior who meets his familiar spirit to Joseph's successful divination in the Old Testament."[98] Hawkes and Woolley: "To a very large extent the development of religious ideas amongst the primitive groups of mankind was conditioned by the social organization of each group,"[99] and the social organization was conditioned, in turn, by the individuals that comprised it and the environment in which they lived.

Though I am not an anthropologist or a scientist, I, too, have lived among the primitives, enjoyed their antics, their unadulterated and warm hospitality, their foods, dances, music, social life, and intense sincerities and wholesomeness, as well as their little conniveries, genuinely refreshing after the all-too-often superficial and artificial ways of civilized cultures. I have watched their magical and religious ceremonies and realized how important and indispensable are these modes of using magic to influence nature to be kind and gracious to them, of trying to pierce the mystery of death and to live on in some fashion *in their vicinity,* in their village, as their ancestors and the ancestors they will become to the generations that follow them. A fashion that allows them to feel and breathe and sense and see and hear the song of the bird, the bowing of the palm in the strong wind, the symphonic sounds of the stream tumbling over the rocks and circling swiftly around the bend, the freshness of the new grass, the flower before the fruit; to witness the planting and harvesting of the crops, the cycles of the rice or the corn; to join in the gaieties of their festivals and lament with the lamenters when one of them dies; to live "forever" this *good* existence they are conscious of, to be always with their loved ones, even in spirit to join in the battle of their children against their enemies: All this pageantry of life and its little dramas from birth to death was given to them, at least in its acceptance as truth and with the confidence that it is not merely a hope but a certainty. As we read Malinowski's apologetics for religion, we can readily see how, sharing with the primitives their daily existence, one can come to feel the "necessity" and the "pragmatic need" of these things. So did William James.

We on the more civilized plane are not so far behind these primitives as we suppose. We still believe in ratio to our indoctrination, our emotions, our intelligence. As we become more free of this indoctrination, our intelligence will enlighten us more and more to the *reality* of our being, and to its limited yet extensive potential. In realizing our limited potential, our sense of our own value in limited time will become more precious and more valuable to us. The primitives will gradually become closer to us, and when they will be like us, they will think as we do and behave as we do, perhaps better. Time, experience, and education dilute ignorance, as they have always done. The necessities of today become the obsolescences of tomorrow, and the actualities of these transferences can be fairly foreseen but not accurately predicted. One thing we do know: Man will always dream and hope and try to extend his own being, as best he can and as long as he can, notwithstanding all other factors.

It seems evident that primitive mentality did not meditate, to any great extent, on the past or the future; any such meditation and contemplation were spent practically on the immediate present. Most people today are not much different. The primitive came to think this way because of the "cold war" that nature and his enemies waged against him day and night at all times of the year. While his memories relived the experiences and effects of the past, he was not able to reflect, to foresee the future and plan for the months or years ahead, as the modern civilized man does today. The primitive was more practical, more realistic in many ways, more resigned and adapted to his state than the modern, whose present time is consumed and dissipated with remorse for the past and filled with fears for the future.

The primitive was satisfied to live well, if he could. The civilized man is satisfied to die rich, famous, and powerful. The primitive, with the little he had of everything we have so much of today, found compatibility with his surroundings, and activated his natural freedom as much as his nature and the field would allow, whereas modern man has created an environment in which to cultivate his own neuroses, brought about mechanical and psychological conditions that have often sadly and adversely affected his natural freedom. He had done this without any more or fewer encroachments from nature than the primitive met with, and in spite of all the accomplishments of science and material progress. The primitive faced the pressing image of nature; the modern faces the pressing image of himself.

The primitive, aware of death and in awe of its mysteries, lamented his beloved ones and revered the memory of the departed, as much as, if not more than, we do today, but his whole nature was not so sensitized in his attitude toward death as is that of modern man. The primitive accepted it and understood it, as witnessed in all the things about and around him: the seasons of the year, the cyclic changes and the waning of the moon, the rising and setting sun, the cycle of the seed to plant, the plant to decay, and from the decay the rising sprout of new life. He saw all the living creatures about him get born, live, and die, just as he himself; he saw the trees and plants, the fish in the waters and the life of the various creatures along its shores, all come and go and come back again. This was the picture that nature, in motion and cycles, constantly screened before him, closely part of his very existence. Today, Andreas Feininger notes the same process is going on and is destined to go on as long as Nature lasts: "Nothing is permanent. Everything is in constant flux and change. Through day and night, through summer and winter, year after year, from birth to death, life flows in a timeless cycle—life in the soil and on the ground, in water and air, life of man and animal and plant—always in change and transformation, in rise and fall, in growth and decline, so that in all nature nothing is the same at day's end as it was at day's beginning."[100]

The modern man is separated from nature to a considerable degree; he is enclosed within mechanical systems, and walks not on grass but on pavements; he does not see this other life around him as openly and constantly as the primitive. The modern is concerned more or less wholly with *himself.* As civilizations rose higher and higher, man's cosmologies and theogonies concentrated more and more on man; the natural elements of the world receded from him and faded more from view, the great cathedrals and skyscrapers took over. The primitive was continually made conscious of the natural field in which he lived; the civilized man became more and more conscious of a fabricated field that reflected, not the natural field, but an incarceration in which he saw only his own image in stone and steel and all their products.

This is no appeal to return to the cave, nor should we, nor can we; but we need to realize that man's body and mind must find some solution that will afford him the natural freedom they both require, that man's physiology cannot find healthful and happy compatibility with only man-made things. In the city we can hardly see the rising sun or the setting sun, nor do we have time or thought to lift our eyes to see it. The stars hang over the factories and the cities, but people are too busy to look up to see the stars and spend a moment in enjoyable meditation of the natural wonders about them. These are the *only* and *real* "miracles" man has ever known. Man is slowly becoming artificial, his body reeked with diseases unknown in the past. Humanity is slowly becoming neurotic. The primitive, with all his struggles, sang with the birds and understood them; the civilized man understands the world "better," but not himself or his life. The Machine Age, with its boring and crunching of men's time and lives, has built new cities of Troy upon the openness and freshness of free animal life, sealed it with asphalt and stone, and upon this new pavement built man's mausoleum, with art and magnificence.[101]

If the primitive had fears, he also had the fortitude and natural courage to feel that he was not alone in fear; all else about him had fears, too, yet played their parts as only they could and as best they could. There was nothing else they could really do. The primitive could only see what he did see and his thoughts were thus more or less limited to this, his life and habitat. He remained in the only world he knew, alive and dead. St. Peter was not yet at Heaven's gates awaiting his arrival. Modern man, with an acutely sensitized ego and with a greater awareness of his ephemeral life, of death, in relation to his increased knowledge of phenomena, shudders at the natural field, and creates heavens and paradises as far into the celestial realms as his eyes and imagination can possibly reach. The only conciliation to the natural field was to allow hell to occupy it—below it, with the help of Satan, on the surface, with the help of man.

Thus, it can be seen how Malinowski, with a deep affection for

the primitives among whom he lived, and with an even higher
sympathy for his civilized brethren of his time, like Boas, had
an intense disgust for Hitlerian dictators and fought with all he
had against totalitarianism and authoritarian rule. It reminds me
of Richard Coudenhove-Kalergi and his *Crusade for Pan-Europe,*
in which he wrote that "Catholicism is the fascist form of Christianity." Himmler admitted that he "fashioned his entire department of Gestapo and the SS along the pattern of the Jesuit order
itself."[102] Malinowski should have known that the very essence
and lifeblood of religion and all its subsidiaries are contained in
its dictatorial, dogmatic, arbitrary, and psychological power, the
same kind of play upon the emotions of people as the Hitlers
have made to achieve their ends.

Yet, with it all, there are many brilliant men, like Malinowski,
who, after a life of association with the "desperate little people,"
feel that it would be cruel and unjustified, all circumstances considered, to take this hope and dream of final rewards and compensations away from them. With all that the primitive has to
struggle against and with all that his civilized brothers have to
cope with, between the increasing strain for peace and security,
on one hand, and the depressing, compressing, and overbearing
defreeing processes of totalitarianism on the other, is it any wonder that Malinowski, himself an agnostic and unable to accept any
positive religion, Christian or otherwise,[103] still felt that if it
meant only a pragramtic relief, it is still good for humans to be
religious and derive some kind of comfort in the belief that
eventually God in his heaven or some spirit will have mercy and
wise judgment and give them eternal life in a happier and more
peaceful sphere? He looked upon religion as a forgivably equitable
device to comfort and solace man, without which the ego of man
would, considering its awareness of death and the finity of life,
break down into personal anarchy and a nihilistic view of life.
He wrote: "Religion, even at its worst, is never completely useless or wholly evil. Even in its lowest forms it has a divine spark,
and when I speak of 'divine' I express simply the point of view
of the believer and not my own. As an anthropologist, I can
speak of the 'divine' only as it manifests itself to man and in
man."[104]

Malinowski argues the utilitarian view of religion further: "Religion promises immortality for man, and it reveals to him his God or his gods. It is this active or creative side of religion which seems to me to be the most important, and on which I have placed the greatest emphasis. Thus, the comparative science of religion compels us to recognize religion as the master-force of human culture. Religion makes man do the biggest things he is capable of, and it does what nothing else can do; it gives him peace and happiness, harmony and a sense of purpose; and it gives all this in an absolute form."[105] He speaks for himself thusly: "The rationalist and agnostic must admit that even if he himself cannot accept these truths, he must at least recognize them as indispensable pragmatic figments without which civilization cannot exist."[106]

Yet our ancestors *did* exist for millions of years before magic and religion, and they lived in a greater and more severe struggle for sustenance and survival. The fact that we are here today proves they were successful. Yet all the other creatures in the world, wild and domesticated, live in a religion-less atmosphere, and who can say absolutely and in the ultimate that our civilization is greater, wiser and better than their way of life? I do not recommend going wild or retreating into the jungle. We are the products of past and present civilizations, and we, in turn, are the progenitors of the civilizations to come. We cannot rationally presume that our judgments can speak for all creation and for all times. What our minds think or wish to think out does not absolutely or necessarily establish any truth based on the premise that thought, in itself, by the very act of thinking, establishes a truth. What it does establish, a priori, is that we are thinking, not *that* which we are thinking about. It does not imply that any thought, as a result of objective verification, does not possibly identify a truth; it does mean that thinking, as a process in itself and by itself does not arbitrarily, *ipso facto,* establish a truth. Szczesny pursues this point: "It would be false thinking and formulation were we to say that nature has endowed man with intelligence in order to allow him to survive after death."[107] "In deed, it is quite impossible to think meaningfully of life after death without bearing strictly in mind at all times that the principle of individuation and the law of becoming are inseparable."[108] In the last analysis, the history of socioreligious cultures, and the history, in particular, of the last two thousand years in Europe, the Near East, and other parts of the world, including the few hundred years of settlement and history on the American continents, reveal the sad exposure of the effects of religion upon mankind. Epictetus wisely counseled: "Where are you going? It cannot be into a place of suffering; there is no hell. You are going to be again peaceably associated with the elements from which you have parted."

For millions of years our protohominid begetters were born, begot, lived and died, without magic and religion, and we are here today because they begot successfully. The other animals are here for the same reasons. Their natural freedoms were not yet to be influenced and metamorphosed into self-incarcerated elements. Actually, today, the intensity of religious adherence is waning as freer education, economic freedom and world communication are increasingly spreading around the world. "A religion which is reduced to defending its ethical solicitation is already moribund. Its name cannot be saved merely by associating it with contemporary aspirations typical of humanity everywhere."[109] "If the Christian metaphysic must be abandoned from its foundation to its superstructure, the only choice remaining is to investigate man as he actually is."[110]

Does religion give man the peace and solace that Malinowski hopes for so fervently? Our prison records clearly show that most of our criminals and murderers are of the religious kind, and the greater percentage of these belong to the more orthodox and obscurantic forms of religion. Our mental institutions and hospitals clearly prove by their records that the greatest percentage of their inmates and patients come from the very religious. "Most Christian wars were found among Christian peoples."[111] "In the eternal theater of carnage and death that was Aztec, one had to conform."[112] Regarding the Christian missionary work in the Pacific islands: "The rivalry between the Protestantism and Catholicism of that era may be gauged by the fact that, on Bougainville Island, Methodist and Catholic native converts were burning down each other's chapels as late as 1930—to the considerable embarrassment of their spiritual mentors."[113]

For many tens of thousands of years our preprimitives and primitives, acquiring magic and its rituals to assist them in the natural field where they could not, in their limited and relative knowledge, assist themselves, carried on without religion. Religion came with *leadership*, with the psychological rule of the one or the few over the many and, later, with arbitrary and naked rule over whole peoples, and, as we shall see, came about through *economic* causes and reasons rather than through celestial effects. As such, the futility-philosophy of Malinowski resigns itself to a premise that it is not possible for man to live happily and peacefully within the *actual truth* and not "accepted truths," when history reveals the constant butchery, massacre, war, strife, prejudice, hate and slavery in its periods of greater religious intensity and density. Mark Twain says of Christianity: "Ours is a terrible religion. The fleets of the world could swim in spacious comfort in the innocent blood it has spilt."[114]

The religious Abyssinian culture is almost wholly devoted to laziness, cruelty, banditry, and to having slaves work for it. Henry Darley, who witnessed these things, wrote: "Behind them is starvation and hunger, for while a single slave can be captured, the Abyssinian will not work."[115] He continues to tell us how the Christian Abyssinians treat their Shangalla neighbors: "It was pitiful to see the state to which the unfortunate Shangallas had been reduced. Murdered, robbed of all their possessions, and carried off into slavery by the thousand, they were now living in the densest forests, and prayed only for the arrival of the white man, a being whom so few of them have ever seen."[116] Darley watched the lines of unfortunate captives moving past his house, en route to the slave markets: "To my amazement I saw an unbroken string of slaves, the men roped together, the women and children walking alongside, while the little babies unable to walk, and whose mothers were exhausted, were strapped on the backs of mules, three or four at a time. . . . I gazed in astonishment at this throng, and tried to count them, but the number seemed endless, so I took my armchair out of my compound and sat there counting them as they filed past. . . . Each soldier conducted his own little mob. I marked the hundreds by throwing bits of stick on the ground. . . . At nightfall the procession of misery halted, and camped on the spot, marching on again at break of day. . . . For nearly four days they streamed along. I counted six thousand in the first two days. . . . I can lay no claim to being a philanthropist, far from it, but I can say with truth that I have never seen a more heartrending sight. I only wish I could write so as to make every reader of this record realize it as I did at the time. It was worse than war. . . . I remember, after the last had gone by, I saw an old woman supporting herself with a stick, hobbling along after them. I said to her in Amharic: 'Where are you going to, mother? Do you want the Abyssinians to catch you?' She answered, 'What do I care? They have killed my husband, and carried off my children and grandchildren. I have no home left, so I follow them to wherever they go.' "[117]

Thus the black Christians, like their white Christian brothers, enslave and enslave more mercilessly and relentlessly. Grzimek: "If you travel by railroad from Dar-es-Salaam to Lake Victoria, via Tabora and Mwanza, you cannot tell that the land all around has been fertilized by the blood, flesh and bones of slaves who collapsed by the road, under Arab whips, during their endless marches, and that the soil has been wetted by the tears of mothers separated from their husbands and children."[118] "The Arab slave hunts in East Africa never reached the frightful proportions of the similar trade in human beings carried out by Europeans and Americans on the West Coast."[119] Herbert J. Muller: "With organized warfare civilization promoted the growth of slavery—the major threats thereafter to the freedom of whole peoples."[120] Should we go into the history of the slave traffic of the Episcopalian English, the Catholic Portuguese and Spaniard, and relate the same story over and over again tens of thousands of times over a period of many *centuries?* To this very day the good Moslems who have just finished their prayers to Allah go on with their slave traffic and when successful, no doubt give thanks to Mahomet, the Prophet, for his kind blessings. Robert Lopez: "As late as the mid eleventh century the Bishop of Chur saw nothing wrong in collecting twopence per head for slaves sold in his market."[121] Roger Bastide: "When Christians tried to justify slavery, they claimed black skin was a punishment from God. . . . Against the background of this symbolism, they invented causes for the malady, intended to justify in their own eyes a process of production based upon the exploitation of Negro labor."[122]

Away off in the Pacific, Oliver writes about the good Christian ethics of the Europeans who did a thriving business "blackbirding" natives into slavery: "The Pacific blackbirders were as proficient a band of slavers as ever shocked an abolition society. They captured savage chiefs and their families and held them hostages until enough able-bodied followers had signed on."[123] "Most blackbirding took place in the western islands, but the central and eastern islands did not escape altogether. Shiploads of Micronesians and Polynesians were taken to Peru and sold at so much a head to the planters and guano-deposit owners. The islanders proved unsuited to the work and large numbers of them died."[124] Catholic plunderers and enslavers selling human booty to Catholic planters and farmers; here is where the formal and well-instituted religion had a greater spiritual influence upon its adherents than the jungle magic of the Polynesian shaman.

Malinowski feels that it is not possible for man to regain his natural freedom, to find life justification on the premises of life itself, to find his heaven on earth and therefore he might as well be happy "thinking" that there is a heaven awaiting him in the sky. This very pathetic philosophy has kept man from justifying his life in normal terms, has kept man from rebelling against the rulers in all their forms and personalities, who have pawned and enslaved him for their own ambitions and securities, and has kept man from reasserting his natural freedom. It has, with apologetics, joined forces unwittingly with the religious rulers and hierarchies to keep man a slave unto himself, to look only to the skies and not at what is below his feet and around him. Meantime these rulers actually, realistically, and practically build greater temples of gold and silver, create empires of finance and profit, organize wider, higher, and deeper penetration of the multitudes to abide in ignorance, credulity, and obedience, while they meekly but firmly join ranks with dictators and oligarchies, so long as their own rule can be maintained and impregnated. These religious rulers praise poverty and humility *for their followers* so that they should happily part with the little they have to give to these rulers, who do all things possible to make sure that they, through their gods, never feel poverty or want, being considered within their catechismic rule as deities of a sort, while the indoctrinated masses follow, like docile sheep behind them, content to inhale the musk of celestial promise and immortal desire the Judas-goat rulers exude behind them.

What Malinowski overlooked, in his subjective analysis of these things, is that wherever religion and magic are interwoven into the living fabric of the social life of a people, among the primitives as well as moderns, individuals and groups alike have become adjusted and adapted to them, and any other offered adjustment or adaptation could not be received unless new living factors came about that brought, within themselves, new symbologies, new more acceptable values, new symbiotic chains of cohesiveness of purpose and meaning that could possibly, suddenly or gradually, induce people to depart from or modify their cultures and beliefs. All things are *in transito*. Malinowski overlooked the constant subjection of people to change and adjustment in matters of magic and religion; these "spiritual" processes have constantly changed within themselves as people became subjected to new conditions. Sometimes this change came about by external factors alone, as in many of the far South Pacific islands during the last war; the natives now can ride in jeeps, wear jeans, smoke cigars, drink coke, and cook on gas stoves. I would not be surprised to find a shaman using a typewriter inside some broken-down airplane left behind as decoration for somebody's backyard. Another war or two and they should be completely civilized to use a machine-gun, radio, have television, and throw the old magic back into the shaman's teeth! But by then a wise shaman will be the local distributor for the new transistor radios!

Sometimes cultural changes take place because of internal factors within the fabric of the society, and most often by a combination of both internal and external factors. When changes become sufficient to eliminate the need for magic and religion, and this process has been progressively going on for a long time, other factors of value and meaningfulness will have already come into the fabric and consciousness of people, for better or worse, which may possibly fulfill or destroy the hopes of man insofar as his knowledge and nature can possibly offer.

Even in the history of religion itself we can see the constant overlapping of one culture into another, of one religion into another, of one philosophy into another, the same determinism that goes on in the very process of experience, in the sciences, in social organizations. Religion, in particular, has been the master copycat, the zealous plagiarist, even the most "honest" forger and falsifier. God will always forgive the method so long as the end is achieved, that another god should not get there first.

The word *pagan* comes from *pagani,* peasants. Barrows Dunham relates how the early Church became *paganized:* "What the *pagani* of A.D. 400 believed was the old magic, the power of familiar demons and local divinities. All this it had been the intent and striving of Christianity to supersede; but one may doubt whether, in the process of accommodation, paganism did not leave more imprint upon Christianity than Christianity upon paganism. In time the saints and their relics came to do what demons had long done, but perhaps on this level they behaved more like demons than saints. Magic falsifies the actual causality in nature, and has its effects, not in the objective world, but in the mind of the believer. Consequently, there cannot have been much difference between a pagan thaumaturge and a Christian miracle worker in respect of science or even of intent."[125] Joseph Campbell: "And there was a great deal more religious lore being carried to Europe in those centuries from the relic-fertile East than is represented merely in the arrival of such holy marvels as the bones, arms, and legs of apostles, splinters of the true cross, little vials of the Virgin's milk, Saint Joseph's breath, and the Lord's tears, several prepuces of Jesus, parts of the burning bush, feathers from the angel Gabriel's wings."[126] Theodor Reik: "Most of the Christmas customs are not originally Christian, but heathen customs absorbed by the Church. The cradle of Christ, for instance, is borrowed from the cult of Adonis; the Yule customs come from the concepts of the *wilde Yagd* of the Teutonic god Odin; and so on. According to some scholars, the Feast of Booths (Hebrew) originated in the worship of Adonis or from the ritual drama of the Canaanites."[127] Birket-Smith: "The Jewish Passover was, for instance, the outcome of a merging of the ancient Canaanite harvest feast and the nomads' spring festival at which the newly harvested barley and the newborn lambs were consecrated."[128] "Our own popular Christmas customs have various sources, but their form clearly indicates that they are based partly on fertility rites, partly on the worship of the dead."[129] Samuel Noah Kramer, reflecting upon the implications of the deciphering of Egyptian and Babylonian tablets, writes: "For it soon became evident that some of the Old Testament material was mythological in character, since it presented clear parallels and resemblances to the myths recovered from Egyptian and Babylonian sources."[130]

The evolution of religion, in itself, is the story from the simple to the complex, from the earliest shamanism to the great patriarchs, hierarchies, and ecumenical councils of today. In some countries shamanism still persists strongly, and in other countries it has gone forever. "Shamanism is an extremely prominent feature of both the Buddhism and the Shintoism of Japan as well as of Chinese and Tibetan religious life."[131] Many changes have gone on from the isolated witch-doctor to a periphery of religion that circles the globe with its many millions of priests, monks, and ministers in a multitudinous array of temples in most all the countries of the world. As man has moved, modified and changed, so has all his cultural properties that he has carried, piggyback, with him on his long trail from the earliest babblings of magic tens of thousands of years ago to all the modes, cults, and religions of the present day. To this very day the Dobu Islanders have "the ever-present anxiety born of the belief that all enemies are potential sorcerers or witches, possessing the magical means of inflicting sickness or ruin or death."[132] Change does not necessarily mean progress or improvement, and whether the awe-inspiring minister today, addicted with parsonitis of the throat, is an improvement over the old witch-doctor scattering the smoke of herbs or going about with his net looking for lost souls, is a judgment which the natural freedom of thought has given to each of us to decide. Perhaps civilization is a refining process that has something to do with modifying the quality or appearance of things.

MYTHS AND TALES ABOUT THE WORLD
AND THE CREATION OF MAN

MANY OF THE primitive and ancient cosmogonies and theogonies of the origin of the world and life are very beautiful and artful metaphors, poems, and symbologies, a commendable credit to the seeking, imaginative, contemplative, and interpretative minds of men. Many of the *upanishads* and *sutras* of India are beautiful stories, and the books of old China contain profound philosophy. Even though this occurred because of the relative ignorance and the limited knowledge about themselves and the world, it is still, by far, the mark of distinction which separates man from all his other animal relatives. Some animals, in their peculiar ways, may be considered "scientists," but man alone is a philosopher and a worshipper of the gods. To list and relate the stories of creation of every little tribe and religion would fill a large volume by itself, but with few exceptions they are all very intriguing, dramatic, colorful and distinctive in their variations and explanations. It is like a child reading fairy tales and believing all the things about people and animals to be true and moving. The farther we go back in history and prehistory, the more we find the cosmogonies to be all-inclusive of man and his animal relatives and the scenes of the particular environments involved. As we emerge into the later periods, we find man leaving his animals and plants and focalizing more and more the creation, the gods and spiritual forces upon, for and within *himself*. Tylor wrote about the sacred animals of Ancient Egypt: "Ancient Egypt was a land of sacred cats and jackals and hawks; whose mummies are among us to this day, but the reason of whose worship was a subject too sacred for the Father of History to discuss. Egyptian animal-worship seems to show, in a double line, traces of a savage ancestry extending into ages lying far behind even the remote antiquity of the Pyramids. Deities patronizing special sacred animals, incarnate in their bodies, or represented in their figures, have nowhere better examples than the divine bull-dynasty of Apis, the sacred hawks caged and fed in the temple of Horus, Thoth and his cynocephalus and ibis, Hator the cow and Sebek the crocodile."[133]

In Bali I learned from the priests that "the island rests on the turtle, which floats on the ocean."[134] Adolph E. Jensen reveals another story: "Nine families of mankind came forth in the beginning from Mount Nunusaku, where the people had emerged from clusters of bananas. And these families stopped in West Ceram, at a place known as the 'Nine Dance Grounds,' which is in the jungle between Ahiolo and Varoloin."[135] As the agricultural and agrarian periods advanced, man and woman came from the *soil,* the same soil that gave forth life and food—*adom* the earth, to *adam* the man. Birket-Smith: "On Mangaia in Polynesia . . . there Tangaroa lives, he who created man out of red earth."[136] Claude Lévi-Strauss relates: "When the supreme being, Gonoen-hodi, decided to create humanity, the Guana were the first of the tribes to come forth from the earth; the others came later."[137] The first human being was created by different gods in different ways. The cosmocentricities of peoples all over the world are similar and different in many ways. Yahweh made man out of clay while Atum masturbated at Heliopolis or in the primeval waters of the beginnings of things and created Shu and Tefnut.[138] Some were spat out, blown out, wept out, and some were brought to life by a serpent. The varieties and methods are numerous. These stories represent the beautiful poetry and imagery of the ancient worlds.

Finally, the Age of the Enlightenment lit up the darkness of the previous centuries and exposed it to the scrutiny and courage of science and intellect, "the mythological Creation story in the Old Testament could no longer be accepted as literally true. Already, in the early 17th century the heliocentric universe had been condemned as contrary to Holy Scriptures, both by Luther and by the Roman Catholic Inquisition: in the 19th century the tendency of the learned world was rather to reject Holy Scriptures as contrary to fact. And with the Hebrew Scripture went the Hebrew God, and the Christian claim to divine authority as well."[139] The new consciousness of the Enlightenment changed from a religious and conforming status to one of new ideas about social, political, economic equity and justice, and moved aggressively toward the acceptance of reason to question old ways and beliefs and new possibilities. George F. Thomas: "A theology that can do nothing but repeat the orthodox doctrines inherited from the past cannot even understand and defend them."[140] "Question the Bible at any point, and you are on the way to a complete rejection of it. Question the orthodox doctrines at any point, and the whole structure falls."[141] Explaining Ralph Barton Perry's opinions in his *Puritanism and Democracy,* Roger Bastide comments: "Puritanism taught that men should distrust their own inclinations and their natural faculties, seeking both their origin and their salvation in a supernatural order. It was a religion of misanthropy. The philosophy of the Enlightenment, on the other hand, was human, optimistic, and eudaemonic."[142] Thus, with the general advance of knowledge and its criticisms came the irresistible and inevitable changes and new acceptances.

FEMALE DIVINITIES AND FERTILITY RITES

THE FIRST DEITIES, most archeologists and anthroplogists believe, were females, dedicated and devoted to their conceptual explainables and furtherances of creation, fertility and fruition. Stonehenge in England is indicative of the worship of the fertility goddess. "There is no sign of a male deity until civilization approaches."[143] "Female figures turn up frequently in sites occupied by Neolithic farmers."[144] "The Palaeolithic Mother Goddess persisted and held sway over almost the whole range of primary Neolithic cultures."[145] "The concept of the Mother Goddess may be said to be almost as universal as the religious impulse itself. Whether she is an inherited figure of the human psyche, or one created by the common experience of life itself, we cannot presume to judge, but she seems to have created eternal life. Her power waxes and wanes, sometimes she is almost dispossessed by her son or by the divine father, but she lives on in the mind of man whether he calls her Nentinugga, Ishtar, Hathor, Isis, Hera or Mary."[146] Among the fertility goddesses of the ancient world we have Cerceto, the Great Mother goddess of Asia, Innina, Astarte, Ashtoreth, Aphrodite, Diana, etc. In India she is Maya, the Great Mother of the Universe, described to contain within her all the gods of the Indian pantheon. "There are three aspects of the Cretan Mother Goddess that stand out more clearly than any of the others; these are her roles as goddess of vegetation, Mistress of Animals, and household goddess. In terms of the Greek pantheon these aspects could be identified as Demeter, Artemis, and Athene."[147] "The Greeks invoked her as Artemis, the Romans appealed to Diana, the Buddhists worshipped her as Maya, the Saxons called on Frigga, and the Christian pays homage to the Virgin Mary. But whatever the name she is known under her attributes remain unchanged, for everywhere and always she is the Divine Mother, the feminine Principle of the Deity, the Virgin-goddess, who is yet maternal and fruitful, and bestows fertility even whilst she protects and honours chastity."[148] At the end of the Ecumenical Conference Session in Rome in November, 1964, Pope Paul proclaimed Mary as the "Mother of the Church."

It seems more than coincidental in rhetoric that many religious philosophies were considered in the feminine gender: *Tao* in the Orient, *Maat* in ancient Egypt, *Dharma* in India, *Me* at Sumer, and *Moira* in ancient Greece, all feminine words. "Minoan-Mycenaean religion . . . is a link between the great fertility religions of the Near East and the complex history of the gods of Olympus."[149] "Taking all the evidence together, it looks very much as if the Maltan religion was a specialized branch of the earth mother fertility cult. . . . Up to about 1500 B.C. Malta, with its monumental goddess, was evidently a link in its spread throughout Europe."[150] Robert Graves and Raphael Patai: "Eve, described in *Genesis* as Adam's wife, is identified by historians with the Goddess Heba, wife of a Hittite Storm-god, who rode naked on a lion's back and, among the Greeks, became the Goddess Hebe, Heracles's bride. A prince of Jerusalem in the Tell Amarna period (fourteenth century B.C.) styled himself Abdu-Heba— 'servant of Eve.' Lilith, Eve's predecessor, has been wholly exorcised from Scripture, though she is remembered by Isaiah as inhabiting desolate ruins. She seems, from midrashic accounts of her sexual promiscuity, to have been a fertility-goddess, and appears as Lillake in a Sumerian religious text, *Gilgamesh and the*

Willow Tree."[151] Joseph Campbell:: "No good Catholic would kneel before an image of Isis if he knew that it was she. Yet every one of the mythic motifs now dogmatically attributed to Mary as a historic human being belongs also—and belonged in the period and place of the development of her cult—to that goddess mother of all things, of whom both Mary and Isis were local manifestations: the mother-bride of the dead and resurrected god, whose earliest known representatives must now be assigned to a date as early, at least, as c.5500 B.C."[152] Frank Waters recounts the Hopi Indians' story of the first people: "So the First People kept multiplying and spreading over the face of the land and were happy. Although they were of different colors and spoke different languages, they felt as one and understood one another without talking. It was the same with the birds and animals. They all suckled at the breast of their Mother Earth, who gave them her milk of grass, seeds, fruit, and corn, and they all felt as one people and animals."[153] He continues: "The pit houses and storage cists in which they had stored the corn that gave them life and in which they had buried their dead now began to be used for performances of the sacred ceremonies by which the peoples bridged life and death in an enduring continuity. They became kivas . . . the kiva (world below) . . . was sunk deep, like a womb, into the body of Mother Earth, from which man is born with all that nourishes him."[154]

The idea of the fruitful goddess who always maintains her virginity, and so her eternal youthfulness, freshness and the repetitive cycles of fertility and fulfillment without end, permeated the earliest Neolithic and prehistoric cultures and into the primal stages of the historic periods. Martin A. Larson: "The immaculate conception of Mary became in due course the Catholic equivalent of the Miraculous origin of Dukdaub."[155] The Hopi Indians had their story of a boy who was born of a virgin and became a great chief whose name was Siliomono.[156] The Hummingbird god of the Mexica, *Huitzilopochtli,* for "whom hundreds of thousands of living hearts were torn out of humans, was taken for a god who was born of woman without man."[157] The menstrual fluids being regarded as a magical substance and a concomitant identity of life itself, the retainment of virginity by the goddess was the insurance of the continual supply of life and renewal for man and all the animals and vegetation that man needed constantly for his sustenance and survival. The goddess was immortal, and the idea of degeneration as exhibited in mortal life could not be thought of as attached to the Divine Mother, from whose teats all life flowered and flowed as a continual stream of food and regeneration. Graves and Patai: "Menstruation is ambivalently regarded by most primitive people as both holy and impure: holy, because marking a girl's readiness for motherhood; impure, because men must avoid contact with menstrous women. Some tribes believe that menstruation results from a snake bite; though snake venom is a coagulant. The myth of Eve's defilement by the Serpent was first told, perhaps, to explain the origin of menstruation: as caused by the lecherous Serpent whose bite made her nubile. According to one Talmudic passage, menstrual pains are among the curses that God laid on Eve."[158]

So great was this psychic ideation of the Earth Mother that man did not attach any significance to the sex act as the creator of life, since each female was in many ways the spiritual emissary of the goddess and brought the renewal of life through her mysterious and magical power. As a consequence, primitive mentality could not fully connect the sexual act with life creation. "It was notable that the Arunta did not believe that children were the result of sexual intercourse."[159] Regarding the Australian aborigines, "it was maintained by various authorities that these Australian people did not recognize the function of sexual intercourse in producing children but ascribed conception entirely to the activities of the ancestral spirits."[160] The Balinese think to this day that the ancestors sneak back to mortality and life renewal in the form of dew on fruits and plants which the woman eats and thus becomes pregnant. "The aborigines, while obviously aware that children issue from the mother's womb, did not emphasize the connection between copulation and procreation. . . . In the view of some tribes all human spirits were pre-existent. . . . These spirits entered women's wombs and were subsequently born as human infants."[161]

The magic and miracle of birth and its vehicles of reincarnation, recurrence, and reinhabitation of soul as an eternal cyclic

process awed the magic-minded primitive, and this awe of the
power of woman eventually brought about a growing fear of a
domain beyond man's physical touch and reach. Eventually it
brought on, through the earliest patrilineal kinships and clans,
the resurgence of male dominance and the emergence of patriarchy and its patrilineal genealogies. The menstrual fluids were
used, when placed or sprinkled on doorposts or entrances, to
ward off or dispose of evil spirits, spells, or the power of black
magic.[162] So fearful was man of his mate and womankind in general that the poor women were subjected to cruelties and disposi-
tions unworthy of the "divine goddess" relationship, and gave
history some of its most terrifying and murderous pages: the
witchcraft epidemics in Europe are but one example. Woman was
just "bad," black magic, the origin of the idea that abstinence,
negation of sex, and noncontamination with the female body in
any way was the pathway to purity of body and soul, godly approval and acceptance. Jealous and dominating Monica, the
mother of Augustine, finally had her way of "purifying" her son
by abstaining from sex with his paramours to keep satisfying her
neurotic and conniving ego; thus Augustine became St. Augustine.

Ottaker Nemecek: "In 1703 the Jesuit *Burges* reported that
the *Indians* of *Paraguay*, when they felt themselves very near to
death, strangled their wives so that death might spare them, the
men."[163] "Primitive man's dread of the daemonic power of hy-
meneal blood also gave rise to the custom of having the bride
deflowered by relations or slaves. In *Azimbaland* (Central Africa)
the bride's father had to pay a man to deflower her. Among the
Kipsikis (East Africa) a husband could not have intercourse with
his bride until she had been deflowered by one of her admirers.
Marco Polo reports that in *Tibet* a mother would offer her
daughter to a stranger that he might deprive her of her virginity."[164]

Priests were the defenders of masculine purity from womanly
magic by taking care of the initial defloweration. Somehow they
felt immune to the magic but not to the maiden. "The taboo
nature of the woman, assigned to her by primitive man as a result
of his belief in the venomous and demonic effect of spilt blood
led him to consider every contact with her as fraught with danger,

a fortiori the act of coition."[165] The twisted idea that woman leads man to hell is explained nicely by Brigid Brophy: "At Eleusis the initiate's entering into the mother's body was further symbolized by including in the initiation some form of holy charade in which the initiant visited the dark region of Hell—that is, we can construe, the womb, the secret and forbidden underground bourne in the body of the mother earth, ruled over by Demeter in her Persephone extention."[166] Such ritual and idea evolved the belief that woman leads man to hell. Thus the antinatural notion arose that sex is immoral, sinful, impure, that any attachment to woman is vile. This notion is well annunciated by many Catholic Saints and authorities and is one of the fundamental dogmas of Catholicism.

As a result, a woman who remains a virgin stays "pure" and "undefiled," and the Catholic adoration of virginity became one of its leading tenets. St. Chrysostom held virginity to be high above the married state. Tertullian is claimed to have stated that the distinction made between marriage and whoredom is neither more nor less than a legal fiction. St. Ambrose devoted five of his works to virginity; the list is long and repetitious. Yet medical science has brought out that "prolonged virginity, as a rule, is extraordinarily harmful to woman."[167] Many gynecologists, neurologists, and psychiatrists today stress the physiological and psychological degeneration of a woman who is deeply inflicted with the notion that sex relations are impure, sinful, not respectable, immoral, and contrary to God's wishes; the amount of frustration, misery, frigidity, neuroses, waste of potential and normal happiness is a tragic aberration from the natural freedoms as well as from the real content of any moral value. "Almost every adult in a Christian community is more or less diseased nervously as a result of the taboo on sex knowledge when he or she was young."[168] "Christianity is the religion that made love a sin."[169] John Dewey: "A body of beliefs and practices that are apart from the common and natural relations of mankind must, in the degree in which it is influential, weaken and sap the force of the possibilities inherent in such relations."[170]

Actually, if everyone were able to follow the rule of virginity and remain "pure," the world would come to an end, and there would be neither people nor Catholicism. Thus, as the male became more dominant in religious deities, and, as a consequence, in all other matters including the exclusive management of temples and rites, his gods became bisexual, *he-shes,* and many of these still exist: *Tinga* in Bali is one example. When the priesthood became the *exclusive* agent of the gods, they were then prepared to create the one and only god in the image of the indivisible male with strength, dominance, wisdom, authority, age and whiskers.

THE POWER OF THE PRIEST

BEFORE WE ENTER into a discussion of how the gods came to be, we should look into the nature of the men and ideas that paved the way for their creation. The primitive shaman, the initial formulator of taboo logistics, took the first cut of freedom, and liked it. He must have wondered at the ecstatic acceptance of his chicanery. This acceptance and sometimes success proved the "truth" of his "divine" and magical power. No doubt he came to believe it himself and became a holy man. The shaman's first child, the witch-doctor, kept a sort of social order, but it was within a circle of fear, emotional terror, and psychic subjection. Felice Belloti: "In the primitive mind the witch doctor eventually becomes an element of order. And, however much in our eyes it may seem an order *sui generis,* it is not clear what one could put in its place. . . . A certain man in the prime of his strength, and in perfectly good health, suddenly dies. His relatives repair to the witch doctor, who is already aware of the fact, and beg him to help them find out who has cast the evil eye so that they can avenge him. The witch doctor puts on his magic trappings and consults the sacred amulets, human bones, tripods or the speaking fetich; then he lights an oakum match, and while it burns pronounces the names of the suspects; if at one of these names the match goes out the culprit has been found. He is pointed out to the dead man's family and to the whole tribe as a murderous caster of *daua,* and is put to death with horrible tortures. . . . But a few days later another individual of the same family dies just as mysteriously. Has the witch doctor made a mistake? Not a bit of it. There are many evil individuals among us, and they must all be put to death, otherwise the whole tribe will be destroyed."[171]

The early kingships were the successors of still earlier priest-hoods, who now added secular power to their divine power so that both heaven and earth can mark the mastery and overallness of their scepters. The early priest, like his grandfather shaman, held this mastery by sheer psychological power, the power of fear, and, to this extent, disrobed the primitive and ancient of his natural freedom, and left him almost naked, subjected now to the protective blanket of mysticism that only the specialized priest proclaimed he possessed; later, these blankets metamorphosed into the shining keys to heaven. But the priest realized that there is more to possess than merely spiritual power dealing with things beyond; he became the priest-king, who now took over the past, present, and future of his subjects. The only natural freedom that was allowed to these "free" slaves was the freedom to serve in abjection, willingly or unwillingly. Naked power held by one or a few over the many was initiated with the blessings of the gods. The minds and bodies of the people were thus traditional-ized to the rule of monarchy and monarchism as priestcraft adorned in civil attire and with imperial authority. Herbert J. Muller: "Whatever 'spiritual' freedom it gave the community was purchased at some expense of social, economic and political freedom."[172]

Professor Sabatino Moscati of Rome, writes about the good religious life in ancient Mesopotamia: "In every department of human life religion is the ruling factor. As is the case throughout the ancient Near East, literature, law, and art are envisaged in Mesopotamia only in connection with religious motives, and these motives penetrate every manifestation of life and so make up the innermost substance of that life. This is perhaps the most distinctive feature of ancient Near East civilization. Human values are epitomized in religion; for independent philosophical specu-lation and artistic creation we must await the coming of the Greeks."[173]

The priest-king not only held the reins of protecting the future

life beyond the grave for his people, but deified himself as a god with supernatural power, which became, as a result, the symbol of protective welfare for the security, happiness, salvation, and all good things for his people. The welfare of their lives depended upon his good health and longevity, in life and death, to such an extent that in order to make sure of his welfare at death, they sacrificed their lives to follow him in a common grave, often buried alive, so that they could continue to serve him and reap the reward of eternal security for themselves. R. T. Rundle Clark: "In two ways Egyptian religion is unique—in the elaborate theory which it wove around the monarchy and in its preoccupation with the afterlife. Essentially the pharaonic kingship was concerned with the same things as kingship everywhere. It grew out of the ideas and customs of the prehistoric chieftains of the Neolithic world."[174] Frazer: "The Mexican kings, when they mounted the throne, swore that they would make the sun to shine, the clouds to give rain, the rivers to flow, and the earth to bring forth fruits in abundance."[175] "At a certain stage of early society the king or priest is often thought to be endowed with supernatural powers or to be an incarnation of a deity, and consistently with this belief the course of nature is supposed to be more or less under his control."[176] Regarding the recent dictator of Indonesia, "many of his countrymen believe that Sukarno is blessed with *kesaktian,* a supernatural magic power that protects him from evil and makes him supernatural. Palace servants used to sell bottles of his bath water to peasants, who hoped that by drinking it they would inherit some of his magic."[177]

Felix Marti-Ibañez writes about the rulers in Constantinople during the era of Byzantium: "Life in Constantinople was cloistered. The people, prevented from looking beyond the city because of the surrounding walls, looked up to the heavens and prayed to God. The Byzantine emperor, the Basileus, was regarded as Christ on earth; his political code was the Bible; his parliament, the Holy Apostles; his offices, the basilicas, vast and towering and ablaze with gilded mosaics and stain-glass windows in all the colors of the spectrum. . . . The Basileus appeared in public 'pale as death,' robed in white and surrounded by his twelve apostles. His meals were replicas of the Last Supper; his garments and countenance were replicas of those in sacred icons. His palace was yet another church, where even the doorkeeper was a priest."[178] "The Byzantine Emperors, striving to strengthen their rule with the image of divine protection, issued for the first time in the seventh century coins on which the figure of Christ appears under the inscription *Rex Regnantium* (King of Kings), with the standing figure of the emperor inscribed *Servus Christi* (Servant of Christ) on the other side of the coin."[179] The idea that the welfare of the group depends upon the strength and health of the king or leader might be rooted in biological origins as we find the same tendency even among some animals. "When a common monkey gets rheumatism it is only disturbing to himself, but when a monkey of high standing has rheumatism, it is not only unpleasant for himself, but also exceedingly painful for his companions."[180]

To be a king or high priest is to be endowed with extraterritorial powers not usually the good fortune of the commonplace to possess, and thus the expression and use of these divine powers cultivated and enculturated the belief in miracles, in exotic occurrences, in prophecies, in the superpsychic power of certain selectives who are the agents or the media by which the gods themselves can communicate with the people or have certain people communiacte with them. Magical ritual, recitation, and prayer were not only these means but became militant commands which the gods were bound to obey or fulfill, because the *Word*, the *Logos*, the uttered sacred *Sound* was of such a nature that it *compelled* and *ordained* fulfillment. The gods, like humans, had no alternative or choice. Janheinz Jahn: "All magic is word magic, incantation and exorcism, blessing and curse. Through *Nommo*, the word, man establishes his mastery over things."[181]

The importance of the utterance, the mere ability to give off communicable sound, was interpreted by the primitive man as the spirit of the god residing, and expressing himself in, the body of man. The *word* became the proof that man is the vehicle of the god; actually, it was the other way around. "The Word is the beginning and, probably, the cause of everything."[182] The concept and use of writing as a form of magic was carried on extensively in Ancient Egypt, by the priests in Azteca and Mayan countries, in India by the Brahmins, by the Buddhistic lamas, and among the Africans today. "So far as we know, the Sumerians were the first people to evolve a proper system of writing."[183] Albert Schweitzer, of Lambaréné, says that "they regarded writing as a form of magic."[184]

Because of the *word,* the utterable name of a person was considered to be the spiritual essence of the person, and in ancient times people used to keep their real names secret and use misleading names to void and offset the evil intentions of others in using the curse against them. Three thousand years ago the Babylonians had the well-established custom of "don't give your right name" doctrine. "The giving of the name of an important warrior carried with it magic"[185] among the primitive Germanic tribes. The Machiguenga Indians of Peru to this day keep their own names a secret and never utter them.[186] "Names carry great importance in Vietnam. Often Vietnamese will have secret names, known only to themselves and their parents. If it is given away, the person believes he is exposed to evil spirits."[187] "A Polar Eskimo would never mention himself by name. Doing so could break its magic protection."[188] "The Indian regards his name, not as a mere label, but as a distinct part of his personality, just as much as are his eyes or his teeth, and believes that injury will result as surely from the malicious handling of his name as from a wound inflicted on any part of his physical organism. This belief was found among the various tribes from the Atlantic to the Pacific."[189] The cuneiform scriptures tell us that men commonly had two names: the true one was kept sacred and concealed while the other adopted name was used in their associations with others. The Malay native, when he sneezes, cries out, "Soul (and name), come right back here where you belong!" The commandment "Thou shalt not take the name of the Lord, thy God, in vain" becomes better understood. Joseph Campbell: "In the Hebrew Kabbala, for example, the sounds and forms of the letters of the Hebrew alphabet are regarded as the very elements of reality, so that by correctly pronouncing the names of things, of angels, or even of God, the competent Kabbalist can make sure of their force."[190] Theodor H. Gaster, writing about the folkways of Jewish life, states: "It is considered imprudent to let an infant's name be divulged during those critical days after birth when the demons are still hovering about it."[191]

I have seen and heard the singing, pleading prayers and laments of the Moslem as he speaks to his prophet; I have seen and heard the cantorous wailing of the Sephardic Jews in the temples of Jerusalem, the contemplative mutterings of the Shinto priest at Nikko, the plaintive cries of the Balinese priest at Sanur, the yelling and shedding of crocodile tears of the Amazonian savage pleading for more fish and sex power, and, right here at home, the awe-inspiring, reverential gibbering of the ministers: In all of these one can readily see that not only is the *word* itself important to utter, but the tone and feeling are also essential to send the radar out to the gods with proper dispatch and more favorable acceptance.

Man does not limit the variety of innovation and adapability in any direction. Imagination has no borders and is not devoted to the principles of calculus or physics. When ideality becomes the tool of ego or purpose, there is no telling to what ends the winged chariot can carry us. Imagination is the prehensile, stretchable finger of man that extends him into limitless space and touches images that reflect the ever-potential and ever-penetrating power of mind into realms, real and unreal. It often reveals the path to the discoverable, the awaiting invention, some unknown elixir, some light on possible experiences and events. Imagination has no alliances or self-purposes; it is a complete slave to the possessor and user. While man utilized this unique pneuma that he so uniquely possesses in every direction of the natural world, he did not stop there. He went beyond and added inference and sympathy to the things he wanted and must have: supernatural power and personal immortality.

IMAGINATION AND ITS OFFSPRING

MAN IS CAPABLE of carrying a dream in sleep into a continuity in consciousness. This is because of the complex and psychical forms of imagination, determined out of his tendencies to conceive experience, unpredictables, and even "impossibles" by relating these in multitudinous forms to his wants and drives, which, in turn, create themselves out of his genetic endowment and its effects and countereffects upon cultural acquisition, experience, and event, the association of ideas determined by the personality and its relationship to experience. Because of these processes of reflection and imagination, he not only invented or discovered quantum physics and theoretical mathematics, but also the soul, devils, gods, flying cherubs, harps in heaven, and everlasting fire and tortures in hell: the former, by his growing sense of curiosity; the latter, because of his psychic wants and fears, part of which can be attributed to his ego-desire to live forever and his innate paradoxical images to suffer, deny, and die.

Imagination has been used not only to give solace to endure the mundane miseries of the "little" and "lowly" people, but it has also been used to mislead and defraud them for the benefit of those who profit by it. This process is not merely relegated to the domain of theology and priestcraft, but permeates itself in all the fields of men and women. The television program *Candid Camera* took a perfume spray bottle, filled it with ordinary water, and asked people to express an opinion as to their delight in smelling the fragrance. Dozens of people smelled the pure water and identified the fragrance as sandalwood, jasmine, roses, gardenias, onion, deer meat, and many others.

On the other hand, imagination has given artful and explainable expression in many ways and forms, and many of them very beautiful, with which the human being can be identified, at least until we know of other life in outer space, as the only and supreme artist and poet extant. The Hindu picture of Vishnu sleeping on the coiled cosmic serpent, floating on the cosmic sea, and dreaming of the lotus-interpreted metaphoricalness of the world is very beautiful. The ancient Egyptians also had their cosmic serpent, the Chinese their guardian-angel Dragon; the Aztecs their Great Serpent godhead. It is interesting to note the worldwide mythical poetry of universe explanation, in which the opening scene and drama is the primeval sea and the serpent. These are beautiful stories of primitive imagination. Graves and Patai: "An alleged desire of divine serpents to impregnate mortal women appears in many mythologies. Sacred serpents kept in Egyptian temples acted as the god's procreative agents. The second *Tanis Papyrus* contains a list of sacred titles given to such beneficent serpents housed in the larger temples. Among the Greeks, too, barren women would lie all night on the floor of Asclepius's temple, hoping that the god would appear in serpent shape and impregnate them during sleep. At the Phrygian Mysteries of Sabazius, women ritually married the god by letting live snakes, or golden replicas, slide between their breasts down to the thighs."[192]

It was another story when priestcraft brought about the later fad of miracles, unthought of, and unknown in the primitive world because the primitive thought and knew of one world only, the world he lived in. A miracle must be an unbelievable thing in order to be believed. A very good miracle is one that guarantees to secure the belief by making itself superpreposterous. A. D. White: "When Professor Buckland, the eminent osteologist and geologist, discovered that the relics of St. Rosalia at Palermo, which had for ages cured diseases and warded off epidemics, were the bones of a goat, this fact caused not the slightest diminution in their miraculous power."[193]

Primitive man understood and knew his natural limitations. He saw too well what happens to people when they die: they disappear. But *he* did not want to disappear, and to accomplish this he needed a power that mortality does not possess. "The savage knows by experience that he can make sparks fly by knocking two flints against each other; what more natural, therefore, than that he should imagine the great sparks which we call lightning to be made in the same way by somebody up aloft, and that when he finds chipped flints on the ground he should take them for thunderstones dropped by the maker of thunder and lightning from the clouds? Thus, arguing from his limited experience primitive man creates a multitude of spirits or gods in his own likeness to explain the succession of phenomena in nature of whose true causes he is ignorant, in short, he personifies the phenomena as powerful anthropomorphic spirits, and believing to be more or less dependent on their good will he woos their favor by prayer and sacrifice."[194]

The imagination went to work. The power of another individual could be added to one's own; life means power and life exhibits and identifies itself in a body, whether animal, human, or plant. Therefore the consuming, actually or symbolically, of another body will add new life, more power to the consumer. William Graham Sumner: "Mothers ate their babies, if the latter died, in order to get back the strength which they had lost in bearing them."[195] James B. Griffin: "One special group of people within an Indian tribe, the Choctaw, in the Southeast allowed their fingernails to grow long so they could better pick the decomposing flesh from the skeleton."[196] Robert Redfield: "The Apache scalp taken in a foray is the symbol of the supernatural power brought to the Papago camp by the warrior who killed, a source of spiritual strength, a form of divine power, solemnly to be welcomed into the camp, into the home of the killer."[197]

Such power could be derived from the gods who inhabit the bodies of creatures, from the gods themselves, from the sacrifices of a high priest or king who is supposed to contain supernatural power. Sir Wallis Budge: "The magic of most early nations aimed at causing the transference of power from a supernatural being to man, whereby he was to be enabled to obtain superhuman results had to become for a time as mighty as the original possessor of the power."[198] The sacrifice of the power in animals and people could transfer this power to the growing crops and the general welfare of the society. Writing about bears and Eskimos, Dufresne tells us: "The hunter who killed a polar bear became the village hero, because every part of the animal was shared equally with the neighbors so that all might be brave and strong."[199] The Aztecs sacrificed infants, children, the young, adults, and old people during the various phases of the growing corn, from the sowing to the harvest. J. Eric S. Thompson: "The bodies of [Maya] sacrificed children are known to have been thrown into the sacred cenote as offerings to the rain gods as late as 1560."[200] R. C. Padden, regarding the religious customs of the Mexica: "From February until the rains came, small children and infants were wantonly immolated. If they cried as they were being slain, the priests rejoiced: it would likely be a wet spring."[201] "By the time Montezuma II came to power the sacrificial engine was forging ahead at frantic speed. Zumárraga's guess that 20,000 children were sacrificed annually pales besides Ixtlilxochitl's estimate that one child out of every five was so slain. A lot of nonsense has been written to show that this sacrifice of children was voluntary, that parents were willing, even anxious, to give up their children for the good of the greater number, just as they themselves almost hastened up the pyramid steps to fling their bodies down on the slab, secure in the knowledge that they were casting away their own lives for the benefit of others. Unfortunately, the sources make it abundantly clear that no such socialized altruism functioned, or was even conceived of by the sobbing mothers from whose breasts the infants were wrenched."[202] "The Greeks and Romans sacrificed pregnant victims to the goddesses of the corn and of the earth, doubtless in order that the earth might teem and the corn swell in the ear."[203] Originating in sympathetic and homeopathic magic, the rituals became more spiritualistic as history moved on. Humans can be married to gods, and by intermixing and crossbreeding the gods with people, the flow of supernaturalness and immortality can be more secured. "The custom of marrying gods either to images or to human beings was widespread among the nations of antiquity."[204] Thus man moved closer to the gods, and his imagination ruled that *he* is a Child of God, that God is his Father, and that *he* himself is also *God*.

Charles W. Eliot, President of Harvard University for forty years, wrote: "Every age, barbarous or civilized, happy or unhappy, improving or degenerating, frames its own conception of God within the limits of its own experiences and imaginings."[205] While this is not an all-inclusive explanation of the origin of gods, it is a clear, resounding fact that the creation of the gods was of man's manufacture, regardless of what manifestations, cravings, societal, economic, or imperial factors were involved, and regardless of any pragmatic or utilitarian solutions by which such creations may be justified. Winwood Reade: "A god's moral disposition, his ideas of right and wrong, are those of the people by whom he is created. Wandering tribes do not, as a rule, consider it wrong to rob outside the circle of their clan: their god is therefore a robber like themselves. If they settle in a fertile country, pass into the agricultural state, build towns, and become peaceful citizens with property of their own, they change their views respecting theft, and accordingly their god forbids it in his laws."[206]

The notion of a universal God, considering our general knowledge of religious history, is a modern idea and itself a product of previously related and nurturing notions. Hawkes and Woolley: "The creed that Moses taught was not, properly speaking, monotheistic, but it was uncompromisingly monolatrous. . . . The one thing that could weld them (the Hebrews) together was the patriarchal faith, and that must be exclusive. The Israelites must acknowledge allegiance to no other god; in that they would be a peculiar people distinguished from all others; but their god must be exclusively the god of Israel, the champion of them alone and the enemy of all other peoples and all other gods."[207] In many formal religions today, especially in Brahmanism and Catholicism, we find a similarity with a greater variety of higher, middle, and lesser saints and deities in orders of castes, functions, and values. Even members of the trinities have been placed on higher or secondary status levels and values from time to time. Birket-Smith: "The belief in a Supreme Being undeniably exists among a great number of peoples. But it should be noted that it is *never* a question of monotheism in the proper sense of the word. Not only are there numerous lower spirits and deities besides or under the Supreme Being, but the fundamental idea of monotheism, the belief in a single Divine Will, is also missing."[208]

In many parts of the world today there are tribal cults and even greater religions that do not profess belief in, or contain any knowledge of, a god; in India Jainism contains no god. Though the Judeo-Christian concept of God owes much of its religious origins to ancient Egypt and Sumeria, yet the monotheistic theology as evolved and instituted by the Hebrews and the later Moslems was not a recognized and established belief in Egypt. It should be noted, however, in deference to the monotheistic concept, that the idea of a single overall God was worldwide in many religions, in Mexico, Polynesia, India, the American Indians, in Africa, and in places too numerous to mention. It was not a sudden and miraculous revelation in Judea. Sir Wallis Budge: "The belief in magic, the word being used in its best sense, is older in Egypt than the belief in God, and it is

certain that a very large number of the Egyptian religious ceremonies, which were performed in later times as an integral part
of a highly spiritual worship, had their origin in superstitious
customs which date from a period when God, under any name or
in any form, was unconceived in the minds of the Egyptians."[209]

Frazer relates how out of totemism emerged a transformation
from its myriad composites into the image of a human god: "As
the attribution of human qualities to the totem is of the essence
of totemism, it is plain that a deity generalized from or including
under him a number of distinct animals and plants must, as his
animal and vegetable attributes contradict and cancel each other,
tend more and more to throw them off and to retain only those
human qualities which to the savage apprehension are the common element of all the totems whereof he is the composite product. In short, the tribal totem tends to pass into an anthropomorphic god."[210] This is why Sir Richard Burton wrote that "the
more I study religions, the more I am convinced that man never
worshipped anything but himself."[211] In another way we can say
that this means the transference of the *Ego-Mind* into a *God-
Mind*. In still another way we can say that if man could not overtake the limitations of nature and existence and all its conflicting
problems and compromising elements in societal need and growth,
which the Ego-Mind, as well as the Unconscious, so often rebel
against, he could and did use this Ego-Mind, with its extending
finger of imagination, to cross the natural barriers and sedate
himself with the being of a god and its attributes of omnipotence
and omniscience. Malinowski and Durkheim both err in resign-
ing themselves to some dividing line between man and other
animal life, that is, according divinity and superconsciousness to
man and mere existential recurrence of matter and event to all
else. As Ernest Hooten puts it: "If man insists upon aping the
apes, he ought, at any rate, to quit posing as an angel."[212]

Did man, by aping godhood or through ritual, magic, worship,
and sacrifice, become stronger, freer, live longer, become happier
and more peaceful? Sadly, the answer is *no*. As history, in its most
impartial and humanless objectivity, confirms. Man became an
addict. He left the openness of his naturally free life and confined
his body and mind within the temple walls to inhale the incense,

just as one inhales opium in some dingy Singapore alley and dreams of palaces, of Gardens of Edens, of cosmic paradises and exhilarating heights of grandeur that only a wildcat imagination can bring about for a helplessly opiated mind to revel in. Paul Blanshard: "If ever there was a church which deserved Karl Marx's slur against religion as 'the opium of the people,' it is the Spanish church."[213]

Man became weaker, not stronger, for his mind told the body that the body is filth, nothing, a transient substance placed on trial, that anything of the flesh is vile and impure, that virtue consists in denying the body, in living a constant negation, in proving to the god that one can sacrifice even life, that love in its most beautiful and normal expression is nothing but the demonic temptation to mislead the soul away from its state of blessed purity, whatever this means, that woman is just bad, very bad, any touch of her is Satanic poisoning, that sleeping with her is the same as sleeping with the Devil. Man's body became weaker, not stronger, under the influence of religion because it stressed, and is still stressing, the priority, the top-echelon rank of the spirit, the soul, and the constant gnawing away with dictum and prayer that the body is meaningless and should be neglected, discarded, that it is the soul and the soul alone that is needed, needed to be pure so it can travel to eternity, to blessedness, whatever this means and could mean without a body! The astronomy of Catholicism is typical of its knowledge of nature in general: "It was a walled-in universe like a walled-in medieval town. In the center lies the earth, dark, heavy, and corrupt, surrounded by the concentric spheres of the moon, sun, planets and stars in an ascending order of perfection, up to the sphere of the *primum mobile,* and beyond that the Empyrean dwelling of God."[214]

Man became less free. Whatever free mind he possessed was only free in its choice to sacrifice its own freedom of expression and to devote itself to the principle of suppressing and maintaining a *status quo* of ignorance and nonprogressiveness. The Jesuit Order forbids its members to *think.* It openly states that God has thought it all out and all that is to be done is to *follow,* not think, not question, not calculate, just believe and be led. How it affected man's freedom we shall see more fully as we go on, but religio-royal combines, expressed not only in the ancient king-deity as one person but later in the dual and separate but co-ordinating mutual-assisting roles of kings and popes, and still later departmentalized into the local politicians and ministers each bestowing affection and protectiveness upon each other for the influences upon the common vote, have now, for thousands of years, carried on and maintained themselves by the very principle of holding down, frustrating, "disciplining," indoctrinating, patternizing, and harnessing the natural freedom of man. Primitive man was freer and more scientific than the serf of the Dark Ages. Religion has been a steel curtain of darkness that descended upon the human drama and cut man off from proceeding, on his natural intelligence learned from natural experience, to adjust and adapt patterns and behaviors that freedom itself might have cultivated for the good of individual and group, and which was, in the primeval sense, the natural and empirical reason that formed the earliest social nuclei in the first place. This steel curtain of absolute authority over the minds and bodies, and their lives, of the adherents, instituted by the religio-royalties, was a most unfortunate tragedy that befell the human being, and the greatest depressor and enslaver of the freedom of man. Charles W. Eliot wrote this a long time ago: "The religion of the future will not be based on authority, either spiritual or temporal. The decline of the reliance upon absolute authority is one of the most significant phenomena of the modern world."[215]

Did man live longer because of these beliefs? Did he become happier? All these will be discussed more fully as we proceed. One thing we do know and history constantly reveals: these beliefs never made man more peaceful. On the contrary, they caused to emerge out of the natural constitution of man his worst and most hateful qualities, the qualities that could murder his neighbor and his children, the qualities that made him willing to sacrifice his own children, to forsake his wife and mother, to destroy himself and others, to an extent that no other influence in human history has done. Herbert J. Muller: "Monotheism, commonly regarded as the highest type of religion, was to inspire much more persecution than any other."[216] Joseph Campbell: "The world is now far too small, and men's stake in sanity too great, for any more of those old games of Chosen Folk (whether of Jehovah, Allah, Wotan, Manu, or the Devil) by which tribesmen were sustained against their enemies in the days when the serpent still could talk."[217]

CRIME, WAR, AND HOLOCAUST, IN THE NAME OF GOD

HISTORY REVEALS A dreadful story of unprecedented barbaric cruelty, the deepest of miseries, the worst of serfdom and slavery, merciless and most unjust laws, decrees, dictums patternized into the most inequitable exploitations, the stagnation of any educational advance, the restraint and the taboo and limitations placed on science and knowledge, on art expression, and the worst sadomasochistic punishments meted out for the "sin" of thinking honestly and freely: history reveals that these occurred in the most zealous and fanatical periods of religiosity. "To this day there are Christian states and cultures in which the dissident risks economic security and social standing, if no longer life and freedom."[218] "The religion which exhorts men to love their neighbors as themselves has inspired fanatical hatred and persecution; and although Christians have often been cruel to peoples of entirely different cultures and persuasions, an especial intolerance is reserved for the heretic who professes a faith which is nearly, but not quite, identical with the current orthodoxy."[219] "Heretics are persecuted because they threaten the security of the believer; and the savage punishments which the orthodox have meted out to those who disagree with them bear witness not to the strength of their faith, but to its vulnerability. . . . The heretic is driven to rebellion because he finds his individuality stifled by the orthodoxy of the group. Conformity, based on close identification, at first promises reassurance, but easily becomes a restriction upon freedom to those who need to assert an individual point of view."[220]

To enumerate the cruelties inflicted upon humanity by the gracious hand of religious power, these murders, the inhumanity of man unto himself and his fellow beings, even to the animals around him, would take a library-full of volumes. They are dreadful. They are so horrible that to recount only a few of them is a nauseous ordeal, like the rite of Varuna in India, in which a woman has intercourse with a dead horse.[221] "The more intense has been the religion of any period and the more profound has been the dogmatic belief, the greater has been the cruelty and the worse has been the state of affairs."[222] "Throughout the world the rituals of transformation from infancy to manhood are attended with, and affected by, excruciating ordeals. Scourgings, fastings, the knocking out of teeth, scarifications, finger sacrifices, the removal of a testicle, cicatrization, circumcision, subincision, bitings, and burnings are the general rule."[223]

David Kenyon Webster relates how people made sacrifices to the shark-gods: "Sacrifices have been made to sharks almost since time began. . . . Years ago, certain West African coastal tribes that worshipped the shark under the name of *joujou* celebrated its festival three or four times annually with offerings of goats and chickens and once a year, as a great treat, with a ten-year old child. Raised specially for the purpose, the child was tied to a post on a sandpit at low tide and left there until it ascended to its adults' heaven via drowning and shark bite. . . . The *manu au* followers also sacrificed people to sharks—right into the 1920s. Less than forty years ago, circular altars of coral stone stood on the Solomon Islands of Mala, Ulawa, and San Cristobal, on which victims were strangled. Each altar had a hole or cave mouth in the centre through which the cadaver was dropped to sharks waiting in the water below. . . . It was not likely, however, that sharks elsewhere ever quite enjoyed the repast once furnished them in India, where followers of a macabre cult used to make annual pilgrimage to the sea and there, with what has been called 'that peculiarly Oriental determination to die rather than to live,' offered themselves to the sharks in mass immolation. Hundreds of pilgrims were taken, but more waded in, until the sea turned bright red and the sharks were so sated that they refused to bite at the frustrated devotees thrusting themselves at their mouths. Of all the ways that man has devised for reaching God's throne, this surely ranks as one of the least attractive."[224] The Irish folk even claim that human souls can occupy the body of a shark and prey upon the fisherman or swimmer; that such a shark, when seen, is a sort of barometer indicating stormy weather ahead.[225]

"To this day seven or eight hundred goats are slaughtered in three days in the Kalighat, the principal temple of the goddess in Calcutta, during her autumn festival, the Durga Puja. The heads are piled before the image, and the bodies go to the devotees, to be consumed in contemplative communion. Water buffalo, sheep, pigs, and fowl, likewise, are immolated lavishly in her worship, and before the prohibition of human sacrifices in 1835, she received from every part of the land even richer fare. In the towering Shiva temple of Tanjore a male child was beheaded before the altar of the goddess every Friday at the holy hour of twilight. In the year 1830 a petty monarch of Bastar, desiring her grace, offered on one occasion twenty-five men at her altar in Danteshvari and in the sixteenth century a king of Cooch Behar immolated a hundred and fifty in that place.

"In the Jaintia hills of Assam it was the custom of a certain royal house to offer one human victim at the Durga Puja every year. After having bathed and purified himself, the sacrifice was dressed in new attire, daubed with red sandalwood and vermillion, arrayed with garlands, and, thus bedecked, installed upon a raised dais before the image, where he spent some time in meditation, repeating sacred sounds, and, when ready, made a sign with his finger. The executuner, likewise pronouncing sacred syllables, having elevated the sword, thereupon struck off the man's head, which was immediately presented to the goddess on a golden plate. The lungs, being cooked, were consumed by the yogis, and the royal family partook of a small quantity of rice steeped in the sacrificial blood. Those offered in this sacrifice were normally volunteers. However, when such were lacking, victims were kidnapped from outside the little state; and so it chanced, in 1832, that four men disappeared from the British domain, of whom one escaped to tell his tale, and the following year the kingdom was annexed—without the custom."[226]

"One of the most explicit recorded instances of the offering to the Earth is the hideous sacrifice to the Earth-goddess among the Khonds of Orissa, the tearing of the flesh of the human victim from the bones, the priest burying half of it in a hole in the

earth behind his back without looking around, and each house-
holder carrying off a particle to bury in like manner in his
favourite field."[227] Coastal Hindus very often accelerated disposal
of the dead by consigning it to the sharks; "many Hindus buried
corpses for a day or two to heighten their attraction to the sharks
before launching them on the voyage to eternity."[228] This is religion at work in India.

Let us see the work of religion in old Mexico. Thomas Gann
and J. Erich Thompson tell us of the Aztecs: "Human sacrifice
was never as frequent as among the Aztecs, where on one occasion, it is said, 70,000 victims were sacrificed at the dedication of
a temple. . . . Prisoners of war usually supplied the victims of
sacrifice. However, in times of great stress, when no prisoners
were available a community would subscribe to buy slaves to
sacrifice, and very devout men would even offer their own children. The victims were kept in small wooden cages until they
were required. Before being sacrificed the victim was stripped
of his clothing and painted with a blue unguent, blue being the
sacrificial color. He was led up the steps of the pyramid to the
foot of the temple perched on its summit. In front of the temple
was a small block of limestone and the convex top of the stone
fitted into the small of his back. Two of the Chacs at his head
held his hands firmly, while the other two each held a foot. In
this position he was helpless, with his breast exposed to receive
the sacrificial knife. The officiating priest, cutting open his chest
with a special knife of obsidian or flint, mounted with a richly
decorated handle, plunged his hand into the wound, and tore
out the wretch's heart almost before it had ceased to palpitate.
The heart he placed on an earthen dish and offered up to the
sun after he smeared the idol's face with it. The lifeless carcass
was hurled down the steep sides of the pyramid to the waiting
crowd beneath. Priests and warriors crowded round to snatch a
part of his body, which now partook of the divinity to which it
had been sacrificed. The flesh was taken home and eaten in a
kind of communion service, thereby endowing him who consumed it with divine grace. Special portions such as the hands
and feet were reserved for the officiating priest. This ceremonial
eating of the victim was not cannibalism in the general meaning

of the word, as the flesh was not eaten for its savor, but for the grace with which it endowed the eater. Sometimes, the skin was reserved, and the priest, donning it, took part in the special cere-monial dance, and continued to wear it for several days. If the victim had been a prisoner of war, his captor was awarded the jawbone, and wore this as a proof of his prowess."[229] Is there any similarity of purpose when the breaking of bread and drinking of wine are supposed to give the worshipper a participation in the body of Christ and a "drink" of the Savior's blood?

Nowhere in the history of mankind could we find a more hor-rible example of the complete coalition of religion and state power in wielding authority over life and death than in the his-tory of the Mexica, the Aztecs, especially during the reign of Ahuitzotl, who was under the murderous power-influence of Tlacaellel. Professor Padden in his *The Hummingbird and the Hawk* relates the terrible story of human sacrifice to appease the Mexica hummingbird god: "All was in readiness; the lines of victims were strung out for miles, with great reservoirs at their ends, thousands of trapped humans milling about like cattle, awaiting their turn in the line that was about to move. Suddenly, the brilliantly arrayed kings appeared on the platform and silence fell over the city. Together they approached Huitzilopochtli's chapel and made reverent obeisance. As they turned to join their aides at the four slabs, great snakeskin drums began to throb, announcing that the lines could now begin to move. The lambs were slaughtered with machine-like precision; as the knife wielders fell exhausted, they were replaced by fresh priests who lifted the heavy blade and let it fall in precise and measured stroke until their arms grew weary; others stepped in without losing a beat. A refinement of mass sacrificial technique was apparent; it took but seconds to dispatch each victim. Under such circumstances ceremonial and symbolic niceties were ignored. Rivulets of blood became bright red streams washing over darkening clots, like boulders in a stream; the freshets became rivers of blood, gradu-ally breaking off huge clotted chunks and carrying them down stream as though in height of springtime flood. At the pyramid's base far below, priests wallowed and skidded about as they re-moved the bodies that tumbled down in ceaseless order. Others rescued hearts by the ton. Still others bailed up blood in jars and cups that were then carried by runners to the barrio temples where the faces of the idols were smeared and painted. . . . The holocaust went on unabated for four days and nights, with tens of thousands perishing on the slabs. Most of the sources claim that over 80,000 were sacrificed during those incredible ninety-six hours. It is impossible to be certain because accurate tallies were not kept. The stench grew so overpowering, the revulsion so general, that there was an exodus from the city. When the full impact of what was happening hit the guests, the rose-covered boxes were deserted in haste, as were other seats of honor, the guests joining the plebeians and the mass of the Pipiltin [nobles, lords] in panic-stricken flight. According to some of the sources, Tlacaellel and his sturdier partisans stuck by their knives, and by the end of the ceremonial month it was estimated that they had butchered over 100,000 people in Huitzilopochtli's honor."[230]

We have seen that blood was regarded by the primitives and later by the formal religions of the more or less civilized periods, to be the beverage of the deities, blood itself being the "flow" of the life power. "All militant religions have been involved in bloodletting in one form or another."[231] The color *red,* signifying the life fluid, was and still is almost universally used by natives for decoration expressing power and even supernatural power. Even the dead are often painted red to express some continuity of the blood supply, even in a spiritual or magical sense, and which will serve as blood in the afterlife. Harald Schultz relates of the Craho Indians: "The nude body of the dead boy lies on his straw mat. He is washed by his parents and relatives and then painted with bright red urukú paint. It is the last festive painting. Red is the color of life."[232] In the New Testament (I John 1:17) it is plainly stated that the blood of Jesus, the Son of God, cleanses the believers from sin. S. G. F. Brandon: "It is possible that in those instances in which the corpse was colored with red pigment some action was also taken, by way of sympathetic magic, for its reanimation by restoring to it the sanguine hue of life."[233]

The sacrifice of the god or king to cleanse, purify, absolve, or forgive the sins of the people, or protect them from evil and ill-fortune, is fairly well sprinkled over the later primitive religious systems and firmly established in the ancient formal religions, especially in the Near East, southeastern Europe, and throughout many parts of Asia. These forms of absolution passed into, or became inherited by, the early Christian church. To this day it is still the nuclear core of Catholic belief and confession, and it provides the principal cause and elements of the Catholic Mass. The body and the blood of Christ became the media, substituted by the bread and wine. Birket-Smith: "By sacrificing himself, the god becomes the savior of the entire race, and since in a mystical way one is united with the resurrected deity, one is rescued from the power of death and sure of life eternal."[234] During the Mass, the priest chants:

> Who, the day before He suffered, took bread into His holy and venerable hands, and having raised His eyes to heaven, unto Thee, O God, His Father Almighty, giving thanks to Thee, He blessed, broke it, and gave it to His disciples, saying: Take ye all and eat of this: For this is My Body. . . .

> For this is the chalice of My Blood of the new and eternal covenant: the mystery of faith, which shall be shed for you and for many unto the forgiveness of sins. . . .

> May the peace of the Lord be always with you. And with thy spirit. May this mingling and hallowing of the Body and Blood of our Lord Jesus Christ help us who receive it unto life everlasting. Amen.

Millions of people still think that they can purify themselves by reciting a language that Christ never knew or spoke, and yet almost two thousand years later they are told to believe that they can be forgiven for their sins by partaking of his body and blood! The Catholic Mass is just another of thousands of similar rites and beliefs in many primitive and modern religions that have existed and still exist today; it continues to expose one of the most ancient rituals of self-purification by the use of a scapegoat or by the sacrifice of another's life. Peter Davison gives his poetic version regarding the Mass:

> Yet, in matters Eucharistic,
> Westerner is proved the mystic:
> Though the mystery defeats him,
> If he loves his God, he eats Him.[235]

George C. Valliant: "At the Temple of Quetzalcoatl individuals were buried under the corners as foundation deposits. At both Teotihuacan and Azcapotzalco shallow dishes, cut from the top of skulls, testify to other rituals involving sacrifices and death."[236] Thus victims were sacrificed as "building materials" for temples in order to assure the structures with divine grace, the transference of living power, the everlasting spirit or soul that could only give continuing strength and spiritual permanence to the edifice. There are palaces and churches in Europe today, built in Catholic countries and places, where humans have been buried alive in the foundations as a sacrifice to gain divine endurance for the buildings.

Let us look at Japan: "The custom of the living following the dead has continued in Japan to the very present. In the period of the great feudal wars it was revived in force, and at the death of a *daimyo*, fifteen or twenty of his retainers would disembowel themselves. For centuries thereafter, even against the firm rulings of the Tokugawa Shogunate (1603-1868), heroic players of the old school insisted on playing on. Against orders, for example, a certain Uyemonno Hyoge disemboweled himself in the late seventeenth century at the death of his lord, Okudaura Tadamasa; and the government promptly confiscated the lands of his family, executed two of his sons, and sent the rest of the household into exile. Other loyal followers, when their lords died, would shave their heads and become Buddhist monks. But even as late as 1912, the General Count Nogi, hero of Port Arthur, committed suicide at the precise hour of the burial of the Mikado, Meiji Tenno; and his wife, the Countess Nogi, then killed herself to accompany her spouse. The proper conduct of the female in such a case was to cut her throat, after having tied her legs together with a belt, so that whatever the agonies of her death might be, her body would be found properly composed."[237]

Thus, the same sacrifices in Japan, thousands of miles away

from the Near East, repeated the same rituals and burial sacrifices that occurred in ancient Scythia, Parthia, Iran and Iraq, and many other parts in that part of the world. We find it very prevalent among the Incas and many Indian tribes of the Americas. Even way out in Fiji it was the custom that "upon the death of a great chief his widows were usually strangled, so that they might accompany him to the afterworld."[238] Tylor confirms the Fiji sacrifices: "Till lately, a main part of the ceremony of a great man's funeral was the strangling of wives, friends, and slaves, for the distinct purpose of attending him into the world of spirits."[239] Referring to the Guinea Coast, "after a royal death in 1789 no less than 595 wives, together with soldiers, eunuchs, and court minstrels sacrificed their lives. These performances were repeated on a smaller scale every year."[240]

In Asia Minor "King Moab offered up his eldest son for a burnt-offering on the wall, when the battle was too sore for him. Phoenicians sacrificed their dearest children to propitiate the angry gods."[241] In Southern Asia, "On the accession of certain kings (9th century) a quantity of rice is prepared, which is eaten by some three or four hundred men, who present themselves voluntarily to share it, thereby undertaking to burn themselves at the monarch's death."[242] "The Polynesian deities coming incarnate in the bodies of birds to feed on the meat-offerings and carcasses of human victims set out upon the altar-scaffolds; the well-fed sacred snakes of West Africa, and local fetish animals like the alligator at Dix Cove which will come up at a whistle, and follow a man half a mile if he carries a white fowl in his hands, or the shark at Bonny that comes to the river bank every day to see if a human victim has been provided for his repast"[243] —all these are only a handful of samples of what religion has been doing for mankind all over this world of ours.

Albert Schweitzer reports from Lambaréné about the good religious life in Africa: "It happened by no means seldom that the fetich-doctor revealed to the person who wanted a charm that in order to get it he must kill a near relation. And he generally added that if the murder were not accomplished the applicant himself must die. Many years ago a young man went to his home village for the purpose of killing his father in order to secure a ju-ju. The father suspected the reason for his coming. In the night he got up and shouted round the village. 'There is someone among us who wants to kill me! But here is somebody who is stronger than he!' The next day the son took refuge at a Mission Station, and not long after he died."[244] We must take into account the psychic damage to a person because of his intense resignation to the power of magic-suggestion, the complete sublimation of the individual into states of shock and paralyzing fears that may cause fatal harm. Schweitzer explains this further: "In the eyes of Africans, the fact that individuals still perish by trespassing against their taboos, by curses of which they are the victims, or by magic to which they are exposed is a proof of the truth of their ideas which it is not easy to controvert. It is difficult indeed to make them understand that in these cases the events are determined by psychical conditions."[245] Victor Hugo so wisely wrote: "There is in every village a torch—the schoolmaster; and an extinguisher—the parson."

Europe, with the suffocation of the democratic and empirical spirit in ancient Greece and to some extent in the Roman periphery, and the emergence of Christianity throughout the Continent, from the Bosporus to the former strongholds of the Druids, from the Iberian Cape to the vastnesses of Russia, outdid them all in the ferocity, persecution, ignorance, murder, and negation which followed for the next fifteen hundred or more years. It was at Rome and not at Nazareth or Jerusalem that Christianity established itself. Pierre Grimal: "It was within the [Roman] Empire that Christianity was born, that it won its first victories, formed its hierarchy and, to a certain extent, matured its doctrines."[246] This hierarchy gradually, through a maze of conflicting, falsifying, fraudulent, and concocting innovations, implications, and ambiguities in the interplay of politics, formed a theology that ordained that life is wicked and meaningless except to purify it and prepare it for the trial of judgment before the Christ, that the the best way to heaven is to make hell on earth, to deprive oneself, to humiliate and humble oneself in ashes and sackcloth— it was this theology that submerged Europe in the darkest of ages. Europe was not alone in its theology to place upon life an ephemeral and meaningless value: Jainism in India also designed

itself to block the will to love and to blot out existence—the
eternal nothingness was the ultimate peace and blessedness.[247]
Regarding Buddhism, Campbell sums it up: "If Kapila caused
the object world to vanish, the Buddha wiped out, also, the subject,"[248] for *Nirvana* means just nothing, beyond everything, without breath or wind.

In the ancient European arena, Herbert J. Muller tells us how
the ambiguous and ethereal neither-here-nor-there Platonic idealism laid the groundwork for the anti-naturalism of later Christianity: "Such idealism has profoundly ambiguous implications.
It has led many thinkers to debase the natural world in which
men must carry out their purposes, to divorce the ideal from
natural possibilities of truth, beauty and goodness, and to declare that the human spirit is forever an alien in the only home
it can surely know."[249] This terrible, tragic negation of life,
slavish subservience, and dejection go on to this very day within
the folds of Catholic indoctrination and training. Paul Blanshard:
"For centuries the Spanish people have been accustomed to
thinking of Catholicism and political power as so closely intertwined that they are parts of the same amalgam. No one can tell
where the power of the church leaves off and the power of the
state begins."[250] Arthur Koestler: "From Aristarchus there is,
logically, only one step to Copernicus; from Hippocrates, only a
step to Paracelsus; from Archimedes, only a step to Galileo. And
yet the continuity was broken for a time-span nearly as long as
that from the beginning of the Christian era to our day. Looking
back at the road along which human science travelled, one has
the image of a destroyed bridge with rafters jutting out from both
sides; and in between nothing."[251]

How are the negation of life and abject obedience exemplified
in the Catholic structure itself? A former Catholic priest reveals
how a novice is prepared for the priesthood: "The young Franciscan is trained that when the Provincial Superior greets him he
must kneel on one knee and kiss the lowest knot on the Superior's
cord, and then his hand. It is the token of complete, abject, unreasonable obedience."[252] He goes on to say: "In the senior
seminaries for Franciscan priests in the United States there hangs,
inside the door of each cell or bedroom, a scourge or whip. It is

made of several strands of heavy cord, each knotted at the end. Each Monday, Wednesday, and Friday evening at 5:45 o'clock we closed the doors of our cells; to the chant of the 'Miserere' we disrobed and 'scourged our flesh to bring it into submission.' The Superior patrolled the corridors to listen to the sounds of beating—the assurance of compliance."[253]

If Europe is considered by some as the core of world intellectuality, civilization and general advance, it is also responsible for "the appalling record of Christian persecution—by far the bloodiest, cruelest record in all religions history."[254] Writing about the First Crusade and the capture of Jerusalem, Franc Shor relates: "Daimbert of Pisa, who had replaced Adhemar as religious leader of the First Crusade, reported to the Pope: 'If you desire to know what was done with the enemy who were found there, know that in Solomon's Porch and in his temple our men rode in the blood of saracens up to the knees of their horses."[255] W. Oldfield Howey writes about the Piedmontese, the crusade against the Albigenses, a "crusade" authorized and proclaimed by Pope Innocent III (1198-1208), Vicar of Christ: "The awful narrative of Leger describing the Piedmontese Massacres makes the blood run cold. Infants snatched from their mothers' arms were torn asunder, or their heads were dashed against the rocks. The sick and old were burned alive, in their homes. Some were flayed alive, some were roasted alive, some disemboweled; or fastened to the trees of their own orchards whilst their hearts were torn out. Some were atrociously mutilated and their mangled remains flung on the highways to be devoured by beasts, whilst of others the brains were boiled and eaten by these devils in human shape. Some were fastened into the furrows of their own fields and ploughed into them. Others were buried alive. Fathers were marched to death with the heads of their children suspended from their necks. Deeds too terrible to mention were committed against them. 'My hand trembles,' says Leger, 'so that I can scarce hold the pen, and my tears mingle in torrents with my ink, while I write the deeds of these children of darkness—blacker even than the Prince of Darkness himself."[256]

Howey continues to tell us about witches, cats, and the adoration of the Virgin Mother: "The Church had adopted so much of the ritual and creed of solar and lunar theogonies, it was furiously energetic against those customs it failed to absorb, and all thru the Middle Ages, not only witches, but cats, were persecuted and tortured by the Christian organizations. The older religions had held these animals sacred, and the Churches dreaded a revival of their faiths, and did not want the populace to see the connection between the Virgin Mary and the Virgin Diana, and to realize that the new religion was the same in essentials as the old."[257] "History has recorded the horrible cruelty by which Christianity, in defiance even of its own teachings, established its power and stamped out opposition."[258]

Herbert J. Muller adds additional light about witches, the subjection of Europe by its obedience to, and blind acceptance of, a book, the Bible: "The Old Testament in particular was a mine of harsh texts, for as the record of a religious growth extending over many centuries it naturally contained many relics of a barbarous past. In the savage religious wars between Protestants and Catholics any atrocity could be justified by citing a God who had ordered Saul to slaughter every man, woman, child, and beast in an enemy town, and then punished him for sparing a few. Scores of thousands of old women were burned to death on the authority of as plain a biblical text: 'Thou shalt not suffer a witch to live.' Orthodox religion became the center of opposition to moral as well as intellectual enlightenment. Men entrenched themselves behind the Bible to fight against almost every major cause in the history of Western freedom—freedom of conscience, democratic government, civil liberties, the abolition of slavery, equal rights for women."[259] Joseph Cambell: "The actual point in question, throughout the centuries of Christian persecution, has never been faith in God, but faith in the Bible as the word of God, and in the Church (this Church or that) as the interpreter of that word."[260]

THE SADOMASOCHISM OF HELL

THE CLIMAX OF Christian cruelty is demonstrated in the enthronement of a Satan, the concoction of a hell in which sinners are thrown to be *eternally* damned and punished. Bernard Hart, in his *The Psychology of Insanity,* regarding the notion of insanity during the Medieval Ages, states that "The prevailing views upon the nature and causation of insanity reverted, as a natural consequence, to the demonological conception of the ancients."[261] The idea of a hell dedicated to a *forever* punishment or an endless helplessness to free oneself from torment, is a product of insanity, as no normal and reasonable mind would want to invent or believe in such a hideous nightmare of the imagination. Bertrand Russell: "I do not myself feel that any person who is really profoundly humane can believe in everlasting punishment."[262] James G. Frazer: "Proclaiming the eternal damnation and excruciating torments of the vast majority of mankind has added incalculably to the dread and horror of death."[263] Robert G. Ingersoll asks: "If the devil should die would God make another?" Szczesny recapitulates: "As long as public opinion in the West insists that the world can be saved only by accepting Christian postulates as true, the period of unbelief will be greatly prolonged and ever new generations will be driven to cynicism, superficiality and stupidity."[264]

We cannot honestly credit Christianity with the exclusive "honor" of creating a devil. Devils and demons were popular all over the ancient world and continue to be in many parts of the world to the present day. In Tibet they still continue in their prime. Ancient Judaism, while it did not establish a full generalship to Beezelbub or construct the intricate machinery devoted exclusively to hurting people, including the eternal roasting of babes and children in stoves, boiling and stewing them in cauldrons, did believe in demons, and demonology was widespread in all the peoples of the ancient world; Judea was no exception. We even find demonology taken up in detail, and how to overcome demons, in the Talmud, Berakhoth, folio 6. It seems that no religion or cult in the world can manage to succeed without the help of the devil. D. T. Atkinson: "It is estimated by Samuel Laing that during the eighth century in Germany alone, over one hundred thousand persons suffered excruciating deaths for the crime of maintaining an alliance with the devil."[265] The idea of dualism persisted in the Middle Ages that the Devil was an acceptable and essential part of the celestial hierarchy and ranked only second to God. Lopez: "After all, the Devil has his place in the Gospels and the Lord's Prayer. King of Hell and consequently associated with the Lord in the supreme administration of justice, Satan was conspicuous in all written, painted and sculptural representations of the Last Judgment. Shortly before the Day of Wrath, which might not be too far away, he would be allowed to come very close to victory under the attractive garb of the Antichrist. In daily life he seduced men and women, sometimes begot children on the latter; even St. Thomas Aquinas believed it."[266]

Hell and freedom are not companions, although there are many people, unfortunately, who have enjoyed the freedom to make a hell on earth, who desire to suffer and to make others suffer, forms of paranoia in various degrees, with less or more of the Hitler touch of extreme sadism and masochism. Religion and its scholastic, theology, have made the fear of hell more important in gathering the flock than the promises of heaven. This is cruel and insane. No person in his right mind could conceive of a god, if he wanted to believe in one, who could be so cruel as to invent and operate such a horrendous establishment, a spectral sphere of sulphurous fire and pain without hope or reprieve. Walter Kaufmann: "As long as we cling to the conception of hell, God is not love in any human sense—and least of all, love in the human sense raised to the highest potency of perfection. And if we renounce the belief in hell, then the notion that God gave his son to save those who believed in the incarnation and resurrection loses meaning. The significance of salvation depends on an alternative, and in traditional Christianity this alternative is eternal torment."[267] A. Powell Davies: "We don't want a religion that terrifies children with hell and fills their minds with the horrors of the crucifixion. . . . We need a religion not of escape but of courage. . . . The hell conjured up in the fantasies of religion has no place in the world of modern knowledge; science has got rid of it."[268] Joseph Campbell: "Nor is there anywhere toward the core of this earth a pit of flaming souls, screaming, tortured by devils who are fallen angels all. There never was a Garden of Eden, where the first human pair ate forbidden fruit, seduced by a serpent who could talk, and so brought death into the world; for there had been death here for millenniums before the species Man evolved: the deaths of dinosaurs and of trilobites, of birds, and mammals, and even of creatures that were almost men. Nor could there ever have occurred that Universal Flood to float the toy menagerie of Noah's Ark to a summit of the Elburz range, whence the animals, then, would have studiously crawled, hopped, swum, or galloped to their continents: kangaroos and duck-billed platypuses to far-away Australia, llamas to Peru, guinea pigs to Brazil, polar bears to the farthest north, and ostriches to the south. . . . It is hard to believe today that for doubting such extravagances a philosopher was actually burned alive in the Campo dei Fiori in Rome in the Year of Our Lord 1600; or that as late as the year of Darwin's *Origin of Species,* 1859, men of authority still could quote this kind of lore against a work of science."[269]

Fortunately, as knowledge increases and rationalism becomes more of an operable and freer factor in the daily lives of people, "men no longer cross themselves at the mention of the Devil's name. They smile instead and flippantly use his portrait to advertise potted ham or Pluto water."[270] "Anyone who without bias looks over the last thousand years of Western history is forced to the conclusion that Western man, the more his character matured, as he tried to penetrate the world's pattern not only in a practical way but by systematic and interpretative thought, the more he came into irreconcilable conflict with the Christian point of view."[271]

Man can make a heaven of his life on earth, if he has good luck, and if he accomplishes this the hell that he is offered by theology will disappear with the gust of his own self-enlightenment. He will find that as the old proverb goes, he can choose to make his life either hell or heaven. Joseph Campbell: "Why should it be that whenever men have looked for something solid on which to found their lives, they have chosen not the facts in which the world abounds, but the myths of an immemorial imagination—preferring even to make life a hell for themselves and their neighbors, in the name of some violent god, to accepting gracefully the bounty the world affords?"[272]

THE EXISTENCE OF GOD

Is THERE A God? Human reason and empiricism, experience and knowledge, cannot extend themselves in the unlimited sense as only imagination and wishing can do. But even when the wishes and imagination of people are profiled and placed in some ordinal method of identity with experience and reasonable hope, we find ourselves totally insufficient and incapable to accept or establish the existence of a God on any sane and knowledgeable basis. Hu Shih states: "On the basis of the biological sciences, we should recognize the terrific wastefulness and brutality in the struggle for existence in the biological world, and consequently the untenability of the hypothesis of a benevolent Ruler."[273] Jean Meslier: "Nature, you say, is totally inexplicable without a God; that is to say, in order to explain what you understand so little, you need a cause which you do not understand at all."[274] Bertrand Russell: "I see no reason, therefore, to believe in any sort of God, however vague and however attenuated."[275] "Most people believe in God because they have been taught from early infancy to do it, and that is the main reason."[276] Philip Wylie: "God has been man's excuse for failure. God is his moral alibi. . . . To the extent a man believes, he cannot seek; and so long as he prays, he is not trying his own best. The dignity which is his as an animal, and the genuine humility which has kept all other species honest, can no more belong to a worshipper of God than a Hitler, for God is an idol, man's own image, and human reverence is the fatuous awe of the ape with the mirror."[277] Lopez points out the importance of God in the daily life of people in the Middle Ages: "God was called to witness in every agreement; a blessing was asked on every enterprise; a pious pretext was sought for every amusement; time was measured in canonical hours. There was an exorcism for every illness, a formula to excommunicate the insects which devoured the harvest. God was invoked to establish the truth in legal proceedings, by means of the duel for the nobles, and by the ordeal of red-hot iron, fire or water for the commoners; or if these methods were discarded so as 'not to tempt the Lord,' by the sacred oath of the interested parties on the Gospels or on a relic."[278]

ORIGIN OF THE SOUL

Now WE COME to some analysis of the origin of man's idea of a *soul*. As we have mentioned in previous pages, the savage *dreamed* the soul into existence. Whatever he dreamed about and "saw" in his dreams, had a soul or spirit or etherealized resemblance, which was actually thought to be the "livingness" or "existential power" of whatever he saw in his dreams or imagined to be. "Soul-land is dream-land in its shadowy unreal pictures, for which, nevertheless, material reality so plainly furnished the models."[279] It could be himself, his friends or enemies, insects, animals, birds or fish, or the slithering crocodile or python ready to pounce upon him, but he "knew" because he "saw" them in his sleep, that they, too, like himself, had a spirit. However, the savage saw all this only in his *one* world, his own environment, and he never could imagine that this spirit or soul was completely immaterial; on the contrary, he felt that it had substance, but a substance he could not touch or see, like his very breath or his act of thinking, the joy in laughing or the grief in tragedy. Not only he himself could have felt this; all else must also have these manifestations, like the trees or a stone, a cloud or a mountain, the fruit or the animal he eats; in short, all that he felt and saw and came in contact with had a spirit just as he "knew" he had; this was his own *imprinting* of the spirit-world upon everything by his own natural tendency to anthropomorphize. Similar imprintings have been substantiated among many animals besides man. Levy-Bruhl: "The dream, to them, is of far greater significance than to us. It is first a percept as real as those of the waking state, but above all it is a provision of the future, a communication and intercourse with spirits, souls, divinities, a means of establishing a relation with their own special guardian angel, and even of discovering who this may be. Their confidence in the reality of that which the dreams make known to them is very profound."[280] Julian H. Steward on the Shoshonean Indians: "Every person hoped to acquire a supernatural power or guardian spirit. This power, manifest in the form of animals, plants, clouds, mountains, and other natural phenomena, came to him in dreams and gave him special abilities, such as gambling luck, hunting skill, endurance, and others of benefit to himself alone."[281]

The idea of a clear dualistic cleavage of matter and spirit was unknown to the savage; this cleavage came about much later by the early formulators, still later by the priestcrafts, and still later by the theologians and metaphysicians. "Among rude races, the original conception of the human soul seems to have been that of ethereality, or vaporous materiality, which has held so large a place in human thought ever since. In fact, the later metaphysical notion of immateriality could scarcely have conveyed any meaning to a savage."[282]

During the day another manifestation was always before him that "agreed" with his dreams: his *shadow*. He was not as yet that good a scientist to realize that the sun caused his shadow; all he knew was that it was there and was, or represented, his spirit. So rooted was this concept of *soul-and-shadow* that it was bad if one would step into another's shadow, as that would be tantamount to stepping on his spirit, and, worst of all, if the trespasser was his mother-in-law. There was hardly a thing or creature that did not have a shadow; as a result, they all had spirits or souls. "The shadow, if not equivalent to the soul, is at least regarded as a living part of the man or the animal, so that injury done to the shadow is felt by the person or animal as if it were done to his body."[283] He "knew" and "proved" it by his dreams at night and the shadows of the day. Levy-Bruhl: "In the Fiji Islands, as in many places inhabited by people of a similar stage of development, it is a mortal insult to walk upon anybody else's shadow. In East Africa, murders are sometimes committed by means of a knife or nail thrust through the shadow of a man; if the guilty person is caught in the act he is executed forthwith."[284]

Frazer tells us about the primitive conception of the soul: "If an animal lives and moves, it can only be, he thinks, because there is a little animal inside which moves it; if a man lives and moves, it can only be because he has a little man or animal inside who moves him. The animal inside the animal, the man inside the man, is the soul. And as the activity of an animal or man is explained by the presence of the soul, so the repose of sleep or death is explained by its absence, sleep or trance being the temporary, death being the permanent absence of the soul. Hence if death be the permanent absence of the soul, the way to guard against it is either to prevent the soul from leaving the body, or, if it does depart, to ensure that it shall return. The precautions adopted by savages to secure one or other of these ends take the form of certain prohibitions or taboos, which are nothing but rules intended to ensure either the continued presence or the return of the soul."[285] Willard Z. Park writing on Paviotso Shamanism, states: "It is thought that the soul often leaves the body during sleep. When this happens, serious harm will result if the sleeper is suddenly awakened."[286]

When the savage saw in his dreams his departed relatives, friends, or enemies, or things he ate or killed, he knew that this livingness still existed in some spirit form, and as a result the dream came to be a source of belief in the soul and its continuance after death. "The savage fails to distinguish the visions of sleep from the realities of waking life, and accordingly when he has dreamed of his dead friends, he necessarily concludes that they have not wholly perished, but that their spirits continue to exist in some place and some form, though in the ordinary course of events they elude the perceptions of his senses."[287]

Where did this soul actually reside within the body? The savage thought it could have been in the head or in the chest. The Egyptians believed the heart was its residence because the mind lived there, too, and not in the head as we all know now.[288] The Aztecs and Toltecs undoubtedly thought the same, as the sacrifices and offering the pulsating, not-dead-yet heart to the gods was deemed the greatest sacrifice and most holy offering of all. The Assyrians and Babylonians thought the head was the seat of the soul and, therefore, when people died, their heads were cut off and safeguarded, even in the household itself. Head-hunters in the jungle, whether in the Amazon or in Southeast Asia, undoubtedly feel that the taking of the head is the capturing of the victim's soul or spirit and all its powers, which, now possessed or enslaved, will add its life, magic, and power to the possessor. In many tribes a male is not marriageable until he has first obtained somebody's head; the more heads he has, the

more powerful and immune to evil he is. Edward B. Tylor: "The
Kamchadals held that every creature, even the smallest fly, would
live again in the underworld. The Kukis of Assam think that the
ghost of every animal a Kuki kills in the chase or for the feast
will belong to him in the next life, even as the enemy he slays in
the field will then become his slave. The Karens apply the doctrine of the spirit or personal life-phantom, which is apt to wander from the body and thus suffer injury, equally to men and to
animals. The Zulus say that the cattle they kill come to life
again, and become the property of the dwellers in the world beneath. The Siamese butcher, when in defiance of the very principles of his Buddhism slaughters an ox, before he kills the creature, has at least the grace to beseech its spirit to seek a happier
abode. . . . The Pawnee warrior's horse is slain on his grave to
be ready for him to mount again, the Comanche's best horses are
buried with his favourite weapons and his pipe, all alike to be
used in the distant happy hunting-grounds. . . . Certain eskimos
would lay a dog's head in a child's grave, that the soul of the dog,
who is everywhere at home, might guide the helpless infant to
the land of souls. . . . The Arab sacrifice of a camel on the grave,
for the dead man's spirit to ride upon. . . . The mongols, who
formerly slaughtered camels and horses at their owner's burial,
have been induced to replace the actual sacrifice by a gift of the
cattle to the Lamas. . . . The Hindus offer a black cow to the
Brahmans, in order to secure their passage across the Vaitarani,
the river of death, and will often die grasping the cow's tail as
if to swim across in herdsman's fashion, holding on to a cow."[289]
According to Gaster, in the little villages of Europe, the orthodox
Jews used to provide the deceased with a trowel "so that he may
dig his way to Zion."[290] The Greek story of the dead being ferried across the Styx and the ancient Egyptian story of souls being
ferried across the Nile to get their hearts weighed before Osiris
are just two of the many tales and myths of rivers the dead had
to cross. All types of animals have been used in getting the spirits
to their outerworld destinations; with the Hindus, it was the
cow's tail; with the Egyptians, it was the crocodile or heaven;
with the Greeks, monster dogs were the welcome mats; with the
Chamula, mules. "In a myth that bears an eerie resemblance to

the Greek story of Orpheus, the Chamula tell that upon arriving in hell one has to be ferried across a large river by a black dog."[291]

The primitives and ancients felt that not only has every object or living thing a spirit or soul, but that it can leave and wander off, be hiccupped or coughed out, be vomited out by mistake. Looking at one's image in reflecting water was looking at one's spirit; to this day primitives are wary of cameras for fear the little black box might carry away their images or souls. W. R. Alger: "The barbarian brain seems to have been generally impregnated with the feeling that everything else has a ghost as well as man. . . . The customs of burning or burying things with the dead probably arose, in some cases at least, from the supposition that every object has its *manes*."[292] Among many primitive people, ancient and still extant, every plant, tree, twig, and bush has a soul, and one must be careful, in uprooting it, not to injure its soul. Many people, even today, first apologize to the fruit or plant before eating it, in order to placate its soul. "When a medicine man of eastern Canada gathers roots or leaves or bark for medicine, he is careful to propitiate the soul of each plant by placing a tiny offering at its base. For he believes that without the co-operation of the soul the mere 'body' of the plant can work no cures."[293]

Spirits or souls could be transplanted, exchanged, coaxed out of people, or frothed into them; magic or sacred words could be used to inspire the spirit of man or god to enter into sculptured images of him. "The Kurnai believed in ghosts, some of which were dangerous. They were afraid to name the dead for fear they might be listening. Death was not normal, but was caused by magic and could be averted by countercharms. They often carried a round black pebble with them. When this was buried with the excreta of an enemy, it was supposed to cause the enemy's death. If the hair of an enemy was tied to the end of a throwing-stick with feathers of the eagle hawk and roasted before the fire with some kangaroo fat, it could cause the person to whom it belonged to pine away and die."[294] "In all uncivilized races everywhere, death requires to be explained by other than natural causes."[295] "If a person died from the results of a violent accident it was supposed that the *huecuvus* or evil spirits had occasioned it, frightening the horse to make it throw its rider, loosening a stone so that it might fall and crush the unwary, temporarily blinding a person to cause him to fall over a precipice, or some other expedient equally fatal. In the case of death from disease, it was supposed that witchcraft had been practised and the victim poisoned."[296] "All ailments of every kind, from the simplest to the most serious, are without exception attributed to the malign influence of an enemy in either human or spirit shape."[297]

The ancients who took their wooden and stone gods to war with them most certainly felt that these objects were inhabited with the spirits, that they were not just stone and wood; this psychological acceptance of the concept that objects so manufactured can still become the "outer shell" of the actual living spirit flourished throughout the ancient world, the Phoenician, Greek, Roman periods, and continued without abatement into Christianity, and flowered more than ever in Catholicism, in which *fetichism* is still, in a hundred ways, the subsurface arterial flow of religious practice. Now and then we hear of some "miraculous" statue or picture that begins to shed tears, or that some child reports that a sculpture or carving of the Mother Mary smiled down upon her, moved, or began to cry. Writing about the legends of Japan, Richard M. Dorson reports: "The images of Buddha were said to whine and writhe if robbers carried them off."[298] Levy-Bruhl: "It is a well-known fact that primitives, even members of communities which are already somewhat advanced, regard artificial likenesses, whether painted, carved, or sculptured, as real, as well as the individual they depict."[299] Sir Wallis Budge: "The Egyptians . . . believed that it was possible to transmit to the *figure* of any man, or woman, or animal, or living creature, the soul of the being which it represented, and from time immemorial the people of Egypt believed that every statue and every figure possessed an indwelling spirit. When the Christianized Egyptians made their attacks on the 'idols' of the heathen, they proved that they possessed this belief, for they always endeavored to throw down the statues of the gods of the Greeks and Romans, knowing that if they were once shattered the spirits which dwelt in them would have no place wherein to dwell, and would thereby

be rendered homeless and powerless."[300] Constantine, who legalized Christianity, still could not part with his pagan heritage.
While he had to be politically diplomatic with Christian demands, he kept on sprinkling statues of the old gods all over
Constantinople. Marti-Ibañez writes: "Constantine seems to
have maintained an ambiguous attitude toward religious faith:
he dedicated Constantinople with pagan rites, but erected a gem-
studded, golden cross before the imperial palace which his ad-
mirer Eusebius described as a protection and a divine charm
against the machinations and evil purposes of his enemies. He
spread a whole galaxy of pagan monuments through the city,
which his apologist Eusebius lamely defended as an attempt to
hold the old idols up to ridicule. Besides setting up a bronze
Apollo as his own effigy, Constantine built a temple to the For-
tuna of Rome, erected statutes to the Dioscuri in the Hippodrome,
placed statues of the Muses from Mount Helicon in the senate
house, and at the entrance set up the Zeus of Dodona and the
Athena of Lindos."[301]

The sculptured saints, sepulchres, the carved holy figures auror-
ally adorned with silver and gold, the Russian and Greek orthodox ikons, outside and inside of churches, the preservation of
relics and alleged remnants of saintly remains, even the preserved prepuces of the Christ, attest to this fetichism no different
than the fetichism of the Bororo, Kurulu, or the Mangbetu. Even
the Protestant believes that the Bible is not merely a book, but
a book with a soul, a spirit, that it contains some livingness of
God. Every crucifix is a fetich that is supposed to possess some
protective and guardian power of the original Jesus; merely holding it up will chase away all the devils. While the apologist may
try to persuade us that these things are merely symbols, that the
possessor does not actually believe that the objects are "spirited"
or possessed with "live holiness," yet to the rank-and-file adherents of the creed they are more than symbols, they actually
possess something more than the material involved. This concept
is the accepted way of all religions throughout the world, poly-
theistic and monotheistic. Priestcraft has never relied on thought
alone; in fact, thought has always been discouraged. Christianity's
prime concept in its own religiosity is based on the will to be-

lieve, not the will to think. Fetichism vanishes with intelligence; it increases with belief. The cry of the scholastic fathers was belief before intelligence because they knew that if intelligence came first, belief would not be there behind it.

Souls must be watched, for they often behave in strange ways, like mischievous children; some tribes have a professional soul watcher-catcher who can be hired to bring back meandering souls with his net, all for a fee. "When a Dyak dreams of falling into the water, he supposed that this accident has really befallen his spirit, and he sends for a wizard, who fishes for the spirit with a hand-net in a basin of water till he catches it and restores it to its owner."[302] "When the Karo-Bataks have buried somebody and are filling in the grave, a sorceress runs about beating the air with a stick. This she does in order to drive away the souls of the survivors, for if one of these souls happened to slip into the grave and be covered up with earth, its owner would die."[303] "In some parts of West Africa, wizards are continually setting traps to catch souls that wander from their bodies in sleep. . . . The wizard does not care whose soul he has captured, and will readily restore it to its owner, if only he is paid for doing so. Some sorcerers keep regular asylums for strayed souls, and anybody who has lost or mislaid his own soul can always have another one from the asylum on payment of the usual fee."[304] "The Indians of the Nass River, in British Columbia, are impressed with a belief that a physician may swallow his patient's soul by mistake. A doctor who is believed to have done so is made by the other members of the faculty to stand over the patient, while one of them thrusts his fingers down the doctor's throat, another kneads him in the stomach with his knuckles, and a third slaps him on his back."[305]

When a soul does leave on some rambling little trip to the woods, the body must be cautious to wait until the spreeing soul returns to it, otherwise when it does return and does not find the body, he could become a lost soul without a tag. Ashley Montagu: "Dreams, among non-literate peoples, provide convincing proof of the fact that the soul is capable of leaving the body and traveling to other realms. Hence, one never wakes a sleeper without giving the soul sufficient time to return to the body, for one can never tell where a sleeper's soul may be during his slumbers. In the dream the sleeper sees himself and sometimes other persons whom he knows, doing strange things in strange places. Hence, it is further clear that when a person falls into a sleep from which he does not awaken that his soul has permanently departed for another abode. So that death is not really cessation but translation to another sphere. Indeed, among non-literate peoples death is not considered to be a natural phenomenon at all. No one dies of natural causes. If it were not for the evil acts of other persons everyone would live forever. All deaths are therefore regarded as murders which must be paid for or avenged. When a man is killed by a blow inflicted by another the cause is plain. When he dies after a lingering illness, the cause is equally evident: it is due to sorcery or black magic."[306]

Cannibalism, with a number of exceptions, as a tribal and cultural trait and ritual, is the idea, manifested by eating, that by consuming another human body the spiritual powers contained therein would be transmigrated and transintegrated to the eater. Birket-Smith: "Through this act one not only succeeds in renewing one's own vital forces, but the ancestors go on living in one's person, and the family in the children, in an eternal cycle of life and death. . . . We find the same idea which forms the basis of cannibalism in the sacrament, which was, to begin with, a purely magical act. The deity appears in the shape of beasts or men, and by eating their flesh, the congregation partakes in the divine nature. . . . Not until much later was the sacrament symbolically interpreted as a spiritual union with the deity."[307]

It is very possible that cannibalism was preceded in earlier cultures by a precursor-idea that by eating a certain kind of animal not only does the eater benefit from its food value, but he also adds the spiritual power of the animal to his own. Thus, eating a bear would give man the strength and peculiar habits of the bear; eating a bird would make him speedy and springy afoot, and so on. "The Chavantes, on the Uruguay, eat their dead children to get back the souls. Especially young mothers do this, as they are thought to have given a part of their own souls to their children too soon."[308] "The Wanika consider that the soul of a dead ancestor animates a child, and this is why it resembles its father or mother; in Guinea a child bearing a strong resemblance, physical or mental, to a dead relative, is supposed to have inherited his soul. . . . The belief in the new human birth of the departed soul, which has even led West African negroes to commit suicide when in distant slavery, that they may revive in their own land (thru rebirth)."[309]

The simulation of binding the dead body also binds the soul likewise, which is one of thousands of emergent ideas and rituals oozing out of the primeval homeopathic formulae of magical forms and rituals. This throws added light to the concept that to the primitive both the spirit and the body came out of, live in, and died within the natural world. "Frobenius gives a considerable series of examples from Africa and antiquity of corpses bound in ropes, bandages, or nets to keep their ghosts from roaming, with the orifices of their bodies stopped to keep the ghosts inside, buried under heaps of stones to keep them down, or simply tossed to the wolves and hyenas, with the hope that they will be consumed that very night."[310]

In Catholicism the soul is the only and most important thing and must always be saved and purified; the body is transient occupancy. Conception is when a soul enters into the embryo or fetus and this soul must be duly saved by baptism, dead or alive, even if it means the death of the mother. "In the Catholic Church, it is a mortal sin to preserve the mother instead of the child, when either but only one can be saved, because this would deprive an immortal soul of Catholic baptism, without which the infant must be damned."[311] Dr. Austin O'Malley, in *The Ethics of Medical Homicide and Mutilation,* published under the imprimatur and authority of Cardinal Farley, states: "An innocent fetus an hour old may not be directly killed to save the lives of all the mothers in the world."[312] If a soul could be compared or presumed to be identified as a mind, according to the scientists, such a fetus does not possess any mind at all, and, therefore, could it be possible for any such mindless fetus to receive a baptism? Sir Charles Scott Sherrington (1861-1952), to whom the world is indebted for the basic principles of *neurophysiology,* established clearly that such a fetus is mindless in the sense that it is not capable of receiving or being affected by any form of mentation directed to it. Homer W. Smith, regarding the mind, states: "Yet even in such vertibrates as exhibit it in the adult stage, it is absent in the ovum and spermatozoon, and very meagerly developed, if at all, in the embryo. A newborn human infant cannot be said to have a 'mind' beyond the elementary perception of such things as hunger, discomfort, and fatigue. . . . 'Mind,' unlike body, appears to be biologically discontinuous, or episodic, or as Dr. Sherrington described it as 'phasic.' "[313]

We have seen that in the preprimitive, primitive, and savage periods, in the past and existing today, the soul, the body, the environment, that is, the natural world in which all these are interlinked and interdependent in a kind of irrevocable and resigned symbiotic integration of relationship and coexistence, were not considered as independent ideas or existences. When the soul did emerge as an independent and separable existence and conceived as capable of being apart from and wholly free of the natural world, religion was born and established as forms of installation, communication, and transportation for the new world of souls. Reincarnation, transmigration, and all other kinds of soul-changes according to merit systems, disciplines, purifications, absolutions, baptisms, etc., emerged and established themselves in various creeds, cults, religions, in most of the countries of the world. The ways, methods, and systems of soul-maturation and soul-change are so extensive, varied, and complicated that it would take volumes and volumes to give them ordinal sequence and clarifying enumeration. Let it suffice to state that it created, in general, *two worlds:* the natural and the supernatural, the physical and the metaphysical. The natural freedom of the being was now turned away from the natural world and the instinctive devotion of it to gain a happy and satisfied life, such as every animal struggles for. Man was *disciplined* to devote himself to forsaking the natural world, to gain ascendancy and finality in the supernatural, in God, Nirvana, Brahma, Allah, etc. The mind of man, previously activating itself in the field of immediacy, in the present, now directed itself away from devotion to the body and its world, and toward that which is void of the body and nature, in a field of pure tomorrows, in the future, oculated only towards the ultimate. Thus, *metaphysics* came of age.

The Age of the Enlightenment and the later nineteenth and twentieth centuries have exposed the wide and deep cleavage that metaphysics, as spokesman for theology and theology as spokesman for organized and formal religion, have produced in the human constitution, the havoc they have wrought upon the freedom of man, and the tragedies, hates, massacres, and persecutions that have been perpetrated as a result of them. If the formal religions are now inevitably on the wane, so integrated is the metaphysical substratum in the dualistic-cultured mind of people that now *ersatz* creeds and philosophies appear, like Hitlerism and Communism, replacing in a way, but definitely not curative and therapeutic, emergences that could reinstate the natural freedom that has been sublimated during so many thousands of years of emasculation and cultural authoritarianism. Rationalism, under metaphysical management, has been used to twist and mold the natural world into unidentifiable strange concoctions of imagery and oughtness, of moral vagaries and impotencies, altars dedicated to frustration, which John Dewey called *antinaturalism in extremis*. Such figuration showed ways of counting one and one to make five, with heaven added as a guideline. Bertrand Russell: "Metaphysical separation of soul and body has had disastrous effects upon philosophy."[314] Samuel F. Dunlap: "We have demonstrated the persistence of faith in the dualist philosophy, which rests on the mistaken theory that such a separate unknown quantity as spirit ever existed. The failure of one of the two factors in dualism destroys the theory. Yet it still lies at the foundation of every creed today."[315] Oliver L. Reiser: "To overcome the dualism of matter and mind we must retrace the history of physics and get the secondary qualities back into the objective world."[316] Joseph Ratner: "The echoes of the 'soul' would have completely died out in philosophy long before our century had not Idealism resorted to necromancy and by percussion instruments spread the deafening clamor of ghosts."[317] Harry A. Overstreet: "We may shudder somewhat at the loss of the familiar soul, but the gain in predictability and in the control and direction of life have doubtless been no mean compensation."[318] Gerhard Szczesny: "The absolute dualism of the Christian concept of the world and the concept of deity linked to it, in this view has been done away with."[319]

IMMORTALITY AND THE FUTURE LIFE

THE EMERGENCE OF the soul-idea, as we have seen, did not originally have anything to do with immortality as we understand the term today, to live in a separate sphere away from the natural world. It emerged and matured as a spirit-form potentiated out of the primitive dualistic concept of *seen and unseen natural forces*. Following the line of homeopathic magic ritual, this primitive concept created patterns of thought and thus ritual that favored the coordination of both these factors of seen and unseen powers to bring about favorable sequences. This came about especially with the gradual rise of agrarian and pastoral cultures, in which fertility rites were conducted in the same vein as rites for the dead.[320] E. Cecil Curwen and Gudmund Hatt: "Fertility cults now formed the chief basis of religion, for the chief aim of life was to increase production by improving the fertility of flocks and fields, and the planting of the seed and the subsequent appearance of the seedling gave rise to wistful longings for resurrection and a future life. As food gatherers men had not had such stimuli as these, and their religion had presumably consisted of sympathetic magic and a belief in spirits. Instead, too, of scattered groups of independent food gatherers, we now find communities firmly bound together under the authority of a priest-king."[321] Frazer: "The killing of the god, that is, of his human incarnation, is therefore merely a necessary step to his revival or resurrection in a better form. Far from being an extinction of the divine spirit, it is only the beginning of a purer and stronger manifestation of it."[322] "By no people does the custom of sacrificing the human representative of a god appear to have been observed so commonly and with so much solemnity as by the Aztecs of ancient Mexico. With the ritual of these remarkable sacrifices we are well acquainted, for it has been fully described by the Spaniards who conquered Mexico in the 16th century, and whose curiosity was naturally excited by the discovery in this distant region of a barbarous and cruel religion which presented many curious points of analogy to the doctrine and ritual of their own church."[323] Valliant: "Instances of human sacrifices keep cropping up in the world's religious systems, and we preserve in our own culture the concept of martyrdom, achieved by voluntary or involuntary means, as an act of virtue. The very beautiful example of the Saviour transmutes to the highest spiritual plane this idea of sacrifice for the good of humanity."[324] Frazer: "When we survey the history of this pathetic fallacy (the dying god as a redeemer) from its crude inception in savagery to its full development in the speculative theology of civilized nations, we cannot but wonder at the singular power which the human mind possesses of transmuting the leaden dross of superstition into a glittering semblance of gold. Certainly in nothing is this alchemy of thought more conspicuous than in the process which has refined the base and foolish custom of the scapegoat into the sublime conception of a God who dies to take away the sins of the world."[325]

Inasmuch as the head priest, chief, or king, was either the god himself, the incarnation of the god, or the duly appointed intercessor between the god and his people, the welfare of the king became the welfare of the state, and, in times of desperation, heavy stress, or calamity, no greater honor could possibly be paid to the god than that the king or a substitute should be sacrificed as pennance or appeasement. By the same line of ideation, it was good to keep the king strong and living longer, so young and strong substitute victims became short-period, make-believe kings, who were then killed so that their youth and strength could supplement and extend the life of the real king.

The story of Jesus, true or legendary, is repeated time and time again in numerous religions and cults in many parts of the world, and in practically all of the religions of the ancient world prior to the time of Jesus. It was a kind of "standard formula" for the religion of the Near East, Greece, Crete, and in Egypt long before the advent of Bethlehem. In Egypt, for instance, we have the progenitor-story of Osiris, Horus and Isis. "Osiris . . . is the prototype of the liberation of the human soul from the helplessness of death as well as the symbol for the liberation of the soul from its psychic hindrances in this life. . . . In its comprehensiveness and lasting vitality the symbol of the dying and triumphing Egyptian god was perhaps the greatest imaginative concept of Oriental antiquity."[326] "Osiris is nature itself or, to speak more accurately, nature as experienced by the farmers and stock-breeders of the Ancient Near-east."[327] From the ancient Egyptians' *Book of the Dead,* Budge derives this about their Son of God: "I am the prince, the son of a prince, the sacred essence which hath proceeded from God."[328] The idea of the "Father and the Son" as one identity, one person, one spirit, is very old and preceded the Christian era by thousands of years. In Egypt we see depicted the rising of Horus (the Son) from the body of Osiris (the Father) by the command of Atum (the Creator of Everything, or the Holy Ghost).[329] J. H. Denison: "When the priest of Heliopolis assumed the crown of Egypt at the end of the Fourth Dynasty, it was proclaimed that it was by his right, since he was the son of the god Ra by the priestess of the Sun."[330] Moscati writes about the Babylonian trinity and Ishtar, the prototype of the Christian Mary: "With her (Ishtar) was associated the young god Tammuz, whose nature was at once divine and mortal. He died and was reborn year by year, typifying the death and rebirth of plant-life. A myth rich in religious and poetical significance relates how the goddess Ishtar went down to fetch him from the abode of the dead."[331]

The concept of the trinity was well established throughout the Near East many centuries before the time of Jesus. The Aramaic storm and wind god, Hadad, the Semitic fertility goddess Atargates and their son Simios, represent another triad common in the Near East in the ancient and pre-Christian era. The Ethiopian Semites had also their trinity, Athtar the Supreme Lord of the Sky, Meder the earth mother and fertility goddess, and Mahram. It should be noted, incidentally, that many of the Aramaens worshipped *Yahweh,* the storm and wind god of the Hebrews. *Yahweh,* the God of the Covenant and the Ark, also was identified with *El* (later *Allah* of the Moslems) of the pre-Christian Arabs. *El* was also identified as *Baal,* who was the Supreme God of many of the peoples of the Syropalestinian region, as well as in Mesopotamia. *El,* the Supreme god, was the *Il* of the Akkadians, *El* of the Canaanites, *Elohim* of the Hebrews, *Bel* of the Babylonians, the *Allah* of the later Arabs, the same deity, Supreme Lord and Protector. Today many synagogues are named *Bethel,* the "House of God."

It is considered most likely, if Jesus did live, that he belonged to a monastic cult or brotherhood called the Essenes, an order that grew up for some time before the time of Christ. Martin A. Larson: "The importance of the Essenes in the history of the occident can scarcely be overstated. Had they never existed, there would have been no Christianity and therefore no Catholic Church."[332] This Jewish cult did not fully accept the rule-and-obedience precepts of the then Jewish state religion. The philosophy of the Essenes rested upon a drawing from three or four major religious philosophies of its day. From Egypt they took the idea of the trinity; from the Persians they took the dualistic division of existence into good and evil forces; from the Jews they took the patriarchal and monotheistic elements; from the Hindus they took the Buddhistic escape from the mundane and material ways of living to gain purity by abstinence, asceticism, contemplation, solitude, and in forsaking family and friends to reach a oneness with God or the Universal Whole. In all, it confessed a philosophy of escapism and one that is not meant or fit to give anyone a normal chance in living a normally happy or satisfied life.

Thus, the Essene cult, by its rituals and precepts, parted company from the natural and nurtured a religion away from and aloof from nature and its intuitive and intellectual experiences. The Zoroastrian principle is heavily expressed in the Essene cult, the constant struggle of man in the general tug-of-war between the angelic armies of the good and the terrible ogres of evil. Szczesny explains it further: "In Old Testament times a messiah was an anointed high priest. Later, in expectation of the coming kingdom of fulfillment, the messiah became the future king of the Jews, ruler of salvation's realm. But it was far from Jewish monotheism to conceive this messiah as an embodiment of God. Among the Essenes, however, this same concrete historico-political anticipation, which tied in the messiah idea with Judaism, suffered a transformation, in keeping with their hostile attitude toward history. With them the anointed messiah became God's agent, a leader of the children of light in their war against the children of darkness."[333] Marcello Craveri, in his *Life of Jesus,* writes about the death of Jesus: "The whole story of the death of Jesus is a theological-ritual dramatization. The details (the two thieves, the vinegar, the division of his garments, the spectator's insults, the darkness, the rent veil, the earthquake, the last words of Jesus) are all fulfillments of prophecies or edifying symbols. . . . The reality was simpler and more tragic. Jesus was tried and executed as a political criminal, he died in agony, forsaken by all, even by God, and his sufferings would have no other witnesses than his executioners."[334]

Mary, as the Mother of God, is the Christian concept of a story that was even older than the story of a dying and resurrected god, as depicted in Jesus. "Tlazolteotl (Eater of Filth) was extensively worshipped and was also known as the 'Mother of the Gods.' Primarily as earth-goddess, she, alone of the goddesses, had amoral siginficance, since in eating refuse she consumed the sins of mankind, leaving them pure. A rite of confession developed in her cult."[335] "God the Holy Ghost in the form of a dove approached the Virgin Mary and she—through the ear—conceived God the Son, who was born in a cave, died and was resurrected, is present hypostatically in the bread and wine of the Mass. For the dove, no less than the serpent, was an attribute and companion of the Great Goddess of the pre-Homeric, pre-Mosaic East. . . . As Aphrodite, surrounded by worshipping Erotes, holding a dove in her left hand. Thus, in the world panorama of mythology, God the Father of the Christian trinity, the father-creator of Mary, God the Holy Ghost, her spouse, and God the Son, her slain and resurrected child, reproduce for a later age the Orphic mystery of Zeus in the form of a serpent begetting on his own daughter Persephone his incarnate son Dionysus."[336]

As only a mother can give birth to a baby, so does the Great Mother give birth to the gods, and throughout the world, in most of the ancient cults, creeds, and religions, the female and mother were the earliest known deities, not only because of the cycle of man, but also in the obvious cycles of all other things, the seasons, the day and night, the birth and decay of plants, and the cycles of animals, fish, and insects. The primeval progenitor of all things is one of tenderness, protectiveness, purity of thought, kindness, mercy, supplying the first milk of strength and growth, and to whom even the strongest god is still a babe in her arms.

With the spreading of the Jesus story and the embryological

and conflicting pulsations of early Christianity, the idea of an immortal soul, eternally immortal, subject to admission to heaven or doomed forever in torment, came to a confrontation of the individual and his god. Whereas the Covenant of the Hebrew was a contractual arrangement between a *people* and its god, the Christianized "covenant" became a personal communion and relationship between a *person* and his god. This kind of immortality was a clear departure from the "immortalities" of the primitives as any ideas of life and death that emanated from the primitive cultures were ideas that permeated their natural and mortal life. The Christian was prepared to abrogate life completely. Even in the Brahmin and Buddhistic philosophies the soul, after death, was not in any sense a fixed and eternal thing but a spirit that goes through changes and cycles until it can possibly reach such purity as to be "dissolved" into the wholeness of universality or nothingness, as Brahmin or Buddhist views it. Levy-Bruhl states in his *The "Soul" of the Primitive* that "everywhere primitives believe in survival, but nowhere do they regard it as unending."[337]

Even in ancient Egypt the soul was considered as survivable as long as the body itself can be preserved, and this led to the arts of mummification and the great tombs of antiquity. Ling Roth, writing about the natives of Sarawak, tell us: "The future life does not, in their minds, extend to an immortality. Death is still the inevitable destiny. Some Dyaks say they have to die three times; others, seven times, but all agree in the notion that, after they have become degenerated by these successive dyings, they become practically annihilated by absorption into air and fog, or by a final dissolution into various jungle plants not recognized by any name. Maybe, they lack the mental capacity to imagine an endless state of liveable life."[338] Budge: "The Egyptian declared that he was immortal, and believed that he would enjoy eternal life in a spiritual body; yet he attempted by the performance of magical ceremonies and the recital of words of power to make his corruptible body to endure for ever."[339]

The transference of youth and strength from one body to another, a sort of "soul-transference" and magically sympathetic, was seen in the sacrifice of people, such as in the Aztecan and Toltecan and kindred practices throughout the world, with the sacrifice of victims who were allowed to live and act as the king for periods and then killed, and expressed in the killing of the king or priest, which exhibited the therapeutic cleansing of the people and bestowed, by resurrection, life-giving powers on the people—all these had a specific soul-body association related to life and struggle on earth. Craveri: "Obviously, the Ascension of Jesus into heaven can be accepted as a myth."[340] The Egyptian god of resurrection, Khepera, represented by the beetle and the scarab, was indicated in the belief that the egg-ball of the beetle and the body were identical and proved the cyclic death and resurrection eventualities of life. "To this day the insect is dried, pounded, and mixed with water, and then drunk by women who believe it to be an unfailing specific for the production of large families."[341]

The complete separation of soul *from* body and the division of existence into natural and supernatural spheres of distinct and separate existences were new inventions which matured with the establishment of Christianity. Barrows Dunham: "The supernatural, being 'above' or 'beyond' nature, is a world that science simply cannot get at. Probably its contents are imaginative projections of needs, hopes, wishes in the natural world, which science can really get at. But, except as such a projection, supernature remains impenetrable. Scientific criteria of truth and falsity will not even enable us to know whether there is such a world, though they strongly suggest that a world to which they cannot apply is a world which itself cannot exist."[342]

When the comparative ignorance of the great masses of people in the world is considered, the lives they lead, and all the mundane miseries they struggle with, it is reasonable to understand why Malinowski and others would come to think that it would be tragic to take away, on the premise of what is really true, this dream of immortality wherein all wrongs are righted, all miseries ended, and when they can really begin to enjoy happiness, peace, and bliss, not for a day or a few years, but forever. Sir Thomas Browne, three hundred years ago ,wrote: "It is the heaviest stone that melancholy can throw at a man, to tell him that he is at the end of his nature; or that there is no further state to come."[343] Edward B. Tylor: "Even among the higher savages, however, a

connexion between a man's life and his happiness or misery
after death is often held as a finite article of theology and thence
it is to be traced onward through barbaric religions, and into
the very heart of Christianity."[344] Jung, trying to justify the need
of religion as "hygienic," wrote: "From the standpoint of psycho-
therapy it would be therefore desirable to think of death as only
a transition—one part of a life-process whose extent and duration
escape our knowledge."[345] James G. Frazer: "The mind of man
refuses to acquiesce in the phenomena of sense. By an instinctive,
an irresistible impulse it is driven to seek for something beyond,
something which it assumes to be more real and abiding than
the shifting phantasmagoria of this sensible world. This search
and this assumption are not peculiar to philosophers; they are
shared in varying degrees by every man and woman born into
the world."[346] Ernest Cassirer: "In a certain sense the whole of
mythical thought may be interpreted as a constant and obstinate
negation of the phenomenon of death. By virtue of this conviction of the unbroken unity and continuity of life myth has to
clear away this phenomenon. Primitive religion is perhaps the
strongest and most energetic affirmation of life that we find in
human nature."[347]

Yet Ralph Waldo Emerson felt that "the immortality of the
soul is too good to be believed."[348] Frazer came to these conclusions in his *The Belief in Immortality:* "If there is any natural
knowledge of human immortality, it must be acquired either by
intuition or by experience; there is no other way. Now whether
other men from a simple contemplation of their own nature,
quite apart from reasoning, know or believe themselves intuitively to be immortal, I cannot say; but I can say with some
confidence that for myself I have no such intuition whatever of
my own immortality, and that if I am left to the resources of my
natural faculties alone, I can as little affirm the certain or probable existence of my personality after death as I can affirm the
certain or probable existence of a personal God. And I am bold
enough to suspect that if men could analyze their own ideas they
would generally find themselves to be in a similar predicament
as to both these profound topics. Hence I incline to lay it down
as a probable proposition that men as a rule have no intuitive

knowledge of their own immortality, and that if there is any natural knowledge of such a thing it can only be acquired by a process of reasoning from experience."[349] Regarding the assurance of this immortality and getting to heaven, a former Catholic priest explains a parochial custom: "It is a custom in all parochial schools for the children to receive communion on the first Friday of each month. This custom has its origin in a story of a vision of Jesus Christ received by a nun in which promise was given that anyone who received communion on nine consecutive 'first fridays' was guaranteed passage to heaven."[350]

And what has all this belief wrought, notwithstanding Jung? Frazer, after a life spent in anthropology, states his conclusions: "The belief in immortality has not merely coloured the outlook of the individual upon the world; it has deeply affected the social and political relations of humanity in all ages; for the religious wars and persecutions, which distracted and devastated Europe for ages, were only the civilized equivalents of the battles and murders which the fear of ghosts has instigated amongst almost all races of savages of whom we possess a record. Regarded from this point of view, the faith in a life hereafter has been sown like dragon's teeth on the earth and has brought forth crop after crop of armed men, who have turned their swords against each other."[351]

When rationalism and the sciences are applied to inquire into this belief, both find no basis to support it. On the contrary, all present knowledge tends to disprove it. Fred Hoyle, the astronomer, writes: "If the something we call mind does survive death then this something must be capable of physical detection. For, if the mind were without physical connections, why is it that the mind is so intimately associated with the body? It is true that some Christians claim to imagine an existence without physical connections. If this is so, then Christians must be endowed with a faculty not possessed by others. I would go so far as to suggest that it is impossible to write half a dozen meaningful sentences concerning such an existence that do not involve some reference to the physical world."[352] Bertrand Russell: "It is not rational argument but emotions that cause belief in a future life . . . the emotion of fear of death."[353] Brigid Brophy gives us

a psychoanalytic view: "The life of the Ego represents an attempt
to capture some of the species' immortality, which is only on loan
to individuals and is really embodied in the continuity of the
reproductive chain."[354] And Graham Wallas, from the genetic
and naturalistic view: "If a modern man believes that the particular combination of 'genes' from his maternal and paternal
ancestry which constitutes the personality with which he is born
is immortal, he can hardly prevent himself from believing in the
personal immortality of the anthropoid apes. If an ape is personally immortal, how can we deny that a dog or a jelly-fish or a
bacillus is also immortal? Or if each of us is immortal, would we
not have been immortal if we had died in our mother's womb?
If the generative cells which combined at the moment of our conception had perished like countless millions of millions of others
before they were combined, would each of them have been immortal? If we answer that that which is personally immortal is
only temporarily connected with the visible organism and will
continue to exist after the visible organism has decayed, must not
that also be true of the personally immortal element in the ape
or the jelly-fish or of the uncombined spermatozoon?"[355]

What the contemporary man should take into consideration
is that what we do know today was not known centuries ago;
what the early bishops of the first four or five centuries after
Christ did was not concern themselves with knowledge, or any
explanation of experience, or what is true or false, but what is
needed to consolidate and fasten an orthodox foundation of
Catholicism, and so preserve and continue its fixation upon the
people. "Thus orthodoxy is that corpus of beliefs which will unite
the most members for the longest time and consequently make
the organization formidable against antagonists."[356] "Indeed, if
the truth could be determined by authority only, we could get
along with libraries and we wouldn't need laboratories at all."[357]

Has the belief in immortality really enhanced the happiness
and peace of man? History gives us no affirmative reply, but reveals that periods of greater religious density experienced the
greater waves of constant brutality, persecution, massacre, war,
power politics, and the wider and more extensive enslavement and
exploitation of peoples. Thus the natural freedom of man, to

this extent, was restrained, perverted, misled, and enchained from expressing and activating itself for a better, more peaceful, and a truly happier life. "Happiness is nonetheless true happiness because it must come to an end, nor do thought and love lose their value because they are not everlasting."[358] Theology has set up guards at every entrance to the celestial world, and no one could pass unless he submitted to this theology, including the payment of fees most willingly given—"On the banks of the river of death, a band of priests has stood for ages to bar the passage against all poor souls who cannot satisfy their demands for ceremonies, and formulas, and fees."[359]

However, the psychological fact of man's fear of death and the desire for the belief in a future life to counteract the dreadful realization that death is the end of all, including any form of consciousness, material and immaterial, are a problem that does not resolve itself by rationalism or the sciences, and it remains deep in the recesses of the human psyche. Whether it can ever be rationalized away is only probable because it is in the nature of freedom itself for man to use all his functions and capabilities in any direction he pleases, and it is in his power of imagination that he finds greater solace and comfort in always extending his mind, even with imagery and idea, beyond the beyond, and creating situations and sequences of fantasia and all types of chimera to please his own cravings and immediate need for peace of mind. This is the direction the Ego takes, once the mind has made it aware of death, to deny death and continue to exist because the Ego knows no other way or desire. This is the very nexus that is the sustenance for theology, and which binds people to it, even subconsciously, even knowing that what they are believing in has very little likelihood of being true. Belief is not just believing, but a process of *wanting* to believe and this *want-to-believe* is the determinant of the nature and extent of belief, not what is actually believed. Albert Schweitzer: "When natives in good faith assure us that they have attained to freedom from such ideas (taboos), they are by no means always really so advanced. The ideas are still subconsciously present and with any provocation may come to life again."[360]

Thus, the constant cyclic resurgence of one kind of belief over another is a wantable thing as circumstances play upon the need for any such want. Even today, with the waning of the formal religions and the nonretreatable dissolution of theological foundations through the advances of general education, the sciences, cultural studies, the humanities, and the faster-infiltrating streams of communication between peoples long lost in more or less traditional isolation, with all of this and in the very heart of civilized communities, we can see the emergence of what is called, as we mentioned before, *ersatz* religions, substitutes, or replacements that would continue to fill the emotional and psychic needs of people and which can only be filled through putting aside intelligence, vigilance, and intellectuality, and refusing to inquire into the realities that face them. We find these ersatz religions in Communism, Hitlerism, Fascism, in many neo-Jamesian pragmatic metaphysics of one kind or another, anything that gives people something they want to believe in to fill the inevitable gap of ultimate solutions and present voids, that puts the nimbus around some imaginary figment that becomes a satisfying plenum of irrational sedation, just as a man goes to a bar knowing beforehand that he wants to become intoxicated, yet knowing that he cannot withhold this want because in this way he can live with himself *now*. But we know what intoxication does: it removes reality for a moment, it does not prevent its return with the same problem.

Sedation and intoxication are not the means of deliverance, but facing up to realities and inquiring into the true nature of things may open up for us a new set of perspectives and values. These perspectives and values may free freedom from its own enslavement and allow it to exhibit and express itself without supranatural tendencies of dilution, but with a new re-evaluation of the natural field and all its possibilities of providing us with happiness without neurosis, love without frustration, normalcy without sublimation and subjection, life satisfaction without life forfeiture; life while we are living, without death. If time has to be spent, as we realize its irreplaceability, so will our feeling of sacredness for the time element and the life duration it represents become more and more fastened upon the human mind that will remind itself of what Socrates told his pupils: that whether there is a future life or not is not important and forever speculative; what is important is to live a good and happy life, which can never negate any life, mortal or immortal, and can only justify any continuance of it. Charles W. Eliot, lecturing at the 11th session of the Harvard Summer School of Theology, in July, 1909, told his listeners: "The fear of hell has not proved effective to deter men from wrong-doing, and heaven has never yet been described in terms very attractive to the average man or woman. Both are indeed unimaginable. The great geniuses, like Dante and Swedenborg, have produced only fantastic and incredible pictures of either state. The modern man would hardly feel any appreciable loss of motive-power toward good or away from evil if heaven were burnt and hell quenched. The prevailing Christian conceptions of heaven and hell have hardly any more influence with educated people in these days than Olympus and Hades have. The modern mind craves an immediate motive or leading good for today on this earth. The new religion builds on the actual experience of men and women and of human society as a whole."[361]

PARASITISM IN RELIGIO-POLITICAL STRUCTURE

THE HISTORY OF the past two thousand years, in particular that of the Christianized world, shows that during this period the freedom of man reached a low ebb and it was not until the seventeenth century, when the Age of the Enlightenment began to express itself strongly, that freedom, stilled and exploited for so long, reared its head to breathe the fresh air of reason. The morass of dogmatic authority, blind belief, and intellectual sterility became too overbearing a load, and people rebelled to regain their natural freedom. Andrew W. White wrote of Christianity: "The establishment of Christianity, beginning a new evolution of theology, arrested the normal development of the physical sciences for over fifteen hundred years. The cause of this arrest was twofold. First, there was created an atmosphere in which all seeking in Nature for truth as truth was regarded as futile. The general belief derived from the New Testament Scriptures was, that the end of the world was at hand; that the last judgment was approaching; that all existing physical nature was soon to be destroyed; hence, the greatest thinkers in the Church generally poured contempt upon all investigation into the science of Nature and insisted that everything except the savings of souls was folly."[362] "Religion, in its intransigent or superstitious forms, could be a more redoubtable foe of the physician. When the Church abandoned the practice of medicine to laymen, she did not do so merely for the reasons she alleged but also from a conscious or unconscious feeling that in many cases sickness may be a divine punishment against which no weapon is permissible apart from repentance and prayer."[363] Regarding this continual opposition to science, John Herman Randall, Jr., of Columbia University, writes: "If in the history of science men had resorted to supernatural explanations every time difficulties of explanation cropped up, there would be very little science to speak of."[364] Sigmund Freud: "In the long run nothing can withstand reason and experience. . . . We believe that it is possible for scientific work to discover something about the reality of the world through which we can increase our power and according to which we can regulate our life. . . . Science is no illusion. . . . It would be an illusion to suppose that we could get anywhere else what it cannot give us."[365]

Theology has not sincerely aimed at finding the truth, but merely at trying to sustain its own tenets, its own canons, to retain its own hold on the people, to oppose any liberal attitude that might bring about some release of freedom. Power, regardless of what form it takes, never desires to lessen itself; it only relinquishes power as the pressure of necessity forces it to, as greater resistances of power become generated and overwhelm it or persuade it, for its own existence, to compromise, to adapt or change itself to meet compatibility in order to continue to exist or be accepted. Truth, to theology, is a strange companion, for theology established only those "truths" which are conducive to the continuity of its organization, to the acceptance of its principles and dictums. Only a plastic, flexible attitude or method, willing to review its own convictions in the light of new findings, can be an *instrument* of finding and establishing a truth on any basis. This necessitates the freedom of thought and action, two factors which are taboo to the theologians. George Santayana: "If the argument is rather that these beliefs, whether true or false, make life better in this world, the thing is simply false. To be boosted by an illusion is not to live better than to live in harmony with the truth; it is not nearly so safe, not nearly so sweet, and not nearly so fruitful. These refusals to part with a decayed illusion are really an infection of the mind. Believe, certainly; we cannot help believing; but believe rationally, holding what seems certain for certain, what seems probable for probable, what seems desirable for desirable, and what seems false for false."

Regardless of how old an idea is, or of how widely it is believed, is not, of itself, sufficient to establish whether anything is true or not. St. Vincent thought otherwise, that a thing is true if it is old and traditional, and that "universality, antiquity, and consent" prove that Vincent's *Commonitorium* is true. St. Vincent was actually more of a politician than a theologian because his work indicates clearly that he was more concerned with the continuity of the Catholic hierarchy as an organization than with what is true or false in any of its doctrines. James Harvey Robinson so wisely wrote: "The fact that an idea is ancient and that it has been widely received is no argument in its favor."[366] Goethe felt the need of freedom in thought and action, if man is to find the truth of anything, when he wrote in *Paralipomena to Faust*:

> Truth puts all ignorance to flight;
> Naught can withstand the searching light
> Of intellect set free.

If human beings are to find the essence of reality, the certainty of things and their nature, they must rely on their intelligence, experience and on their objective and impartial scientific method. Bertrand Russell: "It is to intelligence, increasingly widespread, that we must look for the solution of the ills from which our world is suffering."[367] He continues to say: "I am myself a dissenter from all known religions, and I hope that every kind of religious belief will die out. I do not believe that, on the balance, religious belief has been a force for good. Although, I am pre-

pared to admit that in certain times and places it has had some
good effects, I regard it as belonging to the infancy of human
reason, and to a stage of development which we are now out-
growing."[368] James A. Leuba: "Those who continue to think
that humanity cannot proceed on its ascending march unless
ultimate questions are answered in the formulae given when
the world was in its childhood, evince an unjustifiable lack of
faith in man."[369]

When did man begin seriously to want to know the truth instead of just believing what the king and priest told him to believe? Principally, the first popular and wide attempt of people
to want to learn the truth, the nature of things, to pierce through
the belief barrier and to look at things as they really are or appear to be, came about in ancient Greece, the cradle of Democracy, and the attempt to restore the natural freedom of individuals as *persons* was initiated here in a societal and broader sense.
"Crete might truly be called the cradle of Western freedom."[370]
"The life of freedom as we know it in fact began with the
Greeks."[371] But this freedom was not to live too long, first with
the Roman conquest of Greece and then with the Christian conquest of both. As the curtain of dogma and absolutism came down
over the European continent everything became still and all
forms of free expression became sublimated and subjected to the
glory of the papacy and the perverted catechisms and canons
of churchly power now mated harmoniously with royal tyranny
and naked power. The age became dark and gloomy, and the
only thought expressed was the thought of fear that gripped
everyone, the fear of *Dies Irae,* the dread of the yawning, sulphurous pit of fire and eternal damnation that awaited all except the
saints. Ignorance took to her throne and all the people believed
in her and became her slaves. For the next eighteen hundred years
they stood still, turned to wood and stone to adorn cathedrals,
and forgot to live. The only freedom they expressed was the freedom to be willingly and ignorantly enslaved and exploited. In
those Dark and Middle Ages, "One must refuse and deny one
self almost everything in this life if one wishes to win with God
in the life to come. The earth is evil, the flesh is evil, procreation

is wicked, meat and eggs are foul, the organized Church is corrupt."[372]

One might question the need of all this backtracking on well-explored, well-criticized, and well-documented history of the primitive and later formal and institutionalized religions in our quest for a philosophy of freedom. Though freedom manifests itself in what people so often erroneously call the separate and dualistic parts of *body* and *mind,* which is really a body with a consciousness of some degree, yet there is no experience in the history of human personality and society in which the body and its consciousness, that is, its ways and habits of mentation, are not simultaneously affected. Where there is good achieved and where there is evil done, both the body and its "mind" are affected for better or worse. There is no such thing as something which is good for the mind and not for the body and there is no such thing which is good for the body and not for the mind. The body and mind are *one,* not two.

Our reasons for delving into primitive thought and habit and the early emergences of formalized religions become obvious. Actually, in the limited space given to it, we could only scratch the surfaces of this religiosity in the cultural evolution of human society; it goes deeper and wider. And the deeper and wider our objective investigation extends we find that, with more tribal taboo and religious ritual and the later subjection of people to the dogmas of the subsequent priesthoods and hierarchies, individuals lost more and more of their natural freedom, although man in becoming thus indoctrinated, patternized, and inoculated with these dogmas, felt psychologically a greater latitude of his being and a closer union to all else in a cosmic sense. This is what Freud considered the great illusion. Furthermore, where before, in primitive tribal life his magic and customs operated within the periphery of his natural life and environment, he now moved all his religiosity into the extra-natural or supernatural field and its "limitless" domain. In doing so not only did he unwittingly surrender his freedom by forsaking his nature, but he also surrendered his life. This surrender of life was exhibited in his being subjected to economic and social slavery and exploitation by the priest-king, later divided into priests and kings, and the psychic enslavement and subjection of his mind into new spheres, where belief became mandatory and the freedom of the mind and its normal, reasonable requisition of the body, sinful, criminal, and punishable by exclusion, imprisonment, torture, and even death.

We will now discuss how the individual, bereft of much of his freedom, became impregnated and saturated with the idea that the society to which he belonged, considered as a collective mind or consciousness, was to be ordained as his temporal god, when in actuality his society consisted of the leaders, religious and secular, who had everything to gain and the people who had, even with the little allowed them, everything to lose.

Where before each member of a tribe or clan *participated* more or less equitably in the common labor to gain his equitable share, and where equity and economic sharing were not only imposed, because of environmental enclosure and pressure, upon each member, but were necessarily scaled, even crudely, according to one's extent of participation and contribution, at least until the emergence of shamanism, now with the new emergence of the psychological power of the priest and the naked power of the king, both powers so often fused and mutual-assisting, a new period of history rose in the story of human society—the *Age of Parasitism.* An age, that is, when those with power derived the benefits of wealth, property, status and prestige, including a new heritage of blood now colored a royal blue, deriving all these by "leadership" and by divine appointment by the gods. The people accepted this leadership and divine guidance as the nucleus, core and bone structure of their society, a society in which each of them had little to say. They provided the necessary enslavement of themselves, became serfs, their lives and labors exploited to fill in the necessary fat to keep these kingly and prietly well-fed and corpulent.

This societal growth of parasitism still persists today, not as common, publicly exposed, deep or widespread as before, but still substantially persistent in many parts. A true exposure of the assets, nonspiritual and very material, of the well-established formal religions of today, would show that these religions have actually more faith in their very earthly financial and property wealth to keep their religions going than in any profound spiritual dependence with their god or gods. Where kingly or dictatorial rule prevails and where the religious hierarchies are in control, parasitism still has its strong arbitrary and cruel hold; we see this today in Spain, Portugal, Tibet, in the absolute rulers of Arabia, in the Communist countries, where oligarchic power struggles prevail, in many smaller countries, where totalitarianism in some form or other, regardless of how overt or disguised, rules. No country or hamlet where humans live is actually and completely immune or exempt from this parasitism. It festers, like a creeping disease, upon the lives and experiences of people. It is this parasitism which some fine and well-meaning scholars have metamorphosed into grandeurs of "social cohesiveness" and "collective consciousness" and the societal "overall mind" at whose altars man must bring his freedoms and burn them as incense to the gods of the state and in devotion to the delusions of divine reward. The pantheons of the gods were always the billboards of ephemeral and chimerical mirages, through the perforations of which the king, priest, tyrant, and dictator received their daily portions for which they did not labor. They are the great beggars of history. The difference between the king on his throne, the Brahmin begging for alms or the ward-heeling political demagogue yelling himself hoarse as the servant of "his people," is merely one of form and appearance, not of class: they are all beggars who live by contribution, not by participation. One would be committing folly to expect individuals to live orderly, peacefully, and satisfactorily without some form of society, organization, government. Perhaps human nature and its society still need Carlyle's hero-worship, the pageantry and awe and reverence and rule, the cling-and-clang. Perhaps society always reflected to a degree what its constituents wanted, needed, or were given to accept; perhaps not.

Emile Durkheim wrote a very scholarly anthropological work which was published in 1915, titled *"The Elementary Forms of the Religious Life; a study of religious sociology,"* which attempts to find the origins and study the development of religion and society, the cohesive factors of both which infiltrate and influence each other, the beliefs, the rituals of the earliest possible spiritual

life of the aborigines, the evolution of the soul-spirit idea, of
animism and *naturism,* and how these two evolving systems of
early man's religious culture moved, separated, united, and interacted with each other for modifications, changes; and how all of
this evolved, in turn, into the nucleus of the socio-religious entity which is man's. Durkheim concluded, as a result, that all
magical, ritualistic, and symbological forms became a "collective
conscience" or "collective consciousness" that integrated and
slowly built human society, that this "collective consciousness"
is the very fabric and skeletal structure of social order and harmony, that it is essential to any human society and without it a
man becomes as a suspended and purposeless iota, a thing unattached when attachment is its very nature. He concluded further
that all these human experiences in the world of spirits came
about as a natural evolutionary ladder, and whatever man's freedom can mean to him is ideally realized in his being a harmonious
part of this social or collective consciousness and thus finding
happiness, solace, peace, and maturity in so doing.

Durkheim set before us a splendid account of these early experiences and their manifold influences in the primitive organization of family, group, tribal life and structure. Yet it seems
to me that when he parted from the screening of objective material and natural forms and began to deduce from all this the
existence of a collective consciousness from which the individual
is merely a pseudo-identity of its own awareness as a separate unit,
and individualities merely reflect, or are activated by, the mother-
stream of socio-religious collective spirit or consciousness, then
the apparition of the termite nest comes to mind. Perhaps humanity may be going in that direction, if the orthodoxies and
totalitarian nationalisms have their way. "With two hundred
million years behind them, termites have evolved a grimly efficient organization in which the individual has no rights at all
and everything is run for the good of the community as a whole.
Like all social insects, they are ruthless totalitarians."[373] "There
are no strikes or forty-hour weeks in the termite mound."[374]
Eugene Marais, referring to a "group mind" felt that the "termitary is a separate and composite animal," and S. H. Skaife
counters by saying that "This is just nonsense. . . . If the termitary

is 'a separate and composite animal,' then so is London and New York and Cape Town."[375] Each termite is an individual unit, but it has long lost its individuality and its individualsm. The same could happen to people in London, New York, or Cape Town— if the totalitarians and hierarchies had their way.

Let us fervently hope that freedom, which predetermined the experiences related by Durkheim, may find it still possible to restore the more natural, even though less cultural or religious, place of man and moralize his social and political structure for a harmony that contains social justice and equity for both individual and individuals as a group; if he can, to achieve it. Malinowski wrote: "Culture remains sound and capable of further development only in so far as a definite balance between individual interest and social control can be maintained. If this balance be upset or wrongly poised, we have at one end anarchy, and at the other brutal dictatorship."[376]

There is a difference between attempting to establish the premise that individuals exist and that their tendency to group or form communities is a natural trait and absolutely essential to their security and continuity, and Durkheim's attempt to establish that a superconsciousness, or social cosmocentric superorganism, called society or the state, is the Capitoline Wolf from whose teats all humanity flourishes, and that the self-identity of individualism and individuality is a mere illusion of an ant seeing itself on a mirror. There is a dfference between attempting to establish which came first, the chicken or the egg, the society or the individual, and the attempt to establish that there is a definite *relationship* between the society and the individual, and the happy existence of the individuals that can possibly maintain a *happy relationship* because the existence of each depends on the existence of both.

THE FALLACY OF COLLECTIVE OR WORLD CONSCIOUSNESS

A *society* CANNOT be happy, nor can it think, nor is it conscious; only the individuals that comprise it have the possibility of being happy and unhappy, only individuals can think, and only individuals are conscious, from the standpoint, of course, of being physically able to do so. This attempt for a happy and satisfactory relationship exhibited itself in the Greek *polis*, where individuals, realizing a possibly greater security in so doing, formed a free communty in which they all participated in responbility and benefit: thus was born *democracy*—the first attempt of the common man—not the noble, priest, or king—to form a social and political process that is *moral*, that contained an *ethos*, that satisfied the hearts and minds of men to consider themselves as equally good and responsible. This initial step did not wholly succeed, considering human nature and its ramifications, but the seed was born and sprouted. It is still growing here and there to the present day. The Greek *polis* in the eighth and seventh centuries B.C. gave birth to a change in the market place. Everywhere else in the world tyranny reigned, despotism and priestcraft literally ran and owned the people. All were literal slaves save those who were ordained to live in the temples and palaces. True, the Greeks did not follow through with democratic principle as the centuries went on; true, oligarchies and power intoxicants and zealous fanatics ditched the free principles of the early *polis* and gradually lay Greece prostrate for invasion and enslavement. Nevertheless, the *Idea* of democcracy was born and nurtured here and it never completely vanished. Somehow, the *Idea* kept itself alive through thousands of years of ordeal and the pains of this ordeal are still part of the cries of this *Idea* today, to struggle through the present morass, still trying to perfect and strengthen itself for the good of the *common man* and the world in which he manages to live, but usually behind the eight ball.

Not only are there no two fingers alike but there are no two sets of ears alike. Dr. Wagner H. Bridger of the Albert Einstein College of Medicine, of which I happen to be a founder, reported in November, 1963, that "babies are very different at birth, both in the way they behave and in physiologic functions."[377] No two humans come into the world with exactly the same equipment, physiologically and psychologically, and no two humans acquire the same experiences and the same environmental impact upon their being. Joseph Campbell: "If there is any one thing that our modern archives of anthropology, history, physiology, and psychology prove, it is that there is no single human norm."[378] Anthony Storr: "From the moment of birth, each infant is a separate entity, with an individual life of its own. Although helpless and dependent, the baby has within itself, and soon starts to express, its individuality, and the rest of its life will be an increasing affirmation of its uniqueness."[379] Sinnott: "The members of any species, individuals though they may be, show no monotonous uniformity. . . . Human beings are not turned out by a process of mass production but every individual, so to speak, is custom made to his own genetic specifications."[380] Variants and variations are constant and continual. Individuality and individualism, though recognizable and classified according to genus, phylum, order, species and subspecies, whether animal or man, are at the basic root of regeneration and experience. Gavin de Beer: "It is now necessary to realize that the product of evolution is a population with an adapted pattern of genetic inequality."[381] Thus, society is the *result* of collectivity and similarities, not the *cause* of it. The individual cell, with all its peculiar self-identities, is the *beginning* of all things and many such cells the *cause*, by the nature of themselves and their event in experience and their relatedness to all else, of whatever physical and social structures that come about helplessly by the nature of the cause experienced in event. Democracy was born of dissent, not of unifromity. Thomas Jefferson: "Is uniformity attainable? Millions of innocent men, women, and children, since the introduction of Christianity, have been burnt, tortured, fined, imprisoned; yet we have not advanced one inch toward uniformity."[382] Jean-Jacque Rousseau: "I will even venture to say that I am like no one in the whole world. I may be no better, but at least I am different."

Social structure of any kind always has a natural base to begin with, and a cultural frame by acquisition; thus society is a product of natural and cultural factors. Cultural factors, in themselves, are products of natural factors, as all else is. But nature is not necessarily society, nor is there indicated, by our knowledge and observation of nature, that it contains an inherent or collective "consciousness" from which well the natural factors that are to be used to form society emanate.

Thinking in terms of society, Epictetus thought that the common man, the individual, is just another number added to many other numbers to complete a total which is society, "a factor necessary to complete the sum."[383] Man is more than a number or a factor to complete a sum; he has one life to live. While it is not owned by any society, one must also be aware that an individual cannot reasonably exist without his fellow-creatures. He cannot and should not want to be alone. This should not mean that he has to be sacrificed to make a "total," or "fused" to the group, when the group consists only of individuals like himself who are tied more or less to each other by a *relationship* and moved by a coordinative essentiality for self-survival and possible self-betterment. Considering what society or the state may be, Louis XIV of France most emphatically put it down very plainly that *he* was the State—"*L'état c'est moi!*" This has been the usual rule whenever and wherever democratic principle and freedom of conscience did not exist or could not freely express itself. Whenever and wherever the common man, the "factor necessary to complete the sum," existed in a society where he was in reality an obeying, conforming, fearful and abject slave, subject to the rule and whim of king, lord, and priest, the latter three more or less making up the "sum" of the "superconsciousness" of the society, this common man, just another human in the mass, was always, Durkheim notwithstanding, again behind the eight ball. Bertrand Russell: "To believe that there can be good or evil in a collection of human beings, over and above the good and evil in various individuals, is an error; moreover, it is an error which leads straight to totalitarianism, and is therefore dangerous."[384] "It is in the individuals, not in the whole, that ultimate value is to be sought. A good society is a means to a good life for those who compose it, not something having a separate kind of excellence on its own account."[385]

Durkheim stated that society is the divinity-consciousness of its human elements of individuals through whom, as a collective or group force, it manifests itself. Accordingly, we could ask Durkheim: Which came or existed first, the chicken or the egg?

But this is not necessary: we know that some kind of egg preceded the first ancestor of the protochicken, that the cause preceded the effect, that the chicken in its present state is the result of the interacting and continuing flow of experienced events of evolution which led from the first cell or egg through all of its evolutive history to the present product—the chicken as we know and now see it. The same applies to the human animal and his institutions. The history of human society, like the society of any animal or insect, is not from the complex products to the simple elements, but from the simple elements and the simpler elements to the complex products of its experiences.

Society is the culmination of certain basic biological drives in the human animal manifesting themselves through the primeval organic needs and experiences of the individual unit to survive in its best possible form. Ardrey: "It is sufficient to give ourselves over to wonder that at the primate dawn the basic outline of modern society had appeared. Before monkeys were born, before the significant primate brain had more than begun to come into being . . . the lemur had emerged from the primordial mammalian night to establish that most sophisticated of social inventions, the nation."[386] Regardless of the complexity and variation of political and economic forms attributed to culture, human ingenuity and wisdom, all these forms are basically rooted not only in the biological rudiments of mammalian evolution, but also in many lower forms of animal life. The nation, like all else that lives or comes out of living, is a biological mechanism.

Each male and each female, in mating, become the prime nucleus of possible social structure. Each family is in itself a miniature social order. A number of these families, tied by blood relationship and group living, become a kinship. Regarding the origin of community life, Carleton S. Coon states: "From the time that man became a hunter, if not before, he was a social animal living in groups of families with an optimum population somewhere between twenty and forty persons."[387] There are many strange places today in the world where people still live in isolated families and not in the usual tribal village. The Machiguenga along the Vilcabamba River in the hinterland of Peru live in this fashion.[388] With the advent of ancestor-worship, "It is clear that

it becomes a cult with the development of clan or lineage structure."[389] Villages grew out of clans or the clinging of families in
a given area. Regarding the Naqada culture, H. R. Hays writes:
"It seems that each of the towns developing along the Nile Valley
was perhaps inhabited by a single clan."[390] W. Robertson Smith:
"The original religious society was the kindred group, and all
the duties of kinship were part of religion."[391]

Any number of these kinships, tied together in common and
close living, intermarriages, mutual-assisting in food fathering,
crop growing, cattle raising, group foraging, hunting, defending
or invading, common usage and tenancy of a specific area or
migrating food-following pattern, which, in general, can be considered as an habituated or familiarized pattern of group-living
as a solution for greater security and satisfaction to the families
and individuals, became a tribe or a clan. "The connection between religions and kinship is often manifested in forms that
cannot be explained except by reference to a primitive stage of
society, in which the circle of blood relations was also the circle
of all religious and social unity. . . . That all human societies
have been developed from this stage is now generally recognized."[392]

This is the basal process of societal growth, from the simple to
the complex, from the individual to the group; two little man-
grove seedlings in the proper environmental shallow salt water
flats will gradually build a forest tangle of mangroves and make
an island or a *key*. The individual, in his own mental-physical
probing of the wonders, fears, and powers of nature, was his own
tenable and wondering self and became the first priest unto himself, the first patriarch of his own family without any formalized
religious form or belief; these came later, with his first cultural
acquisitions and organizational experience. Religion or any form
of collective worship or instituted and regulatory tribal forms,
such as taboos, came about as a result of group-living, not its
cause or inspiration. Religion was not in man from the beginning; it is a cultural and acquired growth, and as all cultural
acquisitions, it is subject to change, increase or diminishment,
according to the knowledge-quanta of people and their psychic
and emotional values and needs.

A religion, which is so often embodied and patternized into the customs of a country, especially in a country where a certain religion is more or less in control and predominant, is subject to change, perhaps with slower pace or less variation, but religions have always and helplessly been influenced by, and have evolved through, infiltration, economic and political, of situations arising in any contemporary period, or through previous or surrounding religions, and have modified as cultural changes came about by various resistances and pressures. Christ was nailed to the Cross, Prometheus was nailed to the mountain, and Indra was fastened to the lotus stem. Lot's wife was turned into a pillar of salt for looking back, Persephone had a similar sorrow, and in China we have the legend of the lady by the river Yi who was turned into a mulberry tree because she looked behind her. Story, myth, and legend did not stay pure in any one place, but fast or slow it was a sort of "food-chain" of cultural infusion and diffusion that spread its ways in all directions all over the world. The extent of acquisition and the extent of traditionalism depended on the historical sequences of event, accident, invention, discovery, and natural assets, and their interacting relationships. William Lillie: "In all men there are two opposing tendencies which we may label 'Hormic' and 'Mnemic' tendencies, the tendency to be always seeking something new and the tendency to cling firmly to the old."[393] E. E. Fournier D'Albe: "Ethnologists believe that the metamorphosis from beast-like savage to cultured civilian may be proximately explained as the result of accumulated changes that found their initial impulses in a half-a-dozen or so of practical inventions."[394] Where infusion was nil or hardly perceptible, traditionalism became more fastened and more resistant to modification and change. Louise Marie Spaeth: "Zuni women regard the white women on the reservation as exceedingly vulgar because they spank their children. In New Guinea, where the people were until recently cannibalistic, the natives nearly lynched a white trader who was beating his child."[395]

Society in its precultural and preorganizational beginnings was a physiological tie of psychological and biological forces and factors, which came about through the instinctive and instinctively adaptive processes of the animal to survive, and challenge,

by curiosity and need, the potential of extension required by
the nature of the challenge, group coordination, group simultaneity of purpose and action, group reward as a group achievement, and so, individual reward by sharing, thus bringing about
the coalesced idea and habit of mutual-assistance by means of the
group, through which each individual shared by reason of his
participation. We see this at work among many of the animals in
the killing and eating of their prey, as among the lions, wolves,
sharks, etc. Even today, in all primitive societies the degree of
reward is measured by the degree of participation, a factor that is
manifested and accepted in insect, bird, fish, and general animal
life, where gregarious habits and traits are exhibited in some
measure.

The beginnings of human society are rooted in the earliest
transferences of territory and territorial proclamations of an
individual and his immediate family, to become the mutual-shar-
ing territory of a group of individuals and their families. The
nations and peoples of the world today are the culminations of
this process of adaptability and compatibility in the general operation of evolution. This might have occurred from the earlier acceptances and compatibilities of neutral or unproclaimed territory, in which the many shared without or little conflict. However, when such transferences evolved in the nature of the environment and security from enemies and food potential reward
was assured, it gradually "dawned" on individuals that with in-
corporation came greater security, better and less dangerous means
of obtaining food, and the pleasant discovery of a wider range
and variety and abundance of females to choose from in mating.
This last avenue of potential love-making increased in kinships,
deepened and integrated the clan on wider familial and ancestral
lineages, extended the clans into "blood relationships" along
patrilineal or matrilineal lines, and eventuated into a greater tribe
of family-bindings. "Under unilateral descent and the classifica-
tory system of kinship status, parenthood becomes extended into
clan relationship."[396] Thus the individual family became a genea-
logical entity that grew by integration across and into the family
and blood fabric of the clan, creating a kind of tribal family.
When the kinships of any tribe became too close and severe, the

processes of natural desire and selection brought about a greater degree of exogamy, which "mongrelized" communities as they gradually penetrated and became diffused into each other. Mongrelization has been going on all over the world to the present day, and will continue, depending upon the degree of accessibility and receptiveness of any particular community or area.

Thus, *contrary* to Durkheim, society rose from the moving together of individuals, biologically primed by their family-kinship-clan substance, functions, and their consequential experiences and products, to form the primeval segments of social groupism and the eventuated and determined need for organized order of some kind in order to carry on and satisfy the generic stimulants, purposes, and satisfactions of the individuals to become naturally compatible and favorable to the acceptance of group or tribal unity. It seems evident that this came about as a *natural* growth of experiencing, and that the individual primitive mind, in processing the automatic experiences of grouping for individual purposes, was most probably and completely unaware that in so doing there was or might occur any surrender of his natural freedom, or that the group-order, as a newly evolved experience in his extension of himself through coordination and cooperation with others and the extension of his environmental periphery, was to supersede him in power, or that this process of togetherness in the form of collective effort was an existent apart from himself in the view of considering such a collective as an external factor. Besides, in the trait of gregariousness and the instinct to move and live with others was already a naturally evolved function and instinct that came with his particular nature and had already evolved from the time he was arboreal and was more animal than man. The biological and psychological processes involved, if they formed and structured the social and cultural organism, were activated and extended unconsciously by the animal in that direction because of its own evolution, its own potential for, as well as limitation of, adaptability and compatibility with environmental factors and itself, and not because of any "sacred" or "divine" spark that controlled the "profane" or natural field by eminent domain, or preordained a certain sequence of supernatural, divine or deitic arrangements, which is not only an anthropomorphic attempt of man's mind but also a confession of its own cosmocentricity in viewing the universe by looking at himself. "Nothing is so long-lived as absurdity."[397]

Durkheim felt that society is the basic and real substance of human existence, the *materia prima,* the ulterior and positive foundation of the earliest possible human sense, conception, and awareness of the sacred, the divine, of a god. "A society," he stated, "by its very power over the minds of the people, has everything that is necessary to awaken in them the sensation of the divine; for society is to its members what a god is to his faithful." In Christianity this *materia prima* changed radically because of the *human* factor in *individuals* to become more powerful, more wealthy, more influential. Especially was this change recognizable in the centuries following the uneventful *Dies Irae,* which for some reason missed its schedule. The mendicant friars, so activated in the Dominican and Franciscan orders, at home and for the Crusades, began to make themselves a nuisance to the bishops, priests, and the regular Catholic hierarchy. Dunham relates: "Christianity, indeed, had moved a long way from Saint Paul's liberality: salvation in exchange for faith. You could now acquire salvation only in exchange for faith plus fees. There was in fact a fee for every important transaction in life, from birth to burial. Beyond burial, there were fees for the repose of your soul and of as many other souls as were dear to you. . . . The Roman Church was a union of rival parts and powers, in which respect it resembled every other human organization of large size. The priests and bishops—also, indeed, the other monastic orders— resented and rebuffed the mendicants, who moved among the populace, the ultimate source of profit, with a deadly infiltration. What seemed worst was that the populace welcomed them. The extraordinary mixture of novelty, devotions, and economy was irresistible. And so priests and bishops, archbishops and cardinals, appealed to the Vicar of Christ for a surcease of mendicant activity."[398] Thus, within the Catholic structure itself, in the competition of mendicant friar, priest, bishop and cardinal, for the fullest share of profit from the people in the issuance and sale of indulgences, absolutions, services, confessions, etc., rivalry and bitterness became rampant, and priest uttered anathema and imprecation upon priest with the practical solutions of assassinations, depositions, excommunications, and internecine strife and opposition. Even Martin Luther proclaimed in effect that if men only believe enough in Christ, they can commit adultery and murder a thousand times a day without perilling their salvation. Is this Durkheim's *materia prima* for the divine society?

That the power of a society can become so great as to create itself into a divinity before its people is very true and also very sad, for it confesses two things very clearly: that the power of any such society does not actually represent the power of the constituents but the leadership, and this leadership may be a political electorate, or a dictator, or a dictatorial-oligarchic combine, such as exists in the Communist countries, or a leftover kingship, or other forms of arbitrary power. Such a power can become, and often does become, a power indifferent to the actual welfare of the people, growing from the early stages of propaganda, pageantry, patriotism, indicating forms of revolutionary power, and very often gradually evolves into tyrants, *führers* of plain and unadulterated pure naked power, with the constituents turning into fearing mechanisms saluting the leader like a herd of fear-frozen mannequins. Sandifer and Scheman: "Except for their self-avowed motivation, little difference can be discerned between the closed society today and the feudal and monarchical systems against which mankind struggled for centuries."[399]

The second possible result of such a power is the tragic loss of individualism and with it a patternization that runs counter to the biologically-necessary and psychologically-essential content of natural freedom, which is the inherent cogency of a human life and without which his *humanism* is not possible. Durkheim sadly overlooked the historical fact that his viewpoint, regardless of how well intended, often led to tragic and destructive holocausts in the life of humanity. It often led the unwary and the unthinking into situations that paved the way for a blind and emotional caterpillar society submerged to hero-worship, that paved the way for Napoleonism, Hitlerism, Stalinism, and now Castroism. It smacks of that egotistic smoldering of megalomania exhibited by Fichte with an assist from Hegel and put into operation by Hitler and Mussolini. Carlyle once wrote that history is the biography of great men; obviously the rest were the victims. "Those who cause the most blood to flow are the same ones who believe they have right, logic and history on their side."[400]

The actual result of group-mind or collective genius—which is actually a nonexistent synthesis—the adoration of mob strength as exhibited in the Nazi *Wille zur Macht,* the Will to Power, is catastrophe and paranoic destruction of people and the derangement of millions of its unfortunate followers. "The Jack-in-the-box conception of culture, as the self-revelation of an immanent Genius or Deity, has been cultivated in German metaphysics; it reaches its peak in Hegel's Historical Idealism. But its fullest practical application had to wait till the arrival of the latest incarnation of the Absolute—Herr Adolf Hitler."[401] Regarding Hegel and his philosophy, Bertrand Russell states: "It can quite easily be expounded lucidly in words of one syllable, but then its absurdity becomes obvious." Hegel wrote that "we learn from history that we learn nothing from history"—a point on which Hegel was right insofar as Hegel was concerned. Hermann Rauschning: "National Socialism (Nazism) makes use of the masses in its own highly individual and significant way. It makes use of them in connection with the special German situation in two directions. It enlarges upon the importance of the masses, provides them with a quasi-apotheosis in the conception of the *Volksgemeinschaft,* the 'united nation' and emphasizes from time to time the power of this massed body, though it is a nation united only in its intoxication of spirit and is formless except on the march."[402] Bertrand Russell: "Similarly Fascists and Communists, having in their minds a picture of society as a whole, distort individuals as to make them fit into a pattern; those who cannot be adequately distorted are killed or placed into concentration camps. I do not think an outlook of this sort, which totally ignores the spontaneous impulses of the individual, is ethically justifiable, or can, in the long run, be politically successful."[403] The centuries-long Inquisition of the Roman Catholic hierarchy tried the same thing; those who could not be adequately absorbed were killed, robbed, exiled, and otherwise disposed of. Lopez, in his *Birth of Europe,* describes the Inquisition: "Looked at one by one, the methods of the Inquisitors which are most distasteful to modern juridical feeling all possess a precedent in Roman law or mediaeval custom; recourse to anonymous denunciation, torture, solitary confinement, secret trial, no lawyer for the defence, no cross-examination of witnesses, assumption of guilt in the case of any accused who absconds from trial or cannot prove his innocence. Taken as a whole, they constitute a machine capable of annihilating anyone to whom the slightest suspicion attaches."[404]

There is collective *power,* such a unions, alliances, armies, political factions, societies, nations, and there are typical identifiable similarities among individuals of certain areas or countries, but "collective mind" or "collective consciousness" does not really exist except in the leadership which identifies itself as representing this collectiveness. Actually, it is not anything collective at all, but the temporary government over a group, large or small, of individuals, or an order of law and regulation according to a certain kind of philosophy or culture, or, in the case of dictators, the subjection to the power of certain individuals whose power came about by the very process of subjection, psychological and arbitrary, who became temporal deities and, to some people, actual divine deities, to whom complete loyalty, obedience, and sacrifice, even of one's life, are due. Malinowski: "It is not an accident that Spengler's nihilism and defeatism is founded on an entirely anti-deterministic, hence anti-scientific, conception of culture. To Spengler, 'Culture' is an autonomous group-mind or collective genius which expresses its free will in those outward shadowy manifestations which, to the uninitiated and unwary, appear as the substance. The Eye of the Illuminated Seer and Prophet alone perceives that they are but the outer husk, and penetrates beyond to the inner meaning. This grandiose and mystical conception of culture as a Spirit-behind-the-facts has fascinated millions and stultified the work of social science for a generation or two."[405] Hegel, Fichte, Spengler, et al: these led to Nazism.

Durkheim wrote: "Society is not at all the illogical or a-logical, incoherent and fantastic being which it has too often been considered. Quite the contrary, the collective consciousness is the highest form of the psychic life, since it is the consciousness of consciousness."[406] Society, true, is not illogical or a-logical, incoherent or fantastic, not any more fantastic or illogical than the constituent numbers that compose it. However, society is the biological and cultural sequence of man's original struggle to survive, change, extend, and, in general, evolve as he did according to his nature and the environment. He could not have done otherwise. Man *is* a social animal, to begin with, instinctual to his animal nature and nature's evolutional way to protect, even blindly, the species. This is seen in many other animals too numerous to mention and very common in the insect world. When it comes to comparable opinions of societal structure, the termites, ants, and the bees more or less perfected their societal systems long before man left the trees and started to throw stones. The bees and the termites, if they could afford a moment from their labors and express an opinion, may frown upon the claims of *Homo sapiens,* the new arrival, and ridicule our inflated and optimistic ideas of societal progress and perfection. They may, no doubt, still consider us floundering about chaotically in the first stages of natural regimentation and the rebellious versus organizational directions which are still far from the societal structure the termites have, in which individual identity has been completely lost and operates merely as a segment, separated from, but umbilicalized to, a collective operating instinct, an instinct operating as a whole and without which the segmented unit would immediately wither for lack of collective cohesion and instinctual drive fulfillment.

Contrary to Durkheim, society cannot embrace all totality but merely the sum total of *human* elements involved, and even these more subjectively as the instincts and acquired traits of the human animal in any given group or society operate for its own insightedness and anthropomorphic extensions, and even these on a temporary, changing, evolutional basis. While society supplies the "sum," the area or field in which the arts of communication can possibly be operable, language and other communicating arts came about, not from society to man, but from man to society, from man's efforts to create society as a result of his nature and actions. Society is the effect of communication and need, not the cause of it; if the individual human animal were not capable, through his prehensilities, brain, and neural structure and function, both evolving and extending each other, society, as we understand it, could never have been evolved.

The course and nature of a social order rises and falls because of the particular individuals that comprise it: their minds and principles, the consequences, and the complex and interacting behaviors and relationships that make up the common experiences of any group, large or small. When these particular individuals no longer have any voice or choice, in the practical sense, in the exercise of a conscious freedom, protected by, as well as subjected to, democratic and cultural processes of law and order, then a chaotic nihilism, or a termite nest, is the eventual sequence of the deterioration, gradual or sudden, of the biological and acquired freedoms which, as Jefferson stated, are the *inalienable* processes of life and without which man abdicates his humanity and eradicates the historical acquisitions necessary for a truly peaceful and satisfied life and secured by the necessary freedoms to achieve and maintain it. The rise or fall of a society hinges on its individuals and their individualistic concepts, from which generalizations may be taken to indicate a certain type of social organism, mannerism, behavior or philosophy, but any such generalization is a pollster percentage of averages and indications, not a collective or societal aggregate-consciousness. Malinowski: "Society by the collective wielding of the conditioning apparatus molds the individuals into a cultural personality. The individual, with his physiological needs and psychological processes, is the ultimate source and aim of all tradition, activities, and organized behavior."[407]

"The existence of individual cults," wrote Durkheim, "implies nothing which contradicts or embarrasses the sociological interpretation of religion; for the religious forces to which it addresses itself are only the individualized forms of collective forces. Therefore, even when religion seems to be entirely within the individual conscience, it is still in society that it finds the living source from which it is nourished."[408] True, an individual, born and nurtured in any particular society and religion, becomes a product of his heritage and environment, but this does not preclude the historical confirmation of societal and religious change. Indi-

viduals and groups of individuals are at the root of change potential as well as changes brought about by accident and event, man-
made or nature-made. "Today's individualist is canonized
tomorrow."[409]

I believe Durkheim wishfully hoped for something unrealiz-
able except in a society where all minds and hopes of all individuals are identical, agreeable, and cohesive—which never happened.
There are hundreds of different religions and probably thousands
of cults and sects, each with their own religious structures and
catechisms; any one of them, if they had the power and authority,
would undoubtedly be led to dispose of the others. In the past
they have tried to do this, and history portrays no such tolerance
between creeds and religions as Durkheim wishes there to be.
Martin A. Larson: "The struggle between Catholicism on the one
hand and the esoteric mystery-cults on the other proved once and
for all that any religion which becomes the state will most emphatically destroy all its competitors and, at the same time, every
vestige of freedom. And one of the first to fall before the Church
Triumphant was the cult of Mithra, to which Christianity owed
so much."[410] "The Brahmanas insisted on controlling each and
every member of society: no one could escape their rule and they
made some kind of provision for every one. This, of course, is
the fundamental characteristic of the priest-state: A hierarchy may
or may not seek moral improvement, but it always insists on
universal sway, heavy tribute from all, and the extirpation of
every ideology except its own. It proclaims its prerogative to legislate for every phase of human activity, social, political, moral,
domestic, civil, and religious, all by revealed and sacred authority.
In such a society, no human being is permitted to live his own
life, follow his own reason, or earn a living in his own way, asking
merely to live at peace with his fellowmen. Anyone desiring such
independence will be regarded as a dangerous subversive."[411]
Regarding the Vatican's attitude on the principle of separation of
Church and State, Lopez states: "Although popes and emperors,
bishops and princes fought innumerable battles for precedence
and jurisdiction, although their disputes over specific portions of
land or sources of revenue were relentless, not one of them ever
considered untying the knots they so often had to cut. In their

eyes, separating Church from State, establishing one compartment for religion and another for secular life, would have meant divorcing heaven and earth, an act not only impious but in fact impossible."[412]

SUBJECTION OF THE INDIVIDUAL

GEORGE C. VALLIANT, regarding the temple buildings of the Aztecs: "Not even the Pyramids of Egypt present so carefully calculated a plan to dominate the individual with the sheer weight of supernatural power. The modern visitor to Teotihuacan, now in ruins, cannot escape the ancient association of ideas that the greater his temple, the more powerful a god must be."[413] Victor W. von Hagen: "The Andean people were from birth to death tied to the supernatural."[414] H. R. Hays: "An anti-individualist, collectivisit tendency . . . leads to sterile bureaucracy."[415] Gerhard Szczesny: "So dominant is the idea that Christians are made elect by God by unconditional surrender to Christ that the significance of moral effort and loyalty to the law pales besides it, and any intellectual striving to reach the truth seems absurd and even dangerous."[416] Morris Raphael Cohen: "It is often asserted that one of the great contributions of America to the civilized thought of mankind is the notion of a free church in a free society: that is, a society in which everyone is free to develop his own religious conscience without any group controlling the state so as to inter-fere with the freedom of others. In this respect the complete separation of church and state in America is supposed to be an ideal achievement, and we Americans are sorry for those peoples who have no such advantage as we have in this respect."[417]

I know a friend who is an agnostic and possesses a reasonably free mind. His basic desire is to be happy and see others happy, regardless of their beliefs. Wherever he travels he usually brings back, among other things, many religious articles, which he gives to his religious friends only because he feels these gifts make them happy, and they do. A religious Jew, Protestant, Moslem, Brah-man, or Shinto priest would rarely if ever bring Catholic religious articles to his Catholic friends. Only a person with a free mind could do this, because only a free mind respects, in depth, the freedom of other minds to think or worship as they please. Assuming the existence of a benevolent and equitable God, under such a God all people are His people, because God could never have made rules. Only people have made rules, and these rules, contrary and ambiguous on any worldly plane, have merely divided people the world over and have caused hate, persecution, and prejudice. A man who lives by rules and makes no exceptions becomes a rule to measure by, not to live with. Rules have made people unhappy. Any such God could never have made rules because He could not want people to be divided, because He must know that a human's mind wants, or should want, to be free, because He could not want people to hate each other or to be unhappy. The truly religious person would thus hold communion with his God and not with a rule, for in following a rule he is merely following man or men who made them. A good mind and a kind heart and a peaceful spirit and an honest conscience—these are the things any good God would want people to have—if he happens to be a kind, peaceful, intelligent, and honest God. And all four are not rules.

In a society in which a religion has supreme control and authority over the country, where is there room for the individual who desires no religiosity, who wants no part of spirituality? Most certainly, in any democratic state it is the freedom of a person to believe or not to believe, to follow or not to follow, to agree or to disagree. Where is there, then, room for the intellectual freedom of expression for an individual, or even of any given group, which is indispensable and an essentiality of any true form of civilized and democratic society? Durkheim may claim that regardless of whether a person believes or not, whether he agrees or not, he is still part, unknowingly and/or unconsciously, of this "consciousness of consciousness." This is the metaphysical and the ontological attempt to establish a teleological premise. Durkheim or I can specifically and scientifically claim by our deductions such a final disposition of the universe by our own cosmocentric wishes. Nature is mute and she does not even hear us.

Upon Durkheim's premise that the individual conscience, whatever it may contain or form as a base for thought and action and which is alleged to be nourished from the "living source" of the collective consciousness, organism, or socio-religious nucleus, how can we account for the many revolutionary discoveries and inventions which, from time to time, have upset, radically modified, or substantially transformed much of the socioreligious structure and its cultures—and these brought about very often by *few* individuals? Would the "collective consciousness" of Europe for two thousand years have been the same if one individual by the name of Jesus was never heard of? Would the "Supranatural Societal Mind" in nineteenth century America, with part of this "Mind" in the South wanting to keep human beings as slaves and part of this "Mind" in the North wanting to set them free, would this "Collective Consciousness" have remained the same till today were it not for the life of *one individual,* Abraham Lincoln? Referring to the ancient Egyptian Pharaoh Akhnaton, who dared to change the prevailing religion against the then Amon-worshipping priesthood, Dunham writes: "Heresies are thus ideas that disrupt an existing society in such a way as to change, or to threaten to change, the distribution of power within it."[418] Birket-Smith affirms this point well: "Without being too hard on Durkheim and his followers, it is probably safe to say that their knowledge of primitive people derived more from the shelves of the *Bibliothèque nationale* than from personal contact with the tribes they discussed; otherwise, they would probably have understood that heretics, independent spirits who do not automatically go along with the thoughts of the majority, can also be found among primitive people. Were not this the case, all progress would be impossible."[419] William O .Douglas: "A great risk in any age is the tyranny of the majority. Freedom of expression is the weapon of the minority to win over the majority or to temper the policies of those in power." Sandifer and Scheman: "The cry for freedom is directed either against particular forms or demands of culture or else against culture itself. It does not seem as if man could be brought by any sort of influence to change his nature into that of the ants; he will always, one imagines, defend his claim to individual freedom against the will of the multitude."[420] Anthony Storr: "Disagreement, controversy, and even competitive striving have a positive function in human existence. For how can a man know who he is, and what he thinks and believes, unless there are others who think and believe differently? . . . For we define ourselves, psychologically as well as physically, by comparison and differentiation."[421]

Without going into a long line of examples that have changed cultures and religions and people, we will cite two examples. The first is the invention of the steam engine, which ushered in a new world of industry and modified the cultural habit and environment of man in a short period of time, more than most things have done in thousands of years. The second example is the present new world of physics brought about by one individual, Albert Einstein (who happens not to have believed in any gods, in supernaturalism, or that people should subject themselves to any such notions as souls or spirits), who, with a short equation, changed the world and its societies more than anything heretofore imagined or invented by man, and which may become either the salvation or the destruction of humanity and the world it is now trying to create by *superseding* the precultural biological forms. To say that both Watt and Einstein derived their inventive and creative credits from the collective consciousness is to avoid the true solution and merely begs the linguistics of logic to entangle itself in useless debate. Invention and discovery are not usually the consequences of conformance, acceptability, and resignation. On the contrary, they are the results of the daring, the dissident, and the heretical. The creative, the innovator and the inventors are *individuals*, not societies, who dare to challenge, in some way or other, the fatalistic acceptances of organization and society as some deified or sacrosanct situation. "When deities engage in human politics, they must prepare to suffer the twilight and the dark."[422]

Invention and discovery are the results not of the collectiveness of any society or religion but the manifestation of an individual, isolated in his own nonconforming sense of penetration to reach out for something as yet unknown and strange to his kind and group. When Thomas Edison, an atheist, felt in his searching sense the possibility of the electric light bulb or the disc to repeat sound, he may have unconsciously or consciously

felt the impress of the cumulative knowledge of previous individuals, like himself, but he most certainly did not get any assistance from the collective consciousness of his society to consummate his experiments. History shows that the reverse was
much too often true. Society, and especially religion, opposed
innovation, change, liberality of movement and thought, and free
expression in all its many literary, scientific, and art forms. William O. Douglas: "Freedom of movement is basic in our scheme
of values."

The persecution by the churches and social groups of Dr. Morton, who discovered the use of chloroform to eliminate pain in
surgery, is well known; if they could have, they would have quartered him or hanged him from the nearest tree. It is the work
of the few who have not conformed or believed that has reshaped
the world, and thus reshaped, changed, and encultured societies
and even religions in new ways of adjustment and living that
have become almost irreversible. "Individual mind, when free,
will disturb the tranquility of the group-mind; this divergence
is the essence of all progress. The finest things in life, material,
moral, political and economic, were achieved because individuals
were brave enough to dare the traditional organizations of society, to disrupt the lethargy of the group-mind, to awaken it to
newer and better and finer ways of living."[423]

Buddha changed the culture of the East, and Confucius changed
the manners and social ways of the Chinese to a certain extent.
Akhnaton tried and failed, but Jesus succeeded in changing the
history of the Western world for now almost two thousand years,
and the history of Europe is the history of Christianity. Mohammed changed the history, too, of a great part of the world
and fingered his way for more than a thousand years into all the
crevices and crannies of the Asiatic islands and jungles and even
now is penetrating deep into the heart of the African hinterland.
These were *individuals*. True, they grew up in their own societies
and cultures, and reflected their own cultures, but they *moved*
on, in their own ideas, broke down the standard and accepted
dams of belief, and let out much of the waters of previously
accepted usages and dogmas to let in the new streams of belief
and dogma according to their own recorded, revised, or inno-

vated ideas. If we are to understand the dynamic and colloidal processes of livingness, the tissues of which are constantly bathed and nourished with the plasma of freedom, whether we are conscious of it or not, going on within our own bloodstreams, we will also understand that *nothing stands still,* that the existential process of change in all things only confirms one *status quo,* the status quo of movement, regardless how slow or fast, in which the gravitational illusions of our own rooted dogmas and usages make us seem to stand still or to have reached the heights of perfection in our own self-conceived temples of "truth"; that we have arrived at godhood through our own emulation. Religious, social, and political organizations have always tried, by philosophy, dogma, or physical force, to justify their own existence and necessity. "Organizational self-justification has existed since the earliest empires, and it will continue to be needed and practiced so long as human society lasts."[424]

The Durkheim premise offers a concept in which individual tastes, minds, philosophies, are mere phasic particles or Spinozian attributes operating even unconsciously in the totality of cosmic or collective consciousness which encompasses all humanity. If a collective consciousness, which in itself is a pure metaphysicism, could be presumed to exist, then all inspiration, upon which the arts are based, would not have come about in the manner it did and still does. Art, which exposes the sacred fire of the individual spark and the naked frame of the freedom of expression, knows of no such collective impartiality as is indicated in the overall "Cosmic Mind" of Durkheim.

"There can be no such thing as impartiality," wrote Charles Duff. "He who claims it is either a knave or a slave or a fool."[425] Partiality identifies some freedom of *an* individual and partiality exists to some extent and degree in *all* humans as well as in all other forms of life. This in itself exposes the fallacy of considering any realism to be attached to any theory of collective conscience or consciousness. Partiality not only expresses itself in every form of the Arts, but this very expression is the visible identity of a process deep-rooted in the very core of biological beginnings, by which each living thing, conscious or unconscious, seeks, wants, and tends to move toward things and situations that seem to be favorable to itself. Partiality is the initiating and generating force in the implementation and surge in any approach of new possibility and probability, variation and experimentation. The importance of this approach to variation and development by extending the frontiers of the probably possible is stressed by John Dewey: "The development of modern science began when there was recognized in certain technical fields a power to utilize variations as the starting points of new observations, hypotheses and experiments. The growth of the experimental as distinct from the dogmatic habit of mind is due to increased ability to utilize variations for constructive ends instead of suppressing them."[426] Erich Kahler: "The differentiation of man's relation to the universe develops the human mind. The differentiation of man's relation to the community develops the human individual."[427] Loren Eiseley: "The man who learns how difficult it is to step outside the intellectual climate of his or any age has taken the first step on the road to emancipation, to world citizenship of a high order."[428] Bertrand Russell: "New hopes, new beliefs, and new thoughts are at all times necessary to mankind, and it is not out of a dead uniformity that they can be expected to arise."[429] Friedrich Paulsen: "The collective mind is the subject of the mythological conception of the universe; the individual mind, that of philosophy."[430]

If the religious consciousness of man is considered to be part of his individual-group interaction in social evolution, how is it that, as we go back through history and into primitive times, the density of this consciousness was more deeply and more widely and concentratingly diffused in primitive and ancient times, and has become more and more diluted and less diffused with the rise of civilization, the sciences, the evolution of modern societies, and markedly lacking in the "collective consciousness" of modern scientific and secular people and their societies. Religiosity has no doubt dwindled with the rise of science and modern philosophy, and, in actuality, has never been reconciled to them. Whether this is good or bad may be debatable, but the fact remains that, as we go back, we find the individual's dedication to religious forms more severe, and, as we go onward to modern times, we find that the individual has rebelled time and time

again to free himself from the obscurantic and dogmatic rigidities
of the formal religions and to this extent regain the natural freedoms. The Age of the Enlightenment saw the specific trend away
from dogmatisms and orthodoxies and the most hallowed and
sacred scriptures openly questioned. "The old view of the world,
not radically attacked until the seventeenth century A.D., was that
most happenings are intended happenings. Some deity or other,
some superhuman and supernatural personage, purposed them
and produced them."[431] The twilight of the gods thus began and
is still going on, inevitably, steadily. Evolution, even of the mind
of man and his religions, does not know how to turn back, nor
would we want it to.

The nineteenth century saw the clear cleavage as the sciences
and their investigations brought out the factualities of the natural evolution of man and the world about him. The twentieth
century added the new sciences of the mind, of the physiological
sciences, including genetics, embryology, microbotany, biochemistry, zoology, and the new nuclear physics; the advancement and
expansion of the cultural and social sciences, the anthropologies
and the humanities. With the shrinking of distances and the
diffusion of scientists and social explorers all over the world, it is
only a question of time when even the strongest and most deep-
rooted traditional systems will find it "practical" and "progressive" to modify themselves into various adjustments to meet the
new demands and urgencies of science and people, which the
religions have always done under the finality of pressure in order
to survive, when they did survive.

These modifications will gradually increase until, slowly and
definitely, the religions may cease to exist altogether as formal
religions and they may evolve, as everything else evolves that is
man and man-made, into new forms of social and cultural influence and societal guidance. Power, in any form, wants to remain
as power, even if it means the disposition of once sacred dogmatic
tenets and a change of clothing from black sackcloth to pink or
blue. But their historical vestiges as religious power, with which
they have always been identified, and their theologies, will be
gone, and gone forever. Evolution never turns to look back. Its
processes are present and forward processes, and there is no such

thing as reverse gear in the machinery of evolution, biological and cultural. The process may be destroyed by atom bombs or by nature, but it will not turn around to go backwards.

Durkheim's hypothesis of a collective consciousness, which is supposed to represent or act as a general or overall socioreligious mind or consciousness, and which is the activating core of social structure, does not seem to meet the requisites of the common experiences of people and their relationships between themselves and the world they live in. Assuming any such existence or "activity" of a collective consciousness, it must take the form of a chaotic conglomerate of individual consciousnesses which could not possibly form any such collective consciousness as Durkheim wrote about, and far from any harmonious morality which he depicted as the social nucleus. If Durkheim, Plato, Kant, Hegel, and many others of similar mind and temperament grouped themselves together, with Berkeley as chairman, it would be reasonable to expect a group consciousness of similarities and some cohesiveness of purpose and meaning. But the world of people, or the people in any large group, are not all Durkheims, Platos, or Hegels; the various levels from ferocious, insane criminality to the most honest and kindly of people are many and so diversified and on so many levels, variations, degrees and kinds, that the sum of them defies description, ordinal procedure, or classification. In our country, our jails are full from coast to coast; our mental institutions are crowded with new arrivals constantly; the rich have their minds and principles of thinking and living, and the poor, if they have any time to have principles and do some thinking, most probably are not thinking in terms of any beneficent or solacing gratefulness for their condition. Can the Durkheims and Platos assume that their view is the true and normative one and all others merely aberrations, abstractions, just lost sheep who can't find their way back to the collectively-conscious homestead? On the contrary, we find that history and experience indicate that, while the philosophers mused about the great moral imperatives and the "soul" of mankind, those in charge of religion and of society, with or without ideals, looked out for themselves first, and the rest of the collective consciousness had to look out for itself as best it could.

Regardless of the assumed content of any such collective consciousness, how would it fare if law and the enforcement of order
subject to law would be suspended and society left to depend
solely upon this collective consciousness? Especially when we
know that whatever law we have is the result of the thinking of
the few and not of the many, the rational and moral few trying
to hold down the emotional and immoral many? Did not the
priesthoods and the kingships who held the reins over their societies, like the tribal chief and witch doctor over theirs, use
every artifice, including the multitudinous fears of supernatural
and spiritual powers and favors, rewards, and punishments from
the gods, to obtain the conformance and thus an orderly society
of submission, rules, subservience, and even economic slavery?
War between individuals and groups, between peoples, nations,
ideologies, and religions, and the constant boiling cauldron of
differences and indiffences, the cultural artifice by which people
resolve the endless differences and themselves, will always be
the obstacle to any metaphysical hypothesis of any universal moral
principle, or of any kind of cosmic mind or world-humanity-
mind-consciousness, regardless how subtle, mystic, or contemplative of mind be the good intent of those who harbor such visions.

Take a country like India, for example. Here we have had,
for thousands of years, the social structure of various levels or
castes of people, from the "lowest" and "abominable" pariahs to
the "highest" and "noble" Brahman castes. Does each level have
its own collective consciousness, and does the entire society of
the country of India have a tabulated "whole" of such consciousness departmentalized according to caste? Here we are confronted
with an historical and live society and groups within this society,
each caste or group a specific and segregated level with a minimal
of intermarriages. What disposition should we make of these
under the assumption of a collective consciousness? On the contrary, while the rule of social and religious authority, custom,
tradition, and indoctrinated enculteration, maintained these inequitable levels when viewed from any high moral or ethical
principle, it was the rise of the democratic spirit in present-day
India, as in Japan, that has broken the traditional hold of any
such societal or collective consciousness and restored to some de-

gree the sense of awareness of self, the sense of individualism and being that is slowly breaking down the historical caste systems, as the same democratic spirit operating in many other lands. What was a logical and natural evolutionary sequence in aboriginal times cannot be applied in any logical manner to the evolutionary ladder of culture and modern times. The twentieth century has been determined differently than was a century of ten, fifteen, or twenty thousand years ago.

On the other hand, Russia and China show a process in reverse: The individual sense of freedom and its own consciousness are slowly deteriorating and being collectivized to secure the full conformance of the people to abide by those in power, resulting in the stifling of the individual's freedom of expression and ethico-moral action. Or should we remind ourselves of the Dark Ages, when the Roman Church represented the "consciousness" of its peoples all over Europe, and should we again relate the consequence of this consciousness during the Inquisition, the "witchcraft" epidemics, the Crusades, the exterminations in Europe, in Mexico, Peru, the Carribean, and South America? Or relate the dark pall of barbarism of this consciousness over those millions who subordinated their lives to its philosophy and the millions who have suffered and been murdered because of it? Malinowski: "It cannot be too often repeated that any culture which kills individual initiative, and relegates the interests of most of its members to complete insignificance at the expense of a gang-managed totalitarian state, will not be able to develop or even to preserve its cultural patrimony."[432] Malinowski referred to the Hitlers and Mussolinis, and the Dark Ages had theirs, from the mendicant friar to the Lord and Master on the throne.

Fascism and Communism, too, are processes by which the individual consciousnesses are subjugated to the "collective consciousness" as outlined by those in power and authority. Here it is true that the individuals obtain their thinking, consciousness, and spirit from the state which can gradually become a socio-religious entity and the fountain from which the constituents drink their thoughts into being and practice. We know the results.

It seems to me that the major error of Durkheim is that he tried to become the metaphysical mouthpiece for the totality of nature, as if he could represent it by his incursions into the elements of primitive psychology, symbolic and analogic ritual, and then to proceed to fuse the individual mind, elemental as it was, into a purposeful, designful, and ontological Universal Consciousness, Kantian and Hegelian in approach and with their usual a priori fallacies and anthropomorphic syntheses.

The second error is the cosmocentricity of Durkheim himself, who apparently viewed the universe from his own focus and insight, and, as a result, was not satisfied with a particular and personalized view, which may be wrong or right as a matter of procedure, but attempted to build out of this, as Kant had tried and failed, a critique of man's limitations and efforts to penetrate the unpenetrable and to know the unknowable, and then follows, as Kant had done and failed, with the second critique, in which the unpenetrable and the unknowable are accepted as penetrated and known, and then united as the Universal Consciousness, in which the individual consciousness is fused and from which it draws its purpose and motive, and without which the peacefulness, self-satisfaction, and willingness to accept death would not be lived and realized.

Durkheim proceeds to inject into the totality of nature a moralizing structure to such an extent that he confidently overwhelms himself with self-assurance that the very impetus, rise and diffusion of science and its products are the interchangeable spiritualities of deep-rooted religious forms; that science is but a new manifestation of a spiritual rudiment, of primitive religious forms, and that our knowledge of the sciences is but the present sum total of all the continuums of experience that have issued from the womb of religion itself.

Durkheim is not the first of many scholars and apologists who have attempted to rationalize an idealistically categorical form of imperative or moral godhead out of the cosmos. He goes further by affixing to the social instinct of man what he considers the inescapable and ossifused twin of social life, the religions, by which man has worshipped the supernatural in order to placate and make livable the natural and the mundane. The narcotic addict or opium smoker does the same in another way; the *samana* in India does the same; the orthodox, in their frantic, appealing prayers and exhortations to their gods for peace, blessings, for heaven and escape from hell, is still another way; the scholar accepting the historical heritage of his kind and clan as the most "sensible" and "rational" method to peace of mind, enjoyment of the group society and the reward of "belonging" is another way. All these ways come from the same root—the reflecting and anticipating mind of man that reminds the body of death, which both mind and body refuse, under any circumstances, to accept.

Durkheim, with the most benevolent intent, took Plato"s *Idea,* identified the projection of the individual self-identity with the idea of Universal Oneness through Cartesian inference, entered into the Valhallan temples of Kant and Hegel, imbibed the utilitarianism of Mill, James' "will" and pragmatic contentions of justifiability and the dilution of conflict: put them all together and thus found himself a pseudo-Spinozistic God-Mind of which our minds are all little parts constantly fusing and diffusing from the parent well.

Durkheim, we must concede, was an erudite scholar and his narration of primitive possible thinking and an exposition of primitive rituals are fascinating and informative. But Durkheim, I fear, never felt the "benevolence" of human cruelty or the fakery of the prayerful deceptor, or the sting of the forsaken human in the jungle harassed by insect, reptile, parasitic disease, and steam; or the torment of the depressed and frustrated neurotic, sick in mind and body, trying to fulfill idiotic and baseless rules and catechisms; or was waylaid by a robber with a saintly medal hanging from his neck or threatened by an assassin who had just said his prayers to Allah. Did the Moslems hail the moral consciousness of the Universe when the Crusaders rode in and cut them to pieces while they were praying in their temples, or did the Armenians hail this Cosmic Mind when the Turks killed their children, or did the Jews en route to the crematorium in Hitler's gas chambers feel that all's well with the Great Mind and that all progress and civilization stem from deep religious rootings, and that they should be grateful for this progress in their hour of sacrifice; or did the Mayas and Aztecs, the Caribs, Arawaks, and the Incas and hundreds of other peoples through-

out the world hail the coming of the White Warrior with his
Believe Or Die!, and lay down their lives by millions to gratify
his lust for treasure, slave labor, and to carry the cross, the symbol of this religiosity, for the sake of the Universal or Collective
Consciousness; or did the Negroes, pinioned in irons in the stink-
ing holds of bishop-blessed vessels from the godly countries, say
to themselves that they should be happy to contribute to the
great purposes of the Moral Principle by which the world breathes
and moves? Barrows Dunham feels that if the world and its people
could have managed to survive the Inquisition and the Holy
Work of the Holy Office of the Dominicans and Franciscans, then
humanity can survive anything that may be thrown its way.

Alas, life and human nature move by the calling needs of immediacy according to the minds, good and bad, whatever they
may be, of people who are animals, like the other animals, but
who are usually more ferocious, more selfish, more cruel, even
though the art of communication has been cultivated to such
a fine extent that cruelty could be made to appear as benevolent,
inequity to appear as justice, and mass consciousness of the mass
mind of the regimented, indoctrinated, and caterpillared mob
could be made to appear as reflecting the dancing rays of harmony and goodness radiating from the Moral Principle or Godhead of the Universe—and success for those who profit by it!

Alas, there is goodness in man, and there is morality in man,
and there is peace in man, and there is justice in man, but these
belong to a number of us, to the victimized and to the vigilant.
To attribute a great moral consciousness to *all* human creatures
is to attribute something which simply does not exist. "Divinity
is, upon the whole, the most ingenius device that political theory
has ever discovered. It protects the ruler in life and in power, but
more particularly it protects the *office* against the human frailties
of the incumbent."[433] Sidney Hook: "No faith has truth value
or even a high survival value unless it is based on a prior faith
in intelligence. Faith in intelligence excludes fanaticism, for it
is expressed in a willingness to examine all relevant alternatives
to our beliefs and practices. That is why it can lead to conclusions which are firm without being dogmatic, and to actions which

are resolute and yet flexible enough to deal with the inescapably contingent."[434]

It is needless to reiterate that the moralist has the freedom and the equitable right to moralize for himself, and the cosmologist has the freedom and the right to build his cosmogony for himself, or even the cosmopathic theist and pantheist to create "humanized" universals or Gioberti's ontologism that the existence of God becomes knowledgeable by intuition. The theologian has the freedom and the right to spend his life anticipating the reception *he* will get before the throne of *his* God; the pantheist has the freedom and the right to build and explain the totality of nature in *his* own terms of cosmic consciousness, mechanism, design, vitalism, purposefulness, universal harmony, or the entirety of nature as one coordinative, intelligent, or conscious wholeness of which we are segments, attributes, which yieldingly permeate all its parts and, through its consciousness, give it motive, meaning, and value, thriving tied and feeding from its teats inexorably and forever umbilicalized in a spirituality of eventual victory for the good and righteous. They *all* have the freedom and the right to live, to think or do these things for *themselves,* as others have the freedom and the right to do contrariwise. The problem arises when any of these insist that everyone "ought," "should," or "must" (depending on the nature of the principle and how much power there is behind it for enforcement) think or believe or live as they do. So long as there are many of us who may not agree with any of their principles, so much longer will it take for anyone to establish on any real universal basis any of these cosmologies.

George Santayana wrote: "I had no need to adopt the cosmology of Plato—a mythical and metaphysical creation, more or less playful and desperate, designed to buttress his moral philosophy. I was old enough, when I came under his influence, to discount this sort of priestcraft in thought, so familiar in Christian apologists. . . . Moral philosophy is not a science."[435] He goes on to say thusly in his preface to the second edition of *The Life of Reason:* "Why should the verbal ambiguity be more annoying if in reviewing the life of reason I confidently turn to the friendly reader, whom I suppose to be watching the same drama, and say: 'See mind and nature coming on the scene. What a travesty the green-room of fancy has made of them! Here is nature tricked out in will and purpose like a moral being, and mind tumbling about in motley and gibbering!' "[436]

A presumed aggregate or group consciousness, if taken as a premise, can only be considered no more or less than the culture from which it may be observed as coming from individuals out of the group and generalizations deducted therefrom. Philosophers have created deities, have made deities out of humans, and have even created Platonic ideals out of masses of humanity, according to the wishes and dreams of peoples. Whatever the imagination potential of the human race, it has been tremendous; it has paved the various highways of civilization, but it has also covered those highways with victims, and strewn the byways of advancement with tragedies unknown in the rest of the world. Any consciousness, collective or otherwise, is no ultimate or absolute ideal to go by as *any consciousness is transient, typical and fallible.* To apply any general description or principle to any consciousness is merely to describe or presume what we think it maybe, and which can change in a day or in any given period. Any consciousness is the product of past and present; it has not yet been subjected to the constantly oncoming future experiences and its influences upon this consciousness. We think in terms of experience, and the future is never an experienced event. Our present minds are determined by events leading up to us from *behind.* As each coming day becomes a present day and then part of the past, so do our minds and our consciousness subject themselves to these events and the possible changes and convictions these events may possibly bring about. Consciousness, as everything else that is human, is subject to change in its wants, hopes, patterns, and behaviors, as the course of events determine. It is both the constant cause and effect of a status which is forever in some flux.

Durkheim most carefully systematized his data for his deductive purpose of arrangements covering his socioreligious thesis for the human community and its world. His further error is not in the narration of his objective material, of the primitive ways and strange cults, which is a most interesting story. The error, it appears to me, lies in the logical arrangements of interpretation from which issues unreasonable and illogical a priori deductions, which, in reality, become a personal wish. After going through some history of the aborigines and the early tribal beginnings and their socioreligious thinking and ritual, he now closes his eyes and appears to infer: In spite of history, in spite of what others might determine these to mean, that is what I want and wish it to be, this is what it *must* be if it is to satisfy *my* life at all, and, of course, any such satisfaction to all others, this cosmic collective consciousness of spirit must be *It,* individualized as we may appear to be, but actually fastened to the eternal mind of the universe; we are nothing without it, and if man has freedom, it is the freedom to gain the ultimate realization of this child-to-mother mind-nature. We need this to compensate for our natural limitations; we **need it to justify** our worldly miseries and disillusions; we need it to overcome death, finding immortality in the collective or total consciousness of all things. This is his right of inference, but it appears to be his error. Durkheim prophetically hoped for his ideal when he wrote: "A day will come when our societies will know again those hours of creative effervescence, in the course of which new ideas arise and new formulae are found which serve for a while as a guide to humanity."[437] Santayana assists us to clarify: "Error, under the influence of the existing object which it attempts to describe, suffers correction: and those first mythical notions of nature and of mind may be gradually clarified, until nature is seen to be a mechanism, and mind to be pure intelligence."[438]

Another situation that gives us serious reservations regarding the plausibility and acceptance of any moral basis, conscious or otherwise, for any worldly or cosmic plan, is the analysis of nature itself by any application of common sense. How can we, according to Durkheim's hypothesis, explain the continual and immutably-fastened links of the food-chains, of plant, insect, fish, bird, reptile, animal and animal mammals, including us, which have made the living nature and its stages, whatever and wherever they are, a constant and necessary butchery, a killing of each other, of constant vigilance and attack, shock, pain, suffering and death—the helplessly operating *modus vivendi* of nature—how can we explain all this as an identity of any moral sense, base, or purpose? True, there is nothing that is alone in nature or which exists completely by itself, and whether we can exactly call it social, religious, moral or divine is a matter of opinion and wish, but nothing can escape the tie of relationships and connectedness which simply confesses the nature of existence. However, to give this what appears to be a blind and indifferent process of causality, whether conscious, reflective, or brainless, a cosmocentric and anthropomorphic entity, just because our intelligence and desires want it so, has been the perennial and chronic malignancy of human rationalism ever since the first priest or the first king gathered his flock and managed somehow to get them to agree to serve him as slaves, to believe him, and in him, as a god or prophet, and gradually to patternize the people in this manner to such an extent that after thousands of years they have become so used to it that they cannot part with this pattern, this religious pattern of conformance, and, to justify an explanation of its wantability, they have designed this to be called The Soul of Nature, or the Soul of Mankind, or the Will of God manifested through His peoples.

This great Soul or Cosmic (humanized) Will, through its cultural acquisitions, may yet destroy the food-chains, the symbiotic balances in nature, the environments, poisoning the air, the waters and the soils, and finally, through its "collectively conscious" mass hysteria of uncontrollable fears and powers, destroy man. In such a cataclysm what will occur to the chemical residue and organic debris no man will be witness to. And there will be no consciousness, not even in the dead trees, the yellowed waters and the barren hills. Nowhere will there be a sound or anything to hear a sound, a whimper, or the feeblest cry. And all because nature, way back in the Pleistocene, somehow or other mutated or evolved the first stir of self-awareness, the ultimate and final destroyer of itself.

Santayana, commenting on his impressions in reading Hegel's *Phaenomenologie des Geistes,* writes: "It had seemed to me that myth and sophistry there spoilt a very fine subject. The subject was the history of human ideas: the sophistry was imposed on Hegel by his ambition to show that the episodes he happened to review formed a dialectical chain: and the myth sprang from the constant suggestion that this history of human ideas made up the whole of cosmic evolution, and that these episodes were the scattered syllables of a single eternal oracle. It occurred to me that a more honest criticism of progress might be based on tracing the distracted efforts of man to satisfy his natural impulses in his natural environment. Yet if these impulses were infinitely wayward and variable, and if the environment itself was inconstant or undiscoverable, what criterion of progress could it be possible to set up? As for me, I was utterly without the learning and the romantic imagination that might have enabled some emancipated rival of Hegel, some systematic Nietzsche or some dialectical Walt Whitman, to write a history of the Will to Be Everything and Anything. An omnivorous spirit was no spirit for me, and I could not write the life of reason without distinguishing it from madness."[439]

It seems that man will go on and on forever bent to mold the universe to his own desires and forms and hopes. So long as these contain the beautifying creativeness and expressions of poetry to color and exhilarate his stay, brief as it may be, good. It is when these hopes, dreams, and appealing lamentations cry out to exchange the mortal, the finite, and knowable for the immortal, the infinite, and the unknowable that the wastage and misdirection of life takes place, and this is truly lamentable. Santayana sums it up: "The oracles of spirit all have to be discounted; they are uttered in a cave."[440]

REFERENCES—BOOK THREE

1. William McDougall, *Social Psychology,* ch. II, p. 29; see also Introduction to Ethics, Lillie, pp. 24-5.
2. Robert Ardrey, *African Genesis,* p. 37; see also *Emigration, Migration and Nomadism,* Heape.
3. S. H. Skaife, *Dwellers in Darkness,* p. 1.
4. L. White, *The Science of Culture.*
5. Joseph Campbell, *Masks of God: Primitive Mythology,* p. 42.
6. John Dewey, *A Common Faith,* p. 43.
7. H. R. Hays, *In the Beginnings,* p. 288.
8. Gerhard Szczesny, *The Future of Unbelief,* p. 124.
9. Theodosius Dobzhansky, *Mankind Evolving,* p. 22.

10. Gerhard Szczesny, *The Future of Unbelief*, p. 148.
11. Jacqueta Hawkes and Sir Leonard Woolley, *Prehistory and the Beginnings of Civilization*, vol. I, "The History of Mankind," p. 5.
12. James G. Frazer, *Taboo and the Perils of the Soul*, from "The Golden Bough," Part II, pp. 421-2.
13. Gerhard Szczesny, *The Future of Unbelief*, p. 163.
14. Read Bain, *The Fields and Methods of Biological Sociology*, from "Fields and Methods of Sociology," ed. L. L. Bernard, p. 36.
15. Edward B. Tylor, *Religion in Primitive Culture*, p. 446.
16. Arthur Koestler, *The Sleepwalkers*, p. 56.
17. Steve Allen, *The Ground is Our Table*, p. 17.
18. Bernhard and Michael Grzimek, *Serengati Shall Not Die*, p. 246.
19. Erich Kahler, *Man the Measure*, p. 34.
20. George C. Valliant, *Aztecs of Mexico*, p. 181.
21. James G. Frazer, *The Scope of Social Anthropology*, pp. 163-4.
22. Germain Bazin, *A History of Art*, pp. 1-3.
23. H. R. Hays, *In the Beginnings*, p. 82.
24. John Gray, *The Canaanites*, p. 138.
25. Louis A. Reitmeister, *The Gods and My Friends*, p. 30.
26. Regarding the use of stones as gods, Peter Buck states: "Throughout Polynesia, inanimate objects were selected or made to represent the gods. These objects were kept in the religious structures or in the personal charge of the priests. They were always on hand whereas the animate representatives were not always available. Simple natural objects such as stones and shells were utilized."—*Material Representatives of Tongan and Samoan Gods*, from "The Many Faces of Primitive Art, ed. D. Frazer, p. 102.
27. Kaj Birket-Smith, *The Paths of Culture*, p. 338.
28. Ruth Underhill, *Religion Among American Indians*, from "the North American Indians," ed. R. C. Owen, etc., pp. 99-100.
29. Bronislaw Malinowski, *Myth in Primitive Psychology*, p. 81.
30. Kaj Birket-Smith, *The Paths of Culture*, p. 338.
31. Gerhard Szczesny, *The Future of Unbelief*, p. 26.
32. James G. Frazer, *The Belief in Immortality*, from "The Golden Bough," vol. I, p. 23.
33. John Dewey, *Experience and Nature*, p. 3a.
34. Sylvanius G. Morley, *Ancient Maya*, p. 216.
35. George C. Valliant, *Aztecs of Mexico*, p. 170.
36. Joseph K. Hart, *Inside Experience*, pp. 97-8.
37. Herbert J. Muller, *Freedom in the Ancient World*, p. 96.
38. *Ibid.*, p. 312.
39. Gerhard Szczesny, *The Future of Unbelief*, p. 28.
40. Erich Kahler, *Man the Measure*, p. 47.
41. Mark Twain, *Reflections on Religion*, ed. C. Neider, Hudson Review, vol. XVI, no. 3, Autumn, 1963, p. 335.
42. Edward B. Tylor, *Religion in Primitive Culture*, p. 154.
43. Clyde Kluckhohn and Dorothea Leighton, *Navaho*, p. 202.
44. Jacquetta Hawkes and Sir Leonard Woolley, *Prehistory and the Beginnings of Civilization*, vol. I, "The History of Mankind," p. 363.
45. *Ibid.*, p. 207.
46. S. G. F. Brandon, *Time and the Destiny of Man*, from "Voices of Time," ed. J. T. Fraser, pp. 145-56.
47. Elie Metchnikoff, *The Nature of Man*, p. 165.
48. Bernhard and Michael Grzimek, *Serengati Shall Not Die*, p. 263.
49. Lewis Mumford, *The Myth of the Machine*, p. 203.
50. Peter Matthiessen, *The Cloud Forest*, p. 140.
51. Gerhard Szczesny, *The Future of Unbelief*, p. 79.

52. James G. Fraser, *Totemism and Exogamy*, from "The Golden Bough," vol. IV, pp. 3-5.
53. James G. Fraser, *Spirits of the Corn and of the Wild*, from "The Golden Bough," Part V, vol. II, p. 204.
54. Edward B. Tylor, *Religion in Primitive Culture*, p. 53.
55. Wallis Budge, *Egyptian Magic*, p. 232.
56. *Ibid.*, pp. 232-3.
57. Edward B. Tylor, *Religion in Primitive Culture*, pp. 43-4.
58. E. O. James, *Ancient Gods*, p. 58.
59. *Ibid.*, p. 57.
60. Ann C. Crawford, *Customs and Culture of Vietnam*, p. 110.
61. Thomas A. Dooley, *The Edge of Tomorrow*, p. 61.
62. Andreas Lommel, *Prehistoric and Primitive Man*, pp. 10-1.
63. Richard S. MacNeish, *Ancient Mesoamerican Civilization*, Science Magazine, vol. 143, no. 3606, Feb. 7, 1964, p. 531.
64. Thomas A. Dooley, *The Edge of Tomorrow*, p. 97.
65. Kaj Birket-Smith, *The Paths of Culture*, p. 297.
66. Douglas L. Oliver, *The Pacific Islands*, p. 45.
67. George C. Valliant, *Aztecs of Mexico*, pp. 177-8.
68. H. R. Hays, *From Ape to Angel*, p. 124.
69. Michael Grant, *Myths of the Greeks and Romans*, p. 61.
70. Peter Freuchen, *The Book of the Eskimos*, p. 194.
71. Pedro Ramirez Vazquez, *Mexico*, p. 95.
72. R. C. Padden, *The Hummingbird and the Hawk*, preface vii.
73. Bengt Danielsson, *Love in the South Seas*, p. 52.
74. Lewis Mumford, *The Myth of the Machine*, p. 176.
75. H. R. Hays, *In the Beginnings*, pp. 534-5.
76. Lewis Mumford, *The Myth of the Machine*, p. 171.
77. Joseph Campbell, *Masks of God: Oriental Mythology*, p. 168.
78. Lewis Mumford, *The Myth of the Machine*, p. 152.
79. Ubbelohde-Doering, *On the Royal Highways of the Inca*, p. 11.
80. Peter Farb, *Man's Rise to Civilization*, pp. 128-9.
81. Bronislaw Malinowski, *Sex, Culture and Myth*, p. 262.
82. *Ibid.*, p. 261.
83. *Ibid.*, p. 260.
84. Jean Guiart, *Arts of the South Pacific*, p. 49.
85. Victor W. von Hagen, *The Ancient Sun Kingdoms of the Americas*, pp. 116-7.
86. Henry E. Sigerist, *A History of Medicine*, p. 27.
87. *Ibid.*, pp. 21-2.
88. Felix Marti-Ibañez, *Magic and Drama of Byzantium*, MD Medical Magazine, vol. II, no. 2, pp. 11-2.
89. see chapter on *Religion*, Marett, from "Notes and Queries on Anthropology," 4th ed., London, 1912.
90. Bronislaw Malinowski, *Sex, Culture and Myth*, p. 256.
91. *Ibid.*, p. 190.
92. *Ibid.*, p. 221.
93. *Ibid.*, p. 200.
94. Herbert J. Muller, *Freedom in the Ancient World*, p. 71.
95. Victor W. von Hagen, *The Ancient Sun Kingdoms of the Americas*, p. 364.
96. C. A. Burland, *Peru Under the Incas*, p. 65.
97. William O. Douglas, Look Magazine, Dec. 31, 1962.
98. H. R. Hays, *In the Beginnings*, p. 528.
99. Jacquetta Hawkes and Sir Leonard Woolley, *Prehistory and the Beginnings of Civilization*, vol. I, "The History of Mankind," p. 700.
100. Andreas Feininger, *Forms of Nature and Life*, p. 19.
101. see *A World on the Wane*, Lévi-Strauss, p. 127.

102. see *The Deputy,* Hochhuth, p. 310; also *The Labyrinth: Memoirs of Walter Schellenberg.*
103. see Bronislaw Malinowski, *Sex, Culture and Myth,* p. 263.
104. *Ibid.,* p. 263.
105. *Ibid.,* p. 262.
106. *Ibid.,* p. 336.
107. Gerhard Szczesny, *The Future of Unbelief,* p. 175.
108. *Ibid.,* p. 160.
109. *Ibid.,* p. 74.
110. *Ibid.,* p. 185.
111. *Ibid.,* p. 68.
112. Victor W. von Hagen, *The Ancient Sun Kingdoms of the Americas,* p. 108.
113. Douglas L. Oliver, *The Pacific Islands,* p. 113.
114. Mark Twain, *Reflections on Religion,* ed. C. Neider, Hudson Review, vol. XVI, no. 3, Autumn, 1963, p. 338.
115. Henry Darley, *Slaves and Ivory in Abyssinia,* p. 65.
116. *Ibid.,* p. 96.
117. *Ibid.,* pp. 130-1.
118. Bernhard and Michael Grzimek, *Serengati Shall Not Die,* p. 94.
119. *Ibid., p.* 94.
120. Herbert J. Muller, *Freedom in the Ancient World,* p. 73.
121. Robert Lopez, *The Birth of Europe,* p. 144.
122. Roger Bastide, *Color, Racism, and Christianity,* Daedalus Magazine, Spring, 1967, p. 314.
123. Douglas L. Oliver, *The Pacific Islands,* p. 127.
124. *Ibid.,* p. 128.
125. Barrows Dunham, *Heroes and Heretics,* p. 134.
126. Joseph Campbell, *Masks of God: Creative Mytholgoy,* p. 165.
127. Theodor Reik, *Pagan Rites in Judaism,* p. 5.
128. Kaj Birket-Smith, *The Paths of Culture,* p. 379.
129. *Ibid.,* p. 378.
130. Samuel Noah Kramer, *Sumerian Mythology,* p. 26.
131. Joseph Campbell, *Masks of God: Oriental Mythology,* p. 399.
132. Douglas L. Oliver, *The Pacific Islands.*
133. Edward B. Tylor, *Religion in Primitive Culture,* pp. 323-4.
134. Miguel Covarrubias, *Island of Bali,* p. 7.
135. Joseph Campbell, *Masks of God:Primitive Mythology,* p. 173; see also *Die mythische Weltbetrachtung der alten Pflanzer-Volker,* Adolf E. Jensen, Branos-Jahrbuch, Zurich, Rhein-Verlag, 1950, pp. 34-38.
136. Kaj Birket-Smith, *The Paths of Culture,* p. 388.
137. Claude Lévi-Strauss, *A World on the Wane,* p. 164.
138. see "Pyramid Utterance 527," cited in *Myth and Symbol in Ancient Egypt,* Rundle Clark, p. 42.
139. Joseph Campbell, *Masks of God: Primitive Mythology,* p. 10.
140. George F. Thomas, *New Forms for Old Faith,* from "Changing Patterns in American Civilization," p. 136.
141. *Ibid.,* p. 133.
142. Roger Bastide, *Color, Racism, and Christianity,* Daedalus Magazine, Spring, 1967, p. 323.
143. Herbert J. Muller, *Freedom in the Ancient World,* p. 19.
144. H. R. Hays, *In the Beginnings,* p. 52.
145. Jacquetta Hawkes and Sir Leonard Woolley, *Prehistory and the Beginnings of Civilization,* vol. I, "The History of Mankind," p. 350.
146. *Ibid.,* pp. 213-4.
147. William Taylour, *The Mycenaeans,* p. 63.
148. W. Oldfield Howey, *The Cat in Religion and Magic,* p. 66.

149. H. R. Hays, *In the Beginnings*, p. 106.
150. *Ibid.*, pp. 122-3.
151. Robert Graves and Raphael Patai, *Hebrew Myths*, p. 12.
152. Joseph Campbell, *Masks of God: Occidental Mythology*, p. 43.
153. Frank Waters, *The Book of the Hopi*, p. 12.
154. *Ibid.*, pp. 126-7.
155. Martin A. Larson, *The Religion of the Occident*, p. 87.
156. see *The Book of the Hopi*, Waters, p. 240.
157. R. C. Padden, *The Hummingbird and the Hawk*, p. 51.
158. Robert Graves and Raphael Patai, *Hebrew Myths*, p. 87.
159. H. R. Hays, *From Ape to Angel*, p. 96.
160. H. R. Hays, *In the Beginnings*, p. 48.
161. Douglas L. Oliver, *The Pacific Islands*, p. 31.
162. see *From Ape to Angel*, Hays, pp. 172-3.
163. Ottaker Nemecek, *Virginity*, p. 43.
164. *Ibid.*, p. 38.
165. *Ibid.*, p. 33.
166. Brigid Brophy, *Black Ship to Hell*, p. 435.
167. Bertrand Russell, *Why I am not a Christian*, p. 68.
168. *Ibid.*, p. 29.
169. Walter Kaufmann, *Critique of Religion and Philosophy*, p. 180.
170. John Dewey, *A Common Faith*, p. 27.
171. Felice Belloti, *Fabulous Congo*, p. 49.
172. Herbert J. Muller, *Freedom in the Ancient World*, p. 27.
173. Sabatino Moscati, *Ancient Semitic Civilizations*, p. 57.
174. R. T. Rundle Clark, *Myth and Symbol in Ancient Egypt*, p. 30.
175. James G. Frazer, *The Golden Bough*, 1 vol. ed., p. 101.
176. *Ibid.*, p. 194.
177. Time Magazine, July 15, 1966.
178. Felix Marti-Ibañez, *Magic and Drama of Byzantium*, MD Medical Magazine, vol. II, no. 2, p. 11.
179. Felix Marti-Ibañez, *Byzantine Art*, *op. cit.*, pp. 11-2.
180. Manfred Kyber, *Among Animals*, p. 115.
181. Janheinz Jahn, *Muntu*, p. 132.
182. R. T. Rundle Clark, *Myth and Symbol in Ancient Egypt*, p. 79.
183. Jacquetta Hawkes and Sir Leonard Woolley, *Prehistory and the Beginnings of Civilization*, vol. I, "The History of Mankind," p. 632.
184. Albert Schweitzer, *African Notebook*, p. 37.
185. H. R. Hays, *In the Beginnings*, pp. 164-5.
186. see *By Parachute Into Peru's Lost World*, G. Brooks Baekeland, National Geographic Magazine, vol. 126, no. 2, August, 1964.
187. Ann C. Crawford, *Customs and Culture of Vietnam*, p. 108.
188. Peter Freuchen, *The Book of the Eskimos*, p. 208.
189. J. Mooney, *The Sacred Formulas of the Cherokees*, from "Primitive Heritage," p. 37.
190. Joseph Campbell, *Masks of God: Primitive Mythology*, p. 85.
191. Theodor H. Gaster, *Customs and Folkways of Jewish Life*, p. 34.
192. Robert Graves and Raphael Patai, *Hebrew Myths*, p. 86.
193. A. D. White, *The History of the Warfare of Science with Theology*, vol. II, p. 29.
194. James G. Frazer, *The Belief in Immortality*, from "The Golden Bough," vol. I, p. 23.
195. William Graham Sumner, *Folkways*, p. 285.
196. James B. Griffin, *The Study of Early Cultures*, from "Man, Culture and Society," ed. Harry L. Shapiro, p. 25.

197. Robert Redfield, *How Human Society Operates*, from "Man, Culture and Society," ed. Harry L. Shapiro, p. 348.
198. Wallis Budge, *Egyptian Magic*, preface ix.
199. Frank Dufresne, *No Room for Bears*, p. 57.
200. J. Eric S. Thompson, *Maya Archaeologist*, p. 20.
201. R. C. Padden, *The Hummingbird and the Hawk*, p. 96.
202. *Ibid.*, p. 96.
203. James G. Frazer, *The Golden Bough*, 1 vol. ed., p. 32.
204. *Ibid.*, p. 166.
205. Charles W. Eliot, *The Durable Satisfactions of Life*, p. 584.
206. Winwood Reade, *Martyrdom of Man*, p. 145.
207. Jacquetta Hawkes and Sir Leonard Woolley, *Prehistory and the Beginnings of Civilization*, vol. I, "The History of Mankind," p. 745.
208. Kaj Birket-Smith, *The Paths of Culture*, p. 356.
209. Wallis Budge, *Egyptian Magic*, preface ix.
210. James G. Frazer, *Totemism and Exogamy*, from "The Golden Bough," vol. I, pp. 81-2.
211. see *The Jewel in the Lotus*, Edwardes, quoting Richard Burton, preface xx.
212. Ernest Hooton, *Man's Poor Relations*, p. 391.
213. Paul Blanshard, *Freedom and Catholic Power in Spain and Portugal*, p. 32.
214. Arthur Koestler, *The Sleepwalkers*, p. 94.
215. Charles W. Eliot, *The Durable Satisfactions of Life*, p. 579.
216. Herbert J. Muller, *Freedom in the Ancient World*, p. 66.
217. Joseph Campbell, *Masks of God: Primitive Mythology*, p. 12.
218. Gerhard Szczesny, *The Future of Unbelief*, p. 73.
219. Anthony Storr, *Human Aggression*, p. 55.
220. *Ibid.*, p. 56.
221. Joseph Campbell, *Masks of God: Oriental Mythology*, p. 194.
222. Bertrand Russell, *Why I am not a Christian*, p. 20.
223. Joseph Campbell, *Masks of God: Primitive Mythology*, p. 117.
224. David Kenyon Webster, *Myth and Maneater, The Story of the Shark*, pp. 28-9.
225. *Ibid.*, p. 27.
226. Joseph Campbell, *Masks of God: Oriental Mythology*, pp. 5-6.
227. Edward B. Tylor, *Religion in Primitive Culture*, pp. 463-4.
228. David Kenyon Webster, *Myth and Maneater, The Story of the Shark*, p. 56.
229. Thomas Gann and J. Eric Thompson, *History of the Maya*, pp. 132-4.
230. R. C. Padden, *The Hummingbird and the Hawk*, pp. 73-4.
231. Victor W. von Hagen, *The Ancient Sun Kingdoms of the Americas*, p. 159.
232. Harald Schultz, *Hombu*, p. 30.
233. S. G. F. Brandon, *Time and the Destiny of Man*, from "Voices of Time," ed. J. T. Fraser, p. 144.
234. Kaj Birket-Smith, *The Paths of Culture*, p. 379.
235. Peter Davison, poem *Hunger*, Hudson Review, vol. XVI, no. 3, Autumn, 1963, p. 392.
236. George C. Valliant, *Aztecs of Mexico*, p. 63.
237. Joseph Campbell, *Masks of God: Oriental Mythology*, pp. 499-500.
238. Douglas L. Oliver, *The Pacific Islands*, p. 284.
239. Edward B. Tylor, *Religion in Primitive Culture*, p. 43.
240. Kaj Birket-Smith, *The Paths of Culture*, p. 122.
241. Edward B. Tylor, *Religion in Primitive Culture*, p. 484.
242. *Ibid.*, p. 47.
243. *Ibid.*, p. 465.
244. Albert Schweitzer, *African Notebook*, pp. 66-7.
245. *Ibid.*, p. 88.
246. Pierre Grimal, *The Civilization of Rome*, p. 29.

247. see *Masks of God: Oriental Mythology*, Campbell, p. 232.
248. *Ibid.*, p. 258.
249. Herbert J. Muller, *Freedom in the Ancient World*, p. 211.
250. Paul Blanshard, *Freedom and Catholic Power in Spain and Portugal*, p. 8.
251. Arthur Koestler, *The Sleepwalkers*, p. 51.
252. Emmett McLoughlin, *People's Padre*, p. 15.
253. *Ibid.*, p. 17.
254. Herbert J. Muller, *Freedom in the Ancient World*, p. 144.
255. Franc Shor, *Conquest of the Holy City*, National Geographic Magazine, December, 1963, p. 855.
256. W. Oldfield Howey, *The Cat in Religion and Magic*, p. 106.
257. *Ibid.*, pp. 84-5.
258. *Ibid.*, p. 182.
259. Herbert J. Muller, *Freedom in the Ancient World*, pp. 133-4.
260. Joseph Campbell, *Masks of God: Creative Mythology*, p. 29.
261. Bernard Hart, *The Psychology of Insanity*, p. 3.
262. Bertrand Russell, *Why I am not a Christian*, p. 17.
263. James G. Frazer, *The Dying God*, from "The Golden Bough," Part III, pp. 133-4.
264. Gerhard Szczesny, *The Future of Unbelief*, p. 221.
265. D. T. Atkinson, *Magic, Myth and Medicine*, pp. 87-8.
266. Robert Lopez, *The Birth of Europe*, p. 152.
267. Walter Kaufmann, *Critique of Religion and Philosophy*, p. 144.
268. A. Powell Davies, *The Mind and Faith of A. Powell Davies*, ed. W. O. Douglas.
269. Joseph Campbell, *Masks of God: Creative Mythology*, p. 28.
270. Maxmillian Rudwin, *The Devil in Legend and Literature*, p. 312.
271. Gerhard Szczesny, *The Future of Unbelief*, p. 74.
272. James Campbell, *Masks of God: Primitive Mythology*, p. 4.
273. Hu Shih, *Living Philosophies*, p. 261.
274. Jean Meslier, *Testament*.
275. Bertrand Russell, *Why I am not a Christian*, p. 33.
276. *Ibid.*, p. 14.
277. Philip Wylie, *An Essay on Morals*, p. 15.
278. Robert Lopez, *The Birth of Europe*, p. 150.
279. Edward B. Tylor, *Religion in Primitive Culture*, p. 162.
280. Lucién Lévy-Bruhl, *What the Natives Think of Pictures, Names and Dreams*, from "Primitive Heritage," p. 40.
281. Julian H. Steward, *The Great Basin Shoshonean Indians*, from "The North American Indians," ed. R. C. Owen, etc., p. 253.
282. Edward B. Tylor, *Religion in Primitive Culture*, p. 41.
283. James G. Frazer, *The Golden Bough*, 1 vol. ed., p. 222.
284. Lucién Lévy-Bruhl, *What the Natives Think of Pictures, Names and Dreams*, from "Primitive Heritage," pp. 39-40.
285. James G. Frazer, *Taboo and the Perils of the Soul*, from "The Golden Bough," Part II, p. 26-7.
286. Willard Z. Park, *Paviotso Shamanism*, from "The North American Indians," ed. R. C. Owen, et. al., p. 267.
287. James G. Frazer, *The Spirits of the Corn and of the Wild*, from "The Golden Bough," vol. II, Part V, pp. 260-1.
288. see *Myth and Symbol in Ancient Egypt*, Rundle Clark, p. 62.
289. Edward B. Tylor, *Religion in Primitive Culture*, pp. 54-7.
290. Theodor H. Gaster, *Customs and Folkways of Jewish Life*, p. 141.
291. Patrick Menget, *Death in Chamula*, Natural History Magazine, January, 1968, p. 54.
292. W. R. Alger, *The Future Life*, p. 81.

293. Claude Lévi-Strauss, *The Savage Mind*, p. 43.
294. H. R. Hays, *From Ape to Angel*, p. 90.
295. Lucién Lévy-Bruhl, *The Primitive's Sense of Death*, from "Primitive Heritage," p. 41.
296. R. E. Latcham, *Enthology of the Auracanos*, from "Primitive Heritage," p. 44.
297. B. Spencer and F. J. Gillen, *The Native Tribes of Central Australia*, from "Primitive Heritage," p. 43.
298. Richard M. Dorson, *Folk Legends of Japan*, p. 32.
299. Lucién Lévy-Bruhl, *What the Natives Think of Pictures, Names and Dreams*, from "Primitive Heritage," p. 33.
300. Wallis Budge, *Egyptian Magic*, pp. 65-6.
301. Felix Marti-Ibañez, *Early Christian Art*, MD Medical Magazine, vol. II, no. 2, pp. 180-1.
302. James G. Frazer, *The Golden Bough*, 1 vol. ed., p. 211.
303. *Ibid.*, p. 214.
304. *Ibid.*, p. 217.
305. *Ibid.*, p. 219.
306. Ashley Montagu, *Immortality*, p. 36.
307. Kaj Birket-Smith, *The Paths of Culture*, pp. 305-6.
308. William Graham Sumner, *Folkways*, p. 286.
309. Edward B. Tylor, *Religion in Primitive Culture*, p. 90.
310. Joseph Campbell, *Masks of God: Primitive Mythology*, p. 126; see also *Monumental Africana*, Leo Frobenius, Erlebte Erdteile, Bd. VI, pp. 435-66.
311. Martin A. Larson, *The Religion of the Occident*, p. 619.
312. see *American Freedom and Catholic Power*, Paul Blanshard, p. 113.
313. Homer W. Smith, *From Fish to Philosopher*, p. 199; see also *Man on His Nature*, Sherrington (1941).
314. Bertrand Russell, *Why I am not a Christian*, p. 35.
315. Samuel P. Dunlap, *The Ghebers of Hebron*, p. 999.
316. Oliver L. Reiser, *The Alchemy of Light and Color*, p. 26.
317. Joseph Ratner, *Introduction to the Intelligence in the Modern World*, p. 38.
318. Harry A. Overstreet, *The Enduring Quest*, p. 55.
319. Gerhard Szczesny, *The Future of Unbelief*, p. 77.
320. see *Myth and Symbol in Ancient Egypt*, Rundle Clark, p. 119.
321. E. Cecil Curwen and Gudmund Hatt, *Plough and Pasture*, p. 14.
322. James G. Frazer, *The Golden Bough*, 1 vol. ed., p. 349.
323. *Ibid.*, p. 680.
324. George C. Valliant, *Aztecs of Mexico*, pp. 204-5.
325. James G. Frazer, *The Scapegoat*, from "The Golden Bough," Part VI, preface v.
326. R. T. Rundle Clark, *Myth and Symbol in Ancient Egypt*, p. 180.
327. *Ibid.*, p. 114.
328. Wallis Budge, *Egyptian Magic*, p. 138.
329. *Ibid.*, p. 173.
330. J. H. Denison, *Emotion as the Basis of Civilization*.
331. Sabatino Moscati, *Ancient Semitic Civilizations*, p. 59.
332. Martin A. Larson, *The Religion of the Occident*, p. 291.
333. Gerhard Szczesny, *The Future of Unbelief*, p. 49.
334. Marcello Craveri, *The Life of Jesus*, p. 417.
335. George C. Valliant, *Aztecs of Mexico*, p. 180.
336. Joseph Campbell, *Masks of God: Occidental Mythology*, pp. 27-8.
337. Lévy-Bruhl, *The "Soul" of the Primitive*, p. 313.
338. Ling Roth, *The Natives of Sarawak*, Part I, p. 213.
339. Wallis Budge, *Egyptian Magic*, p. 184.

340. Marcello Craveri, *The Life of Jesus*, p. 429.
341. Wallis Budge, *Egyptian Magic*, p. 39.
342. Barrows Dunham, *Heroes and Heretics*, pp. 165-6.
343. Thomas Browne, *Hydriotaphia or Urne Buriall*, Ch. IV, London, 1685.
344. Edward B. Tylor, *Religion in Primitive Culture*, pp. 169-170.
345. see *Masks of God: Primitive Mythology*, Campbell, p. 124.
346. James G. Frazer, *The Worship of Nature*, from "The Golden Bough," vol. I, pp. 1-3.
347. Ernst Cassirer, *An Essay on Man*, p. 84.
348. Ralph Waldo Emerson, *Essay on Friendship*.
349. James G. Fraser, *The Belief in Immortality*, from "The Golden Bough," vol. I, pp. 23-9.
350. Emmett McLoughlin, *People's Padre*, p. 38.
351. James G. Frazer, *The Belief in Immortality*, from "The Golden Bough," vol. I.
352. Fred Hoyle, *Nature of the Universe*, p. 140.
353. Bertrand Russell, *Why I am not a Christian*, p. 90.
354. Brigid Brophy, *Black Ship to Hell*, p. 427.
355. Graham Wallas, *Social Judgment*, pp. 162-3.
356. Barrows Dunham, *Heroes and Heretics*, p. 167.
357. *Ibid.*, p. 165.
358. Bertrand Russell, *Why I am not a Christian*, p. 54.
359. Edward B. Tylor, *Religion in Primitive Culture*, p. 192.
360. Albert Schweitzer, *African Notebook*, pp. 88-9.
361. Charles W. Eliot, *Durable Satisfactions of Life*, p. 602.
362. A. D. White, *History of the Warfare of Science with Theology*, vol. I, p. 375.
363. Robert Lopez, *The Birth of Europe*, p. 378.
364. John Herman Randall, Jr., *Introduction to Philosophy*, p. 170.
365. Sigmund Freud, *The Future of an Illusion*, pp. 94-5, 98.
366. James Harvey Robinson, *The Mind in the Making*, p. 48.
367. Bertrand Russell, *Sceptical Essays*, p. 54.
368. *Ibid.*, pp. 149-150.
369. James A. Leuba, *The Belief in God and Immortality*.
370. Herbert J. Muller, *Freedom in the Ancient World*, p. 81.
371. *Ibid.*, p. 145.
372. Robert Lopez, *The Birth of Europe*, p. 152.
373. S. H. Skaife, *Dwellers in Darkness*, p. 5.
374. *Ibid.*, p. 161.
375. *Ibid.*, p. 161.
376. Bronislaw Malinowski, *Sex, Culture and Myth*, p. 243.
377. Wagner H. Bridger, New York Eve. Post, Nov. 18, 1963.
378. Joseph Campbell, *Masks of God: Creative Mythology*, p. 32.
379. Anthony Storr, *Human Aggression*, pp. 42-3.
380. Edmund W. Sinnott, *The Bridge of Life*, p. 130.
381. Gavin de Beer, *Darwin's "Origin" Today*, Natural History Magazine, Aug.-Sept., 1966, p. 71.
382. Thomas Jefferson, *The Writings of Jefferson*, Memorial ed., p. 223.
383. see *The Ancient Sun Kingdoms of the Americas*, von Hagen, p. 438.
384. Bertrand Russell, *Authority and the Individual*, p. 74.
385. *Ibid.*, p. 73.
386. Robert Ardrey, *The Territorial Imperative*, p. 200.
387. Carleton S. Coon, *The Origin of Races*, p. 39.
388. see *By Parachute into Peru's Lost World*, G. Brooks Baekeland, National Geographic Magazine, vol. 126, no. 2, August, 1964.
389. H. R. Hays, *In the Beginnings*, p. 531.

390. *Ibid.*, pp. 247-8.
391. W. Robertson Smith, *The Religion of the Semites*, p. 47.
392. *Ibid.*, p. 51.
393. William Lillie, *Introduction to Ethics*, p. 62.
394. E. E. Fournier, *Hephaestus, or the Soul of the Machine*, p. 1.
395. Louise Marie Spaeth, *Marriage and Family Life Among Strange Peoples*, p. 77.
396. Bronislaw Malinowski, *Sex, Culture and Myth*, p. 182.
397. J. Henri Fabre, *The Insect World*, p. 188.
398. Barrows Dunham, *Heroes and Heretics*, pp. 205-6.
399. Durward V. Sandifer and L. Ronald Scheman, *The Foundations of Freedom*, p. 40.
400. *Ibid.*, p. 29.
401. Bronislaw Malinowski, *Sex, Culture and Myth*, p. 170.
402. Hermann Rauschning, *The Revolution of Nihilism*, pp. 83-4.
403. Bertrand Russell, *In Praise of Idleness*, p. 135.
404. Robert Lopez, *The Birth of Europe*, p. 355.
405. Bronislaw Malinowski, *Sex, Culture and Myth*, p. 170.
406. Emile Durkheim, *The Elementary Forms of the Religious Life*, p. 472.
407. Bronislaw Malinowski, *Sex, Culture and Myth*, p. 242.
408. Emile Durkheim, *The Elementary Forms of the Religious Life*, p. 472.
409. Walter Kaufmann, *Critique of Religion and Philosophy*, p. 68.
410. Martin A. Larson, *The Religion of the Occident*, p. 192.
411. *Ibid.*, p. 120.
412. Robert Lopez, *The Birth of Europe*, pp. 149-150.
413. George C. Valliant, *Aztecs of Mexico*, p. 157.
414. Victor W. von Hagen, *The Ancient Sun Kingdoms of the Americas*, p. 482.
415. H. R. Hays, *From Ape to Angel*, p. 389.
416. Gerhard Szczesny, *The Future of Unbelief*, p. 61.
417. Morris R. Cohen, *American Thought: A Critical Sketch*, p. 229.
418. Barrows Dunham, *Heroes and Heretics*, p. 5.
419. Kaj Birket-Smith, *The Paths of Culture*, p. 30.
420. Durward V. Sandifer and L. Ronald Scheman, *The Foundations of Freedom*, p. 39.
421. Anthony Storr, *Human Aggression*, p. 57.
422. Barrows Dunham, *Heroes and Heretics*, p. 5.
423. Louis A. Reitmeister, *The Gods and My Friends*, p. 21.
424. Barrows Dunham, *Heroes and Heretics*, p. 9.
425. Charles Duff, *This Human Nature*, p. 8.
426. John Dewey, *Experience and Nature*, preface vii.
427. Erich Kahler, *Man the Measure*, p. 19.
428. Loren Eiseley, *The Firmament of Time*, p. 7.
429. Bertrand Russell, *Why I am not a Christian*, p. 192.
430. Friedrich Paulsen, *Introduction to Philosophy*, p. 3.
431. Barrows Dunham, *Heroes and Heretics*, p. 6.
432. Bronislaw Malinowski, *Sex, Culture and Myth*, p. 244.
433. Barrows Dunham, *Heroes and Heretics*, p. 7.
434. Sidney Hook, *Political Power and Personal Freedom*, p. 12.
435. George Santayana, *Reason in Common Sense*, vol. I, "Life of Reason," preface to 2nd ed., p. 11.
436. *Ibid.*, pp. 9-10.
437. Emile Durkheim, *The Elementary Forms of the Religious Life*, p. 475.
438. George Santayana, *Reason in Common Sense*, vol. I, "Life of Reason," preface to 2nd ed., p. 10.
439. *Ibid.*, p. 10.
440. *Ibid.*, p. 8.

I am surrounded by priests who repeat incessantly that their kingdom is not of this world and yet they lay hands on everything they can get.

—NAPOLEON

Those who expect to reap the blessings of freedom, must, like men, undergo the fatigue of supporting it.

—THOMAS PAINE, *The Crisis,* No. iv

A man should never put on his best trousers when he goes out to battle for freedom and truth.

—HENRIK IBSEN, *An Enemy of the People,* Act V

BOOK FOUR

THE RISE AND EVOLUTION OF AUTHORITY-POWER FORMS

THE RISE AND EVOLUTION OF
AUTHORITY-POWER FORMS

A GOVERNMENT, LARGE as the government of the United States, England, France, or Russia, or small as Cyprus or the tiny kinship tribe of some cranny of the Amazon tributary stream, is a contrivance by which hundreds of millions of people or merely a few families of individuals, allow themselves to be supervised, controlled, regulated so that these people can live in a *legal* manner as laid down by the rules, dicta, or principles of such a government. A government implies that certain individuals or groups of individuals possess the *authority* to *lead* the people, and they thus become *leaders*. The authority vested in these leaders or groups of leaders might have been obtained by rebellion, force, fraud, ethical and honest selection and elections, merit systems, seniorities, calamity, accident, or expediency, depending upon the nature and culture of the people, the locality, events within the country, historical circumstances within and without it. Actually, in a biological sense, a number of people surrender their personal sovereignty of freedom to one or more other persons who, having gathered these individual sovereignties, have "materialized," by the establishment of authority, a collective or central *power* to which the people, willingly or unwillingly, are induced or ordered to submit.

It seems evident that the protoprimitive groups were made up of their immediate families, and any leaderships there were came into being through natural factors of seniority, either patrilineal or matrilineal. Birket-Smith: "Nor do we ever find that the *individual* is sufficient unto himself; the real economic unit is at least the familly, and very often, even among quite primitive groups, it is an even larger group, the *camp*. Nor is the individual solitary in time; the experiences of innumerable generations are hidden away in everyone's consciousness and thereby also forge him in as a link in the great social chain."[1]

413

This is affirmed in the earliest cultures (5000 to 7500 B.C.) found in pre-Colombian Mexico and South America, as well as in many other parts of the world. It is so in the animal world, and there is no reason why it should not have been so among humans. This type of leadership continues in every family today, to a lesser or greater degree, its exercise and exhibition expressed themselves in many and varying forms. Thus, the biological parental desire to protect the young made itself felt in the earliest forms of social order. The very old are respected for their oldness, which indirectly is a respect for their longer experiences and possibly greater wisdom; this is seen today in many tribes all over the world, in the social and cultural systems of the Orient, as in China and Japan. In Bali I noted the authority of the older people over the local village life and order.

As the individual became more of an independent thinker, respect of the younger for the older weakened. This becomes more pronounced as the intelligence of the individual rises. In America the exaggeration of this trend can be seen in the younger people, who seem to feel that their parents are "obsolete," "living in the Stone Age," "nonscientific," "antibiological," "not with it." What they do not grasp and cannot until they grow up and have children of their own, is that this attempt of the parents to express leadership has nothing to do with culture or politics, but with the biological urge to protect and guide their "own," which is an instinctive and normal process of the more or less normal parent.

As the isolated group of one or more families grew in numbers and formed blood kinships, and these grew into familial clans, this parental instinct and guardian drive continued and resolved itself in control by the oldest and wisest, creating the earliest *chieftainship*. This control was probably expressed in the formation by a number of the oldest of a *council*, with the rest of the tribe or clan accepting the general *counseling* of this aboriginal cabinet, which acted to protect and further the welfare of the tribe, elaborate on its myths, organize its festivals, and establish some sort of ethical order by which the natural and normal wants and needs of the individual and tribe are collated and satisfied. From this sprouted the first *intuitiva* of a sense of power, following the line of the natural aggressiveness of the ego/personality. This degree of aggressiveness of the ego/personality varied more or less with different members of the councils; where this drive was more tenacious and ambitious in certain individuals, these individuals became more and more aware of a sense of power, of being looked up to, of *authority*. This inevitably led to the supremacy of the few over the many, and then the possible *one leader* and his immediate family, the earliest form of premonarchial emergences.

Such leadership of the few or of one over the many came about, no doubt, as the familial group patterns expanded and evolved into the early *village* or *tribal* conglomerates, containing a number of familial patterns or "clans" tied to each other by intermarriage and exogamous interfamilial integration. And so the leader and leaders became power expressions, which changed from the original *parental* instinctively natural drive of protective authority over the children to the first glimpses of *cultural* or *social* authority over a number of families, interwoven by blood relationships and intermarriages from within and without. Thus, each such group of leaders or a single leader became the fathers or the "father" of all.

When the awareness and anticipation of death emerged as an antinatural and magic-induced phenomenon, the reverence due the parents gradually transcended to the leaders or leader of the group and the "power and wisdom" of their protectiveness and security. This led to a natural desire for its continuance and affluences after the physical departure of these "fathers," and for their magical sympathies to aid the living in their constant struggle against unseen and spiritually evil forces. After all, in the primitive field and mind there was no such thing as a clear cleavage between life and death, but a continuation and merging of one into the other as a constant intermixture, recurrence, and interdependence of the living and the dead. The dead "father" continued to aid his living relatives and his posthumous authority continued to express itself in the appeal of the new councils or leaders to these dead fathers and leaders and held council with them, even allowing spaces between themselves where the spirits of the dead were supposed to sit and converse with them. "The dead man's ghost maintained an interest in the tribe [the Iroquois]. Special wintertime feasts were held for the ghosts, who were thought to participate unseen in the dancing and the games; they also accompanied raiding parties, even though they could only watch and not fight."[2] "The dead [the Incas] in their graves were more richly equipped than the living. Between the world of the dead and the world of the living there was a magical and spiritual coexistence."[3] "In some parts of the world, such as Africa and China, dead ancestors are treated like members of the family and scolded or praised according to whether they seem harmful or helpful."[4]

Thus, the worship of the dead and of ancestors fastened itself upon the clan or tribe as a cultural habit and spawned the early embryos of spiritual belief. We can readily visualize the evolution from an animalistic and natural parental drive to the cultural beginnings of the *establishment,* alive and dead, of the authority of the father or parental leader and protector of the extrafamilial tribe. In Bali, roaming about the island, I always found in the "backyard" of every little household the *templum,* a small raised stand overcapped with reed or stone, like a bird-feeding station, where the living members each day put a little rice, a flower or two, and a slice of fruit, as food and as a token of respect for the departed, ancestral spirit or spirits of the household. "The Wankia of East Africa set a coco-nut shell full of rice and tembo near the grave for the 'komo' or shade, which cannot exist without food and drink. . . . In the Congo district the custom has been described of making a channel into the tomb to the head or mouth of the corpse, whereby to send down month by month the offerings of food and drink. . . . Among Turanian races, the Chuwash put food and napkins on the grave, saying 'Rise at night and eat your fill, and there you have napkins to wipe your mouths.' "[5] Donald Harden: "Phoenician interments, like most ancient pagan ones, usually had objects deposited with them. These could be pottery or metal vessels to hold food and drink, small wooden, ivory, or glass containers for perfume, cosmetics and the like, combs, spoons, razors and other implements for toilet or other use, and lamps."[6]

THE SPECIALIST IS BORN

THE FIRST OLIGARCHY, or leadership over a tribe, was now born. Whether such leadership originated as a *shaman* we do not know nor will we ever know, but we do know that the shaman evolved as the belief in spirits and magical forms arose and grew into complicated and complex "technologies," and gradually became the *specialist* in these matters. This specialist became the first shaman, the first leader-priest, on whom a number of people depended for magical support and defense against magical forces directed against them. Birket-Smith: "The more complicated the ritual and the greater the emphasis placed on its being performed faultlessly, even to the minutest details, the more the priests' power increases."[7] Over a period of many generations and long stretches of "slow" time the power-authority *fixation* became more and more impregnated until eventually the idea arose that through its lineal descendancy such leadership was "ordained" by spiritual ancestors or forces. From this idea the concept of monarchial power by *divine* right germinated. Writing about the early Hawaiians, W. Storr Lee states: "The slaves owned nothing; the commoners owned nothing; neither the *kahunas* nor the chiefs actually owned anything. All property in the realm was in the name of the king, from the last square rod of terrain and shore front to the most personal chattel in the hands of a subject. The king alone held the power of life and death. He owned all and ruled all. And Hawaiians would have it no other way. They believed implicitly in the divine right of kings."[8]

The leader became not only a king but also a god-king, as we have seen before, upon whom the general welfare and group continuance depended. He superseded the shaman (a mere specialist in magical formulae) by being elevated to the role of *intercessor* or *agent* of the spirits and gods, in some instances, the spirit of the god himself in carnate form. This brought about a "logical" sequence of thought and belief in the slave subjects that the god-king had supranatural power, to which they desired no alternative save to worship and protect him, give their lives for him, be exploited by him, in order that he should divinely protect them and assure them a satisfied and peaceful existence. It was a reciprocal program brought about by blind belief in the idea that the king was either the god himself or represented the god in such a status that he was the equivalent or pervading power of the god. C. A. Burland: "The peoples of the Inca empire were involved in a mesh of government which penetrated right down into family organization. The diffusion of power was a matter of religion because it derived ultimately from Inti, the Sun God. Therefore the Sapa Inca [the king], being the closest in descent from the great Father in the Sky, was the source of all earthly power."[9] Thus, from a purely and instinctively driven parental and biological urge to protect the young and the family group arose the cultural product of the divine king endowed with the divine right not only to rule his subjects but to "own" them as "his" subjects and "children." The economic and psychological results of this ordainment we shall examine later.

It is important to note the gradual psychological replacement of the parental father by a father who would protect his "children" *forever,* that is, now and after the transitional stage of death. Max Muller: "There was nothing that could be told of the sky that was not in some form or other ascribed to Zeus. It was Zeus who rained, who thundered, who snowed, who hailed, who sent the lightning, who gathered the clouds, who let loose the winds, who held the rainbow. It was Zeus who orders the day and nights, the months, seasons, and years. It is he who watches over the fields, who sends rich harvests, and who tends the flocks. Like the sky, Zeus dwells on the highest mountains; like the sky, Zeus embraces the earth; like the sky, Zeus is eternal, unchanging, the highest god. For good and for evil, Zeus the sky and Zeus the god are wedded together in the Greek mind, language triumphing over thought, tradition over religion."[10] "The same Aryan Heaven-father is Jupiter, in that original name and nature which he bore in Rome long before they arrayed him in the borrowed garments of Greek myth, and adapted him to the ideas of classic philosophy. Thus, in nation after nation, took place the great religious development by which the Father-heaven became the Father in heaven."[11] "Myth has always served as a succinct validation of puzzling laws, rites and social customs."[12]

The king or king-god needed adjutants to represent both him and the god. The priests or temple-keepers were charged with the duty and authority of establishing rules of law and usage that gave them the power to enforce the conformity of the people, and of inciting in them sufficient belief regarding the sacrosanct status of the king-god-religion that they would readily adhere to these usages and rules, and be punished if they did not. Of this ancient "machine," the mass groups of human subjects enslaved to toil their lives away for their priest-king combines, to build colossal monuments for their palaces and tombs, Lewis Mumford writes: "Two devices were essential to make the machine work: a reliable organization of knowledge, natural and supernatural; and an elaborate structure for giving orders, carrying them out, and following them through. The first was incorporated in the priesthood, without whose active aid the institution of divine kingship could not have come into existence: the second, in a bureaucracy. Both were hierarchical organizations at whose apex stood the high priest and the king. Without their combined efforts the power complex could not operate effectively. This condition remains true today, though the existence of automated factories and computer-regulated units conceals both the human components and the religious ideology essential even to current automation."[13] "The Inca rule depended on the acceptance of uniformity in religion as well as in social usage."[14] Kenneth E. Boulding brings out this point in another way, by stressing the necessity and importance of divine approval for king, priest, royalties and other leading-people organizations so that the people would come to obey, serve and even worship them: "God is the great legitimator. A man who believes he is performing a divine role sanctioned by the Lord of the Universe and in conformity with ultimate truth will not have any problems of morale or self-doubt. If he can persuade others likewise that his role is divinely ordained, he will find it easy to obtain external acceptance. This unquestionably is why we find the alliance of priest and king throughout history and why even in our more secular age the British monarch is crowned by the Archbishop and even the American president is sworn in on the Bible, in spite of the fact that if he were to follow its precepts he would probably

soon find himself impeached or at least out of office. Even Napoleon sought legitimacy by having himself crowned by the Pope.
. . . In the modern world indeed the state is probably the most
legitimate of all organizations, and the church has derived
legitimacy from the state by supporting it just as, in the beginning, the state had derived legitimacy from the church."[15]

Whether the Incas, Mayas, Toltecs, Aztecs, Zapotecs, Tlalt-
cans, Olmecs, the Polynesian chieftains, the Judean kingdoms and
priesthoods, the pharaonic dynasties of ancient Egypt, Babylon,
Assyria, Sumeria, the Near East and European Catholic hier-
archial-monarchial tie-ins, clichés, and interplay, economic and
political as well as religious, the Brahman-Rajah interdependencies in India and other parts of Asia and Southeast Asia, they
all represented one consistent pattern throughout the world:
the emergence and coalition of the king and priest to cultivate
their centralized and individual power over the people and its
consequential exploitation. Birket-Smith: "In Polynesia, for example, on Tahiti, where ancestor worship also occupied a prominent position, the priests formed a hereditary class which was
derived from the highest nobility and the royal family."[16] "In so
far as 'Church' and 'State' can be distinguished in ancient Egypt
it is clear that each supported the other. . . . Egyptian mythology
can therefore be interpreted as an attempt to bolster up the
authority of the king, and certainly some changes in religious
belief can be traced to the opening of a new dynasty or a shift
of power from one part of the country to another. . . . The ancient Egyptian really believed that his king had divine authority,
not merely that he claimed it as a justification for his rule. He
believed that the king was the direct intermediary between the
gods and men, and that without the king the divine benefits
could not extend to the ordinary inhabitants of the country. The
king's actions and his welfare were therefore of prime importance
to every one of his subjects."[17]

The king and priest became one coherent and coalesced organization, which maintained itself by the unity and coordination
of both. Ahknaton tried it without the priesthood and failed;
it outlived him and restored the old status of power. "In short,
as in the Sumerian version, man was created as a convenience to

minister to the gods, a fairly clear rationalization of the citizens' duty to support the divine household of the god which included the priesthood and the king, a justification of the Mesopotamian social system."[18] "It is necessary for the king as the agent of national unity, to accept the worship and offerings of his people, and to live with his associates on a scale of magnificence apart from the common herd. This is the price they pay for the unity and peace that makes their civilization possible."[19] Thomas Jefferson wrote: "The day will come when the mystical generation of Jesus by the Supreme Being or his Father, in the womb of a virgin, will be classed with the fables of the generation of Minerva in the brain of Jupiter."[20]

The kings and priests knew very well that the gods who ordained their power over their subjects were as vulnerable and earthly as their armor and armies, not only within their own order but also against possible invasion and conquest by other kings, priests, and gods. So kings went out to conquer other peoples and where the kings conquered the priests followed, to establish their gods, loyalty, and devotion to their victorious king. Every victory and conquest only proved that the king was more divine, that his incarnate god-spirit or power, originally a biological parental protective instinct and prerogative, now moved with the approval and imprimatur of the divine pantheon. "The one cardinal sin was to disregard the authority of the Church."[21] André Gide: "The world will be saved, only by the *unsubmissive.*"[22] C. P. Snow: "Far more, and far more hideous crimes have been committed in the name of obedience than in the name of rebellion."[23] It was St. Augustine who wrote: "Justice being taken away, then, what are kingdoms but great robberies? For what are robberies themselves but little kingdoms?"[24]

Basically, monarchy has not changed since, change showing itself merely in different characters, circumstances, events, directions, places, power struggles and ambitions. Never did monarchy dissociate itself from its twin partner, the priestcraft in the name of caliph, minister, wizard, priest, or pope. The connecting link to the believing masses is important. Even Hitler and Mussolini realized that they must not abrogate, in their rise to power and its maintenance, the authority of the Church, and thereby risk a rebellion against them because of their desire to overthrow the Church. Both made concordats with the Vatican. With monarchies only can the divine or ordained character of the blood be made thus to appear *blue,* only by the constant baptismal dyeing of theological benediction and assent. Now the king and his nobility, on one hand, and the priesthood, on the other, had achieved the necessity of organization and unity in order to retain power and assure continuance of their orders. "Every individual desire or opinion or plan was repressed save as it harmonized with the king's will. The strength and wealth and life of each subject were at the king's disposal to carry out his will."[25]

With organization, the previous Siamese twin-type physical cohesion and inseparatedness of king and priest became no longer essential. Moreover, each had cultivated and extended its own power and organization to express such power, naked and psychological, with and without the pooling of each with the other, although each depended upon the other's support to achieve its ends. It worked out nicely for them—and still does. It never worked out for the people. They remained, as ever they had been, behind the eight ball! "The final developments in barbaric religion, once it has become a business carried on by a state-supported class of specialists, take place in the urban stage of culture. Theology now goes into politics and rationalizes the power of structure of the society. In this case the king and priesthood cooperate, with either high priest and king upholding each other's divine authority, or the two functions combined in one."[26] "When the Wajagga of East Africa desire to make a covenant, the two parties will sometimes sit down with a bowl of milk or beer between them, and after uttering an incantation over the beverage they each take a mouthful of the milk or beer and spit it into the other's mouth. In urgent cases, where there is no time to spend on ceremony, the two will simply spit into each other's mouth, which seals the covenant as well."[27] The historical king-priest alliance is really similar to the Wajagga, and the people usually get it between the eyes! Such an intimate and heartwarming coalition always existed between royalty and priestcraft, and whenever they spat at or upon each other, they managed to realize the importance of one to the existence of the other.

Then something stirred in the minds of some Greeks about three thousand years ago. For the first time since protoprimitive times an attempt was made to *restore* the independence and the rights of the individual within an orderly social, economic, and political system. They created the first *polis*—the parent of democracy! All individuals were equal in their rights to assert their opinions, and they met in the village "campus" and *voted* upon resolutions, procedures, and transactions. While this was an attempt to restore and reassert basic biological cravings of natural freedom, it was already infected with the cultural acquisitions of many thousands of years of king-priest-god influences, and with the traditional greed and misery of a half-free and half-slave state. These influences eventually caused the deterioration of the *polis* into various status and social levels, and these, in turn, became groups opposing groups. The idea of freedom itself became the very tool to destroy itself by the dissensions it had had the freedom to create. Imperialistic ambitions, the gods and their retinues of priests and temple-keepers moved in and eventuated disaster in the many centuries of the tragic story of Greece—when Greek opposed Greek. In the long run, invaders came and overran the country. The Olympian priests merely changed their clothes and worshipped Jupiter instead of Zeus, and when the Romans lost their hold, the priests changed their clothes again and worshipped Mithra, the Sun god. When the Christian god was "legalized" by Constantine, Mithraism was outlawed, and the Mithraic priests changed their clothes and became Catholic theologians; when Protestantism came fifteen hundred years later, many of the Catholic priests changed their clothes and became "reformers," and in many ways and in many places they have kept on changing their clothes to meet changing situations. As a matter of fact, this is religiously advocated in the Sacred Books of India, the principle of Maya, the justified use of chicanery, fraud, deception, and finesse that are to be used by people to get along in this world.

During all this time the people merely changed their positions of prayer—East, West, North, South—and remained poor and miserable, looking forward to heaven and reward. To this day, theologians all over the world, wherever they may be and whatever religion or cult they represent, keep changing their clothes, abruptly or imperceptibly, depending on the situation, and they will keep on changing their clothes so long as they can get somebody to believe in what they say and keep them in comfort and good supply, and free of the labors and struggles demanded of those who are not theologians. Peter Cooper: "In their ignorance and fear, men built altars. Religion became a trade. The preachers ate roast beef, and the people starved. This is religious history."

CONTINUITIES IN CULTURAL EVOLUTION

There is no such thing as a religion or culture original and pure in itself, just as there is no such thing as a pure race, spontaneously generated without any influence, continuance, or acceptance, wholly or partially, modified or reinterpreted, openly or discreetly adopted, from previous or surrounding religions and cultures. The procession and interchange of ideas and usages are a constant process of the historical diffusion of human relationships. "Archeology had destroyed the old image of the virgin birth of Greek culture. We know now that the Hittites, the Canaanites, the Egyptians and the Greeks, bordering as they did on the Mediterranean, formed an international community, all aware of each other's cultures very much as France, England and America are today. In the past the mobility of ancient peoples has been underestimated. We must remember that they were as active in pursuit of pleasure and profit as we. Their business and sightseeing trips took them from one country to another; they hawked their gadgets and gaped at the sights and sometimes brought back strange customs, new ideas and foreign goods."[28] "The old goddesses of Crete are linked to the new deities in various ways. Athena's owl relates her to the old fertility entity who had bird attributes. Athena's snake is reminiscent of those who attended the guardian goddess of the palace of Knossos. Artemis is clearly the ancient mistress of animals. . . . The familiar Demeter and Persephone myth stems from the Ashtar-Tammuz story."[29] "The Sumerian did not evolve the gods from his inner consciousness, he encountered them; they revealed themselves to him in and through the phenomena of the physical world, and his conception of them is proportioned by the degree to which they affected him in that revelation."[30] "The myth of Man's creation from earth, clay or dust is widely current. In Egypt, either the God Khnum or the God Ptah created man on a potter's wheel; in Babylonia, either the Goddess Aruru or the God Ea kneaded man from clay. According to a Phoenician Greek myth, Prometheus used a certain red clay at Panopeus; what was left there continued for centuries to exude an odour of human flesh."[31] "Two ancient myths parallel the *Genesis* Deluge: one Greek, one Akkadian. The Akkadian, found in the *Gilgamesh Epic,* was current also among the Sumerians, the Hurrians and the Hittites."[32] "Seven planetary deities, borrowed from Babylon and Egypt, are commemorated in the seven branches of the Menorah, or sacred candlestick."[33] "And what to some will perhaps be still more amazing is the fact that from the period of Confucius onward there was such a doctoring of texts that even the most learned scholarship, whether of Europe, Japan, or China, has been at a loss, up to now, to reconstruct with assurance even the work of Confucius himself."[34] "The demons and sorcerers of the Christianized Finns were the gods and priests of the older religion which was so cruelly misrepresented and persecuted by Christian intolerance."[35]

Regarding the Christian transformation of Scandinavian gods and goddesses into witches and devils: "Freya herself, like almost all the ancient divinities, was branded as a demon, or witch, and banished to the mountain tops of the lands that had formerly held her sacred. She figures in medieval German stories as old and wrinkled, insatiable and cruel. Her priestesses share her doom. No longer the beautiful daughters of the Mother of Life; they are now deformed, withered and wicked, fit offsprings of Hell. But even so they are not unrecognizable, for the cats that once drew Freya's chariot have become the steeds on which the witches ride through the air, or their companions in daily life, which are said by the Christians to be attendant devils."[36] "Both baptism and the eucharist, like the ethics of the New Testament, were all of pagan origin. And so after six hundred years, the

Catholic Church reduced its worship into a ritual very similar to one which had been practiced in Egypt for more than three thousand years before the advent of Christianity; in Thrace for two thousand; at Eleusis for fifteen hundred; by the Orphic-Pythagorean societies for six hundred; by the devotees of Mithra for two hundred; and by the Essenes for a hundred and fifty. And so the religion of Jesus Christ became an almost exact replica of the universal pagan mystery by which the communicant became divine and immortal by essential union with his savior-god."[37]

Again things began to stir in the hearts and minds of men. It was the seventeenth century. The Reformation and the Renaissance had released new energies to supply the freer and more courageous minds to systematize their doubts, reestablish the power of reason to free them from their slavery and allow the natural freedoms of humanity to emerge. Revolutions expressed the common desire to banish lordship, feudalism, and clericalism in America and in Europe. These revolutions continued through the nineteenth century and continue today in many ways, not necessarily violent or radical, but in every form of extension of education, the sciences, and the generally freer expression of thought and liberal enlightenment. In the eighteenth century people realized for the first time that divinities can be guillotined and disposed of, that the most sacred scriptures can be openly questioned. The sciences revealed that all religion is *man-made* and *cultural,* that kings have the same color of blood as their pet dogs and cats, that the world is much older than Bishop Ussher declared it to be as "divine truth"; they learned that all "truths" are *human* truths, and only the sciences might bring about some sort of certainties about the actual realities of life.

Tyranny, like most other things, repeats itself in the condition and nature of human beings. The nineteenth century, with its turbulent and radical changes, saw the rise of industry, opening of mines, exploitation of natural resources on a grand and unrestricted scale; railroads began to extend themselves through Europe and America. Even then the aristocratic and powerful élite "resigned" themselves to a sort of "divine" division between themselves and the common people. The Duke of Wellington, when told about the new railroads, remarked: "Railroads will only encourage the lower classes to move about needlessly."[38] The widening and expanding concentrates of urbanization felt the violence of many revolutions. There were also many nonviolent yet provocative revolutions beyond the barricades and pitchfork uprisings. "While the labouring poor stirred, the increasing weakness and obsolescence of the old régimes of Europe multiplied crises within the world of the rich and influential."[39] Referring to the causes of the Mexican revolution against Diaz in 1910, "a chaotic, spontaneous, uncoordinated explosion took place as the Mexican people lashed out against everything that reminded them of the past: against the continued imitation of Europe, against the semi-feudal landholding system, against the preferred positions of the Catholic Church, the army, the foreigners, and the government officials permanently in power. Zapata, Carranza, Villa, and Obregón were among the leaders of the revolution. Each one of them was murdered by the traditional forces in power. And the traditional, anti-liberal, anti-democratic powers in Mexico were the usual partners of the old Mexican Establishment: the so-called 'aristocracy' of army leaders, the landowners of vast estates, and the hierarchy of the Catholic Church. Between all three they owned practically the whole country and the millions of peones were left to starve and suffer for so many years and generations."[40]

The sciences broke out with a swelling rash and showered the civilized world with shudders and shattered the age-long idea that man was especially created by God a few thousand years ago. Man was now an *animal* evolved like all other kinds of life, that life itself evolved over a period of thousands of millions of years. In medicine, botany, geology, astronomy, and a hundred other sciences, man and his scientific approach breathed more freely and broke through in every possible direction to seek the truth about the world and himself. Political systems had to change from the naked power of monarchs to parliaments, elections, and representatives chosen by the popular vote of individuals who were now called *citizens*.

In America, England, France, democracy, with all its tribulations and labor pains, fastened itself to the nature of government. The growing philosophy of democratic processes indicated that equity and the basic inalienable rights of individuals, born to natural freedom and the pursuit of happiness, are the foundations upon which government justifies its existence and purpose. Sandifer and Scheman: "Freedom and self-government are fundamental to an enduring system of economic and social justice."[41]

Art and artists, freed from the more contained and traditionally restricted *pietas*, Madonna and Child, and the Temptation of St. Anthony pictures and figures, also broke away from the old trend. Expressionism and impressionism, and even the perplexed abstractionists, coming from a free-flowing and uninhibited issuance of ideas and sentiment, are more and more allowing a freer communication between artist and his work, and from both to the esthete. Wherever you turn you see a freer change, more so in Europe and America, less in other parts of the world, but the movement toward greater freedom is there and with it always the accompanying wider latitude of individual and group expression.

Tyranny in some form, latent or expressed in different times and places, raises its ugly head without surcease whenever the beast in human nature, regardless of how fancy or Maya-draped its physical outlines and appearances, halts this advance of freedom or gives false concepts to people to think they are more free, when, in fact, they are more enslaved, if by new lords and techniques. The cleric has turned politician and the monarch has turned to high finance, top echelon management of capital and industry, or else is wandering around the world with his title and chiseling whenever and wherever he can, a traveling parasite. The cleric has turned statesman and the king has turned banker, but the persistence of certain people not to work and to live off the fat of the land continues under different costumes and different titles and methods. They still find it feasible and good sense to work together for their common parasitism. The people? As usual, we know where to find them, behind the eight ball!

DEMOCRACY

DEMOCRACY, AS A living philosophy and as a political order within which people are sufficiently enlightened to express their freed consciences and to allow themselves and each other to try to live peacefully, to seek and enjoy happiness, to use their power of reason to understand the *reciprocity* value of ethics and the *reprisal* threat when ethics are discarded, is the opening door to any governmental or organizational entity which denotes a *process,* not an object. It identifies a *way,* not a belief or determination; a *method,* not a set of rituals and dogmas; a *movement* of constant flexibilities, like our eyes, heliotropic to light, new experiences, new desires and enjoyments, a *free thinking* that can only make possible a wider choice of actions even though limited within the periphery of our mundane existence and limited to our own natures. Democracy is not a *person* but a *way of life* within a person. "The organized life of the community is necessary, but it is necessary as a mechanism, not something to be valued on its own account."[42] Sandifer and Scheman: "The right to liberty is not only a fundamental condition of democracy; democracy is a condition of liberty."[43]

Democracy is the attempt of man to break away from the pressure and brewing dissatisfactions of the human psyche that cannot permanently stand conformity and uniformity. It thrives on the search for new horizons, newer truths, new thoughts and experiences. People have conformed and become addicted to uniformity either because they were so indoctrinated at an early age as to be patternized and emasculated, or because they were forced by fear and power to do so, and had little choice without placing their security and lives in jeopardy. John Adams: "It will never be pretended that the men who set up the American government had interviews with the gods, or were in any degree under the inspiration of Heaven."[44]

Democracy allows man to give himself the freedom to think or not to think, as he pleases, sometimes with the unfortunate result of thinking how to destroy democracy with good or evil intent. Democracy is the organized effort of people to restore to themselves the privileges and processes of living a *natural* life. Democratic principle or the process of thinking in democratic terms may show man that it is possible to live both a *natural* life and a *good* life simultaneously, as a coadunative and confluent process. Democracy is part of the evolution of social, political, economic, and cultural factors resolving themselves in a biological and natural manner into *compatibilities*, which are, in themselves, *eventual* efforts to allow life and living to continue under certain minimal and necessary conditions in certain ways because of certain situations and events brought on by the historical ascendancy and experience of mankind. The sheer weight of numbers countered by worldly limitations of one kind or another can only point in two directions: extermination or compatibility through adjustment and reasonable control. Tyranny, the blind intoxicant, can only lead to extermination. Democracy, the freedom of choice to adjust and find compatibility, *the free process of self-change through reason, science,* and *ethical judgment,* remains at present as our only vehicle for survival without slavery. "We should realize, from general history as well as from the experiences of everyday life, that all humans, though similar, are nevertheless different in many ways and moods. One need not compromise unwillingly with the benefits or ideas of another in order to preserve a free and individualistic community such as democracy. The main purpose is to understand the nature of difference and differences and the nature of experience."[45]

Democracy is not the establishment of any *particular* philosophy but a dedication in principle that man has arrived at a philosophy that gives him the freedom to philosophize freely. In this way, one might say that democracy is a philosophy of freedom and concerns itself with ways and means to extend the freedom of man, as an individual, more and still more so that he need be governed less and less by any restrictive organized and arbitrary power.

Democracy is a sensible and equitable *way* of harnessing the forces of human nature and *attempting* to convert and channel this force for the good of *the* individual and *all* individuals, if possible. It cannot change the basic rudiments of the human drive, but it might be able to give it a *directional guidance* for its own possible good. This could come about only by activating to the greatest feasible extent the free exercise of an individual's mind and freeing it as much as possible from indoctrinating and dominating influences that are antinatural and detrimental to this human drive, and anti-political in that obscurantic, despotic, and tyrannical forms of government and organized religion exercising arbitrary, psychological, and naked power over people tend to diminish or prevent in some degree this freedom of the mind and body of the individual to live a naturally normal and freely expressive life and try to better himself in a better and happier society. The more a country is democratic and allows a better, happier, and more natural social order, the more we find its social order to be peaceful. Peace comes with emotional, intellectual, and economic security. Europe has barely known a peaceful day since the first Phoenician stepped ashore on Sicily, Spain, or Gaul. If democracy allows itself to be aligned with the persistent remnants of orthodox traditionalism—stranglers of the freedoms of man—to this extent democratic processes will remain contaminated and mired in the morass of decrepit and disproved theologies and philosophies, and to this extent it will endanger its own fullness of process and even possibly its very existence. Paul Blanshard: "Washington, in spite of the official separation of church and state, is a pro-religious capital."[46] Herbert J. Muller: "Today I know of no evidence that orthodox or fundamentalist Christians are the staunchest champions of democracy, but I have read considerable evidence that they are not very staunch defenders of civil liberties."[47] V. T. Thayer: "Freedom of conscience is thus secure as long as the Constitution endures, and Americans are reasonably safe from the evils of sectarian government."[48]

Bertrand Russell states that "democracy is successful in so far as the Government is obliged to respect public opinion."[49] This is obviously good, provided public opinion has not become opinionated to suit those in power and thus valueless as a constructively critical process of choice and determination. Regarding the use of propaganda methods, concealments, and the release of half-truths by governmental agencies to a country's own people, Henry Steele Commager writes: "Without intellectual freedom—

uncontaminated, unimpeachable, and categorical—we cannot achieve the ends to which our society is dedicated. This is ultimately why we cannot tolerate activities of governmental agencies which, whatever their alleged justification, repudiate and paralyze the principles of freedom."[50]

Julia Peterkin states: "If democracy gives morons and defectives an equal economic, political, social and biological opportunity with better human beings, this fact alone is bound to make democracy destructive sooner or later, for heredity counts in men just as it counts in animals and trees and grass."[51] Julia Peterkin, with good intent, I think, is wrong and seems to miss the very nexus of the democratic field which is a freely competitive, participating and compensating interplay of individual forces, in which morons and defectives can succeed only by inheritance of a fortune. History does not show any attempt in any part of the world to equalize the sum total of any country's or peoples' wealth with morons and defectives.

Sir James Jeans states: "Democracy is ever eager for rapid progress, and the only progress which can be rapid is progress downhill. For this reason I suspect that all democracies carry within them the seeds of their own destruction, and I cannot believe that democracy is to be our final form of government."[52] The democratic process, by the nature of itself, precludes any finality in its structures; it is opposite to the historically traditional forms. The despot rarely modifies existing laws or makes new ones; if he does, the changes or additives are rarely beneficial to the people. In democracy there are constant legislative changes; whether such changes are good or bad depends upon the individuals authorized to create them, and their selection depends upon the good or poor judgment of the voters. If the constituents, by their selection, opinion, and voting, find that they do not like or desire an existing law or regulation, they can change or remove it by these same processes. This possibility of modification, change, and improvisation of new ideas to meet situations is not inherent in the traditional political forms. Yet the democratic process is a *human* and a *humanistic* process, and if humans create a process for themselves, what it may be will always reflect the human beings themselves. Whether mankind, at any time and with any process, can actually fulfill the expectations of the wise and the ethical to resolve democratic processes on a successful basis is a conjecture difficult to predict; human factors are too paradoxical to assure sensible and calculable predetermination. If democracy in any society should not succeed in its expectations, it is not because of the fallacy of the process but of the inability of human beings and their animal habits to cope with it effectively. "Inflexible capital, undisciplined labor, mass despair—are doing more for the disintegration of democracy than all the paid agents of Communism and Fascism."[53] H. F. Amiel: "I do not deny the rights of Democracy, but I have no illusions as to the uses that will be made of those rights so long as wisdom is rare and pride abundant."

A state only reflects the nature of its constituents or of the leaders who may be in power and control the state, but in any event any state or institution is the outward impression and expression of its people, and therefore is *human* in its judgments and actions. Thus, it is vulnerable to change, as are people. The more a state is subject to change with less potential turmoil and violence, the more democratic is its structure and procedure. The less a state is subject to change by peaceful means and choice, the more it is vulnerable to change only through violence, and to this extent less democratic. As times and conditions change, people are moved to change, and forcefully or gradually find themselves involved in new conditions, events, and confrontations which of themselves *necessitate* change. Where this necessity-change is realized peacefully and cooperatively there is more democracy; where this necessity-change is halted or thwarted by arbitrary power and other forces of persuasion, then to this extent we can reasonably say that a state of democratic procedure does not exist. Whether those in leadership or those controlling the state itself are good or bad are concepts of judgment, contemporary and historical; and these are at all times *human* judgments, which can never be established, by any democratic political philosophy, as an *absolute* nature that, because of its absoluteness, is not subject to crticism, change, or complete disposal and replacement. Paul Weiss, of Yale University, writing of *The Right to Disobey,* states: "A state is not an absolute good.

It is without justification if its structure, design, and operation involve the denial of the basic rights of life, health, education, speech, assembly, and the like."[54] Regarding the rights of the young to dissent even though they do not vote, Representative Lester L. Wolff of New York delivered an address in Congress on *The Responsibilities of Dissent:* "We teach the young one thing; we practice another. We assert that we are fighting for freedom in Vietnam, yet we make slight effort to secure it for our own people in Mississippi. We preach love of our neighbor, and are in the process of killing him. We claim that we are a democracy, yet we know that the great mass of people have no control over the policies which directly affect their lives."[55]

In human nature there is both good and bad, and what is good and bad, at any particular time and place, is a particular viewpoint. As humans we have no sensible choice but to have a certain faith in ourselves; to despair is to dilute life and make it more valueless in a neurotic well of cynicism. John Dewey: "The foundation of democracy is faith in the capacities of human nature; faith in human intelligence and in the power of pooled and cooperative experience."[56] W. W. Aldrich: "The essence of the democratic idea is first of all the inviolability of the fundamental rights of the individuals so that each individual may be free to develop the best that is in him. To make this liberty effective, we must have opportunity to do those things we wish to do, provided they are not harmful to others. We must have freedom of speech, of conscience and of thought. We must have tolerance for all races, all creeds, and all minority interests. We must recognize the equality of all citizens before the law. This does not imply a simple and crude equalitarianism, because that is impossible, human nature and capabilities being what they are, but it does mean equality of opportunity for all. To make this liberty effective we must have a free educational system which will produce men and women who can think logically, dispassionately, and objectively, and will produce leaders who can direct the affairs of the state wisely and well."[57] Sidney Hook: "Historically, democracy, as understood and practiced in the West, is the process by which freedoms are institutionalized."[58] And all institutions are vulnerable and subject to extension, restriction, containment or destruction from resistances and pressures of the powers that be from within and from without. "No man can win freedom and peace unless he conquers his fear of death. No nation can preserve its freedom unless it is willing to risk destruction in its defense. To do otherwise is to break faith with those who died to keep it free."[59] Bertrand Russell ends up his book on *Power:* "This is the task of a liberal education: to give a sense of the value of things other than domination, to help create wise citizens of a free community, and through the combination of citizenship with liberty in individual creativeness to enable men to give to human life that splendour which some few have shown that it can achieve."[60]

That human nature must be governed and controlled to some necessary extent all practical and intelligent people recognize and accept. If it were left to human nature we would hardly have any other animals left on earth; as it is, man has exterminated hundreds of fine creatures and would have exterminated many hundreds more if it were not for certain governmental controls that stopped the slaughter. But for the psychological and real power of the law and its punishments, the police and the penitentiaries, the thin veneer of morality, peacefulness, and ethics that covers civilization would vaporize quickly and the world turned into a vast insane asylum of murdering, robbing, burning, despoiling maniacs in which the few peaceful and actually good people (who would probably be just as good and peaceful if there were not any police and laws) would have to scramble to the highest peaks or into the deepest caverns of the earth to escape the holocaust of destruction and self-destruction that would continue ceaselessly until peace returned. At it is, even with all the law and enforcement agencies, crime is rampant, increasing, the jails are loaded, and people throughout the world keep killing, mutilating, and robbing each other on any pretext of religious difference, prejudice, fanatical nationalism, sectarian creed, or inflamed by some incapable but revered leader. This last is well exemplified by Archbishop Makarios in Cyprus, where the people recently fought hard and courageously to obtain their independence from England. Once this freedom was achieved, Makarios the Greek Orthodox cleric could not see why Moslem

Turks should occupy any part of the world, especially Cyprus,
and so inflamed the Greeks against their neighbor Turkish
Cypriots. As a result, the Greeks and Turks have been killing
each other's neighbors, houses are barricaded in fear and hate,
and killings go on daily while Makarios prays to his God and eats
his evening meal in comfortable safety. Makarios "lives in a
grandiose new archiepiscopal palace fitted with Greek and Cypriot
furniture and 19th century French religious art. The church owns
nearly 20 percent of the island's farm land and controls the
profitable Cyprus Wine & Spirits Co., which makes beer, wine and
brandy."[61]

On the other side of the world, we had a secular type of
tyrant, Sukarno of Indonesia, who loves power and women, an
egomaniac who will not tolerate any peace anywhere if violence,
intrigue and expansion will make the Indonesians and the world
look up to him as a "towering power." These fools, who, like
Canute, try to hold back the tides that will eventually overwhelm
them and their ambitions, always end up leaving the beach sand
flat and clean, and they gone. One reason for the woes of mankind
is that those who possess fine talent with intent of honest analysis
and projection, write excellent articles for special magazines
which very few read, while the hams and the robbers rule the
world.

No rational observer of human nature and events could possibly see any culture or society without the imperative and constant need of law, police enforcement, and the more soft and
acceptable usages, to keep the *law* as an authoritative and practical factor in the management of human behavior and association. What is needed is the constant examination of this cultural
and societal jurisprudence to see that it meets the moving exigencies and basic fulfillments of the *constituents* of a society and not
the *society* itself as a supra-organism.

It is needless to reiterate that so long as humans are not isolated from each other—nor should they be—unbridled and unrestricted freedom of choice and action cannot be equitably and
reasonably extended to each without inviting chaos, insecurity,
destruction, and hysteria. As it is, with all the law and policing
of societal ordinance of any nation in the world today, there is

abundance of crime, civil violations of the rights and properties of individuals, unethical practices from top to bottom rampant in ratio to what people can get away with without punishment or exposure: the constant reality of the innate kleptomania and cruelty which is in the very core of human behavior. If this is not exhibited or actively expressed by a number of us, it is simply that our experiences and needs have not led us to such expression and activities.

The cold wars between nations and peoples are in fact ritualized warfares which reveal the deep-rooted and biological traits of aggression and self-preservation, the predatory urge, and the fear of being harmed or destroyed. This has evolved among men as it has among many animals, the psychological weapon to dominate, rule, and overwhelm, as well as submission out of self-preservation and need of security, to bow, obey, and comply with the conventionalized terms of propitiation. The origins of the king, priest, and religion are tied in, and evolved out of, the primeval predatory and self-preserving instincts of the human animal. Throughout all animaldom, including our own species, the biological rule seems to have been to *overwhelm or submit.* Compromises to bring about compatibilities of antipathetic and sympathetic symbiosis are legion and vary within the micro- and macro-experiences of individuals, kinds, groups, and classes. Each living creature seems to go through this process of development and envelopment. Individuals form groups, and groups form nations and societies. The nature of the part is related to the whole, and the whole reflects the nature of its parts. We cannot change the nature of ourselves but we might be able to channel our predatory drives into more wholesome and exploratory pursuits, and our instinct for security and existence, instead of resignation, despair, and submission, into a realistic understanding and evaluation of the time-factor in the significance of life-value and to the enjoyment and fulfillment of this life-value as long as we possibly can. Unless this can come to pass, man, continuing his animal traits of the *drive to overwhelm* and the fear in submission, with civilized haberdashery, will overwhelm himself with his aggressive instinct, and his fears of insecurity, intensified and fanaticized through his submissiveness in religion and superstition, will dilute and thus waste away the time-factor and the life-value of the very precious and irreplaceable life that happens to be his.

What is the gap composed of, which makes the individual and his society so fearful of each other? Which makes it so imperative for the group to protect itself from the individual? Or the futility and distrust of the individual who refuses to be just another termite without the intellectual, esthetic, and economic freedoms society so often denies to the individual in one way or another, or that the individual feels are being denied to him by the society in which he so often helplessly finds himself? It is reasonable to think that if any growing society is ever to reach a point of successful maturity, meaning, and purpose, then this society must *somehow* succeed in allowing the individual the necessary quantum of freedom needed for the individual to achieve reasonable life satisfaction. This means that the *first principles* of any organizational *polis* or culture must proceed from the needs of individuals, the prime purpose for which organization itself has been seeded, grown, and maintained, and not from the needs of the organization, regardless of the needs of the individuals. Perhaps this would bring about some abeyance of this kleptomania and cruelty, and our jails would contain fewer inmates. What then is needed to produce individuals who, in turn, could possibly evolve or mature their society in such a way as to allow this reasonable possibility? The answer involves many factors, both external and internal to the human constitution, its progression or regression, or intermixtures of both. Many of these are unpredictable factors, subject to the whim of accident and spontaneous generation of human conflagration.

There are various kinds, classes, levels, and degrees of kleptomania, domination, cruelty, and tyranny. To enumerate them in any detail requires voluminous space. But whether it is Castro or some other self-bloated power-intoxicant, or some high social "Castillian" landowner or mine operator or high finance manipulator of South America, who sees the Alliance for Progress as a continuing fund for himself and his ilk, all forms of tyranny are oppressors of freedom and the withholders of the equities they have stolen or defrauded from the common people, who lack and do not understand the freedoms to which they are attached by their *natural* place in the world and which have been usurped from them, with or without their consent, to make them the miserable slaves they are and will continue to be until these freedoms and equities are restored to them. Thomas Jefferson: "The mass of mankind has not been born with saddles on their back, nor a favored few booted and spurred, ready to ride them legitimately, by the grace of God."

Throughout Central and South America the landowners and military cliques run their countries practically in the same tyrannical way as the kings and royalties of Spain and Portugal in former colonial days. Unless just land agrarian reforms, more equitable industrial labor wages, decent and healthful living conditions, wider and more integrated public schools systems, and down-to-earth democratic principles are applied and activated throughout the political, economic, and social life for and within the people, we can only expect a most tragic and revolutionary upheaval of destruction and violent change. Referring to the northeast provinces of Brazil, where millions of peasants and workers live in filth and utter poverty, Josué de Castro informs us: "The most important of the relationships that must be destroyed is the colonial-feudal land monopoly with its concentration of ownership in the great estates. Even where families have decayed and ancient ownerships fallen to corporations, the master-slave relation between the *patrao* and the *parceiro* persists. No permanent good can be achieved when a few fancy themselves lords of creation and beyond responsibility; they are capable of watching empty-eyed as thousands strain and die."[62] Referring to the pyramids of ancient Egypt, Mumford states: "By a combination of divine command and ruthless military coercion, a large population was made to endure grinding poverty and forced labor at dull repetitive tasks, in order to ensure 'life, prosperity, and health' for the divine or semidivine ruler and his entourage."[63]

Everything that exists, animate and inanimate, contains within itself an active or passive quantum of power. Power, in ertia or inertia, becomes ert or inert in ratio to the nature of the power within itself toward the outside and the nature of the power

directed toward and within it from the outside. Human beings
apparently operate on the same physical and psychological basis.
So long as the despot, lord, landowner, politician, cleric, or what-
not, *knows* that he has a certain power—whether this power be
in terms of military force, legalized ownership of vast properties
and its resources, the power of authority in the politician, whether
elected or self-appointed, or the power of the cleric in terms of
reverence as well as property and wealth—these powers can only
be modified by an opposing power directed toward them from
the outside. This direction of power toward them may not be
necessarily violent. History proves more often that such a direction brought, with violence, less change and new tyrants rather
than beneficence and freedom. On the other hand, through *ideas,*
the power of thought, came the freedom of thought, and as this
freedom of thought expressed itself at the windows of reason,
the ego and personality of man came to look out to see things
in their truer light, in a knowledgeable way which revealed the
fraud, the societal swindle, the enslavement, and the inequities.
But ideas and the power of thought alone could not pierce
through and break down these feudal fortresses of naked and
psychological power. They prepared the way, sometimes out of
sheer pain and sometimes out of the inner desire for relief from
obscurantism and its stifling odors, the craving for the fresh air
of freedom and its invigorating naturalness for the animalistic
and humanistic spirit in man.

FREEDOM OF THOUGHT AND ITS PRODUCTS

THE FREE THOUGHT of man has moved more mountains that
have barred the human march to a more free and equitable
civilization than anything else. It has created philosophies which,
in turn, created more democratic forms of government, and
when so created, the free thought continued and still continues
to modify and adjust to meet new situations and contingencies.
Free thought created the sciences and all they have produced
and effected, good and bad. Free thought is a process, like freedom itself; it is not a product or a particular principle, philoso-

phy, aim or goal. *Freedom is a natural, conspecific, concomitant, concurrent and synchronal process of causation of life itself and evolved with it accordingly; without it the processes of evolution could not have taken place.* Free thought *reveals* the natural basis of this freedom, as it also reveals the many historical injustices and cruelties imposed on mankind in the diminishment of this natural freedom, and the many types of rebellious struggles, violent and intellectual, the suffering and sacrifices necessitated in the attempt to restore them to people.

Freedom of thought does not necessarily mean that man can think as a god, as a super- or supra-organism beyond his own nature. Even the Greeks *made* their gods behave like the Greeks and reflect as they did, and so *humanized* them. In many ways, whether or not we recognize it, theology and its religions and all its myths and imaginings never went beyond the nature of man and all their gods are the reflections of men and their environments. What happened is that they misled man to believe that myth and imaginings *are* reality. The obscurantist principle that a man can think beyond his own nature, or be so free as to be able to choose and think beyond his own nature and his world, is based on the obsolete superstition of rewards and punishments on which theology is based. However, this takes us into the realm of the freedom of the will, morals, ethics, and responsibilities, the discussion of which we will withhold until we come to its place in the next chapter. Here we are concerned primarily with the misleading of man and the taking away from him of his natural freedom to obtain a more or less normal and satisfied life; defrauding and robbing him of the securities and freedom of movement provided him by the world into which he was born, with all its limitations and potentials. If the nature of man requires the necessity of orderliness, this is a matter of enlightenment, knowledge, and cohesion which only the freedom of thought can reasonably mature; it does not necessarily mean that the few self-selected and self-appointed by fraud, force, or by the gods shall have the authority and power to rule over the rest, that the rest shall believe and not think for themselves according to their nature and their natural freedom to do so, that the rest shall remain as devotees dedicating their only lives to what the "ordained" few shall find it "wise," "sacred," or "mandatory" for them to do. Until man frees himself from the traditional laissez-faire spongers, intoxicants, and dreamers, he will not be able to think well enough to see through the swindles of the past, nor will he be able to visualize and evaluate, because of his indoctrinated and constricted beliefs and reflections, the need for the restoration of his *natural* place and his *natural* right without which he cannot be *really* free.

Free thought does not necessarily mean a modern mind or a mind intellectualized in literature, the arts, or any of the high cultural sequences of the present day. The protoprimitive, the primitive, and the savage had their free thought also, in their own limited and embryonic way, as many in the world today, even in civilized places. Whatever the thoughts of the savage yesterday or today, they were free enough for him to enjoy the gathering of his family, his clan, around the festival fire, just as the American or Swede enjoys the gathering of his family and relatives in his church or home at Christmas time, feeling they all belong to each other. Even many animals, as we have seen, enjoy this common "ownership," the gathering of the troop, pride, or herd: this is their type of society. "A society may be an animal aggregation, which holds together as an interacting group, and among the members of which exists an awareness of belonging together—the 'consciousness of kind.' . . . A human society is also an animal aggregation with just these qualities. In the case of human beings, however, almost all social interrelations are dominated by existing culture. We do not know of any groups of cultureless men."[64] Who can say that the social behavior of animals is purely biological and the social behavior of humans purely cultural? The difficulty of man is that he has been looking at himself most of the time and has not spent enough time looking at his animal neighbors and the world. When he comes to know more about them he will realize that his cultures emanated from the same porridge as the "cultures" of the general animal world, and that these animal cultures should not be underestimated or divided away from the cultural pool of all animal life, of which man is just one member. "Man is an out-and-out social animal, not a solitary one. The human environment is before all else the society to which a person belongs, and a society is a complex of individuals bound by cooperative interactions that serve to maintain a common life."[65] This is exactly what we find in many kinds of animals, including insects and inhabitants of the seas, all over the world.

A man and his family have a sort of society tied by blood relationship, and within this family-society each member feels he belongs, that there is a sort of physical as well as psychological attachment and affinity involved. An American and his people are also a society in the same manner. A New Yorker, driving his car in the backhills of Mexico and seeing another New York car, immediately gets a "bang" out of it; he feels an affinity that he is not "alone," that another segment of *his* society is present. In the same way an Englishman feels a natural affinity to the English, the Hindu to the Hindu people, and the Tahitian to the Tahitian people. The primitive or the modern does not have to *acquire* anything to get this feeling, merely to be born in a certain place. True, one grows up in any locality within a certain culture, but this culture is in a particular natural habit of a certain people. A black man feels an affinity for black people whether he meets them in New York or Uganda; a Jew feels an affinity for Jewish people whether he meets them in Tucson or Tel Aviv, two distinctly different cultural places. Being born a Jew may be a matter of chance, but so is being born Chinese, or black, or an American Indian. The basic root of affinity for similarities of kind, class or color remains a *natural* tendency and is not actually based on any intellectual, moral, or ethical values.

A black man feels more at home with black people; brown people feel more at home among their own kind; yellow and white people feel the same. This is a biological, animalistic, and natural expression of affinity, which may be "perfumed" a bit by culture. As man rises to higher intellectual and ethical levels and values, he leaves the narrow boundaries behind and becomes a *world-man*. Thus, the human being not only finds and accepts *humanity* as his family, he belongs to the world itself and all that lives in it. One becomes a world-man when he rises above his particular culture and takes a *world-view* of things and accepts the world as it really is, as a whole for his society, his home, and his philosophy. The individual, who has but one life to live (and brief enough it is!), shortchanges himself by restricting his horizon to a periphery within his local and provincial circle. The world is *his* to enjoy, and he should have the freedom, by life right, to do so. It does not matter whether he can actually and physically reach the moon or Venus or Mars. This he might eventually do. But he has now, and always had, the freedom to *wonder* at the universe about him and its mysteries, its vastness, and its physical laws, mindless and purposeless as they may be, but there they are. That he has evolved the mind to see and think about it is the miracle of every moment of his life. As Albert Schweitzer has constantly taught, it is the *reverence for all life,* including our own, that may pave the way for man to know *one* society—the world itself. Thus peace may come to man with unanimity as man accepts the world as his family and comes to understand the common biological rootings of all life and his participation in it. Thus, the selfish and divisive aggressiveness of the ego, misled before to dilute itself for ethereal bliss or the soma of power, may now restore its own natural value in finding greater life-value by the realization of the cyclic recurrence of things and the sacredness of the irreplaceable and uncertain time he may be able to express and live this value. He does not have to *fear* the universe, for there is really nothing to fear; he does not have to fear any gods because his fear of the gods is an *image* and a *shadow* he created by himself in his own ignorance of things and in a futile attempt to reach the unreachable, the unreal, the nebulous and the fictitious.

THE BIOLOGICAL ROOTS OF CULTURE

WE HAVE NOTED that man, because of his nature, created society, religion, government, and the cultures involved with them; society, governments, and cultures did not create him. Culture and all its offspring evolved because of biological factors rooted in man and his environment and of the interplay of both. The cultural period of man is a tiny fraction in the total period of man's existence. "49/50ths of this time (period of 1,000,000

years), man was in the Old Stone Age, or Paleolithic and Meso-
lithic stages of cultural development."[66] Culture and its products
are the result of the biological capacity of the human animal to
evolve as such; discovery preceded invention; nature preceded
nurture. *Existence did not precede essence; they both came and
evolved together.* Man had the freedom of his nature to produce
genetic beginnings of culture and its pool wherever he migrated
or settled throughout the world. "In less than one million years
man, by contrast, has advanced from the rawest savagery to
civilization and has proliferated at least three thousand distinctive cultures."[67] "The earliest migrants into the New World in
all likelihood came into Alaska from Siberia some fifteen or
twenty thousand years ago during the latter part of, or after,
the last Ice Age."[68] "Some 35,000 or 40,000 years ago men whose
bones were much like our own and who are therefore classified
as *Homo sapiens sapiens,* appeared in Europe. It seems that by
at least 24,000 years ago modern man was living in North America; his camp sites have been found in Nevada. When modern
man populated the American and Australian continents, his geographic distribution became nearly world-wide."[69] "Stone Age
man had begun the process of creating man-made cultural environments. Because nothing is left of his works except those
made of durable materials, we do not know what he had invented
in social organization, in rules of marriage, or in religion or
folklore. It may have been much; it may have been surprisingly
little. We do know that with his handling of fire, language, and
flint implements he had adopted unique human methods of invention and learning. From that day to this, man has followed
this path."[70] "The great upward surge of progress in technology
of which man can rightly boast, therefore, is an evolution from
unplanned discovery to planned invention."[71]

We must avoid the traditional error that considers the biological and the cultural as two distinct and separated entities apart
from each other. This is the same error that the ancient formal
religions made in establishing the separation of body and soul,
material and spiritual, besides separating or "elevating" man
from the rest of the animal life on earth as well as from the earth
itself. There is nothing that one may consider *purely* cultural

that is not related to or transcended from some biological cause. "In producing the genetic basis of culture, biological evolution has transcended itself."[72] This Dobzhansky called the "super-organic," which is to say that it is organic of a different state or quality or size. We are not merely the stuff the stars may be made of. We do not know the composition of the stars, but we do know something about *our* composition, and we are organic, including the soul, spirit, and the capacity to learn algebra or preach a sermon. "The human capacity for culture is a consequence of man's complex and plastic nervous system. It enables man to make adjustments in behavior without going through a biological modification of his organism."[73] "Human evolution has biological and cultural components. Man's biological evolution changes his nature; cultural evolution changes his nurture. . . . A person is what he is because of his nature and his nurture. His genes are his nature, his upbringing is his nurture. The same is true of mankind as a whole: its nature is its gene pool, its nurture is its environment and its culture."[74] All in all, were it not for man's neuronal capacity, which is biological and a product at any particular time of his state of evolution, he would not be what he is, including any culture that may determine itself as a result of the human being and his experiences.

Everything that rose in the cultural sense, that is, acquired techniques and technologies, advanced social, religious and political forms and usages, emanated from the nuclear source of biological nature itself. If we keep this in mind as a *constant* "square root" we can trace the diminishment of natural freedom in the rise from animalism to animism and from animism to primitive barbaric stages, and then suffered its greatest diminishment in the rise of the ancient and later kingdoms (5000 B.C. to A.D. 1600), with its concurrent priestcrafts, religions, and dogmas, except for a brief flare of democratic surge in ancient Greece. Whatever discoveries and inventions came about in this latter period hardly benefited the common people, but accrued to the wealth, authority, and power of the kings, nobles, emperors, lords, and their coexistents in the religious and theological fields. As for the use of metals and various other natural resources and the crafts and inventions of transforming them into power vehicles and wealth, J. O. Brew states: "Regarding the use of metals in prehistoric times, it must be realized and remembered, however, that the benefits of all this were not applied to a very great extent to people as a whole but were restricted largely to members of the ruling classes."[75]

While it is evident that culture is the result of acquired traits exhibited in any particular society by its members, in contradistinction to the biological and genetic nature of man, which is inherited, the constant interplay and interactivity of both, that is, between the animal and its environment, results in a certain product and over long periods of time modifies both. Man's biological equipment in evolution has made possible his rise in toolmaking, invention, intelligence, agriculture, urbanization and his civilizations. As a result, man is gradually changing his habitat, the world, his environment, and thereby modifying to some extent his biological system. "To a very large extent the development of religious ideas amongst the primitive groups of mankind was conditioned by the social organization of each group."[76]

Thus, culture becomes the complement of man's animal nature; his culture may increase, change, or disappear but not his nature, so long as he exists. While individuals can change due to social invention and heritage, through the processes, that is, of enculturation and existence within a certain culture, cultures themselves can change to hinder or favor the natural tendencies of the biological organism in man. "Whenever man's way of life is altered, his whole cultural pattern changes and with it his religious preoccupations."[77] The process of evolution goes on relentlessly, altering both the organism and its culture, depending upon the resistances and pressures exerted from within and from without the animal and its cultural level. Custom and culture are subject to changeabilities of individuals, and individuals change becase of customs and cultures. "The ensemble of a people's customs has always its particular style; they form into systems. I am convinced that the number of these systems is not unlimited and that human societies, like individual human beings, never create *absolutely:* all they can do is to choose certain combinations from a repertory of ideas which it should be possible to reconstitute."[78] "It is doubtful whether there is a single

culture known to history or anthropology that has not owed at
least ninety per cent of its constituent elements to cultural bor-
rowing."[79] "Modern Japan is ancient Japan attired in borrowed
clothing."[80]

The diffusion of culture has been constantly operating for
thousands of years; how far back it goes no one really knows.
Archeology keeps digging up artifacts and other evidence that
set the cultural beginnings farther and farther back. We now
know that cultural and societal organizations were established in
Mexico and South America more than fifteen thousand years ago;
the immigration of Asiatics by way of Siberia over the Aleutian
Straits into the Americas now goes back 25,000 to 30,000 years.
The Eskimo-domed igloo is an architectural and cultural product from Asia; the Romans put two arches together from Babylonia and created the two-arched forms which later led to the
Romanesque and Gothic types. The Mayas of Yucatan invented
the *Zero* sign as well as other positional values of numbers, yet
did not get the idea from the zero figure to invent a wheel; the
ancient Egyptians, Greeks, and Romans had the wheel but did
not think of creating the zero; it took time before they finally
got to each other. And so the constant diffusion of ideas, cultural
products, and social inventions went on everywhere and whenever infiltration and accessibility were possible. Inventions are
the results of *individualistic* creativeness, as ideas themselves can
emanate only from individuals, but even these come about from
the cumulative and diffusing effects of the intercommunication
and suggestibilities in the continual experience of and between
individuals and the environmental influences upon them. The
story of the Flood and the Ark comes from the Babylonian story
of Gilgamesh,* and the story of the Trinity of Christianity comes

---

*According to C. W. Ceram, "they [Sumerians] foreshadowed the Mosaic laws
before 3000 B.C., and the tale of the Flood, a late retelling of which was found in
Nineveh, is Sumerian in origin."[81] Regarding the manifold myths of the Flood,
Ericson and Wollin state: "The story of a fearful deluge appears in the legendary
history and folklore of many ancient peoples. A Chaldean legend recorded on
tablets found in the ruins of Nineveh is so similar in detail to the biblical story
as surely to have had a common origin. In turn the biblical account echoes the
Greek myth of Deucalion, who, forewarned by his father Prometheus, survived the
futile attempt by Zeus to destroy mankind by drowning. In the *Zend-Avesta,* the
sacred book of the old Persian religion, the story of a similar punishment by a
deluge occurs. Almost lost in the jungle of Cambodia, the sculpture and bas-

from most of the ancient religions of the Middle East. People do not cease remembering and start creating; they create because they remember.

It is evident from whatever knowledge we have of primitive cultures and those of the present that are not "Westernized" or "Christianized," that myth and ritual fulfilled a cohesive and therapeutic service and need antecedent to the rise of the formal priesthoods, kingships, and subsequent politico-religio-imperial forms of power and authority. These myths and rituals no doubt preserved the social entity of a family, clan, or tribe and gave vent to communication, chants, singing, dances, and various ceremonies which made life socially and culturally enjoyable and unifying. Wherever you go in Southeast Asia you will find the legend of Ramayana and Sita portrayed in many ways in dramas, dances, ceremonies, pictures, and so on. In Sanur I witnessed one evening this legend narrated in the village square by the use of a small sheet, oil lamps, and the shadowing of one's hands and fingers to create characters and figures; the squatting Balinese, though most of them have surely seen this done hundreds of times, were as exhilarated by the performance as if they were seeing it for the first time. Richard M. Dorson: "In closely knit communities a legend lives on through constant repetition. This repeated telling of the legend over the generations insures its folklore quality."[83]

Moreover, its elements—not merely religious or magical, but also interpretative of their origins and the protectiveness of ancestors and environment—provided the psychological security and power that primitive groups needed in order to stay together, share food and the environment peacefully, and protect each

reliefs of the ancient people of Ankor Vat vividly bring to life the Hindu legend that tells how Manu, one of the fourteen progenitors of mankind, saved the life of a fish—for which kind deed the creature rescued him when rising waters overwhelmed the world. Among the far off South Sea Islands they tell of the fisherman who caught his hooks in the water god's hair, which so angered the god that he drowned mankind, but strange to say spared the fisherman. Among northern people the Sagas tell of the Cimbrian flood. The almost worldwide persistence of a deluge myth suggests some common origin. More than ninety years ago Edward Clodd, in his scholarly book *The Childhood of Religion,* conjectured that fossil sea shells imbedded in rocks now many hundreds of feet above the level of the sea stimulated the imaginations of primitive men to invent stories of a universal flood."[82]

other against their common enemies. "In sum, myths and rituals jointly provide systematic protection against supernatural dangers, the threats of ill health and of the physical environment, antisocial tensions, and the pressures of a more powerful society. In the absence of a codified law and of an authoritarian chief, it is only through the myth-ritual system that the Navahos can present a unified front to all these disintegrating pressures. The all-pervasive configurations of word-symbols (myths) and of act-symbols (rituals) preserve the cohesion of the society and sustain the individual, protecting both from intolerable conflct."[84]

There is no question that this mutual-assistance pact evolved out of the causes and effects of evolving and living together, carrying on from generation to generation over long periods of time, became a *compatible necessity* without which the society or tribe could not continue to exist as such. In such an existence the individual, although naturally and culturally tied to his family, clan, or tribe, felt and expressed his natural freedom within a field that exacted no personal sense or sensitivity of a restricting or enslaving nature as it did later with the establishment of the arbitrary and militant power of the priesthood and imperialism. The Indian did not feel that he was *forced* to do this or that, or that he would be punished or killed if he did not believe in some new ideology, such as that expounded by the Spanish Catholic missionaries and the Protestant Puritans in early America. In studying the cultural forms of human history we must differentiate the protoprimitive and primitive forms of social order, wherein man was more naturally tied and integrated as a *participating* member of the rest of nature, his agricultural environment, and the animals he needed for food and those that preyed upon. Man, then, could not imagine a division between himself and *this* world in which he lived. All these aspects of nature and all these animals were parts of his family, spirited with his own spirit without status levels; he communicated with them constantly and they with him. The world was his kinship and his life was its life. The tragic diminishment of natural freedom came with the power and authority of those who were ideologically, fraudulently, or forcefully raised to *higher* levels for *their* good only and not for the good of the common man.

The padre-chief became the *Fatherland* and the common man became the *patriot,* emotionally and physically enslaved to serve and give his life for those higher levels who sought only to contain and expand their power and authority over him until he was helpless, willingly or unwillingly, but realistically helpless, a victim of resignation, futility, imposed acceptance, or patternization. Man thus ceased to be the *naturally free* animal and gradually became a "civilized" slave.

Human history is the story of this transition from early to modern forms, and democratic principle is the attempt to restore the early freedom forms in a modern compatibility in which man can express his intelligence without lessening his *naturalness,* his evolved ethics without lessening his *humanness,* his political and social orderliness without becoming an exploited slave or a confused nihilist, or a pawn to power-authority propaganda of a thousand shapes and colors; in which he can preserve a nonpsychotic and nonpathological ego to attain and fulfill a *naturally* happy, secure and satisfied life. This is not easy to attain, even with freedom, but at least we have the chance life has given us the right to by being born to it. Man can continue to have his dances, his songs and poetry, his legends and dreams and imaginings that are so colorful and inspiring, without end or limit of type, variety, or kind; he can still be the dreamer, the poet, the creator, which he will always be, anyway; he can still be curiosity's paramour and stretch his eyesight and his mechanisms to pierce the mysteries of the universe. He can still do all these things as part of *his life* as a human and as an animal, compatibly and rationally freed and free to enjoy what he has and might have, to extend it where he seeks farther, but all within *his world* and *his universe.* He can do this without exchanging the *only* life he really *knows* for something self-delusional and an acquired product of history.

Culture is an emergence from the biological assets of a creature which is the result of its particular evolution, its particular relationship to its particular environment, and the constant interplay of all these factors. Culture, it seems, did not emerge from any group psyche or collective consciousness, as was proposed in the writings of Durkheim and others, but in the evolved traits and habits of *individual creatures living together* in numbers of their own kind, in their relationships to each other, and in their peripheral environments and experiences. The individuality and individualism of living things verify themselves in the relationships of their experiences, and thus make possible the sequences, the continual play, of evolutional forces.

Evolution cannot turn back its own clock. It cannot repeat itself; evolution is nonrepeatable. The continuums and combinations of experiences cannot re-experience themselves *exactly*. The stream of experience is *constantly* new, though similarities and parallelisms continually give the impression of commonalities. Evolution, being the parent title of all nature in flux, verifies the individuality of all living things. It is the biological substratum of this individuality that made possible the evolution of noninherited acquisitions and the very core of cultural development.[85] Denzaburo Miyadi relates his observation of Japanese monkeys: "The monkey troop is undoubtedly a society of mutual acquaintance: each monkey knows every other monkey—its rank, status, mother-child relationship, and so on. Some of the infants, for example, are ranked high because they are the children of influential mothers. In these senses, each monkey troop has its own troop peculiarity and cultural trend, and each member of the troop differs from the other members in personality and life history."[86] Even here, we note the biological-into-cultural beginnings of the evolution of the authority-power drive of these animals, close cousins to *Homo*. "Man's capacity for culture did not appear all at once, complete and finished. The germs of this capacity, or raw materials from which it could be formed, exist in the animal world."[87] Sol Tax: "Culture is part of the biology of man, of course, even though it is passed on socially and not through genes. . . . Culture is part of the evolution of man. Man is evolving continually as a species, perhaps more rapidly now than any other species."[88] Dobzhansky: "Culture arose and developed in the human evolutionary sequence hand in hand with the genetic basis which made it possible. . . . To exclude in advance any consideration of the genetic basis from the study of culture is contrary to elementary rules of scientific procedure."[89]

We have seen that culture, its tendencies and products, depend on the relationship of an animal, such as the human being, to its environment. The primitive hunters, migratory food-gatherers (like the Bushmen in Kalahari today) living in mutual-assisting families or small groups in communalities of territory, produced animism, magical ritual, totemism, relativeness, and the interdependencies of individuals upon each other as a mode of survival. When the primitive became a farmer, stayed more or less in one place, carried on husbandry, agricultural plantings, raised and bred herds of cattle, these people evolved cultures leading to fertility rites, ancestor-worship, gods, dualism of spirit and matter, formalized religion. E. Cecil Curwen and Gudmund Hatt: "Agriculture arose very early as a kind of symbiosis between man and certain plants."[99] "The first steps in actual cultivation may be inferred from the remains of some of the earliest settlements in Egypt. Here we find a definite Neolithic culture the date of which has been estimated as between 6000 and 5000 B.C., mainly on geological grounds. Three manifestations of this culture have been observed, their authors being known respectively as the Tasians, the people of the Fayum, and the Merimdians, after the places where their remains have been found."[91] "The earliest traces of material civilization are found in Egypt, Syria, Mesopotamia, and the Indus Valley, with extensions over Persia and Baluchistan and as far north as Turkestan. These areas form one continuous block, the situation of which corresponds more or less with the area of distribution of the wild prototypes of wheat and barley, and the various cultures concerned are all based on agriculture."[92] "We can now see in broad outline a picture of man's cultural evolution and of the fundamental importance of the food quest as its determining factor. In fact, the rise of material civilization has been made possible at all only by the discovery of the possibilities of food production in the twin forms of agriculture and stockbreeding, accelerated by the division of labor involved in its industrial exploitation."[93] Tylor: "South Sea Islanders, though not a very rude people, when visited by Captain Cook, used only stone hatchets and knives, being indeed so ignorant of metal that they planted the first iron nails they got from the English sailors, in the hope of raising a new crop."[94]

Above it all, it created a growing sense of *property*. Property gave birth to *power of ownership,* and with this power came a whole gamut of cultures leading to the *civilized*-type culture. Civilized culture is a mixed porridge of various degrees. *Apparent* culture is what it seems to people through pretensions or the art of connivery, as through Maya. The *Ideal* culture is what some people *think up* as the world or the universe *appears to them,* as a result of reflecting *their* desires onto the cosmic screen culminating in the principle that people should or *ought* to live in certain ways but actually cannot because it would be impossible to fulfill the "ideal" and live sensibly at the same time. The *Real* culture is what they *actually* do. *Selective* culture is that which an individual adopts from his own and other cultures as a personal way of living his own life. *Mass* culture is the observable group-actions, motivations, and patterns of "mass" or group behavior in which individualistic selective or *free* approach has been diminished or negated.

The growth of authority and power was purchased through the sale of certain quanta of freedoms of people, and to this extent the people were subjected or enslaved and their lives denied the free and intelligent expression of living natural and normal lives. The cohesive agent used by those ambitious rulers in the secular and priestly castes was *fear*. A witty anecdote on what fear consists of is related by a former priest describing the effect of the Church upon little children: "I can recall many occasions when the babes were so frightened by the size of the church, the darkness of the confessional and their own sinfulness that they became incontinent. Then I would step outside, and signal the nearest nun, who rebuked the child and called someone to clean up the confessional."[95]

From the primitive little tribe, wherein all members participated and were compensated in a mutual-assistance pact, gradually modifying itself with the rise of agriculture, early urbanization, and walled-in fortified towns, arose the authority and power of the select few, who put reins upon their peoples and held them fast by the fears instituted by "sovereign" and "divine" power, the psychological powers of kingship and priestcraft. Between them they literally owned the people in this life and in the imaginary life to follow; in seamen's language, they were anchored down and held fast aft, forward, by the mid-beams, bow, and keel. Thus the ancient man, the Dark Ages man, the Middle Ages man, up to and including Modern man, the enculturated and indoctrinated fears institutionalized by king and priest, from the palatial balcony and the pulpit, conforming and abiding in the negation of the natural sense of freedom, became *caterpillars,* mindless, following, resigned caterpillars.

This has always brought on, in most people, a sort of help-lessness against social, political, and economic conditions, which made them into various kinds of masochists, to be used and ex-ploited by those in power. Regarding the old and the aged infirm who are institutionalized, and as a result find nonentity and a loss of their own beings as individuals, as *persons,* Jules Henry has a point that can be applied to the impact resulting from the constant pressures that sooner or later patternize people into a state of lethargic indifference to their own being, too weak to recover the spark and rebellious power of freedom, and thus try to recover the value, physical and intellectual, of their lives as *persons,* as beings. "Human beings everywhere," writes Henry, "are required to acquiesce in their material conditions of life and in the way they are socially defined, and the social definition of a person always imposes an attitude toward him by those who define his position in society. . . . Thus it comes about that acquiescence runs a gamut from social conformity to terror-stricken appeasement. Actually, in our culture, the problem of acquiescence is the problem of masochism, for the masochistic approach to life is merely an assent to life. . . . Hopelessness is the parent of acquiescence."[96] Here, the spirit of freedom is lost because only with a continued spirited sense of freedom does the self-identity of a person as an individual continue and with it the desire to pursue, to follow, to reach out one's being in trying to fulfill itself. *So long as fear exists, there is a loss of security,* and with it the restrictive and retarding effects of a lack of courage to reactivate the processes of freedom for reasser-tion and reconstruction. Clyde Kluckhohn: "So long as no se-curity exists for nations, just so long will insecurity and frustra-tion exist for the individuals comprising those nations. The sources of personal and social disorganization are fundamentally the same and inextricably interrelated."[97]

ACCRETION AND USES OF POWER AND THEIR EFFECTS

IT IS THE natural tendency of any form of power to accrue more power by widening its area of influence and control, or at least to try to maintain its already established or traditional power. In both the former and the latter the effect is in the diminishment of freedom to express and innovate idea and change, and to habituate a degenerating and deteriorating process in the behavior of people to resign themselves to a state of slavery and submission and to drift further and further away from the natural force and expression of freedom which is in the biological nuclear root of each living creature, as a life-unit and as an individual personality, whether a non-human or human animal. Bertrand Russell: "The rulers, in a theocracy, are likely to be fanatics; being fanatics they will be severe; being severe, they will be opposed; being opposed they will become more severe. Their power impulses will wear, even to themselves, the cloak of religious zeal, and will therefore be subject to no restraint. Hence the rack and the stake, the Gestapo and the Cheka."[98] Jawaharlal Nehru stated: "Whether it is from the point of view of some religion, or ideology, they are not troubled with the mental conflicts which are always the accompaniment of great ages of transition. And yet, even though it may be more comfortable to have fixed ideas and be complacent, surely that is not to be commended, and that can only lead to stagnation and decay."[99]

The expression of power is natural and normal in existential things; it is in the nature of the illogical pressures and resistances generated by these powers that so often bring conflict and misery. When a primitive ate the flesh of an animal, he thought he not only maintained his own "power" as a form of survival but also added the "spiritual" power of the victuals to the spiritual inventory of his own: to him this was an accretion of power. In a relative sense, the modern industrialist or financier, by building a greater fortune and a wider influence of prestige and power, is employing the same process as the primitive—the psychological effects and their resultant impetus are the same. To the ego of *Homo* the horizon is no marker of limitation; it will create and live in both heaven and hell under one roof to achieve its random and unpredictable desires, whatever they may be from time to time or at any moment. Thus the illogically-directed sense of power is extremist; it knows no moderation so long as its pressure is more powerful than the resistances it encounters. The now all-powerful egomaniac has convinced himself that the world has recognized his "divine" or "destined" role of beneficence to mankind and that the means he has used to reach this apex of power has been justified by the leading hand of the angels, or some gold tablet, some sign in the sky, or of some neurotic discovery of self-divinity or the elevation of oneself to supreme leadership out of the celestial purpose of the zodiac. For the rest of the people their "divine" and "destined" role is to be good little children and abide by what the "Great Father" tells them to do. "Some men's characters lead them always to command, others always to obey; between these extremes lie the mass of average human beings."[100] "Men who allow their love of power to give them a distorted view of the world are to be found in every asylum: one man will think he is the Governor of the Bank of England, another will think he is the King, and yet another will think he is God."[101] "Human life being a perpetual interaction between volition and uncontrollable facts, the philosopher who is guided by his power impulses seeks to minimize or decry the part played by facts that are not the result of our own will. I am thinking now not merely of men who glorify naked power, like Machiavelli and Thrasymachus in *The Republic;* I am thinking of men who invent theories which veil their own love of power beneath a garment of metaphysics or ethics. The first of such philosophers in modern times, and also the most thoroughgoing, is Fichte."[102] "Alexander and Augustus asserted that they were gods, and compelled others to pretend agreement; Fichte, not being in control of the government, lost his job on a charge of atheism, since he could not well proclaim his own divinity."[103] Mussolini, Hitler, Stalin and others expressed an approval of their "divinity" in leadership, exercising their "moral" means of executing those who opposed them. Sukarno of Indonesia, Nkrumah in Ghana, Castro in Cuba, and many others repeat the same process today. Franco of Spain is an excellent example of the rapprochement of church and secular leadership to benefit each other by the maintenance of the power weapon over the Spanish people. Herbert L. Matthews writes of the struggle for freedom in Spain today: "The genius is there. So is the spirit. So is the urge to freedom. But they are not universal. The rulers of Spain since Ferdinand and Isabel have been the traditionalists—the kings, the aristocrats, the generals and the priests. Each time the people rose or freedom asserted itself, one or the other of them, or all together, would clamp the lid back again. This is what happened after the Napoleonic War when a perfidious and wicked king—Ferdinand VII—returned to the throne. That is what happened in 1939 when a *caudillo*—Generalissimo Francisco Franco—slammed another lid down and sat on it."[104] "One of the aims of the rebellion by the generals was to crush the upsurge of workers and peasants."[105] "The landowners and employers were supported by the Army and the Church. All four supported the Monarchy as long as it lasted and tried to make the Monarchy a shield for their interests. But the protection was against the people—the peasants, the workers and the intellectuals."[106] "The combination of a powerful Catholic lobby in Washington and the prevailing isolationism were more than enough to keep the United States 'neutral' in the Spanish War and to maintain the arms embargo."[107] I have always had a great regard and respect for the liberal innovations and progressive ideas of Franklin D. Roosevelt, but he seems in this instance to be a practical politician, and he safeguarded the vote he needed for re-election in the larger and Catholic cities by submitting to the will of the Catholic hierarchy in America to initiate and maintain an arms embargo against the Spanish people, who were fighting and giving up their lives in order to free themselves from the tyrannical intentions of both dictatorship and clericalism and to maintain their first attempt to create for themselves a democratic and reasonably free society.

Regarding the rise of Hitlerism in Germany, Jesuit Father Delph (against whose murder by the Nazis in Plötzensee the

Vatican did not lift a finger) said: "An honest . . . cultural history will have to include some bitter chapters about the churches' contributions to the creation of mass man, of collectivism, of dictatorial forms of government."[108] Before Garibaldi, Mazzini, and others liberated Italy from Papal tyranny and foreign domination, the Church, following principles established long before Metternich, opposed any freedom for the people. "In the Papal States the main cause of complaint was the failure of the Papacy to restore municipal liberties, and its refusal to allow laymen to play any part in government."[109] Cardinal Antonelli would rather see the Italian dead piled high on the barricades in the streets of Rome than to see them free and the Papal power diminished.

The effects of European authority-power psychoses, created by the imperial-clerical combines continued and evolved over many centuries and, nurtured by the general ignorance and fears of people, were tragic, cruel, and merciless whenever and wherever they cast their shadow over the homes and lives of millions of innocent people. Thomas Jefferson: "Millions of innocent men, women and children, since the introduction of Christianity, have been burnt, tortured, fined, imprisoned, yet we have not advanced one inch toward uniformity. What has been the effect of coercion? To make one-half the world fools, and the other half hypocrites."[110] James Bryce, in his *The American Commonwealth,* wrote: "Half the wars of Europe, half the internal troubles that have vexed European states, from the Monophysite controversies in the Roman Empire of the fifth century down to the Kulturkampf in the German Empire of the nineteenth, have arisen from theological differences or from the rival claims of church and state."[111] "After four hundred years of Church dominance in Mexico the people it had 'educated' were ignorant beyond belief."[112]

In his historical account of the Hopi Indians Frank Waters writes: "The hated (Spanish Catholic) mission at Oraibi is still referred to as the 'slave church.' The huge logs used as its roof beams had to be dragged by Hopis from the hills around Kísiwu, forty miles northeast, or from the San Francisco mountains, nearly a hundred miles south. Still today the Hopis point out the great ruts scraped into the soft sandstone of the mesa top by the ends of the heavy logs as they were dragged into place. Enforced labor not only built the church but supplied all the needs of the priests. Tradition recalls that one *padre* would not drink water from any of the springs around Oraibi: he demanded that a runner bring his water from White Sands Spring near Moencopi, fifty miles away. The *padres'* illicit relations with young Hopi girls were common in all villages, and the punishment given Hopis for sacrilege and insubordination added to the growing resentment. It is recorded that at Oraibi in 1655, when Friar Salvador de Guerra caught a Hopi in 'an act of idolatry,' he thrashed the Hopi in the presence of the whole village till he was bathed in blood, and then poured over him burning turpentine. Under these strict measures the Hopis adopted Christianity."[113]

This was the "grace" of the Cross, its humble humility and the champion of the oppressed! Juan Comas: "The exploitation by the whites of agriculture and mining in the newly-discovered countries from the fifteenth century onwards created slavery, particularly the enslavement of Negroes and American Indians. . . . In point of fact, the causes of white aggression were fundamentally economic; the whites seized the richer lands inhabited by coloured populations and reduced the latter to slavery to secure a ready source of labor which would increase the value of their recent acquisitions."[114] "Too often the Negro is still in a position of economic semi-slavery, he is enmeshed in a network of restrictions, partly legal and partly not. Poverty, contempt and disease have made him what he is today."[115]

Bertrand Russell defined power as "the production of intended effects."[116] Accordingly, it would follow that the effects of such intentions in the history of man's political, social, economic and religious institutions have not been very salubrious to mankind and to its freedom. On the subject of religion's *intended effects,* we find the sequences have been disastrous to freedom and to the life of man. "On the whole, the gods behave badly. Even Jehovah, who inspires so much enthusiasm among monotheists, when stripped of modern interpretation, is found to be ruthlessly intolerant and as bloody as any Aztec war god. The gods behave precisely as they do because they are gods. They are immune to the price that ordinary men must pay for living in a social situa-

tion. They are therefore at liberty to be heroically priapic, cannibalistic, castrators and castrated; anarchists of sex, they commit
incest gaily and do not shrink from sodomy, bestiality or copro-
philia. Indeed blood and sex seem to be the stuff from which
ritual is made."[117]—the conclusion of *In the Beginnings* by H. R.
Hays.

Herbert J. Muller states: "The Church can hardly be blamed
for welcoming the power it got from Constantine, but in the
exercise of this power it can be charged with betraying its Christian faith."[118] Bertrand Russell: "The Catholic Church, after
three centuries of persuasion, captured the State in the time of
Constantine, and then, by force, established a system of propaganda which converted almost all the pagans and enabled Christianity to survive the barbarian invasion."[119] Before the expected
Dies Irae (the world's end in the year A.D. 1000) the hysteria of
people to dispose of their property was practically in a state of
panic; everyone was preparing to meet the Lord in a cataclysm
that was to destroy the world. Martin A. Larson: "For years,
thousands had been selling their possessions or had conveyed their
lands, slaves, and serfs to the less believing but more practical
prelates of the Church, which, as a result, became the wealthiest
landowner and exploiter in the world."[120] These *intended effects*
were further exposed by Henry Charles Lea, in his *History of
Auricular Confession:* "Through the instrumentality of the confessional, the sodality and the indulgence, its matchless organization (that is, the Church's) is thus enabled to concentrate in the
Vatican a power greater than has ever before been wielded by
human hands."[121]

These *intended effects* in the fields of education, science, medicine are further explained by A. D. White: "Here we have survivals of that same oppression of thought by theology which has
cost the modern world so dear; the system which forced great
numbers of professors, under penalty of deprivation, to teach
that the sun and planets revolve around the earth; that comets
are fireballs flung by an angry God at a wicked world; that insanity is a diabolic possession; that anatomical investigation of
the human frame is sin against the Holy Ghost; that chemistry
leads to sorcery; that taking interest for money is forbidden by

Scripture; that geology must conform to ancient Hebrew poetry. From the same source came in Austria the rule of the 'Immaculate Oath,' under which university professors, long before the dogma of the Immaculate Conception was defined by the Church, were obliged to swear to their belief in that dogma before they were permitted to teach even arithmetic or geometry; in England, the denunciation of inoculation against smallpox; in Scotland, the protests against using chloroform in childbirth as 'vitiating the primal curse against woman'; in France, the use in clerical schools of a historical textbook from which Napoleon was left out; and in America, the use of Catholic manuals in which the Inquisition is declared to have been a purely civil tribunal, or Protestant manuals in which the Puritans are shown to have been all we could now wish they had been."[122]

Here are a few more *intended effects:* Herbert J. Muller informs us: "In England the Anglican Church was in the vanguard of the violent Tory reaction against democratic ideals that dominated politics in the Napoleonic and post-Waterloo era. The Archbishop of Canterbury expressed its temper by helping to defeat a bill providing for elementary schools: Protestant as well as Catholic churchmen were long fearful of public education as a threat to the traditional order."[123] "Christians have yet to learn the plainest lesson of history, that the churches have always consecrated some particular temporal order or ideology, in effect committed themselves to idolatry, in order to support their worldly interests. As medieval Catholicism blessed the feudal order, so Protestantism came to bless the bourgeois order, likewise without a serious, sustained effort to judge or transform it."[124] "In the reactionary era following Waterloo, the major churches everywhere supported Prince Metternich's policy of restoring all the traditional powers of monarchs and the nobility, or 'gentlemen,' and his relentless warfare on all popular agitation for more liberty and equality."[125] "The Roman Catholic Church met this challenge just as it had dealt with the Protestant Reformation, by an absolute refusal to a compromise. The papacy rejected the whole democratic creed, while calling more insistently for the complete obedience of all Catholics to its decrees. Pope Gregory XVI denounced the 'deadly and execrable liberty' of the press, and with it 'the absurd and erroneous maxim, or rather insanity' of liberty of conscience."[126] Philip Wylie: "Liberty—the room for honesty—is everywhere a confining chamber, a theory but not much a practice, a condition believed to exist hugely until its measurements are examined. The intolerant churches have compressed it. Or they have kept it from expanding. This is an incessant catastrophe; it has given the churches their power —swelled up religious pride where freedom ought to grow—and slain conscience everywhere in the name of Christ."[127] Paul Blanshard: "The Church is a sustaining partner in the whole economic scheme of repression and control. While professing to stand for free trade unionism and free enterprise in the United States and in Northern Europe, the hierarchy gives sanction and respectability to a labor-capital straitjacket which denies and contradicts the basic requirements of freedom [in Spain]."[128] "Even the Church's collaboration with the Franco dictatorship in Spain, one of the most notorious facts in contemporary politics, is almost never mentioned in Congress although it has special religious significance for the American people. American money is keeping Franco's government alive, and that government is openly destroying religious liberty in Spain with Catholic support."[129]

The story of the robber-baron-kings, their exploitation of the people and their "divinely" free hand in murdering opposition, competitors, and heresy on pretext in order to confiscate possessions and property of the victims, and their collusion and collaboration with, and support of, the Church that shared in the spoils, is a most tragic and nauseating history, which often becomes unprintable; the story of Clovis and how he was accepted and favored by the Church is in itself so vile that it is best for it to be hidden and forgotten.[130] Brigadier General F. P. Crozier confesses to the use of churches for arousing the soldier and citizen to war and bestiality: "The Christian churches are the finest blood-lust creators we have and of them we made free use."[131]

Evaluating the *intended effects* of the missionaries in South America, Dr. Herbert S. Dickey writes: "South Americans are long suffering, they put up with much, especially from North Americans, and I sometimes wonder what would happen in our country if a band of priests from the southern continent were to visit the vicinity of one of our churches and exercise a little reciprocity."[132] Regarding these missionaries, Peter Mathiessen adds: "The exposure of a primitive tribe to missionaries, however successful—because of the care, generosity, and devotion of the missionaries, the tribe is almost always benefited at the outset— is followed more often than not by its extinction, through the subsequent exploitation, mixed breeding, alcohol, and disease that arrive not with the advent of the Word but with civilization."[133] "How affecting it is to see the Indian, unchanged by the intervening centuries, paying to Mass the same mindless coca-numbed obeisance that his forebears awarded the Temple of the Sun. There he kneels, ragged and hunched against the cold, before the same gold and silver, now long since refashioned into the panoply of the Church."[134] "One wonders at times why the Communist Party hasn't made more progress, Church or no Church, because its the peasants who are getting it in the neck. But one forgets about the appalling ignorance which stands in the way of constructive resistance, an ignorance which the Church itself, with its use of mystique and sacrament, tends to perpetuate —I hate to say 'encourage,' but the fact is that in backward countries or communities ignorance appears to be the Church's hand-maiden: at the very least, the two are often seen in company."[135]

Not only was the Indian and the African exploited in his very compound but even mail-order tactics have been used to squeeze every last nickel out of them even from afar. The Churches and their commercial agents kept selling anything that these poor people would buy, superstitional things, luck charms, miracle medals, saintly bottles of blessed waters, and many others. Albert Schweitzer tells us: "Probably every one of them—and one and another more than once—has sent his month's wages to Europe to receive in exchange his horoscope or a talisman."[136] These are a few instances; many volumes could be added in regard to the *intended effects* of organized religion upon the freedom of man. Barrows Dunham: "With what astonishment did the Renaissance mind discover that the world could be known and controlled and enjoyed without the smallest use of Christian eschatology. The discovery was as vast as it was astounding, but it had taken fifteen hundred years!"[137]

COMMUNISM AND FASCISM

Let us take a brief look at the *intended effects* of the socio-politico-religious forms of authority and power. We have noted that the primitive little village of kinships was a cooperative in which participatng and compensating equities were simply entered into as a group of individuals, functioning as a mutual-assisting group, maintained itself for survival. Later the kingships and priestcrafts took over, usurped authority and power, and subjected and exploited the people to their will and dominion. Here and there rebellious attempts were made to break down these yokes; some succeeded, most of them failed. Then came the Age of Revolution, beginning with America and France breaking through the armor of the privileged and self-appointed few. *Republics* were formed, that is, democratic forms of government by which the people could ordain the kind of rule by which they should abide in living together as a society and nation. But the Industrial Revolution brought new problems: power expressed itself through wealth and finance and formed invisible kingships and economic nobilities over workers. "There is an important difference," writes Bertrand Russell, "between the dynamics of organizations embodying sentiments to be realized by cooperation and that of those whose purposes essentially involve conflict."[138] Karl Marx and others wrote manifestos calling for the workers to rebel against their exploiters. What Karl Marx overlooked was that *principles* fly out of the window when the intoxicants of power and authority come in through the front door. Out of the rebellious rise of the workers, crying out for relief and reform, came leaders, and these leaders were humans, and these humans became powerful and authoritarian. Again the power and authority of the one or the few held sway and still hold sway over the peoples of present-day Communist countries. The Communist manifestos were supposed to free the peasants and the farmers from their bondage, but the peasants found a new enslavement under the oligarchic rule of arbitary and naked power. David Mitrany: "In every instance, in fact, the Marxist agrarian idea has had to be applied by force and to rely on force for its survival, while the Socialists who wanted to remain democrats have in every instance had to abandon it."[139]—revealing the fallacious approach of Communism to the peasant and the agrarian problem in general.

Communist, Fascist, and other dictatorial-authoritarian police states have one thing in common: the principle that people exist to maintain and strengthen the *State,* that is, to maintain the power and authority of the leader or leaders who hold and control the State as their *personal* power. Again we see the recurrence of this power form from its former expression in the regencies of king and priest (who also held, and still hold, that the people live for the State, that is, for the King, and for God, that is, for the priests). "This is the essential difference between the liberal outlook and that of the totalitarian State, that the former regards the welfare of the State as residing ultimately in the welfare of the individual, while the latter regards the State as the end and individuals merely as indispensable ingredients, whose welfare must be subordinated to a mystical totality which is a cloak for the interests of the rulers."[140] Karl Shapiro, in his essay on Henry Miller, writes: "To place the individual before the state, whether the Russian state or the American state, is the first need of modern man. . . . Modern life, having made everyone state conscious, has destroyed the individual."[141]

Jawaharlal Nehru writes about Communism: "We see the growing contradictions within the rigid framework of communism itself. Its suppression of individual freedom brings about powerful reactions. Its contempt for what might be called the moral and spiritual side of life not only ignores something that is basic in man but also deprives human behavior of standards and values. Its unfortunate association with violence encourages a certain evil tendency in human beings."[142] John Dewey, referring to Communism: "It is ironical that the theory which has made the most display and the greatest pretense of having a scientific foundation should be the one which has violated most systematically every principle of scientific method."[143] "Marxism systematically neglects everything on the side of human nature with respect to its being a factor having efficacy, save as it is previously determined by the state of the forces of production. . . . Marxism throws out psychological as well as moral considerations."[144]

On the other hand, Fascists and dictators use the wolfcry of

Communism to frighten people into allowing them to take over the control of peoples and nations. Referring to the Franco rebellion in Spain, Herbert L. Matthews states: "The charge that the Republicans were planning or would have succumbed to a Communist revolution is nonsense. . . . The Spanish Communists were of no importance before the war or when it began. The Republican leaders were good men in the moral sense, well-intentioned, liberal and democratic."[145] In another way, the diseases of Communism and Fascism are invited to infiltrate because of the greed and shortsightedness of even the democratic countries, who complacently or stupidly allow these ailments to enter into the political and social life of a neighbor. Economic greed is too often found to be the basic and rooted cause of those who, while professing to be democrats, do business with any Communist or Fascist régime so long as profits can thus accrue to them, or else pretend to be intellectuals while getting richer and richer by exploiting, enslaving, and misleading their own native people and keeping these natives poor, ignorant, and religious. How this brought Fascism in Italy, in Germany, Communism in China and now in Cuba, are matters too clear for any student to bypass. Fred J. Cook states: "Not Russia, but the Chinese, took China from Chiang. Not Russia, but the Cubans, took Cuba from Batista. Communism did not win a battle ninety miles from our shores; we lost it. We lost it because we had insisted for years on supporting the horribly brutal Batista dictatorship, in intensifying the misery of Cuba, until, in the final and inevitable and violent explosion, that tragic country was afflicted with Castro."[146]

USES OF POWER TO CONVERT, ENSLAVE, EXPLOIT, AND MASSACRE

EVEN TODAY, WITH all the good intentions of the United States to assist the people of Latin America, to further industrial and agrarian reforms, push better housing, cleaner and better standards of living, lessen exploitation of the *peones* and workers, our moneys and hopes stop at the doorsteps of the political and military aristocrats and *stay there*. Little, if any, finds its proper and honest way to the common people; thus the wealth, prestige, and power of the great landowners stay intact. In almost all Latin American countries we will usually find a small number of wealthy families and cliques getting richer and richer while the people get poorer and poorer.

In many parts of the Brazilian hinterland and in the backhills of Peru and Chile, the Indians, realizing that the politicians, military brass oligarchies, and landowners work together, are slowly returning to the hills, back to the jungles to renew some form of primitive life having only wild animals and the jungle to contend with, lesser and more compatible enemies than the power-thirsty, enslaving, and thieving "civilized" patrons of the arts and the oratorical politicians who have kept them enslaved and who have emasculated them for centuries, and will continue to do so until they are stopped by force and eliminated. Hitler and Mussolini had to be disposed of in this manner, also. Fascism, being a disease, cannot be talked into leaving our minds and bodies. Like a disease, it has to be treated as such and its germs have to be destroyed. Bertrand Russell: "Fascism is not an ordered set of beliefs, like *laissez-faire* or Socialism or Communism; it is essentially an emotional protest, partly of those members of the middle class (such as small shopkeepers) who suffer from modern economic development, partly of anarchic industrial magnates whose love of power has grown into megalomania. It is irrational, in the sense that it cannot achieve what its supporters desire; there is no philosophy of Fascism, but only a psychoanalysis. If it could succeed, the result would be widespread misery; but its inability to find a solution for the problem of war makes it impossible that it should succeed for more than a brief moment."[147]

It is no wonder that any philosopher or political observer becomes disillusioned about the optimum dreams of those who feel that humans are continually "progressing" and that their "civilizations" are "greater" and "higher." In a way, Everett Dean Martin writes hopefully: "Revolutions have their passing hour and are gone. They come like dreams of horror, they pass and leave but exhaustion and sad awakening. But the stream of wisdom coursing through the centuries flows steadily on. Lost for a time it reappears richer and deeper than before. It has brought with it such freedom and civilization as man has not yet known. It is the life of reason which will yet create the republic of the free."[148] Bertrand Russell gives his version: "In the visible world, the Milky Way is a tiny fragment; within this fragment, the Solar System is an infinitesimal speck, and of this speck our planet is a microscopic dot. On this dot tiny lumps of impure carbon and water, of complicated structure, with somewhat unusual physical and chemical properties, crawl about for a few years, until they are dissolved again into the elements of which they are compounded. They divide their time between labor designed to postpone the moment of dissolution for themselves and frantic struggles to hasten it for others of their kind. Natural convulsions periodically destroy some thousands or millions of them, and disease prematurely sweeps away many more. These events are considered to be misfortune; but when men succeed in inflicting similar destruction by their own efforts, they rejoice, and give thanks to God. In the life of the solar system the period during which the existence of man will have been physically possible is a minute portion of the whole; but there is some reason to hope that even before this period is ended man will have set a term to his own existence by his efforts at mutual annihilation."[149] It may come to pass that Martin and Russell were both right: man may build the "perfect" society that would be just too good for humans and in which there would be neither freedom nor humanity, just a perfect, meaningless dream, like an empty star that illuminates the heavens that no one can see.

When a philosopher studies the nature of man and his history, it is not difficult for him to summarize the human being as a cruel and merciless animal. True, we know that many people are good, kind, gracious, whether rich or poor, whether weak or powerful, but these seem to be the negligible few compared with the many. Only education, continued enlightenment, the enculturation of ethics in the young, and their training to think properly, reasonable standards of living and security in order to enjoy the more or less normal satisfactions of life: these might divert the predatory instincts and traits of human nature to more enjoyable and peaceful modes of living. Let us reflect upon

a few events in human history, so that we can better understand
the attitude of Russell and his dim outlook for any genuine
progressiveness in the nature of man and his societies.

The Spaniards began to build their empire in the sixteenth
century. Prescott and others have written enough about them
and what they did in Mexico and South America and in the
Southwest of the United States. William Brandon tells us how
they built their empire in the West Indies and the Carib area:
"Spain persisted in laboriously fulfilling her destiny of constructing, from the world of Indians, that greatest of empires. However,
the people who were that empire were oddly ungrateful for their
destiny. Their gods and homes were shattered, and from an enjoyment of living they were turned into working for it. They
lost their subtle, mystic pride and forgot their very names, so that
they called themselves by the Spanish names for Big Ears or
Short Hairs. They died in massive numbers from measles, smallpox, cholera, and tuberculosis, from starvation, incredible over-
work, from desperation, from sheer horror at inhumanities they
could not believe even while they were happening. They died
drunk, they died insane, they died by their own hands; they
died, they said, because their souls were stolen. They vanished
in such numbers that African Negroes could not be shipped fast
enough to take their places. Their children were born dead,
from syphilis; or their women, rotted with syphilis, became unable to bear children at all."[150]

Brandon's description of Spanish "kindness" to the Caribs and
Arawaks continues: "In his bitter attacks on Spanish brutality,
Las Casas apparently did not exaggerate the details. Population
estimates for Indians in Cuba, Puerto Rico, Española, and Jamaica at the time of the Spanish arrival vary widely, from 200,000
to 4,000,000. What is known, however, is that by the end of the
16th century a great part of these Indians had been wiped out,
directly or indirectly, by the conquerors."[151] Peter Farb: "The
Spaniards set the loving and gentle Arawak to labor in mines and
on plantations. Whole Arawak villages disappeared through slavery, disease, and warfare, as well as by flight into the mountains.
As a result, the native population of Haiti, for example, declined
from an estimated 200,000 in 1492 to a mere 29,000 only twenty-

two years later."[152] Spanish "kindness" to Spaniards also expressed itself: "The spectacle of priests inciting Indians to murder settlers and settlers inciting Indians to murder priests was not unknown. Each courted the Indians with one eye and winked at subterfuge slavery with the other."[153]

Regarding the decimation of the natives in Mexico, Benjamin Keen informs us: "The Indian population of Mexico, according to a recent estimate based on published tribute records, declined from approximately 16,871,406 in 1532 to 2,649,573 in 1568; 1,372,228 in 1595, and 1,069,255 in 1608."[154] The number of Indian servants available for the Spaniards no doubt dwindled in time but the times allowed a free exploitation of the local human supply. "Indians built the countless churches and monasteries of New Spain and provided for the wants of the numerous clergy. In one convent alone, the *visitador* Valderrama found more than one hundred and ninety Indian servants."[155]

Regarding the historical relations between the whites and the Indians, Alvin M. Josephy, Jr.: "No one will ever know how many Indians of how many tribes were enslaved, tortured, debauched, and killed. No one can ever reckon the dimensions of the human tragedy that cost, in addition to lives, the loss of homes, dignity, cultural institutions, and liberty and freedom to millions upon millions of people. The stain is made all the darker by the realization that the conflict was forced upon those who suffered; the aggressors were the whites, the scenes of tragedy the very homelands of the victims. . . . In the bitter narrative of man's suppression and extermination of his fellow man in the Americas, no single European nation or special group of whites was more—or less—blameworthy than others."[156] Bartolomé de Las Casas, a contemporary of those times, wrote of his observations: "They [the Spaniards] came with their Horsemen well armed with Sword and Launce, making most cruel havocks and slaughters. . . . Overrunning Cities and Villages, where they spared no sex nor age; neither would their cruelty pity Women with childe, whose bellies they would rip up, taking out the Infant to hew it in pieces. They would often lay wagers who should with most dexterity either cleave or cut a man in the middle. . . . The children they would take by the feet and dash their innocent heads against the rocks, and when they were fallen into the water, with a strange and cruel derision they would call upon them to swim. . . . They erected certain Gallowses . . . upon every one of which they would hang thirteen persons, blasphemously affirming that they did it in honour of our Redeemer and his Apostles, and then putting fire under them, they burnt the poor wretches alive. Those whom their pity did think to spare, they would send away with their hands half cut off, and so hanging by the skin."[157] These deeds were done by whites, Christians, with crosses on their armor, in the name of their God and His saints.

Claude Lévi-Strauss throws some light on the introduction of European civilization and religion among the Brazilian tribes for the Portuguese: "The Portuguese colonists in the sixteenth century were a brutal, money-grubbing lot. . . . They used to grab hold of the Indians, tie them to the cannons' mouth and blow them to pieces."[158] Peter Matthiessen also informs us about the gradual extermination of the Indians who inhabited the Tierra del Fuego area at the southern end of South America: "The seven to nine thousand Indians thought to inhabit Tierra del Fuego at the time of the settlement of Ushuaia were reduced eighty years later to fewer than two hundred pure-breds; today not more than one hundred Alacalufes eke out an existence in the Chilean islands, and the Yahgans and Onas, a handful of old people excepted, are gone."[159] Matthiessen continues to expose the white man's gentility towards the Indians in the rubber regions of South America: "Someone has estimated that the number of Indians butchered in the few decades of the rubber boom exceeded all the lives lost in World War I—this figure entirely apart from the thousands who died in slavery. To this day the wild peoples of the interior rivers are considered by most South Americans as subhuman creatures, to be shot on sight—not, it should be said, that North Americans are in a very good position to bewail the matter."[160] Josephy, Jr.: "Conflicts among the white men often arose over whether Indians were more valuable free and alive, or enslaved, or dead. Looters, exploiters, and adventurers argued in an attempt to prove that since Indians were not acquisitive, did not hunt gold for themselves, and resisted doing more work than was necessary to feed themselves, they therefore were not normal people but rather members of a subhuman or animal species, lacking souls."[161] The "civilizing" process goes on today in the Amazon: "Today the savages of the Amazonian forests are caught, like game-birds, in the trap of our mechanistic civilization. . . . To have destroyed the Indians is not enough—the public may, indeed, not realize that the destruction has taken place—and what the reader wants is to satisfy, in some sort, the cannibal-instincts of the historical process to which the Indians have already succumbed."[162]

The God-fearing and God-worshipping Americans did *their* share for the native Indians throughout the country. The "civilizing" process goes on today with the result that every act of civilization leaves the Indians with less land and more poverty. With the land boom and settlement expansion now going on in Alaska, every attempt is being made and every kind of pretext used by land exploiters to wrest more reservation land away from the Indians and Eskimos. Brandon relates a few instances of the protection of the Indians by the Great White Father: "As the Indians were increasingly cowed there was the usual increase of lawlessness on the part of opportunistic whites, which goaded new wars into being. Military commanders, sent to Oregon to protect American settlers, found that they had to spend much of their effort vainly trying to protect the Indians from outrages by white men. These outrages were sometimes deliberately intended to keep the hostilities burning, due to a quite sincere belief in many quarters (and an eye on profit in others) that the Indians should be wholly exterminated. 'Let our motto be extermination and death to all opposers,' said a newspaper in Yreka, a trading town in the California-Oregon border country—whose merchants, incidentally, sold goods to a volunteer Indian-chasing expedition in 1854 at such exorbitant prices that the commanding general on the Pacific Coast sent a protest to Washington against paying the expedition's expenses, alleging that the expedition was unnecessary and had only been drummed up as a speculation to benefit the suppliers."[163] Referring to Chief Joseph and his efforts to conciliate peace for his Indian tribe, General Howard revealed the result: "I think that, in his long career, Joseph cannot accuse the Government of the United States of one single act of justice."[164] General George Crook describes his personal opinion of Indians: "I have never yet seen one so demoralized that he was not an example in honor and nobility compared to the wretches who plunder him of the little our government appropriates for him."[165] Yet "General Phil Sheridan had urged the destruction of the bison herds, correctly predicting that when they disappeared the Indians would disappear along with them; by 1885 the bison were virtually extinct, and the Indians were starving to death on the plains."[166]

The Pilgrims and Puritans, with their Bibles, having escaped from persecution so they could think and believe freely in accord with their consciences, which had been denied them by the traditional Catholicism in Europe, felt that the Indians were animals and therefore were not to be considered as people with consciences. The Puritans were "honest" people, yet they did not consider it dishonest to take away the lands of the Indians, burning their homes and killing their women and children in the name of the Lord. This is what the Plymouth governor wrote in his memoirs regarding such an attack by the Pilgrims upon a Pequot Indian village: "It was a fearful sight to see them frying in the fire . . . and horrible was the stink and stench thereof. . . . But the victory seemed a sweet sacrifice and they have praise thereof to God."[167] "Cotton Mather was grateful to the Lord that 'on this day we have sent six hundred heathen souls to hell.' "[168]

Frank Waters: "The Anglo-Protestants were cold-blooded, deeply inhibited, and bound by their Puritan traditions, they began a program of complete extermination of all Indians almost from the day they landed on Plymouth Rock. . . . The precedent was set by a Pequot massacre shortly after the *Mayflower* arrived. Of this Cotton Mather wrote proudly: 'The woods were almost cleared of those pernicious creatures, to make room for a better growth.' . . . A century and a half later Benjamin Franklin echoed this opinion when he wrote of 'the design of Providence to extirpate those savages in order to make room for the cultivators of the earth.' "[169]

The Puritan descendants in the nineteenth century were even worse. To take into account any abbreviated narration of the crimes committed against all the American Indian tribes within the United States and the Polynesians in the Hawaiian Islands, among many other places, by the white civilized people of America and Europe would take volumes, and a stout heart to read them. Regarding the Hawaiians, W. Storrs Lee states: "Along with the Bible, the alphabet, and clever gadgets, foreigners also imported all the diseases and disorders their ancestors had been hatching for thousands of years, as well as enough bacteria and insect life to keep the Islanders everlastingly supplied with afflictions."[170]

If I had to recommend just one book to read, I would suggest *Ishi*. Theodora Kroeber, wife of the anthropologist, did a meritorious work in this great epitaph to the last "wild" Indian in California. In this book Sim Moak describes the manner in which some whites costumed themselves with the scalps of Indians they had killed: "After Good had taken all the scalps, he took a buckskin string and sack needle and tied a knot in the end and salted the scalp and run [sic] the needle through it down to the knot, then tied another knot about two inches above the scalp and it was ready for the next one. The string was fastened to his belt and you can imagine a great tall man with a string of scalps from his belt to his ankle."[171] Frank Waters tell us about the great morals and civilizing influences of the Great White Father: "As early as 1641, New Netherlands began offering bounties for Indian scalps. The practice was adopted in 1704 by Connecticut, and then by Massachusetts, where the Reverend Solomon Stoddard of Northampton urged settlers to hunt Indians with dogs as they did bears. Virginia and Pennsylvania followed suit, the latter in 1764, offering rewards for scalps of Indian bucks, squaws, and boys under ten years of age. . . . In 1814 a fifty-dollar reward for Indian scalps was proclaimed by the Territory of Indiana. In Colorado, legislation was offered placing bounties for the 'destruction of Indians and skunks.' By 1876, in Deadwood, Dakota Territory, the price of scalps had jumped to two hundred dollars. In Oregon a bounty was placed on Indians and coyotes. Indians were trailed with hounds, their springs poisoned. Women were clubbed to death, and children had their brains knocked out against trees to save the expense of lead and powder. . . . Massacres of entire tribes and villages such as that of Sand Creek, Colorado, in 1864, were not uncommon. Here a village of Cheyennes and Arapahoe were asleep in their lodges when the Reverend J. M. Chivington, a minister of the Methodist Church and a presiding elder in Denver, rode up with a troop of volunteers. 'Kill and scalp all Indians, big and little,' he ordered, 'since nits make lice.' Without warning, every Indian was killed—75 men, 225 old people, women and children. Scalps were then taken to Denver and exhibited on the stage of a theater. . . . Wholesale removal of whole tribes from reservations granted them by solemn treaties was in order whenever their land was found to be valuable. The Cherokee Nation was the largest of the Iroquois tribes; its people had invented an alphabet and had written a constitution, establishing a legislature, a judiciary, and executive branch. In 1794, in accordance with a treaty made with the United States, the Cherokees were confined to seven million acres of mountain country in Georgia, North Carolina, and Tennessee. In 1828 gold was discovered on their land. The Georgia legislature passed an act confiscating all Cherokee lands, declaring all laws of the Cherokee Nation to be null and void, and forbidding Indians to testify in court against whites. The confiscated lands were distributed by lottery to whites. . . . The case of the Cherokee Nation came up before the Supreme Court. The Chief Justice rendered his decision, upholding the Cherokee rights to their land. Retorted President Jackson, 'John Marshall has rendered his decision; now let him enforce it.' "[172]

This story of the Christian and white man's cruelty to the American Indians could go on for volumes and would only nauseate every intelligent and just person with any sense of right and wrong. Thus it is within the nature of authority and power to disregard ethics and justice whenever and wherever they deem it "proper" for them to do so to gain their ends; behind the superficial screen of "morals" and "Christian justice" lay the rooted greed of simple economics, to take by force, duress, and coercion what rightfully and equitably belongs to others. This is the story of Christianity, throughout the early centuries, the Crusades, and up to the present day wherever traditional power holds sway over people. People have written books about the black peril, the red peril, the yellow peril, the brown perils, and all sorts of colorful perils; someday someone should write about the *white* peril. It would be a revolting awakening to our sense of considering ourselves civilized.

William Brandon describes the white man's treatment of the Indians in the glorious state of California in the mid-nineteenth century: "Prostitution and venereal disease ran rampant among gold-country Indians and gang rapes of Indian women became so flagrant that even the white press took cognizance. Kidnapping of Indian children to be sold as servants or laborers was common —one recent authority, in a careful calculation from such records as exist, has estimated that between 3,000 and 4,000 Indian children were stolen in the years from 1852 to 1867, 'not including women taken for concubinage or adults for field labor.' "[173] Brandon continues to relate the "Westernization" of these Indians: "The debauched ex-Mission Indians of Los Angeles furnished a revolving slave-labor force for years, regularly arrested for drunkenness on Saturday night in Nigger Alley and bailed out on Monday morning for $2 or $3 a head by anyone who could use an Indian for a week's work."[174] "Indians in pre-gold rush days numbered something more than 100,000 (in California) by conservative estimates. They were killed off in what seems to have been the biggest single spree of massacring in American history. Some guesses say 30,000 were left by 1859. These had dwindled to roughly 15,000 by the end of the 19th century."[175] Regarding the Choctaw, Chickasaw, Cherokee and Creek Indians, he writes: "As the tribal leaders began to accept treaties providing for eventual allotment of their lands and removal to the West, white squatters and land speculators moved in by the swarm to jump the gun on the land allotments, stripping the Indians of their lands and properties by fraud, liquor, or force. Large numbers of Indians, many of whom had been comfortable or prosperous, took to the woods or the swamps in terror, divested of their possessions and driven from their homes. Occasionally they were divested of the clothes they were wearing by frolicking white men armed with writs or rifles."[176] Brandon summarizes: "The Indian world was devoted to living, the European world to getting."[177]

"So mile by mile westward, and year by year through the 'Cen-

tury of Dishonor,' the United States pursued on all levels its
policy of virtual extermination of Indians, accompanied by a
folk saying that served as a national motto: 'The only good Indian
is a dead Indian.' "[178] For more than three hundred years, the
white and Christian man has murdered the Indian, robbed him,
plagued him, and this cruelty continues relentlessly to this very
day. And after the holocaust we will continue to send anthropologists and sociologists to dig up their pots and bones and make
every fastidious effort to preserve their folkways in colorful books.

Bernhard Grzimek, in *Serengati*, gives his estimate of the depra-
vation and exploitation of Africa by the Europeans and Christianity: "Our grandchildren, as well as those of the Africans,
should see what Africa was like before we Europeans brought
Christianity, slavery, human rights and machine-guns, medicine
and motor-cars."[179] Here, too, the African world was devoted to
living, no matter how primitive and crude, but they lived in the
best manner they could in their environment. Besides, they "respected" their environments and the animal life they were associated with, at least until the white man taught them how to be
poachers. They never killed animals for the pleasure of killing
as the white man has done and is still doing. The Europeans and
later the American slavers came to Africa not to do the Africans
any good but to enslave them, rob them, exploit them, cheat
them. The social, political, and economic crimes committed by
the whites (and this includes the Moslems) against the Africans
are horrendous and sickening. The exploitation of these ignorant
and primitive people by supposedly intelligent and godly people
is the story of voracious and unrelenting greed unsurpassed in all
human history. The slave traffic, exposing the opportunity of
money and its power, even engaged Africans themselves to enter
into this sickening business of stealing their own kind for a few
pieces of silver or a yard of calico cloth. Albert Schweitzer relates
his own experiences: "Members of a family were almost invariably separated from each other. Often the parents were drowned
and only the children taken. . . . Old people have told me that
parents from certain regions in the interior sold their children
into slavery less for the sake of gain than to get the children away
to a country where they would get enough to eat."[180] The exploi-

tation continued without abatement, and even when slavery was "legally" abolished, the traffic continued to operate. Where slaves became "technically" free, they remained with their masters or "owners" 'to avoid starvation and to safeguard themselves with some security against re-enslavement and deportation to strange and unpredictable places. Schweitzer tells us about it: "When I came to the country in 1913, there were still a fair number of natives living as slaves. By law indeed they were free. But they made no use of their freedom, but stayed with their masters, serving them without wages, because they were accustomed to live in that way and did not think they could devise a better means of existence."[181] Thus civilization came to Africa.

It is needless to repeat at length the sad history of the slave traffic in Africa, and it is also needless to repeat what people usually in time forget or wish to forget. But James Wellard, in his *The Great Sahara*, exposes again for us the deep tragedy that overtook Africa when the Arabs and Europeans became partners in the rape of Africa. Relating to the part played in this crime by the Arabs from early times, Wellard states: "The exploitation of black labour was the contribution of the Arabs to mankind, for it was they who organized the vast traffic in human merchandise out of Africa to the Atlantic and Mediterranean ports. In short, the slave trade became the corner-stone of Sahara economy for the next thousand years. It made the desert an exceedingly busy place, with tens of thousands of men and animals crawling every day across the immense wasteland, since by the eighteenth century the demand for negro slaves had become insatiable in almost every corner of the globe. Who else was to work the salt mines in the Sahara Desert itself, who the sugar plantations in the Barbados, who the cotton fields in Virginia, who the American, British, French, Portuguese, Spanish, and Turkish mines and factories, if not the docile African negro?"[182]

During the long marches across the Sahara from Timbuktu and Lake Chad en route to the slave markets of the coastal cities, the captive children and the aged who could not survive the long trek of many months in the sun died on the hot sands and the Sahara slave routes were well marked with the bleached remains of the victims. Wellard tells us about them: "The sufferings of these slave children dying from starvation after they had crawled to the wells had long been justified by the Church, both Catholic and Protestant: the slave trade, said the divines, gave Christians an opportunity of saving negro souls. With the blessings, then, of both the Moslem and the Christian religions, the trade continued unabated until the British decided to abolish it. The first result was that the slave ships, chased by Royal Navy gunboats, crowded on all sail and jettisoned their cargo. In the meantime the overland caravans plodded across the Sahara Desert under the whips of their Moslem masters. In both cases the priests were proved correct. The Africans bound for the Americas were converted to Christianity; those for the Middle East to Islam."[183]

What was the great toll of slaves that was wrenched from the jungles and plains of Africa to feed the greed of the Arabs, Europeans and Americans? "During the great days of the slave trade Africans were being brought out of the interior at the rate of at least 100,000 a year. In some cases we have fairly exact statistics: for instance, the records show that 300,000 African slaves were imported into British colonies between 1680 and 1700. Between 1700 and 1786, 610,000 were imported into Jamaica. The *total* number of Africans sent overseas as slaves from 1510 (when the first negroes were shipped to the Spanish gold mines in Hispañiola) to 1865 when the United States, last among the Christian countries, abolished slavery by a constitutional amendment, was, at a minimum, 12,000,000. If we accept Dr. Livingstone's estimate that at least ten lives were lost for every one that reached the coast the figure of Africans who were captured, killed, or exported during the four and a half centuries of the slave trade is almost inconceivable."[184]

Man, in his nature, is born with a potential for cruelty, and cruel institutions only make him worse. Institutions, cultures, nationalisms, civilizations, and their various and nefarious philosophies and tendencies can and do bring out the good in man or the evil in man. Usually history has shown that they have more often brought about the evil than the good. With few exceptions the leaders, in any form or degree, have primarily looked out for themselves. Any leader who wanted to do good, or did good, for the people usually got it in the neck. History is strewn with the victims, celebrated and common, who have given their lives or had their lives taken from them because they were good, honest, idealistic, and had the courage, ethic, and intellectuality to express their freedom in challenging traditional and unjust forms of authority and power. Jesus, Thomas Paine, Abraham Lincoln, and, recently, Martin Luther King, are just four examples that come to mind. The *intended effects* of their contemporary cultures paid them off for their good intentions. The power they desired to express is the power of their freedom to face up to opposing cultures and usages, challenge their values and validities, create and activate new motives in the behavior of people to bring about a more equitable, just, and ethical stage for mankind to play its part upon, for its own good and for the good of the world it has to exist in. Frazer: "It is the practice of the mob first to stone and then erect useless memorials to their greatest benefactors. All who set themselves to replace ancient error and superstition by truth and reason must lay their account with brickbats in their life and a marble monument after death."[185]

Martin Luther, who threw a bottle of ink at the imaginary devil in a single-handed combat, could not have thought like Jesus, Paine, Lincoln, or King. He found it more feasible, to gain and hold his power, to side with the robber-barons against the peasants and workers. He cried out, "The civil sword shall and must be red and bloody!"[186] "Gregory VII was no pacifist. His favourite text was: 'Cursed be the man that keepeth back his sword from blood.'"[187] In the Americas, "the military superiority of the white man to the American Indian is an even more undeniable example of the power of the sword."[188] The invention of the iron sword, which, they say, first appeared in Eastern Europe circa 1500 B.C., certainly extended the power of the warrior or killer and paved the way for greater power and authority of the kings and later on the Catholic Inquisitors, but it did humanity no good. "Man is a predator whose natural instinct is to kill with a weapon."[189] The desire to kill, overwhelm, overcome and master situations and peoples by violence and ruthlessness is the continual and repetitive expression of the history of civilizations. Benjamin Keen, in his introduction to Zorita's *Breve y sumaria relación de los Señores de la Nueva*

España, writes about the cruelties and waste of human lives that plagued the Aztec culture in Mexico: "Chronic warfare was a deadly scourge of ancient Mexico. The loss of life and attendant destruction from this source must have been very heavy. War joined hands with religion to promote human sacrifice in monstrous numbers. During the reign of Moctesuma alone, between twenty-five thousand and sixty thousand prisoners of war were sacrificed. Members of the Aztec tribe were also sacrificed on the altars of Tenochtitlán."[190]

In Argentina today the Nazi members first salute the Crucifix before convening their councils or before engaging in some offensive against their "enemies." A Reverend Julio Meinvielle, a Roman Catholic priest, refers to himself as the "spiritual leader" of these Nazis who call themselves the "Guardia." These sick fanatics dedicate themselves to violence, to the "eventual" war that "must" come. Hitler and Mussolini did the same. We also know the dreadful results. Leo Kalmer: "Convicts as a class seem to be the most religious people in the country."[191] Mark Twain remarked that civilization produces cowards and hypocrites;[192] in this instance he may have been correct.

Napoleon Bonaparte loved his power and authority more than anything he could possibly own or possess in the world. He rightly claimed: "My power depends on my glory, and my glory on my victories. Conquest has made me what I am, and conquest alone can maintain me." But what happens when such egomaniacs find no more adversaries, no need for further violence, all having been conquered and enslaved? "Persecution may be so pleasant to the persecutor that he would find a world without heretics intolerably dull. Similarly, Hitler and Mussolini, since they taught that war is the noblest of human activities, could not be happy if they had conquered the world and had no enemies left to fight. In like manner, party politics become uninteresting as soon as one party has unquestionable supremacy."[193]

When man has no more enemies and finds things dull and boring, he can always fall back on his own fear of hell to keep his spirit warm in a state of shock, anxiety, frustration, expectation, sadomasochism. Brigid Brophy: "Hell is an emotional hypothesis—in other words, a fantasy; and so emotionally satisfactory that men will cling to it at the cost of distorting their intellectual processes. If men conceived, believed and, by every kind of casuistic rationalizing, persisted in the idea that there is a God who condemns sinners to everlasting torture, it was not by error but because they wanted it to be true. The myth of Hell is the classic repository of mankind's daydreams about torture. It leads us straight into the most pressing problem civilization has to face, the problem of violence."[194]

The violent trait in man is psychologically an aid and an evil to the expression and activity of freedom no different from the cause and effect of violence in any wild animal. Man, too, in spite of the veneer of clothes and civilization, remains, basically and actively, a wild animal. It all depends upon certain circumstances, conditions and events to bring out the violence and wildness in him. Robert Ardrey: "Man is a wild species, and every baby born is a wild young thing. Advancing age, weakening vitality, and a long accumulation of fears and experiences may at last work a general inhibition on certain animal sources of human behavior. But the dilemma of any society, closed or free, finds its chief place of residence in the birthrate. Every *accouchement* delivers to society a creature who somehow must be tamed. Every *accouchement*—today, tomorrow, and until the end of our species' time—presents civilization with an aspiring candidate for the hangman's noose. Yet truly to domesticate him means probably to destroy him."[195]

So strong is the innate desire to kill or to be heralded a hero by killing that myths, legends, customs, and codes regarding soldiers and warriors are impregnated throughout the folklore of practically all cultures in the world. In many primitive societies existing today a man must cut off another's head before he can be considered a full-blooded man and suitable for marriage. The ants have them, why not humans? The *Sumerai* in Japan have a history all their own, and all bloody. Referring to the use of *mana* among primitives to induce bravery and sacrifice, H. R. Hays writes: "As sometimes happened before a battle, if a warrior lost his nerve (he was naturally bewitched), the cure was to crawl between the legs of a great chief whose penis would thus shed its strength upon the victim of battle fatigue."[196]

Even today, though the scenes have changed and the *mana* has new forms, statesmen *know* that ultimate solutions to problems are resolved finally and effectively by resorting to war. The world today is more war conscious than ever before. "With the all-consuming passion of the Warfare State for the tensions and gadgets of war, insanity has become no drawback to reality. It has, indeed, become our way of life."[197] "The ultra-conservative classes that rule our 'military-industrial complex' and dominate our society have led us into an age of social upheaval and revolution, obsessed by a paranoid phobia of change and revolution. We have exported our money, our Military Brass, our nuclear bombers and our missiles; but we have exported precious few ideals. We have generalized vaguely and grandiloquently about the 'free world' and 'free enterprise'; but our enterprise is no longer free, it is the captive creature of the Warfare State."[198]

Thus the rise of civilization, with all its authority-power forms, expressions and complexes, has not lessened strife and war, but increased them. Besides its regimenting tendencies to the diminishment of individual freedom, it has more and more urged the use of force as the more expedient "political" weapon in destroying other peoples and themselves. "Conquest by force of arms has had more to do with the spread of civilization than any other single agency."[199] Violence, force, war thus become the "logical" expressions of statesmanship and leadership strength and wisdom. Logic alone, used to justify pretext and pretense, will not save the world. John Dewey so aptly wrote: "The present-day mathematical logician may present the structure of mathematics as if it had sprung all at once from the brain of Zeus whose anatomy is that of pure logic."[200]

A beautiful philosophical tale taken from the legends of the Hopi Indians, gives us a primitive version of the origin of war, and is indicative and applicable to the very causes and *intended effects* of modern times and warfare. The legend tells us the story of the various "worlds" or phases of the emergence of mankind, that is, of the Hopi Indians. In the first phase or emergence, people and the other animals and creatures lived together, spoke to each other and understood each other, and all creation was just one big happy family in nature. Then a cataclysm occurred and the second emergence of man formed on a different plane—the cultural. In this plane "they did not have the privilege of living with the animals, though, for the animals were wild and kept apart. Being separated from the animals, the people tended to their own affairs. They built homes, then villages and trails between them. They made things with their hands and stored food like the Ant People. Then they began to trade and barter with one another. This was when the trouble started. Everything they needed was on this Second World, but they began to want more. More and more they traded for things they did not need, and the more goods they got, the more they wanted. This was very serious. For they did not realize they were drawing away, step by step, from the good life given them. They just forgot to sing joyful praise to the Creator and soon began to sing praises for the goods they bartered and stored. Before long it happened as it had to happen. The people began to quarrel and fight, and then wars between villages began."[201]

Thus, from a natural society, primarily concerned with subsistence and survival, with the rise of tools and techniques there was born the cultural embryo of economic and political power (the rise of civilization) with its resultant and accentuated growths of authority and power, generating within itself the *intended effects* of strife and warfare. Bertrand Russell: "Ever since the dawn of civilization most people in civilized communities have led lives full of misery; glory, adventure, initiative were for the privileged few, while for the multitude there was a life of severe toil with occasional harsh cruelty."[202]

While human nature has not really changed since *Homo sapiens* began to build its historical cultures and marked its way to modern times, the primitives had no imperial ambitions to any extent such as has been expressed during the later periods. While all creatures may defend or extend their "territories," their prime object was to assure security and survival. "War can only be defined as the use of organized force between two politically independent units, in the pursuit of a tribal policy. War in this sense enters fairly late into the development of human societies."[203] Power had not yet become an intoxicant or a means of psychological power except in the use of magic and tribal forms and superstitions by the early shamans. "Fawcett claims, no doubt correctly, that few of the Indian tribes were warlike until the white man enslaved, exploited, and murdered them for his own ends."[204] One must have neighbors to fight with. War necessitates something to fight over and about. Those who have what they need usually do not fight. Those who have not usually fight against those who have, or to regain something they had previously lost. "Since the polar and central Eskimos have no neighbors, nor yet any cause for internal quarrels and dissensions, they cannot have military institutions."[205] Modern nations, through their leaders, *generate* the violence of war, not for the good of their peoples but to impregnate and maintain their own authority-power hold from within and without. Dictators actually stay alive and maintain their power through naked force to subdue their own people and others, or else purposely bring about conditions that can only produce war. Sukarno, Castro, Mao, and others are present-day examples.

The rise of civilization is the history of the rise of these authority-power forms and abuses, with or without the consent of people. Without the consent of the people we encounter the plain unadulterated force of violence, intimidation, fraud, threat and brutality; with the consent of the people we encounter all the many ways and means of modern public relations and propaganda on the part of some individuals to gain power and authority that may be good or bad for the people but always means power for the appointed or elect. As a result, in the former the people find themselves holding a gun or somebody else holding a gun pointed at them; in the latter we find the people holding a vote. While a vote is more indicative of the expression of freedom, yet in the practical and real sense people somehow and for some inexplainable reason find themselves persistently behind the eight ball. Democracy, to date, seems to be the only process which can stand as a defender of individual freedom against the battering offensives of the modern civilizations. Reinhold Niebuhr certainly makes a keen observation when he wrote that "man's capacity for justice makes democracy possible; but man's inclination to injustice makes democracy necessary." "Modern warfare has become nothing but an unmitigated disease of civilization."[206] Ralph Waldo Emerson concludes: "The end of the human race will be that it will eventually die of civilization."

ORGANIZATION

Organization, LIKE GOVERNMENT, is essential in the various fields of human existence, effort, and association. Otherwise there would be a chaotic nihilism everywhere and a gradual or fast deterioration of human forces; this would be the beginning of the end. Organizations of human beings go back to the primeval wandering families of hunters and food-gatherers. We see organization at work among multitudinous types of animals, in the schools of fishes, the insects, the birds, in mammals. The many comparable and relative similarities between human organization and other bird, insect, and animal organizations are not merely coincidental. It is not the sole idea or property of man. Natural and generic forms of organization appear almost everywhere in the biological spread of organics. The importance of the group-need for relationship is essential to the expression and enjoyment of natural force or power for the individual; without a societal and social arena and frame the individual expression of freedom and power would have no reflecting screen for identity and the satisfactions necessary for the ego-psyche makeup of the human animal. C. Wright Mills: "If we took the one hundred most powerful men in America, the one hundred wealthiest, and the one hundred most celebrated away from the institutional positions they now occupy, away from their resources of men and women and money, away from the media of mass communication that are now focused upon them—then they would be powerless and poor and uncelebrated. For power is not of a man. Wealth does not center in the person of the wealthy. Celebrity is not inherent in any personality. To be celebrated, to be wealthy, to have power requires access to major institutions, for the institutional positions men occupy determine in large part their chances to have and to hold these valued experiences."[207]

Organization was not exactly acquired with culture; it may have been advanced or degenerated by culture and all its social,

political, economic, and religious forms, but it did not originate
with culture. Culture extended it, gave it specialization and
particularization, but it did not give birth to it. It was born in
the natural arena of existentials within the biological frame of
living creatures evolving it. Regardless how technical, complicated, mechanized, and civilized various organizations become,
their biological root cannot be removed without cutting off the
sperm-flow of humanness that makes it possible to exist. Therefore, all forms of organization reflect, in one way or another,
its human elements and the principles and cultures these elements reflect. Barrows Dunham: "Human organizations are
founded and built by human beings, and their ideologies have
precisely that same human source."[208] We should keep in mind,
in the general study of human organization, the kindred and related forms in the extra-human world of living creatures, that all
life and its modes of experiences constantly reflect the continual
and ceaseless relativism in which all being is inexorably tied in
what some might call a world symbiosis, others an organic cosmogony; but related we are and shall be, and tied to it, from
birth to death, we are and shall be. From the study of this relativism we can take lessons to advance; from the study of some
parts of it, such as the termites, we can take heed and vigilance
not to become as they have become. There is no perfection in
any form of organization, as there is no perfection in any of the
parts that compose it, primitive, ancient, historical, or modern,
and yet organizations, at any particular time, have often taken
on the robes of perfection and the proclamation that the highest
possible good and goal have been reached. "It is only the slow-
ness of the process that hides the movement from our eyes and
suggests the conclusion, so flattering to human vanity, that nature
has reached her consummation in us and can no further go."[209]

As all organizations contain individuals, and as all individuals
vary in some degree from each other, some aspiring to lead and
others willing and disposed to be led, as in the hen-pecking system or in the dominant-to-dominated arrangements in the monkey and baboon troops: there is no such thing as *true* or *actual*
equality of all individuals. Because certain individuals want to
be *more* and others *less*. It all depends what the equality is about,

to suffer or to be happy. Equality means the same measure for all, but all individuals have not the same measure of themselves or desires. There is no such thing as natural or actual uniformity of equality in the nature of men. What is important is a societal *process* by which an individual can express the freedom and endeavor to aspire to the satisfactions and fullness of his being in whatever direction it takes, provided it does not hinder or injure the same process of freedom and its effects for others. C. H. Arndt: "The optimal social structure would seem to be that which will provide the greatest possible opportunity for the individual to develop his talents commensurate with the welfare of the society of which he is a member."[210] It is the essence of *equity* in the democratic process that makes its value felt by all freedom-loving people. Bertrand Russell: "A society in which each is the slave of all is only a little better than one in which each is the slave of a despot. There is equality where all are slaves, as well as where all are free. This shows that equality, by itself, is not enough to make a good society."[211]

In a democratic order there is, or should be, the opportunity to aspire and express oneself freely, and there are, or should be, the same privileges accorded to each and all to establish a just equity, this being essential to an honest and ethical distribution and expression of the natural freedom to all individuals so long as they *regard* this order of things among themselves as a *process* to maintain this natural flow of freedom. This *regard* takes the form of *acceptance* by law, common or otherwise, tradition, usages, ideals, and various principles by which this democratic process may be established and carried on. "A healthy and progressive society requires both central control and individual and group initiative: without control there is anarchy, and without initiative there is stagnation."[212] John Dewey: "Government, business, art, religion, all social institutions have a meaning, a purpose. That purpose is to set free and to develop the capacities of human individuals without respect to race, sex, class or economic status. And this is all one with saying that the test of their value is the extent to which they educate every individual into the full stature of his possibility. Democracy has many meanings, but if it has a moral meaning, it is found in resolving that the supreme test of all political institutions and industrial arrangements shall be the contribution they make to the all-around growth of every member of society."[213]

Yet all these laws, traditions, institutions, ideals and principles continue to modify themselves, take on new interpretations, are applied and used anew in some changed form, because the individuals have also modified, their cultures changed to meet new trends, new situations and circumstances heretofore not experienced or met with. We see these traditions, often imperceptible and then at other times revolutionary and radical, in the organizations of the sciences, in those of religion, of social, educational, and cultural types of organized associations, in politics, in the constant need of newer forms of legislation and controls, in the military. Inasmuch as the democratic process, in itself, is a vehicle of procedure rather than a standard of rule or dogma, opposition to change is not severe; the democratic process in itself denotes and implies a peaceful and equitable procedure on an amenable level. In the autocratic, dictatorial, and totalitarian states the philosophy of organization becomes far less of a process and more of an *end*, and the *end* is the *State*; that is, the leader and leaders who comprise the State are dissociated from any power and authority that the people might contain for themselves; thus, eventual and inevitable conflict is generated with its usual inevitable and tragic predictabilities. In such a situation a *natural compatibility* becomes less possible, and the greater the impossibility, the greater the diminishment of freedom. The power and authority of the State become oppressors and depressors of freedom, and whatever privileges and freedom of action are accorded the individuals or constituents are controlled in such a manner that the people become the medium of thought and action *for the State* and not for themselves as individuals; they, as a *mass*, identify the organization, not themselves as beings. Here there is no longer *regard* for a set of principles by which they can live as more or less free individuals; instead there is *conformance*, a resigned cohesion, encultured, brainwashed, ordained, decreed or enforced, to which the individual must adhere and cohere in order to avoid placing his security in danger. The State has created, by its authority and power, a mass of *futilitarians*. The individual's relationship is no longer one of voluntary participation, of individual *to* individual, but of the ordered submission of the individual to the State for the express purpose of maintaining and furthering the State as his own warden, of preserving the State as an end unto itself. The human loses his freedom and becomes a termite, without light, self-identity, or awareness of its own being. Niccolò Machiavelli was at least honest when he wrote: "A wise prince ought to adopt such a course that his citizens will always in every sort and kind of circumstance have need of the State and of him, and then he will always find them faithful." This "need" of the State is the Maya, or camouflage, that ordains conformance, or else!

Authoritarian and totalitarian organizations received their rudimentary ideology from the historical orthodox and formal religions. The teacher was made to order for the pupil. Brand Blanshard, reviewing Dunham's *Heroes and Heretics,* gives his version of what orthodoxy is: "Orthodoxy is not loyalty to truth but loyalty to an organization. Suppose, for example, that you believe in the creation story, or in miracles, or in the Trinity; why do you do so? Is it because you have looked at the evidence and found it compelling? Almost certainly not. It is because you belong to a church whose power and prestige are behind these beliefs and presses them upon you with a force that is hardly resistible even when unperceived. And where did the organization itself get the beliefs? From science? From critical history or critical reflection? Not at all. It drew most of them from primitive poetry and the rest from expediency. The men who wrote the creation story knew nothing of critical history; they imagined how things might have happened and wrote it down in all innocence as what presumably did happen. The men who reported the Biblical miracles knew nothing of science and its laws and wrote with a naïve freedom from our rules of probability."[214] Bertrand Russell, in his critique of William James, *The Will to Believe,* stated that "what is wanted is not the will to believe, but the wish to find out, which is the exact opposite."[215]

Orthodoxy is even more than belief. It means that there are no longer such acknowledgments as *persons* with a *free conscience* (which the orthodox religions always opposed strenuously), or *individuals* with the *freedom of thought and expression* (which the orthodoxies opposed even more strenuously), but believers, followers, servants, subjects who are to accept the established orthodox dogma and dicta and to abide by them, all other factors notwithstanding. In many cases the orthodox religion and the political state are a composite structure, like the Emperor of Japan; in other cases the leader or dictator mesmerizes the people to believe in him as some sort of divinity. Thus, an orthodox organization, religious or political, becomes something that has the *intended effects* of stagnation, the delusion of nonchangeability, of rigidity, and the illusion of a fixed status that become more important, more sacred and paramount than any attempt of the individual to express freely any point of view that may be critical of the "divine" structure. As a result, the disease of obscurantism enters into the social life of people and the acceptance of the idea that a "normal" and "good" person is one who abides and coheres as a thoughtless brick in this Tower of Babel. As Dunham points out, "the Catholic God, however, is a projection not so much of personal conscience as of organizational unity."[216] Oliver L. Reiser tells us that "a sane or normal person is one who conforms to the standards set by the average man. The norm is established by what the majority sees and believes"[217] and unfortunately the majority are the *futilitarians* of belief and blind conformance. This is the crux of the modern totalitarian state. The only difference is not in the nature of the organization but merely in the identity of the Godhead; in the religious orthodoxy the godhead may be in the Trinity or in Jesus Himself, or in the Sun-god or in Brahma, Yahweh, Amon-Ra, Mazdao, or Buddha; in the modern Communist, Fascist, or Police State, the godhead is the State, that is, Khrushchev, Mao Tse-tung, Nkruma, Sukarno, General de Gaulle or Castro, for in each case *they are the State*. Regarding the freedom of thought and expression, Sandifer and Scheman write: "The patent lessons of history are that the state itself is the major threat to public order, safety, and freedom."[218] Even Toynbee senses the dangers of nationalism and sovereignties. "Modern nationalism," he writes, "is the ancient idolatrous worship of collective human power raised to an unprecedented degree of intensity by the infusion into it of post-Christian fanaticism. . . . Will allegiance to the fatal ideal of national sovereignty be transferred to the ideal of world government in time to save mankind from self-destruction? . . . The cult of sovereignty has become mankind's major religion. Its god demands human sacrifice."[219]

Whatever the form of authority and power, where the State or organizational structure (it could be a lodge, a business corporation, an institution, or a code) has become "personalized" so as to present itself as an end unto itself, that is, when it ceases to become a medium and process to serve those who constitute it and becomes, instead, a dedication of the people to serve *It*, then to this extent the natural freedom of the people involved has been diminished or eliminated. In this sense the termite has no freedom. James Clark Moloney writes about *Understanding the Japanese Mind:* "We should think about the fact that the Japanese government is not constituted as an instrument to serve the Japanese people. Instead the Japanese people are considered instruments to serve the Japanese government. The popular rights of the Japanese people *(minken)* are subordinated to the nationalistic institution *(kokken)* epitomized in the regality of the emperor."[220] Bertrand Russell explains the problem further: "In a totalitarian state an innovator whose ideas are disliked by the government is not merely put to death, which is a matter to which a brave man may remain indifferent, but is totally prevented from causing his doctrine to be known. . . . This is a new fact in human history, brought about by the much increased control over individuals which the modern technique of government has made possible. It is a very grave fact, and one which shows how fatal a totalitarian regime must be to every kind of moral progress."[221] "Modern techniques have made possible a new intensity of governmental control, and this possibility has been exploited very fully in totalitarian states. It may be that under the stress of war, or the fear of war, or as a result of totalitarian conquest, the parts of the world where some degree of individual liberty survives may grow fewer, and even in them liberty may come to be more and more restricted. There is not much reason to suppose that the resulting system would be unstable, but it would almost certainly be static and unprogressive. And it would bring with it a recrudescence of ancient evils: slavery, bigotry, intolerance, and abject misery for the majority of mankind. . . . For this reason, emphasis upon the value of the individual is even more necessary now than at any former time."[222] "There has never in past history been any large state that controlled its citizens as completely as they are controlled in the Soviet Republic, or even in the countries of Western Europe."[223]

Whatever form an organization takes, its prime foundation should be its medium as a process to serve the needs of its members, to allow them to express their biological and cultural freedoms, to favor individual initiative and expression, to afford them the exercise of their *natural right* to enjoy and fulfill their lives in an equitably processed order that can make, or try to make, this possible. The basic root principle is that a number of individuals constitute a society and not that a society is a composite or collective mass of people. Without the reasonable freedom of the individual there can only be more frustration, tyranny, and some form of enslavement. Where the individual was subjected to serve the state for the ends of the state to the exclusion of the rights of the individual, theocratic, monarchical, and otherwise, the freedom of man was suppressed and the life of the individual made to suffer or to be destroyed. G. C. Valliant describes how the life of an individual fared in the Aztec society: "The boys in the religious-training school . . . their little legs and faces lacerated by maguey spines, their bodies thin from fasts and penance and their eyes dulled by the monotony of self-denial, these children were chanting strophes from a ritualistic chant. Their preceptor, who led the singing, showed by his own scarred and emaciated body that the propitiation of the gods was a relentless and never-ending task. Priest, chief, warrior or husband, every Aztec, from boyhood on, spent much of his life either in a kind of beseeching penance, to ensure his future, or in a state of grateful atonement for not having had a worst past."[224] Japan had felt the same way about its people: "The Japanese insist upon the *insignificance of the individual,* the 'not to be free' concept; while American political theory stresses individualism, the 'to be free' idea."[225] It is good to see that the New Japan has brought about an increase of democratic ideology and practice and the Japanese people are beginning to sense themselves as individuals; even the Emperor himself has discovered his own humanness, sought relief and release from his own imprisonment and lack of normal freedom, and has become a person instead of a divine figment not to be looked upon. As the intelligence of man increases and his plaintive cry for freedom becomes more aroused, the philosophy of the individual moves toward a better and more sensible enjoyment of his life. Erich Fromm: "The depersonalization, the emptiness, the meaninglessness of life, the automatization of the individual result in a growing dissatisfaction and in a need to search for a more adequate way of living and for norms which could guide man to this end."[226] Bertrand Russell: "If life is to be saved from boredom relieved only by disaster, means must be found of restoring individual initiative, not only in things that are trivial, but in the things that really matter. I do not mean that we should destroy those parts of modern organization upon which the very existence of large populations depends, but I do mean that organization should be more flexible, more relieved by local autonomy, and less oppressive to the human spirit through its impersonal vastness, than it has become through its unbearably rapid growth and centralization, with which our ways of thought and feeling have been unable to keep pace."[227]

The resurgence of individualism and the reassertion of individuals that the State exists for them and not that they exist for the State have brought about a fresh maturation of the intellect and a thirst for knowledge and a return to earthiness in a growing number of people throughout the world. "What is needed is not this or that specific piece of information, but such knowledge as inspires a conception of the ends of human life as a whole: art and history, acquaintance with the lives of heroic individuals, and some understanding of the strangely accidental and ephemeral position of man in the cosmos—all this touched with an emotion of pride in what is distinctively human, the power to see and to know, to feel magnanimously and to think with understanding. It is from large perceptions combined with impersonal emotion that wisdom most readily springs."[228] Walter Kaufmann: "The aspiration for truth . . . involves self-assertion and rebellion. We refuse to be imposed upon; we refuse to be like objects; we aspire to a higher state of being."[229] John Dewey: "If past history teaches anything, it is that with intelltectual order we have the surest possible promise of advancement to practical order."[230] Albert Einstein: "Intellectual individualism and the thirst for scientific knowledge emerged simultaneously in history and have remained inseparable."[231] To achieve this the teachers in the world must also reassert their intellectual right and freedom to teach honestly not only the substance of whatever knowledge has been achieved, but also the ways and means of thinking freely, openly, and logically, that is, teach a way of attaining and processing *intelligence*. To *know* is better than to believe without knowing. Bertrand Russell: "One of the chief obstacles to intelligence is credulity, and credulity could be enormously diminished by instruction as to the prevalent forms of mendacity."[232] "It must not be supposed that the officials in charge of education desire the young to become educated. On the contrary, their problem is to impart information without imparting intelligence."[233] Education, the caretakers and process of education, must be *liberalized* and *naturalized* to dispose of the morass and obscurantisms of stagnated and obsolete forms and beliefs if the individual is to find himself, and find for himself, an orderly yet sufficiently free society that can afford him the opportunity for a happy life and a peaceful world to be happy in.

NECESSITY AND SURVIVAL

THE INTELLECT, THE mind, cannot live by the wine of inspiration and knowledge alone; it needs bread, too, just as the most ingenious invention requires some fuel or energy form to process its intended function. It is axiomatic that the necessities of subsistence—water, food, shelter, security—are basic in order to live and survive; all other factors may be relevant or irrelevant, but without these we cannot continue to exist. Even in modern times the jungle savage has to compromise against his own desires and face the elimination of the weak, the sick, and the aged in order to maintain a practical and realistic balance of his economic supply and environment potential for survival. This "elimination" process is very common among many animals and in the insect world, where the needless and the decrepit are disposed of out of evolved necessity. Bees kill off the senile drones, and many American Indian tribes carried off the very old and helpless to some cave or into the woods where they could be alone to die and no longer continue to be a burden to the tribe. Herbert S. Dickey relates: "It is evident that each male member of the tribe [the Guaharibos] has quite enough to do in supporting own family, which in its turn is sufficiently occupied in farming and in the upbringing of the children. The maimed and the old and chronically infirm have no place in the Guaharibo economy. They are excess baggage. They must die. The Quirichaua selects the victims of this tribal law. With his assistants he attends to their demise. The shrinking, trembling unfortunate is taken to the deep forest. He is placed on a little platform built well off the ground and his body is shot full of poisoned arrows. When the flesh disappears, the bones are wrapped in baskets made of leaves and placed underground. No ritual attends the taking off of the old and useless. They have ceased being useful, they must cease existence. Their execution is an economic matter of course."[234]

As we have already noted, the territory proclamation, the neutral grounds, the mutual-assisting groups of animals for food and protectiveness, and the early family stick-together traits both in humans and many other animals, all these are rooted in the simple and elemental craving of the organism for continued absorption of external things and factors in order to live. This is the *economics* of life, biological in origin and evolution, of which culture and the rise of civilization are phasic and ecological complexities of the same need and drive. When we analyze a tribal custom, a tradition, religion, polis, various levels or castes, political and social, sooner or later we hit the *economic chord* that is either hidden or interrelated in the surfaces of things and operating below the surfaces with its interconnecting links to our appearances and ideologies. Each creature must seek, obtain, or beg sufficient *security* in some form, regardless of degree, or else suffer or perish.

In the beginning the environment was an open ground to

human and other animal life subject to extension, dominance and subjection in accord with the animal instincts. These instincts have not changed basically; they have new names, forms, degrees, but in kind they remain the same and are with us to the present day; they identify our frame and nature. To eliminate them we must eliminate life itself. Protohominids used weapons to obtain food or in combat to defend their mates from being stolen or in stealing females from others, or in the conflicts of dominance and territory acquisition. Whether they were aware of any *possessiveness* or *property right* we have no way of knowing, but we do know that as *Homo sapiens* emerged the awareness of property emerged. Thomas and Hamm: "Probably the first things that were treated as private property were weapons and tools."[235] Thus, the idea of property and the right to retain possession by *owning* something became an acquired nurturing element which supplemented the biological competitiveness in the nature of the animal for survival and extension. Robert Ardrey: "If man is a part of the natural world then his competitive drive cannot be erased by the elimination of private property, an institution itself derived from his animal ancestry; the drive can only be shifted— as happens in those social animals holding territory in common —from an expression of individuality through dominance over his fellow beings."[236]

The idea or awareness of *wealth* or *capital*, as a survival and security element, emerged later with the advent of settlements, villages, and some sort of agricultural, agrarian stabilization. The idea of wealth, capital, or property, as a source of *power* came still later, and with power came the means to exploit others in order to increase this power—the vehicle of *authority*. As the form and degree of power increased, the idea, furtherance, and establishment of authority emerged and took its various forms from the force of naked conquest and confiscation to the "divine" right of the god through the priest, who "owned" not only all the material things but also the bodies, labors and lives of the people. Thus *rulerships* came of age, evolved out of the primeval competitiveness to survive and the processes of natural selection that was good for the strong, dominant, and the cunning, and bad for the weak, the illiterate and the subjected. However, the "divine" king, "divine" priest, or "divine" god tied to either or all together, separately, jointly, or compositely, became a firmer and better means of getting the people to *accept* their own subjection because they were psychologically *equated* to the same "high" levels as the god, king and priest by being made to feel and believe that they are umbilically united to all three and derive their own substance, life, welfare and dream of immortality from being part of them. As a result, the king and priest became the greatest exploiters of humanity throughout history. Communism, Fascism, totalitarianism are merely more militant and discreet forms of the same power, psychologically or violently obtained, but they have not changed the process. What may have changed is merely the appearance-identity of the source of social and psychic nourishment: instead of from a god, king or priest, the people can now suckle from the teats of the State, which also ordains, by its form of power and authority, that it literally owns its people and to this extent the sense and spirit of natural freedom has been diminished or eliminated or mischanneled and misled in both cases, both ancient and modern.

The basic manner in which power and authority forms seem to grow, extend, and establish themselves as continuing forms of impersonal power-fear-persuasion vehicles has been, and will always be, the supporting and necessary possession and security of wealth—*money*. The shaman, witch-doctor, medicine man, and priest are not altruistic gems of humility and poverty, as they keep proclaiming with crocodile tears streaming down their faces, as they fill their purses. Without the *economics* factor no religion can survive. Jesus was a rebel against the money changers in and out of the Temple but the people who established Christianity became the money changers. Buddha denounced ritual and ceremony, did not recognize any gods, supernaturalism, souls, etc., but his followers created Buddhism with thousands of temples, hundreds of thousands of lamas wholly devoted to ritual, prayer and ceremony and, whether beggar or prime minister of Lhasa, keep asking and taking whatever they can put their hands on. No organization, religious or nonreligious, can survive without the *economics* factor of power through wealth, property, and finance in order to maintain itself and continue its establishment. This exposes the hypocrisy of the theologians, who keep haranguing that they are interested only in the spiritual, that the worldly and the material things belong to the constant parade of the demons who hinder the people from purifying their souls. While the illiterates have been emptying their pockets for thousands of years in their efforts to "purify" their souls, the religions that received their contributions have become vast and incredibly gigantic financial institutions, some of the greatest and most powerful in the world. Religious organization is still a *human* organization, and humans all need nourishment, not the kind that emanates from ectoplasmic ideals of eternity, of the heavens or from any leasehold on hell, but plain and simple cold cash or its equivalent in liquidity potential.

I remember visiting the Cathedral of Guadalupe, the constant pilgrimage of Indians, mestizos, *peones* from country and city, poor, barefoot, and poverty-stricken, continues around the clock, day and night, as they enter and leave the cathedral. Wherever you move within the church you will find slots, hundreds of them, to accept coins; the pipe system throughout the structure must be quite intricate and extensive. This is typical of the Latin-American church. These cathedrals are smothered with gold and silver miscellany from the altars to the stairways, and the people continue to pour their few coins into the slots and continue to live like pigs, or worse. I remember the cathedral in Panama City, laden with gold, silver, and precious jewels, surrounded by the hovels of the wretched. In Oaxaca I went through several of its beautiful cathedrals, possessing some of the finest gold and silver work in Mexico, and the neo-Zapotecs of today, including their little children of three or four years of age already weaving for the tourist trade, giving a considerable amount of their earnings to the church and continuing to live in dirt and alleyways. To make sure the wretches pay continually, almost every day of the year is devoted to the commemoration of some saint or religious holiday and so they must continually go to the church and give and give and give. As Jesus would say, this is not the road to paradise! *"En verdad que esta no es la via del paraiso!"*—so wrote Guillermo Dellhora, the great fighter for freedom in Mexico in his classic *"La Iglesia Catolica ante la Critica en el Pensamiento y en el Arte."*[237]

The arts of religion throughout the world are tremendous and most fascinating: so far as art is concerned, they often reveal man at his best. The temples of India, Siam, China, and Japan, the mosques of the Moslems, the churches of the Christianized world, even the men's clubs of New Guinea, they are wonderful to see and inspire an exhilarating sense of appreciation for the crafts and expressions of man as *artist*. But let us look around and beyond, for there we will find poverty, ignorance, misery, and the hallucination of unfortunate creatures who have surrendered their true and natural freedom, and with it the best years of their lives. Clyde Kluckhohn writes of the Navahos: "Averages of amounts spent for ceremonials are deceptive in that they tend to obscure the great variation from family to family. Still it is instructive to know that in the Ramah area, on the average, 20 percent of total family income goes into 'religion.' . . . We cannot follow out all of the interconnections between the 'economic' and the 'religious' systems, but it is worthwhile to point out that the seasons when ceremonials are held are those when time and money are free."[238]

Whether the king demanded tribute, tithe or tax, or whether the priest "begged" for alms, contributions, subsidies, donations, material offerings, services in the form of some kind of labor, sacrifice, or offering, does not matter. The result is the *economic* parting with something valuable and necessary by one human being to give another, regardless of whether the giver is a common herdsman or serf and the taker robed in majestic raiments or dressed in the temple garb of the gods. Whether the transactions have been consummated by the sincerity or trickery of either does not matter; the only thing that matters economically is the *parting with,* and the *taking of,* something that is usable, desirable, and valuable. Sometimes the type of offering is surprisingly not so valuable. Cowan cites the following story from Torquemada "respecting the revenue of Moctecsuma which consisted of the natural products of the country, and what was produced by the industry of his subjects. During the abode of Moctecsuma among the Spaniards, in the palace of his father, Alonzo de Ojeda one day espied in a certain apartment of the building a number of small bags tied up. He imagined at first that they were filled with gold dust but on opening one of them, what was his astonishment to find it quite full of lice! Ojeda, greatly surprised at the discovery he had made, immediately communicated what he had seen to Cortes, who then asked Marina and Aguilar for some explanation. They informed him that the Mexicans had such a sense of their duty to pay tribute to their monarch that the poorest and meanest of the inhabitants if they possessed nothing better to present to their king, daily cleaned their persons and saved all the lice they caught, and that when they had a good store of them, they laid them in bags at the feet of their monarch."[239]

In Peru, where the Inca was the embodiment of the god himself, a female had to pay a tax to the government-religion for just being married. "Each woman—once married—owed a finished garment a year to the government."[240] In the Arab countries "the pilgrimage to Mecca began as a concession to the Koreish (tribe) who made great profits from the pilgrims who came to their shrine of the Black Stone, and who feared that the new religion would cut off the source of their wealth."[241] In ancient Egypt "the priesthood devised some new forms of magic (for example, selling passports to the hereafter that got around the moral requirements for admission by issuing verdicts of acquittal in advance), but out of its ranks never came an apostle of popular enlightenment or of either social or religious reform. Prophets were as unheard of in Mesopotamia."[242] In Sumeria the temples of the gods turned into banks and the priests became cashiers in the regular commerce of loaning money at usurious rates, no different from the Roman hierarchy in Italy with all its substantial and widespread financial and commercial investments throughout the Italian economy. "From first to last the religion of Egypt was grossly materialistic . . . in their service of these gods the Sumerians had purely mundane motives, since they had no immortal souls to save. Their temples appropriately served as banks, charging high rates of interest."[243]

In ancient Israel the social law legalized commerce in slaves, as in all the other countries around it. The nations around the Mediterranean in those days considered slavery as quite moral and equitable, and the temples shared the profit spoils of this sinister traffic. All ancient societies accepted the existence of slavery as "legal" and socially favorable to the country; this included the Egyptians, Babylonians, Greeks, Romans, and later the Moslems, who are still engaged in the slave traffic today, with the blessings of Allah. The Hebrew prophets, with all their idealism about the One and Only God, "did not attack the institution of slavery or the inferior status of women. They proposed no concrete measures of reform, made no effort to change the social or political system of Israel in order to assure more equity. In their own time they accomplished little if any improvement in the lot of the poor."[244] In all ancient lands, no matter where, one had to be careful, to protect his security and his very life, not to express any doubts of or opposition to the formal and institutionalized religion of the priesthood. "People who are not well-to-do dare not be frank about their religious beliefs."[245] Socrates did not, and drank hemlock. The Greek people, like Aristotle himself, felt that only certain "high" or "aristocratic" people should enjoy economic abundance, wealth, and luxury and that the common, or ordinary, people were to make out as best as they could with the little they had. "I think you will discover," writes Dunham, "that men who object to abundance for all are remarkably concerned with the spiritual welfare of the underprivileged."[246]

The cults and religions that followed the periods after Christ were not any different than those before. Any priesthood had to accumulate power in the very practical and realistic way, which is to become strong by wealth, property, and collaboration with, and whatever imperial authority and power existed in any particular area. Without Constantine's acceptance of Christianity as the "official" religion of the State and with it the power of the Church to dispose of heretics and heresies, that is, to dispose of *people* who disagreed with it or who had other religious beliefs— and this meant exile, confiscation of property, and often death— it is doubtful whether Christianity would have had the historical impetus and power to spread and establish itself as it did, God's wishes notwithstanding. Without collaboration with imperial and monarchical power the Church could not have lasted, and col-

laboration meant not to favor any principles or actions which
may be favorable to the life and economy of the common people,
and the common people in those days meant the poor and the
enslaved.

Referring to the Greek Orthodox Church, Herbert J. Muller
writes: "While supporting autocracy and war, the Holy Orthodox
Church did little to Christianize life in the temporal social world.
No influential saint echoed the indignation of John Chrysostom
over the misery of the poor; no high churchman led any popular
movement for social or political reform. As a privileged institution, the Church not only acquiesced in the *status quo* but took
advantage of its opportunities for exploitation. Monasteries—
havens from the evil world—accumulated vast wealth by expro-
priating peasants as well as cashing in on the magical virtues of
their ikons and their relics. Monks generally offered the most
determined and successful resistance to the emperors, but principally to those emperors who tried to curb their power or limit
their worldly possessions."[247] Regarding the saints, "Few Christian saints cried out insistently against social injustice. St. Thomas
Aquinas could write very calmly about the naturalness of serfdom, while even gentle St. Francis stressed mainly the blessings
of poverty—blessings that a saint may appreciate, but that few of
the poor can."[248] So avaricious was the Church that even Martin
Luther exclaimed that "Everything is permitted in Rome except
to be an honest man!" Philip Wylie: "The Church of Rome—
this House of God has existed for a thousand years on the bodies
of exploited human beings."[249] "One finds among naked savages,
and the nearly-as-naked savages on Park Avenue in New York
City, that religion owns and controls all human biological procedure. When a man is born, the church must baptize him. When
he is adolescent, the church must confirm the baptism. When he
mates, the church must marry him. When he reproduces, the
church must be handed the offspring, that the cycle may start
again. If he would put his wife away from himself, the church
must assent—or refuse to assent. If he sins, the church must forgive him. If he is sick, the church must take the advantages of
comfort. If he is dying, the church must supply prayers and unc-
tions. And when he dies, the church must bury him. Each of

these steps costs money. A benediction will stoop to extort a farthing. And after a man is dead, the church expects a portion of his estate. Some churches put a posthumous levy on the entrance to Heaven. The sumptuousness of these offices is scaled by price; there is every class of baptism, wedding and funeral—even two-pants suits for the dead, one to wear in the church and a more durable pair evidently needed for a head start on eternity, in the grave."[250]

Emmett McLoughlin, a former priest, writes about the situation today in America: "In Franciscan churches and in those of the secular clergy, the race for money goes far beyond the abuse of the ideal of poverty: it approaches greed. There are always churches and schools to build, shrines to be developed, and priests to be sent to visit their relatives in Ireland. Every priest who is sincere deplores the financial exploitation of the laity that is permitted—even promoted—by the Roman Catholic hierarchy."[251] "Some Catholics in their wills leave thousands of dollars for thousands of masses for their own souls. The fee for a low mass is one dollar. A low mass is recited, not sung. The offering for a high mass is from five dollars up. This provides singing of parts of the mass by the priest and parts by a choir. A solemn mass requires three priests, and the fee is from twenty-five dollars up. It is a shocking thing to visit urban eastern churches and observe high masses whipped through in thirty minutes, with the priest chanting so fast that even an expert in Latin can hardly follow, and with the choir consisting of one person who doubles as organist and singer. Some of these churches will perform ten or twelve high masses a day."[252] McLoughlin continues: "The Church provides no stimulus for man to rise above poverty and struggle to better his housing or lot in life. It canonized poverty and insists that men humbly accept their lot in this world as ordained by God and as a test of their worthiness for a better life to come. It fails to teach its members to think, to doubt, to question, to probe, to inquire, to want and to fight for a better world for their children than their parents gave to them."[253]

Regarding the opposition of the Church in America to the Child Labor Amendment prohibiting the use of children's labor in factories and sweatshops, Paul Blanshard writes: "The leaders of the Catholic hierarchy were largely responsible for the defeat of the proposed child labor amendment in 1924, on the ground that it would interfere with parents' control of their children."[254] Morris Raphael Cohen: "It was the union of manufacturers, farmers and the Catholic Church that defeated the Child Labor Amendment."[255] "That the churches have not kept out of politics, is attested by our national experience in regard to prohibition. The defeat of the Child Labor Amendment to the Constitution, the defeat of the plan for a Federal Department of Education, and even the defeat of the President's Court Plan, were largely due to the influence of the Catholic Church; and the influence of Protestantism in our educational institutions is not confined to anti-evolution laws."[256] These are only a handful of references regarding the general opposition, contrary to popular belief, of organized religion to help lift the standards of living in their localities, not by word of mouth but in actuality to diminish the gnawing ogres of poverty and its twin-sister, ignorance. The history of Mexico and Latin America since the Conquistadores came with Sword and Cross is in itself as thorough an indictment of the Catholic hierarchy as ever there could be one. Besides, it does not take too much intelligence to see that all these theologians do not think that their God is capable of seeing through their hypocrisy and silly little man-made ceremonies.

When one gets around this world and observes the peoples, their homes and home life, their occupations, festivities, arts, music, it is amazing to see what goes on among them with the little they have. It seems the poor get more out of life with practically not much more than their simple and hardy spirits, in contradistinction to the very privileged rich, who so often become confused neurotics and die earlier worrying about their fortunes and properties. Power is not a sobering element in the spirit of man. Often misery and poverty awaken in us a feeling of evaluation of the more important things that sustain us and bring us happiness. Not that it is good to be poor or bad to be rich; it is simply that somehow compensating factors, which we might call necessitated compatibilities, for want of a better term, come about in both sectors. In a world of so much science, so many mechanical miracles, great cities and towering structures, all the vast producing machines and crafts, the rolling plains of wheat and corn, the valleys with millions of livestock, and then to see the many *Tobacco Roads* in our very backyards and back-hills and in other countries, the broken-down shacks, the ignorance and malnutrition, the starved, anguished faces staring with *angst,* the emaciated breasts of the young mother, the forlorn look of a father fogged with despair and defeatism, and with it all, to hear the slow sweet broken notes of some broken-down guitar, one must cry out that all this is not good, that it should not be when there is so much around us.

When I go shopping in the supermarket and see the carts loaded with food of all kinds and I think of those families in the hills with a bare, battered, worn wooden table empty even of a crust of bread, and the children silent and speaking only with their eyes, I cannot help crying out that this is merciless, that it is wrong, that our intelligence must find some way to channel the things they need so that these humans can have at least the same chance to live and be sustained as nature offers even the wild beasts in the jungle. What I have seen in our own country, held up to be the strongest, richest, most advanced in the world, I have seen in Hong Kong, in Indonesia, India, in the Mediterranean countries, in Mexico, in the West Indies, in all of South America. I remember seeing starved little children in the back alleys of Macao lying in the mud-street making fire-crackers to earn seven cents a day! The press of the world herald on their front pages and in their important special columns all the grandiose power struggles of world statesmanship, authority opposing authority and power opposing power, and though it all seems very logical, I still see these millions, the great majority of the world, wallowing in filth, poverty, illiteracy, duped by all these grand structures of politics, high finance, and opulent, gold-encrusted religions. *What price civilization?*

The percentage of poor people in the world today is the confession that the civilization of authority and power is a dismal failure so far as the many are concerned. Perhaps, as the Age of Civilization recedes in its own dusk of the future, the new Age of *Homomundo*—World Humanism—may yet arise to herald the day when the world-view would be that our earth belongs to

all, not to the few alone. When one reads *La Vida* by Oscar
Lewis, he will more compassionately understand the need for this
hopeful change. Scott Buchanan wrote that "the best of all possible worlds is yet to be found, if Satan is to be confounded and
God to be justified."[257]

Civilization, if it ever finds good reason to justify its own
meaning in terms of simple equity, in terms of betterment for
mankind, must somehow overcome poverty and ignorance and
give the impoverished and the illiterate a chance to gain their
natural freedom to help themselves through enlightened and
freed minds, to build for themselves the securities and satisfactions that are the inalienable rights of living things in a world
they did not choose, but in which they find themselves. If civilization is not to destroy mankind and itself, then it must restore
to the common man his natural order of being, his natural freedom, and his natural ability to obtain from his environment
what once he *did* obtain, though a primitive, and which has now
been taken away from him, though a modern.

We must also give food and education to those peoples in
faraway places steeped in the folly of superstitions and engulfed
in economic slavery. Ritchie Calder: "This is the misery-go-round
of poverty: because the peasant is poor he is undernourished;
because he is undernourished he underproduces; because he
underproduces he is poor, and because he is sick, poor and hungry, he is ignorant . . . and because of poverty, these people are
condemned to live like animals, and they breed like animals."[258]
The traditional religions, like those in India with their reincarna-
tions and transmigrations and ancestor rebirths, and like Catholicism with its absoluteness against birth control, only increase
the threat of overpopulation, more widespread poverty, and continued illiteracy. All this can but lead, in time, to a disaster-
ridden and suffering human race. The dream of immortality can
yet destroy the *real* thing, the only mortal life we know. Margaret
Sanger warns: "Unless we recognize and constructively attack the
population problem now, we shall suffer the consequences of a
world so crowded and so inadequate in resources that it may well
be impossible for a free society to meet the ensuing needs."[259]
"Hungry people affect our consciences. Hungry nations affect our

future. Thus, the population explosion presents a global threat which transcends national boundaries, endangering the freedom of all mankind. It must be checked before the damage becomes irreparable, for if free institutions cannot provide the essential needs of the people they will inevitably seek another way out, even at the sacrifice of their freedom."[260] "It is a tragic fact that expanding populations are frustrating efforts on the part of the developing nations to expand their economy. Even with massive foreign aid, they cannot grow enough food, build enough housing or schools or hospitals, or provide enough jobs to keep pace with their growing populations, to whom a life without hope is no longer either inevitable or acceptable."[261] Father James Kavanaugh confesses the outdatedness of his Catholic Church: "One day, history will record the madness of my Church and amend the rules made by monks and celibates. Meanwhile, the weak and ignorant listen to the archaic arguments that support our views on birth control. They do not even sense the irony of our law. The Pope visits India, weeps for its poverty and condemns the only sensible plan to control its teeming population. He comes to the United Nations to speak of peace and takes time for an irrelevant commercial to chastise birth control. I might believe his concern for the warring world if he would relieve the misery of the weak and warring within his Church. We do not need his blessing, we need his openness to honest reform."[262]

The expanding populations of Africa today continue to increase the problems thrown on ill-equipped, newly-free nationalisms to form orderly and sound economies and societal structure. These countries are only going deeper in poverty, being already burdened with insufficient capital for production, lack of skills, insecure governments on the brink of rebellion by the ignorant, impatient, and child-brained natives demanding satisfactions and living area that can come only as a result of education, sound economy, agricultural expansion and industrial increase of technology, producing machinery and products.

Japan has already applied some controls over her population expansion; other countries might follow suit. In Africa the situation is more threatening, perhaps, than elsewhere. These African nations, just hatched to gain their independence, are bursting at

the seams with increased numbers. From lack of sufficient nur-
series, clinics, hospitals, schools, teachers, and above all, lack of
funds and economic productive sufficiency, it may follow that a
few of their leaders, educated in England, France, and America,
may become their masters, turn into dictators, power intoxicants,
and withhold free elections and proper participation of the people to choose freely and democratically their leaders. Some of
these leaders and dictators, as Nkrumah of Ghana, are actually
applying the same pernicious techniques of the Hitlers and
Mussolinis, and are bent on eliminating any freedom in their
lands except to worship, serve, and slave for the new masters.
If the populations of Africa continue to increase, and they will,
and if the economies and political orders are such that they cannot cope with this human pressure, chaos and tragedy can only
result. If the poor and underprivileged all over the world continue to increase their numbers without reasonable controls bearable in ratio to the supply of space and food, the rich and
priviliged who have been exploiting them will not have space for
themselves to enjoy their wealth. If intelligence cannot be added
to the advances of science and civilization, then perhaps the
sheer weight of pressure and resistance, of necessity, might bring
about some forced balance for survival or else extinction. This
natural process has always operated, with and without man, and
it has no choice or discretion but to continue, even blindly, as
it always has.

Greed is a product of the civilizing process. Animals do not
ordinarily possess it, neither did the aborigines, protoprimitives,
and primitives. It came with the awareness of *ownership*. It is
doubtful that the aborigine, in shaping weapons for his own use,
thought of them as we think of *property*. It is more probable
that the only thought he might have had of it was their *use*, not
the title to them. His ideology was too integrated into the tribal
wholeness of mutual-dependence and living-togetherness to create
the awareness of property that implies a *division*, or *fence*, psychological as well as real, of what belongs to one and another. If
property rights are established in some of the primitive peoples
of today, they got a few lessons from the white trader and missionary. Even the earliest forms of agriculture and cattle-raising

were communalities in which all who participated shared accordingly. The only thing that could have expressed, in those dim periods, some sense of possessiveness, was the male for the female, to guard her from being stolen from him and to maintain her for his own use, no different from the expression of males and the receptiveness of females in most of the animal world. Another thing that could have a defensive or offensive attitude of possessiveness was the proclamation of, and claim to, territory. But even in these two primal traits it is doubtful that the *idea of property* enters into the compulsions and drives of this nature; rather, the automatic process of the instinctive drives and pressures in which the awareness of holding and possessing is the natural process of *wanting-it, needing-it, using-it,* and thus *processing* both the animal and its experiences according to its nature. This primeval substratum in the nature of the animal to possess for use and against trespass by others exhibits itself in the poor and illiterate as well as in the most civilized, wealthy and intellectual people today. The underlying neurotic drive to be possessive of others to a degree that eliminates any intelligent and ethical approach to the freedoms and rights of a living thing which, in a way, does not even possess itself, lives according to its nature unchosen and in an environment to which it is unalterably tied.

The study of greed in its many manifestations in the economic history of people and institutions exposes the tragic drain on the natural freedoms, satisfactions, and even the very lives of people for thousands of years. Greed, as we understand the term, is not really part of the rudimentary and primitive nature of man. The more animal the human was the more he was primarily interested in his immediate needs; the more human the animal became, the more he became interested in what he could accumulate, not for today but for tomorrow, always tomorrow. I believe it was Mark Twain who remarked that if one feeds a dog, the dog won't bite him, and that is the difference between a dog and a man. Greed, when it becomes a craving for power, has only a lens which projects into the unreachable future. When greed becomes an obsession and a compulsive intoxicant, the beast in man emerges and atrocity in some form results. Greed does not necessarily mean an attitude toward money; it can mean an attitude of misconception as to the *real* value of something, and a series of misconcepts and confusions as to many basic foundations of ethics and equity, of human kindness. Greed is an acquired, cultural intoxicant; it is rarely known among aborigines; it is well known and very common in civilized places and people. Carthage was destroyed by Rome because of greed. Cato the Elder cried out in the Roman Senate, *"Delenda est Carthage!"*—Carthage must be destroyed! "It is noteworthy that in the Senate he waved, not the traditional sword, but a bunch of figs; the threat of Carthage was not military but economic, Carthage must be destroyed because it had learned the arts of peace too well. They who lived by the plow must perish by the plow. Militarily helpless, the Carthaginians were crushed in the Third Punic War, that ancient piece of Hitlerism. The Romans razed the proud city to the ground and symbolically drove a plow through the ruins."[263]

Greed thus becomes an accelerant to power and authority; all dictators and despots want *all* of the world if they can only put their hands on it, no matter what the cost in human lives and desolation. It is the economics of the temporarily insane, the mentally sick, the pathological miser, the power intoxicant; it is the concomitant and conspecific crystallizer of financial, industrial, political and even religious paranoia. H. R. Schoolcraft, the great American Indian investigator, wrote regarding the Hudson Bay Fur Company allowing its traders to sell wiskey to the Indians: "Little does the spirit of commerce care how many Indians die inebriated if it can be assured of its beaver skins."[264] General George Crook, considered the most experienced of Western Indian fighters, wrote a long time ago: "Greed and avarice on the part of the whites—in other words, the Almighty Dollar, is at the bottom of nine-tenths of all our Indian troubles."[265] Frazier Hunt, in his *Bewildered World,* writes about India before she became an independent nation: "Despite the vast and complicated problems of India, nowhere in the world is the tyranny of profit and uncontrolled exploitation more violently and horribly pictured."[266] "Those whose ears are attuned to the clink of gold never hear the mutterings of a mob until it becomes a roar."[267]

Greed is a robber of people's freedoms, including the misconception and abuse of this natural element in the robber himself. Greed is a kind of sadomasochistic mechanism generated by cultural consequences and the processes of civilization, which extended in a million ways the newly-found "necessity" of the *more-drive,* which means one "must" have more than another. The more this intoxicant processes itself into the daily lives of people, the more life and natural freedoms that could bring satisfaction, peace, and healthful happiness are deteriorated, and life becomes a *medium* of racing somewhere, running, expanding, extending, until the personality itself is lost in the whirlpool of awayness-from-life and becomes a whirling object, lifelike but lifeless, and the finest values and deepest satisfactions of existence are thrust aside by the centrifugal confusions of its own making.

The economic misconception is not merely of individuals or political entities; it has become the nucleus of industrial enterprise, even forced the subservience of the sciences and some of its most brilliant contributors, and has become standard procedure in any competitive enterprise in order to grow always bigger and higher and wider. John Dewey: "It is foolish to regard the political state as the only agency now endowed with coercive power. Its exercise of power is pale in contrast with that exercised by concentrated and organized property interests."[268] Bertrand Russell: "The supreme principle, both in politics and in private life, should be to promote all that is creative, and so to diminish the impulses and desires to center round possession."[269] Herbert J. Muller: "The rise to civilization again meant the rise to power and privilege of the few, at some expense to the many."[270] Jerome Davis: "The ethics of service and sacrifice for the common good cannot be harmonized with exploitation of the people, large profits for the few, and special privilege."[271] Barrows Dunham: "For the freedom which reactionaries admire is the freedom to produce cheaply and sell dear; the equality which they admire is that of equally low wages; and the fraternity they admire is that of millions of obedient workers, toiling contentedly from sunrise to sunset at machines which they do not own, making goods they will never possess."[272]

For some reason or other, probably unknown to the processors, a business "must" get bigger and bigger. Economic overextension among individuals and enterprises is often the cause of their downfall. Pyramiding of finance and production keeps going on until something gives way; in the interim human values, human happiness, and even humanness itself are often clouded and overshadowed. Life becomes a business; to this extent the natural freedoms of people to express the truer values of livingness are lost, abbreviated, twisted and forgotten. Sometimes they are recovered, but often when it is too late. At such time we strangely discover that *time* has passed us by and left us old, wiser, perhaps, and helpless to recover the unrecoverable.

One should differentiate between the natural competitiveness in man to accomplish, create, and produce, to advance himself, on the one hand, and the drive to overwhelm, overcome, overpower, to diminish the creative and personal initiative of the individual and coerce him by pressing circumstances and helpless necessity to lose this individuality to the colossus of organization. The culture gives birth to superficial, mechanical, and humanless values. No longer is there any sense of equity or enjoyment either in employing or in being employed; occupations are considered "so-and-so," just necessary in order to keep going. The advertising field, or to be more modern, the art of public relations, concerns itself not necessarily with what is good, wholesome, honest, and healthful for people, but with what is practical and "smart" for them to put something "across," in a general contour of principles that the ends, disregarding ethics or the public welfare, justify the means. J. H. Denison: "He who pays more than is necessary is regarded by his fellow men and women as an imbecile; and he who gets the best result with the minimum of expenditure is regarded as a genius."[273] F. O. Matthiessen: "We have reached the point where the next best seller could be turned out on the assembly line."[274] Janheinz Jahn: "The age of technology has produced on earth conditions from which it is no longer possible for any nation to escape."[275] Loren Eiseley: "Science is not enough for man. It is not the road back to the waiting Garden, for that road lies through the heart of man. Only when man has recognized this fact will science become what it was for Bacon, something to speak of as 'touching upon Hope.' Only then will man be truly human."[276] Bertrand Russell: "The difficulty is that, as free competition in business dies out, the victors more and more seek to use their economic power in the mental and moral sphere, and to insist upon right living and right thinking as a condition of being allowed to earn a living. This is unfortunate, as 'right living' means hypocrisy and 'right thinking' means stupidity."[277] Carl L. Becker: "Both in domestic and in foreign affairs the horse-and-buggy days are gone, and in a world in which a man can travel from New York to India in less time than it took Benjamin Franklin to travel from Philadelphia to New York the attempt to escape into the Golden Age of Normalcy is an invitation to chaos."[278] Bronislaw Malinowski: "For all this (the benefits of culture) there is a price to be paid in terms of obedience to tradition. Man must submit to a number of rules and determinants that do not come from his organism but from submission to his own artifact and machinery, to co-operation, and to the tyranny of words and other symbols. The oft-repeated opposition as between man and machine, in which man is often described as the slave of his self-produced mechanism, his Frankenstein monster, contains an essential truth."[279] "While we have become the masters of inanimate nature, we have connived at the complete enslavement of man by machine. The greatest need of today is to establish a balance between the stupendous power of natural science and its application, and the self-inflicted backwardness of social science and the consequent impotence of social engineering. . . . We have failed to develop the really scientific spirit in humanism."[280] "Modern civilization is a gigantic hypertrophy of material objects, and contemporary man will still have to fight his battle in order to assert his dominance over the Thing."[281]

As pointed out elsewhere in this book, and as many alert and thinking people, especially the younger and student classes, are growingly aware, the processes of civilization, by the impact and growing pressures of greater numbers, the ensuing necessitating mechanizations of control, and the greater requirements of restriction and limitation for order, are bringing about more rapid and compelling changes in the cultural evolution of man. These changes, in turn, are affecting his biological substratum of basic animal expression and need and thus affecting his natural freedom. Man is gradually becoming brainwashed with the whitewash of cultures; he is becoming "whiter," but diluted, cellophane-packed without strength. Whatever energy he has left becomes the vitality of societal order and greater efficiency. Somewhere he has lost himself within the very coils of his own inventive genius, and the very spirit of his life has dwindled into the porridge of collective non-being.

Today, and probably more so tomorrow, man is becoming a slave of civilization, ostensibly thinking he has more freedom because he has more gadgets. In actuality, he has become more dependent upon other things than himself. Lost in the whirl of routine and submission to obscurantism and the more modern pseudo-theologies, he has forgotten to live the moment, the hour and the day, forever sacrificing foolishly and needlessly today for tomorrow. Man is not his *natural self*. He is less self-sufficient. The more his individuality becomes lost in numbers, conveniences, and orderly routines, the less his individuality has the mood, the chance, or the will to review itself as a born-free animal, detached from cultural impressment, a born-free animal with one life to live that we are sure of and know of. Every catastrophe of mechanical failure affecting great numbers of people proves the growing helplessness of people and the failing cry of the individual to find his natural bearings in the increasing stampede of things and machines which are growing and extending far beyond the power and will of individuals and even groups. As Henry Miller says, "The future belongs to the machines, the robots." Man is gradually becoming the slave of his own creations. Where it may lead is anyone's guess. Man must increasingly submit to the Master Control, the Computer, the Machine, the Routine. These are the new four horsemen that grind their mechanical wheels over the destinies of people.

There are still many places in the Carribean where one can find little homes in the countryside where a family has its own donkey or burro, chickens, a few pigs, a dog or two, a litter of kittens, a patch of banana trees, perhaps a mango and a few coconut palms. These people, as a rule, do not live with the radio, television, or electric power. They live with the stars, the moon, the sunshine, the wind, and fresh, tree-ripened fruits. They are part of the natural household, simple and limited, often even severe and cruel. Most assuredly many a Carib peasant would fly, if he could, to change places with the Madison Avenue penthouse New Yorker, and most assuredly the Madison Avenue man finds escape and relief under a coconut palm swaying gently in the breeze by the sea. These are the recurrent reminders of human nature that the next man's garden may be greener and more fruitful. Whether the peasant enjoys more natural freedom than the mechanical *homo* on Madison Avenue may be judged by anyone. Time alone can tell who was more fortunate, regardless of ignorance or wisdom, regardless of lowness or greatness.

While we cannot retreat or escape from civilization, or its continual penetration into all corners of the habitable world (where the other animals will manage to live and survive is a nightmare of every humane human as well as to the zoologists), it continues to take its toll of human freedom as well as the freedom of almost everything else on earth. Mechanization continues relentlessly, like some Juggernaut pressing into vanishment the naturalness of things and the personalities of human beings, leaving behind structures of steel and blocks of concrete, filthy and dead rivers, polluted skies, and human robots scrambling among all this trying to overtake each other. The drive to exceed and supersede may yet make Nietzsche, one of the founding fathers of modern Nazism, a sounding prophet: "This secret spoke Life herself unto me: 'Behold,' said she, 'I am that which must ever surpass itself!' "[282]

If man is to restore to himself and preserve the freedoms with which nature has endowed him, then it becomes highly relevant that he preserve the parent-endowment, Nature itself. Besides, it is the first and ultimate cupboard of his economy, his own bionomy. Should the basal ecological frame within which man's life exists and upon which it depends for life be changed or destroyed to such an extent that it cannot recover the minimal sufficiencies, then man has sealed his own doom, built his own

mausoleum with his sciences and ingenuities of economic and
political chimeras, and the last human, before closing the door,
can rightly clamor to the skies that he *did* surpass himself!

However, there are many who feel that somehow man will
recover from his errors,, apply his sciences to *assist* Nature and
himself. Glenn T. Seaborg feels that there may be a growing
rapprochement between the sciences and the humanities, that
eventually newer interpretations and applications of the sciences
will lead to a better, freer, and more peaceful world. He writes:
"Today there are encouraging indications—still modest perhaps,
but plainly evident—of a growing rapprochement between science
and the humanities and arts. . . . It seems likely that, as more is
learned about the fine structure of matter in relation to biological processes and, at the other end of the scale, about the relations
between nuclear processes and events in the far reaches of the
universe, there may be renewed efforts to achieve a philosophical
integration of science."[283] . . . "Science and the humanities had
their beginnings during the same era of Western cultural growth.
The remarkable intellectual achievements of the Renaissance that
contained the seeds of modern science were accompanied by lasting achievements in the arts. In certain individuals—Leonardo da
Vinci, Albrecht Dürer, Andrea del Verrocchio, and Sandro Botti-
celli—talents for the arts and science were mutually supporting,
and the great masterpieces of these artists could hardly have been
created in the absence of this duality of interests."[284] . . . "The
growing body of scientific knowledge has, by changing man's
view of reality, modified in an irreversible fashion the earlier
boundaries of the imagination and its limits of freedom."[285]

Nature is a blind mother. She is all we have and yet she expresses no feelings or concern for us. She gives birth to the good
and bad alike *not knowing* which is either, allows them to make
of her what they please, and ultimately swallows them up anyway. She strikes lightning that she cannot see, but we can. She
sends thunderbolts that she cannot hear, but we can. And we
live within her, are part of her. She makes no rules, but we do.
She always exposes herself in the nude, yet the only shame is
ours. We can use our knowledge and skill to modify her appearance, her gifts and products. Neglected or unopposed, subjected

to the pressures and resistances which always keep her in helpless motion, she will act only as her nature directs, indifferently and blindly. Albert Schweitzer: "In Europe man is lord over the earth. In the primeval forest of Equatorial Africa he is a creature that with difficulty wrests a bit of land from the wilderness. His plantation is always surrounded by forest and sooner or later the forest will swallow it up again."[286] And yet if we wastefully destroy the forests and pollute the rivers and thereby destroy the life in both, we, to this extent, destroy the only home we can ever have—this planet. Rachel L. Carson: "The problem of water pollution by pesticides can be understood only in context, as part of the whole to which it belongs—the pollution of the total environment of mankind."[287] "Along with the possibility of the extinction of mankind by nuclear war, the central problem of our age has therefore become the contamination of man's total environment with such substances of incredible potential for harm—substances that accumulate in the tissues of plants and animals and even penetrate the germ cells to shatter or alter the very material of heredity upon which the shape of the future depends."[288]

Mark Graubard wrote that "God did not give us truth ready-made, any more than he gave us bread."[289] Thus, it is up to us to make use of our knowledge, our sciences, and our judgment for sheer survival, to make use of nature without doing irreparable damage; to better her for us by using parts or combinations of her elements, not to destroy but to bolster the natural household; to enjoy her beauty and regard it as worldly treasure, not to despoil it with desecrating billboards or cruelly litter her with our wastes and discards.

For billions of years the animal and plant life that perished went back into the nature of things without infesting the soil and water; but ever since man came to *know* of death he has wanted to preserve himself in death—as if he could! With the growing explosion of human numbers, if man continues to insist on "preserving" himself in the ground, there will be, no doubt, as a result, more graves than homes for the living. Necessity has invoked the need of cremation instead of burial wherever there was no choice if any land were to be left for the living. Japan and India are two examples where there is hardly any

room for the living, let alone the dead; so they managed to receive divine revelation from the gods that to cremate the body
is to purify the spirit. Many peoples in history cremated their
dead, not because they lacked spare land for burial grounds, but
because people did not stay put for any length of time in any
particular place and as a result did not want to leave their dead
to the vultures or wild animals. Yet in many parts of the world
primitive people still take the dead into the jungle so that the
wild beasts can consume them more quickly. "Oddly enough, in
the period which began about 1000 B.C. all the Germanic peoples
began to practice cremation."[290]

The idea of burial in a good number of countries rose with
stabilized settlements and in the cultural and religious acceptance
of the concept that preservation of the body preserves the existence of the soul. In America funerals and burials have built a
gigantic disposal system invested with charm and covered with
flowers. ". . . 65 to 70 percent of the flower industry's revenue, or
$414 million a year, derives from the sale of funeral flowers."[291]
So much money spent for cut flowers when there are millions of
poor children who have not a little flower pot with a single
geranium, and millions more who have not the chance of smelling
a loaf of fresh bread. The affluent society does not wish to be
told about the poor surrounding them; it is distasteful to them
and would mar the enjoyment of an evening at the theater.
George Bernard Shaw so wisely said: "Dead bodies can be cremated. All of them ought to be; for each burial, a horrible practice, will some day be prohibited by law, not because it is
hideously unaesthetic, but because the dead would crowd the
living off the earth if it could be carried out to its end of preserving our bodies for their resurrection on an imaginary Day
of Judgment (in sober fact, every day is a day of judgment)."[292]

It may be good to revere the departed, to have memories of
their love and good deeds, of their devotion and meaning to us.
This is natural and wholesome. It is also natural and more wholesome to express reverence for those we love *whle they live,* while
they can enjoy our affection and our appreciation of what they
have done for us—to hold in mind that whatever we do and feel,
after they are gone, is to console *ourselves* or plague us with

guilts. Let us be conscionable in terms of the living, and if we do, we will be revering the dead in the best manner the dead, if they could talk, would want, if they were alive and with us. Freedom can be expressed only among the living; the dead have no need of it.

As an animal in its wilder state, the aborigine was probably unconscious of any division of power and authority between himself and the environment. He went about like any other wild animal, eating, drinking, moving, gibbering and jabbering with his fellow creatures, mating to fulfill his instinctual drive. The dominance of some over others expressed itself as it does in all animaldom where the drive is so expressed. But this dominance, in the strict sense, was not a cultural acquisition; it was part of the evolved socio-biological framework of the species and operated and processed natural selection and the survival of the fittest in nature's automatic and mechanical way. In many ways, it manifests itself in man to this very day and remains, will always remain, the basic skeletal frame of the human animal and his race.

Even the sense of *time* is unknown in the natural field; time is an invention of man; it identifies itself with his acquired characteristics and philosophies, with his sciences, and with the human concepts of the sense and value of authority and power. Because man gives something a name does not necessarily identify for certain the nature of its substance or the exact dimensional relatedness of it to all else. Leslie Spier: "Time is man-made; nature knows only change. . . . Man is aware of changes in his body and in the outer world—changes through day and night, the succession of the seasons, and their recurrent nature. But the reckoning of periods of change, by hour, day, or year, is a human concept, projected on the world, and known to no other animal."[293]

The economics of the ecology of man preceded his sense of power, authority, and the awareness of property, wealth, and the possession of things beyond his instinctual and animal needs. The sense and the gravitational pull toward power and all its offspring came as leadership emerged in man, as man realized that there were other things besides food, mate, and shelter that man needed, "invisible" or psychological factors which such leadership more or less resolved for others, who thus became psychologically dependent upon it. This was no longer an expression of dominance, of brute strength or better weapon. Leadership disarmed men by the weapon of *fear* and the constant cultivation and acquisition of more things to fear. Thus, by *fearing*, man surrendered to this extent his natural and individual freedom, pawned his simple and natural animal drive, and began to acquire the cultural-psychic products by which power and authority of the few over the many impregnated itself more and more as man entered more and more into known and cultural history.

The rewards of power and authority were great because their extensions encompassed the growing sense of property, wealth, kingship, and divinity, and this growing sense of leadership, regardless of its kind, whether king, priest, or military conqueror, or integrated combinations of all three, acknowledged to itself the "natural" or "godly" justice of their owning and subjecting other people as slaves. The acquired awareness that one human can actually own another human and use him for services and sacrifice on a conscionable basis, without benefit of his natural freedom for volitional choice, reared its ugly head and *slavery* entered human history. No established, orthodox, and formal religion, ancient and throughout history, opposed the custom, principle, and institution of slavery within the lands where any of these religions operated, whether in the Orient, the Near East, Africa, Europe or the Americas. Slavery was worldwide, and still exists in many areas. In some places where it has been legally and socially and politically abolished, it persists today in various forms. Prejudice is born within the cell of religiosity, and all the religious crimes and massacres throughout history identify the fierce hate, partiality, and biogtry generated and endured for thousands of years. Thus, slavery was accepted, and is still accepted, and *exploitation* of people by one or a few on a "just" or "ordained" basis was nurtured and established.

We should hold in mind that cultural products rise out of biological beginnings. That a certain cultural acquisition is completely remote from the "dividing" line "separating" the biological from the cultural is a human invention and viewpoint, as likewise the separation of body and soul, material and immaterial. Santayana: "Everything ideal has a natural basis and everything natural an ideal development." The pure culturist, that is, like the theologian who "separates" mind and body, is like the child who refuses to acknowledge that he was born of parents. Accordingly, if we analyze the problem of slavery and exploitation, we come to see that the potential of such things is innate in the human psyche. Where man has achieved the institution of slavery through cultural emergence, the ant has perfected it by instinctual drive; the ant, in age, was a great-great-grandfather when man was not even a sparkle in the shrew's retina. Perhaps if man can survive and exist as long as the ant, human slavery might become a "natural instinct" "nurtured" from a "cultural acquisition" having its beginnings in biological evolution. It seems more probable that culture is a certain phasic process in the evolution of man, and the evolution of man is tied to the evolution of all else on earth as *one* integrated, interdependent, and related process. When we examine the economics of man in this light, the emergence of various forms of power and authority, we begin to realize that they are transitional, modifying processes and products operating within the realm and potential of natural freedom that make transition and change possible.

The same freedom that has established slavery can be eliminated by the same freedom that finds slavery repugnant to it. Irreconcilables identify forms of opposing kinds of freedom, and as far as Nature is concerned, she does not care who is furthest and who the devil takes as the hindmost. Culture and civilization alone will not save man. The sooner we realize it and restore to ourselves the simple elements of natural freedom operating in a limited world, the sooner our knowledge can be applied to better ourselves and create a more peaceful and happy world. Dobzhansky: "Man's future inexorably depends on the interactions of biological and social forces. Understanding these forces and their interactions may, in the fullness of time, prove to be the main achievement of science."[294] Lester F. Ward: "This ideal solution will be realized through a long series of slight advances which constitute true social progress, which will take place in

strict proportion to the increase and diffusion of sound knowledge of the true nature of man and society."[295]

Accordingly, we come to understand, as we study the history
of man in a clearer, analytical light, that, while it is natural and
logical that man cannot live as an isolated being, the satisfactions
of his whole existence are interrelated and dependent upon some
form of human organization to provide some security in an orderly society, the invention has become the controller, the
few over the many, power and authority have superseded the
very purposes of organization and have become *the* organization.
The individuals who, for biological and cultural reasons, created
it, have become in many ways not necessarily identified with it.
They have become slaves, exploited and regimented to suit the
intended effects of the privileged few, the leaders, the public relations man, the top echelon managements, dictators, the industrial, financial, and commercial impersonalities, and the good old
stand-bys of theologies and theogonies, all operating to make man
feel "civilized," "cultured," and "free," while all the time making him gradually into a nonentity, a robot, depriving him of the
natural freedom of his own awareness as a person, an individual,
a mere adjunct to silly rule and sedentary routine. Whatever
creativeness he might possess is dissipated in a drifting of the
stamina of life-expression away from its natural ways, losing itself
somewhere between the crevices of machines, numbers, files, and
organizational purposes. The picture the painter has made has
come to life, moved out of its frame, and broken the brushes.

Man cannot wholly detach himself from his cultural past and
the good and evil it has brought him. But he can use his freedom
to lift himself out of it by accepting the principle that, although
he is a product of what has been, *the past does not exist* save as he
expresses freedom to hold onto it, modify it for betterment or
some change, or forget it. Whatever it is, it is still within the
constitution of man's freedom to allow change, and better change
will come with better education, with more knowledge of ourselves and our creations. Nothing is ordained forever, and it is
within man's right to force the emergence of newer forms *more
compatible* with his biological and cultural wants and needs,
which could allow a field wherein the individual might be able

to find himself *enjoying life,* his own being, even within an order of reasonable and natural cohesion to group and organization, which should exist not for its own expression of power and authority but to use these vehicles to preserve and secure the means by which the natural power and the compatible authority of the individual can sense and fulfill itself.

So long as these things do not come about as fully as they should and withhold fruition of the natural drives of freedom itself, man will remain the rebel, and human existence will continue to be a rebellion in some form or manner. It seems reasonable that man, even in a more nearly perfect society or order of things, can never completely dispose of his rebellious spirit, his restlessness for change, his emotional curiosity to reach beyond his horizons for things unknown and unattained. This is the very fire of freedom itself, and as long as man exists it is not possible for this fire to go out completely. It can only go out with extinction. What the eventual outcome might be is anyone's guess: one way is ultimate destruction or transition into things and termites; the other way is a restoration of enlightened freedom and democratic process to bring peace and conscious enjoyment of life as *beings,* not as things. Kenneth E. Boulding, writing about his hope of a "post-civilization" age to evolve from or supersede the "civilization" age, gives us his cautiously modest projection: "The characteristic institutions of civilization are, as we have seen, first agriculture, then the city, then war, in the sense of clash of organized armed forces, and finally, inequality, the sharp contrast between the rich and the poor, between the city and the country, between the urbane and the rustic. The state is based very fundamentally on violence and exploitation, and the culture tends to be spiritually monolithic. . . . On the whole, though, I will not shed tears over the grave of civilization any more than I will over pre-civilized society. The credit balance of post-civilization is large. It at least gives us a chance of a modest utopia in which slavery, poverty, exploitation, gross inequality, war and disease —these prime costs of civilization—will fall to the vanishing point."[296]

The rebels in history usually got it in the neck, and rebels are bound to keep getting it in the neck. Jesus rebelled against

the money changers in the Temple and was crucified for his
efforts to free his fellow Jews from the bondage of king and priest.
Millions have since suffered and died for the same cause in all
the countries and histories of the world. Hundreds of great men
have been persecuted and murdered because they felt it was wrong
that one should have so much so that so many should have to
suffer with little. The disarrangements of the natural ecology of
human existence have come about through the distortions and
abuses of power and authority in its many manifestations and
because of the obscurantisms that have blinded people to accept
their privations as the "Will of God"! In 1932, when the Great
Depression saw the world disarranged because of these factors,
the cupboards stuffed with food and material, on the one hand,
and a starving, unemployed world on the other, Pope Pius XI
issued his encyclical in which he appealed to the people to accept
privation and suffering as the Divine Will that ordained starvation in an "ever-loving" caress of affection. Pope Pius XI proclaimed: "Let the poor and all those who at this time are facing
the hard trial of want of work and scarcity of food, let them in a
like spirit of penance suffer with greater resignation the privations imposed upon them by these hard times and the state of
society, which Divine Providence in an ever-loving but inscrut-
able plan has assigned them. Let them accept with a humble and
trustful heart from the hand of God the effects of poverty, rendered harder by the distress in which mankind now is struggling.
. . . Let them take comfort in the certainty that their sacrifices
and troubles borne in a Christian spirit will concur efficaciously
to hasten the hour of mercy and peace."[297]

I am sure that after the issuance of the encyclical, the Pope
was able to eat a comfortable meal without fear that some insurance company was going to foreclose on his home and put him
out. It reminds me of the Buddhist monks in Ceylon, who beg
the people to give and give while they readily exhibit vast treasures of wealth. When they exhibit one of Buddha's teeth, the
populace goes wild and gives more—and the people stay poor
and wretched. All this belongs to the tyranny of words, as Stuart
Chase has put it, and indicates the cruel use of language to mislead millions of people from doing something to prevent such

privation and reconstruct some reasonable basis upon which they can achieve and sustain some economic equilibrium in a world that has and offers it. The fallacy and hypocrisy of such utterances only reveal their real intent of using psychological power over people to persuade them to accept unjust situations, when any thoughtful person can easily see that the concept of fate or fatalism, that is, to accept whatever happens as destined and pre-ordained and irrevocable, and the concept of free will advocated by the dogma of the Church, upon which the entire essence of sin and the "justifiable" punishment thereof is based, become contradictory and silly.[298]

The expression, play, and abuse of power and authority go beyond the recognized and acknowledged forms of religious and political leadership, societal law, and cultural implications and pressures; they penetrate into the expressions and activities of the "little people," the rank-and-file constituents of any society or organization. Being psychological intoxicants and human-trait depressors of freedom, they exhibit themselves in myriad ways and forms in the daily occupations, movements, and even in the very homes of people. Whether it be the manic dominance by a wife or the inconsiderate and cruel domination by a husband, or the unjust and biased exhibitions of the foreman or forelady, the department manager, top executive, or employer who knows beforehand the fears of subordinates to protest or stand up for their rights as people, or the car driver who is unfair and discourteous on the road, or the cruel human beast who kicks a dog or a cat, or the hunter who cannot resist shooting a bird off a branch or cutting off a zebra's tail to show off his "bravado" to the folks back home, or the man who thinks he is entitled to *more* respect just because he is older and that power and authority go with seniority irregardless of competence, intelligence, ingenuity, and individual drive—all these are expressions of authority or pseudo-authority, with one central theme common to all: *insecurity* and *inferiority,* the two problems that somehow enter into almost every man born into the world. The toll these exact all over the world is awesome in needless misery, frustration, and unhappiness. The need for power reveals the innate fear of insecurity, and the need of authority reveals the innate fear of inferiority. The psychological expression of power and authority pervades all the experiences of people, young and old, men and women, and leaves its imprint in almost endless ways upon them, from the time of birth to the end of life.

Whether it is the psychic compulsion of the organism to move to the higher light, to extend itself by exceeding, overwhelming, or overcoming others in the process, or the psychic compulsion to escape or withdraw from the darkness, from the depths to avoid absorption, we do not actually know. The nature of these neural and psychic processes upon the expression and livingness of freedom depends upon the nature and experience eventuated in the use of this power and authority, and its causative sequences. One principle, therefore, that power and authority do not usually recognize is that freedom belongs to *each* individual and *all* individuals, and that power and authority are *processes*, like everything else in the life and in the cosmos, necessitated or cultured in the experience of group or mass living and producing some form or sort of maintenance and continuity of this freedom. Unfortunately, we have become the victims of our own inventions and institutions.

No one in his right mind would argue that human nature does not necessitate control and guidance for its own good, without which the chaos that would immediately ensue would last until the entire human race perished by its own hand. And this control and guidance cannot be accomplished without some established power and authority to *process* and direct these controls. This *process* of power and authority, if it is not to become the master and enslaver, must be fully understood and accepted as the *servant* of the people, not the people as servants to the images of power and authority. Security and a normative sense of being cannot be obtained or nurtured so long as humans continue to contain the acceptance of the concept of fear toward situations and philosophies they themselves had created. We must stop building our own prisons, stop sitting upon the mythic stools of sovereignty warden-intoxicants to subject us to experiences that tend to destroy us. We must renovate what needs renovating and bury the obscurantisms and theologies that have kept us prisoners in this imaginary cage of self-delusion and stupid depressants.

Attempting to explain the *Hostile Mind,* Leon J. Saul writes: "Each individual in our society is activated by strong asocial and antisocial motivations, as well as by social ones. Only by understanding these two sets of motives, the one against life, and the other for it, can we implement those that are prohuman and reduce those that are antihuman; only in this way we can avoid the terror, tyranny, war and want that threaten us all."[299]

NECESSITY, LAW, AND DEMOCRACY

IN RECOGNIZING THE need of control and guidance, no one in his right mind could believe that the arbitrary use of such controls and guidances by individuals also endowed with human nature, or the use of psychological control and authority as exhibited in the religions by those also endowed with human nature, are the keys to such solutions. On the contrary, these have brought upon mankind untold harm, misery, slavery, and exploitation. Power and authority must be understood and established as *vehicles* upon which mankind can ride, move forward, or of which it can avail itself in many ways; they are not to make of mankind the vehicle itself, to be harnessed and subjected to a philosophy which only tends to eliminate the natural sense of being through the diminishment of the natural sense of freedom. The *vehicles* of power and authority allow people to control themselves, and these vehicles are not authoritarian in structure but pliable and subject to change to meet the necessities of change in a world that constantly changes. Power and authority must be considered as an *employment of law,* whose enforcement is a *protective necessity* and whose guidance belongs to the people and their freedom, a public evolved into a *polis* of mutual considerations and concepts based upon the reality of the world and life as revealed through the sciences and the knowledge they impart to us.

Power and authority *over* people must be depersonalized, derigidified, and desanctified so that the power and authority processes should be *for* the people and not instruments of despotism and tyranny. They should emphasize, and be concomitant to, the general process of living on *this* earth, and not allow or accept the silliness of the traditional promises of theology to glorify the suffering of privation and poverty *here* in order to become millionaires on some clouds, yet parting with the little we have to those who profit by these heavenly promises and threatening punishments and batten rich and richer as we get poor and poorer. Humanity must become *humanized* again, not deified. It must become *humanistic* and while we live. Corliss Lamont: "If human beings are to be happy and enjoy life, it must always be during some period of time describable as *now*."[300] Humanity must rise above the past saturated with kingship, priestcraft, dictatorship and imperial saviors who fatten themselves upon the misled masses of humanity. Humanity must restore to itself the natural freedom of rediscovering its own consciousness as *beings* and the irreplaceable values in *being*—if we still want the chance to prove to ourselves and to those who will come after us that we are able to become better and wiser and kinder animals than those around us.

What are the means by which this can be brought about? Here are some of them: *controls* by equitable and democratic jurisprudence and processes and their protective enforcement agencies; *guidance* by education in all its phases, teaching the very young and growing adolescents *how to think* sensibly and freely, how to think and act *ethically* and *why;* the use of *reason* and the inculcation of the history and knowledge of the processes of democratic thought and action in all the departments of human expression and endeavor; the use of *science* to improve upon nature, not destroy it, to preserve our environment, not to waste it; the *realization* that it is only by preserving the freedom of all that we can preserve the freedom of each. Only when *all* are actually *free* can human beings combine the natural freedoms of their earthly heritage and the intellective cumulation and its products throughout history into a restoration and advance in which man can find naturally free expression and possible fulfillment in his restless nature and peace by understanding and congruity, an equitable maturation of his ethics and sciences, and a just commensal and compensational economic system permitting the general welfare to participate in the general abundance. If man is to better himself, he must depend upon himself to do it; if he is to destroy himself, it will be by his own hand. "The Humanist requires no cosmic spokesman to inform or remind him of the dignity of man and the ideal of human brotherhood. The most democratic countries certainly are not and have not been those steeped in supernatural religion. Humanist belief in democracy as the goal and in democratic processes as the method is not derivative from extra-human sources; it stands on its own feet."[301] And man will not be free enough until he is allowed to stand on his own feet; he will not know and enjoy the dignity of being and living until he can look down and see that he *is* standing on his own feet.

Democracy seems at present to be the only philosophy (social, economic, political, religious, and international) that expresses and processes a *means* rather than an end unto itself. It is the means by which a human being can restore to himself and express the natural freedoms that are his life's property and right, his own eminent domain, the sovereignty of his being. No group, society or theology has any right to take this away from him or to discolor it or mislead him with their nonsense. Max Lerner: "For in the end it is man who is the root—not ideologies, not parties, not slogans, not races or religions, but man himself, and the human nexus that ties him to his fellow man."[302]

If democracy has not succeeded as it should have, it is not that there are fundamental fallacies in its philosophy, but such unsuccessfulness or failure reveals that people are not yet fully cognizant of its values, and that human nature has not attained to an intellectual and practical level of wisdom to accept it as the key to the restoration of their own freedoms. If the human race is to survive, it can survive only as *individuals,* and if there is any value in surviving, it can be only as *free individuals.* Democracy is the only process evolved in the societal experiences of people and in the mind of man that can reasonably assure the preservation and continuance of the individual as a free animal. "The democratic spirit is not dogmatic, for it recognizes the value of constant challenges to basic assumptions. . . . These basic forms of democracy are crucial because they provide the central mechanisms for orderly change and progress."[303]

Democracy is a *process*, not an establishment of any absolute forms or an attempt to create an absolute form. It has existed as *natural freedom* in the nature of human and other animal life, necessitating continual *compatibilities* to satisfy want and desire. It preceded the emergence of culture and its priestcrafts and kingships and all their forms of psychological and arbitrary powers and authorities. It is for man *now* to apply his *reason* and his *knowledge* accumulated over the prehistorical and historical periods, to *restore* and apply this natural freedom to express its processes, not for *its* own good (which is impossible), but for *his* own individual good, for his survival and life satisfaction in a constantly changing and eventful world. As Lamont concludes his book on humanism, *man must be his own savior and his own redeemer*—"Humanism assigns to man nothing less than the task of being his own saviour and redeemer."[304]

I repeat: it is not our prayers and our glorification of altars and books, our adoration of stones and wood and jeweled ikons, our flattering epitaphs today for people murdered yesterday, our soothsaying and reverently epistled encyclicals that will redeem us. All these are meaningless and mere pageantry. It is what we actually *do* to make this world a happier, more just, more honest, more peaceful, and healthier home for ourselves and our environmental relatives and fauna; it is this actual doing that could be really appraised as a morality if we intend to stop kidding ourselves with words and gestures and determine to be honest and realistic.

Already the younger and newer generations are beginning to see through the clouding obscurantisms and false prophets and misleading and enslaving ideologies. They intend to *live*, not to be sacrificed for ideals that should have been buried away thousands of years ago and not carried on the backs of the living. The young demand and need the natural freedom to live happy and secure lives. This want is the primary and rooted nucleus of every living thing. Here justice begins.

Margaret Mead, in summarizing a symposium on the study of personality, struck a clarion call for this beginning: "We are going to be fashioning children who are going to be different from any human beings who have ever been—from whom we are going to have to be able to learn things that we would not otherwise know. Although there have been premonitions of it in the past, this is going to be a totally new model of human experience. For millenia it has been the experience of the elders, passed on to the children, that has bound culture together. Now we have got to tie in with this experience of the elders an ability (we do not know how to cultivate yet) to learn from the children who will have an experience that no one has ever had before. We must do so if we are to design the kinds of society for which there have been no precursors and for which we have no models."[305] Joseph Campbell: "We today, willy-nilly, *must* enter the forest *là ou nos la voions plus espesse:* and, like it or not, the pathless way is the only way now before us."[306]

The *new* future will be more of an uncharted sea than any previous future of any previous generations of youth had ever had to sail through. More than ever before, the cultural rigidity and continuity of conventional and traditional sociocultural structures will be looked upon by the young, not with awe and fear, stress and anxiety, but with the now more free, creative, curious, and inventive ways and eyes of the newborn to seek means of peacefully, perhaps reluctantly, but determinedly, to destroy the strictures of repression and life-wastage that cultural history has, by twists and turns of thousands of years of neuropsychological influences upon the human psyche, brought about, and the continuing plague of psychotic and psychosomatic pathologies, pathetic politics, and sickening, tragic ideologies, individually and collectvely, it has perpetuated.

What was yesteryear considered necessarily proper and respectable can now be understood and explained as necessarily incongruous with human sentiment and capacity to find identity, reality, and fulfillment of life satisfactions. Master Culture, with its priestly fairy tales and secular royalties of dyed bloods, did truly change human nature from a less fearless and a freer primitive into a civilized victim and slave. But human nature has remained changeable, as all else on earth is changeable and changing.

The new seed, in freer soil, will change the leaf and the fruit from the same roots. It will take time, but we are on the *new*

A Philosophy of Freedom

way. I know I shall not be here to witness the vanguard fringe penetrations of the new uncharted sea. At present we *know* we have left behind the cruel Scyllas and Charybdises with their Circean illusions. We are in the thick fog before us and around us, but we *know* that beyond the fog we can hear, even distantly, the buoy bells that may guide us into the clearing of a better world and a humanity of happier and healthier people.

The courage of the young, nurtured by a restoration of natural freedom, will build a world, not of hunters and the hunted, but one in which the aggression and no longer transgression and competitive personality-deteriorating compulsions is transformed into individuated and intelligent forms of *necessary* and *compatible* participations for individual, mutual, and world ends by the constant and continuing *means* of realization that no future belongs to the present, that the present must find its own happiness, security, and peace within itself *now*. The impact of this realization means the regeneration of youthfulness, and youthfulness, however old, is a condition that takes time longer to overcome. The youth of today refuse to be sacrificed for the youth of tomorrow, and the youth of tomorrow will be happier and wiser because of the courage of the youth of today.

Only the restoration of the natural freedom given by birth can bring this about. Though the historical priestly and political barricades stand in the way, these are doomed to fade, as they are already doing. The young will trample over their debris of glorified marble, and in their place create the true natural law that must ultimately abide if natural freedom is to emerge and be made secure to endure. Sovereignty, religious and secular, will give way to human sovereignty, to world law and world government, and thus world peace. True, this is a hope, but a hope that knowledge and courage may miraculously bring to reality. Only the young and the coming young can have the courage to save themselves and humanity from unrecoverable disaster and destruction. Only the young can have the courage and knowledge to make this realizable.

REFERENCES—BOOK FOUR

1. Kaj Birket-Smith, *The Paths of Culture*, pp. 119-120.
2. Peter Farb, *Man's Rise to Civilization*, p. 107.
3. H. Ubbelohde-Doering, *On the Royal Highways of the Inca*, p. 11.
4. H. R. Hays, *In the Beginnings*, p. 20.
5. Edward B. Tylor, *Religion in Primitive Culture*, pp. 117-9.
6. Donald Harden, *The Phoenicians*, pp. 113-4.
7. Kaj Birket-Smith, *The Paths of Culture*, p. 376.
8. W. Storrs Lee, *The Islands*, p. 12.
9. C. A. Burland, *Peru Under the Incas*, p. 41.
10. Max Müller, see *Lectures*, 2nd Series, p. 425.
11. Edward B. Tylor, *Religion in Primitive Culture*, pp. 344-5.
12. Robert Graves and Raphael Patai, *Hebrew Myths*, p. 11.
13. Lewis Mumford, *The Myth of the Machine*, p. 199.
14. C. A. Burland, *Peru Under the Incas*, p. 46.
15. Kenneth E. Boulding, *Divine Legitimation and the Defense Establishment*, Humanist Magazine, Jan.-Feb., 1968, p. 24.
16. Kaj Birket-Smith, *The Paths of Culture*, p. 376.
17. see *Egyptian Mythology*, trans. Delano Ames, from "Mythologie Generale," Larousse, pp. 10-11.
18. H. R. Hays, *In the Beginnings*, p. 76.
19. J. H. Denison, *Emotion as the Basis of Civilization*, p. 63.
20. Thomas Jefferson, see *Views of Religion*, ed. Rufus K. Noyes, p. 407.
21. Martin A. Larson, *The Religion of the Occident*, p. 511.
22. André Gide.
23. C. P. Snow, quoted in *Freedom in the Modern World*, Muller, p. 118.
24. St. Augustine, *The City of God*, Book IV, Chapter IV.
25. J. H. Denison, *Emotion as the Basis of Civilization*, p. 62.
26. H. R. Hays, *In the Beginnings*, p. 536.
27. James G. Frazer, *The Golden Bough*, 1 vol. ed., p. 277.
28. H. R. Hays, *In the Beginnings*, p. 107.
29. *Ibid.*, p. 108.
30. Jacquetta Hawkes and Sir Leonard Woolley, *Prehistory and the Beginnings of Civilization*, vol. I, "The History of Mankind," p. 701.
31. Robert Graves and Raphael Patai, *Hebrew Myths*, p. 63.
32. *Ibid.*, p. 116.
33. *Ibid.*, p. 13.
34. Joseph Campbell, *Masks of God: Oriental Mythology*, pp. 379-380.
35. W. Oldfield Howey, *The Cat in Religion and Magic*, p. 72.
36. *Ibid.*, p. 60.
37. Martin A. Larson, *The Religion of the Occident*, p. 662.
38. Frederic Morton, *The Rothschilds*, p. 110.
39. E. J. Hobsbawn, *The Age of Revolution*, p. 305.
40. Walter Hanf, *Mexico*, pp. 44-5.
41. Durward V. Sandifer and L. Ronald Scheman, *The Foundations of Freedom*, p. 8.
42. Bertrand Russell, *Power*, p. 204.
43. Durward V. Sandifer and L. Ronald Scheman, *The Foundations of Freedom*, p. 46.
44. John Adams, quoted in *Freedom in the Modern World*, Muller, p. 8.
45. Louis A. Reitmeister, *The Gods and My Friends*, p. 18.
46. Paul Blanshard, *God and Man in Washington*, p. 211.
47. Herbert J. Muller, *Freedom in the Modern World*, p. 38.

48. V. T. Thayer, *Religion in Public Education,* p. 26.
49. Bertrand Russell, *Power,* p. 130.
50. Henry Steele Commager, *On the Way to 1984,* Saturday Review, April 15, 1967, p. 82.
51. Julia Peterkin, *Living Philosophies,* p. 200.
52. James Jeans, *ibid.,* p. 113.
53. Rabbi Morris S. Lazaron, *Some Challenges to American Democracy,* Proceedings of Congress on Education for Democracy, Columbia University, August, 1939, pp. 86-7.
54. Paul Weiss, *The Right to Disobey,* from "Law and Philosophy," ed. Sidney Hook, p. 99.
55. Lester L. Wolff, *The Responsibilities of Dissent,* Congressional Record, March 16, 1967.
56. John Dewey, address *Democracy and Educational Administration,* Feb. 22, 1937.
57. W. W. Aldrich, *The Incompatibility of Democracy and a Planned Economy.*
58. Sidney Hook, *Political Power and Personal Freedom,* p. 11.
59. *Ibid.,* p. 517.
60. Bertrand Russell, *Power,* p. 206.
61. Makarios, Time Magazine, Sept. 18, 1964.
62. Josue de Castro, *Death in the Northeast,* p. 84.
63. Lewis Mumford, *Technics and the Nature of Man,* from "Knowledge Among Men," p. 135.
64. E. Adamson Hoebel, *The Nature of Culture,* from "Man, Culture and Society," ed. Harry L. Shapiro, p. 171.
65. Theodosius Dobzhansky, *Mankind Evolving,* p. 58.
66. H. L. Movius, Jr., *The Old Stone Age,* from "Man, Culture and Society," ed. Harry L. Shapiro, p. 49.
67. George Peter Murdock, *How Culture Changes,* from "Man, Culture and Society," ed. Harry L. Shapiro, p. 247.
68. L. S .Cressman, *Man in the New World,* from "Man, Culture and Society," ed. Harry L. Shapiro, p. 140.
69. Theodosius Dobzhansky, *Mankind Evolving,* p. 189.
70. Ruth Benedict, *The Growth of Culture,* from "Man, Culture and Society," ed. Harry L. Shapiro, p. 184.
71. *Ibid.,* p. 193.
72. Theodosius Dobzhansky, *Mankind Evolving,* p. 20.
73. E. Adamson Hoebel, *The Nature of Culture,* from "Man, Culture and Society," ed. Harry L. Shapiro, p. 169.
74. Theodosius Dobzhansky, *Mankind Evolving,* p. 23.
75. J. O. Brew, *The Metal Ages: Copper, Bronze and Iron,* from "Man, Culture and Society," ed. Harry L. Shapiro, p. 138.
76. Jacquetta Hawkes and Sir Leonard Woolley, *Prehistory and the Beginnings of Civilization,* vol. I, "The History of Mankind," p. 700.
77. H. R. Hays, *In the Beginnings,* p. 46.
78. Claude Lévi-Strauss, *A World on the Wane,* p. 160.
79. George Peter Murdock, *How Culture Changes,* from "Man, Culture and Society," ed. Harry L. Shapiro, p. 254.
80. James Clark Moloney, *Understanding the Japanese Mind,* p. 10.
81. C. W. Ceram, *The March of Archaeology,* p. 245.
82. David B. Ericson and Goesta Wollin, *The Ever-Changing Sea,* p. 119.
83. Richard A. Dorson, *Folk Legends of Japan,* p. 20.
84. Clyde Kluckhohn and Dorothea Leighton, *Navaho,* p. 240.
85. see *The Nonprevalence of Humanoids,* George Gaylord Simpson, Science Magazine, vol. 143, no. 3608, Feb. 21, 1964, pp. 773-4.

86. Denzaburo Miyadi, *Social Life of Japanese Monkeys*, Science Magazine, vol. 143, no. 3608, Feb. 21, 1964, p. 786.
87. Theodosius Dobzhansky, *Mankind Evolving*, p. 19.
88. Sol Tax, *Evolution After Darwin*, vol. 3, pp. 271-282.
89. Theodosius Dobzhansky, *Mankind Evolving*, p. 75.
90. E. Cecil Curwen and Gudmund Hatt, *Plough and Pasture*, p. 233.
91. *Ibid.*, p. 27.
92. *Ibid.*, p. 26.
93. *Ibid.*, p. 14.
94. Edward B. Tylor, *Anthropology*, p. 20.
95. Emmett McLoughlin, *Crime and Immorality in the Catholic Church*, p. 218.
96. Jules Henry, *Culture Against Man*, p. 426.
97. Clyde Kluckhohn, *Mirror for Man*, p. 225.
98. Bertrand Russell, *Power*, p. 129.
99. Jawaharlal Nehru, New York Times Magazine, Sept. 7, 1958.
100. Bertrand Russell, *Power*, p. 13.
101. *Ibid.*, pp. 175-6.
102. *Ibid.*, p. 173.
103. *Ibid.*, p. 173.
104. Herbert L. Matthews, *The Yoke and the Arrows*, p. 25.
105. *Ibid.*, p. 26.
106. *Ibid.*, p. 38.
107. *Ibid.*, p. 43.
108. Rolf Hochhuth, *The Deputy*, p. 296. For further references, Friedrich Heer, *Die Deutschen der Nationalsozialismus und die Gegenwart*. Bielefeld, Ger., 1960.
109. Christopher Hibbert, *Garibaldi*, p. 11.
110. Thomas Jefferson, *Notes on the State of Virginia;* see also *Religion in Public Education*, Thayer, p. 18.
111. James Bryce, *The American Commonwealth*, p. 643.
112. Emmett McLoughlin, *People's Padre*, p. 85.
113. Frank Waters, *The Book of the Hopi*, p. 253.
114. Juan Comas, *Racial Myths*, p. 21.
115. *Ibid.*, p. 25.
116. Bertrand Russell, *Power*, p. 25.
117. H. R. Hays, *In the Beginnings*, p. 537.
118. Herbert J. Muller, *Freedom in the Ancient World*, p. 311.
119. Bertrand Russell, *Power*, p. 94.
120. Martin A. Larson, *The Religion of the Occident*, p. 488.
121. Henry Charles Lea, *A History of Auricular Confession*, vol. I, p. vi.
122. A. D. White, *History of the Warfare of Science with Theology*, vol. I, p. 319.
123. Herbert J. Muller, *Freedom in the Ancient World*, pp. 15-6.
124. *Ibid.*, p. 116.
125. *Ibid.*, p. 10.
126. *Ibid.*, p. 11.
127. Philip Wylie, *An Essay on Morals*, pp. 128-9.
128. Paul Blanshard, *Freedom and Catholic Power in Spain and Portugal*, p. 173.
129. Paul Blanshard, *God and Man in Washington*, p. 126.
130. J. H. Denison, *Emotion as the Basis of Civilization*, pp. 302-3.
131. Brig. Gen. F. P. Crozier, *A Brass Hat in No Man's Land*.
132. Herbert S. Dickey, *My Jungle Book*, p. 38.
133. Peter Matthiessen, *The Cloud Forest*, pp. 132-3.
134. *Ibid.*, p. 63.
135. *Ibid.*, p. 122.
136. Albert Schweitzer, *African Notebook*, p. 89.

137. Barrows Dunham, *Heroes and Heretics*, p. 304.
138. Bertrand Russell, *Power*, p. 120.
139. David Mitrany, *Marx Against the Peasant*, pp. 214-5.
140. Bertrand Russell, *Power*, p. 205.
141. Karl Shapiro, *In Defense of Ignorance*, pp. 332-3.
142. Jawaharlal Nehru, *India*, New York Times Magazine, Sept. 7, 1958.
143. John Dewey, *Freedom and Culture*, p. 101.
144. *Ibid.*, p. 98.
145. Herbert L. Matthews, *The Yoke and the Arrows*, p. 37.
146. Fred J. Cook, *The Warfare State*, p. 353.
147. Bertrand Russell, *In Praise of Idleness*, pp. 133-4.
148. Everett Dean Martin, *Farewell to Revolution*, p. 371.
149. Bertrand Russell, *Sceptical Essays*, pp. 31-2.
150. William Brandon, *American Heritage Book of Indians*, p. 138.
151. *Ibid.*, p. 99.
152. Peter Farb, *Man's Rise to Civilization*, p. 243.
153. William Brandon, *American Heritage Book of Indians*, p. 143.
154. Benjamin Keen, *Life and Labor in Ancient Mexico*, p. 9; see also *The Indian Population of Central Mexico, 1531-1610,* Cook and Borah.
155. *Ibid.*, p. 14; see also *El Tributo indigena en la Nueva España durante el siglo XVI,* José Miranda, p. 136.
156. Alvin M. Josephy, Jr., *The Indian Heritage of America*, pp. 278-9.
157. Bartolomé de Las Casas, *Historia de las Indias*, ed. Gonzalo de Reparaz.
158. Claude Lévi-Strauss, *A World on the Wane*, pp. 50-1.
159. Peter Matthiessen, *The Cloud Forest*, p. 105.
160. *Ibid.*, p. 235.
161. Alvin M. Josephy, Jr., *The Indian Heritage of America*, p. 281.
162. Claude Lévi-Strauss, *A World on the Wane*, pp. 42-3.
163. William Brandon, *American Heritage Book of Indians*, pp. 311-2.
164. *Ibid.*, p. 316.
165. *Ibid.*, p. 388.
166. Peter Farb, *Man's Rise to Civilization*, p. 256.
167. William Brandon, *American Heritage Book of Indians*, p. 172.
168. Peter Farb, *Man's Rise to Civilization*, p. 247.
169. Frank Waters, *The Book of the Hopi*, p. 278.
170. W. Storrs Lee, *The Islands*, p. 173.
171. Theodora Kroeber, *Ishi*, pp. 65-6.
172. Frank Waters, *The Book of the Hopi*, pp. 278-9.
173. William Brandon, *American Heritage Book of Indians*, p. 305.
174. *Ibid.*, p. 305.
175. *Ibid.*, pp. 304-5.
176. *Ibid.*, p. 222.
177. *Ibid.*, p. 244.
178. Frank Waters, *The Book of the Hopi*, p. 280.
179. Bernard and Michael Grzimek, *Serengati Shall Not Die*, p. 146.
180. Albert Schweitzer, *African Notebook*, p. 27.
181. *Ibid.*, p. 32.
182. James Wellard, *The Great Sahara*, p. 113.
183. *Ibid.*, p. 131.
184. *Ibid.*, p. 118.
185. James G. Frazer, *The Scope of Social Anthropology*, pp. 166-8.
186. see Martin Luther, *Essay on Commerce and Usury*, pub. as *Vonkaufshandlung und Wuchen;* also *Religion and the Rise of Capitalism*, Tawney, p. 102.
187. Bertrand Russell, *Power*, p. 42.
188. *Ibid.*, p. 27.

189. Robert Ardrey, *African Genesis*, p. 316.
190. Benjamin Keen, *Life and Labor in Ancient Mexico*, Introd. p. 73.
191. Leo Kalmer, *Crime and Religion*, pp. 19-20.
192. see *The Mysterious Stranger*, Mark Twain, p. 112.
193. Bertrand Russell, *Power*, p. 119.
194. Brigid Brophy, *Black Ship to Hell*, p. 21.
195. Robert Ardrey, *African Genesis*, pp. 336-7.
196. H. R. Hays, *In the Beginnings*, p. 393.
197. Fred J. Cook, *The Warfare State*, p. 348.
198. *Ibid.*, pp. 351-2.
199. Bertrand Russell, *Power*, pp. 27-8.
200. John Dewey, *Reconstruction in Philosophy*, p. 137.
201. Frank Waters, *The Book of the Hopi*, p. 15.
202. Bertrand Russell, *Authority and the Individual*, p. 47.
203. Bronislaw Malinowski, *Sex, Culture and Myth*, p. 179.
204. Peter Matthiessen, *The Cloud Forest*, p. 31.
205. Bronislaw Malinowski, *Sex, Culture and Myth*, p. 178.
206. *Ibid.*, p. 179.
207. C. Wright Mills, *The Power Elite*, from "America as a Mass Society," ed. Philip Olson, p. 89.
208. Barrows Dunham, *Heroes and Heretics*, p. 17.
209. James G. Frazer, *Man, God and Immortality*, pp. 7-8.
210. C. H. Arndt, *A Biological Concept of Religion*, Humanist Magazine, Sept.-Oct., 1964, p. 138.
211. Bertrand Russell, *Authority and the Individual*, p. 49.
212. *Ibid.*, p. 54.
213. John Dewey, *Reconstruction in Philosophy*, p. 186.
214. Brand Blanshard, New York Times Book Review, Jan. 12, 1964, p. 3.
215. Bertrand Russell, *The Will to Doubt*, p. 23.
216. Barrows Dunham, *Heroes and Heretics*, p. 274.
217. Oliver L. Reiser, *The Alchemy of Light and Color*, p. 14.
218. Durward V. Sandifer and L. Ronald Scheman, *The Foundations of Freedom*, p. 74.
219. Arnold J. Toynbee, *The Reluctant Death of Sovereignty*, Center Magazine, March, 1968, pp. 29-30.
220. James Clark Moloney, *Understanding the Japanese Mind*, p. 217.
221. Bertrand Russell, *Authority and the Individual*, p. 29.
222. *Ibid.*, pp. 23-4.
223. *Ibid.*, p. 22.
224. George C. Valliant, *Aztecs of Mexico*, p. 233.
225. James Clark Moloney, *Understanding the Japanese Mind*, p. 2.
226. Erich Fromm, *The Marketing Orientation*, from "America as a Mass Society," ed. Philip Olson, p. 576.
227. Bertrand Russell, *Authority and the Individual*, p. 36.
228. Bertrand Russell, *The Will to Doubt*, p. 80.
229. Walter Kaufmann, *Critique of Religion and Philosophy*, p. 47.
230. John Dewey, New Republic Magazine, July 29, 1931.
231. Albert Einstein, *Essays*.
232. Bertrand Russell, *The Will to Doubt*, p. 35.
233. *Ibid.*, p. 28.
234. Herbert S. Dickey, *My Jungle Book*, p. 265.
235. H. C. Thomas and W. A. Hamm, *The Foundations of Civilization*, p. 15.
236. Robert Ardrey, *African Genesis*, p. 160.
237. Guillermo Dellhora, *La Iglesia Catolica ante la Critica en en Pensamiento y en el Arte*, p. 110.

238. Clyde Kluckhohn and Dorothea Leighton, *Navaho*, p. 227.
239. Cowan, *Curious Facts in the History of Insects*, 1865.
240. John V. Murra, *Guamán Poma de Ayala*, Natural History Magazine, Aug.-Sept., 1961, p. 41.
241. J. H. Denison, *Emotion as the Basis of Civilization*, p. 275.
242. Herbert J. Muller, *Freedom in the Ancient World*, p. 67.
243. *Ibid.*, p. 63.
244. *Ibid.*, p. 135.
245. Bertrand Russell, *The Will to Doubt*, p. 21.
246. Barrows Dunham, *Man Against Myth*, p. 21.
247. Herbert J. Muller, *Freedom in the Ancient World*, p. 345.
248. *Ibid.*, p. 122.
249. Philip Wylie, *An Essay on Morals*, p. 133.
250. *Ibid.*, pp. 126-7.
251. Emmett McLoughlin, *People's Padre*, p. 76.
252. *Ibid.*, p. 78.
253. Emmett McLoughlin, *Crime and Immorality in the Catholic Church*, p. 38.
254. Paul Blanshard, *God and Man in Washington*, p. 135.
255. Morris R. Cohen, *American Thought: A Critical Sketch*, p. 72.
256. *Ibid.*, pp. 230-1.
257. Scott Buchanan, *A Message to the Young*, Center Magazine, vol. i, no. 3, March, 1968, p. 10.
258. Ritchie Calder, *After the Seventh Day*, pp. 355-6.
259. Margaret Sanger, *Appeal*, June 18, 1962.
260. *Ibid.*
261. *Ibid.*
262. Father James Kavanaugh, *A Modern Priest Looks at His Outdated Church*, Sat. Eve. Post, June 13, 1967, p. 66.
263. Ritchie Calder, *After the Seventh Day*, p. 40.
264. H. R. Schoolcraft, quoted in *From Ape to Angel*, Hays, p. 9.
265. see *American Heritage Book of Indians*, Brandon, p. 342.
266. Frazier Hunt, *This Bewildered World*, p. 146.
267. *Ibid.*, p. 8.
268. John Dewey, *Liberalism and Social Action*.
269. Bertrand Russell, *Why Men Fight*, p. 258.
270. Herbert J. Muller, *Freedom in the Ancient World*, p. 74.
271. Jerome Davis, *Capitalism and Its Culture*, p. 516.
272. Barrows Dunham, *Man Against Myth*, pp. 22-3.
273. J. H. Denison, *This Human Nature*, p. 303.
274. F. O. Matthiessen, *The Pattern of Literature*, from "Changing Patterns in American Civilization," p. 35.
275. Janheinz Jahn, *Muntu*, p. 12.
276. Loren Eiseley, *The Firmament of Time*, p. 186.
277. Bertrand Russell, *Sceptical Essays*, p. 186.
278. Carl L. Becker, *How New Will the Better World Be?*, p. 43.
279. Bronislaw Malinowski, *Sex, Culture and Myth*, pp. 101-2.
280. *Ibid.*, p. 195.
281. *Ibid.*, pp. 181-2.
282. Nietzsche, *Thus Spake Zarathustra*.
283. Glenn T. Seaborg, *Science and the Humanities, A New Level of Symbiosis*, Science Magazine, vol. 144, no. 3623, June 5, 1964, p. 1199.
284. *Ibid.*, p. 1199.
285. *Ibid.*, p. 1199.
286. Albert Schweitzer, *African Notebook*, p. 144.
287. Rachel L. Carson, *Silent Spring*, p. 39.

288. *Ibid.*, p. 8.
289. Mark Graubard, *Man the Slave and Master*, p. 22.
290. H. R. Hays, *In the Beginnings*, p. 162.
291. Jessica Mitford, *The American Way of Death*, p. 110.
292. *Ibid.*, pp. 162-3.
293. Leslie Spier, *Inventions and Human Society*, from "Man, Culture and Society," ed. Harry L. Shapiro, pp. 242-3.
294. Theodosius Dobzhansky, *Mankind Evolving*, p. 287.
295. Lester F. Ward, *The Great Social Problem* (unpub. essay, 1893).
296. Kenneth E. Boulding, *Post-Civilization*, from "Seeds of Liberation," ed. Paul Goodman, pp. 16-7.
297. see *Philosophy of Humanism*, Lamont, p. 190.
298. see *Myths of the Greeks and Romans*, Michael Grant, p. 68.
299. Leon J. Saul, *The Hostile Mind*, p. 5.
300. Corliss Lamont, *The Philisophy of Humanism*, p. 199.
301. *Ibid.*, p. 219.
302. Max Lerner, New York Eve. Post, Sept. 4, 1968.
303. Corliss Lamont, *The Philosophy of Humanism*, p. 219.
304. *Ibid.*, p. 236.
305. Margaret Mead, *Closing Address*, from "The Study of Personality," ed. Norbeck, *et al.*, pp. 380-1.
306. Joseph Campbell, *Masks of God:Creative Mythology*, p. 37.

They're coming here?
  Be not afraid. Those are the
booming sounds of spring:
  Spring is coming here.
Come then to me.
  Quick, give me your lips.
Are they smashing down the door?
            *   *   *
No monument stands over Babi Yar

—Yevgeny Yevtushenko

The literal following of the Sermon on the Mount would destroy order, morality, law and human nature itself.

—Henry Ward Beecher

Regarding the right to question the authority of the pope and judge any of his actions: "Who are we, anyway, that we dare criticize the highest spiritual authority of the century? Nothing, in fact, but the simple defenders of the spirit, who yet have a right to expect the most from those whose mission it is to represent the spirit."

—ALBERT CAMUS

"For the past week
I have been burning the dead ten hours a day.
And with every human body that I burn
a portion of my faith burns also.
God burns.
Corpses—a conveyor belt of corpses. . . .
History is a highway paved with carrion. . . .
If I knew that He looks on—
I would have to—hate Him."

—FATHER RICCARDO, in *The Deputy*
by Rolf Hochhuth

MORALS, ETHICS, AND RESPONSIBILITIES

MORALS, ETHICS, AND RESPONSIBILITIES

PART I

BEFORE PROCEEDING TO the more important considerations of this chapter—*Ethics* and *Responsibilities*—we shall first undertake the discussion and analysis of *Morals*. How morals came to exist and to exert such control over people is a matter of historical investigation of the experiences of mankind. "It would be ridiculous," writes Bertrand Russell, "to warp the philosophy of nature in order to bring out results that are pleasing to the tiny parasites in this insignificant planet."[1] "Superstition is the origin of moral rules."[2]

Before morals and puritans came to be, primitive man got along very well, it seems, in handling the physical relationships between male and female, but upon the ascension of kings and priests, laws were decreed and usages innovated that would protect their female property. Therefore, while it was permissible for a nobleman or a priest to have an affair with a commoner, it was usually a capital crime, punishable by death, when a common man had an affair with a regal lady. This particular custom is fairly widespread, and its influence persists even among royalty today, though today, when a noble lady marries a commoner, there is likely to be scandal, but no capital punishment. Among the "aristocracy," that is, the political, economic, and social élite, it is the usual expectancy and custom for kind to marry its own kind or status. Prestige, the extent of land ownership, and the bank balance seem to be the determinants of marriage proposals and arrangements among the "higher" classes, even in our own America. Bengt Danielsson writes about the Pacific South Seas: "Parents of humble descent considered it a great honour if a high-born chief seduced their daughters. . . . If a chief showed the same mark of respect to a married woman of particularly low birth her husband was almost equally flattered. . . . But if the roles were reversed, so that a man from a lower stratum of society engaged in a liaison with a married noblewoman, it was regarded as a serious crime."[3]

Morals were initiated, not for establishing what may be right or wrong, but merely to establish *property rights* and boundaries as to who can do what with whom. All over the world girls and women were, and still are, salable and purchasable properties. Among the Klamath River Indian tribes it takes a number of "strings" (the Indian money), to make a deal. If a man cannot afford to buy a wife for full time, he can still make a "partial" purchase for a quarter-marriage or half-marriage, and thus share the woman with other "shareholders." Deals and arrangements are usually made with the father of the girl. With variations the sale of females, daughters, sisters, and slaves goes on all over the world; if virginity means that a virgin will bring more money and other considerations and is therefore more in demand and purchasable, it can easily be seen why the fathers got the idea that virginity is sacred. It seems that greater value goes with greater purity (new and unused property), which, in turn, depends upon different opinions, customs, and cultural variations regarding value and purity.[4] Robert Ardrey concludes: "The territorial imperative—just one, it is true, of the evolutionary forces playing upon our lives—is the biological law on which we have founded our edifices of human morality. Our capacities for sacrifice, for altruism, for sympathy, for trust, for responsibilities to other than self-interest, for honesty, for charity, for friendship and love, for social amity and mutual interdependence have evolved just as surely as the flatness of our feet, the muscularity of our buttocks, and the enlargement of our brains, out of the encounter on ancient African savannahs between the primate potential and the hominid circumstance."[5]

Women had hardly any voice in the making of morals; they were the props and the causes of such rules. Since morals came solely from men, even if they were kings and priests, the ordinary man might still get ideas, so revelations from on high and the very mouths of the gods ordained that the adulterer (meaning one who uses someone else's property) should be punished and condemned, and any woman who has been so "soiled" must also be punished and condemned.

The whole realm of sex prohibitions came out of monarchial and priestly men, who intended to make the most use of them for themselves, or to deny others to suit their own misconcepts. The temples of India, Babylonia, Egypt, Greece, and Rome, practically all the ancient religious temples, had their regular saintly prostitutes, who were devoted to the gods and profit-making for the priesthoods. Making use of women for religious and "non-religious" purposes is a *practical* custom in most religions and cults; the work that women can do and the purposes they can be put to have not been overlooked by institutions in history. Even Roman Catholicism, while it condemned woman as the cause of original sin and the downfall of man, the temptress, and the accomplice of the Devil, has created many female saints, has instituted and carried on various orders of sisters, that is, women who are "married" to Christ, but who serve out their lives, in actuality, as servants for the priests. It may be unpleasant to recall, but history reveals that the Church in Rome built St. Peter's out of its receipts from the licensing of brothels and contributions from the ladies attached to them. As one historian of sexual customs writes, if they could only have drawn off a little more revenue from the prostitutes, the Church would not have been forced to sell indulgences in Germany.

The kings, emperors, and all their top managements had their regular retinues of female consorts, and if all this were not enough, the lords had the right of nuptial enjoyment with every bride, royal or common, within their domain, and why not? "The greatest of human blessings was the possibility that the Sapa Inca [the king] should take a woman to his bed. Thereby she was glorified and her children became members of the Inca clan."[6] Did not the very gods of Olympus have their Casanovian affairs regularly? As for the common man, he was fortunate if he could afford *one* wife, and then he had to watch out that the common man next door did not steal her away from him, leaving behind, when polite, a lamb for consolation and "fair" exchange. We must realize, as history shows us, that sexual indulgence and perversions were at their lowest levels during periods of intense religious conformance, if we mean by morals a higher level of conduct.

Most religions, Roman Catholicism excepted, do not harp on sex as a carnal sin, as something to be avoided, nor do they consider it as something sacred or prohibited. Taboos and prohibitions regarding sex were, in the main, regulatory to fit societal orderliness and to prevent conflict and confusion regarding sexual property. Roman Catholicism ordained sex as "soul pollution," and established it as an ungodly act subject to purification, penance, confession, and absolution. The antinatural attitude of Catholicism toward sex is the most senseless principle in all religious perfidy. To ordain that people, in the process of intercourse, should not derive any pleasure and that the sex act must be consciously considered, during coitus, as a process solely for procreation, is a fantastic idea. This fantasy still persists among millions of Catholics today, who follow this principle in good faith, although they derive much pleasure from sex notwithstanding. These people obviously never give any serious thought to how any god could be so illogical, hypocritical, and self-contradictory as to create sex (which produces more people to worship him) and then condemn it as an act against his wishes. "If God knew in advance the sins of which man would be guilty, He was clearly responsible for all the consequences of those sins when He decided to create man."[7] Swinburne could not understand a God "who makes desire, and slays desire with shame." It stands to reason that if every Catholic would seriously adhere to this psychotic principle and *succeed*, there would be, in due time, no Catholics to sin, believe, or confess anything. "The teaching of the church has been, and still is, that virginity is best, but that for those who find this impossible marriage is permissible."[8]

THE ILLUSION OF EVIL IN SEX

THE HYPOCRISY OF the Church lies in the naked and constantly exposed fact of one certain consistency: that all its theories are constantly opposed and negated by all its practices, or what

John Dewey called "the tragic division of theory and practice."[9] Bertrand Russell wrote: "We have two kinds of morality side by side: one which we preach but do not practice, and another which we practice but seldom preach."[10] "In 1490, according to the great historian Henri Pirenne, there were at least 6,800 courtesans in the Holy City. The pope and his cardinals 'consorted publicly with their mistresses, acknowledged their bastards,' Pirenne says, and endowed them with riches stolen from the coffers of the Church. The conduct of the clergy outside Rome was hardly better, as Erasmus and Sir Thomas More, men who died faithful to their church, repeatedly pointed out."[11]

Mark Twain reveals his rebellious spirit against the antinatural and insane impositions indoctrinated into man by obscurantic religions: "Man is not to blame for what he is. He didn't make himself. He has no control over himself. All the control is vested in his temperament—which he did not create—and in the circumstances which hedge him around from the cradle to the grave and which he did not devise and cannot change by any act of his will, for the reason that he has no will. He is as purely a piece of automatic mechanism as is a watch, and can no more dictate or influence his actions than can the watch. He is a subject for pity, not blame—and not contempt. He is flung head over heels into this world without ever a chance to decline, and straightway he conceives and accepts the notion that he is in some mysterious way under obligation to the unknown Power that inflicted this outrage upon him—and henceforth he considers himself responsible for such of his acts as do not meet with the approval of that Power—yet that same man would argue quite differently if a human tyrant should capture him and put chains upon him of any kind and require obedience; that the tyrant had no right to do that; that the tyrant had no right to put commands upon him of any kind and require obedience; that the tyrant had no right to compel him to commit murder and then put the responsibility for the murder upon him. Man constantly makes a most strange distinction between man and his Maker in the matter of morals. He requires of his fellow man obedience to a very creditable code of morals but he observes without shame or disapproval his God's utter destitution of morals."[12]

Alvan L. Barach: "Almost from the start, the Christian concept of the sinful nature of man has aroused opposition. . . . Fierce as has been the attack on man's animal nature—his so-called innate depravity—the rebuttal has been almost equally intense. The path to salvation through repentance has been condemned and man's instincts porclaimed innocent and natural. . . . They rather challenged the value of renouncing the instinctive life and the joys of this world in favor of the world to come. Samuel Butler called the concept of immortality immoral because it gave secondary importance to life on earth. . . . The neuroses and poignant discontents acquired by civilized man represent too high a price for his morality. . . . Since the goal of ascetic Christianity was clearly the elimination of the black principle, some men and women felt an urge to become exclusively pure. The natural inclinations that originated from the black principle were presented as deadly sins. As a result, a continuously rcinforced sense of guilt became the source of a widely prevalent anxiety. Repentance was consequently employed to relieve feelings of culpability and expectations of punishment. Self-criticism became universal. But self-criticism has frequently deflected man from legitimate creative enterprises and tended to transmute self-development into preoccupation with personal sin."[13] Anthony Storr: "Christianity has for so long taught us to conceive of love in terms of self-sacrifice and gentleness that there are many couples who have never experienced the full splendour of sexuality. Innumerable manuals have instructed husbands to be so restrained, or so careful in their love-making that they have inhibited the aggressive component in sexual congress with the result that their wives cannot fully respond to them, and they themselves fail to gain complete satisfaction."[14] "The normal person, if such exists, constantly renews a sense of value through loving and being loved; and the object of physical passion is thus not only a means whereby the drive of sexuality can be expressed and assuaged, but also a vital source of self-esteem. We cannot escape our physical natures; and a proper pride in oneself as a human being is rooted in the body through which love is given and taken."[15]

The primitive could not possibly have seen evil in the sex

act; he craved it, fought for it, and got it like any other sexual animal. Any taboos and regulatory customs merely emerged out of family, clan, and tribal experience as *protective* elements of sexual property, order of inheritance, and social status, and the necessary essentialities of some sort of marital responsibility to maintain, in turn, some stability in the social order. The primitive could not possibly have conceived any state of sin or evil in courtship, sexual desire, and copulation: primitive tribes still extant do not possess any concepts of sin or shame attached to sexual intercourse, nor are there any absolutions or purifications necessary. Peter Freuchen: "More important in understanding the Eskimos' sexual ethic is their point of view that sexual desire is entirely natural and normal, something like the desire for food and sleep. . . . Among the Eskimos, sexual life is not directly connected with marriage, and the simple biological need for the opposite sex is recognized in both men and women, young and old."[16]

Christianity, both Catholic and Protestant, innovated the idea that sex is "bad," "disrespectful," "sinful," "vulgar," etc., and perpetrated the greatest stupidity and hypocrisy in the history of human cultures and religions. They have steadfastly closed their eyes to what the rest of themselves were occupied in doing. The Christian attitude toward sex is ridiculous and preposterous; it holds as evil the prime biological process that has made possible the continued existence of people, of the very people who hold this view. It is self-contradictory, for it is in most of the Catholic countries that the greatest number of illegitimate children are born. In nature there is no distinction between "legitimate" and "illegitimate" children, but to the Church there definitely is.

One should keep in mind that what people *think* or *believe* about sex is not exactly what people *do* about sex. Intelligent and sensible people see no vulgarity, shame, evil, or immorality in the sexual act itself; they might find vulgarity, evil, and immorality in the abuses and unnecessary forebearances of it, in the ascetic and masochistic habits and patterns of Christian people who find it very "respectful" to frustrate themselves and bring upon themselves many neurotic and psychotic ailments that have expressed themselves in hate and crime throughout Christian history. Dr. William S. Kroger, the psychiatrist, calls this pitiful ailment *Ecclesiogenic neurosis* and is most prevalent where children "are subject to the 'fire-and-brimstone' type of strict religious upbringing." In adolescent and adult years this neurosis brings about chronic depression, guilt feelings, various psychosomatic physical dysfunctions, and frigidity. Millions of lives in history and in the present day have been, and are being, wasted in folly, fear, and in ignorance because of the fears, superstitions, and antinatural restraints inoculated into the innocent young by orthodox religious dogma.

In Sicily, as in so many countries of the Mediterranean periphery, the tradition is one of honor *between men;* the women are just between. Here the more ancient social customs regarding sexual property, of wife, sister, fiancée, daughter, gradually changed into a tradition of "honor" of the father, husband, brother, or prospective bridegroom to protect his honor by protecting his females. The loss of virginity on the part of an unmarried female is catastrophic and calls for *vendetta.* This is not really because the female has "lost" something, rather that the men to whom the female belonged have lost "face" or "honor" among the men of the community, and this must be recovered at all costs if they are to retain their "honorable" status. The men are thus concerned about themselves; no one seems to be concerned about the women as *people,* as *selves,* as *beings,* as naturally and reasonably free individuals in the same sense as the men deem themselves free in their society. The Mediterranean common denominator of "honor and family" often means the destruction of those who compose the family, lifelong tragedy, misery, bitterness, and deepest hates. Whatever honor one could attach to such a status of living condition cannot be honor on any genuinely moral or ethical basis.

No sensible and reasonable person would deny the proposition that a monk, for example, has the freedom to deny sex to himself, to consider this life as a preparation or trial for the afterlife; or deny to the idealist his freedom to think and believe in universal goodness, in ultimate perfection, that man is superior to all else on earth, that there is a supernatural force or core of morality superimposed by either God or some psychic revelation given to man alone by nature. Nor should he deny the freedom for an individual to think or hold all these concepts to be untrue and false. What the sensible and reasonable man has is his own freedom not to accept them and to protest the imposition of any of these ideas upon him or his children, to oppose any prosecution of effort, or the validity of this effort, to coerce or force him to accept them. If society is to constitute itself as a democratic, equitable, and meaningful order of association, it must establish as a fundamental premise, and as the basis to justify its own existence as a social process, the principle of freedom of the mind and conscience as prerequisites of this social process.

No reasonable man could deny the freedom of the exhibitionists who stroll up and down the Via Veneto or the freedom of the pseudo-intellectuals who consider themselves the "élite," the "superior," the "high and lonely intelligentsia" (whatever that means). No one could deny the freedom of those who sit and watch this pageantry of egocentrics and egomaniacs and *enjoy* it. No one could deny the freedom of the chiselers and thieves, from the Moslem taxi-driver and the Syrian rug merchant to the Parisian waiter who invariably tries to rob the unsuspecting tourist, and no one could deny the freedom of the victims to be willing suckers. No one could reasonably deny the freedom of whores all over the world and in every large city to peddle their assets for the enjoyment and relief of the lonely traveler, or deny the freedom of these males to buy this enjoyment. Freedom is amoral and a-ethical; it exposes the process of motility and expression in *any* direction by which living things, helplessly devoted to their natures, move according to the pressures and resistances that influence, affect, manifest, and so determine this movement.

If sex is to be considered immoral in its nature, then all of nature is immoral, and all life and all living things, animals and plants. This is truly a mighty accusation for any puny puritan to make against the whole world. Something is "cockeyed" about such an approach. Man may be considered capable of abuse and excess, but this can be a question of underemphasis or overemphasis, depending upon the person doing the emphasizing. It cannot be put down as a prescription for, or description of, all humanity, or be set out as some guiding principle for all people. Every life has the natural freedom as well as the moral and ethical right to fulfill its own life as its own life directs it so long as no one else is injured or hindered thereby. While others have the freedom to deprive others of this natural right, it does not follow that their disposition to do so is to be considered moral, ethical, and righteous. The prude may be subnormal or abnormal, but he is certainly not normal. No one should be considered normal who suppresses himself or herself by denying to others what both of them really and honestly and *naturally* want. Such suppression and denial are misguidances encultured in them by cultural antinatural factors.

Morals are concepts that only humans have created. No other animal feels, thinks, or knows of morals. In the realm of nature itself morals are nonexistent, irrelevant, and inconceivable. George Gaylord Simpson: "The evolutionary process is not moral —but it has finally produced a moral animal."[17] Man, as a result, being a moral animal, is forced to be the sole hypocrite in the universe. Herbert Wendt: "Animals continue to live in a state of sexual innocence. . . . Today it is generally agreed that no group of animals is more moral than any other. We recognize that our human conceptions of vice and virtue are irrelevant for passing judgment in the world of animals. It is as foolish to draw an analogy between a stupid, rough, violent human being and an animal as it is to contrast a brutal, excessive, or degenerate sex life with the same sexuality of animals. Animals are neither good nor evil, neither moral nor immoral. Each species obeys its predetermined laws. But man departed from this pattern once he had tasted of the tree of knowledge,"[18]—man's sense of shame.

Babies and the young do not understand morals, intuitively, instinctively or intellectually, any more than the other animals in the world. Morals are products of man's thinking, and as changeable, flexible, and varied as his thoughts; and thoughts are not necessarily all good or all bad, granting that we have some capacity to understand and recognize *what* is good or bad for ourselves and for all others—something no one has ever *absolutely* understood or known. Man's thoughts are no better than his nature, his imperfections, and his experiences, and, as a result, his

concepts are as natural and imperfect as he is. If this were not so
man could not have had the possibility of *change* in *any* direction, nor the desire for it. Morals are not ideas or things extraterritorial to mundane existence; they are merely thoughts, traditions, and customs which have become part of the indoctrinated
and cultural habit of any particular group or person. Robert
Graves and Raphael Patai give us a point on evolutionary morality: "*Genesis*, which is far more closely linked with Greek,
Phoenician, Hittite, Ugaritic, Sumerian and other bodies of
myth than most pious Jews and Christians care to admit, was
thereafter edited and re-edited from perhaps the sixth century B.C.
onwards, for moralistic ends."[19] Marcello Craveri, the author of
the *Life of Jesus*, states that "it is in the nature of the religious
homily to treat moral symbols as historical facts."[20]

Whether any of these morals merit rational or biological justification in relation to the best possible interests of life satisfaction,
and whether they are aligned with natural freedom, are problems
relating, in turn, to the desires of any individual or group and
their effects upon other individuals and groups. Morals and
morality usages and customs obviously and naturally vary in
different localities and cultures, and even within these cultures
there are variations of some degree in different cities, towns, and
even in the little villages and hamlets, which are the effects of
long periods of provincialism. Civilized countries bordering each
other, with an interrelating and associative history, have their
particular traditional concepts and customs of morals and morality.
Those of Paris are not common to the countryside of France;
New Yorkers, and Chicagoans differ from the rural people of
their states. Therefore, morals and morality, although proclaimed
from the housetops of the formal religions and institutions as the
universality of their moral dicta, differ in the actual concepts of
people, depending on where they live and the people they live
with.

We have noted that the so-called "moral" rules dating from
ancient times were actually rules made by men to protect their
sexual property. Yet, while man could not get along without the
satisfactions of sex provided by women, his religious usages and
convictions caused him to fear them because of the long line of

cultural evolution in primitive man's concepts of magic governing reproduction, supernatural powers, mana, and a host of others, different attributes which woman possessed in her peculiar ability to give birth to new life and to spill blood periodically, blood being the power of life. These fears of woman nurtured mysogynistic magic formulae to protect man from being swallowed up by the specter of the vulva, which constantly beckoned him to surrender himself to it. The puritanical attitudes of Protestantism and the abstinence doctrines of Catholicism emanate from this long line of antisexual and antinatural attitudes, which predate the Hebrew and Christian periods by thousands of years. Géza Róheim summed it up well in his Riddle of the Sphinx,[21] how man, as far back as we can trace, had come to fear woman and how he considered sexual maturity as some awful misfortune metaphorical of and almost conspecific with dying and death itself. Even Hesiod prosed that woman is the "unescapable snare" for man. The Maori say: "That which destroys man is the vulva. The vagina is very hot, it is fire and each time the penis goes in it dies."[22] Strange as it is, this is the kind of death that most men usually hope for. H. R. Hays: "The Polynesians, who possessed a priesthood, an organized body of mythology transmitted by rote memory, and on the whole, a fairly elaborate ceremonial culture, divided the world into two parts: all good was male and all bad female. . . . Good mana was male and bad mana was female. The attributes of maleness were light, the sun, the east, secret religious knowledge, the strong right side. Conversely the female was passive, associated with the west, ignorance, the weak left side, darkness and death. The goddess of the underworld was female. In Hawaii she was Pele, the spirit of the volcano sending forth destruction from beneath the earth."[23] From the ancient Chinese *Shih-ching* we find what they thought about *Yin* and *Yang:* "These were two concrete categories and at the same time were active forces. *Yang* corresponds to male, heavens, bright, and light; *Yin* to female, earth, dark, and heavy."[24]

Mr. Hays goes on to tell us: "The production of the live being from a woman's body undoubtedly endows her with the supernatural properties of mana. . . . Garcilaso de la Vega, the Chronicler of the ancient Incas, wrote that no one must help a woman in childbirth, and any who did would be regarded as witches. Among the Hebrews the midwife was regarded as unclean."[25] Walter Sorell: "An orthodox Jew will not touch the hand of a woman, for blood is unclean to the Jew, and he does not know whether these are her unclean days."[26] Joseph Campbell: "Woman —earthly, actual woman, that is—awakened to her nature, was *janua diaboli,* 'the devil's door.' "[27] Is this one of the cultural reasons why the Christian churches were so much against the use of anaesthesia for women giving birth and fought so strenuously and continuously against any surcease of pain during the act of giving birth?

Man's attitude to the menstrual period has also been loaded to the gills with fears of a million kinds all over the world. The periodical blood has been used in all kinds of magic and potions, and the varieties of its uses to gain ends or cause evil by magical means are legion. "Among the Dogon of East Africa the menstrual taboo is so strong that a woman in this condition brings misfortune to everything she touches. Not only is she segregated in an isolated hut and provided with special eating utensils, but if she is seen passing through a village a general purification must take place. The Wogeo of South Australia believe that if a man has contact with a menstruating woman he will die from a wasting disease against which there is no remedy whatsover." "The Hindus observe an endless number of prohibitions during the first three days of a woman's period. She must not weep, mount a horse, an ox or an elephant, be carried in a palanquin or drive in a vehicle." "In Hebrew tradition the menstruating woman is forbidden to work in a kitchen, sit at meals with other people, or drink from a glass used by others. Any contact with her husband is a sin and the penalty for intercourse during her period is death for both. Indeed the misfortunes which men suffer when they break the menstrual taboo vary but they are always severe. A Uganda Bantu woman by touching her husband's effects makes him sick; if she lays a hand on his weapons, he will be killed in the next fight. The natives of Malacca believe that coitus, or even contact, will cause the man to lose his virility." "The peasants of eastern Europe believe that a woman must not bake bread, make pickles, churn butter or spin thread during her period or all will go wrong."[28]

Do culture and history provide a long list of taboos created by *women*, to protect themselves against the "evil" of men? It's a man's world, to be sure. "Testimony of history leaves no doubt that both the primitive and civilized world has been a man's world. In the past, male dominance has been unchallenged. The majority of ideas and symbols which have shaped culture have always been masculine; even when women were allowed to appear on the stage of society they have been as men have made them."[29]

Hays continues: "An example of purification ceremonies is the bathing of Hebrew women in special bathhouses *(mikvahs)* in which both menstruating and parturient women were cleansed. After her time of sequestration was over, the Hebrew woman was required to send a lamb and a dove to the priest as sacrifices."[30] Why were there not any special regulations regarding the cleansing and purification of men? Lucy S. Dawidowicz, in her brilliant little essay *On Being a Woman in Shul*, states: "Judaism is a man's religion not only in substance and in practice, but also in its symbolic theology."[31] The orthodox Hebrew thanks the Lord each morning that he was not born a woman. Upon rising he gives his thanks to the Lord and one of these is: "Blessed art thou, O Lord, our God, King of the Universe, who hast not made me a woman."[32]

Whom should the woman give thanks to that she was born to be subjected and enslaved by man, ruled by man how she should serve him, placate him, soothe him, relax him, comfort him, and, to boot, be considered as an evil, as unclean, as a polluting agent and a destroyer of man's "purity"? The misogynist mythologies and magic-misogyny formulae are widespread throughout the world; probably no other factors are so imbedded into the cultural frame of peoples all over the earth as are these two acquired customs and usages.

The advent of Christianity not only continued man's fear of women but intensified it to a degree that today would be considered insane. Poor Eve (whose story is taken from previous stories of similar content and direction), became the scapegoat for the escape of all the evils on earth out of Pandora's box. "The Fall of Man should rightly be called the fall of woman because once more the second sex is blamed for all the trouble in the world."[33] Everywhere woman was condemned as the destroyer of men, and is to this day by many mentally-sick people. "A Benedictine monk, Bernard de Moraix, announced flatly in his poem, *De Contemptu mondi,* that there was no good woman on earth."[34] Jean de Meung wrote that "Though you seek her, here, there, everywhere, every woman is a whore."[35] St. Paul exclaimed: "It is good for a man not to touch a woman . . . but if they cannot contain, let them marry: for it is better to marry than to burn." St. Bernard: "What more beautiful thing could be imagined than the sublime virtue of chastity" and St. Basil: "Continence is the ruin of sin, the despoiling of the vicious affections, the mortification of the passions and even of the natural desires of our bodies, the augmentation of merit, the work of God, the school of virtue, and the possession of all blessings!"[36] Thus, the Christians carried on and continued the same misogynist cultures of the earlier and surrounding religions, that women are unclean, evil, that sex is the destroyer of man, and the more a man stays away from sex and woman, so much more pure will he be in the eyes of God. When man should take a bath, or stop masturbating away his "chastity," is not found in the book of rules.

"Paul, a Hellenized Jew with a Greek education, was a Roman citizen living in Tarsus. He was unattractive physically, small, somewhat deformed, with poor eyesight. He was also a prey to hallucinatory experiences, almost epileptic in character; in short, he was the typical shaman."[37] Paul of Tarsus wrote that the greatest of the three virtues was love, but what could he have meant by love? To forsake one's parents, brothers, sisters, forsake all one's friends and run to a cave to contemplate the purity of one's soul?

These have been the miserable "escapes" of people filled with antinatural dogmas, causing endless anxieties and nervous disorders, very often insanity of the weirdest kinds, the causes of terrible crimes against others and themselves, all this in preference to the deep and wonderful exhilaration that comes when a man and a woman make love, when they look into each other's eyes and kiss softly and give of each other to each other. To love one must give so that another can receive and give in return. Did St. Paul follow this principle? He was too much occupied, history reveals, with organization, power politics, intrigue to gain monarchial approval and support, with revamping pagan fiestas into Catholic rites, giving the pagans all they had been accustomed to but with different names. Pagan idols still adorn the religious architecture of Europe as they do in other religions in other parts of the world. St. Paul was too much of a power aspirant and a political organizer to think of love in more than farfetched, transcendental, and nebulous connotations. Love is a participation in *actuality*, not a dedication to self-glorification by life negation. Love is life, and loving is living it well.

All this nonsense has inflicted upon womankind iniquities of every description. The witchcraft epidemics were but one result of centuries of misogynist doctrine enculturated into the hearts and minds of men. Besides, it brought on needless and widespread hypocrisies, and turned the Western world into a house of shame and sham, of prudery, perversion, and sexual criminality. Edith Simon tells us about the order of the Knights Templars in the Middle Ages: "Sodomy was not rare in the Middle Ages, and no stigma of effeminacy was attached to practices which numbered many adherents among the doughty crusaders and distinguished princes such as (probably) Coeur de Lion and Edward II."[38] The Templars of the Medieval period indicate the extent to which the culture and religion of that era held woman in contempt, a tool of the devil, and to keep aloof from her would ensure a greater service to God as well as a more purified state of the soul. "Taboos against women were particularly strong; they were prohibited even from kissing their female relatives."[39]

Sidney Painter writes about the legendary high standards of the "chivalrous" knights of feudal times: "The feudal male was absorbed in war and in the chase. His wife bore him sons, his mistress satisfied his lust. Beyond this women had no place and he had no interest in them. They were freely beaten and in general treated with calloused brutality."[40] Out of these centuries arose the "grandeur" and "respectablity" of puritanical prudery, sickening frustration, and hypocritical social orders. In those centuries of darkness and ignorance, "Ascetic monks fled to the desert to avoid the sight of women, at the same time mortifying their flesh by refraining from washing and encouraging sores and putrefaction. Bathing, involving the baring of the body, was particularly frowned on by the Church, since it was supposed to lead to thoughts of lust, and thus Christian idealism produced an era of medieval filth."[41]

Thus, the religions of the world, from preancient, ancient, and historical periods to the present, have cultured and nurtured the greatest trend of sadomasochism in the story of needless human suffering, denial and life negation. Referring to the Catholic and "civilized" impositions upon marriage and the natural freedoms in Tahiti, Gauguin wrote: "If ever a society was cruel and barbarous, surely it is modern society; this hypocritical society which in the name of Christian morality thus orders the fate of women and causes so much suffering."[42] Many intelligent and reasonable persons cannot understand how people can still believe in the obscurantisms and superstitions reminiscent of the Dark Ages. Gauguin continues: "But what is really incredible is that even today, when the truth is plain to all who can see and read, there should be intelligent and cultivated people who still adhere to the Church. Can we regard them as men of good faith without accusing them of insanity?"[43]

Before we begin to analyze the essence and various concepts of morals and morality and their relationship to, and influence upon, the freedom of man, we should distinguish them from what we identify as *responsibilities,* or what some people may consider a sense of *duty,* the reasonable, expected characteristics of people who take upon themselves certain natural, rational, or cultural obligations or prerogatives toward others as well as themselves. The sense of responsibility very often does not appear the same to a person expressing it as it appears to others judging him, and vice versa. Therefore, from the analytical viewpoint the sense of expression of responsibility is relative; about this we shall speak later.

The farther back we trace primitive and preprimitive mentality and behavior, living, social, and religious usages and traditions, the more we find that whatever "morals" were established were natural "codes" that rarely imposed an antinatural restriction upon the individual, but merely "institutionalized" by tribal custom the behavior exhibited by the surrounding animal and plant life and the naïve concepts of origins and continuances of themselves and their environment, the magical forms of similarities and sympathetic relativism involved. Because it was their nature to do so, because they considered their environment on the same relative and expressive basis as their own nature, they maintained a free-flowing, existential status for all the members of any particular tribe in a peripheral of unopposed interplay with the environment. Rather than cause ideas of restriction, these situations established what the primitives considered as the "true" and therefore "sacred" coalition, or interflowing and interdependent unity, of all living things, animal and plant, of which they themselves were a part. These accepted "truths" became the basis of their later magics, mythologies, legends, dances, and ceremonies. Today the Balinese husband and wife go to their rice paddies and have intercourse beneath the stars to incite the gods of fertility to grant them good harvests and thus protect their precious food supply. Among the so-called primitives still extant we find this free-flowing and uninhibited sway of non-restrictive "moral" life.

With the rise of the totem clans, patrilineal and matrilineal societies, and the rise of the new innovation of *property,* the concepts of moral values began to become affected by *economic* and *power* values. Gradually they began to change to fit into the ensuing concepts of *position, wealth, status, prestige, nobility* or *common, caste,* etc., which, in turn, established traditional acceptances and prohibitions in morality in order to maintain the status quo and the modus vivendi.

Ethics deals not only with the conduct of a person toward others but also the conduct of others toward him. We must differentiate between morality and ethics. Morality concerns itself chiefly with human behavior as it pertains to sex and sexual property and the various ramifications surrounding them. Ethics concerns itself with conduct that pertains to *anything* involving association with others or living within a group or society. From the position of natural freedom, any moral code or established ethical code of behavior, procedure, and practices is voluntary, and cultivated to be accepted or rejected by any individual by his natural right of freedom to do so. However, association and living together, in all their manifold expressions and activities, have evolved certain *necessary compatibilities* that are empathic and congruous with the processes of compatibleness and mutual regard as *practical* and *protective* norms and enhancements of the participants. There is a difference between recognizing, by experience and rationalization, the basic elements required to sustain an orderly and more or less equitable society by volitionally legalized or cultivated acceptances and, on the other hand, the imposition of some form or another upon individuals and groups to accept certain procedures of conduct as a forced, enculturated, or indoctrinated set of rules or dogmas of some ruling power. In the former, natural freedom has been rationally and traditionally established and expressed by the free acceptance of certain compromises and compatibilities rising out of experience which people may find "good" for them to accept and live by. In the latter, however, the people are coerced or ordered to abide by certain procedures of conduct whether it agrees with their best interests or not. In the former, freedom has found a state of natural compatibility; in the latter, freedom has been diminished by surrendering it, willingly or unwillingly, to inhibitions, modes, or edicts, regardless of their being good or bad for the individual concerned.

The analysis of morals and moralities may be classified under two principal categories: *natural* morals (operating unconsciously and functioning without purpose or reflection) and *cultural* morals. In the cultural we may again consider the *societal* and the *religious,* although in many places where a thorough and all-pervading theocracy has been established, the social and religious are so intertwined and coalesced that it would be difficult to separate the behaviors and usages of such people into social and religious spheres; rather they must be considered as a *socio-religious* organism. It is not imperative or absolute that each category be a separate evolution of its type. We will often find that the natural is intermixed and compatible to some degree with the cultural and even with the societal and religious, but more often cultural moralities have conflicted, negated, and opposed the natural. All in all, we should accept the premise that all cultural classes, types, and degrees of morals and moralities are products of *human* experience, not of the rest of nature, and that therefore they are *man*-made, *man*-cultured, *man*-maintained, and *man*-violated. All morals are *human* concepts and carried on by *humans* only. Being of human origin all of them are necessarily imperfect, non-imperative, transitional, and subject to change as humans and their cultures change in themselves. *Morals and moralities are not absolutes,* nor were they ever or ever could be.

Natural morals are the human identities of behavior which, whether humans are cognizant of them or not, would still operate instinctively and biologically in order for a living thing to fulfill its wants and desires and by this process make possible the continuance of its own kind. Natural morals mean that the *sense* of morals, or any *thought* that morals exist, *actually does not exist,* because in any state of nature or specifically biological behavior and expression there seems to be no identity of what is considered as morality—morality meaning, in the cultural, religious, or civilized sense or viewpoint, some form of restrictive, imposed, self-disciplined, self-controlled, indoctrinated, or acquired pattern that restrains, reinterprets, attempts to control, or regulate such sexual behavior and its ordinarily free exercise and expression as activated and carried on in a state of nature. An animal or plant acts or lives as its nature "directs" it to act and live, and there is no such thing as "conscience" or "guilt" in the expression and effects of such behavior. Neurosis among animals is rare if not practically unknown in the natural ecological environment; neuroses of nonhuman animals occur when they are subjected to living in the human habitat and among humans, and their natural environment in its fullness is not available to them; it is a *human* disease acquired with culture and its deterrence of natural living. No animal has evolved that could accept or participate in an antinatural way of living; when coerced or forced to do so, the ensuing neurosis is the effect of the animal's physical inability to absorb or cope with a pattern foreign to its innate way of expressing and activating its natural freedom to live a life as its nature desires and needs in order to satisfy its biological, emotional, and intellectual (where existent) wants. The only restrictive elements, if one desires to seek restrictions, are the limitations put upon each animal, through its evolutionary history and in its present state of adaptability to environment, to behave and carry out its sexual expressions and wants in accordance with its nature at any given point in order to continue its own kind without any acquired or cultural influences.

There is no question that some degree of cultural and societal usages, controls, and restraints is necessary in the moral association of people; otherwise, a chaotic submergence of unbridled and arbitrary, inequitable and even antinatural conditions of living would deteriorate the essential degree or level of orderliness permitting people to live satisfactorily, even happily, without any diminishment of the same potential for others. We are not concerned here with what constitutes happiness or even life satisfaction for any particular person or group; we are here concerned with the "field" of freedom that affords some reasonable opportunity for this realization under conditions that are equitable to *all* individuals. Happiness, success, and satisfaction, are concepts and conditions, viewpoints or goals of each individual. Inasmuch as each individual viewpoint must necessarily vary to some degree from that of other individuals, there are no *universal standards* or categorical imperatives for concepts.

Though it is natural for a man not to allow another man to covet or "sleep" with his wife, there are many men, thanks to culture, who derive sexual satisfaction by observing another man having a sexual affair with the observer's wife. On the other hand, a culture where the wife or female property is purely a materialistic commodity to be enjoyed without emotional involvement, it is a cultural standard to offer one's wife or another female of the household to a guest, stranger, relative, or friend without batting an eye, as among the Eskimos, the Polynesians, and even in some Scandinavian countries. Birket-Smith: "Precisely because sexual life is generally considered normal, situations can arise which call for something other than the customary. When ill luck in hunting or sickness have shaken the Eskimo society to its very roots, the inner coherence of the community is strengthened by mutual exchange of wives."[44]

All sorts of situations arise in the private and intimate affairs of people. That is their private concern. We find some "perversions" in other animals, especially among the monkeys, but not to any great or common extent. However, man is the artist, par excellence, in sexual diversification, and that is his concern. Here we are primarily interested in recognizing the need of some animal and natural discipline, protectiveness and sense of regard for those we love, especially our own sexual property. For all cultural and societal usages and restrictions, whether religious, social, or political, are based on the idea of the property right of man over woman and not vice versa (at least in all ancient and historical cultures in most of the world and predominantly in Europe today). Of course, in any country where the philosophy of democracy has reasonably penetrated, culturally and legally, we find a more equitable attitude toward woman and her equal rights of freedom and the protection of society from the abuses of man. In these countries we find also a diminishment of the previously absolute power of religion and a nominal- or non-acceptance of the dogmas of outmoded and cruel dicta and traditions which unfortunately still deny natural freedom to people and, because of this denial, lead to a worldwide psychotic and neurotic and tragic entanglement of hundreds of millions of people to this very day.

In a previous little book, *The Gods and My Friends,* I wrote that "only a free individual can adopt ethical principles as a guide for action, thought, and association."[45] As democratic philosophy becomes more and more integrated in the freer countries, we can note more and more the demand of the individual to his right of privacy. This should be reasonable to expect in an individual who realizes his natural freedom as a life right. However, as man is a social animal and usually lives among others of his kind, he has evolved, because of the thousands of years of human association, a certain "tolerance," or *compatibility,* just as it has evolved in other animals, and this compatibility or compromise has made such association *tolerable.* Often this tolerance has been too severe for him; when this occurs, the *affirmative want* of the individual forces him to become a hypocrite and continue to carry on as best as he can to fulfill this want, though it may be publicly not desirable or "respectable." The hypocrisy involved should not really be considered "evil," for what is considered evil by the public may often be found to be good for the individual, especially in matters of sex. When Mandeville wrote that public virtues are often private vices, perhaps he meant that private virtues are too often considered public vices.

Every religion and almost every philosophy have maintained that their particular judgments on morality and ethics are either ordained by some divine revelation or uttered by God himself, or by inexplicable intuition, or by "logical" reasoning proving their precepts to be the "laws" of right and wrong for the universe. Religions and philosophies are the products of people, and their hopes and intentions are *in* the people. It is within the freedom and jurisdiction per se of anyone to indicate for himself and the world what *he* thinks morality and ethics should be. This is the way the helplessly egotistic nature of human beings operates. What most people overlook in establishing their principles and dogmas is whether their judgments arise from their personal wishes, and these from the natures they have acquired in their surroundings, which may or may not be realistically applicable, or from the common nature of man.

Man seems to be the only animal who establishes moral and ethical codes and continuously and thoroughly manages to violate every one of them. In the interplay of thought and deed, he has been, and will probably remain, the *Supreme Faker*. No other animal knows of morals or ethics, in the human sense, and therefore on this premise remains, in the human sense, a sincere, truthful, and honest individual. As man's mind grew, his art of faking matured, and today there is no finer faker. Bernard Malamud has Yakov, in *The Fixer*, say: "As for those that look like they got class, take another look."

Let us venture to explore this "art," in deed and word, as practiced by the theologians and philosophers. Whether we can actually find the acceptance of these dogmas and principles in the common experiences of people is something that only investigation could disclose. This is not to state categorically a priori that all these "divine" judgments or observations are wrong or right; that would be presumptuous and only repeat their error. While all people are incapable of pure impartiality, and this partiality identifies freedom in expression, including the view-points of the author, we shall at least try to analyze the ideas and substances of morality and ethics and *try* to find some sensible and more earthly or existential observations of their origins and present-day operability in the daily lives of real, living people.

It has been said over and over again that the road to hell is paved with good intentions. It still stands as the most outstanding truism of human history. What these "good intentions" have achieved is the needless, deepest, and most awesome of human suffering and tragedy and the greatest and widest range of human and world misery. The periods during which most of the foundations of religion emerged, especially in the Near East, Asia Minor, and the Mediterranean periphery, show that every habitation of any reasonable size was a *walled-in* fortress-city. This reveals not only the multiplicity and varieties of gods and goddesses, but also to what extent people in those ages trusted one another and the general "goodwill" and "peaceful" intent of the people in those long historical periods. Invasion routes were well marked and trodden during the many thousands of years of ancient warfare. Though the religions of today are either continuances or off-shoots in some form, or else founded upon the religions of those periods, ancient history reveals hardly any ethics, no real morality, no equitable responsibilities. It does reveal the constant and furious flow and flame of power politics, monarchial and prietly ambitions and aggrandizements, the foulest of intrigues, crimes, betrayals, political blackmail, and the lowest perverted depths of immorality, sexual criminality, and a lack of social, economic, and political justice unequaled in the later periods and in modern times. The creeds of today were born of the tyrannies, chicaneries and ignorance of ancient times. Stendhal, visiting Rome, wrote his observations in his *Roman Journal:* "The pope's government is a pure despotism . . . the gallows in this world and hell in the next. . . . The moment a father sees a child of his manifesting a spark of intelligence, he makes a priest of him. . . . Who knows? he may become pope. . . . The profound immortality that reigned in the Sacred College in 1800 has gradually disappeared, and so has all wit. In Rome, as elsewhere, it is the most stupid who govern."

The Essene cult, to which, it is said, Jesus belonged, considered sex and the desire for sex shameful and sinful, an idea that eventually made its way into the early foundations of Christianity. "The Essene character of this myth (the idea of shame and sin in sex) is unmistakable: marital embraces being here called 'ugly things'; and marital desire 'the fire of sin.' "[46] Any creed, religion, or principle which tends to inculcate antinatural traits and habits, restrictions and repressions in the life of people is not only detrimental to the mental and physical health of these people but a deterrent and destroyer of the very potential of life happiness, peace of mind, and general life satisfactions. There is a wide difference between opposing natural and normative ways of living and, on the other side, enlightenment so that the individual remains a biologically free animal within a sensibly enlightened, rationally nurtured and coordinated society in which this biological freedom is understood, protected, and controllably manifested for the mutual regard and protection of all its members. "Outside human desires there is no moral standard,"[47] and it is the understanding of these normal desires, their benefits and possible abuses, that should be the undertaking of education and knowledge so that the potential of personal happiness can be reasonably maintained or reached. It is high time to stop analyzing imperatives and commands in expositions of morality and begin teaching the children the nature, identities, forms, and happier consequences of goodness and good living, and how to think in order to possibly recognize goodness and good living as such. "Moral rules ought not to be such as to make instinctive happiness impossible."[48] And yet it is necessary in any societal structure to channel these instincts into normal expressions in order to maintain an orderly and peaceful process, not impose abnormal or subnormal deterrents and depressants that bring about conflict and abuse within this process.

"What is the meaning of moral?" asks Moritz Schlick. It is "that conduct which society believes will best further its own welfare."[49] But this contention of such "welfare" must be pliable and flexible, a nondogmatic process, not a standard, by which the naturalness of the individual can be held as a free and educable unit within an order that is as flexible and changeable as the human being himself is or is moved to be. Ward H. Goodenough: "For any rule. . . . the rule must be workable within the limitations of human nature and of people's resources and capacities. It must be compatible with other rules, so that honoring it does not interfere with honoring the others. . . . It must be in keeping with people's self-ideals. . . . Most important of all, people must have some commitment to membership in the community governed by the rule."[50] John Stuart Mill: "The only freedom which deserves the name is that of pursuing our own good in our own way, so long as we do not attempt to deprive others of theirs, or impede their efforts to obtain it."[51]

The history of man's religions has brought no such order. On the contrary, it has promulgated and advanced asceticism in all its ugly forms—needless self-denial, revulsion of the body as filth, lust, and vulgarity—has heaped abuse and condemnation upon the processes of procreation and its procreator, woman, considered her both as valuable property and as the evildoer, the devil himself, full of demons, demons translatable as desires most appetizing to those who condemned her.

According to the Judea-Christian concept, *Innocent Man* was corrupted by *Sinister Woman,* who thus caused the *Fall of Man,* and, as a result, this terrible Mother of All Living Things had to be punished forever! Social history shows us the continual pleasure and use man has derived from "punishing" her for her "evil" ways, that have always been a delightful and delectable joy and relief for man to participate in, before and after prayers. No intelligent and equitable person believes this fairy tale. Anthropology and its kindred sciences and investigations have exposed the historical data that prove this myth to have existed for thousands of years in many prior cultures and religions, in parallel or similar forms, from which porridge the Hebrews and later the Christians made up their own stories with a little dip and dab here and there to adjust to their own cultures and cults.

We have seen that the earliest deities were not male-gods but female fertility goddesses. With the ascendancy of the patriarchal cultures the male-gods took to their thrones and began the gradual and historical demotion of womankind from deified motherhood to a symbol and tool of the devil, the cause of the spoilage of man's "divine" nature and "purity" of soul, a mere chattel in the home and a slave animal in the field. "Tabernacles, a Canaanite vintage feast, could not be suppressed but only purged of sexual abandon, and converted to the joyful worship of a Supreme God by being associated with the Israelite use of tents in the Wilderness; even so, the lightheadedness of women devotees continued to trouble Pharisee sages. The Canaanite feast of unleavened bread was similarly converted into a commemoration of Israel's Exodus from Egypt. . . . A main theme of Greek myth is the gradual reduction of women from sacred beings to chattels. Similarly, Jehovah punishes Eve for causing the Fall of Man. . . . The Greeks, too, made woman responsible for man's unhappy lot by adopting Hesiod's fable of Pandora's jar, from which a Titan's foolish wife let loose the combined spites of sickness, old age, and vice. 'Pandora'—'all gifts'—it should be observed, was once a title of the Creatrix (Eve)."[52] "Some elements of the Fall of Man myth in *Genesis* are of great antiquity; but the composition is late, and even in places suggests Greek influence. The *Gilgamesh Epic*, the earliest version of which can be dated about 2000 B.C., describes how the Sumerian Love-goddess Aruru created from clay a noble savage named Enkidu (who after a series of episodes) sadly resigned himself to death. . . . Adam calls Eve 'the Mother of All Living' (*Genesis*, III.20), a title of this same Love-goddess Aruru, or Ishtar; and she confers wisdom on him, just as Aruru's priestess did on Enkidu. . . . Another source of the *Genesis* Fall of Man is the Akkadian myth of Adapa, found on a tablet at Tell Amarna, Pharaoh Akenaton's capital. . . . Another possible source of the *Genesis* Fall of Man is an ancient Persian myth: Meshia and Meshiane at first live on fruit alone, but are then persuaded by the Demon Ahriman to deny God. They lose their purity, fell trees, kill animals, and commit further evil. . . . The *Genesis* story, in which agricultural work is represented as a cure laid upon man because of Eve's inquisitiveness and disobedient mischief, mythically expresses the age-old Mediterranean point of view which regards physical labour (symbolized and exemplified by tillage of the soil) as an unmitigated and unavoidable hardship. This view continues to be shared in the Middle East. . . . Eden as a peaceful rural retreat, where man lives at his ease among wild animals, occurs not only in the story of Enkidu but in Greek and Latin legends of the Golden Age. . . . All gardens of delight are originally ruled by goddesses; at the change from matriarchy to patriarchy, male gods usurp them. A serpent is almost always present. . . . The Serpent is widely regarded as an enemy of man, and of woman."[53] "Gilgamesh is man seeking immortality."[54]

From a purely physical and humanist view it appears silly for people to consider seriously that an antinatural, antiworldly, and antihappiness concept would be the reasonable predeterminant of any creation of a world in which all these things are innate expressions of the very nature of life and the world, and then try to maintain that natural ways of living and the natural needs and desires of people should be condemned as "bad," "evil," and "sinful." We do know that a god or gods did not create the world and the life upon it, and that it was people who created the myths of its origin and who gradually cultured the various concepts of morals and rules by which they ordained people "must" live by not living naturally. Joseph Campbell: "The world is full of origin myths, and all are factually false."[55]

We also know that this antinatural persuasion upon people by theologies in regard to sex has brought about untold disharmonies in their lives, endless miseries and tragedies, and has withheld from people the biological freedom to live and express their lives as natural and rational beings; they have twisted and aborted their minds and bodies to conform to sadistic and masochistic aberrations of normal and intelligent living. Phyllis and Eberhard Kronhausen wrote: "From a mental point of view, it is established that such negative sex attitudes are not only regrettable, but can, indeed, be dangerous. . . . All the clinical evidence indicates that guilt-based sexual inhibitions, restrictions and repressions result in perversions of the sexual impulse, general intellectual dulling, sadomasochistic inclinations, unreasonable (paranoid) suspiciousness, and a long list of neurotic and psychotic defense reactions with unmistakable sexual content or overtones. . . . For the welfare of society then, no less than for individual mental health, it is incomprehensible why one would not want to accept the normal sex drive rather than to try to remove all temptation toward it, even if that were possible. But anti-sexualists cannot contemplate with equanimity the free acceptance of man's sexual role, nor any literature which tends to inform, educate or increase interest in that role."[56] Bertrand Russell: "You find as you look around the world that every single bit of progress in humane feelings, every improvement in criminal law, every step toward the diminution of war, every step toward better treatment of the colored races, or every mitigation of slavery, every progress there has been in the world, has been consistently opposed by the organized churches of the world. I say quite deliberately that the Christian religion, as organized in the churches, has been and still is the principal enemy of *moral* progress in the world."[57] "Religion teaches ethical codes which are not conducive to human happiness. . . . The worst feature of the Christian religion is its attitude toward sex—an attitude so morbid and so unnatural that it can be understood only when taken in relation to the sickness of the civilized world at the time the Roman Empire was decaying."[58] "A man or woman who has been thwarted sexually is apt to be full of envy; this generally takes the form of moral condemnation of the more fortunate."[59] John J. Honigmann: "When a culture prescribes an excessive load of taboos upon women without proper compensations of prestige, as among some North African societies, it has been shown (Lewin, 1958) that mental disorders in women are common."[60] Ottaker Nemecek: "Moral philosophy is confronted with the grotesque phenomenon represented by the fact that most zealous advocates of morality are themselves neurotics."[61] Philip Wylie: "The men and women and children of broken homes, the whores and homosexuals and murderers and drunkards and drug addicts, are the true church martyrs—human beings who paid out of ignorance the price which the churches exact to keep the reins of biology in their proud, merciless grasp."[62] Emmett McLoughlin, a former priest: "Another thing that became more clear as my years lengthened in the priesthood was that some of the Roman Catholic teachings affecting the moral lives of its members, far from bringing them closer to the religious peace of life which is divine, actually tore their lives asunder, ruined their families, and in many cases drove them into neuroses and even insanity."⁶³ . . . "I was personally convinced that doctrines of the Roman Catholic Church, if sincerely believed, and the hierarchy's laws, if rigidly adhered to, were productive not of peace of mind but of anguish of soul—not of normal creative life but of barrenness of spirit and bleakness of ignorance."⁶⁴ . . . "Alcoholism among the clergy is embarrassingly common—the sacramental wine being always available. One priest I knew commonly said, 'The Pope won't let me have a wife, so I have married this bottle.' "⁶⁵ Considering what may be termed true religious values, that is, values that are humanistic and natural and the oppositions advocated by antinatural theologies, John Dewey wrote: "The opposition between religious values as I conceive them and religions is not to be bridged. Just because the release of these values is so important, their identification with the creeds and cults of religion must be dissolved."⁶⁶

Religion is basically an emotional experience of an individual, while morals and ethics are derived from the lessons of experience of the nature and association of *many* individuals, of what is "good" for the individual or for the group, or for both. Human experiences come from the world and not from heaven. Religion is more or less an experience between the self and the *unknown*, the *unexperienced*. Morals and ethics emerge from the social, relating and relativistic experiences rising out of the processes and consequences of living.

The *theologically* religious man usually considers morality as a path toward his god, a necessary appendage of various restraints, asceticisms, deprivations, for the purpose of meriting a better and higher status after death or avoiding possible punishment in the hereafter. On these premises morality is apt to be far from truly volitional, and therefore the whole fabric of moral behavior becomes superficial and ceremonial, based on some compensational or bartering arrangement. From the standpoint of real and rational value, this is a meaningless trade. A purist is one who insists that the rest of the world should be as bored as he is. At least he seems to be sincere, but the person who thinks that he or she will be brighter in God's eyes because of participation in a hundred thousand masses for $2.50 takes God for an idiot and foolishly parts with $2.50. Besides, to our present knowledge, computers and the Univac have not yet arrived in the heavenly record-keeping offices.

On the other hand, morals and ethical principles directed to man himself, of and for himself, as an individual and as part of a community, become an empirical process that may lead to an intelligent analysis of behavior and conduct, so that these analyses might bring about a possible scale of value and meaning that might make possible, in turn, a volitional procedure based on a truer understanding and appreciation of the natural factors involved, from which all these values emanate and upon which they should be based. Corliss Lamont: "It is an ethics in which conscience does not merely play the role of a vetoing censor, but is creative in the sense of bringing to the fore new and higher values. This system of morality recommends the greater and more frequent enjoyment of earthly goods on the part of all men everywhere; it repudiates ascetic other-worldliness in favor of buoyant this-worldliness; it is against all defeatist systems which either postpone happiness to an after-existence or recommend acquiescence to social injustice in this existence."[67]

Those who continue to regard moral and ethical imperatives as coming from a divine source do not take into account that, if this were so, there would be no justication, moral goodness, or ethical judgment in *death,* also created or bestowed upon man by such divine powers. To say that *death* is pleasant or desirable to the one doing the dying is to commit to folly and silliness the whole gamut of morality based on divine or supernatural origin.

I can see no moral value in the glorification of death. St. Peter's in Rome is a housed cemetery of deified priests and martyrs encased in marble. Wherever one moves he is reminded of death. The morbidity of religion is a sword of Damocles that man himself suspends over his own head. The variety of *articulos* sold in the name of religion outside the Vatican is almost endless. If the Church would allow it, the vendors of religious articles would sell you a signed certificate that you shall be delivered and welcomed in heaven after you die, or Vatican postal stamps for advance money deposits by number in a celestial "Swiss" bank. I would rather watch the swallows sweep high and low over the Via Ludovisi early in the morning or even sit on the Via Veneto and see the queers go parading by making affectionate eyes at each other than to gaze upon this constant, self-indulgent morbidity and solemnness that is an unmoving cloud of grayness over the lives of people.

There seems little doubt that freedom is a two-way street. Freedom, as a natural biological trait, innate in all anima, is not concerned with what one does with it, with what one "ought" or "should" do, or what is "proper" or "nice," or what is expected of "respectable," "fine," "civilized," or "intellectual" people. If we are to presume that it may be just for one individual or group to follow and live by the precepts, principles, or directions, voluntarily or involuntarily, of another individual or group, even though these are not beneficent or acceptive, then we can reasonably conclude that it is natural and inevitable that man must be, in some form or other, to some degree or other, a slave, and that he should no more try to escape from his slavery that from himself or the earth on which he fearfully crawls.

The history of man's attempt to restore natural freedom, with all its concomitant, conscious and subconscious sense of limitations, potentials, and probabilities, is strewn with the courage and lives of people who ideally or out of sheer necessity felt that the individual can be free, free in the widest and fullest natural sense, and still enjoy existence and coexistence within a periphery of human associations and social belongings and in appreciation of the realities upon which and in which all this is existential and recurring.

CULTURE, CRUELTY, AND CATEGORICAL IMPERATIVES

CULTURE AND CIVILIZATION have not tamed or tranquillized the innate aggressiveness, cruelty, and hostility of the human animal. They have, in many ways, merely made him into a greater killer and a wiser criminal. They have given him a shrewder and more cunning way of screening terrible crimes and cruelties with prayer, propaganda, crusades, personal and group revolts against society. They have given him almost endless and intricate laws and varied customs by which he can find a loophole and a rationale to justify his hostile behavior and cool his conscience into self-pity. They have given him the "right" to kill because the "enemy" does not agree or is of another religion or wears a shirt of another color, or is of another shade of skin. Six million Jews were murdered by people who were mesmerized by the loud clamor of buffoonery and rank gangsterism. And still today the few survivors in Israel are surrounded by Arabs who, justified by their Koran, vent their hate upon the Jews and would like to slaughter every one of them. The victims of Musa Dagh lay bare the confession of cruelty fired by religious and ethnic differences.

Civilized white man, in white shirt and buckled shoes, murdered, robbed, defrauded the American Indian, and the white man thanked his God for deliverance from the naked "savage" and felt morally justified in his noble work of extermination. Just as the "sportsman" travels far today with high-powered rifles to shoot from planes the polar bears below like sitting ducks so that he can adorn his floor with the animal's skin and boast how "brave" he was. As our Federal government, made up of civilized statesmen with high hats and intellectual protocol, sanctioned and encouraged the slaughter of millions of buffalo so that the Indians could be starved out and driven from the plains to the bleak wilderness. Even today the civilized gentry of Alaska are plotting to defraud and dispossess the Eskimos of their land. Did not civilized England with Blackstonian law and Magna Carta ethics threaten the arts of India and thus enslave several hundred million people for more than three hundred years?

It is needless to retrace history which, after all, is in itself an almost endless narration of crime, murder, robbery and enslavement. In the quiet high corridors of the temple, mosque, and cathedral, in the whisper of the prayer and the appealing cry to the Lord, were seeded again and again the horrors of massacre, pogrom, prejudice, and hate. Friar Peter's plaintive pleading preceded the march of the plundering Crusaders, who could hardly be considered a gentle, kindly lot. Luther, himself a rebel against the Vatican and Romanism, harangued the lords and barons to exterminate the Anabaptists at Münster: "Rebellion brings with it a land full of murder," he proclaimed in 1492, condemning those who undermined the secular order. "Let everyone who can, smite, slay, and stab . . . remembering that nothing can be more poisonous, hurtful, or devilish than a rebel!" Although the original leaders of the Anabaptists were cruel and merciless Hitlerian dictators, "the direct survivors of the Anabaptists today are the peaceful Mennonites and Amish of the Pennsylvania countryside."[68]

The precultural and hominid lived and evolved by instinctual drives to preserve his shelter, his area of existence, his domain, and within it the subsistence that made possible his survival and the continuance of his kind. That is why we are here today. Human society rose from animal society, and for the same reasons. The social and societal organism and structure evolved out of the exigencies of *necessity*, all of it biological.

The advent and acquisition of cultural and theological pervasives tended to separate him from his natural abode in the same way as it took away his tenacity and natural wisdom and gave in return an ethereal soul and the willingness to slave for others. The beginnings of civilization saw the beginnings of biological confusions. Culture and theology, in reality the statuses, structures, and functions of master and slave, *institutionalized* and *legalized* the human animal and made him into subject and servant, into a dejected, defeatist and resigned slave, mired in ignorance, poverty, emasculation, submission, and without courage.

The values of living and the preciousness of life itself—Schweitzer's *reverence for life*—have become lost in societal ends which derogate the natural processes of a happy existence into dogmatic "immoralities," to false and stupid obscurantisms. The simplicity and congruity of animal morality gave way to societal and theological morality, which has vulgarized the human constitution, made shame and prudery dark curtains to shade and depress natural feelings and inclinations. The world was full of iron curtains long before Churchill's coinage of the phrase. And when, as I hope, these iron curtains will be lifted from the faces of the future generations, the sun again will cast its warmth and truth upon the happy bodies, to live as life *wants* them to live, within the affirmative compatibility that the prime force of living substance itself *necessitates* and *wants*.

If there must be a morality it must be a *naked* morality free of the black and dismal robes of prudery, exposed to the light, the fresh air, and joyful color. If there must be a morality, it must be *dedicated* and *devoted* to living and to life, not to pre-dying and death. The new morality must be an awareness of the preciousness of the moment, the hour, the day, and to the truth that the hands of time do not go back, retrace our own little uncertain allotment of whatever time may be ours. The new morality must be based on the recovery of man's natural alignment with *this* world and all that lives on it, and with us, for it is on this that our persistence and existence depend. The new morality must give back to man his true *identity*. Man must re-create and restore this identity and thus be able to *want* again to reevaluate it for his satisfactions and life fulfillment. *Man must regain his natural freedom.*

Let us probe a little into the nature of categorical imperatives, moral directives, eminent domains, religious and societal mores and usages, "divine" rules and dogmas, the multifarious theo-sophical beliefs designed to sustain and feed the cosmocentricities and egocentricities of people, to which man has submitted himself in one way or other. Let us try to detect, if we can, the impact of these upon the natural freedoms of man, whether any of them are essential, justifiable, wise, equitable, satisfying, and really successful.

Freedom is completely amoral in itself, but the acts of freedom are and can be judged by the freedom of different perspectives and needs. Freedom is a *means,* as life itself is the means of living. Freedom is a capability, a sense of being oneself, a self. Freedom identifies the sense of being *detached yet related, apart yet with affinity,* as well as the desire to be attached yet feeling and sensing that the idea of the attachment as well as the physical attachment itself is a free vehicle of voluntary choice and want within the natural elements of its potential, limitation, and possible extension.

Freedom is not a standard because life-movements do not standardize themselves in actuality. Standardization requires the acceptance of anything *as is,* which implies the freedom to accept it or not to accept it as is. The implication of freedom as an acceptance of something does not standardize it. The standardization can last only as long as the acceptance lasts. So long as man retains the freedom to change things, then such stabilizations which might be construed as "standards" are always open to change, and should be, and they *do* change. Since life itself is *process,* as well as the universe itself being constantly in process, any idea of an absolute standard is an illusion and false.

Inasmuch as we are holding in mind the essence of freedom and not the moral, ethical, or intellectual use of it, we can admit that certain "standards" and usages might be of value to the individual and group, but here again we have to contend with particular viewpoints of certain individuals, groups, and cultures. When a rule of conduct is set up by organizational necessity for the "security" of all, the psychological effect of its authoritarian procedure becomes inadmissible to the essence of freedom, though in many instances necessary for the *real* security of individuals between themselves and as a society. The violence, brutality, dishonesty, evil, and oppressing characteristics of individuals reflect themselves in the character and acts of the group; so do the affirmative and positive characteristics of goodness. Most often combinations of both to some degree are present in the individual and group. Standardization will not undo the evil; we can only build more prisons, hang more criminals and provide more victims.

Nor does the Church lessen "sin" in the violations of their dogmas by threat of eternal damnation. We find more cruelty, dishonesty, and sexual perversion in Catholic countries than in non-Catholic areas: Latin America is certainly no model of equity, honesty, chastity, or monogamy; neither was Catholic Germany in history and under Hitler a model for humaneness, sympathy and love; or the Vatican-Hitler Concordat in which the Roman Catholic Church "played up" for its own existence while Hitler murdered thousands of its priests; nor the silence of Pope Pius XII in refusing to protest the murder of millions of Jews; neither were the Poles with their pogroms years ago. Spain with her autos-da-fé, the Inquisition, with its historical program of keeping people ignorant, impoverished, enslaved, is nothing to admire in terms of morality. Only Catholic countries hold bullfights, and to see the butchery and the bloodied sand as I have seen them (the bullfights in the smaller towns, such as San Miguel de Allende in Mexico, are often frightful), is but to conclude that Catholicism has not been very effective in teaching her subjects kindness to animals. What happens is that people keep on "sinning" because it is in their nature to do so, and to become neurotics and subject to stress and psychosomatic ailments due to their frustrations and repressions and the fears of eternal punishment in hell. The degree of "sinning" and the degree of neurosis depend upon the particular attitude of the adherent and the depth of religiosity involved.

Freedom is the ability to make standardization *soft* and flexible, even to liquefy it into modified or new forms and this is what has actually taken place in history. Otherwise there could have been no progress or change in any endeavor of man, be it in the arts, the sciences, invention, exploration, or the general progress of knowledge and material advance. It was once the "standard" to view the world as flat, the body as filth, and both of no value; to believe that to touch the wristbone of a saint would heal the sick. We now know, because certain people expressed their freedom, that the world is round, that the body is not foul, that it should be clean if there is to be any kind of clean spirit, and that if we are sick we should call a doctor. The Pope today when sick does call a doctor—which, in fact, is a defiance of the "Will of God" and evidence of lack of faith, of depending solely upon God and his spiritual elixirs. There was a time when the Pope did have faith and depended for his well-being solely upon prayer and the intercession of the saints; this "standard" has changed for the popes, as well as for the rest of us, and today we both try to live as long as possible with the aid of whatever medical science can offer to keep us alive.

Freedom, to a more or less normal person, means the ability to operate in a field than can bring certain satisfactions, rewards, acquisitions, requisitions, compensations, psychological and otherwise, which are conducive and meaningful to a potential that is the natural expression of whatever motility of thought, expression, and activity possible to a living thing, even though constrained and limited by the world in which it finds itself, by the nature of its relatedness to external factors and by the impact of cultures upon it.

Freedom is not an end unto itself any more than the rotation of the earth around the sun is an end unto itself. It is essential to know how it operates and what we do with it. *"Der Mensch ist frei geschaffen, ist frei"*—"Man is created free, is free," wrote the poet Friedrich Schiller.[69] Freedom is not for freedom's sake but for *our* sakes. Freedom has meaning when we begin to know what it can do for us or against us and how we might control it, as we control other things, for our own possible good and as a protection of humanity and humanism against the possible deleterious effects of human nature. We have the freedom to restrain our own miseries and ultimate destruction as we have the freedom to destroy ourselves. It is for each to choose, and if the choice is wise, it will be the freedom to choose love and its nutrients and moistures, for without love life is just dry sand in a cold, deathly, and lightless world.

FIRST PRINCIPLES OF LOVE

EPICTETUS, THE ANCIENT sage of Stoicism, said: "If you love an earthen vessel, say it is an earthen vessel which you love; for when it has been broken, you will not be disturbed. If you are kissing your child or wife, say that it is a human being whom you are kissing, for when the wife or child dies, you will not be disturbed."[70] The trouble with Epictetus is that he could not tell the difference between an earthen pot and a human being, between a lump of clay and the human heart. When one loses the one he loves he cannot help being not only disturbed but deeply grieved. There is a difference between understanding, even expecting, the eventualities of life, bearing them when they do occur, and trying to make oneself feel like a piece of wood or a clay pot. Animal mothers grieve for their babies, and animal babies, in their whimpering way, grieve for their mothers. An earthen pot does not love or receive love. Humans have the added

quality of memories and memories in a way can stop our departed
and loved ones at the bridge and can always bring them back to
us. It is as silly to dehumanize a human into a pot as it is to
dehumanize a human into a god.

Love is the greatest experience because it demands so often
the greatest courage—the courage to give of oneself to another
unstintingly and notwithstanding any and all other factors that
might stand in the way, be it religion, law, custom, family, culture, fortune, prestige, reputation, position, even security.

Love is a naked thing. It transcends all ornament, appearance
and impression. Love has no pride or fear of or for the world. It
has only dignity for itself, and this dignity supersedes and precedes all else because love entails an attitude which is nakedly
free, a way of life that for this love indicates a state of freedom.
It is a way of thinking and acting that has nothing to do with
rules, regulations, and rewards. Love, within the nature of itself,
is its own reward. Love is the compensation for living.

Love exudes out of the very essence of freedom. It is not just
a matter between a man and a woman; it is a matter of one's attitude toward another, or others, or things. Or it may be the expression of an artist painting or a composer composing, or it may
be the one who views the painting or hears the music. Without
freedom these cannot exist, nor can love in the expression of it.
Anything that suppresses, represses, undervalues, or frustrates
freedom also frustrates the potential and the flow of love.

There is no such thing as an unfree love. Love can remain only
love so long as it is free, because *only as a free agent can one
really love.* Law and creed and obscurantisms may regulate and
institutionalize relationships such as marriage, which may be
beneficent or harmful, but only love can maintain a happy,
meaningful tie, a true *moral* state of being, a *satisfied* sense of
being. People in love may get married, but marriage does not of
itself preconclude a state of love. There is *honor* in love; a marriage without love is without honor; where there is no honor a
contract or a dogma to assure it is folly and tragedy. The com-
petency and the moral structure of marriage are not made possible by creed and law; these may force a continuance, an unholy
tie, but never affirmatively affect a status of love. Marriage with-

out love is just a begetting process, which may be good, or the
same process without begetting, and often for one or the other,
or both, agony. Yet religious rule demands that even in the absence of love and therefore in the absence of freedom such an
unholy alliance "must" continue in folly and tragedy. Marriage
is a *social* and a natural institution; love is a *personal* as well as
a natural enjoyment of a process.

Love does not necessarily recognize or identify itself with such
regulatory and societal factors. Love is a natural and biological
factor, not a cultural factor, exhibited in many ways, not only
in humans, but in most all other warm-blooded animals: it
exhibits itself more and more as an animal rises in its consciousness of its sense of being attached to the being of others. Love
finds itself in its own need for attachment, for being part of the
being and life of another or others or things. This consciousness
preceded all law and creed and is always apart from and above
these mere contractual manifestations of organizational and societal need and acquisition. It may have started in the wonder in
the primitive's eyes looking at the rainbow, or it may have started
in the bundling together of animals and humanoids to endure
the wind and the storm, but it existed long before the first shaman
laid down the first rule—to make himself king to make rules.

Creed and religion have too often injured love, imprisoned
the sense of freedom and the uninhibited sway of human consciousness and the necessary absence of duress in matters of love.
Law and creed may have forced people to stay united—in chains,
in bitterness, resignation, submission, futility, and blind and
ignorant surrender of life to the fulfillment of their silly rules,
of blind faith in superficial and man-made dogmas and rituals.
Creed and religion and the customs they have given birth to have
been the greatest prostitutors of what is traded as love in the
affairs of people.

Love, as freedom itself, cannot breathe and move in an atmosphere where vulgarized and polluted involuntary factors and
blind caterpillar obedience are the forced, necessary or accepted
processes to maintain a relationship.

Love is not the fear of these societal impositions or the fear
of what others might think or say. It contains the courage to face

these factors squarely and indifferently. *The fears we fear become nothing when love shows its strength.* Life demands and deserves this. Nothing less is worthy of the freedom that can produce the ecstasy and the deepest joys that emanate from inhaling the nectar of love. Unfortunately, most people would rather breathe the pollution of needless frustration and stagnant darkness than to expose themselves to the light and the free air and its compensating freshness. Love is not a sin; the denial of love is a sin, if one must retain any idea of sin. Virtue may abide in the happy person, and vice versa, but virtue, for itself and by itself, is not happiness, nor is it rationally justifiable. It may serve the purposes of egocentricity for public approval or the self-delusion of "purity," but this is hardly socially justifiable or desirable.

Many people say that "God is love." If this be so, then God is the greatest heretic of all and the strongest and most persistent rebel against anything that opposes the free flow of this most necessary of all needs to fulfill a satisfying life, without which life becomes a mere coming and going, of growing, subsisting, and dying. Love gives meaning, purpose, and joy to living *while* we live, not to the after-end of it. The only "prayer" needed is to possess and feel its presence within and around us. The only "ritual" needed is to express it. The only "altar" needed is one's open and free heart to give, to give of oneself in order to receive the fullness that life should seek for itself. The only "heavenly reward" is its own endowment—here, now, on earth—while we live! Happiness is something more often created than found; it is within us, and love is the key that can allow it to permeate our senses, our personalities, to relax us and *see* the realities of life and its values. When we find these we also find the courage that love needs to show us the way.

To do this one must feel and be free. Married people, *in love,* remain free, free to want each other, to give of each other joyfully and to make life what it should be, a continual joy and the desire to welcome each coming day and be grateful for each day we live. Marriage does not preclude love, neither does it preconclude such a state, neither does the marriage license or contract mandatory in a particular culture or society. These are cultural, societal, and legal needs in certain localities to give order, decorum, and responsibility to securities, equities, and property rights involved, to the rearing and care of children, that is, they relate to the *economics* of marriage, not the psychic unity of people and their sentiments for each other. Married people who are still in love have no need of parting nor desire to and thus remain voluntarily free people.

Married people who are not in love are not free any longer and should part to regain this freedom. Married people who resent each other and stay married are sick people, who are not only unfree but slaves to maladies that have changed them into sadists and masochists. Besides, they are wasting time and thus wasting their lives. Many of the religions, especially Roman Catholicism with its silly dogmas on sex, woman, and marriage, and the Puritan-Prude Protestants with their guilts and shames, have been the direct causes of the tragic misery of hundreds of millions of people and still continue to spread their poisons to pollute the freshness, the honesty, and natural freedoms that are so essential to health, love, happiness, and peace of mind.

CONCEPTS OF VIRTUE AND GOODNESS

WILLIAM LILLIE STATES that "we are forced to admit that good is indefinable."[71] Virtue, as a universal, is indefinable; so is a "good" indefinable on the same basis. This is true because goodness or badness cannot be upheld in any shape or form as a universal principle applying alike to all existence. Or, as George Jean Nathan said in a moment of facetious wit: "What makes for pleasure and consequent happiness? Each man to his own poison."[72] So be it with *virtue* which, as a universal is also indefinable in the same manner as *good* is indefinable. Socrates taught that "virtue is knowledge." What is knowledgeable may lead to virtue, whatever this may be conceived to be, but knowledge in itself, which is an element of what has been realized out of experience and learning, or both, does not necessarily preconclude an acquisition of a state of virtue or its opposite. If Socrates sensed any true form of biological morality existent in the experiences of people, he could only have sensed it as part of the natural realm and not in the changeable modes and usages of different people of his time. Yet in the biological we can see no evidence of the existence of morals and morality as these terms are generally considered by the concepts of people and their societies. Lillie states: "It is not known whether Socrates himself ever made an explicit statement that morality is a matter of nature and not of custom, but this was almost certainly his view."[73]

Virtue is a pliable, opinionated viewpoint of any individual or culture, and whether it is virtue or whether it is good or bad can only be judged on the same basis. There is no universal ground to establish an abstract and subjective sense of virtue. As Campbell states: "In the central nervous systems of all animals there exist innate structures that are somehow counterparts of the proper environment of the species."[74] Each living thing simply *has* to live according to its nature and its long evolved adaptation to its environment or else perish, and any principles that do not take into full view the ecology of a living thing and intend to act counterwise in their efforts to induce or force unnatural and antinatural thinking and behaving upon people are detrimental and injurious to the existence of those who are so influenced or are submissive to them. The infant and child know of no morals; they simply act as their natures direct; morals are either indoctrinated, imposed, or taught them as they keep growing up, and whether they are good or bad is reflected in their adult behaviors. John Dewey: "The reason a baby can know little and an experienced adult know much when confronting the same things is not because the latter has a 'mind' which the former has not, but because one has already formed habits which the other has still to acquire."[75]

The freedom that is within the child is often lost with the man. Somehow, in the process of growing up the freedom of the child fades away and the duties and responsibilities of adulthood take over. This is not only explainable and understandable, but becomes obviously necessary when people live within their cultures and societies. Order is essential, not merely to contain a peaceful society, but to protect the individuals from themselves and others. The pity of it all is that eventually order so often deteriorates into subjects instead of free men.

The child, unperturbed by the multitudinous complexities and pressures of culture, is *naturally* more free. The problem of the man in necessarily arranging his own compatibility with culture and societal acquisitions, requisitions and patterns, is to attempt some reasonable and equitable compromise to retain his individuality as a *naturally free being* and still be a *participant* in whatever cultural and societal values and usages he deems acceptable, compatible, and adaptable for his satisfaction and happiness. Insofar as the social, economic, and cultural structures of a society tend to *process* this course of compatibility of the individual as a naturally free being, and the needs of the society to maintain itself as the *process* to serve and manifest itself *for* the individual, to this extent we can say that the society is continuing the natural evolution of itself as the biological and cultural needs of individuals to form groups to express the natural tendency for mutual-assistance and togetherness in terms of the free expression and action of individuals. In this way the limited containment of nature freely directs itself as its particular evolutional state at any given point is determined by all of its own controllable factors, which seem also to operate as free agents in a general natural process of experience.

Political, social, and economic systems ultimately break down when they fail to fulfill within reasonable limits this naturally and biologically free process and when the controllable factors have deteriorated to pure animalism through the individual's opposing himself and other individuals with illogical, irrational, and unjudicious patterns of principle and behavior. The great paradox of human experience is that man has accomplished what he has accomplished under the constantly opposing pressures and resistances of human nature itself, to achieve for itself the reasonably good and the pressing need and quantum of some desire for peace.

Freedom, being a *process*, the *anima* of life itself, takes all possible forms and variations of experience. There are people who will dominate, according to their nature, and people who desire to be dominated, according to their nature. Very often these people may be considered "suited" to each other on the basis of compatibility, even drawn to each other. Often those who desire to dominate are impelled to "purchase" the submission of those willing to "sell" from a desire to achieve a better status, more security, luxury, wealth, escape from insecurity. Again, those who desire to be dominated seek out the one who can be cruel to them, who can master them, allow them to become subservient slaves. All these variations of dominance and meekness express themselves in the animal world, and we witness them readily in almost conspecific identities in the monkey, baboon and many other societies. I have even noticed it in the little fishes, clusters of tropical guppies right in my own home. The psychological weapon of "pecking" is not restricted to hens, and societal variations of status, of master and slave, are not peculiar to humans alone.

For those of us who desire the *equity* of freedom for ourselves as well as for all others, even if our goal may not be completely and ideally realized and established, at least we are *moving* and living in some *sensible* direction of our desired choice. The stage of human existence across which we all must travel from birth to death, even if we are pushed, is a parade of endless variations of personality and experience, each of us molding in our strange ways the nature of one another. For us, let travel from nothing to nothingness be *something*, so long as we have the consciousness, the intelligence, the awareness, the goodness of heart, and whatever potential of choice we may be fortunate enough to express and live by, to make this something a meaningful experience while we *do* live, and as happy and satisfied an experience as the magic wand of freedom may permit.

Many people seem to be gravely concerned with their duties and responsibilities to their society, yet rarely think for a moment just what this society consists of, what it contains or acts like, as a *whole,* how it grows, thrives, changes, and declines. If we give reasonable thought to it, we may find that society as a "whole" cannot be pointed at and identified as such; it consists of others like ourselves: *individuals* patternized more or less into custom, usage and habit similarities, which, regardless of our motives, are constantly changing, slowly or quickly, to meet events and circumstances to which we are continually subjected each day and over periods of time.

As a result, we may become more conscious and aware of its sphere of containment and its influences in other societal spheres, its lack of identifiable rigidity of form, structure, and function. *Society,* as well as the individuals who comprise it, as well as all existence, is *process* and a *process.* We may understand more and more *what* it is; *why* it is, is something our minds may find it difficult to apprehend in the *ultimate* and *certain* sense. All we can do is to apply whatever knowledge may come our way to our own lives as such, to rationalize meanings and values so that these can possibly lead us from the "what" of the sciences to the "what-for" of philosophy to give some value and meaning to our aims and actions.

The metaphysicians and theologians will continue to forego, avoid, evade, and run from the "what" and "what-for," continue to query and answer themselves in the Talmudic fashion that will give them the egocentric and anthropomorphic dream replies they seek, and build for themselves the mirages and fantasies they always need in their unsuccessful and frustrating attempts to escape from the biological roots, functions, and processes from which they can *never* really escape, and from which, when they become wise philosophers, they would not want to escape. Instead, they will try to stay alive, well and well-fed as long as possible.

Prayers never stopped a plague or revealed to man that cleanliness is the approaching road to health. The saints stank in their filth and reflected minds astray and bodies made haggard and smelly in their fantastic idea that by destroying themselves or forcing their natures to suffer, their souls, as a result, would become purer before their gods.

Now that the gods have descended past the twilight into nonentity, the restlessness of man begins to repeat the same metaphysical grind of subjectivism by attempting to replace the gods with "patterns" and "purposes," not only to be indicated a priori in the very processes of "purposive directionalism" (which Simpson rightly terms "evolutionary theology") in the "progressive" (from lower to higher) development by evolution of all micro- and macroorganisms, including man, of course, but that the entire universe may, with its totality and as a totality, indicate within the nature and operationalism of itself a "purpose," a "plan," a specifiable direction, which can, like a person, "intuitively" and "objectively" (now twinned in the classical usage of dualism) "mold" itself in some mystical fashion into a self-directed purpose.

It is not unusual for people of means to feel that they are superior to those of less means, that they and their level of neighbors and associations are more refined, more intellectual, more civilized, and more-to-be-looked-up-to than the less fortunate members in their society. It is seen wherever one goes throughout the world, even in primitive, savage, and semi-primitive tribes. It seems that there is an incontestable ego that, by its own nature, is determined to climb higher, overwhelm, and overcome people, things, and circumstances, an ego of which wealth, power, and prestige are the identifying marks. It is, in actuality, the relentless drive of the human psyche to overwhelm *itself,* to imprison its own natural freedom of being free by the intoxicating influences of approval, distinction, and subjection of the being to the pleasant dominance of external factors.

Freedom implies some ratio and nature of association with other beings and things. This does not mean that to be free one should or could eliminate this degree and nature of biological and cultural symbiosis: this can never be eliminated, alive or dead; we are part of, and tied to, our world inevitably and forever. The problem is how can this degree and nature of relativism and relationship be expressed without diminishing the natural freedoms, of which cultural and intellectual freedom are parts, so that a being, according to its being, might be able to fulfill itself as a life and gain for itself, without taking away from others, the deep and wholesome satisfactions and senses of joy and reasonable fulfillments that existence, linked and frail and brief as it maybe, can possibly make available to us. Only in the ethical maturation of individuals, whether alone or in groups, can there be any possible solution and resolution in transisting the ethical understanding and sympathies of people into individual and group peace and security. The world-view can only be a personal view and a number of personal views. Albert Schweitzer: "We must be men of the future who allow their hearts to speak along with their reason. Only then will we develop into what we are meant to be: not supermen but real men, living and acting in the spirit of profound humanism."[76] A great mind can discover the world, but only a great heart can move it.

As has been stated before and emphasized again, freedom is a process or activity that identifies itself out of the very process and processes of relationships and interdependencies. Directly or indirectly, by closeness or by farness, each part is related to everything else. All the moral, esthetic, ethical, and social mores and sentiments of people rise out of their natural and cultured affinities. *In everything we are a part; in nothing are we strictly alone.* We sophisticates know the heart to be just a muscle of the body, even if it is the most important one. We also know quite definitely that when something "touches the spot," whether it be pity for an old woman, a cry of pain from somewhere, the serfdom of aged men, the subtle whimpering of the child, the innocent courage of youth, or the sweet adolescent smile of a girl meandering along the road, the lazy cruise of leaves upon a quiet rambling stream, the impatient tinting with pastels of the setting sun on a forest of bare trees, or the inexplainable repose that comes from good music, we know quite definitely that there is a feeling of something, perhaps of goodness, of softness, of some kind of fine expression in our hearts, a compelling tenderness, symbolical though it may be, but there it is. For want of a better word I call this friendship—for therein is the seed of realization that we are never alone.

THE NATURE OF MORAL JUDGMENTS

WHETHER THIS VIEW can be sufficiently expressive and influential in controlling man's innate hostility, his cruelty, in diverting the sadomasochistic psyche of humanity into ethical streams of self-knowledge to the point of intellectual discovery and realization that life itself is sacred, as Schweitzer points out to us, and that power, wealth, prestige, and admiration, although naturally enjoyable factors, which must be categorized and considered as servants and processes of life and not its goals, ends, and masters, cannot be fairly and clearly predicted. Yet, with all the learning and knowledge of people, there must be some way to necessitate a catalystic *ethos* that would ensure, by the principle of necessity itself, a reasonably free and natural life, a naturally and rationally free individual and a socio-politico-economic process that can be a means, sufficiently flexible, changeable and adjustable to meet the forming needs for compatibility within new experiences and the various emerging compromises and adaptabilities that rise as determining agents in a constantly changing world.

There is a wide and deep cleavage between intuitive metaphysics and the pursuit of knowledge or the *knowable* based on the nature of man, his experiences, and the world in which he lives. Maimonides describes this emotional and "sympathetic introspection" in the idea of "death through the kiss of God": "The more the powers of the body subside and the fires of passion ebb, the stronger the spirit becomes, the brighter its radiance, the purer its knowledge, and the greater its joy over what it knows. When the perfect man grows old and approaches death, this knowledge increases by leaps and bounds, and his happiness over his knowledge, and his love for what he has come to know, are heightened and intensified until his soul departs from his body at the moment of greatest delight."[77] This sad philosophy reveals the fallacy of being happy over knowledge for its own sake, the fallacy of happiness in dying, and the fallacy of withdrawing from earthly joys and living values. For the life of me, I cannot see anything wrong in passion and sexual enjoyment, or in wanting to drink to quench one's thirst, or to eat, to sleep, to rest or invigorate oneself by some form of activity. What the satisfaction of one's passions, in fulfillment of one's normal nature, has to do with purification by dying or a process of dying throughout life I also cannot see, nor can I visualize any such psychotic arrangements created or desired by any lovable and benevolent god who is honest with his own intentions of creation. What Maimonides accomplishes is the exposure of the deplorable state of human emotion in its egocentric madness to achieve equality in, and union with, some ethereal, perfect state, an inconceivable state in any event, and is an abortion of whatever knowledge man may have or can apply to better and *elongate his actual life* on

earth. This "perfect state," which truly depicts a state of pure
boredom without reprieve, is described in the Talmud regarding
the life beyond the grave: "There is neither eating nor drinking;
the good sit there with crowns on their heads and see God in
Bliss."[78] Even if such a state could be true, and we know it to
be false, such an existence would reek chaos upon the human
personality, which wants to drink and eat and sense the various
appreciations and sympathties as it experienced and *knew* during
its mortal life; it could not endure, by the very nature of itself,
such a total loss of freedom and habit and such an endless unchangeable existence and such a meaningless arrangement of
blissful adoration for its own sake *without end*.

Edward Westermarck has firmly established by his principle of
ethical relativity that moral judgments have their origin in emotions. "There is no need to dispute Westermarck's view that moral
judgments may have their origin in emotions."[79] Lillie explains
further: "The theory that morality depends on human likes and
dislikes has been developed in the modern theory of ethical relativity by Westermarck, who takes full advantage of the evolutionary study of the development of sentiments."[80] "The mnemic
tendency by itself favors the continuance of the level of custom,
and the hormic tendency may lead to new ways of conduct that
refuse to be subordinated to moral standards at all; this is the
reason why moralists so often distrust those with new ideas. It is
the struggle between these two tendencies within the individual
which arouses in him individual reflection and so raises him from
the level of custom to the level of conscience. It may only be
in one or two matters that the two tendencies conflict in any individual, but when he does face that conflict reflectively even on a
single issue, he has passed from the level of custom to the level of
conscience."[81] It is this level of conscience, and its freedom to
be so, that marks the departure of the blind and submissive conformist, which theology militantly requires for its own continuity,
and the beginning of freedom of thought, new ideas, and the
application of this freedom to pursue and determine the knowledgeable and the natural elements upon which life is actually
based. Freedom of conscience depends upon freedom of thought,

and freedom of thought can be achieved by freedom from the necessity of conformance and obedience for its own ends.

We should reemphasize the importance of differentiating between morals and moralities as concepts and responsibilities, or what people call "moral" responsibilities. The former may be ideas or conformances of individuals and groups that people "must" or "ought" to adhere to in order to fulfill the customs, usages, and dogmas of any social order or institutionalized organization, and which may be good or bad for the individual depending upon the nature and intent of the moral. In the latter the concept and the acceptance or nonacceptance of responsibility is based upon what is deemed or considered to be the true nature of people and their natural needs and drives and the necessary compatibilities of these needs and drives within societal grouping, organization, and relationship as a process of allowing the satisfaction of these needs and drives to be reasonably reached as well as controlled, the nature of the process involved necessitating certain responsibilities. The nature of these responsibilities does not really belong in a discussion of morals and will be treated later in this chapter.

Lillie states that "It is the mind as a whole which makes moral judgments,"[82] and we must admit that the mind appears to be wholly attached to a body, and the entire body, including the mind, remains inexorably one piece and forever part of the biological field. Where the mind takes it upon itself, which it has the freedom to do, to make judgments that run contrary to the basic biological needs, some form of conflict has to result, and the history of morals exposes this continual conflict. James G. Frazer: "God may pardon sin, but Nature cannot."[83] This can be taken both ways. It is true that living together as groups necessitates equitable protectiveness evolved out of the very experiences of such living and the exercise of some controls over the unbridled compulsions of people, and that such controls are forms of compromises and compatibilities, which, in turn, form themselves in the nature of group existence, whether volitional, customable, or statutory, and act as deterrents against certain deleterious behaviors emanating either from the group against the individual or the individual against others. Brigid Brophy: "The taboo rules protect the savage from his own unconscious sexual wishes."[84] John Herman Randall: "It is a mistake to believe, as supernaturalists so often do, that materialism sanctions universal license and moral chaos. . . . Materialism does not necessarily entail the abolition of (true moral) values."[85]

There are, of course, certain innovations created and nurtured by various creeds, religions, and tribal cults, which rose out of the experience of group living, whether small or large, and many of these moral rules or disciplines were salubrious for a peaceful coexistence of the individuals involved. Such disciplines, if analyzed, would be seen to have no real significance or relationship to supernatural beliefs and factors, although the practical adherence of these rules become realizable when "ordered" by the gods. Many of the Hebraic Ten Commandments are such, the commandment not to steal or to kill or to covet another's mate, and these commandments were common to the historical period of that time and handed down through many cultures existing long before the Hebraic period. We find them even in India with King Asoka and in many other places far from the Middle East. However, so long as these commandments were rigid and compulsory, the common people could only adhere to them as a religious conformance, not as an intellectual and ethical principle arrived at by education and the cultivation of the freedom of the mind.

The end result has always been that man never progressed intellectually and ethically without this freedom of the mind, nor morally either in the truer and better sense of the word. Robert Briffault: "What man has achieved has been set down to his religion, his morals, to his innate benevolence, to everything, in fact, except to his intelligence."[86] Martin A. Larson writes that "Jesus proclaimed that outward observances or formal respectability would mean nothing in His Kingdom; that social justice is worth more than religious ceremonials; and that hypocrisy is the ultimate sin."[87] John Herman Randall: "The social morality of Western society rests on one ethical tradition in particular, the Hebrew-Christian. We saw that this tradition is based on the assumption of supernaturalism, and that this in turn finds all ethical distinctions set forth in God's Word. Moral standards of a fixed, permanent character are laid down, to observe which is morally correct, to transgress which is morally evil. These rules are authoritarian. We cannot ask, when confronted with a moral prohibition or command, Why? To conform is a duty not to be questioned or analyzed. The point of reference is not man but God. The extreme authoritarian position is sometimes formulated: Had God chosen to legislate the very opposite of his present commandments, the former would have been the morally correct ones."[88] John Dewey: "Rigid moral codes that attempt to lay down definite injunctions and prohibitions for every occasion in life turn out in fact loose and slack. Stretch ten commandments or any other number as far as you will by ingenious exegesis, yet acts unprovided for by them will occur."[89] Mark Twain: "The Christian religion, which requires everybody to be moral and to obey the laws, has its very beginning in immorality and in disobedience to law. You couldn't purify a tomcat by the Immaculate Conception process."[90] Corliss Lamont gives us the *Humanist* position: "The Humanist refuses to accept any Ten Commandments or other ethical precepts as immutable and universal laws never to be challenged or questioned. He bows down to no alleged supreme moral authority either past or present."[91]

Authority and power never furthered education or the whys and wherefores of social behavior and of morality; they merely ordained what was considered "right" for the authority and power to sustain and perpetuate itself, regardless of the consequences to individuals and their lives. Joseph Campbell: "In the broadest view of the history of world mythology, the chief creative development in the period of the waning Middle Ages and approaching Reformation was the rise of the principle of individual conscience over ecclesiastical authority."[92] The Roman Catholic Church forbids freedom of conscience; Protestantism allows freedom of the conscience, but a freedom solely subjected to the acceptance of the Bible as the Word of God and a source of reference and authority for morals. Professor Hightower, formerly on the faculty of the University of Iowa, wrote that "mere knowledge of the Bible is not in itself sufficient to insure character growth."[93]

The free mind of today maintains not only a freedom of conscience but one sufficiently free to admit new ideas and knowledge allowing expression to the biological and the rational, to life and reason. In actual experience, as Samuel Chugerman writes, "When emotionalism tries to feed a starving world with prayers, fancies, esthetics or abstract ideals of love, it is as efficient as a sermon on vegetarianism to a tiger, or the printed word oats served to a horse for dinner."[94] Bertrand Russell: "Conventional Christians think an adulterer more wicked than a politician who takes bribes, although the latter probably does a thousand times more harm."[95] As stated, the Roman Catholic Church denies the right to freedom of conscience. The "duty" of every good Catholic is to conform, not to question. The word *"conscience"* does not appear in the Old Testament because the idea of a person using his own mind to determine for himself what is right and wrong was not thought of as a natural prerogative of an individual, or as a need of a mind designed to think, not conform. The net historical result, as Barrows Dunham sums it up, is that "In any contest with morality, organizations are doomed. The world's tragedy lies in the fact that organizations do not yet know this."[96]

If humans are to cultivate real and true moralities they will never do it by conformance or by authoritarian order or by the fear of supernatural punishment. John Herman Randall: "Conventional morality might well be called authoritarian morality; and critical morality, scientific morality. In the former the emphasis is on conservation, conformity, tradition, law; in the latter, it is on criticism, investigation, comparison, the absence of dogmatsm or conclusiveness."[97] Bertrand Russell: "There is no short-cut to the good life, whether individual or social. To build up the good life, we must build up intelligence, self-control, and sympathy."[98] "We could begin to build a new morality, not based on envy and restriction, but on the wish for a full life and the realization that other beings are a help and not a hindrance when once the madness of envy has been cured. This is not a Utopian hope . . . it could be realized tomorrow if men would learn to pursue their own happiness rather than the misery of others."[99] James G. Frazer: "More and more, as time goes on, morality shifts its ground from the sands of superstition to the rock of reason, from the imaginary to the real, from the supernatural to the natural."[100]

As stated at the outset, morals, as we ordinarily and usually accept the word, are primarily concerned with sex and sexual property; other considerations erroneously classified as morals really belong to the subjects of ethics and responsibilities. Sexual customs and concepts vary all over the world, just as other customs and cultural distinctions. In ancient Maya it was a distinction to be cross-eyed. "Mark of distinction was to be cross-eyed, and mothers deliberately tried to bring about this condition by hanging little balls of resin to the hairs falling between their children's eyes."[101] The maidens of the Huari Indians of South America always go about in the nude but yet blush and feel ashamed if they are asked to part with their nose-rods.[102] The provincial Japanese girls do not mind at all bathing nude in the public baths with men, women, and children, yet on the village street feel embarrassed if their legs above their ankles are exposed. The Polynesian and the Balinese women go about with their breasts exposed to the fresh air, yet feel that the European and American way of kissing is revolting and shocking.[103] These variations of behavior, exposure, and notion are legion in all the habitats of mankind. The sense of shame, so cultivated in the Western countries, is rarely felt as one goes traveling about the world.

The idea of *virgo intacta,* or any mystical or religious value to a state of virginity, goes back thousands of years before the Christian period. Ottaker Nemecek: "Among all primitive tribes we find the belief that in children and virgins who stand remote from sexual life dwells a force that enables them to ward off evil spirits."[104] "In *Japan* chastity is a capital that must be retained. This capital belongs first to the father, then to the husband. According to one report, a girl who gives herself to a man without her father's consent receives sixty blows of the cudgel, another report states that she may even be killed."[105] Fortunately, this happens rarely in the Japan of today. The ancient Hebraic attitude toward women, taken from the earlier Sumerian, Assyrian, Babylonian and Canaanite cultures, was practically a question of sexual property and contained various rules, religious and other-

wise, to protect this property. This usage predates the Hebrews
and we find this social custom in the more ancient cultures of
the Levant. In the *Book of Moses* we read: "If a maiden be found
to be no virgin she shall be driven forth from the door of her
father's house and the men of the city shall stone her and she
shall die." "The Mosaic death penalty was preserved longest in
the highlands of Abyssinia. Among the Beni-Amer, etc., an unmarried mother suffered death by strangulation and her child
was suffocated."[106]

Somehow the strange idea grew in the ancient religions that
to stay away from a woman makes a man purer in spirit and
closer to his God. What sex has to do with one's adoration of
Yahweh is impossible to figure out, but the idea could have come
out of some need for self-suffering and willingness to part with
what is most precious or in withdrawing from what is so warmly
wanted, in order to prove man's willingness to make the greatest
sacrifices and his faith in God. "Moses enjoined sexual abstinence
on the priests when they celebrated divine service. David had to
prove that he and his followers were in a state of purity before
the priest Abimelech would give them the consecrated bread.
When Jahveh appeared on Mount Sinai the people had to remain
chaste. Abstinence from sexual intercourse was also ordained in
ancient Rome on religious festival days, such as those dedicated
to Ceres and Iris. Gregory the Great did not permit men to enter
a church after they had indulged in sexual intercourse should they
have omitted purification."[107]

When Christianity was established and Catholicism really took
over, indulgence in sexual intercourse came to be considered the
lowest a man could fall and sure damnation of his soul. "During
the first century of Christianity the church fathers raised the state
of virginity to the highest ideal which humanity might attain.
From the same standpoint the Council of Trent pronounced
damnation on any who declared that the marriage state was to be
preferred either to virginity or celibacy."[108] Had they had their
way, there would not be any Catholics living today let alone the
Catholic hierarchy that rules over them. If the Greek Orthodox
monks on Mount Athos had their way there would not be any
Greeks in the world, as no females, human or otherwise, have

ever been allowed to enter this celibate monastic world off the coast of Greece. Established in A.D. 963, at one time during the fifteenth century there were over 50,000 monks living on Athos in their secluded *kelias*. On a more recent visit there I learned that the monks finally allowed themselves the pleasure of keeping some hens for egg-laying, since the food shortage had become acute, the orchards and vineyards having been neglected because the number of inhabitants had greatly declined and most of those remaining were too old and weak to keep them up. This proves that man, sooner or later, cannot get along without females, if only hens. Today the monastic population on Mount Athos has dwindled to about 2,000 aged, bearded, decrepit, and senile monks, and the place is clearly destined for extinction and ruin. People are becoming wiser, more moral, and more worldly; they no longer wish to become monks.

Throughout the early Christian centuries and most of the Dark, or Middle Ages every form of oppression existed, every kind of slavery; religion degenerated into a cashier for the sale of indulgences, bishop turned on bishop, and popes excommunicated and murdered popes. The primitive shaman tinkling his magic sticks and dressed like a scarecrow was a peaceful and benign gentleman compared with these crazed and hell-struck people filled with the terror of demons and smelling sulphurous smoke from morning to night. The skies of Europe were filled with the threatening fumes of hell-fire. These were, indeed, gruesome times. Chastity and abstinence were preached from the gorgon-headed steeples, beneath which criminality and widespread immorality abounded. Herbert J. Muller: "Greed, lust, violence, and cruelty are written all over the medieval record, and the Church itself became scandalously corrupt, to an extent simply unthinkable in the modern secular world. Fornication, for example, seems to have been much more common in the Middle Ages than it is in sex-conscious America today, and for that matter it remains more common in such countries as Mexico, where about half the children are born illegitimate."[109] And we must keep in mind that Catholicism has been the *only* teacher in Latin America for almost five hundred years, at least up to a few years ago when secular education was introduced through rebellion in some parts of Latin America. In recent years Mexico and some of her neighbors have established secular schools and some progress has been made, yet in a good part of Mexico and in most of Central and South America ignorance, dishonesty, poverty and filth, widespread prostitution and immoralities of every description are rampant and the common situation. Where has been the so-called moral teachings of the Church in all these centuries? The "teaching" of the Church has been to collect every possible penny they could grasp from the *peones,* and the products of this "education" are in the gold and silver treasures that adorn the churches. Surely Jesus would say that this is not the road to paradise!

Heavens and paradises have been created by people in all times, climes, and ages, prehistoric, historic, and even today, by individuals and peoples throughout the world. Paradises, obviously, are more desirable, of course, and the descriptions of these wonderful and most secure, pleasurable, and ecstatic imaginings are legion, multitudinous, and highly diversified. On the other end, there are not too many hells, also for obvious reasons, but it took Christianity to perfect the cruelest and most nonsensical hell of all, supervised by a fallen angel who lost favor with God because he had the courage to express his own free opinion about nature and disagreed with the God-view that nature and all earthly desires, which God himself had created, were sinful and impure. Yet God accepts the coalition of the Devil in his cabinet as the medium of punishment for those who continue to disagree with him. What if the Devil should refuse to continue as God's partner in cruelty and punishment? What if the Devil should desire to break the contract and say to God: "Why should I continue to punish those who agree with me? With those whose only desire is to live their natural lives in the manner in which you, yourself, created them? Isn't it ironic that you should condemn your own creations and then expect me to punish them for what you did in creating them as they are? I think this is a case where the Judge is the criminal and the accused are the innocent victims of their own natures concocted by the Judge himself to make a case for those who are his self-appointed agents!" But there is no Judge and there is no Devil, and the trial goes on in the minds of those who forfeit happiness and life satisfaction to merit an ethereal and imagined reward.

Edward Westermarck wrote: "The first object of science is to search for truth, that of religion to give happiness. I can not find happiness in a faith that is founded on the deceptive will to believe."[110] What creates misery for people is not moral. The stigma of original sin that Catholicism has placed upon the brow of man is criminal and immoral. "Modern medicine . . . has demonstrated that many undesirable human traits which used to be ascribed to original sin or bad character are actually attributable to glandular insufficiencies or deep-rooted emotional frustrations."[111]

The stigma attached to motherhood itself, to womankind as the Judas-goat leading men to the gates of hell, is criminal and immoral. The Church has consistently opposed anything and everything that would alleviate pain for woman, opposed the political fight for her rights of suffrage, opposed her fight to make her life brighter, easier, more equitable, even though Catholic women are its most devoted worshippers. Bertrand Russell: "They (clergymen) all condemn sexual relations between unmarried people who are fond of each other but not yet sure that they wish to live together all their lives. . . . I knew a fashionable clergyman whose wife had nine children in nine years. The doctors told him that if she had another she would die. Next year she had another and died, No one condemned him; he retained his beneficence and married again."[112] Gerhard Szczesny: "What arguments can Christianity really offer to prove that it is immoral when two people, after mature deliberation and reasonable trial, conclude that the psychological health of both can be preserved only if one leaves the other's bed and board? Will individual dignity or civilized marriage in general actually be thrown into jeopardy if man sets up a standard freeing human beings from dependencies that make for deformity? Is it immoral to want to help every human being develop a serene and secure character?"[113] "A traditionalist and anthropocentric type of man lies concealed in Christianity's static and theocentric metaphysic. Its inability to see man as a multilayered, constantly changing creature leads to a narrowing of the consciousness of self, a restriction of it to the surface layer of the human personality—the part of it, in short, which constitutes what is called man's character."[114] Bertrand Russell: "People who live a life which is unnatural beyond a point are likely to be filled with envy, malice and all uncharitableness. They may develop strains of cruelty, or, on the other hand, they may so completely lose all joy in life that they have no longer any capacity for effort."[115] John Dewey: "Goodness without happiness, valor and virtue without satisfaction, ends without conscious enjoyment—these things are as intolerable practically as they are self-contradictory in conception."[116]

No person, group, or organization, be it theological, political, or social, has any right, so far as natural freedom is concerned, and apart from the consideration of any particular moral viewpoint, to set up any rule or principle that a state of marriage once consummated must be accepted on an irrevocable and "forever" basis. This is one of the worst offenders of the freedom of conscience and the freedom of a person to retain the natural right to happiness, peace of mind, and life satisfaction. It is also an out-and-out self-evident hypocrisy of any theology that bases its claim to reward and punishment on the "free will" of people to choose between virtue and sin, right and wrong, yet denies them the "free will" to express and live the choice of their "free will." It is so stupidly and outrageously unjust that a theology that maintains such a dogma must appear to any intelligent people asinine and disgusting. Besides, it is plainly immoral; it has forced millions of people into a state of *married prostitution,* sadomasochistic maladies, and even driven people to seek surcease by murder and flight. The annulment process is in itself a fraudulent and hypocritical circumvention of what had already been established as a hypocrisy to begin with.

Bengt Danielsson tells us of the South Pacific islands: "For the Polynesians childhood and youth were a time of preparation in this respect as in others, and they were considered, without doubt rightly, that it was of the greatest importance for everyone to acquire as much sexual knowledge and skill as possible before marriage."[117] "On Easter Island the girls first received oral instruction from older women, after which they had intercourse with an older male relative. So important was this preparation held to be that a young woman who was a virgin was despised by all men."[118] "No promise of fidelity for life was demanded during the marriage ceremony and such an idea was quite foreign to the Polynesian mentality."[119]

Whether in Polynesia, Bali, Turkestan, or Chicago, there is no such thing as unbridled and uncontrolled license to abuse the sacrament and structure of marriage and the home. Everywhere, even in the most savage tribes of the Amazon or the Congo, there are societal usages and customs, laws, and established social acceptances and restrictions that more or less regulate the institution of marriage and the marriage life. Some are good, some bad, some queer, or cruel, depending upon any particular viewpoint, some more free and some more regulatory, some just and some needlessly unilateral and inequitable, but it is difficult to find localities where people who become married cannot part if they find living together intolerable and miserable.

The Communists do their share in depressing freedom, even in sex matters, and emasculating the right of privacy and dignity in individual lives in matters which should only be determined and expressed by individual choice and action. In Communist China, in particular, the idea of birth control is impressed to such an extent that normal sex activities are unnecessarily and unjustly discouraged. If boy meets girl and they enjoy each other sexually, they become "rightists" and as such are to be demerited in their social, economic, and political statuses. If a mother has more than two children while gainfully employed, she may lose her job. While it is commendable that birth control literature and privileges are freely promoted and encouraged, while it is commendable for both unwed and wed pregnant women to have access to abortions and relief without cost or shame, no political or social philosophy should or can successfully undertake to eliminate the deep and natural, romantic, esthetic, and emotional expressions and drives which basically make up the nature of the human being. What should be done is to open up to the young, the mature, and the old all available knowledge and educational material regarding the necessity of controlling population growth and expansion; regarding the symbiotic limitations of all kinds of life on earth, of which human life is one segment; regarding

considerations, by reasonable parental control of births, to the
offspring, their proper care and upbringing, and the assurance
of a place in the sun for those who do come into the world; regarding the prolificacy of seed in all of nature and the balancing
forces inherent therein which man by his sciences has modified,
thus making possible a faster growth of humanity than has heretofore been known or experienced. Education and knowledge, and
constantly more of both, so that people, in putting intelligent
controls into action by self-justified responsibility, will know
they are doing it because they understand why according to their
own sense of responsibility, their sense of equity, their sense of
freedom in doing *freely* what they are doing, their sense of regard
for the lives and well-being of others. Whatever changes and
modifications are found necessary to preserve the freedom of the
individual to live his life as best as possible within his own natural domain should be of themselves free vehicles preserving the
free processes of change and choice, the free processes that could
possibly keep us away from tyranny and possibly bring about some
order making its own process of order a process of possibility.
One has at least a chance to do anything best when he is *fully
free* to do what is best in him. Understanding and knowledge
often allow a free condition to absorb and express responsibility
without duress or imposition of rule. Alvan L. Barach: "The life
histories of original thinkers reveal how often they have been
forced to tolerate suffering and to endure scorn from their con-
temporaries—fellowmen outraged by what they saw as insolent
attempts to change accepted thought or practice. . . . Walt Whitman was to peddle his books from door to door in exchange for
bread."[120]

If the word "moral" has any significance as a measure of value
then it must be an aid in strengthening a person's natural right
to be true and honest unto himself and to allow this integrity of
character to create for itself, whenever and wherever possible, a
state of more peaceful, healthful, and happy existence. Bertrand
Russll: "Moral progress has consisted, in the main, of protest
against cruel customs, and of attempts to enlarge the bounds of
human sympathy."[121] "No man is wholly free, and no man is
wholly a slave. To the extent to which a man has freedom, he

needs a personal morality to guide his conduct."[122] "Without civic morality communities perish; without personal morality their survival has no value. Therefore civic and personal morality are equally necessary to a good world."[123] William Lillie: "One of the first ways in which any individual is likely to assert himself is by using his own judgment in moral matters and, whenever he does so, he has for the moment at least moved from the level of custom to the level of conscience."[124] Russell: "In aiming at a good life the limits of human possibility must be borne in mind."[125] Frazer: "The old view that the principles of right and wrong are immutable and eternal is no longer tenable. The moral world is as little exempt as the physical world from the law of ceaseless change, of perpetual flux."[126] "The mountains, too, are passing away, though we do not see it; nothing is stable and abiding under or above the sun. . . . We can as little arrest the process of moral evolution as we can stay the sweep of the tides or the courses of the stars."[127]

Man must become more free to seek and pursue a higher moral stature and state. The theologies and obscurantisms with their silly and sickening catechisms must go if man is to restore to himself the values of honesty and character that are prerequisites to any moral state of association and behavior. Man must stop becoming his own self-antagonist creating within his emotional, physical, and mental makeup a Zarathustrian battleground on which his body and life are mauled and distorted in affirming and negating both in a confused and ascetic neurosis. Paul Kurtz, the humanist, in his wise little essay, "Joyful Humanism," writes: "There is something sadly lacking in a human personality who is unable to enjoy life fully or to savour the immediacies of experience. If humanism says anything significant to human beings, it calls us back to an appreciation of the possibilities of the good life and of the joyful character of human experience. 'The Kingdom of heaven is within thee,' says the humanist; and he who cannot find this is surely dead."

"Too many theists," Kurtz continues, "have denied this; and they have looked elsewhere for salvation and hope. False prophets of immortality have traded in counterfeit specie; in expectation of a kingdom of heaven, they have repressed many natural de-

sires. Consumed by a sense of sin and guilt, they have abandoned
the joys of the flesh for the sake of empty illusion. . . ."

"Here is an ethic of life: our kingdom is here, to live, to suffer
and enjoy, to take the full measure of what is in store and to
be able to say at the end of one's day: it was great while it lasted.
And this is the sin of sins, the failure of failures: to confess that
while alive I am really dead, and that I have lost the capacity to
find satisfaction, richness and gratification in my daily experience."[128]

Elie Fauré, in his *History of Art,* gives us this view: "The
great man introduces an esthetic state of the intelligence into
the world by means of the law which he dictates, of religion
which he animates, of the success which he assures, of the statue
which he sculptures, or the drama which he writes. He evades
now the environing order, now the environing disorder, here,
by establishing a new order in his heart, there, by forcing his
heart to correct the disorder. Thus all history reveals and records
the antithetical struggle of the individual against the social body
that tends to absorb him or which he tends to destroy, their
alternating victories and the privional equilibrium that each
maintains for an hour by absorbing the powers of the other."[129]
Wilhelm Bolsche gives us a poetical bit of *de profundis:*

> Your profound secrets
> That are spun through you
> Like a dark net of fate,
> Like a black cobweb,
> To which your tears cling
> Like dewdrops.[130]

As stated, it is historically and scientifically obvious that morals
and moralities are purely products of humans, not of the general
order of animal life or of nature itself. Any attempt to metamorphose a human moral rule or custom into a natural law must
fail because of the impossibility of substantiating or establishing
the operation of such moral law as an order of nature. We can
rationalize about nature but nature does not rationalize about
itself or about us. Any such attempt must, as a prior assumption,

consider nature as a *totality* to contain intelligence, preplanned direction, justification for its presumed sense of equity, jurisprudence and its "common statutory" generalizations of procedure for *all* things if it is presumed to be jurisprudent, empirical verification of the concept of progression in biological, physiological, neurophysiological, and sociological history and their reflecting sciences, and a rational and logical explanation of such moral law as the, or part of the, causal origins and evolution of all things. William Lillie: "If the moral law is a law of nature, nature must be a system of relations of moral fittingness as well as of causal relations. It is on the ground of the fundamental rationality of nature that we can go on to regard the moral law as a law of reason."[131] "The whole view of the standard as law, or of goodness consisting in obeying universally applicable rules, has serious limitations. It leaves out the doing of unique acts in particular circumstances, and it suggests a uniformity in good actions, which is not what we find in the richly varied pattern of the moral life at its best. The moral law may keep us from lines of action which are universally bad; it cannot guide us to the full variety of human goodness."[132] "Relative ethics maintains that there are no moral rules that apply to all men as such; there are forms in which what is right for any man is a purely individual matter, so that there is no question of any standard at all."[133]

Morals and moralities are *human* usages and concepts of *human* principles and behaviors which may be termed good or bad, possible or impossible, practical or theoretical, natural or antinatural, verifiable or poetical, as particular viewpoints of any individual or group resulting from, and depending upon, the causal and sequential experiences within a certain time, event, and locality and the association and relativeness of these factors. It does not mean that any such moral or system of morality is not good, beneficent, and a betterment for the individual and conducive to a happy and peaceful society. Whether it is such or not is a matter of analysis and approval of its experiences and their effects upon such possible betterment. It does not necessarily follow that any moral that is good for one or a number of individuals or societies is good a priori for *all* individuals and *all* societies. When the idea of need for a particular moral is conceived, based upon, and emanating from, a series of meanings and values which are verifiably considered as beneficent to the best fulfillment of one's life, then within the purposes of man's limited freedom to choose can be nurtured concepts and usages which, in turn, can possibly lead to such possible fulfillment. On this point Lillie writes: "At the reflective level, we realize that morality is not a law imposed on us by an arbitrary creator or his ministering priests; it is not even a law imposed upon us by our fellow-men. It is a law that we ourselves can understand, and choose for our guidance because we see that it is good sense to do so."[134] John Herman Randall: "The morally desirable is what we would desire after examining the interrelation of all the ends which concern us and as many consequences as we can foresee."[135] Ernest Nagel: "Moral responsibility is correctly ascribed to individuals who possess certain capacities; it is correct to make the ascription for the sufficient reason that this is just the way the phrase 'morally responsible' is used."[136]

Thus, any form of morals and morality should be based upon the *free* nature and the *free* conscience of individuals to *know* its portent and whatever benefit of acceptance there may be contained therein. A moral to be truly a moral could only genuinely exist if it is based upon the free expression and conscience of a person and some knowledgeable meaning of its effect upon the normally necessary biological satisfactions to maintain a good, healthy, and happy body and mind. When it does not issue from the free and voluntary choice of people and is, in fact, one of blind or indoctrinated obedience and antinatural discipline, then it ceases to be a moral but simply a rule, law, dogma or doctrine to be worshipped, obeyed, but not *really* lived.

Freedom is a pre-moral essential to the creation, acceptance and practice of any moral principle. Freedom does not necessarily set up righteousness or wrongfulness; it does make possible the natural processing of intellectual maturation which always seems to give us the insight and courage to express a humility for our relative knowledge and questionable wisdom. It gives us the fortitude to pursue the continual overcoming of our relative ignorance and our inevitable and often paradoxical ways of error. If freedom does lead us, as it so often does, to make mistakes, at least let them be happy ones; and if freedom can lead us to make changes and corrections, at least we can try to make them wiser ones. Judge Learned Hand so wisely said: "Liberty lies in the hearts of men and women. When it dies there, no constitution, no law, no court can save it."

Morals change as people change, and people change as their societies change, and societies change as the generation, diffusion, and the interactivity and interinfluencing of ideas continue to function and reforge themselves out of association and the constant experiences of people and the world about them in its various activities and reflective processes. Whether morals change quickly or slowly or whether they change at all over any period, or whether certain people claim *this* against what others claim *that*, whether those in authority makes rules and those behind obey, whether Sunday morning respectabilities assure a place in heaven for those tired bodies who spent Saturday night in hell, or the other way around, all this is really irrelevant: *sex is wanted, enjoyed, continues and will continue* so long as man and woman have healthy bodies and healthy minds, so that both can live healthy lives. *Sex is not a sin,* nor is it vulgar, shameful and the way to damnation and hell; those who consider it a sin are vulgar people and they have been making a hell on earth for too long a time. Edmund R. Leach: "It is useless to console ourselves with the conventional religious formulas. We ourselves have to decide what is sin and what is virtue, and we must do so on the basis of our modern knowledge and not on the basis of traditional categories."[137]

What morals should consist of, if we must have any, is the consideration of the ethical and responsibility factors involved in them because of particular societies and cultures, and any such consideration, to be realistic, does not belong in any sado-masochistic metaphysicism and theological nonworldliness such as morals and their effects upon possible afterlife rewards and punishments. Any such consideration should not be termed "morals," it belongs in the natural world, here in the very living experiences of people, their needs and abuses, in the everyday associations, and whether any of it is right or wrong, good or bad, belongs to the subject of *ethics* and *responsibilities,* to which we shall now proceed.

PART II

AN ETHIC IS an *opinion* based on experience, usages, customs, traditions, or on some intuitional or rational sense. It is not an absolute deduction to fit all premises. One can say that it is a *perspective* of an individual or of a number of individuals, of a group, faction, religion, cult, people, society. It may be considered as a way of life, like *Tao,* or a *direction* risen out of trial and error, causes and effects. It could be considered as an *attitude,* mental and otherwise, brought about through circumstances and situations, congenital and acquired.

There is no assurance that any ethic can last forever, or that it is unchangeable, or that it will last for any given period with absoluteness, because no one can predict with such absoluteness future events, near or far, and predetermine with exactitude the effects of these events. Man has often considered and changed his ethics as pragmatic symbols of his own securities, wants, and dreams. He has even oftener held his ethics high in one hand for the world to see and with the other hand demolished them in private. Inconsistency, pretension, insincerity, deception, phoniness—these and more have been perfected to a very high degree by the human animal. When we see any of the other animals "pull" these tricks, we usually exclaim how "human" it is!

There appears in civilized man, especially among some of our intellectuals, scholars, and intelligentsia, a quality unknown in the primitive world, a tolerance of unwanted hypocrisy and meekness born of the simple lack of courage to stand up and be counted for what he believes to be right and just. This is, of course, a matter of a man's character and fortitude; whether or not it appertains to ethics is not too important. What is important, for the moment, is that fear for oneself is too often translated into a compromise that forces a sudden suspension of one's principles and identity on the grounds of self-preservation, even though the fears have been caused by events beyond one's control and against one's innermost wishes. It is easier to join the crowd and get lost in it than to stand alone, exposed to the public eye. This may be the safer, even the wiser course, depending on one's character and fears. Yet, were it not for those who have stood alone and apart from the mob, who have dared the powers that be, we would still be ignorant serfs breathing the sulphur and smoke of the Dark Ages.

Sometimes I find it difficult to understand some of my closest friends. I know that they hold principles basically congruous and reasonably similar to mine, granting that no two persons see things through the same pair of eyes. Yet a strain of reasonableness and fairness runs through all of them, if not, I would not be happy with them as my friends. Dissent and differences of opinion are respected and regarded. Different viewpoints create interest and perspective which energize the intellect and spirit in association; still better, they widen the view and extend one's comprehension beyond one's own and limited experiences.

However, I find that, even though they are most assuredly as earnest and sincere in their principles of freedom and justice as I am, when they are confronted with situations they think might endanger their occupational, social, or political status were they to continue to use their freedom of expression and expose themselves for what they really are and stand for, often they lose courage, back down, and neutralize their position like the chameleon, which changes its colors, not to suit itself, but to protect itself against sudden danger appearing to it as threatening. Likewise, people often seem to change their colors, not because they desire to do so, but because of the fear of endangering themselves and the various securities which have become to them far more valuable than the need to express their real selves and stand up fearlessly for their principles.

Whatever freedom and justice it is our fortune to possess are ours because certain courageous people had the stamina to rebel against tyranny and oppression and unjust ideologies, fearlessly, come what may. The strength of character of those who stood up against colossal walls of traditional and deep-rooted opposition, regardless of the risks involved to their securities and even their very lives, is the foundation that provided the new soil in which our freedoms were seeded. To whatever extent we are free today and more secure because of democratic processes to render justice and preserve it we owe to their courage and sacrifices. As Ibsen once wrote, a man, if he believes in freedom, must be ready to soil his best clothes, he must do more than merely believe in freedom if freedom and justice are to flourish and continue for us and for those to come.

There were a number of these brave people at Treblinka. After much emotional patience and suffering, they rebelled and killed their executioners, burned Treblinka to the ground. Most of them died fighting or trying to escape, but if they had not fought the Nazi killers, they would have been gassed and cremated in any event as hundreds of thousands of other Jews murdered at Treblinka.

To believe in freedom and justice sincerely one must be ready to fight for it. To protect our freedom we must be intrepid in standing up and being counted as a freedom-loving person. Fear, supplication and appeasement never brought freedom and justice; they have, too frequently, taken them away. If we really desire to maintain ethics, humanism, and the right of freedom to safeguard and secure them, it will take more than words and parlor talk to preserve them. Good intentions of just and freedom-loving people would have been insufficient to save Israel from being overwhelmed and destroyed by the encircling Arab armies and military power.

THE ETHICAL CASE FOR ISRAEL

EVERY ISRAELI MAN, woman, and child responded instantaneously to the call to oppose the Arabs, to protect their precious gifts of home, their hard-earned land, their freedoms, and their deep-rooted drive for self-identity and self-sufficiency: *the want to be free, to be judged justly, to live in decency,* to desire and demand the right to live in peace and in their own well-earned securities—and willing to fight for these gifts, even to die fighting for them rather than to die later at the hands of hysterical hate that would destroy them. It is this power of morale and determined devotion to their principles that guided their forces to victory against even far greater forces.

Whatever political and religious hates and bigotries people might otherwise harbor, they cannot fail to recognize that this tiny country of Israel not only met the openly-declared threats of the Arabs to exterminate them, but took the offensive, as the Arabs began to fire, with such determination to preserve their homes and lives that the enemy was routed and defeated in a few days, a feat unequaled in all history.

It takes more than principles to reveal the true stuff that men are made of. It takes more than the good intentions of ethics to create and preserve an ethical and just world, without which freedom itself is bereft of its value and becomes meaningless. Otherwise, the drive for wanted justice and peaceful security sinks and succumbs in the quicksands of resignation. It is the insufficiency of honest assertion and the failure of courage and readiness to face up to realities that provide easy intrusion and facility for the robbers and destroyers to rule by the persuasions of hate and greed, and to continue to lead their feudal illiterates to destroy themselves and other people while the medallioned thieves in power and authority intoxicate themselves with their insatiable and sadistic thirsts for more and more power, more hate, which can only lead, as always, to tragedy and disaster.

The mitred caliphs harangue their people, by the command of Allah himself, into the hysterical and uncontrollable compulsion to commit genocide upon a people whose only want is to live in peace. Is it because the Arab leaders want to maintain the feudalism in which their peoples have been subjected for countless centuries; is it because they fear the progress and growth of Israel which is a solitary outpost of democracy with its advanced and modern technologies? Democracy and enlightenment for their people are feared by the Arab political and religious leaders, by the sheiks and kings who find power, security, and wealth by maintaining feudalism, primitivism, and illiteracy for their masses. Israel appears to them a threat to their status quo.

Life is uncertain and brief enough at its luckiest and longest, let us at least enjoy the dignity of self-respecting self-identity, not only in the thought alone, but in the realization and admission to ourselves that without the ready courage to translate these thoughts into action and deeds, whenever and wherever the need may arise, to secure these dignities and life essentials, all becomes meaningless and lost. As Abba Eban so sensibly and brilliantly declared, of what good are principles if courage is not present to secure them when they are actually threatened, if the umbrellas are put away when it really begins to rain?

This lack and absence of honest courage coupled with the subtleties of sub rosa diplomacies mark the beginning of the end for the United Nations as a practical and respected force and authority to preserve the peace of the world. Words being its bartering commodity for existence, its forum has degenerated and succumbed to pretext, pretense, and bland, unadulterated prevarication. Its original principles have been diluted and destroyed by inaction and Machiavellian protocol. It has lacked the courage to stand up and be counted for its principles.

Every person who loves freedom and justice has his own United Nations within himself, within his own character. He can secure them with courage and open, fearless honesty—or he can let them die by his own appeasement of his principles, of his fears, by putting away his umbrella when it begins to rain. He can fold his tent like the Arabs and silently steal away to amuse himself as before with talk about ethics, justice, and freedom, far from those who fight and struggle to uphold and maintain these gifts.

THE NATURE OF ETHICS

THEREFORE, WE CAN reasonably state that an ethic, like all other human products and deductions of human origin and usage, is a *transient* factor, determined as of short- or long-lasting applicability in human experience by the currents and countercurrents of the various and constantly changing manifestations of this experience. The determinability of the goodness, fineness, equitableness, or justice of any particular ethic depends upon how *necessary* it is, upon its potential or limitation in its wantability, desirability, essentiality, in any current flow of human particularized or group experience and enculturation.

An ethic may be natural, as all things are natural, and yet be a nonconductor or a depressor of naturalness or of a satifying life. An ethic may be a law, good or bad, obsolete or activated, but it is not a universal law. It may be a canon of the church, but it is not divine. It may be a rule of procedure, but it can be modified, changed, overruled, and forgotten, in one instance or forever. Matson: "Ethics no more depends on God than arithmetic does."[138]

An ethic is a product of human association and its relativeness to all else. It therefore becomes a *human* thing, thought, or principle, and anything human is not sacred, divine, universal, or absolute. An ethic is human projection of itself against the cosmos; it is not a projection of the cosmos upon a human. Man keeps anthropomorphising the universe, but the universe can only identify the human as a quantum of carbon and other things that somehow, through the processes of chemical interactivity and evolution have brought about an animal, *de anima,* which can move itself, do things, even think and conjure up gods and goddesses, heavens and hells.

The universe may remain forever, but certainly not man or his rules and institutions. Whatever we may conjecture, even most idealistically, regarding the nature of the universe, of the nature of existence of any god or gods, or of any soul that exists by itself; whatever we may dream of immortal souls and faraway heavens—all these do not in any way *really* affect the performance of a good act or a bad act on earth. Regardless of any country's political structure and philosophy, of any group's religion and dogma, of the variances of societies and their environments and localities, there will be good people and bad people, and the various natural desires and instincts of people will continue to express themselves notwithstanding. The difficulty and problem arise in the influences of these factors upon people either as natural or antinatural enculturatives and directives that affect the natural freedom of people to adjust themselves more intelligently to new conditions and situations. Professor Snodgrass, the entomologist, gives us a sight and observation of this through the natural sciences: "An act that is right is one in accord with the nature of the creature performing it; that which is wrong is a contrary act. Hence, what is right for one species of animal may be wrong for another, and the reverse. . . . The difference between human actions and those of other animals is not essentially in the acts themselves, but in the methods by which they are brought about. . . . The general truth is clear, however, that in behavior, as in physiology, there is not just one way of arriving at a common result, and that nature may employ quite different means for determining and activating conduct in her creatures. . . . Particularly will there be a difference in the necessary behavior of species that live as individuals and of those that live as groups of individuals."[139] Further, "All of which goes to show that in the social world, as in the physical world, the end alone justifies the means, so far as nature is concerned. Justice to the individual is a human concept; we strive to equalize the benefits and hardships of the social form of life, and in so far as we achieve this aim our civilization differs from that of the insects."[140]

According to Lillie, "Universalism holds that it is the moral duty of an individual to seek the good of the community as a whole."[141] It is obvious that the human individual, whether he is part of a small primitive tribe along some jungle stream or one of millions in a modern, civilized city, could not exist by himself, nor does he normally desire to. Emotionally, psychologically, physically, and economically, alone he would wither away. Human happiness, pleasure, satisfaction, and even success are consequences of living with and among people, as these are relative factors subsisting and processing themselves out of relationships, associations, and competitive, comparative values. Even some highly creative geniuses are lonely people, who, although expressing their talents and arts as they are impelled to do, lack the fulfillment of the normative life satisfactions rising out of some kind of association. Albert Einstein, when asked if, given the opportunity to be born again, would he repeat the same career, replied that he would prefer to be a simple workman, a plumber, or a peddler, so that he could enjoy the simple and ordinary ways of people.

However, the idea that an individual should sacrifice himself or think only in terms of the community as a whole is *too much* of a sacrifice, as it makes him submissive to society regardless of his own life and any possible good that may accrue to his own life. As Lillie states further: "It suggests the abstract of good of a community rather than the concrete good of particular individuals."[142] The contention that any such sacrifices or submissions on the part of the individual in terms of the community as a whole are unrealistic and unnatural as the biological basis of such a community is that it is a grouping together, out of naturally evolved factors, for the benefit and needs of the *individuals* that comprise it, not that the individuals have to supply the benefit and good of the community, which, as a whole, is abstractive, illusory, and subjective. It does not fit in with the natural cravings and necessities of the individual as *a* life.

The individual actually and always lives in the present, not in any future and the idea that an individual should "invest" his present for some "interest" in the future, that is, sacrifice his life *now* for the hope that the "stock" of the society may rise in the future, is an idea that has been used again and again by those in power and authority, in whatever form they take, religious and political, to coerce the individual into parting with himself and often his whole self, that is, even his very life, for something he may never see or know. There is a difference between a person realizing that in order to live in a community of people it is essential that all the individuals within it cultivate some tolerance of compatibility toward each other conducive to a more peaceful and satisfied coexistence; that by helping each other they are able to gain more than by each one's looking out for himself; that by regarding another's life in the same manner as each would regard his own life, a person becomes *educated* to an understanding that can lead to a better norm, to an appreciation of, and a regard for, one another on a *practical* and *earthly* basis, so that each, by coordination and sensible conduct, can have a less restricted opportunity to gain as much as a possible for himself.

The difference between a bundle of sticks signifying unity and strength and a group of people is that the bundle of sticks is lifeless and mindless, to be manipulated and used, not for themselves as a bundle or for each individual stick, but by some external power who requires their gathered strength for its aggrandizement. In a group of people we are dealing with individual lives and minds, with individual particularizations of personality and their particular heritages and experiences, and we cannot dissolve these into a common pot of groupism or social structure without stirring conflict, dissatisfaction, and the maladies of forced adjustment to factors which the biological, emotional, and mental individualization of each person cannot healthfully and normally accept. We must go back to the prime object of people *wanting* to live together, as families, as kinships, as clans and tribes: the result of the biological urge of the animal-individual to seek its own good on an instinctively self-preservative basis and thus indirectly process the continuity of its kind and the social structure that necessitates this process.

Social ethics must take this into account as a fundamental and natural motive of each individual within a social structure. Whether it be employees within an abstractive entity or "personality" of a corporation, or members of a lodge which has become a symbol of some culture, or followers of a religion which has become a "sacred" spirit to worship and revere, or citizens of a political order, the same fundamentally natural and rational motive should be a conscious interactor in association: that it is the individual and the other individuals and their interests as individuals, associated with each other in any undertaking, that are the prime considerations for the gregarious, coordinating, and associative processes involved.

Concepts about ethics are as various and varied as there are humans around. However, ethicists have gradually systematized, classified, and proposed certain types of concepts which they have attempted to establish as *the* foundation of ethical thought and practice. The difficulty that arises in some of these concepts is that they try to justify ethics as some kind of *standard* emanating or emerging out of a particular concept. The difficulty of standardization is that many try to establish a system of ethics that considers society as an "organic sum" or an "organic entity" or a Durkheimian "collective consciousness," and not a number of organic separates or individuals that form a group and a way of living together as a *naturally compatible social process*. William Lillie: "When a state is called an organic unity, that term is being used loosely and vaguely. The real unit is not the state; the real units are the individuals forming it and it is with their actions we are concerned in ethics."[143] Felix Adler: "The law of the jungle is that life feeds on life. The law of an ethical community is that life shall at the least respect other cognate life, forbear to infringe upon it. . . . The ethical paradox—the paradox is that beings whose claim to independence is recognized must at the same time live in a state of mutual dependence."[144]

On the other extreme we have the concept of *egoism* in ethics which holds that it "is the theory that it is the duty of the individual to seek his own good."[145] This is natural and everyone should seek it. When one does not, there is something wrong with him. For a person not to seek his own good, ignorant or intelligent, is an aberration of naturalness and a misdirection of his physical makeup by a misleading mind that has gone haywire or astray. Whether the priest is seeking his own good because he abstains from any contact with a female body is questionable, and whether a woman is seeking her good when she blindly follows the precept of the church that any sex she may have the pleasure of experiencing is sinful, and as a result she is never able to relax sufficiently to enjoy this relationship, is also questionable. Whether a man is actually seeking his own good by stealing or killing is also questionable, but no one can deny that it is within his natural freedom to do as he pleases—*provided* that by so doing others are not involved, hurt, affected adversely; therefore, stealing or killing is bad, and cannot be accepted as an ethic in any sense. The sense of ethics is not alone in the person himself but in the consequences of his acts as these affect the lives of other people besides himself. Oscar Wilde wisely said that "whenever a man does a thoroughly stupid thing, it is always from the noblest motives."[146] Mr. Chamberlain did so when he went to Munich.

Egoism can take the form of harming others without any guilt of conscience, as many do when they kill, hurt, cheat, and rob others, and the egoist can say that this does not bother him so long as he likes it and feels it is "good" for him to do these things. Norman Kotker relates of Charles Dickens' visit to Rome: "One of the first tourist attractions he attended was a public execution. He was horrified to note that the people in the audience counted the drops of blood that spurted out of the decapitated criminal's neck in order to bet that number in the public lottery."[147] No one doubts the almost inexplicable need of man to enjoy seeing the morbid, the grotesque, the bizarre, and the shocking. The Capuchin Church in Rome, now a tourist attraction for those who enjoy the weird, is a "decoration" of tiers of thousands of skulls of Capuchin monks who wasted away their lives to merit the glory of god. "The Cemetery of the Capuchins, one of Rome's more sensational tourist sights, where the walls are adorned with the skulls of monks who have departed to dwell in the City of God."[148]

"The willful torturing of animals which until a century ago was among the most common of English sports."[149] "Shooting at live things with a .22 rifle—whether they are edible or even re-trievable is a matter of no importance—is considered terrific sport in South America and, as the wildlife of the continent grows scarcer, will become more and more important in the inevitable extinctions."[150] John Dewey: "The optimism that says that the world is already the best possible of all worlds might be regarded as the most cynical of pessimisms. If this is the best possible, what would a world which was fundamentally bad be like."[151]

This is the part of human nature that other individuals have to protect themselves against, and this protection takes the forms of law, social and political principles and structure. The group cannot wholly rely upon the good sense or conscience of the indi-vidual, in the same way as the individual has to have a free mind to protect himself from being absorbed by the social order. The idea is to retain one's mind without surrendering it to the mass-mind.

Then there is what is termed *Egoistic Ethical Hedonism* which "holds that what makes an action right is the fact that it causes the greatest possible amount of pleasantness to the doer of the action."[152] This depends upon what the doer considers pleasant to *him*, what he is *actually* doing and to *whom*. Hitler's maniacs found it very "pleasant" to kill millions of helpless people. Some of these murderers found it "pleasant" to smash the heads of little children against stone walls. Humans have been killing, enslaving, torturing, committing every conceivable crime upon others and finding it "pleasant." In ethics we are not only con-cerned with what a human does with or by or to himself. What we are concerned with is the consequence of this act upon others, and this is where the science of ethics begins and leads us gradually to come upon the meaning and value of responsibility.

John Stuart Mill claimed that "what is good is what men do actually desire." Should we say that what Hitler desired was good? Hitler was also an insane egoist. Once he remarked: "There have been only two great men in the world's history—Jesus Christ and I. And Christ is dead!"[153] Could we reasonably say that what Franco of Spain desired is good? All desires are not good or bad, and all humans and human nature are not good or bad, but we must admit that all desires and all of human nature are not all good. And here is where the task of education and ethical teaching begins.

Ethics are presumed to be expressed and applied not by force or fear, but out of the free exercise of one's understanding and knowledge of any particular thing or act about which the ethic is intended to be applied, ethics being the normative science of conduct, and conduct a collective noun for voluntary actions if any ethic is considered in its prime purpose and effect. This understanding and knowledge need not be the result of formal education and learning. It could arise, and most often does, out of the actual experiences of living and from sensing and observing the experiences of others. Learning, that is, forms of education, enhances our knowledgeable horizon of these experiences, and it is logical and reasonable for us to assume that it would be important for the medium of the educational process to be extended to cultivate and nurture in the very young *how to think* rationally, how to weigh different values, to establish a sort of junior methodology in systematically understanding the meaning and purpose of conduct, its whys and wherefores. Thus the young could get a reasonable and junior start in equitable judgment within their own free minds and grow up in a manner of establishing within themselves, by the cultivation of their reflecting processes, a rational and natural basis for evaluation of the behavior and thinking that would seem to be most beneficial and yet be founded on a conscious sense of ethics and equity. Teaching children how to count, read, and write is essential, no doubt, but we should also teach them *how to think,* and in doing so they will find it equally essential to know themselves better. To teach children to believe or say things by repetition and imitation is to make them into ignorant and jabbering parrots and prepare them to become obedient, even bigoted slaves to obscurantism and those who profit from it.

If we had left the education of the young completely in the hands of the Puritans and the Catholic theologians, the American people would still be burning "witches," children would still be smelling sulphur and stifling fumes of burning flesh in their nightmarish dreams of hell and seeing batwing ogres hovering over their four-posters. The atavistic practices of the Dark Ages would still be popular, and a fiery public exhibition of burning Jews would still be pageantry.

Let us realize now that all this has not been really eliminated. Only a few years ago millions of Jews were murdered, and Christians even hung their slaughtered bodies in Jewish butcher shops as a spectacle for young and old to gape at. The parochial-schooled Catholic child still smells sulphur and is taught contempt for those of other faiths. The Calvinist-schooled child still feels tremors about tearing his flesh, Cotton Mather-style, or trembling before the sure and ominous courtroom, Wigglesworth-style, of God's Judgment Day when the living and the dead, living flesh and dead men's bones, will appear and stand the awful and gruesome destiny of trial. The Puritan-trained child still grows up to be a frustrated neurotic and hypocrite and grows old as a dried-up antinatural prude and product of self-denial and life negation. When President Grant clamored, "Keep the church and state forever separate," he meant to protect the American children from the indoctrinations of religion and sectarianism which have always been, and continue to be, the breeders of contempt, hate, and the separation of man from man and their nurtured desire to oppose and even kill each other. We are not yet free by far in a fully established secularization of our schools; when we are, our children and their children's children will breathe in the fine, fresh, and invigorating air of free education and all its enjoyable and healthful possibilities.

When the natural freedom in a child has not been disturbed or misled by antinatural impositions and ideas, we will usually find the child receptive to any ideas and notions that are honest, open, and exposed to what nature and life really appear to be, without theological and metaphysical decoration. No child ever got hurt by looking at Walt Disney's *Beaver Valley* or any other of his wonderful films devoted to a knowledge and appreciation and sense of affinity of animal life in its own naturally free environments. A child, until indoctrinated, has no sense of separation from his animal relatives, or "superiority" to them. To the child the manifestations of what appears before him—the animals, trees, flowers, streams, clouds—are all wonderfully fascinating to him, as they were to the primitive, and he could never visualize himself as a specially created observer or concoct the notion that all this was created *for him.*

Children should be taught the nature of themselves, the sciences of life, its origins, evolutions, and the human relativism to all other surrounding and symbiotic factors that make this life possible. We should not underestimate the potential of the child's mind: in spite of the *Lord of the Flies,* the world's children, if they could have the power and authority, would no doubt make our planet into a vast playground instead of the battlefield the adults have been making of it constantly for thousands of years. In many ways a child becomes an adult when it is old enough to become adulterated.

In actuality it appears that there are no ethics involved in religious *belief* itself, since religious belief, or religious *faith,* is not a matter of human judgment, judgment being the result of some degree of freedom to reflect and decide according to one's free mind and conscience. Religion requires adherence, obedience, and submission in the form of faith, not judgment or a free mind to question it in any degree, whereas the processes of judgment imply the right to weigh values according to each individual and the acknowledgement that *change is inherent and possible.* Jawaharlal Nehru: "The disciplines of religion and social usage fade away without giving place to other disciplines, moral or spiritual. Religion, as practiced, either deals with matters rather unrelated to our normal lives, and thus adopts an ivory-tower attitude, or is allied to certain social usages which do not fit in with the present age."[154] Ethics is the result of human reason and judgment based on experiences and their consequences.

The Roman Catholic Church has always categorically opposed the principle of freedom of conscience. The Jesuit order tells its members that they must not think because God has done all the thinking and judging: all they have to do is believe in his divine judgment and accept his rules of conduct. Human thought and experience as to what may be fair, just, considerate, bilateral, good or bad are not to be considered, especially if anything should conflict with one's submission to, and belief in, the particular religion. The record in history of the Jesuit order is well known; it can hardly be claimed that it had anything to do with ethics or with justice.

Whatever ethics emerged came about because of the thought of man, his power to weigh values and considerations, his ability to transcend his own status quo and put himself in another's shoes. Reason and experience alone have taught us that by protecting the liberties of all we protect our own. The Golden Rule is the result of human experience, desires, fears, not a rule handed down by some divine pen. Whenever such a "divine" pen handed down a rule, woe betide those who opposed it, argued it, and the wrath of the good Lord went down upon the heads of all those who would not blindly follow it. History shows that whenever and wherever a religion was in control of a state or society, either through the priesthood or the secular rule, or combinations of both, that religion found it highly "ethical," "just," and "proper" to rob, torture, slay, quarter, burn, and massacre the dissidents or those of other faiths. Confiscation of the worldly goods and property of those who opposed was a godly deed: Catholicism and Moslemism have confirmed century after century their divine artistry in taking what does not belong to them. After all, they were merely following the usual procedures of the earlier religions, except that they systematized their confiscations on a greater and more thorough scale. The *Great Deception* is the hypocrisy of a religion which proclaims the virtue of poverty while continually amassing wealth, property, land, treasure: if one were to list the properties and investments of the Catholic Church alone, he would simply be amazed.

The Concordat between the Roman Catholic Church and Hitler in 1933 clearly exposes to the world and history that the

Catholic hierarchy is a power and a business and that it has little to do, in reality, with humility and poverty; that any pretense to ethics is not based on any genuine motive of saving people's souls and lives, but merely of carrying on a mode of adaptability that is directed to the preservation of its wealth, property, and influence. Rolf Hochhuth gives us some "sidelights on history": "A few years ago details on the close collaboration between the clergy and heavy industry reached the press. *Der Spiegel,* for example, said in August, 1958: 'During the Second World War the Society of Jesus made profits from both sides in this essential raw material (mercury). While the Spanish mines supplied chiefly the Allies and Russia, the Italian mines provided for the German armaments industry.' At the same time many persons, and not only Catholics, waited in vain for an official denial. The statement that the Vatican is the largest stockholder in the world has not been contested by Rome."[155]

As such, how can one synchronize the constant echo of its priests expounding the virtue of poverty while doing all they can to gather in the ducats from the faithful and from whatever sources they can tap? The coin slots of the Cathedral of Guadalupe are a maze of pipes leading from almost every statue, from every picture, from every corner; the steady and never-ending line of poor *peones* from all parts of Mexico come to drop in their few pennies to buy for after death what nobody would help them get here on earth. "When Gladstone saw in the Homeric gods a sense of duty and a consciousness of moral responsibility, he exaggerated."[156]

Herbert L. Matthews writes about Spain and the Catholic sacred regard for ethics in the matter of religious freedom: "In a population of 30,000,000, the Government estimates there is a total of only 25,000 Protestants. Of these probably 9,000 are foreigners. Yet Protestantism is treated by the Church and by the Government as though it were a great threat to the Catholic faith of Spain."[157] He continues: "As soon as the conflict ended in 1939, General Franco abrogated the Republic's Law of Religious Confessions and Congregations. Protestant schools were closed, although they had been permitted under the Monarchy. An accord that the Caudillo made with the Holy See reaffirmed four articles of the Concordat of 1851, declaring that Roman Catholicism was the sole religion of the Country."[158] "There is, of course, no freedom of worship in Franco Spain. Politics, even more than religion, made this a necessity. The Spanish Church always supported feudalism, monarchism, centralism, authoritarianism, the aristocracy, wealth. The hierarchy today devolves from the Counter Reformation, when the Catholic Church in Spain was saved by its close alliance to the throne and by a rigid censorship that kept the peasantry ignorant as well as poor."[159]

If the same effort, time, and material consumed by people to connive, cheat, defraud, deprive, and otherwise perform chicanery or prevent these things were utilized instead to equitable, just, and considerate causes, these very people, by this bilateral and mutual attitude, would achieve greater material and more satisfying ends and enjoy while doing so with less fear, stress, anxiety, and regret. The average animal is naturally honest; the average human animal is dishonest. If civilization seems to be the means of cultivating us to be less animal and more human, and thus more cunningly dishonest because of our progressively increased brain power in intelligence, then it is high time for us to pause, take inventory, and reevaluate the direction in which the human race is drifting.

The earliest human deceptionists and connivers were the shamans of primitive religion, who later evolved into the medicine-wizards and leaderships. Thus, where primitive magical ritual was performed to outwit, maneuver, or incite for a unilateral purpose, this culminated into the higher religions, which were, if we want to call things by their proper names, the great deceptions imposed upon humanity. This process of deception, if dissected deeply and carefully, would be found to be economic, the enslavement of the many by the few. The earliest kingships were also the earliest priesthoods. Once the primitive tasted of power and authority and all the economic abundance it brought, he wanted the throngs to cower continually at his feet as he flung his arms toward his self-made alliance with fire and the sky.

This practice of fraud, even with the deepest humility and reverence, flowered into the other fields of human leaderships such as kingships, royalties, nobilities, governments, business leaders, financial wizards, the military brass, and still flourishes all over the world. And all over the world, with few exceptions, the general masses of people, who provide the "fields" for this powercraft to exact its tolls, are, as usual, behind the eight ball!

As stated before, one of the most flagrant examples of this situation is the Roman Catholic Church, which, while enjoying the greatest material and opulent wealth of any single organization in the world, speaks, writes, and prays only in the adoration and acceptance of poverty, humility, charity, and the wonderful grace of the "spiritual" life. The Catholic Church is neither poor nor humble, and as to charity, it encourages it because it is itself the principal recipient of it. The Church gets richer, and the poor get more numerous. The politicos and their friends in Latin America exemplify the Holy Church by ensuring the broadening and the stability of the poverty field. No doubt, the corruption in the world today by its political, military, and economic leaders is very bad; yet during historical periods when the religious leaders were more or less in absolute command, times were even worse, more brutal, more dishonest, and the humanities more enslaved. If the world in general is going more and more in the direction of greater power aggrandizement and less religion, it merely signifies that the levels of operating power have gradually and in part been transferred from the more "spiritual" to the more "earthly" of the here and now. The masses are either deluded by the priests that paradise will reach them after death or by the Communists that their grandchildren will reach paradise on earth sometime in the future. They are being defrauded on both premises and on two fronts.

"Blessed are the meek: for they shall inherit the earth!" is a phrase without meaning or verification in the public and private history of experience. The meek may be "blessed," but they have never inherited the earth. The meek have been used to slave for those who are not meek. Even the Catholic Church, which favors this misleading aphorism, has shown, in actuality, very little meekness. It takes what it can get, from the poor as well as from the rich; it has not become the richest organization in the world by meekness. Banco de Santo Espirito branches are all over Rome; they did not sprout there out of meekness and humility; they deal with money and power. The Church did not impose its catechisms and dogmas throughout Europe and the New World by meekness but by the choice of acceptance or the Sword. It did not carry on the Crusades by meekness, nor the Inquisition, during which countless thousands of people, including children, were tortured, quartered, and burned alive. Its missionaries in the New World did not apply meekness to the Caribs, the Arawaks, the Aztecs, Mayas, Incas, the American Indians, and hundreds of other peoples whom they wantonly and mercilessly first robbed and then slaughtered without pity. Its popes did not apply meekness to spread the gospel, to instill terrible fears of hell and damnation, to poison, kill, and mutilate each other. "By 1377 there were two popes, one in Avignon, one in Rome, each excommunicating each other, until 1409, when a council of cardinals at Pisa elected still another, so that of popes there then were three."[160]

Pope Gregory VII kept tirading: "Cursed be the man who keepeth back his sword from blood!" If Gregory really expected the meek to inherit the earth, no doubt it was intended that the Church should have the harvest. Pope Adrian IV proved that high Catholic priests should have the right to be wealthy and powerful. Nor was there meekness on the part of the Catholic Church when, in conspiracy with Philip IV, it brutally disposed of the Templars wholesale and shared the spoils by robbing the dead. The history of Pope Alexander VI, of his son Cesare and daughter Lucrezia, of their many crimes and murders, including the murder of church officials, such as Cardinal Orsini and others, is so full of the impact of plain, unadulterated, naked power that we can only come to the conclusion that meekness is not of the Church but belongs to its credulous followers who follow its precepts in ignorance, awe, and in the fear of being damned to a mythical hell.

Referring to the people in early Gothic times: "Their lives were controlled by a warrior caste which attempted to give them protection, but battened on their labor; or by priests and monks who controlled the ritual of their existence and taught them that life was as fleeting as the crops they harvested. . . . This curious society of peasant and priest and warrior, which drew its strength from individual men rather than from nations and countries, was held together by the Catholic Church and feudal law."[161] During the Renaissance the criminality and corruption of the Papacy reached its new high: "As the power of the Papacy steadily grew through temporal measures such as war and diplomacy, so did the need for such qualities in a pope seem ever more necessary. This is the explanation of what so many now find difficult to understand—of popes such as Alexander VI or Julius II. Alexander VI, whose lusts repelled even the tolerant age in which he lived. . . . Julius II, even as a pope, loved war, loved to get on his horse and feel the weight of his armor and hear the blood-call of battle. . . . The Renaissance popes were worldly men, pragmatic, tough, concerned with power. And like many hardheaded, ambitious men they did not wish to be outshone by their rivals in the symbolic display of wealth and greatness. . . . Rome was full of priests, monks, nuns, churches, monasteries, convents, holy relics, miraculous shrines, healing images. Every year thousands of pilgrims from all corners of the Western world made their way to it in penitance and in hope. Most were simple people to whom the sight of a piece of the True Cross or a saint's leg justified the dangers and tribulations of their journey. They cared nothing for the whispered rumors of the Pope's children, of his poisonings, murders, or even the alarming sensualities of the Borgias. . . . Humanist criticism of the Church's venality, corruption, immorality, and obscurantism fell on deaf ears."[162]

The record of the Church's use of all kinds of power and influence, accumulation of extraordinary wealth and property, of the ornamentation of churches with gold and silver, the increasing storage of treasures, and the "blessed" demands for more and more donations from its followers, the constant sale of masses, all the secular and financial institutions the Church controls and operates, directly or indirectly, openly or sub rosa—all this is mendacity, not meekness, efficacy, and authoritarian puissance and audacity and an effrontery to any individual or group of individuals concerning themselves with a rational, ethical, and moral approach to the principle of freedom and a realistic approach to a just analysis of the natural rights which alone can lead to an honest and happy society. The Church has continually taken from the poor to increase its wealth, and done so without shame.

Centuries ago the Papacy had its own armies and knights to conquer and overrun many Italian cities and provinces, using the sword to gain territory and property. "The world of armed knights was not cheap; the courts of kings have never tolerated poverty; and though princes of the Church might preach self-denial, they rarely practiced it."[163] "To finance their pet projects and their lavish courts, the popes resorted to virtually any means to fill the papal coffers and their own pockets. Simony ran riot. Nearly every cardinal had purchased his red hat for a liberal amount of gold and was willing to sell his vote in the conclave for even more; Paul II left bishoprics unfilled so that he could collect the revenues himself; Innocent VIII seemed to spend most of his time financing the escapades of his profligate son; and Sextus IV declared, 'a pope needs only pen and ink to get what sum he wants.' The sale of indulgences was another lucrative practice, and the appalling proportions it assumed under Julius II and Leo X gave Martin Luther the final provocation for his ninety-five theses. Those churchmen who had not obtained their positions by bribery were usually the favorites or relatives of popes. This practice of nepotism reached a nadir during the pontificate of Alexander VI, whose ultimate goal, some said, was to make the papal tiara a hereditary crown for his Borgia offspring. . . . Money, not salvation, seemed to be the preoccupation of these worldly pontiffs."[164]

The very beginnings of organized Christianity are full of diplomatic intrigue and plain and unashamed power politics, which in actuality were intimidation and blackmail. Marcello Craveri gives us a little of the history of what took place: "In 311, a few years after Diocletian's abdication, his successor, Galerius (reigned 305-11) was compelled to grant freedom of worship to the Christians, hoping thus to mollify their antagonisms. Finally, Constantine the Great frankly sought their support in his struggle to seize the thrones of Maxentius and Maximian and subsequently against his former ally, Licinius, offering them not only broad guarantees of freedom but high public offices (Edict of Milan, 313). . . . This moment marked the beginning of the real triumph

of the Church as a political organization. It signified also a major
change in the problem of Church relations with the temporal
power. . . . At the same time, the recognition of Christianity as
the state religion made it also the mass religion. Through a mere
imperial edict its followers were expanded overnight by many
millions. . . . However, with its exclusivist character as the *one*
truth faith and its grandiose theocratic aspiration, inherited from
the Jews, to control even politically all the nations of the world 'in
the Lord's name.' Christianity could not long retain this dual
aspect (since in fact the emperor was also the head of the Church)
or tolerate the practice of other religious confessions. Its first
act was to subject the pagans to all the agonies that it had suffered
during the period of persecutions and to try to suppress paganism
altogether . . . it destroyed or appropriated to its own use the
pagan shrines; it redistributed the prerogatives of the old inferior
gods to its own saints; in 416 it obtained the enactment of a law
barring pagans from public employment. . . . Above all, the
Church claimed the right to final determination of the morality
and the legality of every act not only of its members but even
the chief of state himself. The maxim of Jesus: 'Render unto
Caesar the things which are Caesar's and unto God the things that
are God's,' left Caesar now with very little. The Church had begun to dominate the state."[165] Craveri concludes his book, *The
Life of Jesus,* thusly: "And so the 'good tidings' preached by
Jesus, which held the hope of happiness, of peace, of justice for
all men, in this life, have been tortured through the centuries into
this perversion of faith that serves no purpose in life because
indeed it rejects life, it curses life, it condemns life to an agony of
unsureness."[166] What the Church gave to its people was continual misery, never a single year of peace, and a cruel, merciless,
and unrelenting injustice. That nice line about "peace on earth
and good will to all men" remained only a line of words, for, in
its historical trek, the Church obviously never really went out to
use its influence to bring this about.

The Church has been on both sides in every conflict clamoring
for victory; it wants everyone to come to church every day of the
year if possible, and punishes adultery by consignment to hell.
Bertrand Russell: "Christ taught that you should not fight, that

you should not go to church, and that you should not punish adultery."[167]

When the Babylonians conquered Jerusalem and enslaved the Hebrews, the priests of Babylon prayed to their Lord and thanked him for the opportunity of killing the Hebrews. When the Romans overran Carthage and slaughtered the people they no doubt thanked Jupiter for allowing them to perform this sacred deed. When the Catholics murdered the Protestants in France, the spiritual-minded followers of St. Peter no doubt thanked the Lord for giving them this great mission of cleansing the land of heresy. When the Protestants massacred the Catholics, no doubt they held the Bible up in one hand and the bloody sword in the other. To encourage the Crusades, Pope Pius II, even when he was dying, exhorted the people to carry out this noble work against the Moslems, threatening, "Woe befall you if you draw back from God's work!" When the Turks persecuted the Armenians, there is no question that they felt they did what in their place Mohammed himself would do with his own hands. The Crusaders went far to do their killing because of the sacred battle call of God and the Saints to relieve the Moslems of the holy places. Hitler, who probably considered God second in command, dedicated his mission on earth to exterminating millions of innocent people. When the Nazi guards gazed upon the long lines of nude Jewish women, with babies in their arms and little tots fearfully holding on to their mothers' legs, naked, shamed, and terror-stricken, en route to the gas chambers, a picture that breaks one's heart and tears the mind into bits of horror and nausea, no doubt they thought they were carrying out the will of their god, that is, the new Wodin—Hitler. Even this very day, May 20, 1967, as I write these lines, a dispatch from Cairo states that "millions of Moslems flocked to the mosques to hear sermons advocating 'a sacred war to uphold God's cause' to wipe out Israel." The report states further that "students and workers flocked to centers to register as volunteers for what is now termed 'the sacred march on Israel.'" The Coptic Christian churches in Egypt also proclaim it is time to do God's will and wipe out the Israeli people. This is *today*, at this very moment. Throughout history it has been the same; people have prayed and killed and looked up and forward to greater reward in God's busy computers. Man prayed to the Lord before enjoying the body of woman, and then prayed afterward to thank his God that he was born a man and not a woman, woman symbolizing the epitome of evil and uncleanliness. No doubt when the "brave" hunter with his high-powered rifle finally brings down a polar bear from a low-flying plane he too might say, "Thank God, I got him!"

Poor God! When will man see, if he ever could, in the reflection of his own mind the bestiality in himself, and then have the audacity to claim that any decent god could have made man in His image? The fantasy of the Lord is the pretext for man's predatory and sadistic compulsions. Probably, in the end, man may overwhelm himself, destroy himself, and give back to God his natural freedom to free himself from the human paranoia that has drenched the centuries with blood and suffering ever since man has used His name. Do all these things ordain theology to merit the authority and respect to order rules of morality? "Man the destroyer is having his day."[168]

In whatever history we have of primitive tribes, preancient and still extant today, each little tribe, in warring against its neighbors, called upon its tribal gods to lead them against the "aggressors." Throughout history every nation and religion everywhere hailed the "commands" and the "will" of a god or many gods to bring them victory over the "pagans" (anyone is considered a pagan who does not believe as you do). In short, the "will of God" was the excuse for conflict of all religions whenever they had the power and the opportunity. This deflection of "God's will" mirrors the innate evil and cruelty in man himself. There is no evil except *human* evil. There is no hate except *human* hate. Man fears only himself and others like him, and to kill his own fears he kills the others. Man, in his audacious, egocentric claim that he is in the image of God is proof that man is a faker and a forger. If there were a God, I feel sure he could not have picked man for his image, but rather some butterflies, the roses in your garden, or a stray buttercup growing between two stones in some cool shade, the scent of lilies of the valley, the musk of pines after a rain, the play of kittens and pups, the searching glance of the fawn's eyes, a mother robin feeding earthworms into the gaping mouths of *goldfish* to express its maternal emotions and instincts, and the love that permeates unconsciously but sweetly the really divine lovers' knot of cooing swans. The brain of man imaged God to justify its own deprivations and crimes, its innuendos appearing as ethics, and the greed of immortal award appearing as morals, and even a Devil—how could man imagine God without an adversary, since man has always desired one for himself? The "distinguished" gentlemen of the United Nations, well trained in the arts of fabrication, evasion, and indifference to genuine justice and ethics, no doubt have their particular god, the *Logos*—the word devoted to do everything but expose and use the truth. Man has picked a thousand gods or one, but God did not really pick man.

It does not follow that a person is ethical simply because he does not happen to be religious or a follower of any religion. The "bad" ones and the "good" ones are found among the high and low, among the pious and the "sinners," the faithful and the heretical. But it does follow that a religionist will oppose and condemn the heretic, and if he had the temporal power he would destroy him, not on any rational, ethical or reasonable basis of freedom of thought and conscience, but merely upon the simple grounds of emotional, neurotic hate built up to destroy anything that comes between him and his Lord, even to destroy himself, a neurotic hate that is inoculated into the very young when they are more or less incapable of reasoning and making judgments. This parochial insemination into the minds and hearts of little children is one of the most brutal acts of organized religion, and it does not contain within it any semblance of ethical content, nor is it any respecter of the life-rights and the naturally-born freedoms of each new life. One can see such neurotic hate instilled into children by the good, Lord-following people of Dallas. When the assassination of President Kennedy was announced in the classrooms, many of the children cheered spontaneously and screamed with joy! This is the "ethic" of the parents, to poison the minds of little children, to foster hate, to cheer the destruction of life.

At the recent Ecumenical Council in Rome the good bishops found it impossible to withdraw from their belief of blaming the

Jews of today because almost two thousand years ago "they say" certain people crucified their Savior but refuse to admit that Jesus, if he had lived at all, was an Essenian follower, a religious *Jew* and one who did not believe in blaming or hating. Besides, if there were no crucifixion, there would have been no resurrection, and no Christianity. Jules Isaac brings out the constant teaching of contempt for the Jew in the Catholic books for children used in their parochial schools.[169] There seems to be a terribly frustrating feeling in many Christians who realize that they never can possibly change the status of Jesus as a Jew; many Christians hate the Jew because they cannot change the accepted "historical" event that Jesus lived and died as a Jew.

Man is the only animal that *hates*. Other animals may exhibit forbearance, fear, withdrawal, suspicion, depression, futility, resignation, defeatism, and become neurotic, but they do not hate. They may exhibit cruelty, indifference, no feeling of guilt for the predator in killing and eating the prey, immune to the fate or suffering of other animals, but not hate. Man is the only creature that sets up moral codes, ethical systems, has the most remarkable brain in all animaldom, has even nurtured and intellectualized freedom of conscience and the most intricate evaluations of rational and scientific procedures, and, with it all, is the only creature that can hate and hate well. Grzimek: "It is almost unknown for a lion to kill one of his own breed, so that we humans, who murdered millions of our fellow men in Europe during the last war [2nd World War], could well learn decent behavior from them."[170] George B. Schaller depicts the gorilla as the most unferocious of beasts, who lives more peacefully with other gorillas than do most humans with humans. "In many ways," he says, "they have achieved the kind of life man has sought for centuries."[171]

There is no better hater, even with all his pitiful glances toward heaven and a thousand amens a day, than the religious and racial hater. So proficiently has the religious or racial fanatic learned his "art" that sectarianism for thousands of years bred hate and more hate until it was coming out of its own ears. Herbert J. Muller: "The hell on earth that Christianity made on principle, as it directly inspired more hatred than has any other religion."[172]

"Religion still works more obviously to divide man than to unite mankind, in a One World that is still far from being a good neighborhood."[173] Grzimek: "When the Benedictine Bishop, Cassion Spiess, was assassinated together with two monks and two nuns, the German Government sent out two light cruisers, a company of marines and native troops from the Pacific Islands. Nearly 100,000 people are said to have perished as a result of this war which ruined the harvest and drove the cattle away [the rebellion, 1905-1907, in German East Africa]."[174] Herbert J. Muller: "On the whole, the triumph of Christianity resulted in a distinct lowering of its ethical standards. If no established church in a great society could be expected to maintain the revolutionary ideals of Jesus, the misfortune remains that its leaders specifically repudiated much in the social gospel that most clearly distinguishes Christians from pagans, and that might have given ordinary men more real freedom. Thus many early Christians, believing their Lord's teachings about nonviolence, had refused all military service, but in obedience to the powers that be churchmen began to hedge: they accepted 'just' wars, while leaving forever uncertain how to tell them from unjust wars. In the fourth century pacifists were declared heretical. Thereafter the Christian Church would give more open support to war than any other of the higher religions save only Mohammedanism; and while many ordinary Christians would perish by the sword, many more would be oppressed in states organized primarily for military purposes. Similarly the Church grew more tolerant of the possibilities of worshipping both God and mammon: by the fifth century a council condemned the old-fashioned idea that the rich could be saved only by renouncing their wealth. Christian camels could now pass through the eye of a needle."[175] "Until the rise of atheistic communism, the churches placed God squarely on both sides in very war."[176] Bertrand Russell: "The ruling party is supported by the immense majority of ministers of religion, who, with the Pope at their head, have pledged the vast forces of superstition throughout the world to the support of social injustice."[177] A former priest, Emmett McLoughlin: "It is my contention and my sincere conviction, from my experience in the Catholic educational system, my life of fifteen years in the priesthood, and thirteen years of constant observation and intense study since leaving the Church, that its influence on all civilization has been far more of evil than of good."[178] Father DuBay of Santa Monica, writes about his Church: "No longer does it serve the flesh loved and cherished by God as his own. For a long time it has disdained the aspirations and strivings of men. For centuries the greatest obstacle to human progress has been the church itself. In its tremendous organizational potential and investment, the church today remains immobile and resistant to the movement of man. Any gesture it makes simulating an awakening from the centuries-long coma it has suffered creates a storm of interest among men. Any movement in its giant but sclerotic limbs evokes accolades of applause and recognition. Most people choose to ignore its comatose condition; but it wears down on them, nevertheless, an enormous parasite draining their energy and tolerance. The reformers and physicians have tried several times to wake it up, and the present efforts also seemed doomed to failure for the same reasons as earlier ones. It is not only the world's humanity the churches fails to take seriously, but its own humanity. The disease consists not in being too human, but not human enough."[179]

Hate has made it possible for the human animal to enjoy the murder of his own kind, even his own kin. It has marked fences and barriers where others shall and shall not be and go, and others have hated back because of it. Hate has made possible the worst depraved cruelties of people upon people. The words *massacre* and *pogrom* are really adjectives to the noun *hate*. Only those who have experienced the terror of these words and were fortunate enough to survive *know* the impact of what hate can do to make a human animal commit such foul and heinous crimes upon innocent people whom he does not even know and who have never known him or done him any wrong. Hate is the ignorant judge that marks a person guilty and sentences him without a trial, appeal, or common mercy, and then considers the sentence and the punishment as a revelation of divine wisdom or a deed done in the service of the Lord. Martin A. Larson: "Not only are several of the epistles wholly spurious, but those which are genuine were drastically revised."[180] "That various passages were deleted, altered, or interpolated into the Gospels and even more in the Pauline epistles is true beyond any doubt."[181] Joseph Wheless: "The Bible, in its every Book, and in the strictest legal and moral sense, is a huge forgery. . . . Every Book of the New Testament is a forgery of the Christian Church; and every significant passage in those Books, on which the fabric of the Church and its principal dogmas are founded, is a further and conscious later forgery, wrought with definite fraudulent intent. . . . The Christian Church, from its inception in the first little Jewish-Christian religious societies until it reached the apex of its temporal glory and moral degradaton, was a vast and tireless Forgery-mill."[182] "To such an extent are the origins of the Christian religion wrapped in obscurity, due to the labyrinthine confusions and contradictions and forgeries of its early records, that it is quite impossible to extricate, with any degree of confidence, a thread of historic truth from the tangle."[183]

HATE, THE MARK OF HOMO

IF CIVILIZATION MEANS the nurture and cultivation of non-violence, of ethical procedure and consideration, of the recognition of the basic natural freedom of life, of the natural equities innate in it, then man is really audacious to call himself a civilized person, or a good person, or even, in the true sense, a religious person. André Maurois wrote that "It is regrettable but true that hatred is the only thing that can unite mankind."[184] Even though Maurois felt this as a resigned and pessimistic conclusion, hate has not united mankind. Hatred has caused the murder of more human beings than any other factor and still does. Hardly a moment passes by that some human is not being killed, hurt, or deprived because of hate. If anyone presumes that hate can be the true uniting agent for humanity, then it must also be presumed that humanity can only be united as a psychotic mass bent on graduallly destroying itself from within, by conflict, negation, and denial of each member of it by another. V. T. Thayer: "The harsh and inconsiderate treatment accorded the children of Jehovah's Witnesses in some communities today is but a faint reproduction of far more stern and uncompromising handling of Catholic and Jewish children seventy-five to one hundred years ago. In Boston, in 1858, a Catholic child was severely whipped when it refused to read the Protestant Bible. About the same time one hundred Catholic children were expelled from a Boston school as a penalty for refusing to participate in religious exercise. And in the city of brotherly love an irate mob burned Catholic schools, in answer to a Catholic bishop's suggestion that the public schools excuse Catholic children from the necessity of reading the Protestant version of the Bible."[185]

In another way Ed Howe states that "Instead of loving your enemies, treat your friends a little better." Nobody really loves his enemies. I do not think that even Jesus did. Hell was not invented out of affection for those who cross us. The human psyche is not really benevolent to people and things that oppose it or do not allow it to have its full way or vent of action and expression. This is the root of intolerance, and intolerance breeds not only hate but all forms of prejudice and bigotry, religious and racial. According to St. Luke, Jesus is supposed to have said: "If any man cometh unto me and hateth not his own father and mother and wife and children and brethren and sisters, yea, and his own life also, he cannot be my disciple."[186]

The Catholic dogma and rule expose their own contradiction where the principle of tolerance and goodwill among men is concerned; this is especially so in its historic ailment of anti-Semitism. Guenter Lewy: "When Hitler set out on his murderous campaign against the Jews of Europe truth and justice found few defenders. The Deputy of Christ and the German episcopate were not among them."[187] "The policy of accommodation of the German episcopate . . . provides but the most recent striking example of the Church's inability to transcend her institutional interests and to be a guardian of human morality. . . . The Church's hold upon the faithful in many situations is too precarious to risk an open clash with a state trampling upon human dignity and freedom. The situation is worsened when, as in Nazi Germany, the bishops and the clergy are themselves infected with an alien creed. Whenever either of these manifestations is present, many seemingly good reasons can be brought forth to

defend the Church's political quietism and her surrender to
Caesar."[188] Saul Friedlander, in his documentary on Nazi-Church
policies, concludes thusly: "How is it conceivable that at the end
of 1943 the Pope and the highest dignitaries of the Church were
still wishing for victorious resistance by the Nazis in the East and
therefore seemingly accepted by implication the maintenance,
however temporary, of the entire Nazi extermination machine?
How can one explain the manifestations of special predilection
which the Pope continued to lavish on the Germans, even in
1943, when he was aware of the nature of the Hitler regime?"[189]

D. T. Atkinson: "During the Middle Ages . . . the Jews were
not allowed to enter the professions in Europe or to compete
with any non-Jewish person in business. Christians of the period
were forbidden to take interest on money, so the Jews became
the bankers of each country and made loans to Christians. It was
due to this that so many Jews were suspected of poisoning the
wells. An accusation in those Dark Ages amounted in nearly
every case to a conviction, and the plagues gave a golden opportunity to those indebted to the Jews for money to make accusa-
tions which would likely end in a conviction and a cancellation
of their debts."[190] Herbert J. Muller: "I think it important to
remember that anti-Semitism is no recent aberration, but deeply
rooted in Christian tradition. Neither the Catholic Church nor
the Lutheran Church in Germany took the lead in denouncing
Hitler's persecution of the Jews, which could indeed have been
justified by some of Martin Luther's tirades against them."[191]

Martin Luther was a first-class Jew-hater; he would have loved
to hang every Jew with his own hands. Guenter Lewy: "Which
ethical system will best form man's conscience so as to inculcate
a sense of justice and compassion is hard to determine. But one
thing can perhaps be said: the conscience of man must remain
free of entanglements with the interests of a religious institution.
It cannot depend on an ideology. When thousands of German
anti-Nazis were tortured to death in Hitler's concentration camps,
when the Polish intelligentsia was slaughtered, when hundreds of
thousands of Russians died as a result of being treated as Slavic
Untermenschen and when 6,000,000 human beings were murdered for being 'non-Aryan,' Catholic Church officials in Germany

bolstered the regime perpetrating these crimes. The Pope in Rome, the spiritual head and supreme moral teacher of the Roman Catholic Church, remained silent."[192] Abraham Lincoln: "To sin by silence when they should protest makes cowards of men."

"It was not long ago," writes Herbert J. Muller, "that the popular Father Coughlin was stirring up anti-Semitism, together with other Fascist sentiments as congenial to the Protestant Ku Klux Klan. In the South, Protestant churches remain the most highly segregated institutions in the country, and Fundamentalist sects produce the most rabid preachers of Protestant white supremacy. Short of such bigotry, studies of public opinion indicate that churchgoers are less favorable to freedom of speech and press than non-churchgoers."[193] Paul Blanshard: "The Catholic diocesan press of the United States, which constantly protests the Protestant Presidential monopoly, is delighted to condone the laws of Catholic countries like Spain, Argentina and Paraguay which exclude all Protestants and Jews from the highest state offices."[194] Philip Wylie: "The three brains that uncovered the deepest laws of subject and object and human relations were in the heads of despised Jews—Jesus, Freud, and Einstein."[195]

The historical constancy of anti-Semitism in Europe ever since Christianity came into being and the continually recurring waves of torture and murder of innocent people are not pleasant witnesses for Christianity to shuffle its records around in order to make out a code of ethics or of conscience or of morality or of any sense of a state of civilization. Hannah Arendt describes how Christian "ethics" operated in Rumania during the Second World War: "Deportation Rumanian style consisted in herding five thousand people into freight cars and letting them die there of suffocation while the train traveled through the countryside without plan or aim for days on end; a favorite follow-up to these killing operations was to expose the corpses in Jewish butcher shops."[196]

Arendt reveals the sad situation in Europe in which Jews, to save their own lives, became Judas-goats in assisting the Nazis to round up other Jews and gain knowledge of their possessions for confiscation and robbery. On the other hand the Chasidic and optimistic fatalism allowed the Jews to suffer meekness, resignation, Will of God no-matter-what, and the crematorium. Elie Wiesel[197] exposes the Hebraic fatalism and surrender of life to the delusion of togetherness with God and its concomitant willingness to suffer and even die. Yet there are some who revolt against this irrational and masochistic process of religious belief and strike out to regain the breath and color, the openness and encircling horizons that life itself expresses. Thus the Israeli nation was born as a protest, one could say, as a rebellion against the seemingly endless patience of the Jew to await the Messiah who is supposed to deliver him from evil, bring him peace and all kinds of goodies.

If Hitler had won the war there is no doubt that he would have had confiscated all the wealth and property of both the Roman Catholic and the Eastern Orthodox churches, as well as the Protestant sects, and abolished by decree all religions. And yet, the fence-sitter Pope Pius XII will go down in history as the silent accepter of Nazism and the dormant partner in the most cruel of all the cruelest periods of world history—the torture and extermination of millions of people. This, in the modern period, marks as Exhibit I the evidence that the Roman Catholic hierarchy is an arch-trust interested principally in its power, its wealth, its properties, that its ultimate interest in spirituality is secondary and a pretentious stage prop for its historical play of humility and the adoration of poverty. Guenter Lewy: "The Nazis were biding their time, impatiently waiting for the day on which they could afford to settle final accounts with the Church. . . . In fact, much of the regime's hostility was due to the desire to get rid of an unwanted ally whom the Nazis intended to destroy as a force in Germany as soon as the war was over."[198] Himmler said that "We shall not rest until we have rooted out Christianity."[199]

The so-called "natural law" of morality behind which the Church has so often hidden to justify her myriad interpretations and preserve her political and economic power has merely been the pliable and flexible tool that the hierarchy has consistently and historically used to preserve itself first, and then morals, if need be, regardless of injustice, crime, and wholesale murder.

Guenter Lewy: "The German Catholics in 1937 were told that resistance to the Nazi state was sinful; Spanish Catholics at the same time were urged to support the rebellion of General Franco against the Second Spanish Republic. In World War II Catholics serving in both of the warring factions were assured that they were fighting a just war. The institution of slavery was at one time defended by leading theologians as in consonance with natural law; today in an age of colonial revolts and assaults upon all forms of discrimination, the Church stands for full equality. All these positions have been justified on the basis of the same natural law premises."[200]

We find, as we put our lenses of insight and analysis closer, that this "natural law" as ordained by any particular creed is merely an ideology of a priori dimension, and thus a discoloration and distortion of historical events and movements to sustain a *logicality* of appearance that these events and movements identify the "truth" of the particular ideology. It is the old game of reasoning that is preoculated to see and accept the world as the "truism" and "proof" of a particular ideology. This process of self-beguilement and the beguilement of others does not take into account *persons*, individual *humans*, the constituents of humanity as they really are, but what the ideology wants to make them appear, just segments or numbers of a particular "historical" or "divine" order of "consistency." This is how people were induced to believe in the ordinarily impossible, in the supranatural, in the absurdities of miracles; they saw, they accepted, they believed, just as Hoffmann saw his beloved doll through his magical spectacles; what was not there they accepted, an event that never occurred.

This a priori deduction is the weapon the Church has used to uphold, justify, and provoke anti-Semitism from generation to generation; this is how it has been possible for *aggregates* of millions of human beings (in this instance, Jews) to be condemned for an alleged event of two thousand years ago, as a logicality of historical process and continuity that ordained the hating and extermination of people. What is not revealed in the ideology is the sinister and psychotic purposes to maintain a process of mass obedience and blind acceptance to the power, authority, and establishment of an organization that needed the justification of hate and murder to nourish its processes of mass unity and adherence of its followers, not by intelligence or rationalized ethics, but through *emotion,* because only through emotion can hostility prevail.

On this basis and submissiveness to this "natural law," was it possible for the populace and priests to be eager to see and enjoy the burning of heretics, Jews, witches, as a "natural" and "ordained" process of "purification" and "absolution," in which the actual crime of murder and torture of *individual* human beings, as *persons,* was not felt or understood as such.

Hannah Arendt, in her brilliant *The Origins of Totalitarianism,* exposes this very process as seeding dictatorships, the continual resurgences of anti-Semitism, the stirring of mass emotional hysteria, which led, likewise, to the emergence of Hitlerism: "Deism, though it denies divine revelation, does not simply make 'scientific' statements on a God in order to explain the course of the world. . . . An ideology is quite literally what its name indicates: it is the logic of an idea. Its subject matter is history, to which the 'idea' is applied; the result of this application is not a body of statements about something that *is,* but the unfolding of a process which is in constant change. The ideology treats the course of events as though it followed the same 'law' as the logical exposition of the 'idea.' Ideologies pretend to know the mysteries of the whole historical process—the secrets of the past, the intricacies of the present, the uncertainties of the future—because of the logic inherent in their respective ideas. . . . Ideologies are never interested in the miracle of the being. They are historical, concerned with becoming and perishing, with the rise and fall of cultures, even if they try to explain history by some 'law of nature.' The word 'race' in racism does not signify any genuine curiosity about the human race as a field of scientific exploration, but is the 'idea' by which the movement of history is explained as one consistent process."[201]

It should now be better understood why it was more important for another totalitarian state, the Church, to find it more feasible to make a concordat of noninterference with Hitler so long as its own ideology of self-maintenance, considered more important

than the lives of millions of individual human beings, was preserved.

The Israeli nation is the outcome of sheer desperation of people
to regain their natural freedom as *human beings* and the "second
wind" of these people to regain for themselves some dignity as
beings and selves, a protest against the world that they cannot
and will not rely any longer on the tyranny of words and the evading promises of statesmanship. During my last visit to Israel I
seemed to sense some process of compromise, however, between
societal need and the individual desire for freedom of thought and
action, that this compromise has materialized into a gratifying
modus vivendi. The Israeli is a proud and independent individualist, and yet he loves his country with a passion, always fearlessly ready to fight and die to protect it. I cannot call it patriotism; it goes deeper and beyond. I would rather think that the
Israeli, in protecting his country, feels that all of it is *his* to protect. One should differentiate between the typical Israeli man
and woman and the orthodox Jewish man and woman. The
Israeli is not the optimistic, fatalistic expectant that the orthodox
Jew is; he may believe in God, but he has not and does not wait
for God to answer his prayers. He is probably the busiest individual on earth today, furiously building, constantly changing
the landscapes of his little country from "badlands" of sand, stone,
and crag to beautiful vistas of orchards, orange groves, vineyards,
farms of growing food. His *kibbutzim* have become villages, his
villages have become towns, his towns expanding cities. Each year
the returning visitor sees tremendous, unbelievable progress.
All this is the "miracle" of what the restoration of freedom can
do for people, for individuals who have forcefully, at last, determined to free themselves from the political, social, and cultural
claustrophobia of Christian domination, persecution, and hate.
Let's face it: *Christianity has always hated the Jew.* The Catholic
bishops even consider this hate an asset and do not wish to part
with it in spite of growing world opinion against their historical
injustice toward the Jewish people.

Recently a statue of Thomas Paine was erected in his native
English village of Thetford; there will be many Thetfordians
who will no doubt splash this statue with rubbish to continue

their Christian hate for a man who, too, believed in freedom and who spent his life so we might be more free today. The orthodox Jew, such as the Chasidic sect, opposes the Israeli because the Israeli was wise and strong and fearless enough to say "Enough is enough! I want to be free *today*, not always tomorrow, and I will not wait for any Messiah to free me!" The Chasidic Jew has contempt for such insolence, and fatalistically insists on waiting for the Messiah while meantime enjoying the freedom and the security that the Israeli man and woman, and all their sacrifices, have provided him. The Papacy has no thought of rescinding the excommunication of Garibaldi, who took away Italy from the Holy See. Garibaldi, too, could not wait for God to deliver freedom; he fought and won it for himself and his countrymen.

The Israeli, by his actions, has practically said: "For over two thousand years I have prayed to God and *waited* for God to deliver us from our historical and unrelenting enemies who have tortured us, restricted us, robbed us, stockyarded us into ghettos, built walls around us and then blamed us for events outside these walls. The Romans killed us, the Greeks killed us, the Egyptians killed us, the Moslems killed us, the Christians killed us and still hate us, the Hitlers almost exterminated us. We still prayed, but no one raised his hand or head to help us. We could wait no longer. We built a country we could call our own, built it with our bare hands, where we might find some surcease from those who would rather see us dead than alive. How long, indeed, can a people suffer for their prayer and their patience? No one can truly say that we were not patient, devoted to our God, always thanking him for what we got, and *how* we got it! Now we have no walls, no ghettos, no one to push us around, to order us to learn less, see less, even serve less. For a person to be truly free does not require that another be less free; it does require that one should understand his freedom, how to use it, what it means, its value and purpose. In doing so we may possibly attain a reasonable level of peace. This is what we mean, in greeting and departing, when we say *Shalom*. This is what Israel, *my* country, means to me. Like the *sabra* that I am, an outer strength and awareness to intrusion, a most sensitive, prickly awareness that more than two thousand years of persecution has well made its mark—but below the outer skin is the desire for peace, for the sweetness of life, for a world democratic and ethical order that holds the possible key to save mankind from itself." C. L. Sulzberger reports what David Ben-Gurion told him: "Our people cannot understand destiny. They believe in the freedom of choice. Human beings can make their own fate. All history proves this, and most recently and specially the history of Israel. There is no abstract fate or destiny involved. We don't believe in fate." Terence Prittie concludes his book, *Israel, The Miracle in the Desert:* "Israel's role in history . . . implies the transmission of that deep-rooted golden faith of the Jewish people, the realization of the Jewish dream of a rule of honesty, justice, and decency on earth. . . . Israel must and will survive."[202]

If the religions were not enough to brew and maintain hatreds and conflicts, the hate of the racists moves in to keep the cauldron of intolerance and persecution boiling and bubbling over with its tragic and bitter consequences. No single being should be expected to be expendable to the exclusive benefit of others; the fact that he is so often forced by "duty," or the call of the gods for some "holy crusade," to become expendable indicates the extent of the influence of the authority-power form over how his life is to be "lived" and when it is to be stopped. In the "science" of ideologies, in which an ideology becomes more important than people, the leaders in power who maintain such ideology find it highly justified and "necessary" to sustain the ideology with all their authority and influence, even if it means the expendability of all its people.

In his attempt to justify slavery, Juan Ginés de Sepulveda (1550) wrote: "Indians are as different from Spaniards as cruelty is from kindness and as monkeys are from men."[203] And this comes from an obedient and faithful Catholic, devoted to his church and its principles. Juan Comas: "To maintain that a man is an inferior human being because he is black is as ridiculous as contending that a white horse will necessarily be faster than a black horse."[204] George Gaylord Simpson: "There are no biologically superior or inferior races."[205] Comas: "All the evidence of biology, anthropology, evolution and genetics demonstrates that racial discrimination on grounds of color is a myth without the slightest scientific warrant, and hence that the supposed 'racial inferiority of coloured peoples' is untrue. It is unfavourable environment, political and social-economic factors which alone keep these groups in their present levels."[206] Harry L. Shapiro: "The great injustice, after all, that has been placed on the mixed blood is that he is judged, not as an individual, an elementary right to which he is entitled, but as a member of a group about which there is so much prejudice and little understanding."[207] Clyde Kluckhohn: "The physical anthropologist finds no basis for ranking 'races' in relative order of superiority and inferiority."[208] L. C. Dunn: "The persistence of race prejudice where it exists is a cultural acquisition which as we have seen finds no justification in biology."[209] Dunn continues, replying to the query as to *what* is race: "We know now why certain views about race uniformity and purity and the fixity of racial differences were wrong; and why social and political views of race inequality were wrong. Since the former were often used as a justification for the latter, we should as reasonable beings like to believe that, if we get rid of our biological misconceptions, we should thereby cure the social and political ills of injustice and exploitation which appeared to be based upon wrong biology. Eventually we may expect this to happen, but we should not forget that the way in which human beings as individuals and as groups have acted with regard to race differences has more often stemmed from feelings and from prejudice than from knowledge. Knowledge eventually overcomes prejudice, but the delay may be long unless active steps are taken to implement the improvements in knowledge."[210] Ashley Montagu: "There is no such thing as the kind of 'race' in which the layman believes, namely, that there exists an indissoluble association between mental and physical characters which make individual members of certain 'races' either inferior or superior to the members of certain other 'races.' "[211]

In primitive times tribal life went on in some orderly fashion shaped out of rules, not necessarily based on right or wrong, but based on traditions and usages risen out of their common problems of existence, security, food, territorial needs, health, marriage, child-bearing, social togetherness, and the pooling of talents for mutual assistance. These are natural and basic factors with little estehtic or "moral" considerations. Even then, art forms exhibited themselves in their expression of fertility, subsistence, animal pleasures and relationships, mimicking the life around, immediate satisfactions, the chase of the hunter and the nature and relationships of the hunted, and all this without catechisms or parliamentary procedures. Tribal life was in the togetherness of its members as a group; all primitive dances were group or mass dances, which identified the social and clan culture as a coordinating and "all-pull-together" function; this gave each member the psychological mass-power of the tribe itself. Man was then also much more attached to the animal and natural environment and hardly "knew" the divinities, covenants, and priestcraft systems of worship that came much later with the early kingdoms.

Rules came with leadership, royalties, and priesthoods. Standards and moral-religio-socio-political forms rose out of the attempts of the early chieftains to keep the flocks of humans in line, as good hardworking caterpillars, for the sake of maintaining the priesthoods and kingships on a high and opulent level. The earliest codes of morality and law were based on the preservation of the royal or divine maintenance of the few, and whatever happened to the many did not matter so long as their abiding cohesive conduct preserved the religio-kingly status quo or bettered it. The priest-king clique always contained in its own core a devoted empathy for its own continuance and level, and most often little or no sympathy for all else that made it possible. To this very day we find an excellent example in the hierarchy of the Roman Catholic Church which has consistently favored and promoted the old status quo of religio-monarchial dominance over populations closed to intellectual and natural freedoms of expression. So long as its followers are kept in ignorance and blind belief, frozen in fear of eternal damnation, so long can the Catholic hierarchy maintain itself from generation to generation. It has done more harm to humanity than anything else in history, being always more devoted to the maintenance of its power, property, and general wealth than in the happiness and life-satisfactions of its followers and other peoples. Once its precepts infiltrate the mind of a child, it rarely recovers. It has caused more murders, slavery, massacres and needless sacrifices than any other factor. It has nurtured more neuroses of bitterness, sadism, masochism, bigotry, prejudice, misery and drunkenness than any other factor. It still tries to do this because being what it is, possibilities to change and modify itself are difficult even if the leaders actually know and are convinced that these changes are essential to the continuance of its own prestige and the realization of the pressures moving against it for change and modification. It is the World Interferer in the lives of people and a powerful transgressor of human freedom. Bertrand Russell: "There is nothing in human nature that compels us to acquiesce in continual savagery."[212] Lillie: "At the level of custom there is no room for progress or development. . . . The rising level of conscience opens the door for change; this change need not always be for the better, but at least progress is now possible."[213] "Surely the most characteristic expressions of conscience are those where it contradicts the commands of the group. It is true that conscience often bids a man follow the customs of his group, but sometimes it does not, and at this level the deciding factor is always what the man himself regards as right."[214]

THE ILLUSION OF ETHICS IN SOCIETY

ETHICS IS THAT department of philosophy that concerns itself with a person's or a group's principles and activity of conduct within themselves and toward others. Whether the particular principle or activity is actually good or bad is a perspective depending upon the usages, customs, cultures, laws, conventions, mores, and any sum of experiences which have led up to or brought it about. To state that any particular principle of ethics or any action of people, judged by ethical standards, is good or bad is merely to apply a personal, local, transient, or contemporary judgment. It cannot be placed on any universal plane. Time is a universal and is therefore neither before nor after. It is an unknown quantity in the ultimate. We, *particulars,* can never measure it; we can only record it as a measure in which our particular experiences take place. The clock is purely a human invention *for humans.* We cannot look at it as a measure for experiences of a universal nature, for, to ourselves, such does not exist. Corliss Lamont: "A supernatural First Cause or Sustaining Principle is no more necessary in the sphere of ethics than in that of physics or metaphysics."[215] "The self or personality is not a fixed, simple and ready-made entity standing behind a man's activities and directing them; that idea is a holdover from the supernatural doctrine of a divinely created soul—complete in all essentials—entering the body from on high. The human personality is a fluid, developing, growing complex of habits, impulses and ideas that is never finished and is always in the making *through* its activities and interests."[216] William J. Fielding: "So-called supernatural ethics and metaphysical moral codes are mere adaptations, developments, and often perversions, of natural ethics that have evolved through the eons of experience of primitive man."[217] Lillie: "Most people feel that a good action would still be a good action even if it were not commanded by God."[218] Herbert S. Dickey : "The Huitotos, like all Indian tribes I know, have no belief in a beneficent Supreme Being. They believe only in spirits of evil."[219] The savage feared what he could not see; he certainly did not love it. The *fear* of the Lord is primitive, but the *love* of Him is certainly a modern transitional paradox of the complex willy-nilly experiences of man's emotional evolution; *one cannot really fear and love the same thing.* H. R. Hays: "Etruscan belief does not relate ethics to rewards and punishments in the afterworld."[220]

At present the thought of putting to death incurables suffering constant pain, babes contorted and misshapen into suffering monsters, or incurable maniacs, would be considered bad; perhaps in a century or two it may be considered the *duty* to do away with these unfortunates. The farmer and the stockbreeder always desire to pick the best seed and the best bloodline to grow good crops and breed healthy cattle. Yet today in most countries of the world, especially those dominated more or less by Western cultures and in particular by Christianity, to grant a merciful relief to these pitiful accidents of life is illegal or sinful, or both. Therefore we can see that an ethic is a transient viewpoint, not a universal order or dictum.

Savages do not know the meaning of theft, nor do little tots when they take things because they just want to. Neither do they understand the principle of private property as we do. To them the world is a "field" from which each takes what he can. Theodora Kroeber writes of the Mill Creek Indians in California: "They stole and killed to live, not to accumulate herds or wealth, nor did the Indians really understand that what they took was the private property of a single person. Many years later when Ishi was past middle age, he blushed in painful embarrassment whenever he recalled that by white standards he and his brother Yahi had been guilty of stealing."[221]

Thus, with the slow and enveloping rise of civilized influences in any direction, the sense of private property became established and infiltrated wherever the economic field changed from a general to a particularized or personalized area of containment and identity. Janet McCloud, American Northwest Indian, presently fighting to maintain the fishing rights on the Nisqually River for her Indian people, gives her enlightening view: "The native Americans held all land in a communal ownership with free use and occupation of it within their territory. Each tribe was responsible for the preservation of the game, fish and fowl within their jurisdiction. Waste was a crime against natural law. Each tribe was responsible for the health of its land and forests, and the forests were as clean as modern parks. This was done to eliminate the danger of fire, to make hunting easier, and to preserve wild life. They took only as much as they needed from Mother Earth and never wasted it even in the midst of plenty. They were well aware of the penalties which awaited those foolhardy enough to violate nature. They never saw themselves as Europeans did as the dominant species with the power of life and death over every other living creature. . . . After four hundred years of learning white ways, we are more firmly resolved that our way is better."[222]

While theft is not rare in the animal world, especially among the monkeys, the art of stealing evolved to its highest levels of excellence in the human being. Based on voluntary actions and a genuine intellectualization of ethics, honest people are the exceptions. The unwary tourist finds this out readily and continually as he goes about. Wherever he goes he is generally robbed, that is, he is gypped, overcharged, shortchanged, and financially done in. Of course, there are fine and honest people everywhere but it seems very strange that the tourist does not usually meet them. At the moment, I am in Tel Aviv, on Ben Yehuda Road, and I am ordering a drink of grapefruit juice, *skerlotta*. Two natives pay fifteen *groshen* each; the storekeeper spied my camera and the price for me promptly went up to forty-five *groshen*. The Israeli usually considers the Arab, with minor exceptions, a potential crook if given an opportunity to express his talents, and there is no question that this is most often correct. In Paris the waiter simply cannot part with the correct change and in Jakarta the Moslem cabbie never has any change to give you. Crookedness is a relative term that could be applied to many people everywhere. The kleptomaniac human is not far removed from the kleptomaniac monkey; the question as to who is the greater and more proficient thief is mere rhetoric. Human nature, in spite of all the religions, literature, laws, taboos, commandments, does not trust itself. At another moment I am in Italy, in a fashionable hotel in Rome, writing in bed. The rooms have doors with two or three locks, and there are three sets of window enclosures, from the outer shutters to the inner self-locking doors. In Hong Kong "Watch Out For Pick-pocket" signs are all too common. All over the world man protects himself from man more than from anything else. Man fears man more than anything else.

Theft is not limited to the lowly, the desperate, and hungry, the social derelicts and organized crime; we find it among the high and mighty, in the upper strata of dignified, "respectable," and "high class" people and institutions. Relating to *ethos* and applied ethics in the Arts, it seems that every method—"the ends justify the means"—has been utilized, openly and clandestinely, to obtain, pilfer, and pillage the ancient arts and remains from the lands of their origin. Museum directors, tomb robbers, and undercover middlemen in back alleys have long been cooperative and unholy partners in plundering the dead. The Louvre is stuffed with treasures stolen by Napoleon, and the British Museum proudly displays the Greek marbles Lord Elgin stole from the Parthenon. The Peabody Museum in Cambridge somehow got possession of much of the ancient Mayan arts from Chichen Itza and would not give it back to Mexico. Many of our museums contain caches of stolen works of art purchased from well-known crooks and smuggled illegally out of the countries of origin by all kinds of trickery. Often museums become "fences" for stolen art works from many parts of the world. They feel that if they do not grab them up another museum will, so it is a race to see who gets there first with the mostest. When it comes to ethics, some of the "highest" and most "reputable" institutions are willing to stoop very low in their competitive greed of possessiveness to obtain precious works of art by committing the basest violations. "Meanwhile the rape of Turkey goes on. Italian and American yachts, evading Turkish coast guard patrols, have been known to slip inshore, close to the ruins of the Roman town of Side under cover of night, and with their crews, dynamite Greek and Roman antiquities from their setting. . . . In ten years' time in Turkey there will be nothing."[223]

Regarding the *ethos* and sense of justice of the Western countries toward the primitive and semi-primitive people of the more recently historical periods, such as the Eskimos, the American Indians from Hudson Bay to the Magellan Straits, from the Leeward Islands of the Caribbean, the natives of many islands sprinkled over the vast oceanic areas of Polynesia and Melanesia, Khartoum to the Kalahari and the Cape of Good Hope. we have stuffed our museum halls and closets with their many exotic and unique arts and artifacts, preserving their cultural remains, yet never giving much thought to helping them better their lot, considering them as we consider ourselves, extending friendship and cultivating a cordial feeling to foster mutual understanding and assistance. Instead, "civilized" man has robbed both the living and the dead, defrauded, murdered, impoverished, and emasculated the primitives. Civilized man has created a hell on earth for all these people, and his missionaries have provided them with a hell after they die, to make sure they get it both now and forever.

Apart from the obvious fact that freedom does not imply a concomitant measure of discipline or responsibility, it does not even assure that justice and freedom are always attracted to each other. Justice necessitates some surrender of sovereignty to order, to what may be rationally considered to be clearly just, honest and fair. Even when people are freed from a previous state of subjection, it is historically observed in many cases that such new independence brought about a state of irresponsibility, a total lapse of justice, chaos, nihilistic confusion, and a general breakdown of humanity into shivers of paranoic pandemonium. Escape from subjection often exacts its own toll of adjustment, and the price of adjustment is too often and sadly the penalty that the innocents have to pay and suffer. It is not that independence is to be avoided and that slavery is the greater security; man, by his life right, merits independence as by his life right he expresses freedom. What is important is that freedom, although naturally uncommitted to responsibility and justice, necessitates the responsibility and justice to mature its better, finer, and more peaceful expression.

The French Revolution and the emergence of Hitlerism as a form of rebellion are just two instances of many where such cataclysms have so tragically occurred. The Government of the United States and thousands of its so-called civilized white gentry, being free and independent, certainly did not express any concomitance of justice and responsibility when millions of buffalo were wantonly and wastefully slaughtered on the American plains as a means of exterminating the Indians by starvation. Civilization has not yet proven that independence and freedom bring justice, ethics, and humaneness. "Karamojo" Bell, an English white hunter, coming from the highly civilized society of Britannica, writes about the pleasure of killing in Africa: "There is nothing more satisfying than the complete flop of a running elephant shot in the brain!"[224] Jean-Pierre Hallet tells us about the Congolese when they very recently achieved their independence: "During the first days of the Congo's newly granted freedom, more than a thousand elephants were slaughtered in the Albert National Park alone. Buffaloes, antelopes, and hippos died with them, massacred in such incredible numbers that vulture and hyena scavengers couldn't keep up with the corpses. After thirty-five years of complete protection, the animals had forgotten the very meaning of guns. They watched, trustingly, as hordes of native poachers came to shoot them for their tusks, meat, or horns. Mutinous soldiers of the Congolese army joined in the carnage. Some of them, as one mutineer informed me, machine-gunned elephants or blew them up with hand grenades, 'just for the fun of it.' "[225] The civilized and the savage are not too far apart; they are both human. In both we find people from the finest, responsible, and most peaceful to the worst, most cruel, and criminal. And all free.

Civilized man has little justifiable right to talk of ethics and justice. Even though highly improbable and not to be expected, he still might learn the tenets of ethics from the innocents he has despoiled, diseased, and decimated. Not that the primitive is better or finer than the civilized man, but the civilized man has assured for himself a better and finer status, and this status is, when all is said and done, his own self-mirrored concept of what is better and finer. The primitive may be as savage as the civilized man if he tries hard enough, but the primitive with his blowgun can kill only one victim at a time, whereas civilized man, being more intelligent and "progressive," has a high-powered machine-gun that can mow down hundreds in a moment. The primitive, in finding food, must use his spear and hunt his beast in close quarters; the civilized man, being wise, can stay hundreds of yards away in safety and comfort and kill the beast with his rifle. The primitive hunts for food to eat, or for someone's head to increase his spiritual power or make him competent for marriage; the civilized man, being a "sportsman," hunts for trophies, for pleasure, *the pleasure of killing,* and adorns his home with the animal's head and carpets his floor with the animal's skin, just as the primitive savage. One cannot, in all reasonableness, consider one more ethical than the other.

We cannot be a primitive any more than we can turn the clock back and relive time already spent. We would not want to, being already born and patternized in present cultural acquisitions. This does not prevent us, in our vain efforts to be constructively critical and analytical, from seeing the realities of civilization's products, processes, and directions, from noting the thin surface appearances of cultural decorations, below which, when this veneer is penetrated, we can observe that the animalism and primitivism of man has hardly changed, that he is still contained, helplessly, in his basal traits and drives of cruelty, self-beguilement, and the innate emotional tendency to betray himself by refusal or inability, to avoid the acceptance of realities which in the ultimate can be the only basis upon which he may find himself and receive the values of freedom through self-identity.

The primitive may steal a wife from another; the civilized man may covet another's wife, and if successful, as so many are, possess her, momentarily, temporarily, or permanently. Who is more ethical is a matter of judgment, depending upon who's taking whom. The primitive may steal something that belongs to another, not even knowing the meaning of theft or that he is doing anything wrong; the civilized man, if he happens to be a banker, a Wall Street manipulator, a politician, or some high echelon industrial executive, can be found often enough to be an expert in getting money without really working for it, expressing his power of wealth to get more and more, so much so that if he lived five hundred years he could not possibly begin to reduce the principal; yet he still wants more ever increasingly to his dying day. If a civilized man would render judgment, he would consider the primitive a plain, animalistic crook, to be beaten, caged, or eliminated to solve a problem, and he would consider the banker and industrial executive as performing their wizardry always within the outer periphery of what is considered lawful, as a successful, shrewd, and highly qualified genius who must be placed substantially far above the plebeians of his society. The question as to who is more ethical, honest, and fair, the primitive or the banker, is not easy to answer; this depends upon the extent of illiteracy of the primitive and upon the honesty and integrity of the banker and his own ways and opinions of right and wrong. We may enlighten ourselves through the primitive: Claude Lévi-Strauss feels that "a primitive people is not a backward or retarded people; indeed it may possess a genius for invention or action that leaves the achievements of civilized peoples far behind."

It is one thing to know the meaning of ethics, and it is quite another thing to act *ethically*. The primitive, being relatively ignorant, probably has little if any knowledge of the meaning of ethics, and the civilized man may know much about it, but so long as both do not *act* as ethical persons, it does not really matter in ethics whether one is primitive or civilized. The process and the ends are the same. The only difference one can perceive is that the primitive, just as the child, does not seem to know better, to realize and differentiate between right and wrong, but knows merely what he desires or needs. The civilized man, on the other hand, usually knows and realizes the elements of equity yet *pretends* to be ethical while actually *acting* unethically.

Civilization may indicate material progress, all types of advanced and still advancing technologies—air-conditioning, television, and a thousand other things including such civilized toys as atom bombs, supersonic bombers, air pollution, and a list of new diseases born of anxiety, stress, conflict, subconscious rebellion, confusion and endless routine—but many of these things have made men and women more comfortable, their lives more pleasurable because of less physical work. They have hardly made them happier because gradually the individual, in modern society, with its impersonal, unconscious drives to engulf him, Durkheim-wise, has lost to a great extent his sense of self-identity in the maelstrom of numbers and organizations. So long as an individual remains a free individual, he will be able to sense, apply, and carry on because of relationships and associations, to contemplate, analyze ethics, and activate it in his own living experiences due to the responsibilities that self-identity generates and cultivates between individuals.

The termite has no need of ethics, nor does it know of any. All its behaviors and instincts have been consigned to the termite State, of which it is a mere segment. It is a living automaton without self-identity and without even temporary self-sufficiency. It is born, grows, and exists only for the termitary. The fallacy of Durkheim is that so long as humans exist there will be some who will always carry on the torch of freedom to keep the individual free enough to process the society for *his* betterment, not process him to build a society for its own ends of needless and fallacious ideology. Man is more important than ideology, whether it be an ideology of religion, political form, society, or anything else. A human individual *lives*, breathes, exists for a limited period and then *has to die*. Ideologies are born of men's minds and emotions; of themselves they are nothing save what man makes them appear to be. If we must have an ideology, it should be, if ethics prevails, dedicated to bettering man, not subjecting his only life as a sacrifice to any ideology. Man, in being good to *himself* and preserving himself, transcends this inferential reflection to the good of *others,* and enters into the sanctum where ethics can be knowingly and actively applied in one's direction toward his own life and to the world.

No animal in the world talks so much about freedom as the human being and does so much to freeze it, abandon it, enslave it, abort it, discolor it, sell himself short on it, leave it, forget it, manage to get along somehow with little of it. Actually *he is the only animal that talks himself out of it.* So many humans have fought for it and died for it, and when it seemed to be achieved, handed it over to others who enslaved them again. The greatest poets of old and new have given us words on freedom that swept us up like little clouds and floated us across the clear sky toward the fresh wind, the sun and warmth. Many painters have glorified us in color, reminding us of the acts of genius that can operate only in a sphere of uninhibited and relaxed freedom. Many composers have given us the beauty of song and sound that have sweetened our ears and inspired our minds and requited our anxieties. Many great sculptors have cut and carved out of wood, stone, and metal, and created images that have communicated to us the lowness and greatness, and the simplicities of both, of ourselves and the world about us. Yet we do not seem to understand that all the energy that moved all these creators and creations came out of the surging, helpless whirlpool of life, which continues its motion out of a process that is, at its root, a free process, free in the sense that it operates freely in a limited or unlimited field, whatever and whichever view we take, but still operates, to this extent, freely. Every great character in history, every great poet, painter, philosopher, or even every great lover, attempted to express and attain a higher individuality, to portray himself through the medium of his genius. Bertrand Russell: "Respectability, regularity, and routine—the whole cast-iron discipline of a modern industrial society—have atrophied the artistic impulse, and imprisoned love so that it can no longer be generous and free and creative, but must be either stuffy or furtive."[226] "The decay of art in our times is not only due to the fact that the social function of the artist is not as important as in former days; it is due also to the fact that spontaneous delight is no longer felt as something which it is important to be able to enjoy. Among comparatively unsophisticated populations folk dances and popular music still flourish, and something of the poet exists in very many men. But as men grow more industrialized and regimented, the kind of delight that is common in children becomes impossible to adults, because they are always thinking of the next thing, and cannot let themselves be absorbed in the moment. This habit of thinking of the 'next thing' is more fatal to any kind of aesthetic excellence than any other habit of mind can be imagined, and if art, in any important sense, is to survive, it will not be by the foundation of solemn academies, but by recapturing the capacity for wholehearted joys and sorrows which prudence and foresight have all but destroyed."[227] Janheinz Jahn: "African philosophy consistently stands on the side of the artist; for it the finished work as it stands in the museum has nothing more to do with art; it is a 'thing,' it is wood, vocable, lead, ivory, glass, colour—nothing more. It is not the artistic product that is important in African philosophy, but the fashion in which the creative, form-giving process takes effect."[228]

When any inequitable act, custom, dogma, pattern, or law turns into a restraint upon this freedom of creativeness and individuality, chills it, retards it, misconstrues it, prevents it, to this extent life, the precious and only life we really know of, is injured, wasted, mischanneled. Must we continue to go about as dismal, ascetic monks or mechanized and regimented segments of industrialization, trying to escape from what is rightfully the inalienable right of everyone; to turn our faces from the joyful, from the sun, from whatever happiness time and event may be fortunate to give us within our all-too-brief and limited time? Can the human being overcome the tendency, cultured by culture and all its offspring, to be stone-deaf to his inner nature to want to be happy, to be peaceful, to be creative and uninhibited, to be satisfied? Must we all our lives be "Sammies" running but not knowing where? Is the trait of human indifference and cruelty so deep-rooted in us that we deserve no better destination than eventual self-extermination? And what is the ultimate end of all cruelty? Yet there is something fine in many of us, something that wants us to look up to the sun, to be tolerant, helpful, peaceful, sympathetic, hospitable, kind, and generous. Must humanity continue its historical neurosis of defeating its own natural and rational processes and ends? No philosopher can answer these questions. What will be will be. Whether we exist or not is of no concern to the universe or even to our own little world. The ultimate destination should not concern us; we will not be around to think about it. What does concern us is the brief time we happen to be here, without asking to be, but nevertheless here.

History, experiences of individuals and groups, wisdom, all funnel themselves into the realization that man can exist only within some orderly group or organization, and, indeed, this has proved to be the case. Where society disintegrated for some reason or other, the people and their culture also disintegrated, or became absorbed in some new or modified form of organization and culture which eventually rose in its place. The freedom of man should be directed not to destroy organization but to educate himself so that he might understand why it exists, its values and functions; that organization exists or should exist for him and his kind, that its power should be directed to serve, extend, and preserve the greatest potential of freedom for the individual; that the individual has it within his right and intelligence, in the expression of his freedom, to change the organizational structure to meet new challenges, conditions, and situations, and to continue the securities and satisfactions of the individuals within such an order in the solution of common problems affecting them. This was the preprimitive purpose of the clan, kinship, and tribal relationship and "pooling" of fears and securities to form group or societal strength for the individual. Man, in his modern confusions, must try to regain these primordial intentions, elemental as they are, in order to sustain present and new forms of equitable society, in which true ethics can flourish and operate for the meaningful good of each and possibly all.

This latitude of freedom and a philosophy of social, economic, and political ethics cannot emanate from any society which considers itself as an end unto itself, to maintain and expand its power as an impersonalized structure to control, to enslave directly or indirectly if necessary, and to limit the freedom of people merely to secure the maintenance and power of the structure itself. John Dewey: "A society that chiefly esteems order, that finds growth painful and change disturbing, inevitably seeks for a fixed body of superior truths upon which it may depend. It looks backward, to something already in existence, for the source and sanction of truth. It falls back upon what is antecedent, prior, original, *a priori,* for assurance. The thought of looking ahead, toward the eventual, toward consequences, creates uneasiness and fear."[229]

Any form of totalitarianism and authoritarianism as exemplified in the political forms of Communism, Fascism, Nazism, dictatorships, oligarchies, police states, etc., or in the religious forms of dogmatisms, psychological duress, and sterile, antinatural conformance without reason or practical justification, or in the economic forms of expanding corporate growths in which the expressive individuality and personality of people are more or less lost in the labyrinth of helpless and pressured cohesion and loss of self-identity as the result of organizational absorptions—all these forms are depressors of natural and cultural freedom and only tend to lessen the potential of life satisfactions which should be natural and normal expressions in the lives of people.

Ethics is the confession that man has to guard himself against man. Ethical principles are formed so that man can be enculturated with them as acceptable forms of behavior and conduct that would *safeguard* the lives, property, sphere of movement and activity which, according to the ethic, is the *just* and *rightful* prerogative of people. Ethics is a *practical attempt* to foster and allow people to live not only in an orderly manner but also in a peaceful manner in which there is a reasonable regard and respect of individual and mutual privileges and rights. Thus, *democracy* is the political attempt to reach some kind of ethical order in which the societal organization itself is recognized as the *medium* by which the equitable rights of individuals are so respected and regarded and protected. A democratic ethic is the admission that an individual allows himself to be subject to the necessary limitations of democratic society so that he himself may be benefited by the most possible extensions of personal freedom for which the democratic polity is supposed to be dedicated.

THE ESSENTIALITY OF LAW AND ORDER

Law WITHIN A truly democratic society is for the primary protection of individuals against individuals or groups formed by individuals. Without law individuals, left to themselves and to their judgments and actions, would create nihilism and anarchy and thus destroy any order in which an individual can be *really* free and secure from himself and others. Human nature, in *actuality,* considers its immediate needs, impulses, and compulsions; a democratic society, in actuality, considers the preservation of its order and power as a protector for *continuing* order and events. It is the social and political drive of democratic institutions to protect the continuing future against present disintegration that creates in itself, by its precepts and laws, the protective security for the individuals who comprise it. Here again we see the democratic order as a *process,* not as an end unto itself, in contradistinction to the political organizations and self-sustaining elements of the priest-king-divinity forms as they existed in ancient Egypt, Sumeria, Cambodia, and other countries in the past, and exist today in many parts of the world, and the later monarchial and imperial systems in which the constituents or subjects were merely used as a means to sustain the élite few, and the people were practically enslaved by various types of power, psychological and physical, their lives expended for the priest-king echelons and the aristocratic order of "nobilities" they created.

Everything in the universe appears to be related to everything in it. Nothing is really apart from all else. Freedom, in its essence, identifies itself as a process rising out of relationships. To maintain freedom is to maintain the₁ compatible relationship necessary for its expression, process and continuance. Thus, we see the cyclic recurrence of its very life and existence as a regenerating or degenerating activity determined by the pressures and resistances within its constant process of experience.

Compatibility in freedom, therefore, necessitates, in turn, some "sacrifice" in the sovereignty of freedom in order to protect its process. Commitment to some necessary responsibility is the "sacrifice" of some freedom or "sovereignty" in order to assure its beneficence. When this commitment is understood in this light, then such commitment ceases to sense itself as an obligation or duty and becomes a compatible responsibility. The understanding of this necessitated compatibility is the foundation of democracy, which, in itself, seeks to create an *orderly* process within an order of people free enough and wise enough to maintain it.

Disorder destroys freedom. Violence and the nihilistic effects it produces disperse freedom into self-defeating confusions, extreme, irrational, self-destroying, and self-deceiving partialities. Dissent and opposition, within an orderly process of expression and action, will always be a natural and rational stimulant and engaging gear to change, growth, and any possible progress, but when this dissent and opposition become vehicles of folly, neurotic purpose and destruction, then the very freedoms of dissent and opposition become endangered by self-dilution.

Human relationships and the relationships of humans with all else cannot be eliminated without eliminating man; these relationships necessitate social, political, economic, and cutural order, as an orderly process. In order to create such a stabilizing and compatible order, the pillars and structural functions within it must be equated with equity, security, and the potentials that foster the reasonable fulfillment of life satisfactions. Nature, itself, in all its roots and extensions, appears to be an order of compatibility evolved over billions of years; man, a biological infant, must learn this process if he, as Nature itself has helplessly done, will be fortunate to understand it *in time*.

Order does not mean a dogmatism, a rigid absolute, for these are merely *concepts* of order, an ideology, not order itself. There can be no dogma or absolutism so long as freedom expresses itself; there can be no genuine order unless it contains within its process of order the freedoms necessary to flex its structure to change and adjustment. When the processes of change and adjustment are part of the concomitant expression of freedom within order, then we can reasonably say that here we have democracy in process, a process that is capable of peaceful and constructive change within a larger, wider, and peripheral parallel of stability. Such an order seems to be essential to human peace and to the human relationship and direction to all else.

It is reasonable to presume that the purpose of law is the

means of orderly living, by which people, in acknowledging it and submitting to it, bring upon themselves the possibility of various securities for and from each other. Whether it actually accomplishes this depends upon the kind and nature of the law itself, the nature of the people and the relationships and experiences of both upon each other. Eichmann, on trial for his life in Jerusalem, claimed the "law" as his guardian angel to justify his terrible crimes upon the Jewish people. Referring to Eichmann, Hannah Arendt reports: "Whatever he did he did, as far as he could see, as a law-abiding citizen. He did his *duty,* as he told the police and the court over and over again; he not only obeyed *orders,* he also obeyed the *law.*"[230]

Whatever be the nature of people, thousands of years of human experience and association have culminated in certain common and statutory laws essential and mandatory in order to maintain an orderly society. But whether the law or the society, or both, is based on any ethical principle or human sense of justice and goodness, is a question that begs definition depending on those who are doing the defining. Cruel people will enact cruel laws and cruel laws are oppressive to good people. Laws that are anti-natural and irrational, so that they cannot be normally and reasonably operable, become depressors, and the people will find ways to violate them and make them impracticable and meaningless. As people change, the interpretations and meaningfulness and effectiveness of laws also change. All laws are human products, and products made by humans often become obsolete or modify themselves as humans modify themselves. Law should never be dogma, but a *servant* and *guide* serving the best interests of the people. Law, an external factor affecting the thought, conduct, and behavior of people, should also be realistic and reasonable. To be reasonable and practical demands an ever increasing knowledge of ourselves and our environments, the world in which we live; it should not be based on what we idealistically and poetically dream it up to be. Any anthropocentric view is wishful thinking that has only misled us away from life and into spheres of illusions and defraudments. John Dewey: "External reasonableness or adaptation to ends precedes reasonableness of mind."[231] Much of our wishful thinking today regarding crimes and criminals is unrealistic and does not confront with the basic causes and influences that make for crime. Kluckhohn: "Most criminals are not ordinarily neurotic, and do not become candidates for analysis. Society may wish to change them or they may wish to change society, but they rarely wish to change themselves."[232]

Realistic and operable laws that desire to maintain some sense of ethics have to meet up with the basic needs of living and which, more often than not, are economic. Maurice Parmelee: "The criminality of any time and place is conditioned and to a considerable extent determined by the existing economic system."[233] Louis Harris: "The science of criminology is a branch of the science of sociology,"[234] and sociology must be primarily concerned with the economics of life, with the basic essentials necessary to a curriculum of normal factors that can assure a peaceful and healthful community. Albert Schweitzer: "Ethics have materialistic instincts. They want to be concerned with empirical happenings and to transform the circumstances of the empirical world."[235] "My solution to the problem [ethics] is that we must make up our minds to renounce completely the optimistic-ethical interpretation of the world. If we take the world as it is, it is impossible to attribute to it a meaning in which the aims and objects of mankind and of individual men have a meaning also. Neither world- and life-affirmation nor ethics can be founded on what our knowledge of the world can tell us about the world. In the world we can discover nothing of any purposive evolution in which our activities can acquire a meaning. Nor is the ethical to be discovered in any form in the world-process. The only advance in knowledge that we can make is to describe more and more minutely the phenomena which make up the world and their implications. To understand the meaning of the whole— and that is what a world-view demands—is for us an impossibility. The last fact which knowledge can discover is that the world is a manifestation, and in every way a puzzling manifestation, of the universal will to live. . . . We are not meant to unite the world and ourselves in such harmony with one another."[236]

We cannot change the nature of nature; that is what the metaphysicians have been trying to do for thousands of years. What we can do is try to understand more and more the realities of our own ecology as well as the ecology of the life about us, to preserve it and better it if we can and not waste or destroy it. We are tied to the earth not by gravitation alone. By wasting and destroying our own ecological assets, to which other life on which we depend for existence is also tied, we will undermine, by our greed and indifference, the natural formulae that makes life and living possible. Lynn White, Jr., exposes the tendency of Christianity throughout its history to inculcate norms and usages into the cultures of the West which have been, and still are destructive to nature in general and to ecological environments: "Especially in its Western form, Christianity is the most anthropocentric religion the world has seen. . . . Christianity, in absolute contrast to ancient paganism and Asia's religions (except perhaps Zoroastrianism), not only established a dualism of man and nature but also insisted that it is God's will that man exploit nature for his own ends. . . . In antiquity every tree, every spring, every stream, every hill, had its own *genius loci,* its guardian spirit. These spirits were accessible to men, but were very unlike men. Before one cut a tree, mined a mountain, or dammed a brook, it was important to placate the spirit in charge of that particular situation, and to keep it placated. By destroying animism, Christianity made it possible to exploit nature in a mood of indifference to the feelings of natural objects. . . . It is often said that for animism the Church substituted the cult of saints. True; but the cult of saints is functionally quite different from animism. The saint is not *in* natural objects; he may have special shrines, but his citizenship is in heaven. . . . The spirits *in* natural objects, which formerly had protected nature from man, evaporated. Man's effective monopoly of spirit in this world was confirmed, and the old inhibitions to the exploitation of nature crumbled."[237] "Despite Darwin, we are *not,* in our hearts, part of the natural process. We are superior to nature, contemptuous of it, willing to use it for our slightest whim. . . . The whole concept of the sacred grove is alien to Christianity and to the ethos of the West. For nearly two millenniums Christian missionaries have been chopping down sacred groves, considering them idolatrous because they assume spirit in nature. . . . We shall continue to have a worsening ecologic crisis until we reject the Christian axiom that nature has no reason for existence save to serve man. . . . Both our present science and our present technology are so tinctured with orthodox Christian arrogance toward nature that no solution for our ecologic crisis can be expected from them alone."[238] Lynn White sums it up: "Our present combustion of fossil fuels threatens to change the chemistry of the globe's atmosphere as a whole, with consequences that we are only beginning to guess. With the population explosion, the carcinoma of planless urbanism, the now geological deposits of sewage and garbage, surely no creature other than man ever managed to foul its nest in such short order."[239]

Abundance there could be if our own crimes against ourselves and our environment were less abundant. We must realize that whether we have intelligence or not, whether we can write poetry or not, we still must eat, and a satisfied stomach usually makes more possible an ethical mind. As Shakespeare put it:

> Famine is in thy cheeks,
> Need and oppression starveth in thy eyes,
> Upon thy back hangs ragged misery,
> The world is not thy friend, nor the world's law.

Laws are rules people are to abide by and not violate. The continual occurrence of violation does not mean that the law is bad or that the people are good, or the other way around, but it does mean that a law is insufficient for the purpose of societal orderliness and peacefulness when its laws are constantly violated. Whether the law is supposed to operate as a deterrent, that is, punishing the violator to deter others; or whether the law's punishment is reformative, to reorientate or rehabilitate the offender; or whether the law acts as a retributive factor, that is, the offender must suffer for his deed, which comes to us from the old *lex talionis* codes of ancient countries—all of these do not eliminate crime any more than one can eliminate human nature. The retributive theory of punishment is innate and expressive, even compulsive, in the very instincts of people. If one gets hit, it is natural and self-preservative to hit back; the counterattack is justified by the attack. This is the way it has always been in human experience, attack and counterattack. The "ethics" of human nature is such today that the calendars of our courts are heavily overloaded, and all we can possibly do is to make more courts, appoint more judges, make more laws, exact more punishments. Lillie: "It is not only the case that punishment has an instinctive origin, but it appears to be a necessary implication of man's living in society. A social organization requires to have certain rules or laws as we call them; otherwise it will break down. . . . If laws are a necessary condition of our life in organized societies, and they appear to be so, then there must be some penalty for disobeying them."[240] Yet it is also true, as Morris Raphael Cohen states, "That in the long run justice in the law is a matter of faith, not of knowledge. It will certainly not occur so long as men lack complete knowledge and perfect good will."[241]

What could be done is to explore all possible causative facts and try to overcome them. Happy and satisfied people usually do not attack or commit crime; yet often the nature of certain people will lead them to commit crime in any event, whether they are happy or not. However, history proves that wars were generally begun by people who were in need, the have-nots, and those usually attacked were those who "had." There is no denying that wars were often initiated for political and ideological reasons, but the common people rarely supported such wars except when the power-authority forms of leadership succeeded in emotionalizing them to do so. People who were settled were agricultural as a rule, had cattle and raised their own food supply, lived in a beneficent environment, and seldom went out to conquer others.

Crime exposes the lack of something, some dissatisfaction, something needed, or a condition of psychotic, mental, or physical illness. If society for some reason or other provides the stage for the nonfulfillment of needed things, it also provides the crimes. Society provides the environment for its members, or we can say that society *consists* of the environment, and unless this environment is such that the basic natural freedoms are allowed to be reasonably expressed in order to attain satisfactions, then violation, violence, and crime occur. In order to assure the maintenance of some order in an equitable and democratic society, it is essential that the humans in it receive the proper education and freedom of thought so that the individuals can cultivate a

way of conduct and principles of thinking that would create out
of their own enlightenment sufficient ethics to warrant and allow
these natural freedoms to exhibit themselves with less societal
restraint and imposition.

To this must be added a sound economy in which individuals
have at least some reasonable *opportunity* to work and obtain
the necessities of living; a rational process of education that allows
the young to think freely and learn freely without indoctrination;
and usages and laws that, while they are fully cognizant of the
animalism in human nature, are not of a nature that would tend
to coerce people into an unnatural and antinatural way of living;
and the application and organization of scientific approaches to
the diagnoses, analyses, and treatment of those unfortunates who
are afflicted with neurological and organic diseases caused by, or
the direct cause of, abnormal and subnormal behavior making
for misery and crime. Lillie: "The tendency of certain forms of
criminality to occur most commonly among people with a fairly
low intelligence quotient is well established, and this certainly
suggests that a certain amount of ability is advantageous for living a good life."[242] Ernest Renan: "The end of humanity, and
therefore the aim which political conduct should keep before it,
is to realize the highest human culture possible, that is to say, the
most perfect religion, by science, philosophy, art and morality:
in a word by all the means of attaining the ideal which are in the
nature of man."[243] Soterios Nicholson: "He who expects the
achievement of the maximum, the ideally good and perfect, will
be surely disappointed, and bitter tears will shed from the person
who sets his heart upon catching the moon. But he who, shutting
his eyes to schemes of Utopian perfection, aims only at the better,
and from the better moves on to the still better, who is not discouraged by failures, but makes of obstacles stepping stones for
further progress in a path of which he does not see the end, a
practical idealist, in short, will surely not be disappointed."[244]

Regardless of how high man's wisdom may reach, it is still a
pliable and changeable factor, and adjusts and justifies itself in
meeting new situations. Law must act likewise, and it can so act,
not in a dictatorial or authoritarian form of government or as a
rigid and dogmatic theological organization, but as a society

wherein the democratic process is the foundation of the society. The American Constitution is a *process* of principle, recognized and respected by the people (or should be), to interpret properly this process of democratic thought and practice. When a constituted authority ceases to function as a process and becomes an end unto itself, it becomes meaningless to the people and begins to age, to degenerate, and in time brings about its own end by the inertia and rigidity of its psychological structure. The only plausible rule to follow is to informalize all rules and to accept the proposition that all standards are subject to change by newer needs, adjustments, and essentialities, and to subordinate these standards to the flexibility of movement and the operable needs of freedom itself, which means that rules will exist for people and not people for rules. Self-knowledge, increased education in the humanities and the teaching of ethical culture to the young, these things should enculturate people to think in ethical terms and behave intelligently and justly by understanding the purpose and need of any rule for *their* benefit. Man does not come into the world with a book of rules in his hand, and he does not die that way; if between these two points there must be any rules, let them be rules to further and assure his happiness, not his misery. To formalize ethics is to standardize behavior, conduct, and thought into categorical procedures that become, by the nature of the process, stagnant and immobilized to meet new situations, new considerations and judgments. The meeting of new situations should be the continual vigilance and analysis of the actual experiences and their consequences, and this entails both the scientific and rational faculties.

What may seem logical may not really be true or existent and what is real very often appears illogical: this is the result of the human-partiality complex to begin with. Morris Raphael Cohen: "While logic helps us to see the inadequacies of existing rules and the possibility of varying them or departing from them, it cannot by itself determine what new premises are necessary to make the law work more satisfactorily or to satisfy the maximum of human needs."[245] Justice Holmes once stated that "the life of the law has not been logic, it has been experience."[246] Yet logic and experience are both essential to the nature of law; they complement each other. Many laws may be logical but not provable or practically demonstrable in the actual experiences of people. Many experiences of people are such that they appear illogical to the legal philosopher and to the decorum of legal procedure. The legally idealistic need of what seems to be logically required in the mind of the legal philosopher often clashes in a tug-of-war with the paradoxes and incomprehensible behaviors of the human animal, as a unit and as a group of human animals—the *mob*. However, if a democratic process of lawmaking and law-abiding is to be reasonably achieved and successful, then the individuals within the society should be able to have the opportunity of education and economic stability to allow them to understand, appreciate, and coordinate their liberties and privileges within such a society. Professor Cohen adds another note: "Liberties and privileges are part of the legal system. . . . Its realization cuts the ground from the anarchistic error that all law is restraint on freedom, so that the less legislation, the more men are free. Legislation makes a change within the legal system; and if it takes away the liberty of some, it thereby creates liberties for others. Whether the total result is good or bad must be determined by an analysis of all the actual consequences and not by the mere fact that there has been legislation."[247]

Human rights have been classified as the right to live, the right to freedom, the right to hold property, the right of contract, the right to obtain an education, and others. But these rights should include the right of movement, the right of freedom of thought and expression, the freedom of conscience, the right to be happy, the right to be healthy, the right to oppose impressment or conscription to do harm or to injure others. There is the right of the individual to expect the society to respect his right of individual opinion and not to use methods of various types and degrees to oppose the flow and expression of individual opinion.[248] George Gaylord Simpson: "The means of gaining right ends involve both organic and human evolution, but human choice as to what *are* the right ends must be based on human evolution. . . . The old evolution was and is essentially amoral. The new evolution involves knowledge, including the knowledge of good and evil."[249] Yet knowledge, including the knowledge of good and bad concepts, is transitory and changing, always evolving as the organics; everything is always in some engagement of process; therefore, any rational system of learning must be based on particulars, not on the assumption of universals. The door must always be kept open to new ideas; this, too, is part of human evolution.

C. H. Waddington wrote in his book, *The Ethical Animal:* "Values are products of human culture, not of the human genotype. But in order to become an 'ethicizing being' man must be an 'authority acceptor' and talks about a child developing an 'authority-bearing system.' Thus a successfully socialized infant grows to become an effective member of the society."[250] This presupposes that ethics is a cultural imposition upon the biological state, which it is, in order to maintain social stability and order. While it seems logical that a human within a group grows up to accept the usages and even the authority of his order or society because this is the way that people, as they do grow up, patternize themselves according to their particular culture and learn to accept these usages and forms of authority, yet the nature and changeability of authority itself should become knowledgeable and conscious factors to the individual, that this knowledge and consciousness must have the concomitant ability to make such changes within the societal structure and authority that the ends of this authority-form may forever be, not as an end unto its own power, but a means of fulfilling the primordial process of human beings to make for themselves, as living things and not as corporate subjects, a satisfied and a possibly happy existence. Waddington seems to overlook the fact that human experience, of which culture is a consequence, is basically rooted in the biological, and if the socialized infant is not to grow up into a regimented robot without the natural freedom of individuality, then the society must be of such a nature and process as to allow the individual to grow up as one, which necessitates, within the bounds of social compatibility, an essential quantum of flexibility and free-flowing expression to keep this individualism free-flowing and naturally free. The feudal lords liked very much to see their subjects grow up as authority-acceptors; so do the Communist leaders and dictators like Franco and Nkrumah. Authority-acceptors do not, as a rule, threaten the rule over themselves, and those in arbitrary and naked power always idealized the wonderful spirit of the abiding authority-accepting people as almost reverential patriotism. Bertrand Russell: "I do not think the reconciliation of primitive impulses with the civilized way of life is impossible, and the studies of anthropologsts have shown the very wide adaptability of human nature to different culture patterns. But I do not think it can be achieved by complete exclusion of any basic impulse."[251] The most basic impulse within which all the other impulses create themselves is the natural freedom of mind and body, the freedom for the mind and body to live according to their nature, including the freedom to change for the better.

As many have stated, there seems to be little doubt that freedom is a two-way street. Freedom, as a natural biological trait, is not concerned with what one "ought" or "should" do, or what is "proper" or what is expected of "fine," "civilized," or "respectable" people. As a natural, innate factor, it is concerned primarily with what one *can, wants, desires,* or *must* do in order, knowingly or unknowingly, to carry on this expression and activity of freedom. Individualism, according to Lillie, is "the assertion by the individual of his own opinions, beliefs, his own independence and interests as over and against group standards, authority and interests."[252]

HUMANISM AND HUMAN NATURE

"HUMANISM," WRITES CORLISS LAMONT, "reserves the right to disagree with or defy any governmental or other authority. The final court of appeal for the Humanist is his own conscience and intelligence."[253] These are strong words, indeed, and whether they are justified or not depends upon the type and quality of individual expressing them; and whether the society or government or authority merits defiance and denial also depends upon the type and quality of authority involved, but no one can really deny the inherent right of the individual to speak his own mind honestly and to use his intelligence as a critical barrier or acceptor of whatever compatibility the particular form of society or authority allows him to absorb and still remain the individual he wants to be. If we are to presume that it may be just for one individual or group to follow or live by the precepts, principles or directives, voluntarily or involuntarily, of another individual or group, even though these may not be receptive or acceptive, then we can reasonably conclude that it is natural and inevitable that man must be, in some form or other, to some greater or lesser extent, a slave, and that from this he should not even try to escape any more than he can escape from himself or the earth. John Dewey: "The causes remain which brought philosophy into existence as an attempt to find an intelligent substitute for blind custom and blind impulse as guides to life and conduct. The attempt has not been successfully accomplished."[254] But we must keep trying, as we must try to keep living, for living is always *trying,* in a sort of way, and may our intelligence, whatever it is, keep trying to make our lives better so far as we can see and feel what appears to us to be better, and perhaps in doing so bring about a better world for ourselves and for those we leave behind.

The history of man's attempt to restore his natural freedom and still try to maintain some sensible order of society, with all its concomitant conscious and unconscious limitations, potentials and probabilities, is strewn with the courageous lives of people who ideally or pragmatically felt that the individual *can* be free, free in the widest and fullest natural sense, and still enjoy existence within the periphery of human association and social belongings, and with some appreciation of the realities upon which and in which all this is existential and recurring.

Freedom is not a custom but a creator, evolver, and changer of customs. Custom is a cultural product in a natural field, and there are thousands of cultures all over the world; cultures have been born, continued for even long periods of time, and then the custom died, often with its culture. Customs are historical, provincial, local patterns, even to a particular neighborhood or street. Small or large groups may have their special customs, and they become modified in time and place according to the desires of people and changing moods and needs. But freedom remains always the same quantum, as life contains the same quantum.

For the same reasons freedom is not an institution or a code, a constitution or a set of by-laws, although it is imperatively essential for their creation and activities. A person has (or should have) the freedom to believe or disbelieve, but the belief itself is not freedom but a product of it. The Catholic is free to hate the Protestant, and the Protestant is free to hate the Buddhist, and the Buddhist is free to hate the Hindu, and the Hindu is free to hate the Moslem, and the Moslem is free to hate the Jew, but the hate itself is not freedom but a product of it. Everything that man has created by using his freedom, psychological, social, or cultural, can be modified, changed, destroyed, or substituted by newer or different forms. Perhaps some day people may stop hating, and if they should ever accomplish this radical change in human nature, not only could freedom make change possible but perhaps for the better. When one can acknowledge that freedom *can* make changes, it is the beginning of his enlightenment, and of the wisdom to realize that certain things might *warrant* change, and that the freedom of believing means that one can change and believe in something else.

The psychical and physical objectivity of biological foundations have been established through the sciences; it is through the scientific approach in the study of man's natural and cultural needs that human evolution in its various phases may be investigated and possibly controlled for the mutual benefit of man and the world around him. It may be possible, unless humanity destroys itself with hydrogen bombs, that the orderly procedure of the scientific method, not only in the biochemical laboratory but also in the classroom, in the creation of new ideas and forms of organization, might bring about a more ethical animal in *Homo sapiens.*

If this should come to pass, it will be nurtured not so much by the intelligence of man as by the pressures of necessity that intelligence may have to deal with. Hudson Hoagland gives his view: "Societies are built by ideas, and, within limits, the more new ideas there are competing with each other for social acceptance, the more effective social evolution is likely to be. Freedom of individuals to express and develop new ideas is necessary for progress in social evolution, just as many mutations must be screened by natural selection for the development of an improved or a new species of plant or animal. In the case of social evolution the impact of ideas is measurable in years or at least in centuries, while in biological evolution the time scale for mutant genes to establish new forms is measurable in millions of years."[255]

If the individual is to remain one, even in this modern world of increasing complexities, regimented urbanization, exploding populations, economic pressures, the growth of larger and still larger corporate structures, and the lessening of the competitive spirit, then the individual must retain at all costs his character as an independent and reasonably free person, even though this independence and freedom are made more secure by reasonable and appropriate coalescence with a society that justifies its existence and purpose by making possible such independence and freedom. It remains for us to review the purposes of social order and political organization, to try to realign their existences so that the elemental compatibilities essential for free individuals to accept as parts of mass-group societal growth will not deteriorate into the loss of the natural and cultural freedoms without which people no longer remain people but become subjects and numbers and tags to serve abjectly and in resignation to something their natures can never really absorb and still obtain life satisfaction according to their natures.

No one should dismiss the necessity of society or political organization for the purpose of making possible some kind of orderly way for people to live together for mutual benefits without any encroachment upon the securities of its members by any among them. We are also unable to dismiss what history has revealed: that society, once established, most often and with exceptions, impregnated itself as an end unto itself and became an impersonalized power structure, which enslaved, in many ways and forms, its people and diminished in varying degrees the biological and cultural freedoms of the people. It may be true that the judgment of an act as good or bad depends upon its consequences for the individual and society, but when an act is good for the society only and bad for the individuals, then it is time to change the society, since its sole justification to exist is the benefit of the individuals comprising it. We see this one-sidedness at work in the remaining few absolute monarchs in the world today, in the dictatorships of Spain, Portugal, Cuba, in many countries of Latin America and Africa, in the Communist oligarchies of Russia and China: all these are malignant cancers in social, economic, and political structures, and it is the individuals who unfortunately live in these countries who have been bereft of their freedoms and who suffer the ignominy of being slaves and mere numbers, constant sacrifices to the recurring power struggles, constant sacrifices to feed the maintenance of these power structures under the illusion of "good" to come. Hoagland: "The concept of the dignity and brotherhood of man which is common to many ethical systems is a condition necessary to the pursuit of truth. Science leaves no room for the rationalization of quasi-ethical totalitarian ideologies and racial hatreds. These are maintained by coercion and are supported by sacroscanct fictions which are shattered once scientific inquiry is turned upon them."[256]

The bright yellow moon is on the wane and its glow glimmers on the soft hazy ripples of the flats like endless sheets of crumpled glass as I stand on the edge of a long narrow dock fingering itself off the shore in the lunar-lit darkness of the wide ocean. It is in the Florida Keys. The moonlight reveals the clear shallow bottom of the flat, and I see the small blue runners dashing among the minnows, and then suddenly a small cuda charging a busy blue runner and carrying him off crosswise in his tiger-toothed mouth. As I watch this constant drama of sudden death, my mind sees the panorama of all life being just *that,* a continual play of absorption of one thing by another. We humans are a part of this play, and we are stuck with it regardless of our esthetic decoration, emotional sensitivity, and cultural etiquette. In Pasadena a woman weeps for her darling little poodle dog as he is laid to rest in a cushioned bronze casket; in Canton, China, another woman goes to the butcher to see a nice fat chow dog killed fresh and sliced up for the evening meal. In New York a man eats only vegetables and cereals; in Mexico City another man orders a heaping plateful of delicately-roasted locusts to tempt his gourmet desire. In London a peer looks ravishingly at a nicely done quail, and in Singapore another man is seen eating a tenderly-cooked snake, skin, head and all, coiled up to please his genteel taste. There is hardly a living thing, animal or plant, that man has not eaten, including himself. We are truly beasts, free or unfree, and, through the curriculum of a dog-eat-dog way of life, we cannot break our acquired habits to satisfy our conscience or intellectual sense, or our ethically sympathetic feelings. From the truly cruel, from the killing and eating, we cannot escape. We are free in many ways and things, but we are never free from being what we are—*humans.* And humans are killers or eaters of the killed, or both, and if many of us do not have to kill, it is because others kill for us.

When the Ainu took the bear into his household, fed him, played with him, danced around him, revered him, and then killed him for food, we may have considered it circus-like, totemistic, and primitive, but perhaps the Ainu had a finer sense of appreciation and gratitude for the bear's giving up his life so that the Ainu could live than our extinguishing species of fine animals just to sustain our pleasure in killing, not for food, but for trophies and self-emulation as "sportsmen." When the primitive killed a lion it was for security reasons (although kings and princes enjoyed the chase in the good old days as they still do today with safaris), but today a lion is killed so that the hunter can cut off his paws and use them as decorations for his office. When the primitive speared a zebra, he needed it for food, but today zebras are cut down just for their tails, which are sold to tourists as fancy fly-swatters to prove to the folks back home that they traveled to Africa and even went into the bush and saw snakes, crocodiles, and other things, and have pictures to prove it.

Switzerland has been a peaceful country for centuries, geographically well-placed as an easy and close haven for those who seek political refuge, for those who have lost in war, and a money chest for dictators, kings, and police-state leaders from the world over. This traditional security from war allows the Swiss men hardly any outlet for their aggressive drives, so they become hunters! All over this beautiful land the hunters keep shooting and looking for something to shoot at, including much target practice. As a result, many animals once abundant have now disappeared from the Swiss countryside and in the higher mountains. In many parts of the country not even one lonely bear can be found.

Speaking with an official of the Natural History Museum in Chur, I was told that bears no longer exist in the canton.

The extermination of the bear in Europe goes back many centuries. "Emperor Joseph of Austria regarded the bears as outlaw characters and in 1788 decreed their extermination. East Prussia shot its last bear in 1804, and by 1850 bears were wiped out in most parts of Europe."[257] In our own country, unlike the Indians who considered the bears as friends and equals, the white settlers were bent on killing everything in their path in addition to Indians. "Today, hundreds of California communities brag about the big bears they used to have. They point with pride to the golden bear emblem as something special for their state. But a hundred years ago this noblest of all carnivores was treated like the yellow plague and destroyed without mercy. . . . When it was all over, when California had been made safe from all people-killing bears, when a tremendously valuable attraction had gone into oblivion with the great auk and the passenger pigeon—a thoughtful Californian made a remark I shall always remember. 'All the humans slain by California's golden bears in 75 years,' he said, 'probably would not equal the number now killed and maimed on our highways during a holiday weekend.' "[258] "Today, in all the world, only seven kinds of bears survive. It seems strange to surmise—as many naturalists have—that after 25,000,000 years of dominant life on this planet, they may practically all be wiped out of feral existence within the next century; that succeeding generations of humans will know the bears only by peering at stuffed hides in museums."[259] "In the last half of the eighteenth century the Atlas Bear vanished from Morocco, leaving no bears in any part of the great African continent. In North America, the Mendocino grizzly was gone by 1875, Henshaw's grizzly by 1895, the California coast grizzly by 1908, and the Klamath grizzly by 1911. The Tejon and Southern California grizzly both were exterminated by 1916. At least nine other subspecies of grizzly bear, including the great plains grizzly, have vanished in the last hundred and fifty years . . . the polar bear has recently been found to be in danger."[260] "Kotzebue and Point Barrow are crowded in the Spring with big game hunters who seek to bag the vanishing polar bear. . . . At the present rate . . .

polar bears will soon be attractions . . . found only in zoos."[261]

No animal has pushed the rest of the animal kingdom around so much and so indifferently and so heartlessly and with less gratitude as has the human animal. All primitive cultures had a liaison of communication and relationships with, and respect for, their surroundings and surrounding animal and plant life, upon which they depended for survival. True, I have seen savages in the Amazon jungle hold a live monkey by the tail over a fire, and I have seen many other cruelties by man in feeding himself with the lives of others, and this is cruel enough, yet I have never seen a primitive or a savage kill something just for sport. For sport of this kind we must go to the "civilized" man. Man the ethicist still has to eat like the primitive and savage. Whether it is wrong or right, immoral or moral, to kill even for food is something that has to be judged by each individual according to his own esthetic habits and the power of restraint to keep away from a garlic-strewn charcoal-broiled filet mignon. Man has to eat in order to live; this was not his choice but his heritage and nature; no animal or plant has the freedom of choice to be born or not. Freedom comes with one's presence; it is a *fait accompli* of life. Mark Twain explains it this way: "The spider was so contrived that she would not eat grass but must catch flies and such things and inflict a slow and horrible death upon them, unaware that her turn would come next. The wasp was so contrived that he also would decline grass and stab the spider, not conferring upon her a swift and merciful death, but merely half-paralyzing her, then ramming her down into the wasp den, there to live and suffer for days while the wasp babies should chew her legs off at their leisure. In turn, there was a murderer provided for the wasp, and another murderer for the wasp's murderer, and so on throughout the whole scheme of living creatures in the earth. There isn't one of them that was not designed and appointed to inflict misery and murder on some fellow creature and suffer the same in turn from some other murderous fellow creature."[262]

Man the ethicist and moralist has to eat, but let him regain the respect and reverence for life and its symbiotic needs as the Ainu, or the Eskimo in thanking the spirit of the seal for its flesh. The primitive rarely killed needlessly. Needless killing came with "sport" and the desire to be admired for one's acts of "bravery." To the primitive the surrounding country in which he lived was a temple and all its creatures and contents greater or lesser divinities in which he recognized his own place as a *part*. To the primitive, nature itself is his totem and his kin. The modern, in his bedlam-like confusion of mechanization in all directions and in his wild fury for all kinds of power and its indifference to his own kind as well as to other things, has lost touch with these relationships, and with this loss has lost natural freedoms which may possibly never return.

True ethics is based on what we *need* and on the needs of others and what they need of us. Ethics is the science of principles covering human relationships and the things and world in which they create themselves. The respect and wise maintenance of this relating, recurring symbiosis for life satisfaction can be considered the task of ethics. Morals all too often are things which do not exist per se but only in the minds of people, who for some reason or other do not desire to live happily and naturally, and seem often to seek and enjoy seeing other people as miserable as they are themslves.

In society the rights of man are generally amended and interpreted to follow the pattern of their affecting and influencing the common good of the community or social order. However, what the "common good" is at any time is merely the consensus at that particular time, and it has been seen that many laws, usages, and customs, considered indicative and productive of the common good, have been abolished, revised, modified to meet new situations and concepts of the common good. The ability of any social order to make these changes peacefully is indicative of the ability of that particular social order to progress. We have observed in history that individuals who rebelled against the general and common acceptances of their day succeeded in bringing about changes that eventually proved to be increasingly beneficial to the community and the common good, and vice versa.

Many moralists consider the idea of vengeance as something bad, and they may be justified in thinking so, but the affinity and propinquity of moral standards and human nature exigencies depend upon how much the moralist has been wronged or offended. Pain is not a question of choosing nor does it seem to take into account any rational approach to accept it as desirable. There are limits, most assuredly, where even the most altruistic moralist is forced to concern himself with the preservation of his own life and interest. Even Jesus, on the Cross, finally admitted that his God had forsaken him, and so Jesus, too, the supreme altruist, implied the inference of doubt whether his sacrifice was really worthwhile or justified.

It is unfortunate that so many theorists, with the best of hopes and intentions, have, with a great deal of scholarship and erudite detail, arranged and systematized various philosophies on morality, ethics, and conduct, only to reveal that their systems reflected people like themselves who are a very small minority, and who usually have reasonable security, sufficient food, and a comfortable bed, and not the vast hordes of humanity that decide the nature of their morality and ethics by their immediate needs and desires, whither the next meal and where and how to sleep well and securely. Malamud's Yakov in *The Fixer* philosophizes in his humble way: "What choice has a man who doesn't know what his choices are?" It may be all good for one with means, financial and otherwise, to believe in free will because he can make choices and try to carry them out to his satisfaction, but for those without any means, what good are choices when they are incapable of doing anything about them, when they are incarcerated and closed within the narrow limits of trying to survive, enmeshed in sedentary work they despise to squeeze out something hardly better than poverty existence? Many believe that life is what one makes of it, but when they look more honestly and wisely at reality, they may find that for the most part, people are what life makes of them. Most people do not think about choices because they are compelled by too many circumstances, overpowering and overwhelming, to go along with what has no alternative.

This does not mean it is impossible for them to succeed in attaining their hearts' desire. But those who do are far too few, and the great masses of humanity, in their unfortunate ignorance and impoverishment, do not think of choice, but only how they are going to get their next meal or avoid being mauled, pushed around, or killed by the political and war debacles and confusions that so often uproot, harass, and endanger them. Obviously, the gods do not concern themselves seriously with *individual* human problems; they seem to be concerned only with principles, ideologies, dogmas, and the needs of conformance—that's *their* deal. It's like Yakov, The Fixer, who says again: "A meshummed gives up one God for another. I don't want either. We live in a world where the clock ticks fast while he's on his timeless mountain staring in space. He doesn't see us and he doesn't care. Today I want my piece of bread, not in Paradise."[263]

The ability to express and consider inclinations of any kind in the process of producing a judgment or a decision to act is logically forbidden in any categorical moral standard that is theoretically proposed to be of a universal character, which, of course, it cannot be, in any event, as no moral rule or standard can be raised in an inflexible manner to be a guide or obligation to cover all past, present, and future human experience and people.

The fallacy of Kant in his ideas of ethics is that he implied that man exists or should exist, for the means of maintaining Kant's idea of moral law, which is *the* end and an end in itself. It seems wiser to consider that any moral judgment or "law" should be instrumentally the means, and not an end for itself, of bettering man and his condition; in this case, man is the continual end to be considered.

Men are born, live and die not for the purpose of proving or sustaining any particular standard of procedure, thought or rule, but these things are created by men, and create themselves out of their experiences, to sustain and perhaps better their lives. "There is no cure for birth and death," wrote Santayana, "save to enjoy the interval."

Protoplasm is too collodial and motile, even in accepting the principle of similarities, to become a state of any absolute rule to live by. Organics is not a theory but a substantive process of existence, and existence, in the nature of itself, is forever pliable and subject to change. When an individual *knows* how to *think*, how to proceed, how to act, the sense of "duty" is not existent, but, instead, the sense of ethical process may become expressed and operable.

Brand Blanshard writes: "Action impelled by the sense of duty, as Kant perceived, is action on a different level from anything mechanical or associative. But Kant was mistaken in supposing that when we were determined by reason we were not determined at all. This supposition seems to me wholly unwarranted. The determination is still there, but, since it is a determination by the moral necessities of the case, it is just what the moral man wants and thus is the equivalent of freedom. For the moral man, like the logician and the artist, is really seeking self-surrender. Through him as through the others an impersonal ideal is working, and to the extent that this ideal takes possession of him and molds him according to its pattern, he feels free and is free."[264]

DUTY, RESPONSIBILITY, AND FREE WILL

Duty IMPLIES THAT a person "must," "should," or "ought" to do something, regardless of whether he agrees with it or not, or regardless of whether he even gives it any thought or not. As a result, duty may become an involitional obligation which, by the nature of itself, seems to be opposed to *education*, which is a process of self-enlightenment that in the field of ethics enables us to make axiological judgments and to apply our intelligence, supported by this education, to produce decisions for actions that may possibly bring about a sense of greater or truer values, more satisfactions, and possibly less adverse or regretful consequences. Thus, while duty may become an antagonist of freedom, education may promote it and reveal it.

When the nature of a particular duty, in the aggregate or social sense, is considered good by an individual who would have acted accordingly even if such a duty were not an established formal acceptance, his act ceases to be in the nature of a duty, and he performs the act because of *understanding* why he acts in this manner. As a result, the sense of freedom is not so affected but can possibly, consciously or unconsciously, be kept more or less intact. In short, he remains more of an individual and relatively free rather than a caterpillar regimented to follow, with blinders, hardly knowing why. Ethics and responsibilities, to be realistic and good, must rise out of the reflective consciousness of people, from the experience of living and all its concomitant manifestations.

There is a world of difference between duty and responsibility. Duty is what a person is supposed to carry out or perform regardless of his own convictions. Responsibility is what a person has placed upon himself to express or fulfill because he has realized that if he does not fulfill it there would be some kind of personal loss to himself as a person, that the nature of this responsibility has been caused by volitional factors and circumstances in which the person himself is an acknowledged participant. Duty performance is to gratify the outside world, for public approval, to maintain a status or resignation, regardless of whether it gives the person pleasantness, satisfaction, and relief. Responsibility is what a person feels he should fulfill in order to obtain personal satisfaction and relief, whether or not he feels it to be inconsistent with his own convictions and desires. Duty is a cultural acquisition; responsibility is a personal and a biological sequence rising out of biological and cultural events, relationships and experiences. Duty is a thing which the person should not question and which has been ordained for him to perform. Responsibility is what a person *realizes* he should do because of his own sentiments, his personal involvement, his own feelings and thinking. Thus, where duty becomes a rigid cultural or societal order or requisition, responsibility, on the other hand, rises out of the necessity of *compatible* want and desirability. Duty is a social or political order; responsibility is a sense of a personal order. Duty has never actually made people responsible but responsibility has made duty irrelevant. Duty preconcludes the absence of choice; responsibility rises out of choice and becomes its sequence. Explaining John Dewey's principles on this point, Howard W. Hintz wrote: "Each man is *responsible* for making the best choice available to him *within the scope of his limitations and his powers.* That these limitations and powers differ widely among men no one will deny. But to the extent that an individual acts or fails to act responsibly within the range of his capacities, whatever they may be, to that extent he is praiseworthy or blameworthy. It is only because this principle is universally recognized in everyday experience and practice that any type of social order is even possible."[265] Sidney Hook: "No one can live in human society without learning to recognize the distinction between the actions he holds others and himself responsible for and the actions he does not."[266] "What we can make different we are responsible for."[267] Carl R. Rogers: "Personal freedom and responsibility have a crucial signifiance, that one cannot live a complete life without such personal freedom and responsibility, and that self-understanding and responsible choice make a sharp and measurable difference in the behavior of the individual."[268]

William E. Hocking feels that man cannot have freedom without responsibility. He writes: "The tightest of organization depends on individual creativity. When that creativity is limited to a few at the top, we have despotism. . . . Creativity exists as long as the servant has any moral initiative of his own. Individualism grows and spreads with responsibility. You can only make men free when they are inwardly bound by their own sense of responsibility."[269] In nature there is no awareness of the sense of responsibility; neither is this sense a function of the unconscious drives of the human psyche. Responsibility comes with some awareness of things, of relationships, of inclinations and acquired needs and situations. Responsibility does not come in a "package deal" with every human born into the world; it varies according to the character, traits, and potential of intelligence and reflective capacities of each individual and the variations of degree are legion. The sense of responsibility comes with the reflective processes, and these can only initiate themselves and mature reasonably when there is a freedom of conscience and a freedom of expression. The sense of responsibility cannot make itself known and felt and make its impress upon an individual to the extent that the sense of responsibility is actually activated, unless the form of responsibility is made intelligible and rational, no matter in what degree, so that the individual becomes responsible, if he can, by his own awareness of its need and by his own self-justification in pursuing and fulfilling it.

Biological freedom subjects itself to functions, not responsibilities. Responsibilities rise out of the nurturing elements of interdependencies which, in turn, have risen out of the relationships and experiences of cultural habit and living. Freedom and responsibility do not always go hand in hand; the despot is free to look after himself and his sense of responsibility is only toward himself and not to others except insofar as they tend to support his despotism. The egomaniac cannot become aware that others should be considered and have feelings and sentiments that deserve consideration, appreciation, and sympathy. The infant is free, also, to think only in terms of itself; it cannot do otherwise. Responsibility, rising out of the process of maturation in some degree, a product of freedom itself like all other things, is a relative factor varying with all individuals, regardless of the degree of freedom which they may possess and express. Human nature expresses itself by the nature of its own free processes, but the products of this process are not always responsibilities, nor are they always ethical. Life and freedom do go hand in hand, but living experiences and responsibilities are not always companions. The belated vigilance of the slave and the power of the master attest that the sense and awareness of responsibility alleged to be attached to every person who expresses free choice and action is a hope and not a reality.

Freedom, in itself, does not imply or preconclude a need of, or a concomitant or conspecific quantum of, responsibility. The fact of the matter is that when a person expresses any process of freedom in any degree or kind he does so whether he feels or senses a state of some kind of responsibility or not. The adolescents of today, in exhibiting more or less uninhibited sexual liberties as acts of escape from the boredom and pressures of modern society, of defiance against the narrowing of economic barriers that hinder personal and individual expression and initiative, of unadulterated revolt, often called biological, against the prudery, nonsensical puritanism, and irrelevance of sexual matters on any moral plane, these adolescents express a sense of freedom with hardly any sense of responsibility. They feel that the world has been overcast with too much metaphysical morass and religious debris to make possible a normal enjoyment of one's natural right in life. And they are right. But they may be wrong when these acts of freedom emerge and express themselves as attempts to *escape* from their umbilicalized ties to the social organism of which they are parts; disillusion is so often the end result of these compulsions to bypass, overcome, or sidetrack the inevitable sense of commitment to some kind of responsibility that becomes a part of those who are born into, grow up in, and live within a certain kind of society.

Responsibility does not necessarily mean submissiveness or appeasement with factors or principles which the individual may find intolerable or unnecessary. Societies have not changed or modified themselves to meet newer conditions. Individuals with intellect, honesty, courage, and a sense of justice have often changed societies for the better as individuals with emotion, dishonesty, tyranny, and a sense of destruction have changed societies for the worse.

Civilization may have given man many new gadgets, conveniences, faster modes of travel, and miraculous forms of communication; it has taken away his horse and buggy and has given him a racing autocar, plane, and rocket; it has given him many things he could not have dreamed about a short time ago. But I doubt whether it has made him more of a person, or more happy or satisfied.

Freedom and responsibility should harmonize with each other, not race or outrace each other. The turbulent waves of each opposing the other resound around the world, leaving behind too often bewilderment, confusion, and even death. Civilization has given the young more revolt, more defiance, more indifference, even more arrogance and highfalutin-ness, but with these it has given them the seeds of self-effacement, nonentity, boredom, disillusion, and with their fears, often despair. Civilization has given women independence, careers, made them executives, politicians, and scientists, even ambassadors, and they have every right to all these exactly as men have; but it has also given them loneliness, on-their-ownness, less love and less motherhood, less of those inner and finer enjoyments and nourishments which solely belong to the female heart, mind, and body, the stir and the kiss they truly need.

Biologists, behaviorists, psychologists, and various other scientists, in addition to agenda of theologians and pseudo-theologians, keep up a constant barrage against each other on the theories of free will and choice, primarily to establish some sort of responsibility upon an individual for his thoughts and acts. Hudson Hoagland contends that people must be held responsible to some reasonable degree, otherwise chaos would result. He writes: "What would be the social consequences if everyone were convincd that he was an automaton with no freedom of choice? It may be true that he is an automaton, although this contradicts our deepest convictions. In practice it seems to me that it would leave a society in a position in which people could not be held responsible for their acts. This conceivably might be a desirable state of affairs, but I do not think so."[270] Replying to the Hoagland inference that man is captain of his soul and master of his destiny, Burnham P. Beckwith says that "When philosophers assert that men have freedom of will, they mean that choices are uncaused,"[271] and we do know that anything and everything that occurs, including the premise of free will, do have causes, and we are well acquainted, unfortunately, with some of their effects.

Richard A. Yarnell also replies: "It is possible that we are entering an era in which we will require knowledge requisite to influencing many of the cause-and-effect relationships of our own cultural evolution in significant respects but the vision of man *in control* of his own destiny is a dim one and one which has the effect of obscuring, rather than enlightening, our view of ourselves."[272]

Man is not exactly an automaton because man is not just put together as mechanical contrivances are manufactured, even the finely invented electronic cybernetic and calculating machines; man is not exactly fabricated or put together as a product. *Man has evolved as part of the general evolution of all life on earth.* He has not evolved all by himself, but has evolved as *part* of a maze of evolutionary interactivity and interrelationship and interdependence of all living things in an intricate symbiotic chain of causes and effects, and all this has been inexorably tied and related to the nonliving, or chemical and physical conditions and properties on earth and in the universe itself. Man, being what he is, could never be an automaton, but we do understand and continually find more knowledge as to how he came to be what he is, what the world is in which he exists, and what he could possibly do. Within this potential of what man is and what he could possibly do we infer the natural limitations within which the natural freedoms operate. By understanding these limitations and potentials of an evolved animal, we begin to realize that the categorical principle of free will, as expounded and laid down by the theologian, metaphysician, the mystic, and the intuitional philosopher, falls to the ground because they are all basing their premise not on knowledge, not on the sciences, not on the actual experiences of people, not even on the world itself, but merely on their desire to make gods out of animals.

A man and a lion are both animals evolved out of the same stream of animal life. Man has evolved a larger brain capable of many things the lion is not capable of, among which is a reflective brain aware of many things, including death. The lion is capable of things man cannot do, but so far as we can determine it seems that he is not equipped with a reflective and rational brain as man is. Man's brain and his tools made a gun and man can use this gun to shoot the lion; the lion somehow could not evolve to invent a gun to shoot back. The lion cannot be held responsible for not thinking rationally or reflectively, or for not shooting back at the human hunter; man cannot be held responsible for not being able to spring and pounce upon a fast-running zebra and tear him to pieces with his bare hands. Any animal, including man, can only be expected to do what it *can only do* according to its nature, but each animal, including man, has a *particular nature* and is thereby limited to it and to its potential of evolutional change and adaptation. Man is not an omnipotent or omniscient animal, but he does think and reflect according to his nature and the experiences he meets up with, and his nature indicates a potential of choice whether he should go this way or that way, in the same sense that a lion, also limited in choice, can choose to climb up this hill or another hill. Whether they choose wisely or not depends upon the sequences of experience that follow, and this is a matter of chance and accident. Man can use his brain to predict, but he cannot predict with absolute certainty because prediction means implementing a future state, and any future state is not one of experience.

Now there are stronger and wiser lions, and there are stronger and wiser men: young and old lions, inexperienced and experienced lions, young and old men, also inexperienced and experienced men, and each lion-individual and each man-individual varies in heritage and experience, and whatever ability to choose it may have cannot be generalized into a principle applying to all or a principle of free will to be held valid and existent for men and not for the other animals. There are young girls and young boys, and here, too, each individual has a freedom of choice *caused* and *limited* by his particular inheritance and experience. A young boy or girl thinks and acts like a young boy or girl; the grown-ups are expected to do likewise, as grown-ups. The same goes with all the living creatures of the world. Each living thing is not unlimited in its freedom of choice, but limited to its particular nature, and any choice it does make rises as a consequence of its nature and condition.

The whole idea of free will as a general principle is fallacious because the idea of free will itself is a religious and cultural tool based on the theological theory of rewards and punishments, and becomes a self-contradictory metaphysicism when screened against the actual nature of man, his behavior, his experiences, and the world he lives in. Corliss Lamont: "Even the wisest of men hardly possess the knowledge and impartiality to render a Last Judgment on himself or anyone else."[273] William Lillie: "The argument sometimes used that man's will must be free if we are to make any moral judgments at all about his conduct is not valid."[274] "It has been argued that the knowledge that our conduct is determined by causes over which we have no control provides no inducement for moral effort and so morality is likely to suffer. Historically this does not seem to have been the case."[275]

Accordingly, we see that any ethical or moral principle based on responsibility on the assumption that man possesses a free will cannot be placed upon the human being because it exposes merely a wishful claim. Any such theory presupposes that man has some sort of pure, operable will to choose that is external to his mind and body. We see this presupposition in the traditional belief of the separation of body and soul, of material and immaterial, of the impure or earthly and the pure or heavenly. This must be discarded if man is to make any real progress in self-knowledge and his surroundings. It is far better to try to make a better world for himself with the *limited* and the *possible* in his nature than to keep making a hell on earth with his fanciful idea that he possesses some kind of omnipotence and omniscience worthy of God's judgment, when in fact religion itself is "man's confession of impotence in certain matters."[276] If man reaches the full stature of responsibility and if man should become, in actuality, an ethical animal, it will be because of a truer and realistic knowledge of himself, of life, and of the world in which he spends his life.

Carl R. Rogers writes that "freedom is an inner thing. It is the discovery of meaning from within oneself. It is the recognition by a person that he is an emerging process, not a static end product."[277] No doubt man is an emerging process, and evolution goes on relentlessly because of the nature of things, but is the lion less free as a lion whether he can discover its meaning within him, or because he is incapable of recognizing the operational methods of existence? We must try to avoid, even though we cannot be completely successful, the partiality and anthropocentric tool of analysis. *Freedom is a conspecific of life;* we may discover its meaning by *our* mind and nature, even identify it as meaning freedom, but freedom has been with us throughout the eons of evolution; if not we would not have it now with us; we just would not *be*. Freedom exists whether we discover it or not, whether we sense it or not, whether we are conscious of its processes or not. It seems we begin to sense it, discover it, and feel conscious about it when natural freedom is denied to us in some degree and when any of its processes are retarded within us and from without. The human being, eons ago, did not anticipate death, nor was he aware of it, just as any other animal appears not to be. Freedom existed then as it continues to exist in all animal life today. The wild animal fights arrestment and incarceration; the civilized man writes essays against tyranny and slavery, and even sometimes rebels against them. The former fights, but may not be aware of why; the latter fights because he is aware of why, and his reflections and reasoning tell him about natural rights and privileges and responsibilities. Biologically, both operate on the same premise and by the same process.

Carl R. Rogers continues: "Unless, as individuals, and as a society, we can make constructive use of this capacity for freedom and commitment, mankind is set on a collision course with fate."[278] I feel that Mr. Rogers overlooks the fact that man *has* been living for millions of years and *has* always expressed the choice factor according to his nature and ability in making judgments and decisions as pre-states of choice. Man *has* been responsible in his historical experiences also limited to nature and his ability to understand. At the moment the Arab world is aroused by its political leaders and by its mosques to carry out a "holy war" to exterminate the Jews and destroy Israel; this, too, in their viewpoint, is their freedom and their commitment. And Mr. Rogers and I would not be able to change their opinion about commitment. What is important is the nature of the commitment and the kind of judgments that people make and the necessity of enlightenment and education that becomes essential to bring about a coalition of freedom and commitment on an ethical and just basis. Mr. Rogers need not fear a collision course because of the lack of making the proper choice; whatever choices human beings are capable of making, they have made and will continue to make. The problem is not in pedantic debate as to whether man is partially or completely, controllably or absolutely free to express his will and to make a choice; the problem is to educate man to the realities of himself and the world so that he can try, with whatever limited capacity he happens to have, to make his own life happy, healthy, satisfied, and make a better and more peaceful world to live in.

THE OUTLOOK

THE FACT THAT man is an evolved mechanism does not mean that he is a robot. He may be a mechanism, but one that can love, write poetry, carry his thoughts through the stars, and make the rushing stream, the rain, and the furies translate themselves into symphonies. Because man now turns the light of science upon himself, because man now refuses to believe in fantasies and fairy tales that have enslaved him, injured him, made him miserable, and caused him to make needless sacrifices, all this does not mean that he now values his life less and after-death more.

Knowledge and reason have given him new insights, the insights to re-evaluate his life in terms of living, not in dying, to recognize that the brevities and uncertainties of life make life more sacred, more precious. Knowledge and science, by themselves, cannot be depended upon to make men more ethical and responsible, but they can usher in new thoughts, new recapitulations, new rationalizations that may open windows, not to Dantian phantasmagoria, but windows that reveal our surroundings in each precious day in each individual's precious life.

The freedom to think and search and the freedom to understand one's natural right to happiness and satisfaction may make better men, more ethical and responsible men. The old ways simply did not. We know this from our past. History shows us no ethics or responsibilities in the traditions of religion of metaphysical abstractions, and the power-authority forms of kings, emperors, royalties, dictators, and phony and paranoiac egomaniacs. These forms only extracted duties, conformances, obediences, mental and physical slavery, and continue to do so to the present day, except where true democratic process has delivered us from the impressment under these impositions upon our natural freedoms. Any period of more religious and king-emperor-dictator density reveals less ethics and responsibilities and more duties and slavery. Paradoxes there will always be, and even if knowledge and science may show us what the defeatists call "an absurd and meaningless universe," then let there be for man happy paradoxes and healthy absurdities so long as his life, short as it may be, can be longer with less regret and greater satisfaction. John Dewey sounds his philosophic clarion to awaken a new world: "This change of human disposition toward the world does not mean that man ceases to have ideals, or ceases to be primarily a creature of the imagination. But it does signify a radical change in the character and function of the ideal realm which man shapes for himself. In the classic philosophy, the ideal world is essentially a haven in which man finds rest from the

storms of life; it is an asylum in which he takes refuge from the
troubles of existence with the calm assurance that it alone is
supremely real. When the belief that knowledge is active and
operative takes hold of men, the ideal realm is no longer something aloof and separate; it is rather that collection of imagined
possibilities that stimulates men to new efforts and realizations.
It still remains true that the troubles which men undergo are
the forces that lead them to project pictures of a better state of
things. But the picture of the better is shaped so that it may become an instrumentality of action, while in the classic view the
Idea belongs ready-made in a noumenal world. Hence, it is only
an object of personal aspiration or consolation, while to the
modern, an idea is a suggestion of something to be done or a
way of doing."[279]

"We must come to understand," writes Loren Eiseley, "the
fact that learning its endless and that nowhere does it lead us
behind the existent world. It may reduce the prejudices of ignorance, set our bones, build our cities. In itself it will never make
us ethical men."[280] If man is to become a better and finer ethical
animal, and if he is to nurture and establish his own responsibilities within the general frame of natural freedom, it will be
upon what is found to be true and earthly or what John Dewey
called "warranted assertability." Bertrand Russell: "It is not by
prayer and humility that you cause things to go as you wish, but
by acquiring a knowledge of natural laws."[281] It is by applying
this knowledge of nature and existence to a higher and more
equitable level of ethics and responsibilities that we can better
use this knowledge, not because we have to, but because we will
know better to *want* to.

For the beginning of ethics and responsibilities is the cultivation of appreciation, of sympathy, of new insights and a better
understanding of values, a realization of what life may be and
its sacredness. By understanding our own sense of sacredness for
our own life we may come to appreciate the same value for other
living things, including our own kind. And we have the natural
freedom to do this. Andreas Feininger: "For, as I see it, life is
a privilege, a gift bestowed upon us at the expense of other living
things—the animals and plants that give us our food. So that we

may live, others must die—steers and sheep and swine, chicken
and turkeys, lobsters and clams; the grains of wheat and corn that
will never become plants, and countless other living things."[282]
When we understand and appreciate the truism that we are a
part and never separately alone in the fuller sense, we will also
have regard for the value of all the *other parts* without which we
could not live at all. Albert Schweitzer: "How can ethics become
the basis for a world philosophy? When it relates to the entire
world; when it forms and builds our spiritual relationship to the
world. It does that only if it shows us how we are linked with
all living things . . . reverence for all life—the great mystery in
which we find ourselves together with all living things."[283]

The fact that we realize we are a *part of parts* does not make
us less individuals, nor does it mean that each individual has no
potential of individualistic opinion. Each person is *particularized*
so that his mind, being naturally already oculated in a particular
way, can, if reasonably free, express his views and live his actions
without the necessity of being a caterpillar-conformist or being a
blind follower of what is merely ordained by others. J. Bronowski
writes: "The arts and the sciences have changed the values of
the Middle Ages; and this change has been an enrichment, moving towards what makes us more deeply human. . . . The concepts of value are profound and difficult exactly because they do
two things at once: they join men into societies, and yet they preserve for them a freedom which makes them single men. . . . Independence, originality, and therefore dissent: these words show
the progress, they stamp the character of our civilization. . . .
Dissent is not itself an end; it is the surface mark of a deeper
value. Dissent is the mark of freedom, as originality is the mark
of independence of mind. . . . The values by which we are to
survive are not rules for just and unjust conduct, but are those
deeper illuminations in whose light justice and injustice, good
and evil, means and ends are seen in fearful sharpness of outline."[284]

Our consciousness of freedom, in any field or capacity, is merely
our identification of a process which seems to operate and process
itself by capabilities and potentials which we can call the processes
of freedom. There are no freedoms which are not natural; "super-

natural" freedoms only emanate from the consciousness and imagination of some natural field of the human mind.

Human history proceeds from the simple to the complex, from
the singles and individuals to the manys and masses. All human
institutions, including their religions and societies, have been
forming toward mass-multiples, mass-considerations, mass-aggre-
gates. The preponderances of numbers are swallowing up the individuals that tend to create and form these preponderables. Society, created, evolved, and maintained by individuals, is about to
doom the individual as a free creature. Nurture is about to synthesize nature and create a synthetic product, a superficial mass-
personality, a covering over what remains of the natural product.

It is for man to restore to himself his natural freedoms as *a*
person, as a single being and as an individual if all his intellectualization is to find meaning and value in a world wherein numbers and masses have cultivated and forced situations and consequences that tend to make individual meanings and values nebulous and futile. Man must halt the march to multiplicity and
complexity and regain some control and some consciousness of the
simpler elements that reflect the more basic and meaningful
values of *a* person to himself and through himself to others. Unless this can be reasonably accomplished, the march to the future
labyrinthine complex will only consummate bewilderment and
the ultimate termite-complex, in which individual minds, hopes,
and strivings will be gone.

Even to attempt this on any realizable basis man must throw
away his cultured fears that create needless opposition between
men. Fear, both of hell and of people, is the destroyer of freedom.
Man's fear is yesterday's hold upon today's living time, already
forfeited in fear of tomorrow. Thus fear freezes freedom, in-
capacitates it, and in the long run atrophies it beyond repair. Let
us fervently hope that men of today and tomorrow will have the
wisdom and fortitude to reflame and restore the fire of freedom
so that people will enjoy, not fear, to live and to try to live well,
happily, and peacefully whenever and wherever possible, to use
this very freedom to avoid conflict by the realization that life is
sacred yet earthly and specific, irreplaceable even if imaginative,
and the reasonable, ethical and equitable asset of every one, not

because of color, class, or clan, but because every one is born to freedom.

Man will always seek the ultimate, yet, in seeking, let the search live its time; perhaps in so doing the ultimate may be found in the presence of things. Man will always want to imagine and feel beneath his feet some immutable foundation in order to reach and fulfill the horizon of his psychical need, yet he may find that this foundation is in the movement of his life, as in the movement of the earth, as in all the motions of the universe, the constant process of every moment of his life. Andreas Feininger frames his view wisely: "I need the reassurance of something immutable. But to find this immutable something—and we still do not know what it is—man has to be free spiritually—free from taboos and superstition, free from dogmas laid down in fear and ignorance and never revised in the light of added insight; free to pursue the truth wherever the chase may lead. And I am sure—sure as anyone can ever be of anything—that at the end there will be light, the all-pervading light of insight illuminating the entire immense structure of the cosmos, and with it revealing the rightful place and purpose of man."[285]

Let us hope that man will use his freedoms to live better and longer, not to waste or shorten his life, let alone his freedom to destroy himself, others, and the world. Whatever he does, if it is good, it will be *his* good; if it is evil, it will be *his* evil; but whatever happens, Nature herself will not exalt him or shed a tear. Man has the power of his freedom, limited as it is according to his nature and potential to do whatever he eventually will do. Let us hope that reason and equity may wisely guide him to the good, to the peaceful, to the happier, to the better and the finer.

One thing is sure: If there are to be ethical and responsible people with some reasonable and knowledgeable sense of equity, and if the truer and more sustaining values of life and living are to be found and possibly realized, they will never be found by blinding ourselves with wishful and egocentric dreams, but by continuing the search for what seems to be the truer and more certain reality, and upon this apply our minds and hearts to build from it as happy, as satisfying and invigorating, as ecstatic and beautiful a life as we possibly can. And this we can do only if man releases and restores to himself and to his kind the natural freedoms with which nature in her strange and sightless way seeded him.

REFERENCES—BOOK FIVE

1. Bertrand Russell, *Why I am not a Christian,* p. 55.
2. *Ibid.,* p. 65.
3. Bengt Danielsson, *Love in the South Seas,* p. 121.
4. see *Indian Primitive,* Ralph W. Andrews, p. 159.
5. Robert Ardrey, *The Territorial Imperative,* p. 351.
6. C. A. Burland, *Peru Under the Incas,* p. 42.
7. Bertrand Russell, *Why I am not a Christian,* p. 29.
8. *Ibid.,* p. 27.
9. John Dewey, *Reconstruction in Philosophy,* p. 140.
10. Bertrand Russell, *Sceptical Essays,* p. 105.
11. Edmund Stillman, *The Holy Terrors of Münster,* Horizon, Summer, 1967, vol. IX, no. 3, p. 91.
12. Mark Twain, *Reflections on Religion,* ed. Neider, Hudson Review, vol. XVI, no. 3, Autumn, 1963, pp. 351-2.
13. Alvan L. Barach. *Promethean Anxieties,* Part I, Columbia University Forum, Fall, 1966, pp. 25-6.
14. Anthony Storr, *Human Aggression,* p. 63.
15. *Ibid.,* p. 69.
16. Peter Freuchen, *The Book of the Eskimos,* pp. 82 and 121.
17. George Gaylord Simpson, *This View of Life,* p. 25.
18. Herbert Wendt, *The Sexual Life of the Animals,* p. 11.
19. Robert Graves and Raphael Patai, *Hebrew Myths,* p. 14.
20. Marcello Craveri, *Life of Jesus.*
21. Géza Róheim, *The Riddle of the Sphinx,* London, 1934; see also *The Dangerous Sex,* Hays.
22. H. R. Hays, *The Dangerous Sex,* p. 58.
23. *Ibid.,* p. 77.
24. Luigi Pareti, Paolo Brezzi, and Luciano Petech, *The Ancient World,* from "History of Mankind," vol. II, p. 213.
25. H. R. Hays, *The Dangerous Sex,* p. 43.
26. Walter Sorell, *The Story of the Human Hand,* p. 3.
27. Joseph Campbell, *Masks of God: Creative Mythology,* p. 53.
28. H. R. Hays, *The Dangerous Sex,* p. 41.
29. *Ibid.,* p. 17.
30. *Ibid.,* p. 44.
31. Lucy S. Dawidowicz, *On Being a Woman in Shul,* Commentary Magazine, vol. 46, no. 1, July, 1968, p. 72.
32. *Ibid.,* p. 72.
33. H. R. Hays, *The Dangerous Sex,* p. 88.
34. *Ibid.,* p. 121.
35. *Ibid.,* p. 122.
36. Paul LaCroix, *History of Prostitution,* vol. II, p. 63.
37. H. R. Hays, *The Dangerous Sex,* p .109.
38. Edith Simon, *The Piebald Standard: A Biography of the Knights Templars,* London, 1959.

39. H. R. Hays, *The Dangerous Sex,* p. 137.
40. Sidney Painter, *French Chivalry;* see also *Womankind in Western Europe from the Earliest Times to the Seventeenth Century,* Thomas Wright; also *The Dangerous Sex,* Hays, p. 114.
41. H. R. Hays, *The Dangerous Sex,* p. 111.
42. Bengt Danielsson, *Gauguin in the South Seas,* p. 276.
43. *Ibid.,* p. 211.
44. Kaj Birket-Smith, *The Paths of Culture,* p. 232.
45. Louis A. Reitmeister, *The Gods and My Friends,* p. 16.
46. Robert Graves and Raphael Patai, *Hebrew Myths,* p. 89.
47. Bertrand Russell, *Why I am not a Christian,* p. 62.
48. *Ibid.,* p. 70.
49. Moritz Schlick, *Problems of Ethics,* p. 160.
50. Ward H. Goodenough, *Arms Control and Behavior Science,* Science Magazine, vol. 144, no. 3620, May 15, 1964, p. 821.
51. John Stuart Mill, quoted in *Freedom in the Modern World,* Muller, p. 4.
52. Robert Graves and Raphael Patai, *Hebrew Myths,* p. 15.
53. *Ibid.,* pp. 79-81.
54. Sabatino Moscati, *Ancient Semitic Civilizations,* p. 71.
55. Joseph Campbell, *Masks of God: Occidental Mythology,* p. 95.
56. Phyllis and Eberhard Kronhausen, *Pornography and the Law.*
57. Bertrand Russell, *Why I am not a Christian,* pp. 20-1.
58. *Ibid.,* p. 26.
59. *Ibid.,* p. 81.
60. John J. Honigmann, *The Study of Personality in Primitive Societies,* from "The Study of Personality," ed. Norbeck, *et al.,* p. 282.
61. Ottaker Nemecek, *Virginity,* p. 105.
62. Philip Wylie, *An Essay on Morals,* p. 155.
63. Emmett McLoughlin, *People's Padre,* p. 88.
64. *Ibid.,* p. 97.
65. *Ibid.,* p. 95.
66. John Dewey, *A Common Faith,* p. 28.
67. Corliss Lamont, *The Philosophy of Humanism,* p. 190.
68. see *The Literary Road to Rome,* Norman Kotker, Horizon, Summer, 1967, p. 26.
69. Friedrich Schiller, from the poem, *Die Worte des Glaubons.*
70. Epictetus, *Discourses of,* trans. George Lang, p. 423.
71. William Lillie, *Introduction to Ethics,* p. 113.
72. George Jean Nathan, *Living Philosophies,* p. 224.
73. William Lillie, *Introduction to Ethics,* pp. 93-4.
74. Joseph Campbell, *Masks of God: Primitive Mythology,* p. 35.
75. John Dewey, *Human Nature and Conduct,* p. 182.
76. Albert Schweitzer, *The Schweitzer Album,* ed. Erica Anderson, p. 53.
77. Maimonides, from *In Time and Eternity,* ed. Nahum N. Glatzer, p. 63.
78. Talmud, *Traité Bérakhote,* sh. 17.
79. William Lillie, *Introduction to Ethics,* p. 60.
80. *Ibid.,* p. 98.
81. *Ibid.,* p. 63.
82. *Ibid.,* p. 80.
83. James G. Frazer, *Taboo and the Perils of the Soul,* from "The Golden Bough," Part II, p. 218.
84. Brigid Brophy, *Black Ship to Hell,* p. 425.
85. John Herman Randall, Jr., *Introduction to Philosophy,* p. 200.
86. Robert Briffault, *Rational Evolution,* p. 9.
87. Martin A. Larson, *The Religion of the Occident,* p. 327.

88. John Herman Randall, Jr., *Introduction to Philosophy*, p. 249.
89. John Dewey, *Human Nature and Conduct*, p. 103.
90. Mark Twain, *Reflections on Religion*, ed. Neider, Hudson Review, vol. XVI, no. 3, Autumn, 1963, p. 338.
91. Corliss Lamont, *The Philosophy of Humanism*, p. 195.
92. Joseph Campbell, *Masks of God: Occidental Mythology*, p. 504.
93. Hightower, quoted in *Religion in Public Education*, Thayer, p. 111.
94. Samuel Chugerman, *Lester F. Ward*, p. 218.
95. Bertrand Russell, *Why I am not a Christian*, p. 33.
96. Barrows Dunham, *Heroes and Heretics*, p. 335.
97. John Herman Randall, Jr., *Introduction to Philosophy*, p. 249.
98. Bertrand Russell, *Why I am not a Christian*, p. 76.
99. Bertrand Russell, *Sceptical Essays*, p. 25.
100. James G. Frazer, *Psyche's Task*, from "The Golden Bough," pp. 151-3.
101. Sylvanus G. Morley, *The Ancient Maya*, p. 182.
102. Ottaker Nemecek, *Virginity*, p. 100.
103. Bengt Danielsson, *Love in the South Seas*, p. 77.
104. Ottaker Nemecek, *Virginity*, p. 44.
105. *Ibid.*, p. 67.
106. *Ibid.*, p. 64.
107. *Ibid.*, p. 34.
108. *Ibid.*, pp. 50-1.
109. Herbert J. Muller, *Freedom in the Modern World*, p. 42.
110. Edward Westermarck, quoted in *From Ape to Angel*, Hays, p. 162.
111. Corliss Lamont, *The Philosophy of Humanism*, p. 194.
112. Bertrand Russell, *Why I am not a Christian*, p. 68.
113. Gerhard Szczesny, *The Future of Unbelief*, p. 219.
114. *Ibid.*, p. 201.
115. Bertrand Russell, *Authority and the Individual*, p. 8.
116. John Dewey, *Reconstruction in Philosophy*, p. 179.
117. Bengt Danielsson, *Love in the South Seas*, p. 81.
118. *Ibid.*, pp. 89-90.
119. *Ibid.*, p. 115.
120. Alvan L. Barach, *Promethean Anxieties*, Part I, Columbia University Forum, Fall, 1966, pp. 22, 24.
121. Bertrand Russell, *Authority and the Individual*, p. 28.
122. *Ibid.*, p. 68.
123. *Ibid.*, p. 70.
124. William Lillie, *Introduction to Ethics*, p. 64.
125. Bertrand Russell, *Why I am not a Christian*, p. 60.
126. James G. Frazer, *Taboo and the Perils of the Soul*, from "The Golden Bough," Part II, preface pp. vi-viii.
127. *Ibid.*, p. viii.
128. Paul Kurtz, *Joyful Humanism*, Humanist Magazine, vol. XXVII, no. 2, pp. 39-40.
129. Elie Faure, *Spirit of Forms*, vol. V, "History of Art," p. 198.
130. Wilhelm Bolsche, *Love-Life in Nature*, vol. II, p. 7.
131. William Lillie, *Introduction to Ethics*, p. 158.
132. *Ibid.*, p. 87.
133. *Ibid.*, p. 102.
134. *Ibid.*, p. 71.
135. John Herman Randall, Jr., *Introduction to Philosophy*, p. 256.
136. Ernest Nagel, *Some Notes on Determinism*, from "Determinism and Freedom," ed. Sidney Hook, p. 200.
137. Edmund R. Leach, *We Scientists Have the Right to Play God*, Sat. Eve. Post, November, 1968, p. 20.

138. Wallace I. Matson, *The Existence of God,* p. 233.
139. Robert Evans Snodgrass, *Insects, Their Ways and Means of Living,* pp. 126-7.
140. *Ibid.,* p. 151.
141. William Lillie, *Introduction to Ethics,* p. 248.
142. *Ibid.,* p. 248.
143. *Ibid.,* p. 243.
144. Felix Adler, *Personality,* from "Essays in Honor of John Dewey," pp. 7-8.
145. William Lillie, *Introduction to Ethics,* p. 246.
146. Oscar Wilde, *Picture of Dorian Gray,* p. 88.
147. Norman Kotker, *The Literary Road to Rome,* Horizon, Summer, 1967, p. 30.
148. *Ibid.,* p. 29.
149. William Lillie, *Introduction to Ethics,* p. 71.
150. Peter Matthiessen, *The Cloud Forest,* p. 96.
151. John Dewey, *Reconstruction in Philosophy,* p. 178.
152. William Lillie, *Introduction to Ethics,* p. 164.
153. *The Brown Network,* p. 9.
154. Jawaharlal Nehru, *India,* New York Times Magazine, Sept. 7, 1958.
155. Rolf Hochhuth, *The Deputy,* p .350.
156. Michael Grant, *Myths of the Greeks and Romans,* p. 67.
157. Herbert L. Matthews, *The Yoke and the Arrows,* p. 176.
158. *Ibid.,* p. 177.
159. *Ibid.,* p. 163.
160. Joseph Campbell, *Masks of God: Occidental Mythology,* p. 503.
161. *Horizon Book of the Renaissance,* ed. R. M. Ketchum, p. 12.
162. *Ibid.,* pp. 212-3.
163. *Ibid.,* p. 15.
164. *Ibid.,* p. 241.
165. Marcello Craveri, *The Life of Jesus,* pp. 310-12.
166. *Ibid.,* p. 435.
167. Bertrand Russell, *Why I am not a Christian,* p. 25.
168. Roger A. Caras, *Last Chance on Earth,* p. 94.
169. see *The Teaching of Contempt,* Jules Isaac.
170. Bernhard and Michael Grzimek, *Serengati Shall Not Die,* p. 82.
171. George B. Schaller, *The Year of the Gorilla.*
172. Herbert J. Muller, *Freedom in the Ancient World,* p. 315.
173. Herbert J. Muller, *Freedom in the Modern World,* p. 128.
174. Bernhard and Michael Grzimek, *Serengati Shall Not Die,* p. 107.
175. Herbert J. Muller, *Freedom in the Ancient World,* p. 312.
176. Herbert J. Muller, *Freedom in the Modern World,* p. 36.
177. Bertrand Russell, *Why I am not a Christian,* p. 67.
178. Emmett McLoughlin, *Crime and Immorality in the Catholic Church,* p. 20.
179. William H. DuBay, *The Human Church,* p. 38.
180. Martin A. Larson, *The Religion of the Occident,* p. 437.
181. *Ibid.,* p. 507.
182. Joseph Wheless, *Forgery in Christianity,* preface p. xix.
183. *Ibid.,* p. 91.
184. André Maurois, *The War Against the Moon,* p. 19.
185. V. T. Thayer, *Religion in Public Education,* pp. 36-7.
186. St. Luke, quoted in *Freedom in the Ancient World,* Muller, pp. 48-9.
187. Guenter Lewy, *The Catholic Church and Nazi Germany,* p. 308.
188. *Ibid.,* pp. 337-8.
189. Saul Friedlander, *Pius XII and the Third Reich,* pp. 237-8.
190. D. T. Atkinson, *Magic, Myth and Medicine,* pp. 212-3.
191. Herbert J. Muller, *Freedom in the Modern World,* p. 15.
192. Guenter Lewy, *The Catholic Church and Nazi Germany,* p. 341.
193. Herbert J. Muller, *Freedom in the Modern World,* pp. 81-2.

194. Paul Blanshard, *God and Man in Washington*, p. 56.
195. Philip Wylie, *An Essay on Morals*, p. 45.
196. Hannah Arendt, *Eichmann in Jerusalem*, p. 173.
197. see *The Town Beyond the Wall*, Elie Wiesel.
198. Guenter Lewy, *The Catholic Church and Nazi Germany*, p. 257.
199. Rolf Hochhuth, *The Deputy*, p. 305; also *Memoirs*, Ernst Heinrich von Weizsacker, p. 281.
200. Guenter Lewy, *The Catholic Church and Nazi Germany*, p. 339.
201. Hannah Arendt, *The Origins of Totalitarianism*, p. 469.
202. Terence Prittie, *Israel, The Miracle in the Desert*, p. 233.
203. Juan Comas, *Racial Myths*, p. 27.
204. *Ibid.*, p. 21.
205. George Gaylord Simpson, *This View of Life*, p. 39.
206. Juan Comas, *Racial Myths*, p. 27.
207. Harry L. Shapiro, *Race Mixture*, p. 52.
208. Clyde Kluckhohn, *Mirror for Man*, p. 134.
209. L. C. Dunn, *Race and Biology*, p. 42.
210. *Ibid.*, p. 13.
211. Ashley Montagu, *The Concept of Race*, p. 24.
212. Bertrand Russell, *Authority and the Individual*, p. 24.
213. William Lillie, *Introduction to Ethics*, p. 67.
214. *Ibid.*, p. 61.
215. Corliss Lamont, *The Philosophy of Humanism*, p. 193.
216. *Ibid.*, p. 204.
217. William J. Fielding, *The Shackles of the Supernatural*, p. 17.
218. William Lillie, *Introduction to Ethics*, p. 114.
219. Herbert S. Dickey, *My Jungle Book*, p. 211.
220. H. R. Hays, *In the Beginnings*, p. 183.
221. Theodora Kroeber, *Ishi*, p. 61.
222. Janet McCloud, *The Continuing "Last Indian War,"* Humanist Magazine, Fall, 1967, pp. 177-9.
223. Kenneth Pearson and Patricia Connor, *The Strange Case of James Mellaart*, Horizon, Summer, 1967, p. 14.
224. see *Animal Kitabu*, Hallet, pp. 94-5.
225. *Ibid.*, pp. 128-9.
226. Bertrand Russell, *Sceptical Essays*, pp. 24-5.
227. Bertrand Russell, *Authority and the Individual*, p. 27.
228. Janheinz Jahn, *Muntu*, pp. 173-4.
229. John Dewey, *Reconstruction in Philosophy*, p. 159.
230. Hannah Arendt, *Eichmann in Jerusalem*, p. 120.
231. John Dewey, *Human Nature and Conduct*, p. 77.
232. Clyde Kluckhohn, *Mirror for Man*, p. 215.
233. Maurice Parmalee, *The Fields and Problems of Criminology*, from "Fields and Methods of Sociology," ed. L. L. Bernard, p. 177.
234. Louis Harris, *The Story of Crime*, preface, p. ix.
235. Albert Schweitzer, *The Philosophy of Civilization*, p. 187.
236. *Ibid.*, pp. 76-7.
237. Lynn White, Jr., *Saint Francis and the Ecologic Backlash*, Horizon, Summer, 1967, pp. 45-6.
238. *Ibid.*, p. 47.
239. *Ibid.*, p. 43.
240. William Lillie, *Introduction to Ethics*, p. 255.
241. Morris R. Cohen, *Reason and Law*, p. 15.
242. William Lillie, *Introduction to Ethics*, p. 280.
243. Ernest Renan, *The Future of Science*, p. 403.

244. Soterios Nicholson, *Wor or a United World*, pp. 324-5.
245. Morris R. Cohen, *Reason and Law*, p. 14.
246. *Ibid.,* p. 13.
247. *Ibid.,* p. 13.
248. see *Introduction to Ethics*, Lillie, p. 261.
249. George Gaylord Simpson, quoted in *Mankind Evolving*, Dobzhansky, p. 343.
250. C. H. Waddington, *The Ethical Animal;* see also *Mankind Evolving*, Dobzhansky, p. 343.
251. Bertrand Russell, *Authority and the Individual*, pp. 10-11.
252. William Lillie, *Introduction to Ethics*, p. 62.
253. Corliss Lamont, *The Philosophy of Humanism*, p. 215.
254. John Dewey, *Reconstruction in Philosophy*, p. 126.
255. Hudson Hoagland, *Science and the New Humanism*, Science Magazine, vol. 143, no. 3602, Jan. 10, 1964, pp. 111-2.
256. *Ibid.,* p. 112.
257. Frank Dufresne, *No Room for Bears*, p. 105.
258. *Ibid.,* pp. 111-2, 114.
259. *Ibid.,* pp. 44-5.
260. Roger A. Caras, *Last Chance on Earth*, p. 67.
261. Herb and Miriam Hilscher, *Alaska, U.S.A., 1959.*
262. Mark Twain, *Reflections on Religion*, ed. Neider, Hudson Review, vol. XVI, no. 3, Autumn, 1963, p. 347.
263. Bernard Malamud, *The Fixer*, pp. 17 and 32.
264. Brand Blanshard, *The Case for Determinism*, from "Determinism and Freedom," ed. Sidney Hook, p. 29.
265. Howard W. Hintz, *Some Further Reflections on Moral Responsibilities*, from "Determinism and Freedom," ed. Sidney Hook, p. 177.
266. Sidney Hook, *Necessity, Indeterminism and Sentimentalism*, from "Determinism and Freedom," ed. Sidney Hook, p. 188.
267. *Ibid.,* p. 192.
268. Carl R. Rogers, *Freedom and Commitment*, Humanist Magazine, vol. 24, no. 2, Mar.-Apr., 1964, p. 40.
269. William E. Hocking, Time Magazine, May 10, 1963.
270. Hudson Hoagland, Science Magazine, vol. 143, no. 3611, Mar. 13, 1964, p. 1123.
271. Burnham P. Beckwith, Science Magazine, vol. 143, no. 3611, Mar. 13, 1964, p. 1122.
272. Richard A. Yarnell, Science Magazine, vol. 143, no. 3611, Mar. 13, 1964, p. 1122.
273. Corliss Lamont, *The Philosophy of Humanism*, p. 200.
274. William Lillie, *Introduction to Ethics*, p. 43.
275. *Ibid.,* p. 48.
276. Clyde Kluckhohn and Dorothea Leighton, *Navaho*, p. 179.
277. Carl R. Rogers, *Freedom and Commitment*, Humanist Magazine, vol. 24, no. 2, Mar.-Apr., 1964, p. 38.
278. *Ibid.,* p. 39.
279. John Dewey, *Reconstruction in Philosophy*, p. 118.
280. Loren Eiseley, *Nature, Man, and Miracle*, Horizon, July, 1960, p. 27.
281. Bertrand Russell, *The Impact of Science on Society*, from "Exploring the Universe," ed. Louise B. Young, p. 425.
282. Andreas Feininger, *Forms of Nature and Life*, p. 55.
283. Albert Schweitzer, *The Schweitzer Album*, ed. Erica Anderson, p. 40.
284. J. Bronowski, *Science and Human Values;* see also *Exploring the Universe*, ed. Louise B. Young, pp. 428-9, 434.
285. Andreas Feininger, *Forms of Nature and Life*, p. 18.

BIBLIOGRAPHY

Adamson, Joy, *Living Free,* New York: Harcourt, Brace & World, 1961.

Adler, Felix, *Personality,* from "Essays in Honor of John Dewey," New York; Henry Holt, 1929.

Aldrich, W. W., *The Incompatibility of Democracy and a Planned Economy,* Washington, Pa.: address at the Washington and Jefferson College, June 3, 1939.

Alger, W. R., *The Future Life,* Philadelphia: G. W. Childs, 1864.

Allee, W. C., *The Social Life of Animals,* New York: Norton, 1938.

Allen, Arthur A., *The Book of Bird Life,* New York: Van Nostrand, 1961.

Allen, Steve, *The Ground is Our Table,* Garden City: Double day, 1966.

Altizer, Thomas J . J., *Radical Theology and the Death of God,* New York: Bobbs-Merrill, 1966.

Andrews, Ralph W., *Indian Primitive,* New York: Bonanza, 1960.

Appel, Fredric C., *The Intellectual Mammal,* Sat. Eve. Post, Jan. 4, 1964.

Ardrey, Robert, *African Genesis,* New York: Atheneum, 1961.

———, *The Territorial Imperative,* New York: Atheneum, 1966.

Arendt, Hannah, *Eichmann in Jerusalem,* New York: Viking, 1963.

———, *The Origins of Totalitarianism,* New York: Harcourt, Brace & World, 1966.

Arndt, C. H., *A Biological Concept of Religion,* Yellow Springs, Ohio: Humanist Magazine, Sept.-Oct., 1964.

Atkinson, D. T., *Magic, Myth and Medicine,* Cleveland: World, 1956.

Backster, Cleve, article on, Thorn Bacon, Washington, D.C.: National Wildlife Magazine, Feb.-Mar., 1969.

713

Baekeland, G. Brooks, *By Parachute into Peru's Lost World*, Washington, D.C.: National Geographic Magazine, vol. 126, no. 2, August, 1964.

Bain, Read, *The Fields and Methods of Biological Sociology*, from "Fields and Methods of Sociology," ed. L. L. Bernard, New York: Ray Long and R. R. Smith, 1934.

Barach, Alvan L., *Promethean Anxieties*, Part I, New York: Columbia University Forum, vol. IX, no. 4, Fall, 1966.

Bastian, Harmut, *And Then Came Man*, New York: Viking, 1964.

Bastian, Jarvis, *Primate Signaling Systems and Human Languages*, from "Primate Behavior," ed. Irven DeVore, New York: Holt, Rinehart and Winston, 1965.

Bastide, Roger, *Color, Racism, and Christianity*, Cambridge, Mass.: Daedalus Magazine, Proceedings of the American Academy of Arts and Sciences, Spring, 1967.

Baumer, Franklin L., *Religion and the Rise of Scepticism*, New York: Harcourt, Brace, 1960.

Bazin, Germain, *A History of Art*, New York: Bonanza, no date.

Bebel, August, *Woman and Socialism*, New York: Socialist Literature, 1910.

Becker, Carl L., *How New Will the Better World Be?*, New York: Knopf, 1944.

Beckwith, Burnham, Washington, D.C.: Science Magazine, March 13, 1964, vol. 143, no. 3611.

Beer, Gavin de, *Darwin's "Origin" Today*, New York: Natural History Magazine, Aug-Sept., 1966.

Belloti, Felice, *Fabulous Congo*, London: A. Dakers, no date.

Benedict, Ruth, *The Growth of Culture*, from "Man, Culture and Society," ed. Harry L. Shapiro, New York: Oxford Galaxy, 1960.

Bere, Rennie, *The African Elephant*, New York: Golden, 1966.

Berrill, N. J., *The Living Tide*, New York: Dodd, Mead, 1951.

Birket-Smith, Kaj, *The Paths of Culture*, Madison, Wis.: University of Wisconsin Press, 1965.

Blanshard, Brand, *Heritage of Idealism*, from "Changing Patterns in American Civilization," New York: A. S. Barnes, 1962.

———, *The Case for Determinism*, from "Determinism and Freedom," ed. Sidney Hook, New York: Collier, 1961.

Blanshard, Paul, *American Freedom and Catholic Power,* Boston: Beacon, 1958.

———, *Freedom and Catholic Power in Spain and Portugal,* Boston: Beacon, 1962.

———, *God and Man in Washington,* Boston: Beacon, 1960.

Bölsche, Wilhelm, *Love-Life in Nature,* 2 vol., New York: Albert & Charles Boni, 1926.

Boros, Ladislaus, S.J., *The Mystery of Death,* New York: Herder & Herder, 1965.

Boulding, Kenneth E., *Post-Civilization,* from "Seeds of Liberation," ed. Paul Goodman, New York: George Braziller, 1964.

———, *Divine Legitimation and the Defense Establishment,* San Francisco: Humanist Magazine, Jan.-Feb., 1968.

Boulenger, E. G., *Apes and Monkeys,* New York: McBride, no date.

Boyd, William C., *Genetics and the Races of Man,* Boston: Little, Brown, 1956.

Brandon, S. G. F., *Time and the Destiny of Man,* from "Voices of Time," ed. J. T. Fraser, New York: George Braziller, 1966.

Brandon, William, *American Heritage Book of Indians,* New York: American Heritage, 1961.

Brew, J. O., *The Metal Ages: Copper, Bronze and Iron,* from "Man, Culture and Society," ed. Harry L. Shapiro, New York: Oxford Galaxy, 1960.

Briffault, Robert, *Rational Evolution,* New York: Macmillan, 1930.

Bronowski, J., *Science and Human Values,* New York: Messner, 1956.

Brophy, Brigid, *Black Ship to Hell,* New York: Harcourt, Brace & World, 1962.

Brown Network, The Activities of the Nazis in Foreign Countries, New York: Knight, 1936.

Browne, Sir Thomas, *Hydriataphia or Urne Buriall,* London, 1658.

Bruner, Jerome S., *The Perfectibility of Intellect,* from "Knowledge Among Men," New York: Simon and Schuster, 1966.

Bryce, James, *The American Commonwealth,* New York: Commonwealth, 1908.

Buchanan, Scott, *A Message to the Young,* Santa Barbara: Center Magazine, vol. I, no. 3, March, 1968.

Buck, Peter, *Material Representatives of Tongan and Samoan Gods,* from "Many Faces of Primitive Art," ed. Douglas Fraser, Englewood Cliffs, N. J.: Prentice-Hall, 1966.

Budge, Sir Wallis, *Egyptian Magic,* Evanston, Ill.: University Books, no date.

Burkhardt, Dietrich, Wolfgang Schleidt, and Helmut Altner, *Signals in the Animal World,* New York: McGraw-Hill, 1967.

Burland, C. A., *Peru Under the Incas,* New York: Putnam, 1967.

Burnet, Sir MacFarlane, *Natural History of Infectious Diseases,* Cambridge, Eng.: University Press, 1962.

Burtt, Harold E., *The Psychology of Birds,* New York: Macmillan, 1967.

Bustad, Leo K., *Schwein und Mensch sind Brüder* [Pigs and Men are Brothers], Berne, Switzerland: Tier Magazine, no. 7, July, 1967.

Calder, Ritchie, *After the Seventh Day,* New York: Simon and Schuster, 1961.

Campbell, Bernard, *Human Evolution,* Chicago: Aldine, 1966.

Campbell, Joseph, *Masks of God: Occidental Mythology,* New York: Viking, 1964.

———, *Masks of God: Oriental Mythology,* New York: Viking, 1962.

———, *Masks of God: Primitive Mythology,* New York: Viking, 1959.

———, *Masks of God: Creative Mythology,* New York: Viking, 1968.

Caras, Roger A., *Last Chance on Earth,* New York: Chilton, 1966.

Carlson, Anton J., *Physiological Processes,* from "The World and Man as Science Sees Them," ed . Forest Ray Moulton, Garden City: Doubleday, 1937.

Carrington, Richard, *A Biography of the Sea,* New York: Basic, 1960.

Carson, Rachel L., *Silent Spring,* Boston: Houghton, Mifflin, 1962.

Casas, Bartolomé de Las, *Historia de las Indias,* ed. Gonzalo de Reparaz, Madrid, 1927.

Cassirer, Ernst, *An Essay on Man,* New Haven: Yale University Press, 1944.

Castro, Josué de, *Death in the Northeast,* New York: Random House, 1966.

Ceram, C. W., *The March of Archaeology,* New York: Knopf, 1958.

Chardin, Teilhard de, *The Phenomenon of Man,* New York: Harper, 1959.

Chugerman, Samuel, *Lester F. Ward,* Durham, N. C.: Duke University Press, 1939.

Clark, R. T. Rundle, *Myth and Symbol in Ancient Egypt,* New York: Grove, 1960.

Clowes, Royston, *The Structure of Life,* Baltimore: Penguin, 1967.

Cohen, Morris R., *American Thought: A Critical Sketch,* New York: Collier, 1962.

———, *Reason and Law,* New York: Collier, 1961.

Cole, Fay-Cooper, *Man,* from "The World and Man as Science Sees Them," ed. Forest Ray Moulton, Garden City: Doubleday, Doran, 1937.

Comas, Juan, *Racial Myths,* New York: UNESCO, 1958.

Comfort, Alex, *The Nature of Human Nature,* New York: Harper & Row, 1967.

Commager, Henry Steele, *On the Way to 1984,* New York: Saturday Review, April 15, 1967.

Commoner, Barry, *Science and Survival,* New York: Viking Compass, 1967.

Conant, James B., *Man Thinking About Man,* Washington, D.C.: American Scholar, vol. 33, no. 4, Autumn, 1964.

Cook, Fred J., *The Warfare State,* New York: Macmillan, 1962.

Cook, S. F., and Woodrow Borah, *The Indian Population of Central Mexico,* 1531-1610, Berkeley: Ibero-Americana 44, University of California Press, 1960.

Coon, Carleton S., *Origin of Races,* New York: Knopf, 1962.

Covarrubias, Miguel, *Island of Bali,* New York: Knopf, 1937.

Cowan, Ian McTaggart, *Conservation and Man's Environment*, from "Knowledge Among Men," New York: Simon and Schuster, 1966.

Cowan, *Curious Facts in the History of Insects*, New York: Lippincott, 1865.

Cowie, Mervyn, *The African Lion*, New York: Golden, 1966.

Crampton, Henry E., *The Coming and Evolution of Life*, New York: University Series, 2nd Unit, Part II, The University Society, 1931.

Craveri, Marcello, *The Life of Jesus*, New York: Grove, 1967.

Crawford, Ann Caddell, *Customs and Culture of Vietnam*, Rutland, Vt.: Tuttle, 1966.

Cressman, L. S., *Man in the New World*, from "Man, Culture and Society," ed. Harry L. Shapiro, New York: Oxford Galaxy, 1960.

Cromie, William J., *Exploring the Secrets of the Sea*, Englewood Cliffs, N. J.: Prentice-Hall, 1962.

——, *The Living World of the Sea*, Englewood Cliffs, N. J.: Prentice-Hall, 1966.

Curwen, E. Cecil, and Gudmund Hatt, *Plough and Pasture*, New York: Collier, 1961.

Danielsson, Bengt, *Gauguin in the South Seas*, New York: Doubleday, 1966.

——, *Love in the South Seas*, New York: Reynal, 1956.

Darley, Henry, *Slaves and Ivory in Abyssinia*, New York: McBride, 1935.

Darwin, Charles, *Descent of Man*, New York: Appleton, 1930.

Davies, A. Powell, *The Mind and Faith of A. Powell Davies*, ed. William O. Douglas, Garden City, Doubleday, 1959.

Davies, John Langdon, *A Short History of Women*, New York: Viking, 1927.

Davis, Jerome, *Capitalism and Its Culture*, New York: Farrar & Rinehart, 1935.

Davison, Peter, *Hunger, a poem*, New York: Hudson Review, vol. XVI, no. 3, Autumn, 1963.

Dawidowicz, Lucy S., *On Being a Woman in Shul*, New York: Commentary, vol. 46, no. 1, July, 1968.

Dawson, E. Yale, *The Giants of Galapagos,* New York: Natural History Magazine, November, 1962.

Dellhora, Guillermo, *La Iglesia Catolica ante la Critica en el Pensamiento y en el Arte,* Mexico City: Ediciones Dellhora, 1929.

Denison, J. H., *Emotion as the Basis of Civilization,* New York: Scribner's, 1928.

——, *This Human Nature,* New York: Scribner's, 1930.

Dethier, V. G., *Microscopic Brains,* Washington, D.C.: Science Magazine, vol. 143, no. 3611, Mar. 13, 1964.

Devoe, Allan, *This Fascinating Animal World,* New York: McGraw-Hill, 1951.

Dewey, John, *A Common Faith,* New Haven: Yale University Press, 1934.

——, *Antinaturalism in Extremis,* from "Naturalism and the Human Spirit," New York: Columbia University Press, 1944.

——, *Art as Experience,* New York: Minton, Balch, 1934.

——, *Freedom and Culture,* New York: Putnam's, 1939.

——, *Human Nature and Conduct,* New York: Modern Library, 1930.

——, *Individualism, Old and New,* New York: Minton, Balch.

——, *Liberalism and Social Action,* New York: Putnam's, 1935.

——, *Nature and Experience,* New York: Norton, 1929.

——, *Reconstruction in Philosophy,* New York: Henry Holt, 1920.

Dickey, Herbert S., *My Jungle Book,* Boston: Little, Brown, 1932.

Dobzhansky, Theodosius, *Mankind Evolving,* New Haven: Yale University Press, 1962.

Dooley, Thomas A., *The Edge of Tomorrow,* New York: Farrar, Strauss, 1958.

Dorson, Richard M., *Folk Legends of Japan,* Rutland, Vt.: Tuttle, 1962.

Douglas, William O., *Farewell to Texas, A Vanishing Wilderness,* New York: McGraw-Hill, 1967.

——, *My Wilderness: East to Katahdin,* New York: Doubleday, 1961.

———, *The Bible and the Schools,* Boston: Little, Brown, 1966.

DuBay, William H., *The Human Church,* Garden City: Double-day, 1966.

Dubos, René, *Humanistic Biology,* Washington, D.C.: American Scholar, vol. 34, no. 2, Spring, 1965.

———, *So Human an Animal,* New York: Scribner's, 1968.

Ducasse, C. J., *Determinism, Freedom, and Responsibility,* from "Determinism and Freedom," ed. Sidney Hook, New York: Collier, 1961.

Duff, Charles, *This Human Nature,* New York: Cosmopolitan, 1930.

Dufresne, Frank, *No Room for Bears,* New York: Holt, Rinehart & Winston, 1965.

Dunham, Barrows, *Heroes and Heretics,* New York: Knopf, 1964.

———, *Man Against Myth,* Boston: Little, Brown, 1947.

Dunlap, Samuel F., *The Ghebers of Hebron,* New York: J. W. Bouton, 1898.

Dunn, L. C., *Race and Biology,* New York: UNESCO, 1958.

Durkheim, Emile, *Elementary Forms of the Religious Life,* New York: Collier, 1961.

Durrell, Gerald, *A Zoo in My Luggage,* New York: Viking, 1960.

———, *The Whispering Land,* New York: Viking, 1962.

Edwardes, Allen, *The Jewel in the Lotus,* New York: Julian, 1959.

Edwards, Paul, *Hard and Soft Determinism,* from "Determinism and Freedom," ed. Sidney Hook, New York: Collier, 1961.

Eibl-Eibesfeldt, Irenäus, Land of a *Thousand Atolls,* Cleveland: World, 1966.

Einstein, Albert, *The World as I See it,* New York: Philosophical Library, 1949.

Eiseley, Loren, *Epitaph,* a poem, Washington, D.C.: American Scholar, vol. 35, no. 2, Spring, 1966.

———, *Nature, Man and Miracle,* New York: Horizon, July, 1960.

———, *Science and the Unexpected Universe,* Washington, D.C.: American Scholar, vol. 35, no. 3, Summer, 1966.

———, *The Firmament of Time,* New York: Atheneum, 1960.

———, *The Immense Journey,* London: Victor Gollanez, 1958.

Eliot, Charles W., *The Durable Satisfactions of Life,* New York: T. Y. Crowell, 1910.

Engel, Fritz-Martin, *Life Around Us,* New York: T. Y. Crowell, 1965.

Epictetus, *Discourses* of, trans. George Lang, New York: A. L. Burt, no date.

Ericson, David B., and Goesta Wollin, *The Ever-Changing Sea,* New York: Knopf, 1967.

Evans, E. P., *Evolutional Ethics and Animal Psychology,* London: Heinemann, 1898.

Evans, William F., *Communication in the Animal World,* New York: T. Y. Crowell, 1968.

Fabre, J. Henri, *The Insect World,* ed. E. W. Teale, New York: Dodd, Mead, 1949.

——, *Social Life in the Insect World,* London: Penguin, 1911.

Farb, Peter, *Man's Rise to Civilization,* New York: Dutton, 1968.

Faure, Elie, *History of Art,* Garden City: Garden City Pub., 1937.

Feininger, Andreas, *Forms of Nature and Life,* New York: Viking, 1966.

Fielding, William J., *The Shackles of the Supernatural,* Girard, Kan.: Haldeman-Julius, 1938.

Fisher, Allan C., *Nature of the Atom,* Washington, D.C.: National Geographic Magazine, 1958.

Forel, Auguste, *The Social World of the Ants,* 2 vol., New York: Albert & Charles Boni, 1929.

Fournier, E. E., *Hephaestus, or the Soul of the Machine,* New York: Dutton, no date.

Frazer, James G., *The Golden Bough,* 13 vol., New York: Macmillan, 1935.

——, *The Golden Bough,* 1 vol. ed., New York, Macmillan, 1922.

——, *Man, God and Immortality,* New York: Macmillan, 1927.

——, *The Scope of Social Anthropology,* London: P. Lund Humphries, 1938.

Freuchen, Peter, *The Book of the Eskimos,* Cleveland: World, 1961.

Freud, Sigmund, *The Future of an Illusion,* London: Hogarth, 1949.

Friedlander, Saul, *Pius XII and the Third Reich,* New York: Knopf, 1966.

Friedman, Maurice, ed. *The Worlds of Existentialism,* New York: Random House, 1964.

Fromm, Erich, *The Marketing Orientation,* from "America as Mass Society," ed. Philip Olson, Glencoe, Ill.: Free Press, 1963.

Gager, D. Stuart, *The Plant World,* New York: University Series, 1st Unit, Part III, University Society, 1931.

Gann, Thomas, and J. Eric Thompson, *The History of the Maya,* New York: Scribner's, 1931.

Gaster, Theodor H., *Customs and Folkways of Jewish Life,* New York: William Sloane Associates, 1955.

Gesell, Robert, Annals of Allergy, March-April, 1953.

Golding, William, *The Lord of the Flies,* New York: Putnam's, 1959.

Goodenough, Ward H., *Arms Control and Behavior Science,* Washington, D.C.: Science Magazine, vol. 144, no. 3620, May 15, 1964.

Grant, Michael, *Myths of the Greeks and Romans,* Cleveland: World, 1962.

Grant, E. I. Watson, *Mysteries of Natural History,* New York: Stokes, 1937.

Graubard, Mark, *Man the Slave and Master,* New York: Covici-Friede, 1938.

Graves, Robert, and Raphael Patai, *Hebrew Myths,* Garden City: Doubleday, 1964.

Gray, John, *The Canaanites,* New York: Praeger, 1964.

Gregory, William K., and Marcella Roigneau, *Introduction to Human Anatomy,* New York: American Museum of Natural History, Series 86.

Griffin, James B., *The Study of Early Cultures,* from "Man, Culture and Society," ed. Harry L. Shapiro, New York: Oxford Galaxy, 1960.

Grimal, Pierre, *The Civilization of Rome,* New York: Simon and Schuster, 1963.

Gronefeld, Gerhard, *Understanding Animals,* New York: Viking, 1965.

Grzimek, Bernhard and Michael, *Serengati Shall Not Die,* New York: Dutton, 1961.

Grzimek, Bernhard, *Such Agreeable Friends,* New York: Hill and Wang, 1964.

Guiart, Jean, *The Arts of the South Pacific,* New York: Golden, 1963.

Hagen, Victor W. von, *The Ancient Sun Kingdoms of the Americas,* Cleveland: World, 1961.

Hallet, Jean-Pierre, *Animal Kitabu,* New York: Random House, 1968.

Hanf, Walter, *Mexico,* Munich: Wilhelm Anderman Verlag, 1967.

Harden, Donald, *The Phoenicians,* New York: Praeger, 1962.

Harris, Louis, *The Story of Crime,* New Haven: Literary Press, 1929.

Hart, Barnard, *The Psychology of Insanity,* Cambridge, Eng.: University Press, 1928.

Hart, Joseph K., *Inside Experience,* New York: Longmans, Green, 1927.

Hawkes, Jacquetta, and Sir Leonard Woolley, *Prehistory and the Beginnings of Civilization,* from "The History of Mankind," vol. I, New York: Harper & Row, 1963.

Hays, H. R., *From Ape to Angel,* New York: Knopf, 1958.

———, *In the Beginnings,* New York: Putnam's, 1963.

———, *The Dangerous Sex,* New York: Putnam's, 1964.

Headley, F. W., *Problems of Evolution,* New York: T. Y. Crowell, 1931.

Heck, Heinz, *The Future of Animals,* from "The Survival of the Free," New York: Putnam's, 1962.

Hediger, Heini, *Evolution of Territorial Behavior,* from "The Social Life of Early Man," ed. S. L. Washburn, New York: Wenner-Gren Foundation for Anthropological Research, 1961.

Heer, Friedrich, *Die Deutschen der Nationalsozialismus und die Gegenwart,* Bielefeld, Fed. Rep. of Germany: 1960.

Heilner, van Campen, *Salt Water Fishing,* New York: Knopf, 1943.

Heinemann, F. H., *Existentialism and the Modern Predicament,* New York: Harper, 1958.

Hempel, Carl G., *Some Reflections on "The Case for Determinism,"* from "Determinism and Freedom," ed. Sidney Hook, New York: Collier, 1961.

Henry, Jules, *Culture Against Man,* New York: Random House, 1963.

Herzog, Edgar, *Psyche and Death,* New York: Putnam's, 1967.

Hesse, Hermann, *Siddhartha,* New York: New Directions, 1957.

Hibbert, Christopher, *Garibaldi,* Boston: Little, Brown, 1965.

Hilscher, Herb and Miriam, *Alaska, U.S.A.,* Boston: Little, Brown, 1959.

Hingston, R. W. G., *Instinct and Intelligence,* New York: Macmillan, 1929.

Hintz, Howard, *Some Further Reflections on Moral Responsibility,* from "Determinism and Freedom," ed. Sidney Hook, New York: Collier, 1961.

Hoagland, Hudson, *Science and the New Humanism,* Washington, D.C.: Science Magazine, vol. 143, no. 3602, Jan. 10, 1964.

——, *Correspondence,* Science Magazine, vol. 143, no. 3611, March 13, 1964.

Hobsbawn, E. J., *The Age of Revolution,* Cleveland: World, 1962.

Hochhuth, Rolf, *The Deputy,* New York: Grove, 1964.

Hoebel, E. Adamson, *The Nature of Culture,* from "Man, Culture and Society," ed. Harry L. Shapiro, New York: Oxford Galaxy, 1960.

Hoffer, Eric, *The Ordeal of Change,* New York: Harper & Row, 1963.

Hoijer, Harry, *Language and Writing,* from "Man, Culture and Society," ed. Harry L. Shapiro, New York: Oxford Galaxy, 1960.

Honigmann, John J., *The Study of Personality in Primitive Societies,* from "The Study of Personality," ed. Edward Norbeck, *et al.,* New York: Holt, Rinehart & Winston, 1968.

Hook, Sidney, *Necessity, Indeterminism, and Sentimentalism,* from "Determinism and Freedom," ed. Sidney Hook, New York: Collier, 1961.

——, *Political Power and Personal Freedom,* New York: Collier, 1962.

Hooton, E. A., *Apes, Men and Morons,* New York: Putnam's, 1937.

——, *Man's Poor Relations,* Garden City: Doubleday, Doran, 1942.

Howey, W. Oldfield, *The Cat in Religion and Magic,* New York: Castle, 1956.

Hoyle, Fred, *Can We Learn from Other Planets?,* New York: Saturday Review, Nov. 7, 1964.

——, *Nature of the Universe,* New York: Harper, 1950.

Hulse, Fred. S., *The Human Species,* New York: Random House, 1963.

Hunt, Frazier, *This Bewildered World,* New York: Stokes, 1934.

Huxley, Julian, *Ants,* New York: Cape and Ballou, 1930.

——, *Evolution, Cultural and Biological,* New York: Current Anthropology, 1956.

Hylander, C. J., *The World of Plant Life,* New York: Macmillan, 1944.

Idyll, C. P., *Abyss, The Deep Sea and the Creatures That Live in It,* New York: T. Y. Crowell, 1964.

Ingelman-Sundberg, A., *A Child is Born,* New York: Delacorte, 1965.

Isaac, Jules, *The Teaching of Contempt,* New York: Holt, Rinehart & Winston, 1964.

Jahn, Janheinz, *Muntu,* New York: Grove, 1961.

James, E. O., *Ancient Gods,* New York: Putnam's, 1960.

James, William, *Pragmatism,* New York: Longmans, Green, 1909.

Jaspers, Karl, *The Worlds of Existentialism,* ed. Maurice Friedman, New York: Random House, 1964.

Jeans, Sir James, *Living Philosophies,* New York: Simon and Schuster, 1931.

Jefferson, Thomas, *Notes on the State of Virginia.*

——, *Writings of Jefferson,* Memorial Edition, 1903.

Jensen, Adolf E., *Die mythische Weltbetrachtung der alten Pflanzer-Volker,* Zurich: Eranos-Jahrbuch, Rhein-Verlag, 1950.

Joad, Cyril E. M., *Decadence; A Philosophical Inquiry,* London: 1948.

Josephy, Jr., Alvin M., *The Indian Heritage of America,* New York: Knopf, 1968.

Kahler, Erich, *Man the Measure,* New York: Braziller, 1961.

Kallen, Horace M., *How I Bet My Life,* New York: Saturday Review, Oct. 1, 1966.

Kalmer, Leo, *Crime and Religion,* ed. James Meyer, Chicago: Franciscan Herald, 1936.

Kaplan, Abraham, *The New World of Philosophy,* New York: Vintage, 1961.

Kaufmann, Walter, *Critique of Religion and Philosophy,* New York: Harper, 1958.

Kavanaugh, Father James, *A Modern Priest Looks at His Outdated Church,* New York: Sat. Eve. Post, June 13, 1967.

Keen, Benjamin, *Life and Labor in Ancient Mexico,* New Brunswick, N. J.: Rutgers University Press, 1963.

Keith, Sir Arthur, *Living Philosophies,* New York: Simon and Schuster, 1931.

Keller, W. Phillip, *Under Wilderness Skies,* London: Jarrolds, 1966.

Kessler, *Memoirs,* of the St. Petersburg Society of Naturalists, vol. XI, St. Petersburg, Russia, 1880.

Kirchshofer, Rosl, *The World of Zoos,* New York: Viking, 1968.

Kluckhohn, Clyde, *Mirror for Man,* New York: McGraw-Hill, 1949.

———, and Dorothea Leighton, *Navaho,* Garden City: Doubleday, 1962.

Koestler, Arthur, *The Sleepwalkers,* New York: Macmillan, 1959.

Kotker, Norman, *The Literary Road to Rome,* New York: Horizon, vol. IX, no. 3, Summer, 1967.

Kramer, Samuel Noah, *Sumerian Mythology,* New York: Harper & Row, 1961.

Kroeber, Theodora, *Ishi,* Los Angeles; University of California Press, 1961.

Kronhausen, Phyllis and Eberhard, *Pornography and the Law,* New York: Ballantine, 1959.

Kurtz, Paul , *Joyful Humanism,* Yellow Springs, Ohio: Humanist Magazine, vol. XXVII, no. 2, Mar.-Apr., 1967.

Kyber, Manfred, *Among Animals,* Fontwell, Eng.: Centaur, 1967.

LaCroix, Paul, *History of Prostitution,* 3 vol., Chicago: Pascal Covici, 1926.

Lamont, Corliss, *The Philosophy of Humanism,* New York: Philosophical Library, 1949.

——, *Freedom of Choice Affirmed,* New York: Horizon, 1967.

Lane, Frank W., *Kingdom of the Octopus,* New York: Sheridan House, 1960.

Lang, Ernst M., *The Story of Jambo,* Washington, D.C.: National Geographic Magazine, vol. 125, no. 3, March, 1964.

Larson, Martin A., *The Religion of the Occident,* New York: Philosophical Library, 1959.

Latcham, R. E., *Ethnology of the Auracanos,* from "Primitive Heritage," ed. Margaret Mead and Nicolas Calas, New York: Random House, 1953.

Lawick-Goodall, Jane van, *My Friends, the Wild Chimpanzees,* Washington, D.C.: National Geographic Society, 1967.

Lea, Henry Charles, *A History of Auricular Confession,* Philadelphia: Sea Brothers, 1896.

Leakey, L. S. B., *Adam's Ancestors,* New York: Longmans, Green, 1935.

Lecomte, Jacques, *Animals in Our World,* New York: Holt, Rinehart & Winston, 1967.

Lee, W. Storrs, *The Islands,* New York: Holt, Rinehart & Winston, 1966.

Leuba, James A., *The Belief in God and Immortality,* Chicago: Open Court, 1921.

Lévy-Bruhl, Lucién, *The "Soul" of the Primitive,* New York: Macmillan, 1928.

——, *What the Natives Think of Pictures, Names and Dreams,*

from "Primitive Heritage," ed. Margaret Mead and Nicolas Calas, New York; Random House, 1953.

Lévi-Strauss, Claude, *The World on the Wane,* New York: Criterion, 1961.

———, *The Savage Mind,* Chicago: University of Chicago Press, 1966.

Lewis, Oscar, *The Children of Sanchez,* New York: Random House, 1961.

———, *La Vida,* New York: Random House, 1966.

Lewy, Guenter, *The Catholic Church and Nazi Germany,* New York: McGraw-Hill, 1964.

Lillie, William, *Introduction to Ethics,* New York: University Paperbacks, 1961.

Linnér, Birgitta, *Sex and Society in Sweden,* New York: Pantheon, 1967.

Lommel, Andreas, *Prehistoric and Primitive Man,* New York: McGraw-Hill, 1966.

Lopez, Robert, *The Birth of Europe,* Philadelphia: Evans-Lippincott, 1967.

Lust, Peter, *The Last Seal Pup,* Montreal: Harvest House, 1967.

Luther, Martin, *On Commerce and Usury,* from "Religion and the Rise of Capitalism," New York: Harcourt, Brace, 1926.

MacBride, E. W., *Evolution,* New York: R. M. McBride, no date.

MacEvan, Douglas M. C., *Conservation as the Intelligent and Purposeful Control of Human Environment,* Utrecht, Netherlands: International Humanism, vol. III, no. 1, 1968.

MacLeish, Archibald, *The Great American Frustration,* New York: Saturday Review, July 13, 1968.

MacNeish, Richard S., *Ancient Mesoamerican Civilization,* Washington, D.C.: Science Magazine, vol. 143, no. 3606, Feb. 7, 1964.

Maimonides, Moses, *Writings* of, *In Time and Eternity,* ed. Nahum N. Glatzer, New York: Schocken, 1946.

Malamud, Bernard, *The Fixer,* New York: Farrar, Strauss & Giroux, 1966.

Malinowski, Bronislaw, *Myth in Primitive Psychology,* Frazer

Lecture in Social Anthropology for 1925, London: K. Paul, Trench, Trubner, 1926.

———, *Sex, Culture and Myth,* New York: Harcourt, Brace & World, 1962.

Marais, Eugene, *The Soul of the White Ant,* New York: Dodd-Mead, 1937.

Marett, Ronald R., *Religion,* from "Notes and Queries on Anthropology," 4th ed., London: 1912.

Marler, Peter, *Communication in Monkeys and Apes,* from "Primate Behavior," ed. Irven DeVore, New York: Holt, Rinehart & Winston, 1965.

Marti-Ibañez, Felix, *Byzantine Art,* New York: MD Medical Magazine, vol. II, no. 2, February, 1967.

———, *Early Christian Art, loc. cit.*

———, *Magic and Drama of Byzantium, loc. cit.*

Martin, Everett Dean, *Farewell to Revolution,* New York: Norton, 1935.

Martin, Richard A., *Mummies,* Chicago: Natural History Museum, Anthropology, no. 36, 1945.

Mason, William A., *The Social Development of Monkeys and Apes,* from "Primate Behavior," ed. Irven DeVore, New York: Holt, Rinehart & Winston, 1965.

Masserman, Jules H., *The Biodynamic Roots of Psychoanalysis,* from "Modern Psychoanalysis," New York: Basic Books, 1968.

Matson, Wallace I., *The Existence of God,* Ithaca: Cornell University Press, 1965.

Matthews, Herbert L., *The Yoke and the Arrows,* New York: Braziller, 1961.

Matthiessen, Peter, *The Cloud Forest,* New York: Viking, 1961.

———, *Under the Mountain Wall,* New York: Viking, 1962.

Matthiessen, F. O., *The Pattern of Literature,* from "Changing Patterns in American Civilization," New York: A. S. Barnes, 1962.

Maurois, André, *The War Against the Moon,* New York: Dutton, 1928.

Maxwell, Gavin, *Seals of the World,* Boston: Houghton, Mifflin, 1967.

McCloud, Janet, *The Continuing "Last Indian War,"* Yellow Springs, Ohio: Humanist Magazine, vol. XXVII, no. 5-6, Fall, 1967.

McCormack, Jack, *The Living Forest,* New York: Harper, 1959.

McDougall, William, *Social Psychology,* London: 1908.

McGrady, Pat, *The Savage Cell,* New York: Basic Books, 1964.

McLoughlin, Emmett, *People's Padre,* Boston: Beacon, 1954.

———, *Crime and Immorality in the Catholic Church,* New York: Lyle Stuart, 1962.

Mead, Margaret, *Continuities in Cultural Evolution,* New Haven: Yale University Press, 1964.

———, *Closing Address, Problems and Progress in the Study of Personality,* from "The Study of Personality," ed. Edward Norbeck, *et al.,* New York: Holt, Rinehart & Winston, 1968.

Mech, Dave, *The Wolf,* Washington, D.C.: National Wildlife Magazine, Feb.-Mar., 1968.

Menget, Patrick, *Death in Chamula,* New York: Natural History Magazine, vol. LXXVII, no. 1, January, 1968.

Metchnikoff, Élie, *The Nature of Life,* New York: Putnam's, 1906.

Mills, C. Wright, *The Power Elite,* from "America as a Mass Society," ed. Philip Olson, Chicago: Free Press, 1963.

Milne, Lorus and Margery, *The Senses of Animals and Men,* New York: Atheneum, 1962.

Miner, Roy Waldo, *Fragile Creatures of the Deep, The Story of the Hydroids,* New York: American Museum of Natural History, Natural History Magazine, vol. XLII, November, 1938.

Miranda, José, *El Tributo indigena en la Nueva España durante el siglo XVI,* Mexico City: Colegio de Mexico, 1952.

Mitford, Jessica, *The American Way of Death,* New York: Simon and Schuster, 1963.

Mitrany, David, *Marx Against the Peasant,* New York: Collier, 1961.

Miyadi, Denzaburo, *Social Life of Japanese Monkeys,* Washington, D.C.: Science Magazine, vol. 143, no. 3608, Feb. 21, 1964.

Moloney, James Clark, *Understanding the Japanese Mind,* Rutland, Vt.: Tuttle, 1954.

Montagu, Ashley, *Immortality,* New York: Grove, 1955.

———, *The Concept of Race,* Glencoe, Ill.: Free Press, 1964.

Mooney, J., *The Sacred Formulas of the Cherokees,* from "Primitive Heritage," ed. Margaret Mead and Nicolas Calas, New York: Random House, 1953.

Moorehead, Alan, *The Fatal Impact,* New York: Harper & Row, 1966.

Morley, Sylvanus G., *The Ancient Maya,* Stanford: Stanford University Press, 1946.

Morris, Desmond, *The Naked Ape,* New York: McGraw-Hill, 1968.

Morton, Frederic, *The Rothschilds,* New York: Atheneum, 1962.

Moscati, Sabatino, *Ancient Semitic Civilizations,* London: Elek, 1957.

Movius, H. L., Jr., *The Old Stone Age,* from "Man, Culture and Society," ed. Harry L. Shapiro, New York: Oxford Galaxy, 1960.

Mowat, Farley, *Never Cry Wolf,* Boston: Little, Brown, 1963.

Muller, Herbert J., *Freedom in the Ancient World,* New York: Harper, 1961.

———, *Freedom in the Modern World,* Chicago: University of Chicago Press, 1963.

Mumford, Lewis, *Technics and the Nature of Man,* from "Knowledge Among Men," New York: Simon and Schuster, 1966.

———, *The Myth of the Machine,* New York: Harcourt, Brace & World, 1967.

Murdock, George Peter, *How Culture Changes,* from "Man, Culture and Society," ed. Harry L. Shapiro, New York: Oxford Galaxy, 1960.

Murra, John V., *Guamán Poma de Ayala,* New York: Natural History Magazine, Aug.-Sept., 1961.

Nagel, Ernst, *Some Notes on Determinism,* from "Determinism and Freedom," ed. Sidney Hook, New York: Collier, 1961.

Nansen, Fridtjof, *Living Philosophies,* New York: Simon and Schuster, 1931.

Nathan, George Jean, *Living Philosophies,* New York: Simon and Schuster, 1931.

Nemecek, Ottaker, *Virginity, Pre-Nuptial Rites and Rituals*, New York: Citadel, 1962.

Nicholson, Soterios, *War or a United World*, New York: Washington, 1916.

Nietzsche, *Thus Spake Zarathustra*, New York: Macmillan, 1896; Modern Library, 1929.

North, Sterling, *Who is Afraid of a Little Wolf?*, Washington, D.C.: Defenders of Wildlife, Aug.-Sept., 1968.

Noyes, Rufus K., *Views of Religion*, Boston: L. K. Washburn, 1906.

Oliver, Douglas L., *The Pacific Islands*, Garden City: Doubleday, 1961.

Ommanney, F. D., *A Draught of Fishes*, New York: T. Y. Crowell, 1965.

Oparin, A. I., *Origin of Life*, New York: Macmillan, 1938.

Overstreet,, H. A., *The Enduring Quest*, Chautauqua, N. Y.: Chautauqua Press, 1931.

Padden, R. C., *The Hummingbird and the Hawk*, Ohio State University Press, 1967.

Painter, Sidney, *French Chivalry*, Baltimore, 1940.

Pap, Arthur, *Determinism, Freedom, Moral Responsibility and Casual Talk*, from "Determinism and Freedom," ed. Sidney Hook, New York: Collier, 1961.

Pareti, Luigi, Paolo Brezzi and Luciano Petech, *The Ancient World,* from "The History of Mankind," vol. II, New York: Harper & Row, 1965.

Park, Willard Z., *Paviotso Shamanism*, from "The North American Indians," ed. R. C. Owen, *et al.*, New York: Macmillan, 1967.

Parmelee, Maurice, *The Fields and Problems of Criminology*, from "The Fields and Methods of Sociology," ed. L. L. Bernard, New York: Ray Long and R. R. Smith, 1934.

Paulsen, Friedrich, *Introduction to Philosophy*, New York: Holt, 1907.

Pearson, Kenneth, and Patricia Connor, *The Strange Case of*

James Mellaart, New York: Horizon, vol. IX, no. 3, Summer, 1967.

Peattie, Donald Culross, *Flowering Earth,* New York: Putnam's, 1939.

———, *This is Living,* New York: Dodd-Mead, 1938.

Peck, Joseph H., *Life with Women and How to Survive It,* New York: Pocket Books, 1962.

Perry, Richard, *The World of the Polar Bear,* Seattle: University of Washington Press, 1966.

Peterkin, Julia, *Living Philosophies,* New York: Simon and Schuster, 1931.

Pieron, Henri, *Thought and the Brain,* New York: Harcourt, Brace, 1927.

Pimlott, Douglas H., *The Whitecoat in Peril,* New York: Audubon Magazine, vol. 69, no. 5, Sept.-Oct., 1967.

Pinney, Roy, *Vanishing Wildlife,* New York: Dodd-Mead, 1963.

Pomerai, Ralph de, *Marriage,* New York: Richard R. Smith, 1930.

Portmann, Adolf, *Animals as Social Beings,* New York: Viking, 1961.

Pramer, David, *Nematode-Trapping Fungi,* Washington, D.C.: Science Magazine, vol. 144, no. 3617, April 24, 1964.

Prittie, Terence, *Israel, The Miracle in the Desert,* New York: Praeger, 1967.

Proctor, Richard A., *Our Place Among Infinities,* New York: D. Appleton, 1889; London: Longmans, Green, 1897.

Pyramid Utterance no. 527: "Atum was creative in that he proceeded to masturbate with himself in Heliopolis; he put his penis in his hand that he might obtain the pleasure of emission thereby and there was born brother and sister—that is, *Shu* and *Tefnut.*"

Randall, John Herman, Jr., *Introduction to Philosophy,* New York: Barnes & Noble, 1961.

Ratner, Joseph, *Introduction to the Intelligence in the Modern World,* New York: Modern Library, 1939.

Rauschning, Hermann, *The Revolution of Nihilism,* New York: Alliance Book, 1939.

Ray, Carleton, and Elgin Ciampi, *Marine Life,* New York: A. S. Barnes, 1956.

Reade, Winwood, *Martyrdom of Man,* London: Watts, 1924.

Redfield, Robert, *How Human Society Operates,* from "Man, Culture and Society," ed. Harry L. Shapiro, New York: Oxford Galaxy, 1960.

Reid, Leslie, *Earth's Company,* London: John Murray, 1958.

Reik, Theodor, *Pagan Rites in Judaism,* New York: Farrar, Strauss, 1964.

Reiser, Oliver L., *The Alchemy of Light and Color,* New York: Norton, 1928.

Reitmeister, Louis A., *The Gods and My Friends,* New York: Walden Press, 1948.

Renan, Ernst, *The Future of Science,* Boston: Roberts Bros., 1891.

Renaissance, Horizon Book of the, ed. Richard M. Ketchum, New York: American Heritage, 1961.

Reynolds, Vernon, *The Apes,* New York: Dutton, 1967.

Ricketts, Edward F., and Jack Calvin, *Between Pacific Tides,* revised by Joel W. Hedgpeth, Stanford: Stanford University Press, 1968.

Riesman, David, *Individualism Reconsidered,* Garden City, Doubleday, 1955.

Robinson, James Harvey, *The Mind in the Making,* New York: Harper, 1921.

Roedelberger, Franz A., and Vera Groschoff, *The Wonders of Wildlife,* New York: Viking, 1963.

Rogers, Carl R., *Freedom and Commitment,* Yellow Springs, Ohio: Humanist Magazine, vol. 24, no. 2, Mar.-Apr., 1964.

Róheim, Géza, *The Riddle of the Sphinx,* London, 1934.

Roubiczek, Paul, *Existentialism, For and Against,* Cambridge, Eng.: Cambridge University Press, 1964.

Rudd, R. C., *Pesticides and the Living Landscape,* Madison, Wis.: University of Wisconsin Press, 1964.

Rudwin, Maxmillian, *The Devil in Legend and Literature,* La Salle, Ill.: Open Court, 1931.

Rue III, Leonard Lee, *Photographs,* New York: Natural History Magazine, June-July, 1964.

Russell, Bertrand, *Authority and the Individual,* Boston: Beacon, 1960.

——, *The Impact of Science on Society,* from "Exploring the Universe," ed. Louise B. Young, New York: McGraw-Hill, 1963.

——, *In Praise of Idleness,* New York: Norton, 1935.

——, *My Philosophical Development,* London: Allen & Unwin, 1959.

——, *Mysticism and Logic,* New York: Norton, 1929.

——, *Our Knowledge of the External World,* New York: Norton, 1929.

——, *Power,* New York: Barnes & Noble, 1962.

——, *Sceptical Essays,* New York: Norton, 1928.

——, *Why Men Fight,* New York: Century, 1916.

——, *Why I am not a Christian,* New York: Simon and Schuster, 1957.

——, *The Will to Doubt,* New York: Wisdom Library, 1958.

Russell, Walter, *The Universal One,* New York: privately printed.

Sandifer, Durward V., and L. Ronald Scheman, *The Foundations of Freedom,* New York: Praeger, 1966.

Santayana, George, *The Letters of George Santayana,* ed. Daniel Dory, New York: Scribner's, 1955.

——, *The Life of Reason,* 5 vol., New York: Collier, 1962.

Sartre, Jean-Paul, *Existentialism and Human Emotions,* New York: Philosophical Library, 1957.

Saul, Leon J., *The Hostile Mind,* New York: Random House, 1956.

Schaller, George B., *The Year of the Gorilla,* Chicago: University of Chicago Press, 1964.

Schellenberg, Walter, *The Labyrinth: Memoirs of Walter Schellenberg,* New York: Harper, 1956.

Schiller, Friedrich, *The Works of Friedrich Schiller,* vol. *Poems,* ed. Nathan Haskell Dole, Boston: Wyman-Fogg, 1902.

Schlick, Moritz, *Problems of Ethics,* Englewood Cliffs, N. J.: Prentice-Hall, 1939; also Dover, 1962.

Schultz, Harald, *Hombu, Indian Life in the Brazilian Jungle,* New York: Macmillan, 1962.

Schweitzer, Albert, *African Notebook,* Bloomington, Ind.: Indiana University Press, 1958.

———, *The Schweitzer Album,* ed. Erica Anderson, New York: Harper & Row, 1965.

———, *The Philosophy of Civilization,* New York: Macmillan, 1960.

Scott, John Paul, *Animal Behavior,* Garden City: Doubleday, 1963; also Chicago: University of Chicago Press, 1958.

Scriven, Michael, *Primary Philosophy,* New York: McGraw-Hill, 1966.

Seaborg, Glenn T., *Science and the Humanities, A New Level of Symbiosis,* Washington, D.C.: Science Magazine, vol. 144, no. 3623, June 5, 1964.

Shapiro, Harry L., *Human Beginnings,* from "Man, Culture and Society," ed. Harry L. Shapiro, New York: Oxford Galaxy, 1960.

———, *Race Mixture,* New York: UNESCO, 1953.

Shapiro, Karl, *In Defense of Ignorance,* New York: Vintage, 1965.

Sheldrick, Daphne, *The Orphans of Tsavo,* New York: David McKay, 1967.

Sherrington, Sir Charles Scott, *Man on His Nature,* Gifford Lectures, 1937-38, Cambridge, Eng.: University Press, 1940; also New York: Macmillan, 1941.

Shih, Hu, *Living Philosophies,* New York: Simon and Schuster, 1931.

Shor, Franc, *Conquest of the Holy City,* Washington, D.C.: National Geographic Magazine, vol. 124, no. 6, December, 1963.

Sigerist, Henry E., *A History of Medicine,* New York: Oxford University Press, 1961; also Pub. no. 38, Dept. of the History of Medicine, New Haven: Yale University Press, 1959.

Silverberg, Robert, *The Auk, the Dodo, and the Oryx,* New York: T. Y. Crowell, 1967.

Simon, Edith, *The Piebald Standard: A Biography of the Knights Templars,* London, 1959.

Simpson, George Gaylord, *The Major Features of Evolution,* New York: Columbia University Press, 1953.

——, *The Crisis in Biology*, Washington, D.C.: American Scholar, vol. 36, no. 3, Summer, 1967.

——, *The Meaning of Evolution*, Terry Foundation Lecture Series, New Haven: Yale University Press, 1952.

——, *The Nonprevalence of Humanoids*, Washington, D.C.: Science Magazine, vol. 143, no. 3608, Feb. 21, 1964.

——, *This View of Life*, New York: Harcourt, Brace & World, 1964.

Singer, Ronald, *Emerging Man in Africa*, New York: Natural History Magazine, November, 1962.

Sinnott, Edmund W., *The Bridge of Life*, New York: Simon and Schuster, 1966.

Sinsheimer, Robert L., quoted by Joseph Wood Krutch, New York: Saturday Review, May 4, 1968.

Skaife, S. H., *Dwellers in Darkness*, Garden City: Doubleday, 1961.

Slijper, E. J., *Whales*, New York: Basic Books, 1962.

Smith, Homer W., *From Fish to Philosopher*, Garden City: Doubleday, 1961.

——, *Man and His Gods*, New York: Grosset's Universal Library, 1956.

Smith, W. Robertson, *The Religion of the Semites*, New York: Meridian Library, 1956.

Snodgrass, Robert Evans, *Insects, Their Ways and Means of Living*, New York: Dover, 1967; also Smithsonian Institute Lecture Series, Washington, D.C., 1930.

Sorell, Walter, *The Story of the Human Hand*, New York: Bobbs-Merrill, 1967.

Spaeth, Louise Marie, *Marriage and Family Life Among Strange Peoples*, Chicago: T. S. Rockwell, 1931.

Spencer, B., and F. J. Gillen, *The Native Tribes of Central Australia*, from "Primitive Heritage," ed. Margaret Mead and Nicolas Calas, New York: Random House, 1953.

Spier, Leslie, *Inventions and Human Society*, from "Man, Culture and Society," ed. Harry L. Shapiro, New York: Oxford Galaxy, 1960.

Steen, Edwin B., and Ashley Montagu, *Anatomy and Physiology*, vol. I, New York: Barnes & Noble, 1959.

Steinbeck, John, quoted in *The Radical Humanism of John Steinbeck,* Daniel Aaron, New York: Saturday Review, Sept. 28, 1968.

Steiner, Jean-François, *Treblinka,* New York: Simon and Schuster, 1967.

Steward, Julian H., *The Great Basin Shoshonean Indians,* from "The North American Indians, A Sourcebook," New York: Macmillan, 1967.

Stillman, Edmund, *The Holy Terrors of Münster,* New York: Horizon, vol. IX, no. 3, Summer, 1967.

Storr, Anthony, *Human Aggression,* New York: Atheneum, 1968.

Sumner, William Graham, *Folkways,* Boston: Ginn & Co., 1906; also Dover, 1959.

Suzuki, D. T., *Zen Buddhism,* ed. William Barrett, Garden City: Doubleday, 1956.

Szczesny, Gerhard, *The Future of Unbelief,* New York: Braziller, 1961.

Talmud, *Traité Bérakhote, Sheet 17,* Boston: Talmud Society, 1918.

Tax, Sol, *Evolution After Darwin,* vol. III, Chicago: University of Chicago Press, 1960.

Taylour, Lord William, *The Myceneans,* New York: Praeger, 1964.

Teale, Edwin Way, *Strange Lives of Familiar Insects,* New York: Dodd-Mead, 1962.

Thayer, V. T., *Religion in Public Education,* New York: Viking, 1947.

Thomas, George F., *New Forms for Old Faith,* from "Changing Patterns in American Civilization," New York: A. S. Barnes, 1962.

Thomas, H. C., and W. A. Hamm, *The Foundations of Modern Civilization,* New York: Vanguard Press, 1927.

Thompson, Sir D'Arcy, *On Growth and Form,* ed. J. T. Bonner, Cambridge, Eng.: Cambridge University Press, 1961.

Toynbee, Arnold J., *The Reluctant Death of Sovereignty,* Santa Barbara: Center Magazine, vol. I, no. 3, March, 1968.

Twain, Mark, *The Mysterious Stranger,* New York: Harper, 1924.

————, *Reflections on Religion,* ed. Charles Neider, New York: Hudson Review, vol. XVI, no. 3, Autumn, 1963.

Tylor, Edward B., *Anthropology,* New York: Appleton, 1897.

————, *Religion in Primitive Culture,* New York: Harper, 1958; also London, Eng.: John Murray, 1900.

Ubbelohde-Doering, H., *On the Royal Highways of the Inca,* New York: Praeger, 1966.

Underhill, Ruth, *Religion Among American Indians,* from "The North American Indians, A Sourcebook," ed. R. C. Owen, etc., New York: Macmillan, 1967.

Valliant, George C., *Aztecs of Mexico,* Garden City: Doubleday, 1944.

Vazquez, Pedro Ramirez, *Mexico,* Mexico City and New York: Harry N. Abrams, 1968.

Waddington, C. H., *The Ethical Animal,* London: Allen & Unwin, 1960.

Wahl, Jean, *A Short History of Existentialism,* New York: Philosophical Library, 1949; also Editions Club Maintenant, Paris, 1947.

Wallas, Graham, *Social Judgment,* New York: Harcourt, Brace, 1935.

Walsh, John, *Time is Short and the Water Rises,* New York: Dutton, 1967.

Waters, Frank, *The Book of the Hopi,* New York: Viking, 1963.

Webster, David Kenyon, *Myth and Maneater, The Story of the Shark,* New York: Norton, 1963.

Weiss, Paul, *Common Sense and Beyond,* from "Determinism and Freedom," ed. Sidney Hook, New York: Collier, 1961.

————, *The Right to Disobey,* from "Law and Philosophy," ed. Sidney Hook, New York: New York University Press, 1964.

Weizsäcker, Ernst Heinrich von, *Memoirs,* Chicago: Regnery, 1951.

Wellard, James, *The Great Sahara,* New York: Dutton, 1965.

Welty, Joel Carl, *The Life of Birds,* New York: Knopf, 1963.

Wendt, Herbert, *The Sexual Life of the Animals,* New York: Simon and Schuster, 1965.

Westermarck, Edward, *Memories of My Life,* New York: Macaulay, 1927.

Wheless, Joseph, *Forgery in Christianity,* New York: Knopf, 1930.

White, Andrew D., *The History of the Warfare of Science with Theology,* 2 vol., New York: Dover, 1960; originally published 1896.

White, L., *The Science of Culture,* New York: Grove, 1949.

White, Lynn, Jr., *Saint Francis and the Ecologic Backlash,* New York: Horizon, vol. IX, no. 3, Summer, 1967.

Wiesel, Elie, *The Town Beyond the Wall,* New York: Atheneum, 1964.

Wilde, Oscar, *The Picture of Dorian Gray,* New York: Modern Library, 1925.

Wittgenstein, Ludwig, *Tractatus Logico-Philosophicus,* 1922.

Wolff, Lester L., *The Responsibilities of Dissent,* Washington, D.C.: Congressional Record, March 16, 1967.

Wylie, Philip, *An Essay on Morals,* New York: Rinehart, 1947.

Yarnell, Richard A., *Correspondence,* Washington, D.C.: Science Magazine, vol. 143, no. 3611, March 13, 1964.

Zollinger, Peter, *The Political Structure,* New York: Braziller, 1967.

Zorita, Alonzo de, *Breve y Sumaria relación de los Señores de la Nueva España;* see "Life and Labor in Ancient Mexico," ed. Benjamin Keen, New Brunswick, N. J.: Rutgers University Press, 1963.

Zuckerman, S., *Functional Affinities of Man, Monkeys and Apes,* New York: Harcourt, Brace, 1933.

INDEX

752   *Index*

Simpson, George Gaylord, 21, 63, 64, 135, 141, 145-46, 163, 194, 203, 558, 594, 653, 678

Sin, expiation of, 320; as a psychotic concept, 607

Singer, Ronald, 195

Singh, T. C. N., 197

Sinnott, Edmund W., 7, 27, 29, 147, 365

Sinsheimer, Robert L., 74

Skaife, S. H., 172, 208, 248, 362

Slave ships, blessed, 93

Slavery, 56, 381; in Abyssinia, 286; in Africa, 478, 480; in ancient countries, 502; by Arabs, 287; of Negroes, 460; in Micronesia, Polynesia, and Peru, 288

Slijper, E. J., 188, 215, 230

Smith, Homer W., 25, 97, 171, 194, 341

Smith, W. Robertson, 368

Snodgrass, Robert Evans, 148, 151, 621-22

Snow, C. P., 421

Society, illusion of ethics in, 656-68; *versus* the individual, 438; nature of, 367; origins of, 79, 122, 211, 248; process and change in, 384; tendency to oppose change, 383

Socrates, 29, 35, 354, 503, 590

Sorell, Walter, 561

Soul, origins and notions of the, 331-42; in Roman Catholicism, 340; -transference, 348

Sound, *see* Communication

Spaeth, Louise Marie, 369

Spain, absence of religious freedom in, 631-32; church coalition with military, 458; church collaboration with Fascists, 463; freedom in, 18, Roman Catholicism in, 324

Sparta, ancient, 192

Speech, freedom of, 434

Spencer, B., and F. J. Gillen, 336

Spengler, Oswald, 375

Spier, Leslie, 521

Spinoza, Baruch, 33, 35, 79

Spirits, residences of the, 264

Standardization, effects of, 584

State, dominance, 491-94; separation of Church and, 628; totalitarian, 493; *see* Organization

Steinbeck, John, 86

Stendhal, 572

Steward, Julian H., 331

Stillman, Edmund, 553

Storr, Anthony, 182, 314, 365, 381, 554

Sulzberger, C. L., 653

Sumerai, 483

Sumeria, temple banks of, 502

Sumerians, 248

Sumner, William Graham, 308, 339

Supernaturalism, 341

Survival, problems of, 57; ecomonics of, 496

Suzuki, D. T., 52

Swedenborg, Emanuel, 355

Swinburne, Algernon C., 552

Switzerland, hunters in, 685-86

Symbiosis, in nature, 172, 183, 703; among fishes, 184

Symbology, 253; of fire, 255

Synthesis, of Spinoza, Hegel, 79

Szczesny, Gerhard, 20, 31, 165, 199, 249, 250, 257, 259, 262, 284, 314, 327, 342, 346, 379, 607-08

Szymanski, J. S., 168

Taboos, against woman, 561

Talmud, 327, 598

Taylour, William, 295

Tax, Sol, 452

Teale, Edwin Way, 58, 100, 207, 219, 220-21

Ten Commandments, 600

Territorial Imperative, power factor of, 154

Thales, 11

Thayer, V. T., 431, 644-45

Theology, in the pursuit of truth, 356; Christian, 323

Thomas, George F., 95, 294

Thomas, H. C., and W. A. Hamm, 498

Thompson, D'Arcy, 165

Thompson, J. Eric S., 308

Thomson, J. Arthur, 95

Thought, freedom of, 434, 440-44

Tolerance, 17

Toltecs, 333, 348

Tools, among animals, 170

Totalitarianism, 499

Totemism, 262

Toynbee, Arnold J., 492

Traditionalism, *see* Society

Treblinka, 618

Tribal society, evolution of, 368

Trinities, ancient Egyptian, 344; Aramaic, 345; Babylonian, 345; Christian, 345-48; Ethiopian Semitic, 345

Truth, concepts of, 5; existence of, 9

Tummuz, 270, 345

Tylor, Edward B., 251, 259, 262, 264, 292, 316, 322, 331-32, 334, 339, 349, 353, 416, 418, 453